The Birth of California Narrow Gauge

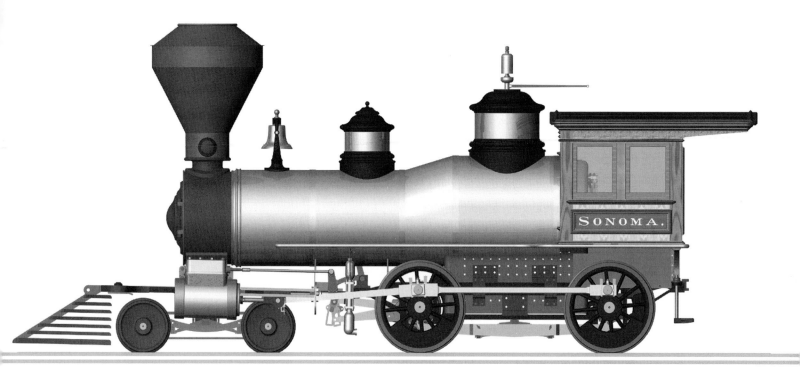

Nearly completed Baldwin 8-18 C *Sonoma*. [Curtis Ferrington]

The Birth of California Narrow Gauge

A Regional Study of the Technology of Thomas and Martin Carter

BRUCE MacGREGOR

Research contributions by Susanne Todd

Illustrated by Curtis Ferrington

Stanford University Press   Stanford, California 2003

Published with the assistance of the
Edgar M. Kahn Memorial Fund.

Stanford University Press
Stanford, California

Printed in the United States of America
on acid-free, archival-quality paper.

Library of Congress Cataloging-in-Publication Data
MacGregor, Bruce A.
The birth of California narrow gauge:
a regional study of the technology of Thomas
and Martin Carter / Bruce MacGregor;
research contributions by Susanne Todd;
illustrated by Curtis Ferrington.
p. cm.
Includes bibliographical references and index.
ISBN 0-8047-3550-6
1. Narrow gauge railroads—California—History. I. Title.
TF24.C3M34 2003
385.5'2'09794—dc21
20022155942

Original Printing 2003

Last figure below indicates year of this printing:
12   11   10   09   08   07   06   05   04   03

Designed and typeset by Julie Allred, B. Williams & Associates
in 10.8/14 Sabon

Front end papers: view of Santa Cruz, ca. 1873, before
the coming of the railroads; from a lithograph by Gifford.
[Museum of Art and History, Santa Cruz]

Rear end papers: view of Santa Cruz, ca. 1877, after the
coming of the Santa Cruz Rail Road and the Santa Cruz &
Felton; from a Dutch lithograph. [Bancroft Library]

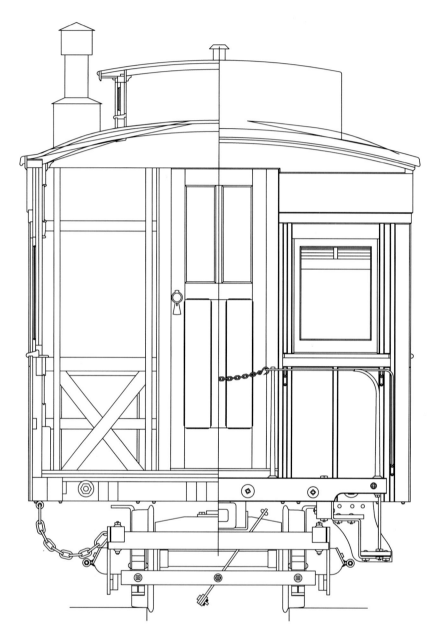

End elevation, Carter Brothers Monterey & Salinas Valley Railroad combination car. [Michael A. Collins]

Contents

South Pacific Coast train crew, location unknown, ca. 1904. [Ken Lorenzen collection]

Acknowledgments

The author would like to acknowledge a long list of individual and organizational contributors who have made this book possible.

Acknowledgment to libraries, institutions, and governmental agencies includes the Alameda Historical Society; Courtney DeAngelis of the Amon Carter Museum; Susan Snyder and Jenny Mullowney of the Bancroft Library; Paul Yon and Lee McLaird of the Center for Archival Collections, Bowling Green State University; Emily Wolff, Jennifer Schaftner, and Pat Keats of the California Historical Society; Walter Gray III of the California State Archives; Gary Kurutz and Ellen Harding, California State Library; William A. Jones, Debbie Besnard, and Pam Bush of Special Collections, Meriam Library, California State University, Chico; David Monahan and Antony Pacey, Canada Science and Technology Museum, Ottawa; Marie-Chantal Anctil and Julie Leclerc of the Canadian Center for Architecture in Montreal; Carolyn Swift of the Capitola Museum; the Church of Latter Day Saints, Lake Oswego, Oregon; Clackamas County Historical Society, Oregon City, Oregon; Kay Bost, DeGolyer Library, Southern Methodist University; Cynthia Lamley, Fairfax Historical Society; the Fremont City Library; Harvard School of Business, Baker Library; Dan Gosnell of the Huckleberry Railroad; William Frank and Dan Lewis, the Huntington Library; Sue Beatty of the Jack Mason Museum, Inverness; Gordon Belt, Kalmback Memorial Library; Jocelyn Moss of the Anne Kent California Room, Marin County Library; Jerry Kozol, Marin Historical Society; Lucinda Walker, Mechanics Institute of San Francisco; Mona Gudgel, Monterey County Historical Society; Dennis Copeland and Joe Johnson, California History Room, Monterey Public Library; Nikki Silva, Rachel McKay, and Barbara Clark, Museum of Art and History, Santa Cruz; John Ballweber and Chris Dewitt, Nevada State Railroad Museum; Maureen Fennie, Niagara Falls Public Library; Dianne Curry, Oakland Museum; Bill Barbour, Bob Cook, Brian Norden, and Dave Garcia, Orange Empire Railway Museum; Andre Charbonneau and Doris Drolet-Dube, Parks Canada; Patricia Johnson, Sacramento Archives and Museum Collections Center; William Kooiman and Irene Stachura, San Francisco Maritime National Historic Park, Shaw Library; Phil Frank, Sausalito Historical Society; Bill Schaumberg, railroad model craftsman; Ed Tyson, Searles Memorial Library, Nevada City; Susan Tolbert, Albert Eggerton, and Craig Orr, Smithsonian Institution; Susan Haas of the Society of California Pioneers; Roberto Trujillo, Linda Long, Maggie Kimball, and Steven Mandeville-Gamble, Department of Special Collections and University Archives, Green Library, Stanford University; Piper Ross Berger, Tiburon Landmark Society; Lois Parks, Tomales Regional History Center; Special Collections, University of California at Davis; Carol Champion and Paul Stubbs, University of California at Santa Cruz, McHenry Library, Special Collections; and Don Walker and Jeneen Ford, Holt-Atherton Department of Special Collections, University of the Pacific Libraries.

In addition, special thanks go to Ellen Halteman and Steven E. Drew of the California State Railroad Museum, for sustained support over the ten-year life span of research; to the men and women of HP (Hewlett-Packard) for their expertise in the theory and practice of manufacturing; and to the volunteers of the Society for the Preservation of Carter Railroad Resources (SPCRR) for sharing twenty years of hands-on experience in railroad car building.

Individuals who contributed to research or illustrations include Frank Allen, Tom Armstrong, Gene Arrillaga, Ted Benson, Henry Boer, E. Bond, David Braun, Jack and Jacque Burgess, Meredith Carter Fisch, John Christensen, Fred Codoni, Hart Corbett, Dale Darney, Jack and William Darrough, Richard C. Datin Jr., Lewis Deasy, Bob Dockery, Rich Dunn, Guy Dunscomb, Emiliano Echeverria, David Eggleston, Jack Farley, Robert Fisher M.D., Malcolm Gaddis, Stuart Geudon, Jack Gibson, Al Graves, Rick Hamman, Paul Hammond, Norman Hansen, Kevin Hassing, Pat Hathaway, John Hemmann, George Hildebrand, Rich Hill, Craig Hoefer, Glen Joesten, Jim Johnson, Don and Jerry Juergenson, Fred Keesaw, Stan Kistler, George and Pria Koerner, John Labbe, Elmer Lagorio, Harold A. Lapham, Robert J. Lee, Dewey Livingston, Kenneth Lorenzen, Don Marenzi, Dan Markoff, Dan and Stephanie Matthews, Greg Maxwell, John Maxwell, Doug MacLeod, Lissa Mckee, Ken Meeker, Arnold Menke, Bob Moulton, Jack Muzio, Rich Nealson, Peter Palmquist, Bob Paoa, Steven Perry, Rich Pitter, Bob Piwarzyk, Ron Powell, Doug Richter, Brook Rother, Vernon Sappers, Nick and Lois Schaeffer, John Schmale, Charles Siebenthal, Henry Sorensen, David Spohr, Louis Stein, Allen Tacy, John Taubeneck, George F. Thagard III, Sam Thompson, Henry Welzel, Bill and Janne Wissel, Bill Wulf, Ted Wurm, Ken Yeo, and Alan Young.

For their skill and knowledge in mechanical drawing, the author would like to acknowledge the contributions of Kevin Bunker, Michael A. Collins, Herman Darr, Dan McGinty, Boone Morrison, Robert Schlechter, Russ Simpson, and project illustrator Curtis Ferrington.

For exceptional support in historical research, and for a critical reading of the manuscript, the author is indebted to Randy Hees, Wendell Huffman, Stanley Stevens, John Stutz, John White, Jr., and Kyle Wyatt. The author takes responsibility for errors in fact or interpretation that remain.

For groundbreaking research into Carter family genealogy and numerous other topics that supported and extended the scope of this project, the author would like to thank Susanne Todd and Nate Shugars.

To my editor at Stanford University Press, Judith Hibbard, to designer and typographer Julie Allred, and to copyeditor Tom Finnegan go thanks for enormous patience and discipline required to produce the finished book.

To the Pope family collectively—Norris, Janet, Geoffrey and Jeremy—go my thanks for friendship and support over the lifetime of the project. To Geoffrey, in particular, goes acknowledgment for suggesting the link between the locomotive *Betsy Jane* and his great-great-great-grandmother, Betsey Webster Pope. And last, to Norris in particular go profound thanks for believing in this project and for sharing the remarkable contents of Fowler Pope's trunk.

The Birth of California Narrow Gauge

In 1911 or 1912 (newspapers do not tell us which), the gabled, Eastlake-style home of Martin Carter burned to the ground in what is today the Irvington District of modern Fremont, California. By that time, both Martin and his older brother, Thomas, had died, and the business that they started together, called Carter Brothers, was long since closed and shuttered.

The contents of the house were previously inventoried in 1908, shortly after Martin's death. The summary, totaling forty pages and accounting for nearly $300,000 in personal and real property, included not only thoroughbred trotters, quarter horses, and draft horses that Carter raised on the surrounding Nutwood Stock Farm but also household goods and personal belongings. Still, nowhere in the inventory is mention made of the company records of Carter Brothers, the business papers that accumulated (along with considerable wealth) from thirty years of operating "the pioneer car building enterprise of the West Coast." Perhaps they escaped the inventory locked away in the attic or the basement of the Irvington mansion, only to fall victim to the fire that destroyed the home some three years later. We know only that except for small caches of drawings and a handful of employee time sheets, the business and personal records of Carter Brothers have vanished without a trace.

What a tale they could tell. They could explain, perhaps, the early phase of an industrial chain reaction that gave birth to a uniquely California version of the narrow gauge railroad movement.

Thomas and Martin Carter, both refugees from the Irish potato famine, achieved almost overnight success providing contracting and engineering services to the first six narrow gauge railroads built in the state: the Monterey & Salinas Valley, the North Pacific Coast, the Santa Cruz Rail Road, the Santa Cruz & Felton, the Nevada County Narrow Gauge, and the South Pacific Coast. Each of these railroads attempted to synthesize local or regional autonomy for investors who believed that railroad monopolies and associated cartels caused, or were prolonging, the worst recession California had experienced since statehood. Most of the narrow gauge railroads that resulted were built with grassroots funding, which is to say on a shoestring, and lacked both money and technical know-how to build even a modest bulwark against the "Octopus": the Central and Southern Pacific Railroads.

The Carter Brothers therefore went into business by commoditizing light railroad construction—by dropping the price and simplifying the technology to the point where it became accessible to regional buyers who saw themselves either as victims of the Octopus or potential competitors, albeit on a small scale.

The narrow gauge movement was sweeping America in the same time period in which Carter began to explore the California marketplace. To be fair, the Carters initiated their unique marketing solution on the shoulders of ex-

Portraits of Thomas Carter (left) and Martin Carter. [Martin G. Carter collection]

isting innovation. A variety of miniaturized locomotives, rolling stock, and rail were suddenly available at costs estimated by the industry at two-thirds those of standard gauge. The American narrow gauge movement was set in motion by the promise of dramatic capital savings in a time of widespread recession. However, in spite of such savings, California proved a stubborn marketing challenge to the eastern U.S. and British sources of early narrow gauge products, because of the extreme transportation costs involved and poor infrastructure. Skilled mechanics, for example, who could assemble and maintain such equipment were in short supply. West Coast iron manufactories had existed since right after the Gold Rush, but the quality of iron they produced was consistently berated as inferior to imported iron, which raised the cost of such staples as rail and cast iron car wheels.

In this hostile economic environment, Carter Brothers survived and grew as a small business because of its ability to adapt local, West Coast manufacturing resources to East Coast designs and products. John Carroll, once Thomas Carter's boss, joined the tiny partnership with experience at Davenport and Bridges, a Boston-area car builder known for commercially successful improvements in early car design. Carroll helped shape a technical strategy for early Carter Brothers car designs. When the business moved into production of narrow gauge rolling stock, they attacked the problem of high factory overhead (a problem that plagued large eastern manufacturers) by keeping their factory small—and at times even portable, setting up "field factories" at the customer site. They solved the problem of iron quality by using locally available iron foundries for all the metal parts on cars *except* wheels, importing wheels from East Coast suppliers such as A. Whitney and Sons of Philadelphia.

Carter's adaptive engineering and manufacturing techniques quickly went head-to-head with a much larger West Coast manufactory named Kimball and won customers away in the key year of 1874, when California's first narrow gauge lines were gaining public attention. For the next two years, Carter Brothers juggled scarce capital, a small core of mechanics, and widely dispersed customer sites to win and hold the business of the first six narrow gauge lines in the state. Each small guerrilla victory furthered the larger war for economic choice being waged throughout California, and (in spite of the failure of half of the railroads on the list) a demonstration that less was more.

The Monterey & Salinas Valley Railroad was the protean example. One hundred wheat farmers succeeded in building a narrow gauge railroad that diverted (at least for a season) the grain harvest of the Salinas Valley away from the Central and Southern Pacific Railroads and onto independent shipping at Monterey. The victory proved instructive to other regions of the state, with their own unique economic hurdles. To each region, Carter offered low-cost railroad hardware whose manufacture and delivery relied on local resources (foundries, lumber suppliers, carpenters, and paint shops) to lower costs. At the same time, Carter reinvested a large part of its revenue in the local economy, reinforcing the regional autonomy of its customers.

The low street price of narrow gauge rolling stock was not the only factor in its surge of popularity on the West Coast. Nathan Rosenberg called revolution of this sort a "compulsive technological sequence" and used the term to describe complex, mutual reinforcement of a new technology and the markets that form its context. (The concept is notably descriptive of today's microchip industry.) Rosenberg's concept explains the ability of a new technology to transform and disrupt adjacent industries and markets, and it is especially appropriate to the period in which California was first becoming a self-sustaining industrial center. Carter did not "invent" the narrow gauge technology that Carter Brothers sold. Instead, they adapted the technology to the context, and just as often adapted the context to the technology. Cases in point:

Shortening the Supply Chain. By working with the foundries and lumber suppliers closest to the place where they assembled rolling stock, Carter minimized the time, distance, and cost of getting raw materials to the manufacturing site. An example is Amner, Morton and Co., a small but complete iron foundry located just twenty miles from Carter's early factory site at Monterey, California. Carter quickly purchased Amner, Morton's entire production capability for a period of about three months and used it to minimize the costs of car building in the Monterey Bay area.

Gifting the Supply Chain. By leaving patterns and other "intellectual property" with the foundry that poured its car castings, Carter gifted that foundry with designs it could reuse. In doing so, the foundry kept its processes and tooling honed to Carter's designs. A year after gifting Amner, Morton with patterns, Carter returned and was able to use the foundry as a source of supply for a second car contract, this one even closer to the foundry. In the meantime, Amner, Morton was able to sell Carter-designed parts to the Santa Cruz Rail Road (which used the parts to manufacture its own cars).

Field Factory. Setting up temporary tooling and subassembly processes in a remote location, Carter in essence built a rudimentary factory close enough to the customer to avoid complicated shipment of parts and finished goods to and from a permanent factory. An example: although the Carter production facility for the Monterey & Salinas Valley Railroad was temporarily operating in Monterey, their permanent factory was established in Saucelito at almost the same time.

"Platform-Based" Product Development. Much as different body types can be put on top of a common, standardized automotive power train, Carter was able to engineer standardized running gear upon which a variety of freight and passenger car bodies could be built. Example: Carter manufactured numerous freight car products on three basic platforms representing eight-, ten-, and fifteen-ton-capacity running gear. By standardizing a platform, Carter was able to spread its design and development costs across multiple products.

Kit Production. In a permanent factory, Carter sometimes produced parts and components, rather than completed cars, and shipped them to a remote customer site for relatively simple assembly. The customer railroad had the option of assembling only the part of the consignment it needed, saving labor costs and stockpiling raw materials for cars that would be assembled after the railroad began to generate traffic. An example is the Nevada County Narrow Gauge, which assembled thirty Carter kits in 1875 but kept about eight additional kits in reserve, unassembled, against future demand.

Permanent Factory. When business finally justified the investment, Carter created what we think of as a facility for taking in raw materials and producing finished goods—in other words, a permanent factory. As an example, Newark, California, was home to Carter Brothers from 1877 until the business closed in 1902; there Carter had the space to migrate most or all of the other manufacturing strategies to a permanent physical site. Several suppliers migrated as well, co-locating in Newark and creating a small but self-sufficient industrial campus.

In a brief period of just three years, from 1874 through 1877, all of these tactics were tried, combined, and retried, refining a production strategy for products that were themselves undergoing change. At first, Carter's car-building technology was simply one component in the piecemeal development of low-cost, light railroads. But other experiments were in progress. The more precocious narrow gauge railroads (the North Pacific Coast was an example) were experimenting with relatively untried combinations of locomotives, cars, and track, testing them on sharper curves and steeper grades than anything yet seen in California. Perhaps Thomas Carter's real breakthrough came when he first grasped the opportunity to bring these components together as a dynamic system—balancing, optimizing, and integrating track, locomotives, and cars into a high-performance railroad.

The opportunity came in 1877 when he found himself in charge of the mechanical specification of the South Pacific Coast Railroad. With the powerful Nevada Bank of San Francisco writing the checks, Carter was in a position to either design or choose elements of the railroad's physical plant

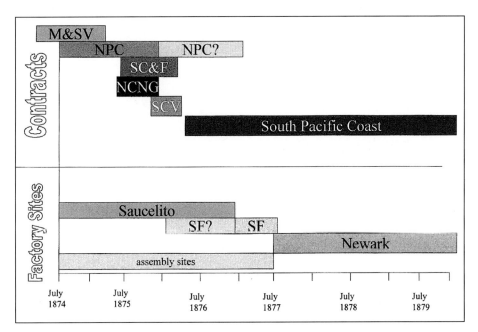

Chronology of Carter Brothers contracts and factory sites, 1874–1880.

that, together, could demonstrate dramatic improvements in speed and load-carrying ability. When someone actually put a stop watch on the result, the *San Francisco Examiner* reported that a South Pacific Coast train had clocked seventy miles per hour on straight track across the San Francisco Bay marsh. For the record, the locomotive engineer wanted the *Examiner* to know that normally he "don't like to run her that fast." But it was Carter, we conclude, who stood to gain from the breakthrough performance of a relatively new, untested technology.

The time scale in which these performance improvements occurred was surprisingly compressed. Carter's design activity, and the manufacturing strategies that Carter applied the designs to, often overlapped. What we think of (and write of) as historiographically unique railroads Carter Brothers saw as a common marketing opportunity to leverage new designs and new production methods across common customer needs. This compression was the key to their survival as a business. They struggled to extend production methods and limited resources (as little as $3,000 in capital and as few as six employees) as widely and profitably as possible. If we look at a time line of Carter's contract activity in the period 1874–1876, what stands out is the telescoping of work: multiple jobs to bid, to staff, to procure, and to execute, piled one on top of the next. At one point, in 1875, four Carter projects overlapped; to meet this challenge with relatively little working capital and a few skilled men, Carter began to try the kind of manufacturing innovations mentioned earlier. This was the strategy not of an old-world cabinet maker but of a calculating entrepreneur, evidence of the engine relentlessly driving Rosenberg's compulsive technological sequence.

Manufacturing flexibility allowed Carter Brothers to hang on in the same period of time, and under the same marketing pressures, that finally drove its chief competitor, the Kimball Carriage and Car Co., to the brink of insolvency and to a virtual cessation of railroad car work, effectively removing them as a competitor when the Bank of California failed in August 1875.

Carter Brothers freight car production, 1874–1880. Car counts show total work per year, for any of these railroads: North Pacific Coast, Monterey & Salinas Valley, Santa Cruz & Felton, Nevada County Narrow Gauge, Santa Clara Valley, and South Pacific Coast. Two hundred additional cars are also shown, ordered in 1880 by the Oregonian Railroad; believed to be the largest order in Carter's history.

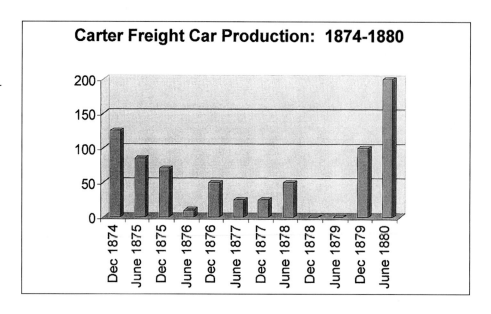

Carter Freight Car Production: 1874–1880

But Carter came close to the same fate. In the deepening recession, its largest customer (the North Pacific Coast) eventually jumped ship to eastern car manufacturers, who were willing to cut their prices below Carter's. Struggling to survive, Carter turned to producing small lots of kits, seeking a way to lower production costs. From the end of 1874 until early 1876, its overall production and sales trended steadily downward, very nearly grinding to a halt before the end of 1875.

Here (the lost records could help us understand exactly how) a reversal of fortune occurred. The Centennial year, the worst year in the recession, began not only with new car work for the South Pacific Coast but also with management positions for both Carter brothers in the railroad's chain of command: for Martin as master mechanic, and for Thomas as superintendent of the railroad. As mentioned earlier, the Carters began to reengineer not just the new rolling stock they would build under contract but the physical plant it ran on as well. The South Pacific Coast's heavier rail and higher speed in turn promoted higher-capacity cars, with smoother running gear, which allowed Carter to overhaul its entire product line. The decade climaxed with a building spurt that confirmed the South Pacific Coast as the only narrow gauge competition to the Southern Pacific and demonstrated the Carter Brothers to be a successful, independent West Coast car manufacturer. As an R. G. Dun and Co. credit report concluded in 1878, Thomas Carter "is a cautious, industrious man of considerable ability in his line and regarded as reliable." He was also on his way to becoming a millionaire.

However, there was a darker side to his success. Half the railroads that Carter supported during this decade were either absorbed by the Southern Pacific or insolvent by the end of the 1870s. The populist uprising against the Southern Pacific, if it were ever embodied by the narrow gauge movement in California, resulted in fewer than 350 individuals owning the stock of every narrow gauge line in the state. Key partners of the narrow gauge movement—such as E. E. Morgan and Sons, a commission banking house that made it possible for the Grange movement to launch the Monterey &

Salinas Valley Railroad—went bankrupt in the process. The public at large, disempowered and frequently unemployed, scapegoated its anger on the Chinese, the source of labor common to California railroads large and small. The result was violence and social upheaval.

The Carters themselves barely survived the startup phase of their business and had trouble adapting to the new growth and complexity that finally sustained them. Even after the South Pacific Coast contract work ended his cash flow problems, Thomas Carter seemed unable to cope with the politics and complexity of the resulting organization. In May 1880, shortly after the South Pacific Coast opened its completed mainline between Alameda and Santa Cruz, human error was probably responsible for a wreck that killed sixteen passengers. Held culpable by a coroner's journey, Thomas Carter resigned as superintendent a few weeks later, bringing a close to the startup phase of his business (and to the 1870s as well). In the aftermath of the accident, the cartels were quick to label the narrow gauge movement in general as a threat to public safety. It was the same year in which the national growth rate of new narrow gauge railroads reached its maximum, when the ratio of narrow gauge miles to total railroad miles built in the United States reached a peak of about one-fourth and began a steep decline.

In a decade whose achievements lay forgotten between the completion of the transcontinental railroad and the takeoff of California urbanization, the contribution of Carter Brothers has remained hidden in alternating layers of myth and exaggeration. The myth was in part the work of Thomas Carter himself, whose known personal writings amount to some six hundred words in a subscription biography, an embellished and self-serving narrative of his life.

The myth grew larger in the distortions of future generations. By the time of his death, contemporary observers confused Carter's accomplishments with the monopolistic business conditions around him. A neighbor family near the Carter ranch, whose daughter had more than a passing interest in Martin Carter's sons, thought the family's good fortune derived from the Pullman Co. Thomas Carter's obituary, written by the *San Francisco Examiner* in 1898, testified that Carter Brothers had built "nearly all the rolling stock of the Central Pacific and Southern Pacific Railroads," which amounts to accusing Carter Brothers of sleeping with the enemy. It was a claim that managed to obviate all the risks, the uniqueness, and the individuality of Carter Brothers and equate it with its ethical opposite. The Southern Pacific made a career of putting the small independents out of business, and more than once Carter was nearly a victim. But to the emerging California conscience, the decade of the "terrible seventies" was one to be buried and forgotten. The death of Thomas Carter marked the growing influence of the generation that nearly tamed the railroad monopolies and would, in 1899, memorialize the onset of railroad reform in Frank Norris's novel *The Octopus*. Those who, a generation earlier, would have been called its victims would soon be buried in the common grave of the ogre.

In reality, Carter Brothers came out of a dark time that perhaps mirrored the darker side of Thomas Carter's character. Fleeing the Irish potato famine at the age of twelve, Carter sought refuge the rest of his life from calamity and human tragedy, first from Ireland, next from the American Civil War, and finally from the economic and social upheaval of 1870s California. Displaced and marginalized all his life, Carter found familiar demons in the California narrow gauge movement. It was railroading for the odd man out, the underdog, and as a startup industry it engaged a part of Thomas Carter that worked best from a minority position, his uniqueness and his product defined by isolation. He eventually branded the confined commercial space he worked in. "Special Attention," his business card read long after the decline of the market he had helped create, "given to Narrow Gauge Work."

This book, then, seeks to explain the surprising success of Thomas and Martin Carter in a time of wrenching dislocation in the social and economic fabric of California. Given the disappearance of virtually all of their personal and business papers, such a study would be impossible without turning the optics of the inquiry around. The lives of the Carter brothers are like a darkened room in which the lens of the camera obscura projects a brightly illuminated, external landscape. We see the Carters through the railroads they helped create, and in the context in which they were built. Through the newly available North Pacific Coast cash books, for example, we are able to reconstruct for the first time a business case, in which the Carters' early activity as independent contractors can be followed in detail by the trail of dollars through the railroad's nearly complete financial records. Through these numbers, we can visualize the shape of their nascent business, its resources, and its plan, and assess the personal risks the brothers assumed.

Through the business papers and day books of Henry and Charley Gorrill, Henry Fairfax Williams, and J. Barr Robertson, we can piece together an understanding of the tightly networked character of the narrow gauge movement, a network from which Thomas Carter frequently brokered the skills and resources he needed from others. Through archeology—literally, the reverse engineering of surviving relics—we begin to understand Carter's "design intent," what today would be described as an engineer's learning curve as he or she creates a new design in response to the technical requirements of the consumer marketplace. In the last twenty years, several professional, museum-quality restorations of early Carter Brothers equipment have yielded a living reconstruction of the technical contribution the Carters made to the industry.

Martin Carter home, in the Irvington District of modern-day Fremont, Calif. [Meredith Carter-Fisch collection]

Through the diary of Fowler Pope, a locomotive engineer on the Santa Cruz & Felton, we understand the end user's perspective, a rare look into the day-to-day operation of one of the short line railroads that relied, exclusively in Pope's case, on rolling stock manufactured by Carter Brothers.

In turn, understanding the contemporary business and technological climate surrounding the Carter Brothers has led to a better grasp of its emotional climate. There was, indeed, an emotional content to these products and services. The regions of California that embraced the narrow gauge movement did so because it gave them hope in a time of severe economic recession and unemployment. The first Carter passenger car to roll out of Monterey, a tiny yellow jewel box that ironically lacked toilet facilities, was a ticket to freedom for the embattled Grangers whose economic livelihood had been held hostage by railroad and grain cartels. The narrow gauge lines that Carter ultimately supplied became a thin but sharp edge of a populist movement, conditioning California politics to the Progressive Era and to its modern political legacies of initiative and referendum.

Little or nothing remains from their own hand to tell us what the Carters knew, felt, or dreamt about the uncertain horizon of California's early railroad industry. In the ashes of Martin Carter's gabled house, better answers may have been lost.

View of Roebling suspension bridge, at Suspension Bridge, N.Y., ca. 1858. [Charles Rand Penney collection]

Landfall

The novelist Evelyn Waugh once remarked that for the Irish desperately trying to escape the potato famine, there were only two possible realities: Hell or the United States.

Off the bow of Carter's ship, anchored in the St. Lawrence River during the summer or early fall of 1848, the United States lay to port. To starboard, where the long, wooded contour of Grosse Isle thrust up like a dark wall along the northern edge of the river, the specter of death seemed to rise with the river mist. The island marked the ship's first mooring in Canadian waters and Canada's quarantine station for ocean traffic coming up the St. Lawrence. The Carter family, exhausted from eight weeks at sea, stared silently at their first landfall in North America, a mass grave containing perhaps ten thousand of their countrymen.[1]

A year before, in May 1847, the ship *Urania* from Cork put into the island with about two hundred passengers, many sick with typhus.[2] Before the end of the first week in June, eighty-four vessels had followed *Urania* up the St. Lawrence from Commonwealth ports in Liverpool, Dublin, Londonderry, Belfast, Sligo, and Galway, all bearing refugees from the Irish famine. All eighty-four ships carried the deadly disease. Soon the line of detained ships stretched two miles along the river, lying in the shallows along the southern edge of the island. Crew members, some stricken themselves, struggled to empty their ships. The living were lowered into rowboats; the dead were pulled from the fetid holds with boat hooks. Hundreds of corpses littered the beaches along the St. Lawrence. A few decrepit sheds on the island were soon overflowing with the dying.

The well were impounded with the sick. The diary of Gerald Keegan chronicled his confinement on the island, where he was trapped after his uncle and wife died in the fever sheds. Heartbroken, on June 6, 1847, Keegan wrote[3]:

> The Almighty will surely have a day of reckoning with the rulers of
> Canada, for it is Canada's territory we are on and it is Canada's quarantine in which we lie bound. The sick are everywhere and neglected.
> I found the body of a man in the thicket where he had crawled like a
> scared beast to die in peace. Bodies are taken from the tents daily where
> the healthy are supposed to lodge. The sheds have become repugnant

to every sense, and the sick are worse off than on the ship, for few have relatives to attend them, and they lie for hours without being helped even to a drink of water. The inmates of a tent told me nobody had been near them for two days, and not one among them able to stand for a minute. Everything is against us, for the weather is windy and wet. I go to spend the night in the old shed. My brain is overburdened with the sorrows of my people, and I would were at rest with Aileen.

That summer, between ten thousand and twenty thousand were estimated to have died on Grosse Isle itself, buried in mass graves near the fever sheds. In spite of the attempt to quarantine the disease on the island, typhus followed the ships when they resumed passage up the river. Six thousand more emigrants died in Quebec City, another two thousand in Kingston, three hundred and fifty miles up the St. Lawrence from Quebec.[4] As tales of morbidity spread, American ports—New York City the prime example—refused to let Commonwealth ships discharge passengers, forcing the vessels north toward the only harbors that would let them anchor: the St. Lawrence ports guarded by Grosse Isle. The record of deaths at the quarantine station continued into 1848, the year of the Carter emigration, when two thousand additional deaths from cholera were reported at Grosse Isle alone.[5]

Even with the fate of the "coffin ships" widely known, by the spring and summer of 1848 the exodus of Irish refugees reached its highest level in the previous two and a half years. The conditions that drove the mass migration —nearly two million Irish departing by ship between 1841 and 1851—were as horrible as the fate that awaited many on Grosse Isle. Of those who stayed behind, a million would die in the same time period. Connaught Province, the most likely birthplace of the Carter children, claimed the highest "excess death rate" of the four Irish provinces, a death rate attributed to cholera and starvation.

To eight-year-old Thomas Carter, the eight-week journey may have seemed especially futile. To a child acutely aware of the adult reactions of fear and flight, the same fate may have appeared to await them at either end of the long, exhausting sea voyage.

Driven by such emotions, the Carter family had chosen to leave their home in County Galway, no matter what the risks.[6] They left as a family: father Thomas; mother Margaret; son John, age fourteen; daughter Margaret, age nine; son Thomas, age eight; and son Martin, age four.[7] It was not unusual for an Irish Catholic family to emigrate together. To secure ship passage and emigration tax (lower in Canada than in the United States), a family would frequently have to liquidate property or business, removing the foundation of the entire family's livelihood. In Connaught Province, including County Galway, the population most displaced by the famine were native Irish-speaking tenant farmers, lacking even minimal ability to speak or write English. The Irish exodus swelled the class of emigrant poor and illiterate who would have to fend for themselves on the other side of the Atlantic, assuming they survived the trip.[8]

But the Thomas Carters may have been better off than most of the Irish who risked their lives to come to North America. Although Galway and its neighboring counties supported mostly small tenant farms, not industry, the later careers of the Carter children suggested a long family tradition in the trades. By 1871, for example, son John was a blacksmith in Chippewa, Ontario,[9] near the U.S.-Canadian border. Young Thomas and Martin both started their careers in the carriage manufacturing trade. Back in Galway, we imagine Thomas senior to have been a resourceful, literate carpenter, cabinet maker, smith, ferrier, carriage maker, pattern maker, wheel wright, millwright, cooper, ship wright, foundryman, or machinist. We know not which.

Still, the feat of getting the entire family out of Ireland must have taken most of Carter's resources. The price of ship's passage varied from two to five pounds but was generally cheaper to British North America than to the United States. In 1847, some 117,000 Irish emigrants booked passage to American ports, but 98,000, the poorest of the poor, sailed to ports inside modern Canada.[10]

The Carters cast their lot with the dregs of the Irish exodus.

Fleeing together, the Carters left few footprints in their flight from famine. The name of their ship, the port of emigration, the possessions they took, the amount of money they carried, tools from their chosen profession—all such facts have been lost to the extant record. Long gaps in the family's annals would continue to fragment their narrative over the next half century, years that included triumph, wealth, public acclaim, tragedy, and scandal, years that left behind few known personal accounts of the same events.

One of the few exceptions is the Lewis Publishing Co.'s seven-hundred-word sketch, printed in *The Bay of San Francisco: A History*, in 1892.[11] Lewis made a living from writing short biographies of prominent area businessmen and, for a fee, publishing them in subscription digests. It is likely that Thomas Carter, then fifty-two years old, provided the basic facts for the sketch, and the subscription fee as well.

But the Lewis digest suffered on two accounts. The first was a lack of balanced input from Martin, who might have elaborated on the roles and contributions of the extended Carter family, so clearly underpinning the partnership of "Carter Brothers." Second, it suffered from Thomas's penchant for hyperbole. What becomes clear, even in the brief narrative, is Tom Carter's flair for assigning himself a starring role in historical dramas that gave him, in reality, only a bit part. For example, Lewis states that "In 1869 . . . [Thomas Carter] took charge of the construction of the road from Portland to Oregon City [the Oregon Central Railroad]."[12] In fact, the Oregon Central employed Thomas Carter as a draftsman, working under a master mechanic named John Carroll, who in turn worked under John Kidder, chief construction superintendent of the railroad.

Or, Lewis states that "Mr. Carter then built the road from Healdsburg to Donahue landing, constructing all bridges and rolling stock." In fact, in February 1872 Carter held the position of foreman of the car department under Superintendent Bean and remained with the San Francisco & North Pacific Railroad less than a year.[13]

Or, Lewis states that "in 1872, [Carter] secured contracts for building the bridges and rolling stock of the North Pacific Coast Railroad." But the fact was that Thomas Carter secured the contract for designing (not building) one bridge and for building the freight cars (not passenger cars) for the North Pacific Coast.

Lewis's exaggerations were not isolated examples. Reporters who interviewed Thomas Carter in the mid-1870s, when he was becoming an innovator in low-cost, on-site railroad manufacture, usually found him to be an innovator on behalf of his own reputation. On the Santa Cruz Rail Road project, for example, a reporter from the *Santa Cruz Sentinel* gratuitously identified Carter as "the Architect of the road"[14] following a conversation over a drafting table during the spring of 1874, on which the plans of the San Lorenzo River Bridge were painstakingly being inked. The job title, and its capitalization, may have been Carter's own invention. Less than six weeks later, he was gone from the project, failing to secure any contracts for new rolling stock.

The boasts continued, reflected in newspaper articles scattered over the next quarter century, usually attributed to Thomas (not Martin) and usually making inflated claims about his role in early California railroad development.

Thomas Carter, in short, created his own mythology. When he died in 1898, at the age of fifty-eight, the *San Francisco Call* saved the biggest exaggeration for his obituary. If Carter had stretched the truth during his lifetime, the *Call* took it beyond its elastic limit: "[Carter Brothers] is known from one end of the United States to the other. The cars of the Southern Pacific and Central Pacific Railroad are *nearly all* turned out of their workshops" (italics added).[15]

The latter accomplishment would truly have been a mythological feat, since Carter Brothers didn't come into existence until ten years after the Central Pacific was created by California's "Big Four": Leland Stanford, Collis Huntington, Mark Hopkins, and Charles Crocker. Much of the early rolling stock needed to equip the Central and Southern Pacific lines was home-built. Although some eastern car builders were used, the Big Four shunned independent, West Coast builders. Unless the year 1869 is counted (the single year in which Thomas and Martin labored as hourly carpenters in the Central Pacific's Sacramento shops—a fact not mentioned by Lewis), they weren't making large profits from selling their services or their products to the Big Four.

In fact, the Carter fortune ultimately came from a business backlash against the monopolistic practices of the Central and Southern Pacific Railroads, piecemealed from the investments of small, locally funded short lines seeking to break the monopoly's stranglehold on statewide transportation rates.

Tom Carter's real innovation was a simple plan to market railroad hardware to this fragmented, somewhat idealistically motivated business segment. He developed a cost-effective, time-effective alternative to eastern railroad suppliers. He built simple, lightweight railroad cars using local materials and local craftsmen, keeping transportation costs to a minimum by fabricating cars at the customer's site. Local construction translated to faster delivery. Lower costs translated to lower prices, in turn offering competitive advantages over eastern manufacturers.

The estimated ten thousand cars that Carter produced in its thirty-year lifetime paled in comparison to the production of industry giants such as Barney and Smith, Billmeyer and Small, or even the Central Pacific's own Sacramento shops. In 1878 alone, thirty-one thousand cars were built in the United States, the vast majority from established eastern firms.[16]

But the Carters created a marketing niche large enough—and focused enough—to sustain a small revolution in the normally conventional and tradition-bound railroad industry. They began with the premise that the narrow gauge movement, spreading across the United States in the early 1870s, was not an easy transplant to California. Far from its base of supply, seeking root in a state dominated by a single standard gauge railroad, the technology of narrow gauge railroading seemed specialized, immature, and experimental. But in a four-year period between 1873 and 1877, the Carters created a line of products and services that encouraged not one but six narrow gauge start-ups within California. In modern business language, the Carters "productized" narrow gauge railroads and worked diligently to brand their product to a wider audience. In a short time period, they engineered a product line of repeatable, sustainable quality and cost, the foundation of a new business.

The California narrow gauge movement was an overnight phenomenon that appeared to address, or redress, monopolistic conditions linked to complex societal ills ranging from racism to recession. It was perceived as a proactive, grassroots response from the same people the existing railroad monopoly disenfranchised. California's unique social problems, in other words, offered a built-in advertisement for Carter's narrow gauge products, giving Carter an audience, and ultimately a marketing strategy.

Small farming communities pooled scarce dollars to fund locally financed and locally controlled narrow gauge wheat haulers. Timber tracts in the Coast Range, considered too remote for a standard gauge railroad, were tapped with less expensive narrow gauge short lines. The same economics applied to such small communities as Nevada City, Grass Valley, and Santa Cruz, isolated by geography until local financing could afford (to use another modern term) the "connectivity" of narrow gauge railroads. From these isolated examples, Carter extracted the critical elements of a branding strategy, on the basis of common local interests and a more widespread distrust of the prevailing standard gauge market leader to serve them. Even in the 1890s, when the narrow gauge "movement" had run its course, Carter's business cards still signified "Special Attention given to Narrow Gauge Work," a combination of trademark, brand, and social identity.

In proportion, the family fortune, representing more than a million dollars in the probate of Thomas Carter's will alone,[17] offered proof that mythology and hard-edge business acumen merged without a visible parting line. Exaggeration, simply, could be good for business.

It was also good for the soul. To an emigrant whose culture had nearly vanished in a holocaust, the creation of a new personal history, one in which he became not only the survivor but the hero of his own stories, was the start of the path that led Thomas Carter away from early memories of Grosse Isle, and its aftermath.

Those who died on the coffin ships were often the lucky ones. Struggling for subsistence, "Irish emigrants were disproportionately concentrated in the lowest-paid, least-skilled, and most dangerous and insecure employment," wrote Kerby Miller in *Emigrants and Exiles*. They were also the victims of bigotry, discrimination, and greed. In the winter of 1851–52, railroad contractors in upstate New York ran newspaper advertisements for double the number of laborers they actually needed. Bringing their families in hope of finding employment, Irish laborers stood in long lines to apply for available positions, only to be turned away, first by the railroad and finally by the state militia, who drove destitute families into the maw of winter storms to die of starvation.[18]

Thomas Carter was eleven at the time, living perhaps less than a hundred miles away.

The Carters settled in Niagara Falls, Ontario, on the Canadian side of the famous cataracts, due west of the New York state line.[19] Thomas grew up over six feet tall, thin and angular—a patriarchal presence dramatized early on by a bib-length beard. A Carter family tradition has remembered Martin having bright red hair.[20] Thomas probably did as well. He chain-smoked and was not opposed to strong drink, habits that started young. Comfortable around tools, shops, and working men, he also cordoned off a space around himself in which to be alone with ideas. Thomas was an abstract thinker, a designer and a problem solver (the two Carter patents, filed in 1886, were both in Thomas's name[21]). It is doubtful that he had any formal schooling as a civil or mechanical engineer; the Lewis biography would probably have mentioned it.

His insularity kept others from knowing him. Thomas kept few close friends and was perceived by others as quiet, even aloof, not a joiner of political or social causes. A case in point was the rising passion for Irish nationalism. In the early 1850s, the eastern United States became a seedbed for the militant Fenian liberation movement, fomented among an Irish poor, alienated from their homeland and convinced that British policy had forced the exodus on them. Fenian "circles" raised money and bought arms during the 1860s. Recruitment of Irish into the Civil War extended military training to emigrants with Fenian leanings, equipping them to fight in some future, imagined war for Irish liberation.

But without a ticket home, much of the emigrant's anger found vent on U.S. soil. The most visible demonstration was the New York draft riot of 1863, when hoards of "strange, wretched, abandoned creatures . . . flocked out of their dens and lairs" to burn and loot, an unorganized reaction to poverty, prejudice, and unemployment by largely Irish emigrants.[22]

The draft riots may have horrified the Carters as much as the eastern establishment. Because of his family's background as tradesmen and their comparative financial security, the Carters were not good Fenian prospects. Thomas, surrounded by opportunities to be active in the movement during the American Civil War, kept his distance from the Fenians' California branch.

Instead, passion for self-reliance in business, disdain for politics, and a deep-seated fear of poverty ran like hidden veins through his character.

But the deeper frustrations of his family and countrymen, passed down from the horror of the exodus, surfaced in Thomas Carter's instincts for self-sufficiency and an even stronger, personal sense of moral outrage that, perhaps left to fester inside him, hunted for unknown targets.

Tom Carter's business instincts matured early. According to the Lewis biography, at the age of twenty he opened a small carriage manufactory across the Niagara River on the American side of the falls, at Suspension Bridge, New York.[23] Brother Martin, age sixteen at the time, joined him as an apprentice. Lewis dated the business venture from 1860, such an early date that it seems likely Thomas may have expanded, or perhaps transplanted, a business his father or older brother started.

In that year, Suspension Bridge had a population of nearly two thousand, a small commercial and industrial appendage to the larger, more famous city of Niagara Falls. The New York Central Railroad maintained a roundhouse, repair shop, and car shop in town, where the railroad manufactured its own rolling stock. The Carters had a ringside seat to a steady parade of changes in railroad technology—for example, introduction of the passenger car clerestory roof, seen on New York Central rolling stock for the first time in July 1860.[24] Sleeping cars equipped with the new "ventilated roof" were making the regular run between Albany and Niagara Falls.

"The Bridge," as the hamlet was known locally, was a showcase of new railroad technology. The town got its name from what it proudly claimed was the "greatest suspension bridge in the world," an 822-foot combination railroad and highway bridge opened in 1855 to link the New York Central Railroad with the Canadian Great Western Railway. Custom houses were established on both sides of the river, and across the bridge poured thousands of tons of Canadian-U.S. trade goods.

Multiple gauges and gauntlet track mark the portal to the New York Central & Hudson River Railroad's suspension bridge over the Niagara River, near Niagara Falls. [Top, Norris Pope Collection; bottom, Kyle Wyatt collection]

The bridge drew the curiosity, and sometimes skepticism, of a worldwide engineering community. At the time, it was the longest suspension bridge in the world. It cost half a million dollars and took three years to complete. Nine thousand miles of wire were woven into four primary cables, each ten and a half inches thick, capable of supporting more than twelve thousand tons.[25] A heavy freight train of the day, made up of a thirty-five-ton steam engine and eight loaded cattle cars, caused the structure to deflect just eight inches in the middle of the span. Its designer and builder, John A. Roebling, inspected the bridge in 1860,[26] the first year Carter lived in town. Carter might have watched the inspection and, perhaps fascinated by the novel technology, met him. Eight years later, Roebling would begin design work on the Brooklyn Bridge, and fourteen years later Carter would begin designing early railroad bridges in California.

Niagara Falls was a crossroads for travelers on Carter's career path. He may not have been aware that nine years before he opened his carriage works, Theodore Judah had settled in the embryonic town of Suspension Bridge, living in a house on the "ferry road" with his wife, Anna, during the period when Roebling's bridge was under construction. There, Judah hung out a shingle as a practicing civil engineer, his office located in his home.[27] It remains unproven, although likely, that Judah held a contract for a portion of the engineering work on Roebling's bridge.

In 1854, when Tom Carter was just fifteen, Judah moved on, hired to complete a survey for the first railroad in California, the Sacramento Valley.[28] He soon found additional work designing bridges for affiliated lines, work stemming from experience gained in the seminal bridge projects of Niagara Falls. On the basis of a growing reputation as a railroad engineer, Judah remained in California and in 1860 started work on a barometrical survey for a railroad location across the Sierra Nevada range. It is doubtful the Carters knew Judah, but it is more likely they knew engineers or railroad administrators whom Judah knew and worked with, a thread of relationships that may have led Tom Carter to follow Judah's westward footsteps.

Lester L. Robinson, one of the financiers behind the Sacramento Valley Railroad, had also come from upstate New York and like Judah was closely identified with California railroad projects in the mid-1850s. Judah, Robinson, or one of the growing circle of New York railroad engineers who knew them may have afforded a critical career link for Thomas Carter. In just two years, by the end of 1862, Carter would be working for the Sacramento Valley Railroad, reporting to a foreman named John Carroll. Although written seven years before Carter's arrival, a newspaper report on Carroll's activity emphasized the role that New York machinists played in staffing the railroad. The paper noted that car materials had "been landed at the foot of the R Street Levee, where the various parts are now being put together by machinists—brought out from New York for that purpose—under the supervision of the engineer, Mr. Judah."[29] Carroll and Carter's connection prior to the Sacramento Valley Railroad remains speculative, but at the start of the Civil War, with skilled mechanics in short supply, Carter's abilities would not have remained unattached for long.

We know little about the Carter carriage business itself. It was located "in the rear of Colt's Block" in Suspension Bridge, where Carter advertised his services as a wagon maker. Together, Thomas and Martin manufactured buggies, carriages, wagons, and sleighs from "the best of timber, iron &c."[30]

The small business required a necessary pairing of family talents. Tom's older brother, John, six years his senior and an experienced blacksmith, may have been closely involved, but he received no mention in the Lewis biography.

By contrast, Thomas was quick to acknowledge the role of Martin. The middle child in the family, Martin was diplomatic and socially outgoing. Red-haired, blue-eyed, and stocky, he stood almost six feet tall as an adult. Perhaps less conceptual and less creative than Thomas, Martin was the better taskmaster, and better suited to the drill of shop production work. Martin was probably the better manager, a role frequently eclipsed by the prominence, and later notoriety, of his older brother, Thomas. Later in life, Martin would look the part. His youngest son remembered Martin's daily attire for work in the Newark shop: starched white shirt, bow tie, suit coat, and bowler hat, worn routinely as the uniform of leadership over the shop's foreman and workmen.[31]

It would also be easier to see later in life that Martin was more accounted to community, family, and friends. He helped settle the fledgling town site of Newark by serving as its first postmaster. He helped raise money for the town's new schoolhouse. He rounded up a posse and performed a citizen's arrest when a would-be hijacker attempted a getaway on a railroad handcar. He got married, fathered three sons, cared for the aging parents of his wife, and provided foster care for the daughter of his deceased sister.

Thomas Carter never married and had no offspring. He was known for his fierce pride and combustible temper. He made enemies. He gravitated to the city, comfortable in the saloons of San Francisco's financial district, and seldom visited Martin at his country home across San Francisco Bay. Martin's youngest son remembered his uncle shared none of his father's fondness or feel for horses, or land, or country life.[32]

The passion in Thomas's life was a woman named Molly Redmond, whose temper matched his own and with whom he had a long and stormy affair that would propel him to public notoriety and scandal shortly before his death in 1898. The years magnified the differences between the two brothers and—perhaps rewarding patience, generosity, and a temperate attitude toward tobacco and alcohol—were kinder to Martin.

But at Suspension Bridge, Thomas and Martin Carter proved each was an indispensable part of a team. Thomas smelled the storms, read the compass. Thomas identified the markets, found capital, and weighed risks. Martin stayed in the engine room, firing the boilers. When Thomas's risks backfired, his brother picked up the pieces. Martin provided the family that Thomas himself never started, a safety net that more than once saved his older sibling from disaster. Falling from the pinnacle of his career after a disastrous wreck on the South Pacific Coast, a wreck for which he took substantial blame, Thomas Carter may have felt again—as he did in the passage from Ireland—that he had come out of, and would vanish into, catastrophe. A nameless anger, the legacy of the Irish exodus, may well have been directed at himself.

Following the wreck, the name of Carter Brothers disappeared from the San Francisco business directory for three years. It was a sign that Thomas had withdrawn from the car business, from railroading, perhaps from life— leaving Martin to manage the Newark car shops and keep the business alive while he struggled to pull himself back together. Thanks to Martin and perhaps also to Molly Redmond, the siblings emerged intact, still the Carter Brothers, when Thomas returned to lead the business through the enormously successful decade of the 1880s.

In the autumn of 1861, Thomas smelled the first of the storms gathering over the small, untested carriage business in Suspension Bridge. With the outbreak of the Civil War, emigrants in the industrial Northeast faced new pressures, not the gravest of which was a business recession. There were signs the war was already hurting similar businesses in Canadian Niagara

Falls, across the river, when the small car builder C. W. Pierson and Co. failed in February 1861. About the same time, the Canadian press recommended that Ontario businesses decline to accept U.S. treasury notes. A year later, the New York Central car shops at Suspension Bridge were closed and moved to Albany, further evidence that war jitters were affecting the economy of the entire region.[33]

There were also signs that Canada was growing edgy about the security of its border. In late December 1861, the Great Western Railway began demanding an oath of allegiance from is train crews, putting a number of its American employees (as well as American patrons) in an awkward position.[34] A month later, the Canadian War Department advertised for contractors to erect defensive earthworks along the Welland Canal, a commercial shipping artery that paralleled the impassable Niagara River about ten miles to the west. Canadian troop movements increased close to the border.

Initially, Niagara County itself had little trouble finding its share of volunteers for U.S. military service, and when the first national draft act took effect on November 1, 1862, the county stood forty-three recruits over its population-based quota.[35] No draft, as a result, would have to be enforced in the county.

Considerable recruitment effort had already taken place during the preceding eighteen months, with numerous Canadian nationals joining a volunteer company that departed Niagara Falls for Albany on May 4, 1861. The ethnic mix of the company was reported by the May 5 *Niagara Falls Gazette*. In spite of the difficulties of assimilation into the society at large, about 12 percent of the Niagara Company were Irish natives. In November, a recruitment effort was launched for an all-Irish brigade, with an office opened in the Union House in Niagara Falls. Signups, according to the *Gazette*, were steady.

But another stream of U.S.-Canadians had also formed, retreating back across the suspension bridge, convinced that staying could mean military impressment. New York assemblymen were writing legislation in the fall of 1861 that contained strong sanctions against fleeing military service across international borders.[36] Roebling's bridge, literally in Carter's back yard, was the only escape route into Canada for miles up and down the Niagara River. By summer, armed guards would be posted at the bridge to stop "skedaddlers."

Tom Carter sensed his options running out long before D Company of New York's 66th Infantry was posted at The Bridge. In December 1861, before the escape route was cut off, he took out a small advertisement in the *Gazette* (see figure).

In spite of the advertisement's patriotic undercoat, Thomas Carter had no intention of enlisting. After dissolving the small business at Suspension Bridge and making sure his brother Martin was safely across the Canadian border (employed at Clark's Carriage Works in Toronto), Thomas booked passage on a ship for California, by way of the Isthmus of Panama.

The Lewis biography reports his arrival in August 1862.

AUCTION !

Thomas Carter, Wagon Maker, of this place, being about to close out his business, and engage in his Country's Service, will offer an excellent opportunity to procure at auction a good Cutter, Wagon, Gig, &c., all of his own manufacture. We know what his work is, and can recommend it as being made from the best of timber, iron &c.

The sale will take place at his shop in the rear of Oblt's Block on Tuesday next, the 24th inst. at 10 o'clock. Be Wise in time !

Niagara Falls Gazette, December 1861.
[Niagara Falls Public Library]

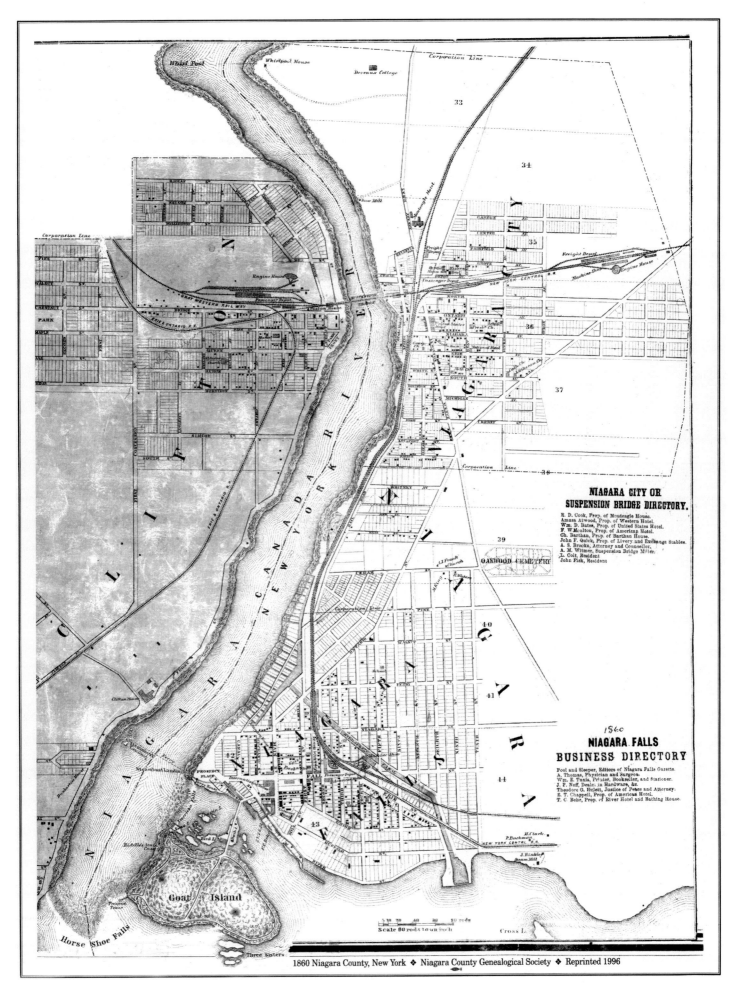

Map of Niagara Falls and Suspension Bridge (then called Niagara City), 1860. [Niagara County Genealogical Society]

San Francisco & San Jose Railroad, unidentified date and location; Eadweard Muybridge photograph. [Bancroft Library]

The "Railroadist"

When Thomas Carter was barely fifteen years old, living on the other side of the continent, John Ambrose Carroll began the industry that would eventually unite them. On July 4, 1856, Carroll noted briefly in his diary: "Wednesday. Very Pleasant. Built the Pioneer Car for California. That will be an Epoch in the History of California. Commenced Board at the National Serpentine."[1]

That day, Carroll laid out the sills of what he believed to be the first railroad car built in the new state of California.[2] Carroll was employed as master car builder for the Sacramento Valley Railroad, temporarily quartered near the Front Street levee in Sacramento, at the foot of R Street. There was no locomotive yet on the line. Except for the rails inside the sweltering shop, no track was laid. John Carroll had begun to assemble the first of three flatcars the Sacramento Valley needed to lay its track.

The materials that Carroll assembled had been shaped, drilled, and cut at a distant factory, components of what today would be called a kit. Carroll arranged the parts to form the car's skeleton, consisting of six long sills laid out on sawhorses like parallel joists in a deck. The sills had names. The two that lay on the outside edges of the skeleton were called *side sills*, thirty-foot-long beams of butter-colored oak, four inches across the top, an estimated ten inches in depth, cut close to the center of the tree.[3] The pair of sills in the middle of the skeleton were called *center sills*, or sometimes *draft sills*. The two remaining beams were called *intermediate sills*.

Like a "story stick" that carpenters traditionally used for locating cuts, gains, or drill-outs in a long beam, the side sill itself acted like a blueprint of the entire car. Spaced along the side sills, square holes, called *mortices*, were chiseled to a depth of about an inch and a half. Their position indicated where the tenons of cross beams would peg in, future supports for decking. *Gains* were located about a quarter of the distance from each end of the sill. These were open-sided mortice cuts, where two cross beams called *bolsters* would find a nesting place locked between the side sills. Like bridge piers, the bolsters were load-bearing members where the car wheels, assembled in a frame called a *truck*, would eventually pivot. Between them, the entire weight of the flatcar, and its load, would be carried over open air by the strength of the frame alone.

The entire assembly was designed much like a bridge. Two side sills, laid

A car frame traditionally consisted of either four or six parallel beams, or sills, running lengthwise, named in pairs (*side sills* on the outside, next *intermediate sills*, and in the middle the *center* or *draft sills*). Two *end sills* enclosed the frame like a box, while two *bolsters* sat crosswise on the frame about a quarter of the way in from each end, acting as attachment points for the car's trucks. *Cross-framing*, or *blocking*, could be added to the frame at the midpoints.

Numerous carpentry techniques existed for joining these elements tightly together. *Mortice and tenon joints* acted like square pegs in square holes, joining (for example) a side sill to an end sill in a form of post-and-beam construction. A bolster could be *gained* into the sill —in other words, keyed into it with a shallow, open-sided notch. A partial gain, where a bolster would nest into a side sill, might be called a *let-in* or sometimes a *rabbet*. All these joining techniques ultimately traded some volume of solid wood for a degree of interlocking, a tradeoff that a good car builder knew how to balance without sacrificing the strength of the finished design.

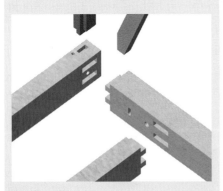

Mortice and tenon joint, as applied to frame members in a South Pacific Coast 28-foot boxcar. [Curtis Ferrington]

out as a mirror image of each other, would clamp together four interior sills, two bolsters, two end beams, and the assortment of blocks and cross beams required to keep the sills parallel. Squeezed tightly together by the compression of a series of threaded iron rods, the sills would support the car the same way a bridge supported the weight of a wagon.

Like a bridge, the design of a railroad car used principles of static engineering that had been understood, and trusted, for thousands of years. Too many mortices chiseled into the side sill would leave cavities like termite dens, eating away the integrity of the beam itself, negating its value as a structural backbone. Too few mortices would limit the number of cross timbers that could be locked into the side sill, eliminating ribs needed to support decking. There were subtleties to a good design. Side sills were often designed larger than necessary, not just to resist the hogging forces of gravity but simply to ensure that tenons cut in the ends would be large enough not to break. The reverse logic applied to end sills, which had to contain enough meat to remain structurally sound after twelve deep mortice cuts were hollowed out to accept the tenons of the side sills.

Car builders practiced many of the same tricks that bridge builders practiced. They placed the *crown* of the sills up, so their natural bow would help the structure resist gravity. They often adapted, in detail, the earlier design work of bridge engineers. Boxcar wall construction, for example, used a modified Pratt or Howe truss design favored by bridge builders.[4]

But unlike bridges of the day, the wooden structure of a flatcar was designed to withstand dynamic stress. *Torsioning*, forced on the rolling car by curves or uneven track, twisted the frame by trying to rotate the ends in opposition. The effect can be understood by extending two fingers from each hand until they touch. When your hands are slowly rotated in opposite directions, the fingers twist in the same way the sills undergo torsion in a moving railroad car. To flex in this fashion, the frame cannot be rigid. The concept of mortice and tenon joints was adapted to railroad car construction from early wagon and carriage manufacture, intended to allow the wooden frame members to experience torsion without fracturing the joints that connected them.

Paradoxically, the parts would have to fit together tightly to ensure that the overall design remains flexible. Violin makers understand the relationship well. Individual parts of a violin are bonded together so the ensemble can vibrate coherently, as a unit. One poorly glued part can cause the case to become discordant, the instrument rendered permanently out of tune. Analogously, a moving flatcar with tightly fitted mortice and tenon joints held under compression by truss rods behaved something like a musical instrument, its members vibrating complementarily. Thus chafing between parts was minimized; wear was spread out more evenly; and unwanted vibration, when the finished car was placed in motion, was reduced.

On sawhorses, John Carroll laid the precut sills next to each other and checked for the accuracy of the layout. Their original manufacturer, probably a Massachusetts car builder named Davenport and Bridges, had taken steps to be sure the parts they had manufactured would fit together after some two hundred days in transit by sailing ship and river schooner.[5] Davenport and Bridges craftsmen, for example, probably painted or primed the sills, preventing the fresh-cut beams from drying out too rapidly and then splitting, or *checking*, during transit. Carroll painstakingly examined the workmanship. He checked the location of holes, gains, and mortices, sometimes cleaning burrs with a rasp, or shaving the chamfer of a tenon with a sharp chisel, allowing its snug insertion into a mortice.

Apparently, the parts fit tightly together. John Carroll completed the car frames and set them on their wheels in six working days. On July 9, according to his diary, he "ran out" three new cars into the blistering Sacramento sun and directed his hardworking shop crew to start work on the boxcars.

<hr />

It is possible Carroll left Davenport and Bridges as its field representative, chaperoning the car kits on their long journey from the East Coast.[6] Loaded onto the clipper ships *Winged Racer* and *Dashing Wave* in February and March 1855, the kits (and a locomotive) sailed from Boston harbor on the arduous four-month ocean journey around Cape Horn.

Carroll's diaries began on May 3, 1855, when he left Boston for California via a shorter route across the Isthmus of Panama. On June 7, slightly over a month after he embarked, Carroll arrived in San Francisco just ahead of the *Winged Racer*, allowing him to supervise unloading of the parts from the two clippers. Three more weeks were consumed in shuttling the parts to Sacramento on a brigade of schooners, among them the *Eagle, Joseph Neswith, A. R. Forbes,* and *Two Brothers.* Each vessel discharged parts at the R and Front streets wharf on the Sacramento levee, adding to the growing stockpile. From these materials, Carroll and his crew would fashion the Sacramento Valley Railroad.

Perhaps intending to return to Boston after assembling the rolling stock, Carroll soon received a more attractive offer. By mid-July, he was filling a permanent position as the Sacramento Valley's car shop foreman. In this role, he used his diary as a timebook, recording the hours he and his crew spent on dozens of individual carpentry projects, many having nothing to do with cars. On July 19, for example, the diary reported that brothers O. H. and Charles Taylor began work on the R Street water tank.

By July 26, Carroll noted that mechanic Ben Welch (who, eight years later, became the master car builder for the Central Pacific) was running a small truck assembly crew. Soon Welch would be specializing in making the railroad's wooden patterns.

The diaries chronicle hardships as well as progress. On July 26, a carpenter named Earl Lawyer fell and hurt himself and was unable to assist the Taylor brothers for several days. His help was sorely missed. Few skilled mechanics were available on the West Coast, virtually none of them with railroad experience.

Far from home and family, John Carroll had left Boston to put together the essential elements of what was probably the first railroad shop on the Pacific Coast, comprising tools, materials, and a skilled crew. Under primitive conditions, the new facility would have to maintain and protect the premium investment the railroad had made in its relatively small fleet of rolling

The Field Notebook: The Inbound and Outbound "Supply Chain"

A factory receives raw materials from its *inbound supply chain* and ships finished goods (as well as replacement parts) through its *outbound supply chain* to the customer. The eight thousand miles of ocean that separated the East Coast from California represented, in 1855, an unusually long outbound supply chain. Typically 120 days away from their West Coast destinations, eastern-manufactured goods such as locomotives and cars grew increasingly costly not because of the labor and materials required to make them but because of the cost to ship finished goods to the customer. As much as 25 percent of the final cost of such goods could be consumed by their transport.

These conditions quickly gave rise to localization of California's railroad industry. However, new West Coast industries, though close to their customers, faced the opposite problem of being far away from sources of raw materials. The length of the inbound supply chain thus increased, also raising the cost of finished goods. An example was the San Francisco iron industry, which (by the mid-1860s) was purchasing scrap iron from Britain to create such products as rail for West Coast customers. This example suggests a fourteen-thousand-mile inbound supply chain—an extreme case. In general, the trend was toward localized manufacturing, shortening the outbound supply chain and in effect creating local skills and jobs in response to local demand.

The 1859 Wason "kit" passenger cars, built for the California Central Railroad, were described as 41'6" long and carrying sixty passengers. They cost $4,000 each. Even though the kits came from Massachusetts, it is interesting that they incorporated local, California-sourced redwood, probably used for "deafening ceiling" (actually a subfloor). Perhaps resembling the kits of Davenport and Bridges, their design was detailed in the *Sacramento Bee* of Aug. 13, 1861:

> The outside panels are of white wood, laid perpendicularly, to avoid absorption and expansion, and lined with heavy canvas, glued on and painted to exclude dust. For the later [latter] purpose, there are also two floors . . . the under one of California redwood, and the upper one of Georgia pine, one inch and a quarter thick. The truck frames are of oak of massive size, and thoroughly bolted and strengthened. They rest on wrought iron axles and eight double plate wheels of Mason [sic] & Co's patent. Each pair of wheels and axle weigh thirteen hundred pounds. The inside paneling below the windows is of oak and walnut; the upper part of the window frames and blinds of curled maple, cherry, bay, mahogany and rosewoods, and heavy guilt moldings and cornices. The ceiling is of enameled cloth, of neat color and pattern. The seats, with revolving backs and cushions, are covered in crimson plush. Each car has three ventilators, and will be lighted by two large brass lamps. Outside, the cars will be painted a light straw color; inside, the wood will be painted and varnished only.

stock. Of $400,000 spent for the railroad's cars and locomotives, $100,000 was spent in getting it all to California.[7] Far from supporting railroad supply houses, or even a neighboring railroad, Carroll would have to assemble and maintain the equipment in an industrial vacuum.

The kit strategy of Davenport and Bridges became crucial to Carroll's achievement. He built the rolling stock from prefabricated components, shipped disassembled in the holds of the clippers *Winged Racer* and *Dashing Wave*. When the *Dashing Wave* arrived on June 20, the *San Francisco Herald* presented a partial listing of the assortment of parts, subassemblies, and crates that made up the car kits: "100 car wheels, 32 car axles, 24 car doors, 32 car steps, 3 car bodies, 6 pairs of wheels, 2095 pcs 287 bdls car stock. . . . "

On August 6, Carroll began to assemble a portion of these parts into the line's first passenger car, a fourteen-window, forty-foot-long, arch-roofed coach. Clearly, a kit design that relied on subassemblies, not just individual component parts, made the work easier. Historian Wendell Huffman has pointed out, however, that the largest physical dimension of any kit component was severely limited by the size of a ship's hold and hatches. A locomotive boiler, stripped of its running gear, was the biggest physical item reported in known shipping manifests.[8] Similarly, cars were broken down into shippable components. In the *Herald* article, "3 car bodies" probably represented partially assembled walls and frames of passenger cars, while "2095 pcs . . . car stock" represented individually milled pieces of eastern oak, the components of freight car frames and walls, shipped on pallets or in crates.

Carroll organized these parts, tooling, and workmen into a small but efficient assembly process. On July 4, the same day he noted completion of the first flatcar at the R Street shop, the *Sacramento Union* wrote:

> Within the past few days the contractors of the Sacramento Valley Railroad have received nearly one hundred thousand dollars worth of the rolling stock for the road. It has been landed at the foot of the R Street Levee, where the various parts are now being put together by machinists—brought out from New York for that purpose—under the supervision of the engineer, Mr. Judah. They have the parts, including frames, woodwork, seats, &c., for putting up forty freight cars, six passenger, and two baggage cars. . . . A large shed building has been erected, under which the workmen are now putting together the cars. The wheels, axles, boxes, &c. make a pile which is well worth a walk to R Street to see.

Carroll quickly became educated on the drawbacks of remote suppliers. Coach number 1 was the first passenger car completed at the R Street shops. Within a year of its assembly, the car grew an unwanted "sowbelly," visibly sagging under its own weight. With little possibility of asking the factory for warranty repairs, Carroll began pulling the siding off the coach on June 16, 1856. On July 11, he described the installation of "30'8" long braces."

A "brace" could refer to an auxiliary wall truss, or possibly a truss plank, installed to stiffen the original design.

By the last week in August, the R Street shops had retrofitted all the coaches in the same way. In the process, John Carroll had acquired skills in reengineering wooden cars.

Historic "firsts" seem to occur regularly in Carroll's diary. On August 8, 1855, the first ties were set in place on the freshly graded Sacramento Valley mainline. On August 12, the first rails, enough to lay five hundred feet of track, were spiked to the ties at Third and R streets, gauged to three and a half inches wider than conventional standard gauge.

That afternoon, John Carroll; the construction contractor, Lester Robinson; and Chief Engineer Theodore Dehone Judah poled themselves over the new track on a push car, the first passengers on the line. Carroll noted simply: "afternoon, had a ride on the railroad."

The "first" that Carroll claimed on August 17, the steam-up of the locomotive *Sacramento*, may have been an exaggeration: "Friday 11½ o'clock the iron horse drew breath for the first time in California. Wrote letter to my wife." In fact, a Boston-built 4-4-0 had been in the state since 1850, imported to assist in filling in parts of San Francisco Bay.[9]

Ransom Bishop faced a similar problem with the line's new locomotives to what Carroll faced with its rolling stock. A close friend who had accompanied Carroll on the steamer from Boston, Bishop reported for duty as master mechanic for the Sacramento Valley Railroad the same week Carroll became resident car shop foreman. In the weeks preceding the steam-up of the *Sacramento*, Bishop worked without factory representatives to set up the locomotive's side rods and bearings.

The first railroad insolvency in California, however, was an unwelcome entry in Carroll's diary. News of a run on eastern banks reached San Francisco by steamer on February 17, 1855, and one day later the threat of scarce credit crippled several San Francisco banks. One of them held large deposits for the Sacramento Valley's construction, extended to Charles Wilson, the principal backer and president of the railroad. In the wake of the panic, Wilson resigned. Carroll, aware of the trouble, felt the organization crumbling around him.

By the following fall, the railroad could no longer meet its obligations to contractors Lester and James Robinson. Carroll was trying to complete a baggage car while rumors of bankruptcy circulated among the employees. "Things look dark," Carroll wrote on October 5. "The cloud must burst soon." On October 6, Carroll suspended work in his shop and furloughed his crew. A week later, Lester and James Robinson suspended work on the railroad and filed a breach of contract suit in the U.S. Circuit Court. Powerless to raise additional funds, the board agreed to execute a deed of trust to the Robinsons, a banker named J. Mora Moss acting as trustee, in effect giving the Robinsons financial control of the railroad.

In spite of Carroll's pessimism, Lester Robinson quickly won the foreman's confidence, perhaps with stories of his own younger days as a car builder in Canada. A friendship was created. New capital (in the form of a $750,000 loan Moss arranged through the bank of Pioche, Bayerque) eased the road's cash flow problems but increased its debt. By New Year's, Carroll was back at work on the line's fifth passenger car.

New firsts continued in Carroll's diary. On January 14, 1856, he directed construction of the first turntable in California, located at the Sacramento R Street terminal, and framed an identical table to be installed at Folsom once the mainline was finished (an event that occurred a month later). The first locomotive was turned at Folsom on February 20. The line opened for business on February 22—followed nine days later by the first derailment when the locomotive *Nevada* hit a steer, damaging passenger car number 4 slightly and damaging the steer beyond repair.

Even with derailment, fatality, and insolvency all occurring in the opening months of the Sacramento Valley Railroad, John Ambrose Carroll viewed the enterprise with pride and keen awareness of his pioneering role. On February 20, 1856, he wrote in his diary: "Mr. Moss and Robinson . . . highly pleased with performance. In after years . . . my descendants can say my father or grandfather built the first car and first turntable in California."

John Carroll was thirty-one years old when he started the diary. His entries were made by oil lamp in his room at the Serpentine House, a room-and-board establishment in Sacramento. His wife, Mary, and daughter were still in Boston, and he wrote openly of missing them, especially on Sunday and especially in winter: "Feb 22, 1855: Sunday. This is a most delightful day. I wish I could enjoy it as I should like but always I cannot. Time which sets all things . . . I must abideth thy time."

The diary often mentioned the letters he sent Mary, and letters received from her, but ironically it made no mention of his wife and daughter's arrival in California. The entries grew noticeably shorter, though, in 1858 and ceased altogether by 1860, an indication that the Carrolls were safely reunited in California before the start of the Civil War.

The U.S. census revealed that in 1860 John Carroll reported $2,000 in real estate assets and $3,000 in savings, the resources of a successful craftsman. When the *Sacramento Union* published personal incomes for the year 1865, Carroll's reported $1,268 actually represented a salary in excess of $2,000, since "$600 for family expenses, and also the actual amount of house-rent paid" was deducted before publication of the net.[10]

Carroll's census listing as "carpenter" did not entirely do him justice. To borrow a term that would become popular in the 1870s, John Carroll could better be described as a "railroadist": a general practitioner who combined the design skills of a mechanical engineer, the practical knowledge of a shop foreman, and the risk taking of an entrepreneur. A little like the notion of a renaissance man, the role owed its uniquely western character first to the extreme length of the railroad supply chain and second to the vision of a few individuals who could specify, purchase, set up, and maintain railroad hardware at locations far outside the normal service areas of established East Coast suppliers.

Perhaps Carroll owed his broad portfolio of skills to his association with Davenport and Bridges. Charles Davenport, a principal in the firm, was responsible for influential patents in American railroad truck design, including metal side frames and swing motion.[11] Davenport and Bridges was also an innovator in rolling stock manufacturing, pioneering the kit manufacturing process in early exports of rolling stock to Cuba.[12] The shipments, taking place in the mid-1840s, were warm-up exercises for the long, complex export of products to California some ten years later.

On the Sacramento Valley, Carroll was quickly identified as an innovator and inventor. Just five years after he began work in Folsom, he was credited with inventing a "self adjusting railroad safety switch," designed to align turnouts with cams tripped by an approaching locomotive. The invention was successfully tested on the Sacramento Valley in January 1861.[13] As mentioned, he improved the structural integrity of cars originally purchased as kits, perhaps from firsthand knowledge of Davenport and Bridge's original designs.

Carroll, and the Sacramento Valley Railroad, prospered. Another daughter and a son were born to the family prior to 1860. John Carroll settled into what were probably the happiest years of his life.

Folsom had become an ideal place to raise a family. Laid out by Theodore Judah as a real estate speculation in 1855, the town had a population of just five hundred souls at the outbreak of the Civil War. The *Folsom Telegraph* liked to satirize the town's modest size[14]: "A fierce dog fight took place on last Sunday afternoon, which intellectual entertainment was attended by a congregation of less than 10,000 people, on Sutter St."

The depot acted as the center of the village and featured an ice cream concession named the Ladies and Gentlemen Refreshment Saloon, helping to balance the alcoholic influence of the Folsom Lager Beer Brewery next door. At the same intersection, the Patterson House, run by Mrs. H. D. Waddilove, was the best hotel in town as well as its social hub, the scene of Christmas parties, railroad shop parties, and meetings of the Fenian Brotherhood, an increasingly militant movement for Irish independence.

At Patterson's, discussions mirrored the political and economic crosscurrents that churned through antebellum California. Barroom grumbling on the topic of mining was normal. Surface (or placer) mining had given way to expensive, deep-rock mining. The flinty independence of the "honest miner" had been replaced by the increasingly complex, sinister presence of corporations, in turn thrusting such capital-intensifying businesses as banks and railroads into the forefront of mining development. California's early dislike of monopoly was a reaction to the tensions between individual and corporation. The Robinson brothers' principal backer, the French bank of Pioche, Bayerque, had provoked outrage in San Francisco when it tried to wrest legal control of the city's inner harbor.

Three times between 1854 and 1856, the bank's treasurer, J. Mora Moss, had tried to ramrod "Parson's Bulkhead Bill" through the state assembly. The bill would have given Pioche, Bayerque a monopoly on wharf rates in the state's largest commercial port. Closely allied with the state's Democrats, Moss and the Robinson brothers had all been tarred with the "Bulkhead" brush and were clearly villains in speeches by the leaders of the emerging California Republican Party, Leland Stanford foremost among them. The Republicans soon became a voice for populist, liberal stands, attacking what today would be called special interests. The bank of Pioche, Bayerque easily made the Republicans' list of social cancers.

Closely tied to Pioche, Bayerque, the Robinson brothers could not escape the political overtones of Republican attack. When Monsieur Bayerque died in 1865, Lester Robinson was named bank director—working his way higher on the list of Republican enemies. California railroad development began to exhibit political as well as regional polarity. If the Democrats coined votes from owning railroads, the Republicans would construct a mint of their own.

But viewed from the perspective of the small, isolated Sacramento Valley Railroad, politics was the least of the Robinsons' worries. Day by day, the railroad struggled for a niche in the transportation trade. Only twenty miles long, the Sacramento Valley hardly claimed a monopoly on freighting to the mines. Teamsters joked they could keep freight on board their wagons from such mining towns as Nevada City, Placerville, Georgetown, and Forest Hill, beating the Sacramento Valley Railroad's rates and its trains to the docks in Sacramento.

Saddled with 30 percent interest on top of the floating debt, the Robinsons needed a practical financial strategy to survive. A new board member, William Ralston, brought banking and investment experience to the short line in 1857. In 1858, the sv's founder, Charles Lincoln Wilson, reentered the picture, financing construction of the California Central Railroad from Folsom north toward the small foothill village that would bear his middle name. The California Central's rails reached their terminal at Lincoln in October 1861, expanding the Sacramento Valley's service area.[15]

Wilson championed the "hub" concept. Using Sacramento Valley Railroad facilities at Folsom, the CCRR would intersect numerous east-west wagon roads coming down from the mining camps, acting as a feeder to the original Sacramento Valley Railroad. In exchange for maintenance and terminal facilities at Folsom, the Robinsons would benefit from an injection of California Central traffic. Still apparently working for Wilson, Theodore Judah surveyed rail routes from the California Central to eastern points in the foothills (for example, Auburn), adding potential east-west spokes to the Folsom hub.

But Judah was working for no one but Judah. A visionary without capital, he schemed to control one of the new spokes himself. A letter written in Judah's hand, entitled "What I Want," detailed loans and terms Judah would need to pay the balance on an $18,000 promissory note he had signed for rail delivered from the New York–based Rensselaer Iron Co. The rail was delivered to San Francisco but held by forwarding agent William Coleman until Judah could settle the balance. There was enough rail in the lot to build the Eastern Extension Railroad, Judah's projected bridge line connecting the California Central with Auburn.[16] But Judah speculated on a shoestring. When he couldn't come up with the cash, the bank of Pioche, Bayerque paid off Coleman's note and used Judah's rails to build the Sacramento, Placer & Nevada Railroad, creating its own bridge line to the foothills.

Frustrated, Judah expanded his search for backing. By 1860, the surveyor was publicly advertising his own contracting business, openly looking for financial support while maintaining the cover of "freight solicitor" for the patient Robinson brothers. In interviews published in the *Sacramento Union*, Judah talked vigorously of extending the reach of the foothill short lines over the High Sierra, the most difficult link in a transcontinental railroad. Republicans, beginning to win office on the promise of protecting California with such a railroad, began to listen to Judah.

Just days after the first major West Coast Republican victory (the election of Oregon Sen. Edward "Ned" Baker, in November 1860), Judah moved quickly to curry Republican favor. He had just completed his first barometric survey of what was then called Truckee, now Donner Pass. One week after Baker's election, Judah gave the senator a copy of the completed maps to take to Washington. Along with the survey, Judah had also crafted an early draft of the articles of incorporation for the Central Pacific Railroad, putting together both the geographical and business parameters of the future transcontinental entity.[17] Judah handed the Republican Party its political coin.

Acutely aware of Judah's movements in the Sierra Nevada range, the Robinsons began to view the surveyor with increasing distrust, frequently writing to Moss of Judah's whereabouts.[18] While Judah grew preoccupied with the Donner Pass survey, the Bank of Pioche, Bayerque began its first tentative steps toward locating a competing railroad over Johnson Pass, following the main commercial artery between Sacramento and the Comstock mines. Pioche, Bayerque hired William J. Lewis and Francis Bishop as location engineers. Lewis, in particular, had earned commendation for the earliest railroad surveys in the state, including, by 1862, the routes of the San Francisco & San Jose and the Western Pacific.

Lewis's hiring was intended as a warning shot across Judah's bow. The Bank of Pioche, Bayerque had found a civil engineer with more local credibility than Judah, threatening a long and protracted battle for California's transcontinental gateway. Lewis and Bishop, in turn, hired a little-known field assistant named John Flint Kidder to drive location work, soon positioning Pioche, Bayerque with the technical ability to start construction ahead of the Central Pacific.[19]

The resulting Placerville & Sacramento Valley Railroad began construction at Folsom in 1862, grading its line southeast toward Placerville, aiming for the summit of Johnson Pass beyond. The P&SV was the most technically difficult and expensive of the railroads off the Folsom hub; despite the nearly steady flow of Virginia City mining traffic along the route, progress was painfully slow. By November 1863, only eight miles of the route were graded. Bishop's location of a four-mile tunnel through the summit of the Sierra was announced in the summer of 1864, which guaranteed that the project would become costly.[20]

By 1862, four short lines—the California Central; the Placerville & Sacramento Valley; the Sacramento, Placer & Nevada; and the original Sacramento Valley Railroad—all grew into spokes off the Folsom hub, and the town's railroad shops were hard pressed to build and repair the rolling stock needed to support the expansion.

Carroll's diary was nearing its conclusion when Lewis began his reconnaissance of Johnson Pass; it offers little insight into the aggressive movement that Pioche, Bayerque took toward surveying a Sierra Nevada crossing. But it is clear that Carroll played a critical role in developing the support system the Robinsons would require to maintain a fleet of new rolling stock. In 1861, during construction of a complete new shop facility in Folsom, Carroll designed a new pattern works, iron foundry, blacksmith shop, machine shop, car shop, and paint shop, the only examples of their distinct railroad crafts in the western United States.

To run them, Carroll needed help badly. In 1862, "Uncle" Ben Welch, one of his most talented woodworkers, quit to take a job on the San Francisco & San Jose Railroad, which was finally under construction along the route of Lewis's early survey. Carroll's friend Ransom Bishop left the Sacramento Valley Railroad in 1865 to become the SF&SJ's master mechanic.

At the height of the expansion, the same year Ben Welch left, Thomas Carter went to work for Carroll as a shop carpenter. Lester Robinson probably liked the fact that both he and Carter had lived and worked in upstate New

York as carpenters, and he took an interest in the young emigrant. Carter was twenty-three, far from home, and single. He boarded at the Patterson House, just across from the shops. His income can be estimated, from a tax assessment in the *Sacramento Union,* as a modest $1,000 per year.[21] The fact that his income was listed at all was a signature of permanent employment and a recognized role in the community.

Even so, for the next three years, till 1866, Carter remained anonymous in the pages of the *Folsom Telegraph.* The Fenian Brotherhood continued to grow in strength and visibility, holding benefit dances in the Folsom Catholic Church, but Carter's name appeared nowhere in its list of organizers.

The shops, by contrast, could easily have laid claim to all of Carter's time. Situated on the steep bluffs of the American River, the facility and surrounding village of Folsom dramatically recreated Carter's home town on the Niagara River, complete with an enormous railroad bridge. The 213-foot, Hall-style truss spanning the American River was designed by Theodore Judah for the new California Central Railroad and completed in 1859 (see pages 34–35). The longest railroad bridge in California at the time of its construction, it was already undergoing major retrofits just one year after Carter arrived, repairs aimed at fixing an embarrassing and potentially dangerous sag. Carter could walk to the bridge, just a quarter mile from the shops, and watch the work. In fact, as part of the carpentry crew, it is likely he participated in its repair.[22]

The Folsom car and machine shop crews now supported four railroads, three of which were under construction. Carter's hiring was symptomatic of the new pressures on the shop, and a sign of accelerating spending. Justifiably, the Robinsons were beginning to get nervous about the financial footing of the P&SV. By late 1862, Charles Wilson was in financial trouble again, this time over repayment of California Central Railroad loans for its rolling stock.

The Robinsons were also getting nervous about the Central Pacific. By 1860, Theodore Judah had forged a partnership with new Republican Senator Baker and begun to craft an elaborate political framework that would become the Pacific Railroad Act. Election of the first Republican president, Abraham Lincoln, ensured the passage of the act in July 1862. It added a critical new railroad network to the Union's war strategy. But it also was living proof of a new alignment between Judah and West Coast Republicans Leland Stanford, Collis Huntington, Charles and E. B. Crocker, and Mark Hopkins.

As governor of California, Stanford shoveled the first earth for the Central Pacific not far from the Sacramento Valley's terminus on Front Street. The final location stakes for the Central Pacific, driven into valley soil by Judah during the summer of 1861, were quickly followed by advancing rail, laid from Front Street toward Auburn, deep into the Robinsons' turf.[23]

Downtown Sacramento became a battleground between the two competitors. In April 1864, the city's board of trustees yielded to pressure from the majority Republicans to enforce a "level grade" ordinance on the Sacramento Valley's Front Street terminal track. Condemning the exposed rails of the SV as a hazard to wagons, the board of trustees ordered the track

Companion views of truss bridge, designed by Theodore Judah, over the American River at Folsom, on the California Central Railroad; by the time of these Thomas Houseworth photographs, taken prior to 1872, the poorly designed bridge had already developed a visible sag. [Both views, Society of California Pioneers]

summarily torn up from P to K streets. "The rails and ties now lie scattered in a confused manner along the desolated route," the *Sacramento Union* reported on April 25.

The same month, the Central Pacific's rails reached and crossed those of the California Central within the city limits of today's Roseville. In one stroke, the California Central's feeder business to Folsom was diverted down the shorter path of the Central Pacific, robbing the Folsom hub of one of its three spokes.

The Robinson lawyers retaliated. In July, a court injunction ordered the Sacramento Valley's rails restored to the Front Street levee. After the track was rebuilt, trains of both the Central Pacific and the sv boarded within a few yards of each other at the foot of K Street, giving the battle the look of a stalemate.

But the Robinsons' strategic position was being slowly undermined. In June, courts foreclosed against Charles Wilson's unpaid debt, clearing the

way for sale of collateral, the California Central's rolling stock. For an attractive price, the principal creditors sold their notes to the Central Pacific Railroad on November 10.[24] The Central Pacific did not foreclose on the unpaid debt, but with its rolling stock held hostage Stanford had virtually neutralized the competitive threat of the California Central. Its giant bridge across the American River at Folsom continued to sag at midspan, a sad relic of the defeat.

Traffic volume on the Placerville spoke had steadily increased on the strength of freight for the Comstock mines, including a fifteen-foot-diameter cast iron cog wheel that traveled by flatcar on September 26, 1865. Business through the Folsom hub actually grew. A Folsom quarry began shipments of granite block via the Sacramento Valley Railroad during the same summer, destined for construction of Fort Winfield Scott at Fort Point in San Francisco. Three daily trains ran from Folsom to Latrobe, the line's temporary terminal. The SV's steam engines were already logging more than 160 miles in a single working day, and as winter approached, its threatened blockage of Johnson Pass increased pressure on the Sacramento Valley to deliver a stockpile of goods to the Latrobe railhead.[25]

Risk to the Folsom operating crews was also growing. Sometime during the week of June 10, conductor Richard Thomas was caught and crushed between two cars at Latrobe, and badly injured.[26]

Stress on the Folsom shop grew in kind. By the summer of 1865, there were seven belt-driven lathes operating in the machine shop, a complete foundry, a blacksmith shop, and a paint shop, busily engaged in manufacturing new rolling stock.[27] "The railroad is doing an immense freight business, every day running short of freight cars," the *Folsom Telegraph* wrote in summarizing the plight.

With the Civil War interfering with delivery of eastern car kits, John Carroll was forced to build new rolling stock from scratch. For the first time, he may have tapped supplies of West Coast Douglas fir to fabricate car sills, and redwood from which to mill siding. He felt new freedom to adapt old kit designs to new materials. That fall, plans were in the works for additional coaches for the Placerville extension, scheduled for completion in Carroll's shop over the winter.

Distracted by the pressures on the shop, Carroll had little warning of the Robinsons' unconditional surrender. On August 12, 1865, at the height of the shop buildup, the Central Pacific's management announced the purchase of the Sacramento Valley Railroad. Stanford had paid the railroad's bond holders and creditors, the Robinsons among them, a reported $300,000 to throw the game and get out.[28] Carroll, a close friend of the Robinsons, was stunned. On top of the personal loss came a professional loss. Carroll was suddenly working for a larger organization, whose own master car builder, Ben Welch, had been Carroll's employee just three years before. Carroll would now be taking orders from his former employee.

The Central Pacific, not the Sacramento Valley, would now dictate the gauge of the Robinsons' entire network. The Sacramento Valley, the California Central, and the P&SV, all five-foot-gauge lines, would have to convert not only their track but all their rolling stock to match the Central Pacific's 4'8½" gauge.

Ironically, it was Carroll who ran the superior shop facility. The Central Pacific's only shop was housed in a temporary 20' × 150' shed, hastily erected in its Sacramento yard in 1863. The crude facility employed just ten full-time mechanics. It was slated for replacement with permanent brick structures sometime after the railroad secured government subsidies, and Welch accepted the fact that in the meantime he would have to tailor his support services to the facility that housed them. For example, the Central Pacific's first rolling stock was delivered in the form of kits from eastern manufacturers. In March 1864, the kits were assembled in the temporary shop without the need for car manufacturing machinery. Although the prefab cars got trains rolling quickly, the kit strategy contributed to delay in constructing a mechanized car shop. The delay lasted five years.

Standard gauging the Folsom short lines meant not only a seamless exchange of cars and freight but also direct access for the Central Pacific to the fully equipped Folsom backshops. It was a prize worthy of note by the CP's directorate. Mark Hopkins wrote to Collis Huntington on February 21, 1866, that "Wilson's track is changed [regauged] from Lincoln to the Junction and nearly completed to Folsom, and enough of the rolling stock is changed for present purposes and will all soon be changed. What they couldn't do themselves has been done in *our* Folsom shops" (italics added).[29]

Until its own Sacramento shop complex could be expanded, the CP counted on the Folsom shops to do much of its major repair and erection work. Regauging the Robinsons' rolling stock began in earnest in the late fall of 1865, and the work fell squarely on the Folsom shop. The decision apparently interrupted a number of Carroll's projects. On January 8, 1866, the *Folsom Telegraph* reported that "a splendid new passenger car has just been finished in the Sacramento Valley Railroad machine shop. . . . We are informed that the trucks of this car will be changed, so as to run on the Central Pacific Railroad, and will not be used on this road, as was first intended."

By the first of January 1866, Carroll had completed a standard gauge smoker and coach, "fine piece[s] of workmanship [that] cannot be surpassed by the Eastern manufacturers," noted the *Telegraph*, further evidence that Carroll was no longer simply assembling eastern kits.

By the beginning of 1866, Carroll was running the largest car manufactory on the West Coast, virtually managing design, procurement, and production of rolling stock on his own. In this pressured, self-sufficient facility, young Thomas Carter not only apprenticed but became Carroll's second in command.

But the circumstances of the takeover had festered in John Carroll. He waited for the Christmas holiday to end before he could face a difficult personal decision. There was an opportunity to go into business for himself. He had been offered contracts for new cars for the San Francisco & San Jose Railroad, which he would fill as an independent supplier at the behest of his friend Ransom Bishop, now SF&SJ's master mechanic. Carroll's contract encompassed half a dozen passenger cars, priced at $3,700 apiece, totaling more than $20,000, and included another $20,000 worth of freight cars.

Other contracts were on the horizon. Several Bay Area short lines, among them the San Francisco & Alameda and the Western Pacific, were under construction. Carroll would take the risk, trading the security of Folsom for a market share in the virtually nonexistent California car manufacturing industry. He had served as a mechanical engineer, a shop foreman, and now an entrepreneur, the three practical facets of the railroadist. Thus he may deserve one last title: first practicing railroadist on the West Coast.

It was a cold winter in Folsom. Snow had come early to the Sierra. On January 27, the whole backshop force crossed the street to the Depot Saloon to celebrate the Carrolls with dinner, a brass band, and generous farewell gifts, including a $150 jeweled watch for John Ambrose and silver napkin rings for Mary.[30] At midnight, the party escorted the Carrolls to their home, drank a toast, and bid tearful good-byes.

Pressure on the Folsom shop crew continued to grow after Carroll's departure. On March 10, the *Telegraph* reported that:

The machine shop and grounds of the Sacramento Valley Railroad, present a scene of great activity at the present time; the running gear of engines and cars is being rapidly altered to correspond with the gauge of the Central Pacific railroad track; a new track has been laid from the turn-table running up the Plaza, on which the cars as soon as finished are temporarily placed, till such time as the main track is fixed to accommodate their change of navigating powers.

By April 7, the mainline was completely converted to standard gauge operation between Folsom and Sacramento, and the now-upgraded *C. K. Garrison* had the honors of piloting the first regauged westbound train.

By the first of September 1866, the backshop was working day and night shifts to complete the gauge conversion of the line's rolling stock. Machine shop and car shop foremen doubtless worked both shifts. Some idea of the volume of work pouring through the shops comes from a simple note about the railroad's foundry output, published in the *Telegraph*. In the first two weeks of October, the in-house foundry turned out twenty thousand pounds of new iron castings to support the conversion work.[31]

The circumstances must have appeared chaotic. At the edge of town, the giant California Central bridge over the American River manifested a new sag, this time a depression of three and a half feet at midspan, continuing the distressing trend first seen in 1862. Tom Carter must have taken note of the root cause of the bridge's problems. Judah had used wood beams, instead of iron rods, as tension members, and it was nearly impossible to keep them tight. Fascinated by the laboratory experiment taking place a short distance from the shop, Carter watched the bridge reach the point of near failure. The structure was condemned that October; six years later, it would fall into the American River under its own weight.[32]

The first physical connection between the Central Pacific and the Sacramento Valley apparently occurred in July 1866 at the foot of K Street in downtown Sacramento. The connection doubled the pressure on the shops by giving an embattled Ben Welch an alternative repair facility to the cramped, temporary Sacramento works of the Central Pacific. He could now channel the work to Folsom.

Tom Carter, promoted to foreman of the Folsom car shops after Carroll's retirement, inherited the onslaught of new work. Probably working both day and swing shifts seven days a week, Carter must have been short on sleep when he lifted the massive door of the Folsom freight house on the evening of Saturday, December 22, 1866. He lost his footing as he ducked under the door, sprawling helplessly as the door came crashing down. Both bones in one leg were broken just above the ankle.

A few days later, in a room at the Patterson House, a Dr. Powell amputated Carter's leg to prevent the spread of gangrene.

Younger brother Martin, living in San Francisco at the time of the accident, came to his older sibling's rescue.

The Lewis biography places Martin in San Francisco in 1863, working for an unnamed carriage manufacturer. But with steamer passage made hazardous by the Civil War, Lewis's date may be suspect. We know for certain only that Martin was in California nine months before the accident. In the frontispiece of an 1856 edition of Webster's Dictionary, he inscribed the earliest authenticated date of his residence on the Pacific Coast: March 3, 1866.[33]

In any event, with family close by Thomas had a place to recuperate, physically and emotionally, after the accident. He probably stayed with Martin at his residence at 800 Howard Street.

Thomas had nowhere to turn his temper but on himself. All the jobs he had held demanded strength and physical agility. With only one leg, he was a danger to himself and others on the floor of a railroad shop. The year was spent searching—himself and the world around him—for answers. It was the first of two episodes in Carter's life when he retreated into a long period of reflection and isolation. Forced to confront his physical limitations, he began to count, like cans of preserves in the winter pantry, the intellectual resources that remained.

Carter may have brooded for more than a year after the accident. It was not until February 1868 that he surfaced again, apparently with purpose restored to his life. The charity may have galled him, but Carter returned to the Folsom shop to accept what amounted to the only insurance coverage he could claim. The *Folsom Telegraph* of February 1 described the loyalty of the shop toward a fallen foreman: "He came to bid the boys good-bye, and while here a subscription was started for his benefit, and in twenty five minutes the sum of one hundred and seventeen dollars was given him by the employees of the works."

The trip east was brief. He was soon back on the West Coast, and the *Telegraph* of August 8 reported the charity well-spent: "While in the east, he procured one of the celebrated Springfield wooden legs, which he is now using. Mr. C. desires to return his thanks to the S.V.R.R. Co. and their employees for the many personal acts of kindness rendered him."

Along with public expression of gratitude came rekindling of his own sense of direction. A month later, in September 1868, Carter was naturalized as a U.S. citizen in a Sacramento district court, an agreement he might have struck with himself as a condition of return to normal life. With the artificial limb came increased mobility. Thomas now walked with the use of a cane—perhaps one turned from California oak on a lathe by Martin.

The cane soon became a trademark on long walks that Carter took all over San Francisco.

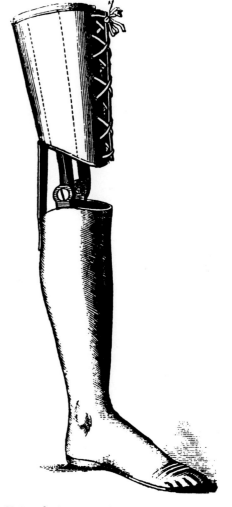

[*Scientific American*, Apr. 15, 1865]

In the autumn of 1868, the City by the Bay had started its second growth spurt by recycling the artifacts of its first. Hulls of abandoned ships, beached at the water's edge on Montgomery Street or First Street, were now surrounded by fill and made into hardware stores, hotels, and even brothels. The hull of the beached *Niantic* served as all three. Slowly, San Francisco's economy began to climb out of the recession that followed the end of California placer mining in the early 1850s. A second economic wind, blowing in on the force of the Comstock discovery and the industries it spawned, was breathing new life into the city's manufacturing sector.

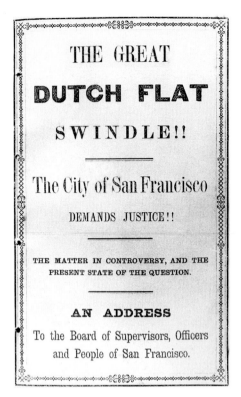

Anticipating completion of the transcontinental railroad (and in some cases
fearing it), large and small businesses had begun to orient themselves to the
distant magnetism of the Central Pacific. Wells Fargo, the California Steam
Navigation Co., and the Bank of Pioche, to name just three, all had strong
vested interests in obstructing the onset of a publicly funded railroad system.
The Robinson brothers were apparently behind a thinly disguised pamphlet
attack on the Central Pacific, entitled "The Great Dutch Flat Swindle," stir-
ring up memories of the 1856 San Francisco Bulkhead plot, ironically funded
by the Bank of Pioche. Now the political winds were blowing from the opposite direction. Would Leland Stanford, once the political opponent of monopolists, try to position the Central Pacific inside an impregnable fortress
created within the city's wharves? Many San Franciscans, in 1868, braced
for the next onslaught of Bulkheaders.

Many braced for new profits.

With cane in hand, Tom Carter ventured out to explore the city in the
early autumn of 1868, testing his prosthesis by walking a little further each
day. In a circuit of less than three miles, Carter could have strolled past virtually every player in the new California railroad game.

Leaving his brother's apartment in the 800 block of Howard Street, Carter would have reached Market Street three blocks north, near the current
site of City Hall. Heading down Market toward the bay, he was soon making footprints in the sawdust of Henry Casebolt's carriage works at the corner of Fifth Street. Wind and time had carried the drifting sawdust up and
down the board sidewalks. Through open windows, the sharp odor of
glue, varnish, and paint mixed with the sweet aroma of milled oak and fir,
soaking the air with the smells of wood craft. Carter's pace slowed as he
walked past Casebolt's factory, a San Francisco institution for nearly ten
years.[34]

Casebolt had started one of the earliest carriage manufactories in the city
and grown the business by growing a family. By 1867, his eldest son, George,
was operating a wholesale wood business, specializing in carriage and wagon
hardwoods such as oak, ash, and hickory. Middle son Ira was a carriage
hardware wholesaler, stocking hubs, spokes, whiffles, lamps, and silver- and
gold-plated carriage mountings. The youngest Casebolt son, Jacob, was a
foreman in his father's works. The elder Casebolt bought lumber and trimmings from his sons and then combined the materials into finished vehicles,
keeping most of the profits inside the family.

As early as 1866, Casebolt experimented with assembling eastern-manufactured horsecars. Instead of constructing cars from scratch, he purchased
disassembled car kits from John Stephenson, an established New York horsecar builder.[35] It was an early example of a manufacturing strategy that would
today be called original equipment manufacture, or "OEM-ing" (see the accompanying Field Notebook). Casebolt assembled the kits at his Fifth and
Market shop, added a few improvements of his own (for example antichat-
ter brass window springs), painted the cars, and then sold them to the Omnibus Railway and the Market Street Railroad, which owned extensive
horsecar lines. A completed car retailed for about $900.

If Tom Carter peered through Casebolt's windows in 1868, it's likely he
would have seen rows of the "delicate green" Stephenson car bodies, trimmed

On the North Beach & Mission St. Railway in San Francisco; thought to be a Stephenson horsecar assembled by Casebolt; Muybridge photo. [Bancroft Library]

The Field Notebook:
The OEM Strategy

Today, the concept of "OEM-ing" applies to manufactured goods that incorporate a major component or subsystem made by another manufacturer. A good example is the mechanism inside a Hewlett-Packard color laserjet printer. The mechanism is actually manufactured by Canon, which agrees by contract to let its manufactured goods be incorporated into an HP-branded product.

One hundred fifty years before the laserjet example, the horsecars of John Stephenson arrived in San Francisco from New York only partly assembled. Easier to ship in ocean-going vessels as kits, it was also easier to have another manufacturer modify, paint, and complete them. At his San Francisco factory, Henry Casebolt was able to install his own hardware to complete Stephenson's cars (such as the anti-chatter window spring mentioned in the text) as well as paint and decorate them to suit the San Francisco markets Casebolt catered to. In this approach, the primary manufacturer, Casebolt, used a secondary manufacturer, Stephenson, to provide "original equipment" for Casebolt's products.

Unlike modern examples of OEM-ing, Stephenson did not hide his brand name but routinely advertised in San Francisco business directories, gaining exposure and brand identification considerably more credible than Casebolt's own. The period of Stephenson "original equipment" sold into California ended in the early 1870s with the accelerating capability of California's own manufacturers.

in red. The branding of the work, however, remained with Stephenson. San Francisco business observers praised the cars as traditional, quality eastern products. Without mentioning Casebolt's own technical innovations, the Omnibus Railway was singled out by the editor of the 1877 Langley's San Francisco Directory for having "30 of the most elegant, best constructed, most thoroughly equipped, excellently lighted, convenient and comfortable horsecars that the skill and taste of that veteran car-builder, John Stephenson, could construct."

Casebolt's own brand may not have fared so well in the public eye. His reputation was closely associated with the cars he built for the Sutter Street Railway, formally incorporated as the Front Street, Mission & Ocean Railroad Co. As its general contractor in 1865, Casebolt capitalized on his position by building the line's twelve horsecars himself, keeping the profits undivided within his family. But Casebolt's own products became the object of considerable public scorn as the original Sutter Street rolling stock began to age in the early 1870s[36]: "People who patronize the Bush St. Branch of the Sutter St. line are indignant at the leaky condition of the cars. If the storm continues much longer the roofs of the cars ought to be shingled."

Public inconvenience turned to outrage when the cars' brake systems began to fail in 1875:

Restored standard gauge horsecar, San Jose Trolley Museum; thought to be a Casebolt assembly of a John Stephenson horsecar body, built for San Francisco's Omnibus Railroad in 1862 or 1863. Shipping eastern-manufactured railroad cars to California by clipper during the Civil War represented a high-risk commercial venture, which inspired West Coast craftsmen such as Henry Casebolt and Kimball Carriage and Car Mfg. Co. to start complete manufactories. [Bruce MacGregor]

The cars of the Sutter St. railroad are in a deplorable condition. . . . The general rickety condition of the cars was demonstrated in a rather unpleasant manner about 6 o'clock last evening. As car No. 13 was coming down Sutter street, the brake broke at the Stockton St. crossing, and the car dashed with alarming speed down the hill. Michael Maloney, the driver, who has been in the employ of the company for six years, immediately applied the lash, and the affrighted horses careered down Sutter street, which was crowded with vehicles, as usual. Michael has lungs like a pair of bellows, using them to good purpose, his shouts clearing the way in advance. At Kearny street crossing the car narrowly escaped collision with several vehicles and flew down toward Montgomery street with fearful velocity. . . . One man succeeded in leaving the car opposite the Lick House, and as a result rolled like a football after the car. On the lower crossing of Montgomery street the car collided with the buggy of Captain Baker, breaking the pole into splinters and dashing horses, buggy and occupant into a heap. By this collision the car was thrown from the track, running upon the prostrate horses, one of which had his legs broken. This is the second accident of the kind that has occurred recently. Fortunately no one was hurt either time. The bloated carcuse of the horse killed was not removed from the scene of the disaster until a late hour this morning.[37]

After the run of bad luck, the San Francisco press began referring to the cars' builder as "Coffin Casebolt."[38]

In its entire active lifespan, the sum of Casebolt's factory production, an estimated two hundred cars built for the San Francisco street railway system addressed only a tiny niche in the growing railroad rolling stock market.[39] Even within that niche, competition had become keen by the late 1860s. When it first appeared, the "bobtail" horsecar achieved instant popularity with San Francisco street railways. Designed without a traditional rear platform, the bobtail car eliminated the haunt of smokers and stowaways, making the cars more attractive to women passengers. But George Kimball, not Casebolt, got the contract for the first batch of bobtails, delivered to the Oakland Street Railway system in 1871.[40] In 1868, Carter would witness firsthand the inroads Kimball was making into the West Coast car trade and dismiss Casebolt as a relic of California's early dependence on eastern suppliers.

To save his good leg, Carter could have boarded an eastbound horsecar on the Market Street Railway and ridden it as far as First Street. Again on foot, he would walk heel-and-cane down the board sidewalks into the South of Market district, locally known as "Tar Flat." The acrid smell was all Carter needed to find his way.

A square mile of waterfront, bounded by Mission, Front, Folsom, and First streets, fairly reeked from the largest concentration of iron foundries on the Pacific Coast. Risdon and Coffey's Iron Works, Union Iron Works (by 1868 known as H. J. Booth), Miner's Foundry, Golden State Iron Works, Vulcan, Pacific Rolling Mills, Aetna Foundry, Fulton Foundry, Pacific Iron Works, Pracy's Machine Works, and the San Francisco Boiler Works—and dozens of smaller foundries, machine shops, rolling mills, hammer works, pattern shops, pig iron suppliers, and fabrication yards—crowded into the corrosive landscape of Tar Flat.[41]

Peter Donahue's Union Iron Works was the first of the Tar Flat foundries, and when it located at First and Mission streets in 1849 the tidal waters of Yerba Buena Cove lapped at its back door.[42] Steamships beached in the cove at high tide, dropped their broken propellers, shafts, cylinder heads, and valves, and were fitted with new castings poured and machined in Donahue's works. By 1860, the Comstock boom had channeled the foundry business into commercial mining machinery. To meet the growth, Tar Flat was forced to expand, mostly onto "made land" (fill and rubble dumped into the tidelands), creating the blocks bounded today by First, Folsom, and Mission streets.

New foundries crowded in next door to the Union. Like organisms adapting to the forces of natural selection, the industries on Tar Flat began to interleave, juxtaposing competition and cooperation in interdependent business relationships. The Miner's Foundry, for example, was organized in 1859 as the first cooperative iron works in San Francisco, and the first West Coast source of machinery for the Comstock Lode mines. Small groups of self-employed molders, even single operators, shared the cost and maintenance of a pair of coke-fired cupolas, together melting about fifteen tons of iron in the common furnace each day. From the white-hot river of metal, individual foundrymen created a variety of products and often competed in selling them. If he had visited the floor of the Miner's Foundry in 1868, Tom Carter could have seen stationary steam engines, stamp mills, shoes and dies for stamp mills, ore amalgamators, pans, barrels and settlers, diamond drill engines, sugar mill machinery, and saw mill and cotton mill machinery.[43]

Through coal-sooted windows, Tom Carter could watch the molders of the Miner's Foundry move through their jobs in heavy-footed dance step. Piles of black sand were shoveled into screen-bottomed pans and sifted like flour to create consistency and smoothness. Maple or oak patterns were pulled from lofts, checked for splits or cracks, filled with putty and sanded smooth. Dividing the pattern into an upper and a lower half allowed the mold to be split into two parts, called the *cope* and the *drag*, wooden boxes that each contained a half of the pattern, packed in black sand.

Carefully, without moving a grain of the compressed sand, the molder withdrew each half of the pattern—one from the cope and one from the drag—leaving a hollow imprint in each the shape of half the finished part. When the cope and the drag were gently set atop each other, the cavity inside represented the volume of the entire part. *Gates* were then cut like chimneys into the interior of the mold, allowing a path for molten iron to reach the cavity.

The *pour*, done twice a day in the larger foundries, was pyrotechnic. Each molder poured his own work, returning time after time to the cupola to fill fifty-pound ladles with molten iron. The yellow-hot metal was poured carefully into gates in the cope. Coursing through the moist sand, the iron would push scalding clouds of steam out vent holes, often creating enough heat to cause the wooden boxes to burst into flame. Boys with water buckets ran from mold to mold, extinguishing small fires until the molten metal cooled.

The molds glowed and simmered through the night, lighting the dark interior of the Miner's Foundry in a ruddy afterglow. In the morning, mold-

This cartoon in *The Wasp*, published in San Francisco on Sept. 16, 1876 (two years after Henry Casebolt introduced the balloon car to San Francisco), criticized Casebolt for animal abuse. [California State Library]

West Coast foundry advertisements at the peak of the Comstock excitement; the Miner's Foundry would later play a key role as a founderer to Carter Brothers. [Top, California State Library; bottom, Guy Dunscomb collection]

Making a mold for a Miller coupler reproduction; Sunset Foundry, Newark, California, 1994. [Bruce MacGregor]

ers would break open the molds, and inspect the work. The only telltale sign of the long, painstaking process was a thin line around the part, marking the location where the cope and drag had met. For a skilled molder, the part-line was almost invisible.

Tom Carter recognized many of the castings that cooled, silver gray, on the earthen floor of the Miner's Foundry. By 1868, several of Tar Flat foundries had begun to routinely manufacture railroad hardware, and most of these early foundries quickly evolved interdependent relationships with the growing railroad industry. Peter Donahue's Union Iron Works was building locomotives as early as 1865, for example, and soon Donahue would become a developer of new railroads in Marin and Sonoma counties, vertically integrating railroad and foundry businesses.[44]

By 1868, Pacific Rolling Mills was producing rail for the Central Pacific on eleven acres of bayside land in Tar Flat. PRM typified the problem common to all Tar Flat industries, the lack of a predictable supply of high-quality iron. Scrap rail, purchased from England, was a common starting point for raw material (an example of reliance on an extremely long inbound supply chain). Forged into billets and extruded through dies, the raw materials were fashioned by PRM into nearly thirty tons of new rail each day. Track bolts, fish plates, and bar iron for car trucks was forged at the same works, often destined for machining and finishing at other foundries such as Risdon Iron.[45]

Risdon, in turn, specialized in car wheels, producing the so-called chilled car wheel by inserting an inch-thick iron ring around the circumference of each wheel mold. Unlike sand, the thick iron collar acted as a heat sink when the molten iron touched it, hardening the first quarter inch of the tread and toughening its surface against wear. Risdon chilled wheels were being sold to the Kimball car works (as well as the Central Pacific) prior to 1870.[46]

San Francisco locomotive builders experimented with cooperative business models. Vulcan Iron Works, located deep in Tar Flat in the 100 block of First Street, soon entered into a version of the co-op pioneered by the Miner's Foundry. In 1868, Vulcan was hosting one of three San Francisco car builders listed in the city directory. Next to Casebolt and Kimball, the name of Palmer Cox appeared in Langley's Directory, in residence at Vulcan. His ad promised "passenger, freight and construction cars on the shortest notice and most reasonable terms." Cox listed just two customers in his portfolio: the Napa Valley Railroad and the company that John Carroll had intended to contract for when he left Folsom, the San Francisco & San Jose Railroad. In the ad, Cox used Carroll's old boss, Ransom Bishop, as a reference, suggesting that Carroll may not have continued long in the role of private contractor. Ironically, Carroll's name was no longer connected with the SF&SJ at all, but with a tiny horsecar railroad operating in the new South of Market district in the city.

Palmer Cox seemed to appear out of thin air, bursting in on the San Francisco car manufacturing scene perhaps as a manufacturing rep for Wason, which had contracted for San Francisco streetcars for the Omnibus Railway in 1862. Cox had left Wason with several large trunks full of car pat-

Thought to be a Pittsburg Railroad standard gauge locomotive manufactured by Union Iron Works in San Francisco, ca. 1866–1867. [Guy Dunscomb collection]

terns and used the collection, with or without Wason's permission, as the basis for starting his West Coast business.[47]

Details of the arrangement between Cox and Vulcan are unknown. But both struck advantages from the bargain: for Cox, possibly free or reduced rent, a handy foundry, and a vast assortment of machine tools and mechanics to run them; for Vulcan, a close, steady customer for its castings and forgings, and a means to broaden their railroad portfolio to include rolling stock. Cox and Vulcan were an early example of a strategic shortening of the supply chain, made possible by the proximity of a growing car manufacturing trade and the city iron works that supported it.

From acquaintance with Cox, Tom Carter would have begun to understand the business advantages of tightly clustered industries and a short supply chain. In 1868, Carter could have observed the Cox project at Fremont, First, and Beale streets, perhaps even met Cox himself, and watched examples of arch-roofed passenger cars being assembled, already an anachronism compared to East Coast styles.

Pittsburg Railroad coal operations at Somersville, near Mt. Diablo; locomotives and coal cars were probably manufactured by Union Iron Works in San Francisco, increasingly prominent as a West Coast railroad supplier. [Both, Norris Pope Collection]

Roughly half way around his circumnavigation of San Francisco's industrial south side, Carter could have stopped for lunch. The Miner's Hotel at First and Folsom beckoned like an oasis in the heart of Tar Flat. The Miner's was a foundryman's hostel, serving its patrons steaming, hearty fare on thick white institutional china. Here, Irish foundry workers gathered in the ethnic enclave of South of Market, one of the few urban settings in 1868 where Irish laborers found job security and comparative freedom from discrimination.[48] In part, the California economy made a difference. By the end of the Civil War, the foundries were booming with demand for machinery from the Comstock mines. But by the end of the decade, thousands of furloughed Chinese railroad workers would enter the state's job market, adding dramatically to unemployment and giving the Irish laborer new, unwelcome competition. The year of Carter's imagined walk, 1868, was the last one of full economic employment before the first effects of recession were felt.

From the Miner's menu, Carter could order a molder's lunch: rump steak at twenty-five cents; porterhouse steak at thirty-seven cents; beef stew for twelve cents; salmon steak, fried or boiled, for twelve cents; corned beef hash for twelve cents; pig's feet in batter for twelve cents; or quail on toast for twelve cents. All were served with corn bread and potatoes at no extra charge.[49] For six bits, Carter would not have left the Miner's hungry.

With fog breaching the hills at Twin Peaks and descending slowly into the city, Tom Carter would have finally turned west, skirting the northern edge of Rincon Hill up Folsom Street. Turning south on Third Street, he would have walked to the fringe of tidewater on Mission Bay, turned west again on Bryant, and followed the rapidly changing shoreline of Mission Bay as it cupped into the San Francisco peninsula. As Tar Flat continued to expand in the late sixties and early seventies, its industries were trapped between Market Street on the north and the mud flats of Mission Bay on the south. There was only one practical outlet for further expansion: filling Mission Bay.

By law, tidelands belonged to the state of California, and their sale and ultimate use was left to the discretion of the state legislature. The process of selling Mission Bay tidelands had already begun when land speculators proposed grading Rincon Hill to the level of Market Street, creating one real estate development on top of the flattened hill and another in Mission Bay, filled with Rincon Hill's rock. As Carter might have surveyed the scene from a westerly stroll along Bryant Street, the underwater lots closest to Rincon Hill were being filled first, and filled again and again as the rock settled into the seemingly bottomless tidal mud.

The filling would continue, with more and more urgency, as the largest tenant prepared to move in. The Central Pacific, in 1868, had been deeded one hundred and fifty acres of the Mission Bay tidal basin by the legislature, creating a beachhead for future terminal activities and a distribution point for the cornucopia of goods that would pour from the completed transcontinental railroad. The Central Pacific still lacked a connection between its railhead in Sacramento and the new Mission Bay terminal, but it was just a matter of time until it bridged the last hundred miles to the critical coastal port.

Kimball plant at Fourth and Bryant streets in San Francisco, ca. 1868. [California Historical Society]

Control of even this small beachhead gave the CP a sinister presence in San Francisco. The controversy was already reaching a low boil by the late summer of 1868. San Francisco newspapers bemoaned the "notorious politicians and schemers" who had given away public real estate to "the new bulkheaders."[50] Carter walked the fringes of the bay at the beginning of what would become known as the terminal wars.

Hobbling down the long, muddy reaches of Bryant Street, Carter's stump was certainly beginning to ache by the time he reached the tracks of the Potrero & Bay View Railroad at Fourth Street. The horsecar line was a strategic part of the Mission Bay development, passing from downtown directly along Fourth Street to the edge of Mission Bay, and then across its neck on the five-thousand-foot, elbow-shaped "Long Bridge" to the southern bank, and ultimately on to the Potrero District and Hunter's Point. As Mission Bay was slowly filled in, its made lands steadily increased in value, attracting powerful speculators. Eventually, the P&BV's developers—Henry Fairfax Williams prominent among them—would use the horsecar to tie the Mission Bay development together into a vast new industrial tract within Mission Bay itself, accessible by ship through a draw section in Long Bridge. It was on the Potrero & Bay View that John Carroll had found employment in 1867, building horsecars for the line.[51] Carter no doubt saw Carroll occasionally and joined him for a drink. This day, Carter would watch a Carroll-crafted car roll by on Fourth Street and admire the workmanship.

There was another venture car builder in the neighborhood. One block off Bryant and Fourth, toward Brannan Street, Duncan McLean and Co. opened the San Francisco Railroad Car Factory in 1867. McLean had been Henry Casebolt's shop foreman at the Fifth and Market factory but quit to start his own works. McLean's shop must have been small, and marginally capitalized. His published notice appeared just once, in the 1867–68 Langley's Directory, before it vanished, a victim of the looming recession.

From the tracks of the Potrero & Bay View, Carter could look across Fourth Street at a sight he had walked miles to see: the colossal new factory of the Kimball Carriage and Car Co. The businesses of McLean, Cox, and even Casebolt paled in comparison. Rising three stories high, Kimball's works became, with its construction in 1868, the largest car manufacturing facility on the West Coast.

Kimball, like Casebolt, had been a carriage manufacturer in the city in the fifties but launched his new facility with a war chest no other San Francisco car builder could ever hope to match. The public, and even the R. G. Dun credit reporters, had to guess about the size and source of the capital.[52] The figures would not be public knowledge until 1875, when loan papers came to light in the aftermath of William Ralston's death. In 1868, Kimball and his partner Richard Ogden had borrowed $578,580 from Ralston's Bank of California.[53] A loan of this magnitude should have guaranteed their preeminence in Pacific Coast railroad manufacturing.

But the loan should also have triggered concerns about the solvency of the partners. Not until five years later, on May 28, 1873, did the R. G. Dun agency publish the adverse credit history of Richard Ogden:

> We learn that when Ogden of this firm was a U.S. Quarter Master he was a defaulter to the Government to about $100,000 and was ordered East where he made sufficient to settle his accounts. Previous to going into present business was engaged in shipping carriages and other articles from the East and is reported to be owing still on account of that business. When he joined Kimball he bought out the latter's partnership one night, giving in payment his notes, endorsed by W. C. Ralston Cashier of the Bank of California who paid them as they fell due, Ogden at that time being with little or [no resources] and the impression is that neither he nor Kimball has made anything worth mentioning since and many think they have gone behind and are no doubt sustained by some capitalists who are looked on as the real owners of the concern.[54]

The loan should also have triggered deep concerns about conflict of interest. The president of the Bank of California, William Ralston, was also a member of Kimball's board of directors. Ralston perhaps rationalized the loan as collateral on an even larger loan, extended to the Central Pacific when Stanford was desperate for cash. Ralston assumed that Stanford's railroad, already the largest transportation company in the state, could offer Kimball the car manufacturing business that would justify the credit. Ralston's circular logic was based in part on the modest status of the Central Pacific's own shop capacity. Before 1868, its Sacramento shop complex remained housed in temporary quarters in the capital, much of its car building need met by kits from eastern suppliers.

Ralston, George Kimball, and Richard Ogden had become partners in the hope of becoming Stanford's preferred source for thousands of new cars. "The concern is an immense one as to capability of turning out work," reported the R. G. Dun credit agency in November 1869. In fact, the loan had

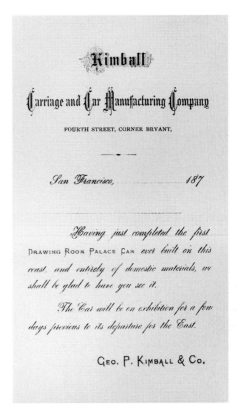

Announcement of Kimball's luxury sleeper, *Siempre Viva*, ca. May 1871; less than six months later, the car was destroyed in the Great Chicago Fire. [California Historical Society]

purchased a facility big enough to meet the immediate rolling stock needs of the entire West Coast, as well as agricultural implements, carriages, and wagons. In a 275-foot-square lot, an L-shaped three-story brick building enclosed nearly two acres of lumber yards and parts stores.

Although written several years after the opening of the facility, the San Francisco *Trade Circular* gave a detailed account of what Tom Carter might have seen in 1868:

> On the first floor of the main or principle [sic] building, which is three stories high and measures 275 × 50 feet, are located the steam room, the iron work and black-smithing department. On one side of this room are ranged twenty forges, which are kept constantly at work. . . .
>
> On the second floor of the main building are the business and private offices of the company. Here, also, is the principal depository for newly finished work, and the show-room for harness, robes, blankets, etc. Here are ranged every conceivable variety of carriage, buggy, wagon, landeau, and brougham, including one hundred and fifty different varieties or styles of vehicles, exquisitely finished, and many of them already sold to customers in California, Nevada, Oregon, Peru, Chile, Bolivia and Japan.
>
> At the further end of this room is situated the nickel-plating establishment. Of this branch of the business the Kimball Company makes a specialty, being prepared to plate articles of *all descriptions* of *any metal.* All articles of household hardware are plated on short notice and warranted.
>
> From here we approach, on the second floor, a room measuring 100 × 50 feet, where all the painting is executed for carriage gearings, etc, etc. At the further end of this room is another, 75 × 150 feet, used for giving the last coat of varnish, and general finishing.
>
> On the third floor is the manufactory of wood work, such as body-making, wheels, gears, etc. At the back or west end of this room is done the ornamental work, including gold, silver and nickel.
>
> . . . From the third floor the visitor passes on to a bridge connecting the two buildings. This platform, similar to the one on the floor below, is used for drying carriage bodies. Proceeding on, we come to a room measuring 80 × 50 feet, where the bodies are painted and varnished. Beyond this is a room fifty feet square, where the trimming and upholstering is attended to.
>
> . . . A large portion of the first floor of the building, approached from the yard, entered from Fourth Street, is devoted to the manufacture of street cars. It was here that forty-four cars were lately built for Mr. Woodward, of Woodward's Gardens, the whole order being completed within ninety days from date of commencement.
>
> In consequence of the late horse disease, which has recently been so general on this coast, business has been comparatively quiet, and the number of men employed has been reduced to about 150, the usual staff, during brisk times, amounting to 230.
>
> The payroll of this extensive factory amounts to about $3,500 a week.

We may notice that in the horse-car manufactory there are orders for Oregon and Japan in course of completion. The cars built for Woodward cost that enterprising citizen no more than the same class of Eastern-made goods would have done, were acknowledged equally as good, if not better, than those of Eastern make, and had the advantage of being 300 pounds lighter. Every part of those cars were manufactured from California woods, which are accounted the best in the world for car work.[55]

Through branding, Kimball carefully began to curry its public image, and in the process the image of West Coast manufacturing. The annual September San Francisco Mechanics Fair was a showcase for Kimball products, which in turn showcased West Coast raw materials, such as Douglas fir (or Oregon pine, as it was called) and redwood. In 1868, the U.S. Navy, at the local Mare Island shipyards, conducted tests on the strengths of various woods and confirmed that Douglas fir could be substituted for eastern oak with far less expense, less weight, and virtually no loss in strength.[56] Kimball's early combination of Oregon pine frames and redwood sheathing became a West Coast industry standard in horsecar as well as mainline rolling stock manufacture, and a radical departure from eastern car building practice. The emphasis on local woods and locally procured component parts gave Kimball a seminal role in developing California manufacturing to a level of quality, volume, and price that competed successfully with eastern manufacturers.

In 1868, eastern-built railroad car kits were still transported to California by water around Cape Horn. For Kimball, the high transportation costs acted as a trade barrier to eastern products. But scarcely a year later, the national economic playing field would begin to level out. When the Central Pacific was finally completed, the transcontinental railroad would throw the door open to rapid, inexpensive delivery of eastern goods.

As a result, eastern brand names would become household words on the West Coast. John Stephenson's incursion into the California streetcar market was accompanied by full-page ads in the 1866 San Francisco business directories, clearly aimed at establishing brand identification. Salesmen from numerous eastern railroad suppliers and manufacturers, such as Adams and Westlake, established San Francisco sales offices by the early 1870s, aggressively creating a point-of-sale for a new West Coast market.

Overbuilt by West Coast standards, Kimball, at two hundred and fifty employees, was miniscule compared to the eight hundred workers the Barney and Smith car works employed in 1873, the latter being probably the largest railroad car manufacturer in the country.[57] Soon, with the completion of the Central Pacific, the trade barrier that kept Barney and Smith out of the California market would vanish.

Kimball had less than two years to perfect a business strategy before facing the brunt of eastern competition. Its first mainline railroad cars, produced in 1868, were therefore aimed at the transcontinental railroad itself and were built on speculation. Kimball exhibited its first demonstration sleeping car at the Mechanics Institute Fair in San Francisco in August 1868, obviously a marketing pitch to the Central Pacific.[58] Tom Carter undoubtedly saw the exhibit.

Carter could only marvel at Kimball's audacity. In 1868, the year Carter might have first toured the South of Market district in San Francisco, Kimball had created a seemingly impregnable manufacturing fortress in the future heartland of the California railroad industry. Who could compete? Palmer Cox, who was subletting space from Vulcan and building cars with virtually no overhead? Or "Coffin" Casebolt, apparently trapped in a niche market for street railway equipment? Or John Carroll, Carter's mentor and friend, and sadly, a victim of a personal miscalculation about his ability to make a go at railroad car contracting? Carroll's two-year odyssey was especially troubling to Carter, for Carroll had been one of the first to recognize the potential market for California rolling stock, and the unique role that West Coast lumber could play in its manufacture.

By late afternoon, the fog was creeping over Mission Bay and settling, cold and wet, along the flats of upper Market Street, bringing an early twilight to his brother's neighborhood. Tom Carter, no doubt limping badly by the time he reached Martin's rooming house on Howard Street, flung off his patented Springfield wooden leg, poured himself a stiff drink, and considered the possibilities.

That winter, we have to imagine Tom Carter, brother Martin, John Carroll, Ransom Bishop, and Lester Robinson having a drink together in San Francisco's What Cheer House, talking about the strangely distant landscape of old times.

It was a night to be maudlin. Carroll's wife, Mary, had recently died, leaving him with four children to raise.[59] His oldest daughter, May, was about fifteen years old at the time, and she stepped into the role of housekeeper and mother to the young Carroll children. The startup car business had either failed from lack of capital or died from the neglect of worry and grief. John Carroll was further away from being an independent contractor than he had been in Folsom, and by the late 1860s he was supporting his family on day wages from the small Potrero & Bay View horsecar line. Thomas Carter had sought naturalization in 1868, but Carroll had not.[60] To register to vote in San Francisco County, Carroll misrepresented his birthplace as Maryland, rather than New Brunswick, the birthplace Carroll entered in census records.[61] These few anecdotes suggest that Carroll had become disillusioned, perhaps for a time despondent.

Tom Carter still wrestled with self-pity and itched to get back to work.

Lester Robinson, once captain of the Sacramento Valley Railroad's transcontinental dreams, was now vice president of the Potrero & Bay View horsecar line, perhaps not the destiny he had imagined for himself. No sooner had its tracks gotten across Long Bridge into the Potrero than mud slides closed a deep cut just south of the bridge, forcing a winter closure of most of the line. Robinson had no doubt taken John Carroll aboard the P&BV shop when the San Francisco & San Jose Railroad car contracts ran out, and now with Long Bridge shut down he might have faced the distasteful prospect of laying Carroll off. Ransom Bishop was still master mechanic of the SF&SJ, but the Central Pacific had just purchased control of the road,

securing a south door into San Francisco, and Bishop might have joked with Carroll about the continuing anxiety of having Governor Stanford for a new boss.

San Francisco & San Jose Railroad double-header, at a site identified as G. S. Hale's mill. [William Wulf collection]

Stanford's presence was permeating the city. The 150 acres of Mission Bay land deeded to the Stanford interests had been deliberately split up into relatively small parcels, each divided from the others by rights-of-way that would become city streets.[62] Underwater at the time of the grant, the land would soon be filled to create warehouses, yards, and narrowly constricted rail access to wharfage—an attempt to contain the "new Bulkheaders." But even with these restrictions, the impact of the Central Pacific's grant drove speculators to buy and sell made land on the northeast corner of Mission Bay, trading on the growth in industry and shipping that would accompany a large Central Pacific terminal development. Robinson, for example, owned underwater lots in Mission Bay.

But Robinson certainly knew that the underwater lots were worthless without a rail link to the Central Pacific's home base in Sacramento. How, and when, would the connection be made? The sf&sj was only one of three possible avenues Stanford could use to enter San Francisco. But its use also forced the cp to detour south around the bay, creating a 208-mile connection to Sacramento by way of Niles. A shorter link lay through Stockton, Niles, and Oakland, then across the open bay to San Francisco, or 171 miles. But the third alternative was almost an airline: 83.5 miles from Sacramento to a small toehold on the Golden Gate named Saucelito (which would be renamed Sausalito in 1884), thence just four miles across the bay to San Francisco.[63] From the perspective of 1868, cynics speculated that Stanford would soon control all three avenues, encircling San Francisco's Mission Bay

[William Wulf collection]

terminal like a noose. The Bulkheaders, the cynics concluded, were back in force.

With good reason to be cynical themselves, the drinkers might have shared news of other Sacramento Valley alumni caught up in the Central Pacific juggernaut. Two had become notably successful. In 1868, John Flint Kidder was an independent civil engineer, leaving the employ of the Central Pacific to lay out sections of the Virginia & Truckee Railroad between Reno and Carson City.[64]

Uncle Ben Welch had gone to work for Huntington in 1863 and was finally getting a new car facility in Sacramento, one equipped to handle the demands of a transcontinental system (and soon to eclipse Kimball as the largest car manufactory in the West).[65] The new CP car shop was a completely self-contained manufacturing facility. Its main erection hall was two stories high and measured ninety by two hundred feet, with an annex ninety by three hundred feet. The facility was laid out like an assembly line. Fifty thousand board feet of lumber would pour into the building each working day and, in a cloud of sawdust, pass through batteries of planers, morticers, dovetailers, and boring and gaining machines, emerging as a train of six cars, each and every workday.

An on-site blacksmith shop, foundry, and brass and tin works gave the Central Pacific virtually all the resources of Tar Flat, including on-site manufacture of car wheels. Four hundred men would work for Welch in the car shop alone. By 1871, Welch would be filling in-house car orders that the Kimball Co. had only imagined, such as constructing a thousand combination boxcars that were desperately needed by the Central Pacific to meet the expanding California-Liverpool wheat traffic.

In 1866, gearing up for the new car facility, the CP had also performed tests on Oregon pine and, like the Navy, found it as structurally sound as eastern oak. From that point on, Ben Welch had urged Collis Huntington to ship no more oak from the East Coast. The kit era was ending; the era of in-house Central Pacific car manufacturing had begun.[66]

There was a rumor making the rounds that when the new Sacramento shop was finally open, the old Sacramento Valley shops at Folsom would be closed down for good. Everyone at the What Cheer bar except Martin Carter had been in California long enough to understand the legacy of the Sacramento Valley shops, and the first generation of California railroaders — railroadists — it had produced. Independent, knowledgeable, and badly in need of work, the craftsmen at the What Cheer that night were the first of their generation. At the ripe old age of twenty-eight, Thomas Carter may have entertained the nagging doubt that they were also the last.

But that night, deep into their cups, the pessimism didn't last long. There was also a rumor that Uncle Ben Welch was hiring.

For Tom Carter, the sojourning years began. For the next five years, he would live out of a trunk, moving from project to project up and down the West Coast. The living conditions, in general, were dismal. He was a tenant in dormitories, bunk houses, or cheap hotels where track crews and laborers were bivouacked, eating from common board. The projects, requiring water transport of ties, rail, and bulk lumber, all seemed to headquarter on rivers, inlets, or tidelands, cold and wet places in winter and fog-bound in summer. With only two exceptions, the projects lay on the fringe of an urban setting, at the end of a slough, on the wind-battered shore of a bay, off road and beyond the commercial telegraph. In these settings, Carter, lonely, unsure of his physical ability, would learn his craft.

The economic forecasts accompanying his apprentice years seemed as windswept and cold as the landscape. He set a compass through the trailing edge of a storm front created by the Central Pacific, expanding toward Portland, Oregon, on the north, and Los Angeles on the south, creating a system of feeder lines in its wake to supply the transcontinental trunk.

In the expansion phase of the storm, the Central Pacific and its family of corporate mergers, leases, and franchises appeared to control every conceivable dimension of the state's railroad development—its resources and suppliers, markets, government subsidies, the editorial opinions expressed by newspapers, and, most important, the competition. But in slower times, with money in short supply, the Central Pacific instead ceded portions of these activities to the regional or local economy, which, like a microclimate, was sometimes forceful enough to create a locally defined and locally funded transportation system of its own. During these periods, Tom Carter took calculated risks and managed to eke a living out of the whirlwind.

The first risk, and the most foolish, was the belief that he could return to his old job. In 1869, Tom and Martin Carter and John Carroll hired onto Ben Welch's shop as carpenters. They all badly needed work, but for Tom especially the move must have taken physical courage. Welch's Sacramento car shop was a high-pressure, commodity business within a business. Three or four hundred men were employed at a time, organized under dozens of foremen. Tom Carter could not claim seniority and had no way to leverage the foreman's position he had held three years before on the Sacramento Valley. Instead, he probably operated heavy machinery, making the same saw cut or the same drill-out hundreds of times each day. He performed the work balanced on his good leg, unable to prevent a bad spill if a beam shifted or a tool slipped. It must have been a frustrating year, taxing his physical abilities to the limit.

What attracted Carter was Welch's growing reputation as an innovator in railroad technology. By 1865, Welch had already prototyped the first CP bucker snow plow, soon to become the railroad's principal assault weapon in its war to keep the transcontinental mainline open over the Sierra in winter. He invented a tenon machine for speeding the manufacture of railroad car frames. In the late 1860s, he was developing designs for specialized passenger cars for the emigrant trade, the product that had launched Kimball's effort to produce mainline rolling stock, addressing market conditions that would result from completion of the transcontinental railroad in 1869.

Long before Carter joined the shop, Welch was managing the ongoing reengineering of car designs better adapted to the torturous conditions imposed by the Central Pacific's mountain track. A sharp-eyed Mark Hopkins, one of the four well-known partners in the Central Pacific, analyzed one such problem in a letter to Collis Huntington on May 31, 1865:

> Last winter, during the rainy weather, we had much difficulty keeping Box Cars from leaving the track on steep grades and sharp curves, where the new heavy embankments were continually settling out of true line. At the same time no passenger or flat car ever ran off. The cause seems to be attributable to the stiff unyielding character of a box car's side bearings. The rainy season tending to swell the sheathing renders a box car so stiff that a Jack Screw set under one corner can raise the whole end . . . as though the Jack screw was set at the end midway between the corners. Therefore [the truck] being set on side bearers there is no such yield diagonally . . . as to accommodate [sic] an inequality in the track, as a flat car or a passenger car will do. This is an important matter with us in operating a mountain road, high grades, new precipitous banks and continual short curves, though in operating ordinary valley road no great difficulty will be expected. My object in so minutely calling your attention to this matter is to have you ascertain from experienced men upon mountain grades and curves whether there is not some kind of center bearing truck, with or without side rollers, which are better adapted to the wants of our road.

Hopkins's letter sets perhaps the earliest known context to the challenges facing the western car shop foreman, a harsh testing ground for materials, designs, and the alleged "best practices" of eastern car manufacturers. By 1869, under Welch's leadership, the Central Pacific had become a test bed for freight trucks better adapted to the operating conditions that Hopkins described. Welch often adapted eastern designs with features uniquely suited to western operating conditions, as with the Allen patent freight truck, which depended on two longitudinal wooden cross pieces, or transoms, for lateral support.[67] Like the western narrow gauge lines that would adapt similar truck designs at a later date, Welch's preferred truck design incorporated a wooden transom, a response to the demand for mechanical flexibility on undulating right of way. During the year they worked for Welch, Tom and Martin Carter and John Carroll would have been exposed to the new thinking in truck design.

Tom and Martin rented a place together at N.E. Seventh and E streets in Sacramento, in the same block where John Carroll and his children (May, then sixteen; Maggie, eleven; Frank, nine; and Charles, eight) rented a house. Tom, Martin, and John were by then close friends and all working for the Central Pacific at its moment of triumph, on May 10, 1869, when the transcontinental railroad was finished at Promontory Point, Utah. For Ben Welch and the small army of carpenters who worked for him, it was a time to celebrate, but it was hard to imagine the Carters having much of a personal stake in the festivities.

Nor was the celebration long-lived. A flood of eastern-manufactured goods, arriving by train, catalyzed a slow-down in the California economy. Unable to match the abundant supply of eastern goods in price or quantity,

Western manufacturers lost business, which ironically contributed to a slow-down in Central Pacific's own traffic volume. Before the year was out, John Carroll and Tom Carter were probably laid off.

They weren't alone. A contingent of furloughed CP car shop employees followed Carter and Carroll to the Oregon Central Railroad in early October 1869. On the East Side district in Portland, Carter shared quarters in a railroad mess house with other carpenters recruited from the Central Pacific shops in Sacramento: Stephen Cardoff, John Main, H. J. Stephenson, Miche Conley, Michael McDonald, and D. W. Treat.[68] Surplus Central Pacific labor was to play a key role in Carter's business during the 1870s, acting as a temporary labor pool for projects he could not afford to staff with full-time employees. The Oregon Central Railroad mess house gave him an opportunity to start collecting résumés.

The Oregon jobs had probably been brokered by the old Folsom shop fraternity. John Carroll was apparently hired onto the Oregon Central first by John Flint Kidder, once Lester Robinson's assistant chief engineer on the Placerville & Sacramento and now the Oregon Central's chief engineer. Carroll came on board as master mechanic, the highest rank he would ever hold in a railroad organization. Tom Carter, in turn, was hired (presumably by Carroll) as project draftsman, his first job title encompassing mechanical engineering responsibilities and a far better fit to his physical limitations than floor mechanic.

Work on the Oregon Central was in high gear by early November 1869, when Carroll began assembling cars in a machine shop near Portland's East Side railroad wharf. The *Oregonian* mentioned Carroll's growing interest in local woods in an article published on November 2:

> Railroad cars: we visited the car and machine shop of the Oregon Central Railroad (East Side) yesterday, and found a force of men engaged upon the iron work of the turntable which is being constructed near the landing at East Portland. In the car shop are two large and elegant passenger cars of the monitor style, finished, except some . . . painting, and ready to be mounted on wheels. They are built entirely of Oregon wood—the frames of yellow . . . , the inside panel work of plain and curl maple, and . . . of alder. They seem to be very substantial, and will be certainly, when the painting [is] finished, very handsome. The lumber is being put out for eight more cars of the same description.

The tools, the techniques, even the style of passenger car bore a resemblance to the Folsom kit work that Carroll had done fifteen years earlier. But by adapting local woods to the job, Carroll shortened the inbound supply chain, saving money and time. In the process, he began to develop his own skill as a car designer. The kit regimen was broken. Carroll could add value through his own judgment about materials. He could alter the design of rolling stock by altering part size or placement, strengthening and lightening the car at the same time by specifying sills of Douglas fir instead of oak. The mention of a "monitor" style roof suggests a clerestory incorporated into the design, a feature substantiated by early photographs of the Oregon Central. In adapting West Coast materials, Carroll was laying the foundation for

Early Oregon Central Railroad milestone: first train on the Clackamas River Bridge, near Oregon City, 1870. [Clackamas County Historical Society]

a variation in car design—lighter, cheaper, and uniquely western. Whether the variation was better than eastern products, only time and experience would tell.

Tom Carter had a new role. For the first time, he would not have to touch a piece of hardware. His attention was completely devoted to documentation and design. As draftsman, he visualized the design of a car as an exercise on paper and could fathom the reasons for choosing the type and size of a material, for placement of irons, for the size of bolts. At the same time, he also acquired visibility into the choice of outside suppliers, and control of cost. Few details are known about the car work, but the relationship between Carroll and Carter took on a new focus around engineering and business, rather than shop practice.

Carter's later boast of "taking charge" of the construction of the Oregon Central was a legerdemain about acquiring new technical skills and new responsibilities, about taking charge of himself. In reality, Carter remained in a subordinate position to both Carroll and Kidder until his work was finished. But even his personal appearance seemed to give him a new authority. With a bib-length beard, at thirty Carter no longer looked the apprentice to John Kidder's forty years and Carroll's venerable forty-six.

Carter and Carroll remained in Portland for at least seven months. Carroll was listed by the 1870 U.S. census as superintendent of construction, and part of his responsibility was clearly procurement and supply. On March 11, 1870, the *Sacramento Union* interviewed Carroll in transit on a business trip to the East Coast to buy rail, car parts, and locomotives as the Oregon Central's master mechanic.

On July 29, 1870, the U.S. census made the only known mention of Tom Carter in Oregon. He was listed as single, residing in the Oregon Central Railroad mess house, thirty years old, and by profession a "railroad draftsman." The census also noted his considerable resources: Carter claimed $1,000 in personal property, and $1,000 in real estate.

Most of the mess house workmen claimed nothing in either category.

From the time of the 1870 census until early February 1872, Tom Carter vanished from the public record. Following the Oregon Central job, the Lewis biography placed him in Petaluma, California, where it insisted that "Mr. Carter then built the road from Healdsburg to Donahue landing, constructing all bridges and rolling stock."

In reality, Carter became a wage-earning employee of the San Francisco & North Pacific Railroad. A *Petaluma Argus* reporter found Carter at Donahue Landing in February 1872, working as the car shop foreman and probably boarding at the Sonoma House, the only public lodging at the landing. The February 17 article described the gray, forbidding environment at Donahue, a windswept outpost on the Suisun Bay tidelands where Peter Donahue had originally set up the shops for the San Francisco & North Pacific in 1870:

> Donahue as a town may be properly termed a failure. It consists of one hotel, the Company's machine shops, car houses, etc, a long wharf where the steamboat lands, and we believe one hundred acres of land, all of which is the property of the company. Being the landing point of the steam boats, and the southern terminus of the S.F.&N.P. Railroad, it is dignified by a position on railroad maps and time schedules, which might possibly lead strangers into the error of believing Donahue a town. This is not the case. Donahue is not a town, and can never be one, which is all contrary to the expectations of him whose name it bears and whose "first name" is Peter . . . and so its greatness will Peter out.[69]

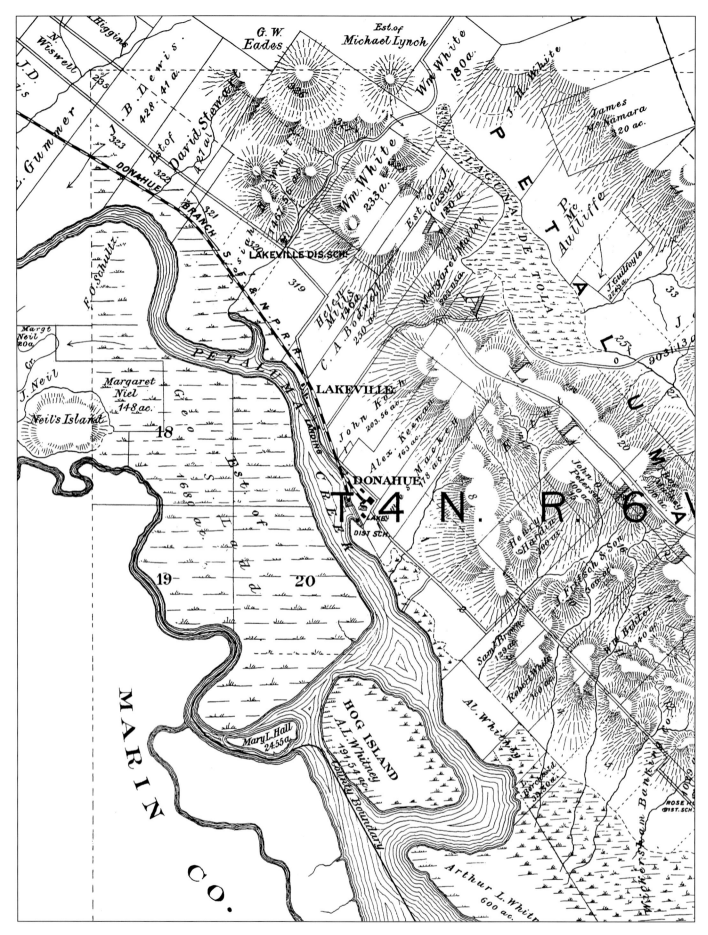

Site of Donahue Landing, from the *Illustrated Atlas of Sonoma County, California,
Published by Reynolds and Proctor, 1897.* [Sonoma County Historical Society]

Donahue Landing, with steamer *James M. Donahue* moored by the trainshed. The Sonoma House appears in the left background. [San Francisco Maritime National Historical Park, Livingston Collection]

In this unlikely setting, Tom Carter discovered himself on the front lines of the terminal wars. For three years, since Peter Donahue had developed the landing as the southern anchor point for a rail route to the redwoods, the outpost on the edge of Petaluma Slough was squarely in the line of fire when Stanford began to strike an airline route from Sacramento to Saucelito. Most of the route had been built by the "Cal P," as the California Pacific was locally known, opening its mainline between Sacramento and Vallejo in 1869. The Cal P's trains reached San Francisco ferry connections nearly twice as fast as Central Pacific trains over the longer route through Stockton. Long before the gold spike was driven in Utah, Stanford had marked the Cal P as the route of choice to reach a new Pacific terminal.

Visualizing Stanford's chess moves before he could make them, a San Francisco investment banker named Milton Slocumb Latham bought control of the Cal P in late 1870.[70] Latham quickly formed a bulwark against Central Pacific incursion. Interlocking presidencies, including that of the London and San Francisco Bank, soon gave Milton Latham vicelike control of the airline route. Latham, however, had no intention of becoming Stanford's competition. Evidence quickly mounted that he intended to bleed the property dry before an inevitable sale to the Central Pacific.

When he took over as the Cal P's president in January 1871, Latham first pressured the railroad's board of directors to approve issuing $1.3 million in bonds, allegedly to repair and reinforce poorly protected track built on levees along the Sacramento River. As president of the London and San Francisco Bank, Latham negotiated the new bonds to English and European investors, selling them for cash. Then (the plaintiffs charged in a subsequent lawsuit) Latham used the proceeds first to line his own pockets and second to purchase control of Peter Donahue's San Francisco & North Pacific Railroad, including its terminal at Donahue Landing. None of the bond money, alleged the suit, was used to repair the Cal P's sagging levees.

As if to prove his innocence, Latham repeated the speculation. On August 9, 1871, ostensibly to raise additional money to reinforce the railroad against floods, Latham encouraged the Cal P's heavily indebted board to authorize an additional $1.5 million in bonds. To avoid the appearance of a second European bond laundering (the first would be sufficient to cause the suit), Latham struck a deal with Leland Stanford. Stanford would buy the bonds and put a generous part of their cash value into Latham's personal bank account. Latham would compensate Stanford for his trouble. Sometime in late 1871, Latham signed a joint traffic agreement with Stanford, granting Central Pacific passenger trains trackage rights over the Cal P from Sacramento to Vallejo. Thus the first overland trains reached Oakland by the airline route in November 1871, allowing Stanford fast and direct access to the Bay Area. At the same time, Central Pacific surveying teams quickly moved into position on the marshy approaches around Donahue Landing, probing for a continuation of the airline route into Saucelito.

When the engorged Sacramento River undermined the Cal P's neglected levees in the winter of 1871–72, Latham refused to produce the dollars to do repair work, and the Cal P closed down its mainline. To complete the takeover, all Stanford had to do was call in the full amount of the bond debt, let the Cal P declare bankruptcy, and buy the defaulting company at a fraction on the dollar. The formal bankruptcy transaction occurred in July 1875.

For virtually no additional cash outlay, Stanford acquired Donahue Landing and the San Francisco & North Pacific. The fact that the Central Pacific controlled the SF&NP from the date of the Cal P bond sale (August 9, 1871) to January 1873 clearly suggests that Thomas Carter had gotten the position of car shop foreman through his Central Pacific connections. Tasked with setting up cars built in Sacramento, Carter was in effect back working for Uncle Ben Welch. The *Argus* continued the narrative of its February 17, 1872, visit to Donahue Landing: "The Rolling stock of the road at present embraces five locomotives and a 'dummy,' seven passenger coaches, two baggage cars, twenty freight cars, thirty-six platform cars, ten hand cars, three large sleeping and dining cars for track laying purposes, five push cars, and building in the shops at present three box cars. Besides these, another engine and twenty five cars are expected soon to arrive from Sacramento."

Tom Carter himself, foreman of the Car Department, escorted the reporter through the facility and took pride in explaining the workings of Westinghouse straight air brakes, a revelation to a public accustomed to the hazards of hand brakes.

The appearance of advanced safety appliances in the SF&NP roster probably originated with the Cal P, not the Central Pacific. A year before Carter was setting up air brakes on the SF&NP, the Cal P Vallejo shops were noted for passenger equipment "superior in finish and comfort to anything in use on the Coast." On June 2, 1871, a Cal P train was the first in California to be equipped with Miller Platform couplers, and the Miller system may have been instituted at Donahue Landing as well when the Cal P acquired the SF&NP.[71] Much like the cross-cultural exchange of technology that had occurred at Folsom, the Central Pacific's acquisition of the Cal P's shops and shopcraft soon catalyzed its own upgrade to Miller platforms and Westinghouse air brakes.

Carter also gained access to the Cal P's capable supply chain. The tiny, virtually unknown Vallejo foundry of McCormick and Lewis had either built or acted as a major supplier for an estimated 14 percent of the Cal P's passenger cars and 85 percent of its freight cars.[72] The foundry's own advertising boldly claimed railroad car manufacturing as a commercial offering. By the time of Carter's employment at Donahue Landing, the foundry may also have provided a connection between Thomas Carter and Thomas McCormick, who would soon be doing business together on the North Pacific Coast.[73]

The Central Pacific's encampment at Donahue Landing, however, resembled an occupying army more than a graduate engineering school. Poised to fortify the airline route to Saucelito, the Central Pacific held the SF&NP for just eighteen months before giving up the ground it had won. With his credit strained to the limit by railroad construction and buyouts, and with revenues diminished by the recession, Stanford took the unprecedented step of selling back a piece of the monopoly he was struggling to create. In January 1873, the Central Pacific sold the SF&NP back to Peter Donahue, restoring the relationship between Donahue Landing and its namesake.[74] It is likely that Carter remained in the position of car shop foreman until the date of the sale. Labeled as the "Central Pacific's man," Carter was vulnerable to replacement by a Donahue insider, perhaps the same car shop foreman that Carter himself had replaced.

But assuming Carter did stay at Donahue Landing for the remainder of 1872, a crucial missing piece in the complex period might be filled by even a chance meeting between Carter and a civil engineer named George Black —who was, in December 1872, working for Stanford as a locating engineer on an extension of the SF&NP toward the Russian River. Donahue Landing was Black's principal supply point, his cache for tools and equipment, and his boat connection to San Francisco. Going and coming from the City, Black would have boarded at the Sonoma House, where Carter roomed. We can imagine them drinking together on a foggy, cold evening at Donahue, the wind howling across the Suisun marsh outside, trying to make sense of the terminal wars raging around them.

If they did meet late in 1872, Black would have been the first to tell Carter details of a small, trouble-ridden project he had just quit in nearby Marin County, a project named the North Pacific Coast. If the meeting took place, Black, ironically, would have warned Tom Carter not to get involved.

Early Central Pacific station at Arbuckle, Calif.; February 2001. [Bruce MacGregor]

More is known about Martin, in the first three years of the new decade, than Thomas.

Martin too worked for others. The census of 1870 found him still employed by the Central Pacific, not in the Sacramento car shop but as a laborer in Yuba City, further evidence that the recession had taken its toll on the skilled crafts at the Central Pacific's Sacramento shops. Martin was then twenty-seven years old, single, with no listed resources in real estate or savings. Before the year was out, he appeared in the San Francisco business di-

Reconstruction of Martin Carter's staircase, State Capitol of California, Sacramento. [Bruce MacGregor]

rectory in the employ of Langland and Cameron. As business expanded, the city directories reflected a change in the name of the firm. In 1871, it was known as N. P. Langland and began to grow into new commercial and residential markets in Sacramento, as well as San Francisco, specializing in cabinetry and stair manufacture.

In 1868, Langland bid on a library staircase for the new State Capitol building in Sacramento and won the job for $3,425.[75] Two years later, Langland successfully bid an additional Capitol contract to construct several five-story stair assemblies, designed to serve the northwest and southwest corners of the Capitol building, as well as the formal "main" western entrance.

The design of the western staircase was a work of art. It consisted of a pair of mirrored stairways, bracing the central doors, rising to the left and to the right half a story each, reaching a landing (or "gallery") before reversing direction to rise to a common meeting point at the floor above, directly above the west entrance doors. Langland designed formal staircase architecture to showcase the entrance: milled rails fitted into newel posts, turned balusters set into rails above and into the "shoe" of the stair tread below, richly executed in rosewood and oak.

On April 4, 1871, San Francisco artisans Bryant and Strahan joined the project to execute ornamental carvings, detailed figures of a California grizzly bear head, mounted to the newel posts, celebrating California's official state animal. The carvings and relief on the newel posts were done in black walnut.

In the deepening recession, the project caused its share of controversy. A new state architect, joining the work on the Capitol building in 1873, referred to the completed staircase as "elegant but uselessly expensive." By this time, Martin had enjoyed almost two years of steady work from Langland, staying aboard long enough to earn a foreman's position and moving from $3.50 to $5.00 a day in the process. Under Martin, a crew assembled the thousands of intricate milled parts into the capitol's grand staircases.

Langland commissioned many of the required moldings from subcontractors and outside scroll saw shops. Ironically, the Central Pacific car shops, much of its capacity unused in the business slump, contracted out as one of Langland's subs, turning balusters on its belt-driven lathes. In a sense, Ben Welch was finally working for Carter.

In the midst of hard times, Martin started a family. On September 25, 1873, with the staircase work completed, Martin Carter was married to Mary Larkin at St. Rose's Church in Sacramento. Mary's father, John Larkin, had worked for Langland during the Capitol stair project. Archibald Hook, another member of the crew, served as a witness at the wedding and would remain a close friend to the Carters over the next thirty years. One year later, Martin and Mary's first son, Thomas Newton Carter, was born in Sacramento, a namesake for the proud, childless Uncle Thomas.

For the next twenty years, Uncle Thomas would struggle, and fail, to start a family of his own. A tradition survived in the Carter family that Thomas remained closely attached to Martin and Mary, adopting their family as his own. Especially after the founding of Carter Brothers in 1873 or 1874, Thomas and Martin alike nurtured the hope that someday the business would be passed along to Martin's children.[76]

Before the year 1873 was out, the Sacramento directory noted another change in the name of the stair builder, this time to Langland and *Carter*, with local offices at Fourth and N streets. It is compelling evidence that Martin had begun to consider himself a craftsman and a businessman as well. By this time, word of the grand staircase in the Capitol had spread, guaranteeing the firm work in residential staircases and cabinetry. In spite of the recession, Martin had earned a measure of success. He built and owned the family's first home at Fifth and N streets, close to the business, but apparently maintained a separate residence at 1707 Market Street in San Francisco, near Langland's main shop.

We can picture the first visit from a proud uncle. Celebrating the birth of his nephew with good whiskey, Thomas toasted his brother's family, his young namesake, and the new Langland partnership.

Over a second whiskey, Thomas no doubt told Martin the strange story of George Black.

JAN	**Via Chicago & Northwestern Railway.**	17 16
FEB	**SPECIAL-LIMITED-TICKET.**	18 15
MAR	Good for One Continuous	19 14
APR	**Third-Class Passage.**	20 13
MAY	**GOOD IN EMIGRANT CARS (ONLY).**	21 12
JUN	Subject to the following Contract:	22 11
JUL	The Passenger for whom this ticket is issued must sign the same in presence of the Agent as a witness. Conductors will not honor the ticket until so signed.	23 10
AUG	Agents will in no case extend time on this ticket. If more than one date be cancelled, it will not be received for passage by conductors.	24 9
SEP	CHECKS TO BE DETACHED BY CONDUCTORS ONLY. No Stop-Over Privileges will be given on this Ticket. *Baggage Checked only to Destination.*	25 8
OCT	In consideration of this ticket being sold at a reduced price from the regular, full, first-class rate, I, *the undersigned, hereby agree that it will not be good for passage after "TEN" (10) days from (and including) the date* indicated by the Agent's Punch Marks in the margin, and that I will go through to place of Destination by the proper train and its connecting trains; also, that this ticket is **"Not Transferable,"** and shall become "Void" if not presented for passage on the trip for which sold, and that I failing to comply with this agreement either of the Companies may refuse to accept this ticket or any coupons (checks) hereof, and demand the full, regular fare, which I agree to pay.	26 7
NOV		27 6
DEC	I hereby agree to all the provisions of the above contract.	28 5
1880	Signature, *A.by d. Wheel* (SIGN IN INK.)	29 4
1881	Witness, *S. Malpas*	30 3
1882	In case of error on part of Agent, or question of doubt between Holder and Conductor, pay latter's claim, take his receipt, and all irregularities reported to the General Office shall be satisfactorily adjusted.	31 2
1883	*E.H. Goodman*	1
1884	Gen. Pass. & Tkt Agt C.P.R.R.	DAY

| 3410 M | 3d CLASS. | **Chicago & Northwestern Railway.**
COUNCIL BLUFFS
TO
CHICAGO.
On Conditions named in Contract.
Form 3d C. 2 \| This Check will not be good
if detached from Ticket.
CP...UP. | CHICAGO | C. & N. W. Ry. |

The Central Pacific's attempts to establish a single Pacific terminal at Goat Island, in the early 1870s, quickly devolved to construction of smaller facilities scattered around the Bay Area—for example, at Davis Street, in San Francisco (facing page, above); as well as a grain port at Vallejo, with the car transfer *Thoroughfare* connecting to the California Pacific mainline across the Carquinez Strait (shown to the left). The largest San Francisco Bay Area terminal became Oakland's Long Wharf (below). [Facing page: above left, Arthur and Evelyn Mac-Gregor; right, Bancroft Library; this page: top, California State Library; below, Society of California Pioneers]

Refusing to sign an agreement with the Pullman Corp. to operate transcontinental sleeper service, the Central Pacific illustrated its early instinct for vertical control of its business. Instead of Pullman service, the CP insisted on having a fleet of *Silver Palace* sleeping cars built by Harlan & Hollingsworth in 1869 and operating them completely on its own. The eastern-built cars (shown in Thomas Houseworth photographs taken at Oakland, this page and facing page, top) marked a dramatic departure from the flat-roofed car architecture of the 1860s, shown facing page, below, at San Jose some time after 1889. [Thomas Houseworth photographs: Society of California Pioneers; facing page, below, William Wulf collection]

A. G. RIFENBURG,   California Scenery.

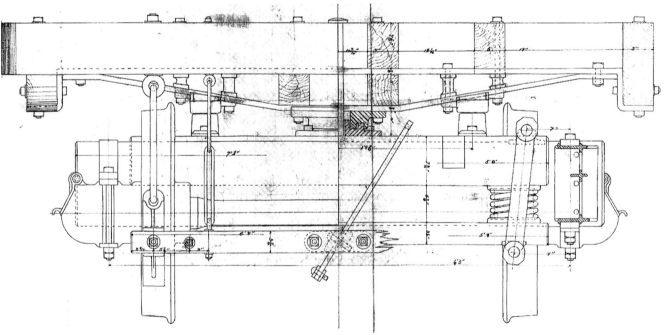

Once the Central Pacific's Sacramento car shop became a high-volume manufacturer of rolling stock, it drove costs down by adopting standardized truck designs, such as the "California" style swing-motion freight truck shown on flanger 923 (above), built in 1875. Drawings of a standard gauge Carter Brothers truck, built for the Eel River & Eureka Railroad in the mid-1880s, show the strong influence of the California-style truck in Carter designs. [Above, Society of California Pioneers; below, California State Railroad Museum]

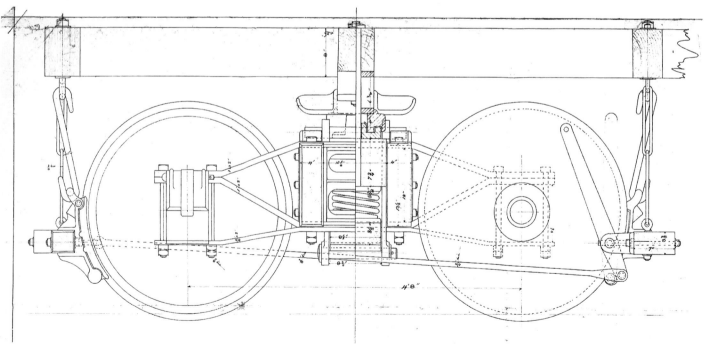

In 1864, the Central Pacific shops were housed in a primitive board and batten shed at Sixth and D Streets in Sacramento, thought to be the building portrayed in the photograph reproduced on the facing page (bottom), after it was apparently moved to the site of the new shops sometime around 1870. Overshadowing the old building, the brick edifice of the Central Pacific's 1868 car shop is portrayed on the facing page (top). Boxcar-sized ricks for seasoning lumber are evidence of the scale of car manufacturing taking place at the Sacramento shops in the 1870s. A Thomas Houseworth view (above) illustrates an early Sacramento-built stock car on the levee near flooded China Slough. [Above, Society of California Pioneers; opposite, above, Sacramento Archives and Museum Collection Center; opposite, below, California State Library]

Already a quarter-century old, the 1874 Baldwin *Olema* posed on the Sausalito pier with its train crew around the turn of the century (above). When the 1875 right-of-way map was plotted (below), the town's name was spelled "Saucelito" and the pier was identified as "the Rail Road Wharf," shown at the extreme left. [Above, California State Railroad Museum; bottom of pages 74–78, California State Archives]

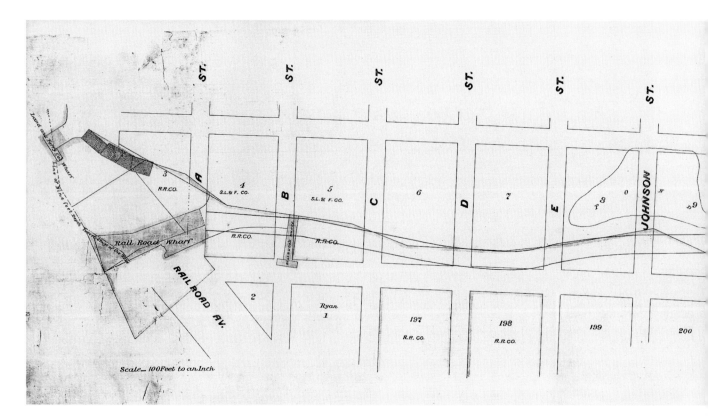

Saucelito: The Kimball Skirmish

George Black was the first of four chief engineers to quit the North Pacific Coast Railroad during its troubled construction, but the only one to leave behind a clear statement why. His resignation, effective at the end of March 1872, was published in the *Marin County Journal* on May 25[1]:

> To the President and Directors of the North Pacific Coast Railroad: gentlemen:
>
> In resigning my position as Chief Engineer of your company, I beg to submit to you the following report of the work which has been done under my directions, and of the future prospects of your enterprise. . . . Having received instructions from you, I proceeded with my party on the 12th of February to San Rafael and commenced the preliminary surveys, which have been completed to Tomales. Two other surveying parties have been put to work by you—one from Saucelito to San Rafael and one from the Russian River to Freestone. There still remains

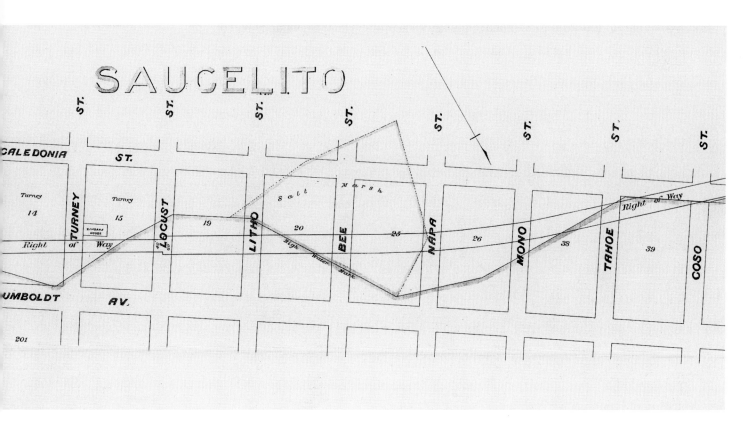

Muybridge view, construction near the wharf area in Saucelito, prior to the building of the train shed, ca. 1873. [Kyle Wyatt collection]

the Division from the Russian River to Walhalla, on which no surveys have yet been made. . . .

. . . Leaving Saucelito, the line traverses a very rough and unfavorable country, through which very heavy earthwork and considerable piling will be required. It will enter San Rafael by a tunnel or very deep cutting through the ridge separating the Ross and San Rafael valleys.

On leaving San Rafael, for the first four miles the line passes over an undulating country, which presents no difficulty whatever. The line here reaches a place known as the "Willow Swamp," a short distance below Mr. Bresson's house, from which there will be an ascending grade of 100 feet per mile for upwards of three miles, to the entrance of the proposed tunnel through White Hill.[2] This hill interposes almost an effectual barrier against the construction of a railroad, unless at enormous cost. It is broken up into sharp ridges, spurs and deep ravines, which are contorted into the most fantastic shapes, and only render construction possible by very heavy cuttings, trestle-work from 50 to 70 feet high, and an uninterrupted succession of the sharpest curves and reverse curves from end to end. Having made the most thorough surveys of this hill and its approaches in all its details, and after having examined five different lines on the south side of it, I have come to the conclusion that the least objectionable line is the one I have recommended. A tunnel fifteen hundred feet in length will be required which will pierce the hill where the Olema road now crosses.[3]

. . . A short distance after leaving the tunnel the line enters a small valley at the head of Arroya San Geronimo (known also as Paper Mill Creek) and continues along it for a distance of five miles with tolerably

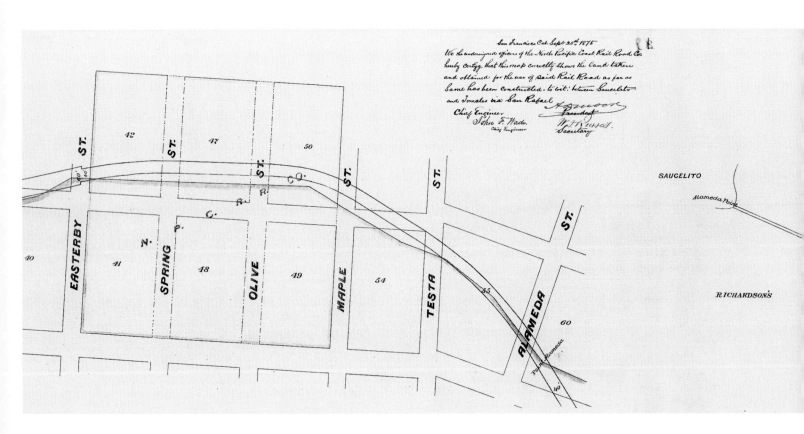

good alignment and grades. It then enters a narrow gorge, following the general direction of the same stream, passing a few wood chopper's huts; then the vestige of what once was a powder mill, and lower down the Paper Mill owned by Mr. S. P. Taylor, and continuing to a point above the Paper Mill warehouse at the head of Tomales Bay, a distance of twenty two miles from the town of San Rafael.

The line then skirts this bay for a distance of about 15 miles to the junction with the Estero de San Antonia which it follows to its junction with Keyes Creek, and continues along the bank of this creek to the town of Tomales, the total distance from San Rafael being about 41 miles.

From Tomales to Valley Ford, a distance of 7 miles, the country assumes a more cultivated aspect, the line passing over undulating ground with two intervening ridges. From Valley Ford to Freestone there is but one ridge to cross, the distance being about 4 miles. From Freestone to Dutch Bill's there will be an ascending grade of from 80 to 100 feet per mile for $3^{1}/_{2}$ miles with very sharp curves, heavy cuttings and high trestle work. From this gap a descending grade of 80 feet to the mile can be obtained over very rough and broken ground which will involve considerable outlay and a continual succession of the sharpest curves. The distance will be about 4 miles. From the end of this grade the line will follow along the banks of Dutch Bill's ravine to its junction with Russian River, thence along the banks of this river to Duncan's Mills. The total distance from Saucelito being 80 miles. . . .

. . . I have made no surveys from Duncan's Mills to Walhalla [Gualala], but from all the information I have obtained from those

Muybridge view, perhaps the earliest known photograph of the North Pacific Coast grade, under construction, near the site of the Saucelito shops, ca. 1873. Below, the 1875 right-of-way map crosses Richardson Bay at the left and continues toward Collins Summit on the right. [Top, Kyle Wyatt collection]

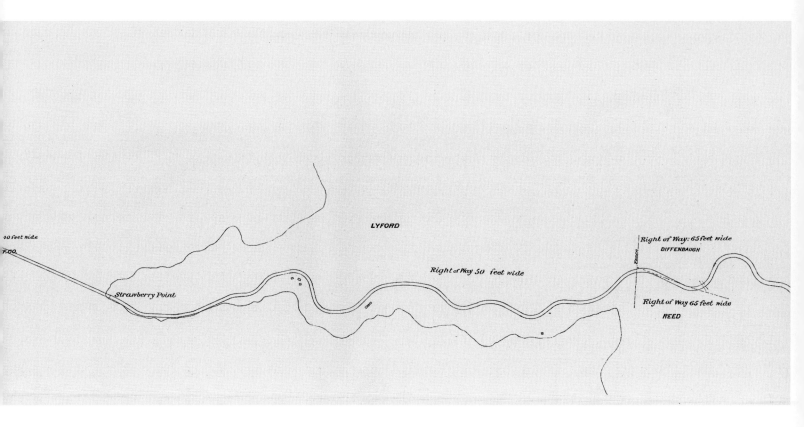

who are perfectly familiar with this section of the country, as well
as private surveys I have examined I entertain no doubt but that if a
railroad is at all practicable it can only be at an enormous outlay, being bounded on one side by the rugged cliffs of the Pacific Ocean and
on the other by a steep mountain side intersected by wide and deep
ravines. Terminating at the Walhalla River, the total distance from
Saucelito will be 115 miles. . . .

. . . The cost of your railroad, as you can see from the estimate,[4] will
be about $23,000 per mile, which may seem large for a narrow gauge
road. Such a road, however, through country as rugged and mountainous as this, will cost more than a broad-gauge road through any of the
valleys of California. . . .

Taking all the foregoing points into consideration, I do not feel myself justified professionally in recommending the construction of the
proposed road as likely ever to make an adequate or any return for the
very large outlay which it will involve. The country through which it
passes from its commencement at the little village of Saucelito on the
Bay of San Francisco to its termination at the mouth of the Walhalla
river, at a distance of 115 miles, is, for the most part, a complete wilderness, unprovided with roads, and entirely unfit for cultivation. The
natural obstacles to its continuance north-ward from the latter point
are such as must effectually bar its further passage at any time.

I am, gentlemen, very respectfully, yours,
Geo. Black, C.E.

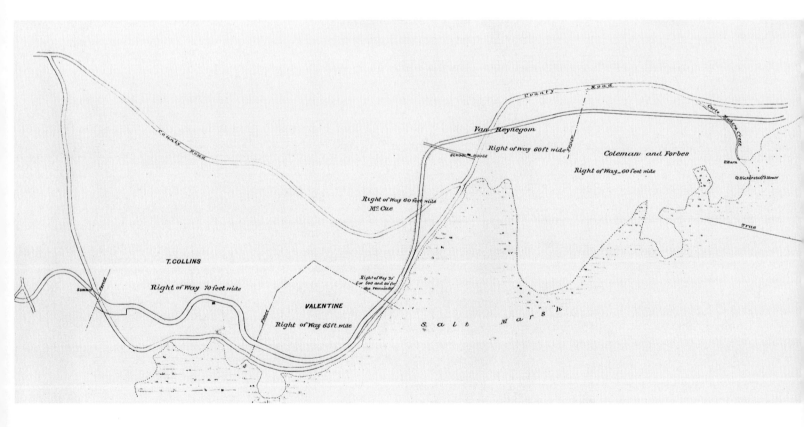

Black wrote the pessimistic resignation during the height of the terminal wars. It was a time after the euphoria of the transcontinental railroad had subsided, leaving most of California still unrewarded by the railroad's direct service or benefits. Instead, like a magnet moving under a roulette wheel, the Central Pacific's search for a Bay Area terminal perturbed the search of smaller investors for a connection. Timber from Marin County, wheat from the Central Valley, and truck-farming crops from Santa Clara Valley all became traffic targeted—and retargeted—at a yet-undetermined city that would act as a portal for the Central Pacific's true Pacific gateway. At the beginning of the terminal wars, signs of a national recession began to appear, tightening capital and creating a sense of urgency in disenfranchised regions of the state, which were anxious to connect with the railroad infrastructure before the resources were simply unavailable.

George Black was outfitted with tents, horses, and chainmen, and sent into the field to establish such a time-critical link. He had been hired by a redwood lumber speculator named Austin Moore, who had most of his capital tied up in a tract of timber he could not profitably harvest without a railroad. Between 1869 and 1871, Moore and his brother, Joseph, had purchased some sixteen thousand acres of timber land at the northern extremity of the Bodega Rancho, in the Coast Range seventy-five miles north of San Francisco.[5] The property included a small mill on Knowles Creek, near its junction with the Russian River. But because of the expense of coastal shipping, the mill remained closed as long as Moore owned the property, its timber reserves largely untouched. In December 1871, the Moore brothers put together a small group of investors to connect the timber land with San Francisco by a narrow gauge railroad, to be called the North Pacific Coast, the only economically viable way of recovering their original investment in the Bodega Rancho. Black was pulled into the project as early as February 1872 and tasked with finding a route through terrain rumpled by the San Andreas Fault.[6]

Austin Moore clearly saw commercial potential in a region larger than the timber preserve he owned. Adjoining first-growth timber stands (such as those that would come under the ownership of the Sonoma Lumber Co.) added market potential to the total reserve along the drainage of Dutch Bill Creek, flowing north into the Russian River. Moore referred to the entire region as "Dutch Bill," after a nearby town, named for its founder, Dutch Bill Howard.[7] On the opposite bank of the Russian River, the sweep of forests continued northward, uninterrupted.

Shortly after Black agreed to run Moore's survey, his transit parties began to cross paths with Central Pacific surveyors in the grassy Marin headlands north of Saucelito, taking meals at adjoining tables in the prematurely christened Railroad Restaurant in Saucelito itself. It was obvious to Black that the two companies would soon be going head-to-head in Marin and Sonoma counties. He struggled with the paradox of the terminal wars: both consort and competition, the Central Pacific was just as likely to build feeder lines as Austin Moore was. They had already poured money into the San Francisco & North Pacific Railroad as a gateway to the Russian River; via its standard gauge rails they were significantly closer to Dutch Bill, at that moment, than

Moore was. In a war of attrition to gain the Russian River timber traffic, the Central Pacific would win.

In November 1871, Black watched the Central Pacific mark its new turf. Stanford's surveyors erected a small brick monument in front of Saucelito's Green Hotel shortly after Stanford bought the California Pacific bonds, gaining control of the SF&NP.[8] The Central Pacific men went about their task in silence, revealing no strategy. But the *Saucelito Weekly Herald* had little trouble predicting that the San Francisco & North Pacific track would be extended across the San Pablo Bay marsh from its terminal at Vallejo, completing the Central Pacific mainline from Sacramento to Saucelito—at eighty-three and a half miles long, the shortest possible "airline" route to its western terminal. A village of just one hundred eighty-one souls, Saucelito regarded the marker as a contract. Editorials published in the *Herald* pictured the village at the extreme reach of the Central Pacific's expansion to the coast, the western gateway to the transcontinental railroad.[9]

Austin Moore, searching for local funding, at first found the brick marker a useful catalyst. It was evidence that the southern end of the county would soon have rail connections to the outside world. He convinced two county commissioners, William Tillinghast and Sam Taylor, that $160,000 invested in twenty-year, 7 percent county bonds would open the Saucelito gateway not only to his own timber interests but to Tillinghast's real estate development at Saucelito and Taylor's paper mill in Lagunitas Canyon. Up the coast, a Bodega potato farmer named Warren Dutton joined the investors. Local politics soon aligned with Moore's backers. On January 28, 1872, two months after the brick marker was cemented into place, the fifty-nine male

An 1872 profile of North Pacific Coast, on mudflats near Saucelito. [Northwestern Pacific Railroad Historical Society]

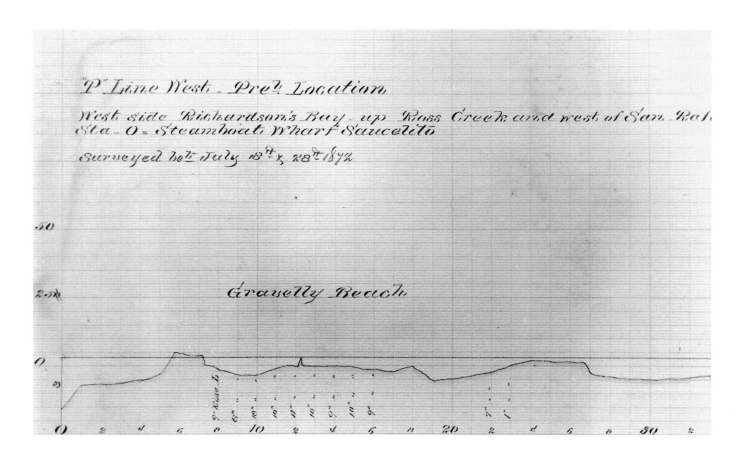

voters in the Saucelito precinct voted *unanimously* in favor of a county railroad bond measure that would tie the northern end of the county to its port at Saucelito. The county commissioners named the North Pacific Coast as the beneficiary of the bonds.

Saucelito suddenly became a redoubt in the terminal wars.

Tucked into the lee side of Mt. Tamalpais, close to the tip of a hilly, narrow peninsula that swept into the bay like the abutment of a bridge, the village began to take on the airs of a major transportation hub. The Railroad Restaurant opened without a railroad anywhere in sight. Old and New Saucelito, joined along four thousand feet of shallow bay frontage, gazed Janus-like at each other, seeing past and future across the seam. The old town, consisting of the ship ways; the Green Hotel; and the store, post office, livery stable, and lumber yard of J. S. Bellrude, had been a commercial harbor since the Gold Rush. In more recent times, it was a weekend anchorage of the San Francisco yacht fraternity, as well as a watering hole for the adventurous Bohemia Club.

The new town was a sluggish real estate development promoted (not very successfully) by Tillinghast's Saucelito Land and Ferry Co. In the early 1870s, its principal marketing strategy had been picnic excursions to a rustic dance pavilion located in the oak-dotted uplands of the property, but the resultant drunken sprees led to an abrupt halt to the excursions and the dismantling, in March 1872, of the dance floor. Instead, the company "hoped to promote a peaceful, residential atmosphere." All that was missing were residents.

But along with the railroad, residents would come. The voters of Saucelito began to see proof. On Sunday, June 30, 1872, the lunch crowd at the Railroad Restaurant pressed their noses to the window glass and stared in amazement as Leland Stanford, Collis Huntington, and H. H. Montague walked the streets outside, causing the restaurant's patrons to speculate about an imminent Central Pacific invasion of the whole north coast.[10] With signs of the recession deepening, the effect of the visit was like a business call from the Holy Trinity.

For the seventeen months the Central Pacific controlled the SF&NP, the brick marker became a cipher for Saucelito's undelivered future, the site of the true western terminal of the transcontinental railroad, and the narrow end of the funnel for forest products flowing south into a huge Central Pacific feeder system.

For the two months he remained chief engineer of the North Pacific Coast, at a salary of $300 per month, George Black regarded the brick marker as evidence of the invincible enemy he faced. The Central Pacific already controlled SF&NP track extending twenty-seven miles north from Donahue Landing, through the broad valleys of Petaluma and Santa Rosa nearly to the Russian River itself.[11] A branch from Fulton would bring SF&NP track within three miles of Austin Moore's mill, rendering the North Pacific Coast useless before it was even built.

Tillinghast's real estate development would benefit from the Saucelito terminal, but Sam Taylor's paper mill lay deep in the narrow canyon of San Geronimo, accessible only by crossing the high, jagged ridge of White's Hill. The North Pacific Coast route, specified in the January bond election, ran through the nether regions of the county. Black was hamstrung by a survey

Lagunitas depot, an example of a first-generation North Pacific Coast station; the store remains a landmark today on Sir Francis Drake Boulevard.

White's Hill landscape at sunrise, May 2001; the original North Pacific Coast grade rounds the promontory in the foreground and heads uphill toward the site of the summit tunnel, now daylighted by highway terraces in the distance. [Bruce MacGregor]

predicated on serving Moore's investors. A long and expensive tunnel would be required to breast the summit. If by some miracle Black succeeded in surveying a commercial line over the labyrinth of White's Hill, he would soon face miles of costly trestling on Tomales Bay to reach the town of Tomales, where Warren Dutton's potato harvests awaited shipment by rail, and he would still be thirty miles shy of Austin Moore's sawmill. Black concluded the worst. His resignation was on Moore's desk by April 1, 1872. Sometime that summer, Black accepted a position with the enemy, signing onto the SF&NP as a locating engineer.

That winter, in the Sonoma House bar, George Black probably told Tom Carter the simple truth that compelled him to quit the North Pacific Coast. The route that the Marin electorate had committed $160,000 to build in the bond election of December 1871, the route that *every* registered voter in Saucelito voted for, the route that would, in President Austin Moore's thinking, become a secure inland pipeline for all the coastal lumber production between San Francisco and Puget Sound, was not the route the North Pacific Coast should take.

If it was not the biggest vaudeville act in the history of U.S. railroad surveying, the North Pacific Coast still could have charged admission.

On August 24, 1872, President Austin Moore followed George Black's resignation with a public confession.[12] He acknowledged the belated discovery of a dramatically better route to the timber belt, bypassing some thirty-five miles of Black's survey up treacherous White's Hill, using instead San Pablo Bay and San Antonio Creek to reach the town of Tomales with minimal grades, no tunnels, and virtually no large bridges. The route would have followed the modern line of highway 101 to the marsh about five miles south of Petaluma and then ascended Arroyo San Antonio an additional ten miles to the town of Tomales. The mistake, Moore insisted, was an honest one. The San Antonio Creek route simply had not been known, much less surveyed, at the time Black did his discouraging work on White's Hill. Moore closed his letter of apology with an amazing offer to build *both* lines, Black's and the San Antonio Creek line, if the county would rescind the old bond measure and pass a new bond measure—this one for $360,000, double the old.

The combination of Black's resignation and Moore's bait-and-switch tactic left the North Pacific Coast Railroad short of the two things it needed most: cash and credibility.

Moore generated his first funding by selling 935 shares of capital stock, at $100 a share, to twenty local businessmen.[13] But the terms of the stock subscription were generous, tailored to the liquidity of small businesses. The investors could pay their debt in modest installments. Just 10 percent of the stock value, for example, was due in the "first assessment" on December 16, 1871. Similar assessments continued throughout 1872. By July of that year, when the summer weather provided the first opportunity to start construction, only four assessments had been made, and less than $40,000 collected.[14] Without capital, construction languished. Two wheelbarrows and some twenty shovelmen were sent to White's Hill in July 1872 as a token effort at keeping the original promise, but their presence was a source of humor, not reassurance, to Marin newspapers.[15] The Marin County bonds remained undelivered, the county supervisors increasingly skeptical of Moore's commitment.[16]

Inside the North Pacific Coast's board of directors, the bungled bond issue did not cause the alarm it should have. To most of the directors, multiple routes simply rationalized multiple business agendas. The board members were all prominent local businessmen, and their individual interests, with one exception, appeared well protected no matter which route was adopted. Austin Moore's Dutch Bill timber holdings have already been discussed. Board member Warren Dutton owned potato farms at Bodega, and his crop would be safely sacked onto the cars at Tomales for shipment to the city, whether by White's Hill or by San Antonio Creek. NPC treasurer William Tillinghast, also vice president of the Saucelito Land and Ferry Co., owned real estate interests at the extreme southern terminal of the railroad, as well as lumber lands in Dutch Bill, all within the scope of Moore's revised proposal.

Tillinghast was betting that Saucelito's slumbering real estate market would take wing once the railroad was built—by either route—and he had potentially invaluable connections with Ralston's Bank of California through the land and ferry company's treasurer, Maurice Dore. There was no banking house yet involved with the railroad, but soon there would have to be. As treasurer of the North Pacific Coast, Tillinghast was looked to for long-term financial guidance, and ultimately a plan for solvency.

Tillinghast had little to lose no matter which route the North Pacific Coast chose. To speed the real estate development along, Saucelito Land and Ferry donated forty acres of its Saucelito development to the narrow gauge for right-of-way, shop, and depot buildings. Tillinghast moved his family into Saucelito's first mansion that July, exuding confidence that the real estate boom was imminent once the terminal was in operation. Local humorists liked to explain Tillinghast's strategy this way: If the North Pacific Coast just connected Saucelito with the county seat at San Rafael, barely seven miles away, it could stop laying track and stop worrying about which route it needed to reach the redwoods. Marin County—and Tillinghast—would be all the better served.

But Sam Taylor would not. Taylor was the only board member who would suffer a large personal loss from the rescinding of the original route. Pioneer developer of the first paper mill on the Pacific Coast, constructed in 1856 just over the seemingly unbreachable barrier of White's Hill, Taylor made no bones about his stake in the original plan. He badly needed direct service from the NPC to meet all-winter contracts for newsprint delivery to San Francisco dailies such as the *Daily Alta California* and the *Bulletin*. When the Paper Mill shattered a cast iron gear in the winter of 1873, a replacement part was cast in San Francisco, entrusted to an express wagon over the muddy roads of White's Hill, and installed in less than three working days. The feat was considered a miracle. Taylor imagined catastrophes that would strand his mill for weeks if the roads became impassable.

At railroad board meetings, Sam Taylor was not shy about pointing out the mutual interests of railroad and paper mill. Taylor's mill was one of the few large on-line industries the railroad would serve before it reached the sawmills of the Russian River, and without it the struggling carrier was bereft of freight revenue for its first fifty miles.

Unable to resolve the sectional issues that frustrated his south county backers, Moore was becoming nervous that the board had forgotten the whole point: to reach *his* timber in Dutch Bill. During the summer of 1872, little surveying work was completed on the track required to ascend Salmon Creek to the edge of the Dutch Bill watershed. Even if it were unanimous in its rejection of the White's Hill route (which it wasn't), the NPC's board still could not accurately forecast the additional capital the railroad would eat up in tunneling out of Tomales and struggling north up the Salmon and Dutch Bill watersheds to reach the Russian River.

Instead, like thousands of other newspaper readers across the country, the board members believed articles they read extolling the unique economies of narrow gauge railroad construction. The publicity appeared with the advent of the Denver & Rio Grande Railroad in February 1871 and began to reach the proportions of a fad by the time the first National Narrow Gauge Convention met in St. Louis on June 19, 1872.[17] Leaders in the movement, such as Howard Schuyler (the chief engineer for the Denver & Rio Grande), authored detailed cost estimates on the basis of experience laying and equipping the first 120 miles of Rio Grande mainline along the edge of the Front Range in Colorado.[18]

Two facts stood out prominently in Schuyler's reports and in the newspaper summaries that followed. First, the Rio Grande was completed for $13,500 per mile (including rolling stock), almost half of the $23,500 per mile required to build the neighboring standard gauge Kansas Pacific, which Schuyler had also helped engineer. Both lines, Schuyler pointed out, were built through comparable country: rolling foothills, not mountains.

Second, Schuyler emphasized what he considered to be an inherent advantage in the design of narrow gauge rolling stock. For standard gauge cars of the time, the ratio of dead weight to payload weight in rolling stock was about one to one. This meant that for every pound of freight hauled, the railroad had to haul one pound as dead weight in the body of the car. But for the early narrow gauge designs Schuyler purchased, the payload-to-dead-weight ratio was at least two to one, and as high as three to one in the case of flatcars.[19] In other words, for every pound of dead weight in rolling stock, at least two pounds of payload could be carried. These arguments, published at the time of the first Narrow Gauge Convention, were repeated in the *Saucelito Weekly Herald* on July 13, 1872.

This apparent improvement in payload-to-dead-weight ratio translated to extremely lightly built narrow gauge cars. Cynical old car builders criticized the logic. A fleet of such cars might save capital expense at the time they were built, but they would wear out quickly under even normal service conditions. Under peak loads, such cars were likely to last about as long as disposable packing crates.

A second false economy was at work. The first American narrow gauge car designs had been inspired by light, rigid, European four-wheel vans, a design rejected thirty years earlier by the industry as too rigid for American track. Yet the first-generation Denver & Rio Grande rolling stock, manufactured by Billmeyer and Small, attempted to preserve the high payload-to-dead-weight ratio by using four-wheel designs, which was an invitation to derailment.[20] In 1871, the American narrow gauge movement was simply downsizing outdated technology.

Most mechanical engineers who considered these arguments agreed that the narrow gauge movement was too new and too untested to reach any reliable conclusions. Only one evolutionary trend was clear. Narrow gauge designs soon began to migrate toward standard U.S. railroad practice. By 1872, Schuyler was applauding the merits of the Rio Grande's new eight-wheel rolling stock, manufactured by Jackson and Sharp and Billmeyer and Small.[21] Billmeyer and Small's second-generation boxcars and flatcars, for example, measured about twenty-four feet long, were built on four sills, used eight-wheel trucks, and were rated at a capacity of 8.8 tons—a miniature standard gauge car. Weight reduction was still a key feature of the design. Schuyler took pride in pointing out that the payload-to-dead-weight ratio in the new eight-wheel cars was still close to two to one. Billmeyer and Small became recognized as a leader in the narrow gauge movement and published extensive explanations of their design philosophy and product approach. In most of these publications, light construction and low body weight were emphasized.[22]

Business conditions in California seemed primed for such technology:

> California undoubtedly needs competition, . . . there is an opening for *some* system as a rival to the existing one . . . while the huge "existing system" might suffice to transport the greater bulks, the through freight, we sorely need another, in the words of the song, to "do up the finer work." While the Central Pacific and its branches strike like great arteries through California, we require an extensive network of local feeders or local rivals to meet our needs. This idea has rooted itself deeply in the minds of the people, and in consequence of it there sprang up an almost innumerable crop of narrow gauge enterprises, which have seemed to choke each other out like grain sown too thick.[23]

The "crop," by 1873, included the Benicia & Red Bluff (soon reborn as the California Central Narrow Gauge Railroad), chartered to build a narrow gauge feeder through the Central Valley wheat belt; the Stockton & Ione (Howard Schuyler's brother, James, was its chief engineer); the San Francisco, San Mateo & Santa Cruz; the San Benito Railroad; the Monterey & Natividad; the Truckee & Plumas; the Los Angeles & Santa Monica; the Colfax & Nevada City; the San Luis Obispo & Santa Maria; and the San Jose & Alviso—not *one* of which was off the drawing boards at the time the North Pacific Coast first struggled to break ground. But looking at maps of the imagined narrow gauge lines, cross-stitched through coastal California, it didn't take long for local developers to imagine a single system of low-cost feeder lines long enough, and integrated enough, to compete with the Central Pacific.[24] Finally breaking ground in July 1872, the North Pacific Coast became the first California narrow gauge railroad to join the contest, and the first to test optimistic assumptions about cost savings.

But more careful survey work along the skirt of Tomales Bay raised doubts about the real costs. Engineering reports on the North Pacific Coast, for example, included the grim scenario of miles of open trestle work along Tomales Bay, demanding an enormous quantity of Douglas fir to construct trestle. Rumors began to churn that the NPC would bypass the county seat at San Rafael in its erratic flight over White's Hill, choosing instead the wide corridor of Ross Valley to reach the base of White's Hill at the modern location of San Anselmo. Angry land owners, such as William Coleman, began to corrode the support of the county board of supervisors, threatening suit if the railroad defaulted on its bond election promise to directly serve the county seat.

It was hard to keep the North Pacific Coast's troubles under wraps. On July 13, 1872, less than four months after Black's departure, Chief Engineer Andrew Jackson Binney, the second man in the position, handed in his resignation with no public explanation. Julius Smith was recruited to take his place.

Sluggish fundraising continued to plague the company. In September, Austin Moore and H. A. Cobb appealed to San Francisco for help, trying to influence the board of supervisors there to mandate an election for $1 million in bonds, issued on the condition that the North Pacific Coast Railroad establish a terminal at North Beach. The promotional pitch, delivered by Moore on September 21, played up the economies of narrow gauge (Moore claimed operating expenses per ton of freight hauled would be half those of broad gauge) and played up the growing fear that the Mission Bay lands owned by the Central Pacific would soon pull the mercantile center of the city away from North Beach, turning it into a ghost town. Moore used the recession as a basis for scare tactics. Without new traffic sources like his, San Francisco would starve.

But the Central Pacific marker at the Green Hotel was still in place, and Stanford's surveyors were still actively at work in upper Marin and Sonoma counties. Moore could hardly guarantee that North Beach would receive the undivided whole of the coastal lumber business. Crumbs, perhaps, if Stanford moved against Moore with a mainline directly from Saucelito to the Russian River. Unmoved by the David-and-Goliath image Moore concocted, the San Francisco Board of Supervisors refused to consider the bond election.

Moore fared little better back in Marin County. An unsigned card appeared in the *San Francisco Bulletin* on September 23, 1872, offering a local assessment of the situation:

> The citizens and tax-payers of Marin County by no means endorse or favor the scheme of the corporation called the North Pacific Coast Railroad. The fact is, the North Pacific Coast Railroad has a very indefinite location in the county. None of us, as yet, have any very distinct notion of its future where-abouts, nor is it very clear that the parties operating this affair know themselves. . . .
>
> . . . The fact is, the county has had quite enough of the North Pacific Coast Railroad, such as it is.

At least, it seems the Marin County Board of Supervisors had had quite enough of Moore's bait-and-switch strategy; they voted unanimously, on October 4, 1872, to reject the railroad's request for "doubling down" on its public bonds. Thus a gun was placed to Moore's head: complete the White's

Hill route, or forfeit the $160,000 in first-election county bonds. By this time, civil engineers Black, Binney, and now Smith were all aware that the North Pacific Coast would burn up $30,000 per mile getting through the hard backbone of White's Hill—the price of two tunnels, six trestles, and nearly continuous cut-and-fill earthworks.

At that rate, even $160,000 worth of Marin County bonds would not take the railroad very far from the Saucelito wharf.

George Black was right. As long as the Central Pacific controlled the San Francisco & North Pacific, no bank in its right mind would lend money to the badly outgunned North Pacific Coast. By December 31, 1872, one full year after incorporation, the only liquidity Moore could lay his hands on was $119,925 in assessments squeezed from twenty Marin and Sonoma County businessmen, a few thousand dollars at a time. The last assessment money the railroad would collect (paid the following April) brought the cash contribution to $163,450.[25] The total represented just 5 percent of the face value of the subscribed stock. The county well had run dry.

Moore needed a miracle, and when it showed up—wrapped for Christmas 1872—he recognized that it would come at a price. Though the press would not publish the story until a month later, Moore probably knew by the middle of December that the Central Pacific was negotiating to sell the SF&NP back to its original owner, Peter Donahue. Beset by the recession, struggling with cash problems of its own, Stanford's engorged organization badly needed to focus its resources on terminal construction in San Francisco and Oakland. It would cede the north coast timber hauling to others. Stanford's army had begun its withdrawal from Marin and Sonoma counties, abandoning the stone marker by Green's Hotel.

It was no coincidence that the first loan from Milton Latham to the North Pacific Coast, a modest $45,000, followed the news by just days. With the Central Pacific out of the picture, Latham wanted back in. Just a year before, he had controlled the SF&NP. Now, with the Central Pacific threat removed, he would invest in its competitor and start the game anew. The loan, entered into the railroad's financial *Journal* no. 1 on December 31, 1872, was a good-faith advance on a package deal Latham extended to Moore.

The deal saved Moore from disaster. More loans from Latham quickly followed. Latham's London and San Francisco Bank would underwrite a North Pacific Coast first mortgage bond issue the following April, worth a total of $3 million. Latham appeared to be generous. Moore was welcome to sell $2 million of the bonds for as much as he could get; the remaining million in bonds, held by the London and San Francisco Bank in a bond hypothecate account, would be converted to cash at thirty-three cents on the dollar. The bank would advance Moore $335,000 while holding, in turn, three times that amount in bonds as collateral.[26] Upon repayment of the loan, Moore would get the bonds back, free to sell them at face value. Similar hypothecate accounts were created at the Bank of British Columbia in August and September 1873, apparently under Latham's guarantee, bringing in an additional $165,000 in advances.

The best part, from Moore's perspective, was that the bank's advance did not represent control of the company. Latham purchased no stock and could not vote on the affairs of the railroad. He would remain a silent partner, and Moore would remain in control.

Although the first cash advance from the London and San Francisco Bank would not be made until April 1873, the impact of the credit was felt immediately inside the cash-starved company. On December 24, 1872, a contract for construction of the railroad between Saucelito and Tomales was signed with A. K. Grim for $1.2 million, to be compensated by equal parts cash and stock. Working on the installment plan, Moore could afford to pay Grim with monies coming in from bond hypothecate transactions, on average about $30,000 every month. At the same rate he garnered cash, Grim took delivery on a like value of stock. Grim thus acquired an average of almost seven hundred shares a month throughout 1873, easily becoming the majority stockholder in the railroad.

Much of the day-to-day bookkeeping for construction became invisible in the railroad's cash journals, subsumed—like his growing control of the railroad—in A. K. Grim's own account books.

But surveyors remained directly under Chief Engineer Julius Smith, and thus securely under Moore's control. New field engineers (E. Y. Buchanan for one) began to drive stakes into gradients only roughly located by Black. Buchanan's field party consisted of a transit man, a rodman, a topographer, two chainmen, two axemen, a flagman, a cook, and a teamster. Charged with developing detailed location maps, Buchanan was also given the critical specification of the earth moving that would be handed to A. K. Grim, from which projections of cost could be developed. Without such data, Moore was blind to the real cost of construction. So critical was engineering data to the railroad's planning that Buchanan was soon sharing field work with civil engineer E. H. Mix, who, by March, was running lines to establish the big tunnel on White's Hill. By late February 1873, Moore even had a locating party in Dutch Bill, doing advance work on the northern end of the line under a civil engineer named John Wade.[27] For the first time in months, Austin Moore must have felt he had Dutch Bill timber in the crosshairs of the railroad's transits.

In lieu of cash, the forwarding house of Falkner and Bell accepted bonds as collateral for rail.[28] The bark *Lapwing* dropped anchor in Saucelito harbor on November 13, 1873, with a thousand tons of British rail on board, and was unloaded by lighters shuttling back and forth to a temporary pier. The rail was stockpiled at the foot of Easterby Street in Saucelito, soon to be the site of the North Pacific Coast's shops. Enough rail was on hand by Christmas to lay twenty miles of track, up over White's Hill and into the Paper Mill Creek canyon, as far as the paper mill itself, bringing season's greetings to Sam Taylor.

The bark *Martha Rideout* brought bridge and tunnel timbers from Puget Sound, from the Renton Smith mill at Port Blakely.[29] The schooner *J. Mora Moss* brought ties from Stewart's Point on the Mendocino coast. Most of the material was stockpiled at the foot of Easterby Street, since the railroad was unable to move it north of the uncompleted Richardson Bay bridge.

Grim, meanwhile, began to assign segments of line to subcontractors, among them James Lemon, who successfully bid the Collins Summit stretch on the opposite side of the uncompleted Richardson Bay bridge—perhaps, it would turn out, at too low a price.[30] Each subcontractor in turn had to hire large Chinese gangs to begin work. By March 1, three hundred men were running scrapers and buckets along the Saucelito-Tomales survey line, a small army compared to the skeleton crew of the previous summer. White and Bugbee got the contract for the 1,250-foot tunnel through the crest of White's Hill, and eighty-five contract Chinese shovelmen went to work on the approaches to the tunnel, split between a day and a night shift.[31]

By early March, bids were being solicited for major bridge work. Boxed in on three sides by water, the railroad chose to make its escape from Saucelito on a four-thousand-foot trestle across Richardson Bay, bridging over the oyster beds and onto the narrow, hilly promontory of Strawberry Point.

From the eastern bridge pier, a steep climb to Collins Summit, near the flourishing Lyford dairy, brought the North Pacific Coast to an overlook of the county seat at San Rafael.

In the rising tide of new work, Thomas Carter got a small engineering job. On the last day of February 1873, the railroad's accountant noted an advance of forty dollars to Carter for a trip from Sacramento to Livermore, where the North Pacific Coast would pay him five dollars a day to make engineering sketches of the stone culverts on the Central Pacific's line over Altamont Pass. The work might be referred to today as "benchmarking," establishing new designs on the basis of the accepted practice of others. Perhaps Smith anticipated the need for similar culverts on the steep ascent of White's Hill. Ironically, as far as we know, no dressed stone culverts were ever constructed on the North Pacific Coast.

The railroad's first journal entry under account 45 shows that Carter was paid for travel by train from Sacramento to Livermore, which suggests he was living with Martin and his family after being furloughed from Donahue Landing—a layoff, we suspect, that occurred six weeks earlier after the Central Pacific decamped from the SF&NP. It remains unclear how Carter got the new assignment. In the first two months of 1873, twenty-five or thirty new names enter Journal no. 1 as civil engineers or engineering assistants, required to support Grim's snowballing construction contract. Smith, in turn, probably knew and respected Black (whose tortuous grade over White's Hill was slowly being repackaged by the Marin press as an "engineering wonder of the world"). Even a referral from Black, not exactly the most celebrated hero in the railroad's growing list of departed chief engineers, might have been enough to land Carter the few days of work in the Livermore hills. Carter quickly produced tracings of the stone culverts, evidence that in spite of the rigorous demands of field work he had the talent and the physical ability to do the job.

The journal testified to Carter's return to the challenging outdoor life of a contract engineer. The proof that survives is not the mechanical drawings themselves but an accountant's line item entered into Journal no. 1 on March 24, 1873. It noted Carter paid four dollars to a stable in Livermore and sent the North Pacific Coast the bill.

Thomas Carter, with just one leg, could now ride a horse.

———

Considering the foul mood of the Marin County Board of Supervisors, it was clear to nearly everyone that the arrival of the narrow gauge in the county seat of San Rafael would be one of the most politically correct moves the company could make. But nearly a mile of open water blocked the way, effectively delaying distribution of supplies, among them the thousand tons of stockpiled rail, to northerly points along the survey. Trapped by the terrain as well as the politics, the NPC's fate seemed linked to the Richardson Bay bridge, and newspapers watched its progress like a kind of bellwether for the general health of the embattled railroad.

As early as March 8, 1873, the *Saucelito Herald* reported reconnaissance activity on Richardson Bay itself. Storms routinely brought rain and cold winds. Small boats, putting out to make soundings for the bridge, bobbed like corks as they worked their way back and forth across the narrows. The soundings were essential for mapping out the depth of Richardson Bay across the nearly mile-long reach of the bridge and were the basis for determining the length of "spiles" (as the *Herald* called piles) as well as the location of the draw span at the deepest point in the channel.

Inside the adolescent company, the bridge project soon became a painful example of growing bureaucracy. A. K. Grim, as general contractor, had the authority to retain and pay a bridge subcontractor. But the railroad, under Chief Engineer Julius Smith, maintained the authority to "design and specify" the work that Grim was contracted to deliver. Such engineering work was often subcontracted to freelance professionals, sometimes (Carter's culvert work is an example) in installments of only a few days work at a time. In addition to these two distinct types of direct contracting work (engineering and construction), there was a third: purchasing. The railroad retained the right to purchase the raw materials its general contractors and subcontractors would use. For example, it was Smith, not Grim, who specified the suppliers for materials the latter would use and paid for them through railroad accounts.

At least three separate layers of bookkeeping were involved in accounting for these activities as they unfolded on the Strawberry Point bridge project: an account (or "folio") for Grim himself, numbered 150; an account for engineering activity, such as an account that would soon be in Thomas Carter's name, numbered 45; and an account for the supplier of procured materials, for example, Renton Smith for timbers, billed to account 92.

Although the distinctions among railroad, contractor, subcontractor, and supplier were not made clear in newspaper articles about the bridge, all of the players made at least a token appearance in the pages of the *Herald*. A site engineer (unnamed in the March 8 article) was busy developing the plans and bills of material for the bridge. Smith, as chief engineer for the railroad, inspected the plans and approved them. In turn, he carried out procurement according to the bill of material and handed the purchase orders and the engineering package over to contractor Grim to execute. Grim, in turn, handed the responsibility for actually building the bridge to a construction subcontractor.

The chain of command between chief engineer, contractor, subcontractors, and suppliers was established with almost military discipline. Field engineering, though assigned to a contractor, would report directly to the chief engineer of the North Pacific Coast. The chief engineer then turned the engineering work into requirements and procurement for a construction contractor. That contractor, in turn, could take the same plans and materials and assign them to a subcontractor. The chain of command had one basic intent: as much as possible, to keep the engineering work under the close control of the railroad's management—represented by Julius Smith.

Perhaps because of the new layers of bureaucracy, the Richardson Bay bridge work seemed to proceed slowly. Not until a month later, on April 5, 1873, did the *Herald* publish an update of the progress on the critical bridge, offering the first details of its design and finally naming the engineer in charge.

Looking like Melville's Captain Ahab, Thomas Carter stood wooden-legged in a dingy, his beard billowing sideways to indicate the prevailing wind.

He was in command of his ship. Thirty-eight times across the narrows, every one hundred feet, he gave the order for two hands to feather their oars. Charles Forrest and Thomas Cassidy would then spring into action, lowering a sounding rod over the side until it touched bottom. Carter navigated, keeping Strawberry Point to the stern and Alameda Point to the bow, dead reckoning a forty-two-hundred-foot course across open water. He made at least two passes, at high tide and low tide. In two working days, his oarsmen rowed nearly four miles.[32]

After two days on the choppy, wind-burned water, Carter had mapped the bottom of Richardson Bay. At the center, the channel was twelve feet, seven inches deep at high tide; its depth shrank to just six feet at low tide. The *Herald* also reported that Carter estimated the depth of mud at twenty-eight feet, concluding that forty-foot spiles—750 of them—would be long enough to be driven through the mud to refusal in the hard pan below.

On Friday, one day before the paper's April 5 publication date, Carter moved his flotilla to the bay shallows just offshore from the village of Saucelito itself and took trial soundings for the projected railroad ferry pier.

Favorably impressed with Carter's work on the Altamont Pass culverts, Smith hired him as a contract engineer to the North Pacific Coast, a "direct" contractor and not a subcontractor to Grim or the Gorrill brothers, who would subsequently build the Strawberry Point bridge under the business entity of the Pacific Bridge Co. Thus Carter—like Buchanan, Mix, and Wade—reported directly to the chief engineer. Although in charge of only four thousand feet of track on the bridge itself, Carter was expected to break through one of the most frustrating bottlenecks on the railroad. The season of good weather was upon them. The bridge would hold up shipments of rail and track material to the north unless finished before winter. Because of the many layers in the organization—linking chief engineer (Smith), field engineer (Carter), construction contractor (Grim), subcontractor (Pacific Bridge Co.), and suppliers (Renton Smith and others), a mistake in specifying the project could hold the railroad hostage for months. Carter was given Smith's trust that there would be no mistakes.

From local accounts in the *Saucelito Herald*, we know Carter's involvement probably unfolded something like this: from the sounding data, he drew scale elevations of the bridge, including a rotating draw span, which opened up a shipping channel to let scows and pleasure craft reach the cove of Richardson Bay. He finished the profiles quickly, for Smith personally rechecked Carter's data about a week after the early April soundings and announced to the *Herald* that the work was free from error.[33]

From elevations, Carter drew up two bills of material (one for iron, one for timber), turning the specifications back over to Smith during the week of April 26. The drawings do not survive, but a Carter elevation of a similar bridge, drawn in 1876, does and suggests that they represented working drawings of sufficient detail to specify both timber and iron parts. This elevation is reproduced in Chapter Ten and is the earliest known Carter mechanical drawing. On the basis of bids received against the bill of material, Smith made arrangements with Renton Smith for bridge piles. He made arrangements with Alexander Duncan, a Russian River mill owner, for bridge timbers.[34] Grim was going through a similar process to find a subcontractor to actually erect the bridge, soliciting bids on the completed plans by the middle of May.[35]

Smith's urgent schedule soon slipped. A successful bidder for the construction subcontract wasn't identified in the newspaper until July 31, three months later, when the *Herald* announced Pacific Bridge Co. of Oakland would get the work. But even the good news, the arrival of Renton Smith spiles aboard the *Martha Rideout* on July 24, brought delays when at least a portion of the spiles were found to be too short—a determination not reported until September 4, when Pacific Bridge pile drivers were in position in Richardson Bay, finally ready for action. With autumn fast approaching, setbacks plagued the notorious bridge.

⸻

If the roles had been reversed—if Carter Brothers and the Pacific Bridge Co. had magically traded places—the two pairs of brothers would have been remarkably at home in each other's worlds. In fact, for a brief time they were. Both pioneered a startup business that transplanted and shortened the eastern supply chain for products that had virtually no western source. Both focused substantially on designing and building hybrid structures of wood and metal, and both entered a western market place almost without competition. But the Carters left behind no known correspondence while Henry and Charlie Gorrill did, and it is from the perspective of Pacific Bridge that the earliest accomplishments of Thomas Carter as an independent engineering contractor can best be judged.[36]

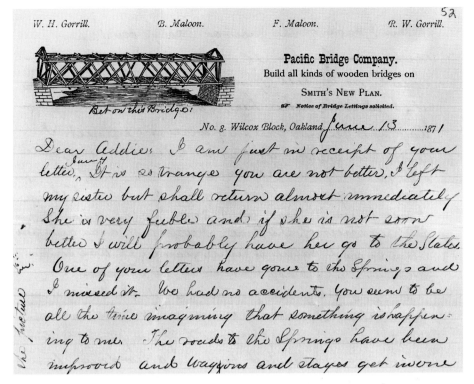

Henry Gorrill (above) founded the Pacific Bridge Co. and, only partly in humor, asked his fiancée, on company stationery, to "bet on this bridge." [Both, Center for Archival Collections, Bowling Green State University]

Ironically, like Carter, William Henry Gorrill had started his business with a serious physical limitation. Wracked by tuberculosis, and perhaps by uncertainties in a relationship, he had left a law partnership in Toledo, delayed his marriage to fiancée Addie Walker, and come west to recuperate. He settled in Vallejo, California, and wrote to Addie, on January 7, 1870, "am glad my photo pleases you. My friends all think it denotes improvement." Feeling better, Gorrill soon began to look for work.

He brought with him a franchise for the "Smith Patent Truss," which he and his brother Charlie had helped market in Ohio primarily as a wagon bridge.[37] The design competed at the low end of a bridge market already characterized by mature, successful designs, including the Howe truss and the Pratt truss, both of which held dominant positions in railroad applications. To position his product, Henry crafted a description of the Robert Smith patent that emphasized economy and simplicity. He described the bridge in a letter to Addie on January 29, 1870:

> The Bridge is a new invention we claim as good as Howe's and
> much cheaper, being composed entirely of wood, while Howe's uses
> much iron which renders it very expensive. Ours will take precedence
> on wagon roads while Howe's still leads us on Rail Roads. Ours is
> the best Wooden Bridge that is built and I am satisfied. I have all the
> [franchise] territory west of the Mountains including Colorado, Montana, Wyoming and Utah. The prospects now are first rate.[38]

It is questionable whether the Smith patent was indeed "as good as Howe's" since it omitted the iron tension rods that the Howe design used to tie the top and bottom chords together. Instead, the Smith design relied on diagonal timbers to perform the same function, introducing the same weakness that had handicapped Judah's bridge over the American River at Folsom.[39]

The Field Notebook:
Howe Versus Smith: Variations on Truss Design

The problem the Gorrills were trying to solve by applying the "Smith Patent Truss" to western bridge design was primarily cost. A 150-foot Howe truss bridge contained about two thousand feet of $1\frac{1}{4}$" iron tension rods, arranged vertically between the top and bottom chords of the bridge and designed to compress the diagonal timbers tightly between nuts and washers. However, the considerable expense of this much iron could be at least partially offset by making the timber diagonals do the same work. By clamping or attaching the ends of the diagonals tightly to the chords, a train rolling over a Smith truss would alternately force one diagonal into compression, while its neighbor was under tension; the two beams would then reverse roles as the load continued to travel across the bridge.

However simple—and cheap— this approach sounded to engineers like Smith or Gorrill, it required that the diagonal timbers be deeply notched to connect them firmly under tension to a chord. Notching, however, removed cross section from the timber, reducing its strength and weakening the design as a whole. In railroad design, the Smith patent never competed successfully against the Howe truss, or its variations.

Although Robert Smith and Henry and Charlie Gorrill promoted the bridge for use in wagon roads, its light construction proved to inhibit interest among railroads. Smith, based in Toledo, provided the main engineering support for the design.[40] Charlie labored unsuccessfully in Toledo to attract the Wabash as the first railroad customer.

But Henry, with a manic burst of energy, began to plan a marketing campaign for the new bridge that would take him south to Los Angeles and north to Oregon, "canvassing the counties as I go," and selling the design to what he sensed was a new, untapped market, including railroads. "I mean to work in the matter," he wrote Addie.[41] In his daybook, he compiled names of potential sales contacts, among them John F. Kidder and John A. Carroll, still employed by the Oregon Central Railroad when Gorrill was actively planning the "canvassing" trip in March 1870.[42] However, the chance of meeting Tom Carter at this early date might not have materialized. When Gorrill actually made the trip to Portland the following August, Carter, Carroll, and Kidder were probably all gone from the project. Still, optimism for the new bridge seemed boundless.

His physical symptoms steadily receded, and he wrote to Addie, on April 23, 1870: "I am confident in my recovery. Would bet on it, and then you will always bet on me, which leaves me two backers."

By the same date, Henry's letterhead changed its title from "Smith Patent Truss Bridge" to "the Pacific Bridge Company," witnessing his legal restructuring of the new business. He actively bid on wagon bridge projects in the Bay Area, sending Robert Smith basic site dimensions and asking Smith to produce elevations and bills of material that Henry, in turn, could use to write a bid.

The limitations of such long-distance engineering became painfully obvious. Smith was sometimes slow in providing the modified drawings, and they often arrived with errors. Henry wrote Charlie on October 10, 1870: "I wish Smith had a clerk who could send one plan in a dozen complete and right. Believe I have had nothing to do with a single one yet but there was more or less errors in it. . . . now I am going to change all this. I will get up my own plans here after from his [Smith's] bills."

Long before he actually won a bridge contract, Henry saw a pressing need to develop his own engineering skills. Coming from a legal background, he admitted to Addie, on June 12, 1870, that he was almost starting from scratch: "I am getting [to be] quite an expert Draughtsman and talk about bridges and Piers and abutments as if it was the only thing I had ever paid any attention to."

By July 1870, he was "getting up his own drawings" and at night reading basic algebra, trigonometry, and geometry textbooks, trying to build up a minimal understanding of the principles of static engineering.

By day, he pursued bids. But the news from Charlie continued to put a damper on hopes for railroad work. Henry summarized Charlie's progress to Addie on July 3, 1870: "The Rail Road Bridge hangs fire. Think the Vice President of the [Wabash] road prevented its being put up. Well we will have to own waggon Road's awhile, and it will keep me busy to do that."[43]

A small wagon bridge, successfully bid in Alameda County, became Henry's first project, in July 1870. He earned a $200 commission on a contract price of \$3,600, most of which would go to the construction contractor, Maloon and Co.

Henry and Addie joked that a little whiskey in his diet might improve his luck, and he wrote to her, on May 5, 1871, of his next success, a large wagon bridge at Oroville: "The Bourbon Whiskey did it. I have won this fight. It is the largest bridge let this year. Main span is 220 feet, shorter one 175. We get \$17,000 for contract of building. . . . have ½ interest in [construction] contract. It was a long hard fight. . . . I shall buy another bottle for the next bridge."

However, the complexities of the Oroville bridge soon suggested that a case of bourbon might be required to actually finish the project. Henry modified one of Smith's drawings himself to produce the elevations and the bills of material, which were needed to quickly engage suppliers and contractors. He found a temporary framing site at Vallejo (suggesting that his first casting work may have come the Vallejo Foundry), ordered timber from Puget Sound, and began to forward the materials to the Maloon brothers, who were by now full-time partners in the business.

Responsibility for project engineering, however, remained with Henry, and the responsibility bore heavily on his conscience. In a letter to Charlie, on May 2, 1871, Henry freely admitted he was out of his depth:

> My letter came back this a.m. wherein I said I had ordered my timber and made the bottom chords of the 214 foot span 2 [pieces] 6×15 and 2 pieces 7×15. To this Smith says the 7×15 should be 8×15. And then you say "Smith says 7×15 is big enough for *short* bridge but is pretty small for long one. If you can do so make it 8×15 for long bridge." I have telegraphed to Puget Sound to have center pieces made 8×15 in long [section] and 8×12 in short [section] but am fearful it cannot be changed. As I have written you these sizes as ordered were materially heavier than those given me by Smith. Call his attention to this fact and tell him that I am exceedingly anxious to have every thing right on the start. That changes here by reason of the long distance we get our timber are made public and impair confidence.
>
> The 175 foot span 21 feet high has heavier chords than the 193 feet span he sent me. Can it be I am mistaken? If I cannot get 8×15 in place of 7×15 it seems to me the chord will answer.

> | | | |
> |---|---|---|
> | The whole areas of each chord is 26×15 | = | 390 |
> | $1\frac{1}{4}$ for each post $\times 6 = 7\frac{1}{2} \times 15 = 112$ | | |
> | 2 inches for the bolts $= 2 \times 26$ | 52 | |
> | 2" at each splice | 30 | 194 |
> | leaves to sustain strain in each chord | | |
> | the sum of . . . . | | 196 |
> | Both chords . . . . | | 392 |

In span is less than 10,000 cubic feet avegs 300,000 pounds. Suppose 40 tons in one point = 80,000 pounds.

> I won't figure it out but with 40 tons at one point I make the strain less than 1800 lbs to inch. The fact is I don't know what the Deuce to do—Smith don't say it won't answer. Three different answers makes it look like guesswork.

All my disappointments has not disheartened me as this does. I am in the dark. If I build as it is will it fail. If I order again we may lose on contract and will get suit on our bond because we aren't on time. I did look for the Devil to make a miss in some way but did not think this would be where he would come.

. . . Talk to Smith and see if any bridge has failed?

Did he test Indiana bridge with 100 tons. Does he find timber bills have been too light? Does he intend to put on more iron? Has any bridge every lost its kimbo? . . .

Your loving Bro.
Henry

The devil, indeed, had paid a call on the Gorrill brothers. Henry wrote Charlie the following day to report that he had intercepted the Puget Sound timber shipment and, "at considerable expense," got the thickness of the middle chords increased from seven to eight inches. But in the process, he had revealed the guesswork at the root of his practice and a deep, troubling uncertainty about even the fundamentals of static engineering. The episode also graphically revealed the difficulty in scaling Smith designs to the higher loadings of railroad use. Even the eye of an untrained railroad procurement officer could tell the Smith design did not include the same number of iron tension rods, or timbers of the same size. Like Kimball, Henry's hopes for engaging the giant Central Pacific went unfulfilled.

Still, the mistakes on the Oroville bridge project had not leaked to the public. Positive reports on the bridge appeared in the mining and scientific press, lauding the 220-foot span as "probably the longest span yet built on the coast" and giving Pacific Bridge credit.[44]

Henry felt he had earned the praise. In November 1871, when the Oroville bridge was finished, he was flush with new confidence in his business and in himself. Early in December, Addie Walker came west by train. Henry and Addie were married in San Francisco on December 11 and settled down in Oakland. Henry's health remained precarious, but he and Addie started a family, celebrating the birth of a son on November 27, 1872.

For the next two years, the Gorrill brothers continued to build wagon bridges but got no known contract for a railroad bridge. Hopes aimed at the standard gauge Central Pacific were misplaced; Henry turned his hope instead on emerging narrow gauge projects, writing to Charlie on January 20, 1872, just before his brother moved west to join him: "Look after Narrow Guage [sic] Roads at Denver, Salt Lake. See what can be done in bridge line. Will at once send you a dozen lithographs at each place."

Narrow gauge construction offered the Gorrills a kind of half step between wagon bridges and those acceptable to a standard gauge railroad. Henry focused on gaining a toehold in the new business niche.

It took eighteen more months of hard work to actually win the first railroad bridge contract, but Henry's instincts were right. Sometime in June 1873, Pacific Bridge took the contract for the North Pacific Coast's Strawberry Point bridge. But there was a caveat: The railroad company, not Pacific Bridge, would provide a complete engineering package, including working drawings and bills of material. Charlie Gorrill reported in his diary, on June 3, 1873, that he "saw engineer on Northern RR who said work would not be let very soon—not for [a] week anyhow"; this was his first reference to Tom Carter and an admission that he did not yet know the engineer's name.

For Carter, the June diary entry marks his first work as an independent designer, and evidence that North Pacific Coast management considered him to be a competent railroad engineer. No detailed photographs or elevations remain of the original Strawberry Point bridge to suggest the provenance of the design. But details of similar Carter bridge projects are captured in early photographs, and they show massive tension rods, some $1\frac{1}{2}$ inches in diameter, holding the timber chords of the structures together in tension, clearly a traditional Howe design.[45] Confident he understood standard railroad bridge practice and armed with at least one notable bridge design to avoid, Carter convinced Julius Smith that he knew—in the words of Henry Gorrill—"what the deuce he was doing."

By 1873, Tom Carter had become the railroadist the Gorrills badly needed. Their relationship would continue, and grow more interdependent, for the remainder of the decade.

The delays in opening the Strawberry Point bridge, approaching six months after the date of Carter's initial soundings, must have seemed to the press and public like one more example of the railroad's lack of intentionality. The bureaucratic processes separating engineering, contracting, and procurement introduced a long delay in communication between source and supply, making mistakes likely and difficult to correct. Blame for the error in spile length, for example, came to rest with Renton Smith, which had loaded the wrong material onto the *Martha Rideout*. Two hundred ninety-two spiles were returned to Puget Sound in August, to be exchanged for the correct material, though it held up completion of the bridge.[46]

But since Julius Smith had resigned as chief engineer on June 1, 1873, the question of blame degenerated into a question of leadership. The engineering department was left rudderless while Moore scrambled to find a fourth candidate for the project's technical lead. In spite of the managerial vacuum, A. K. Grim managed to start the work on the Strawberry Point bridge. Charlie Gorrill's diary indicated that Pacific Bridge had a signed contract for the Strawberry Point project by July 18, reporting directly to Grim, and had a pile driver and a crew of eight in position by the end of the month.

With the bridge subcontractor in place, Thomas Carter's direct involvement in the project appeared to end. His name did not appear in Charlie Gorrill's diary for the remainder of the Strawberry Point project (roughly July through December 1873[47]). His name vanished from newspapers for an even longer period, totaling some nine months, leaving open a period of speculation about his continued involvement with the project, his income as an independent contractor, and even his whereabouts.[48]

Carter's problems seemed to pale in comparison to James Lemon's, the contract grader on the Collins Summit work. The deep cuts and sharp curves of Collins Summit quickly became the railroad's next bottleneck once the bridge was finished and opened to traffic. Under pressure from Grim to

Designed by Thomas Carter and fabricated by the Pacific Bridge Co., the Strawberry Point Bridge crossed the North Pacific Coast's first major geographic obstacle: spanning nearly a mile of open water at Richardson Bay. In the upper painting, by N. Bush (ca. 1883), the original bridge (shown running left to right across the page) is being bypassed by work on the new Corte Madera cutoff; the view below shows the bridge as it appeared in 1877 in a drawing from *Resources of California,* allegedly based on a photograph by Muybridge; in the photograph on the opposite page, the tracks exit the bridge near Lyford's mansion and begin a short, steep climb to Collins Summit. [Top, Sausalito Historical Society; below, Harold A. Lapham collection; opposite, Marin County Historical Society]

NORTH PACIFIC COAST RAILROAD.—CROSSING RICHARDSON'S BAY.

deliver the section, Lemon began to contrive shortcuts. First, in April 1873, came mandatory overtime for his Chinese crews, an increase in the length of the work day from ten to eleven hours. Infuriated, seventy-five of Lemon's Chinese workers went on strike the next day, forcing the contractor to recant.

Unable to institute longer work days, Lemon tried to increase productivity. In early May, his foreman got the bright idea of placing a triple load of California Powder Works no. 1 into a deep drill hole. The results were reported in the *Herald* on May 10:

When the smoke cleared off, [the foreman] rushed up to the point of rock when an infuriated individual met him point blank with a Henry rifle raised to his shoulder, just preparing to draw a bead on "the boss." Not a moment stopped or stayed, but with one wild yell he turned and fled with that "Henry" in swift pursuit. In the course of time he reached Strawberry Point, when he was last seen to take a boat and hurriedly embark, since which the Railroad has known him no more. The result of this blasted blast was a storm of rock down on the house; seriously bruising the proprietor with flying rocks, to break the ribs of a small child belonging to him, to send his wife into duplex hysterics, to knock over half a dozen cows, stampeding a field full of stock, and in short to cause general demoralization and dismay. No more blasting is done on these premises. The line has been changed.[49]

Few were surprised when contractor Lemon declared bankruptcy in late May. The Marin County sheriff foreclosed on his equipment and teams, and chief contractor Grim was forced to pick up the unfinished pieces of Lemon's work on Collins Summit.

Marin newspapers began to see the North Pacific Coast as black comedy. White and Bugbee's use of blind horses on the summit tunnel project was a fresh example, when a black powder blast spooked a sightless animal off a cliff it could not see, breaking its neck in the process.[50]

Bridge supplies continued to pile up on the Saucelito wharf. The barks *Martha Rideout* and *Nicholas Biddle* discharged Puget Sound timber; the schooner *Two Brothers* made weekly trips with ties from Stewart's Point.[51] By September 18, with material for twenty miles of track stockpiled near the wharf, Grim took a cold, hard look at progress on the Strawberry Point bridge. Just seven hundred feet of piling had been driven into Richardson Bay, less than 20 percent of the length of the bridge.[52]

Watching the good weather slip away, Grim came to the conclusion that to move rail and ties north before the winter a drastic stratagem would have to be risked. Late in the month, Pacific Bridge crews began to close the entire gap across the deep channel of Richardson Bay with piles, eliminating the drawbridge.[53] Perhaps at first planned as a temporary expedient, Grim's abridged drawbridge brought instant reprisal from the landowners along the shore of Richardson Bay. S. A. Throckmorton, for example, cut off from access to bay shipping, filed for an injunction in early October to stop construction of the bridge.

Copycat litigation followed. The Morgan Oyster Co., whose beds lay on the west side of Strawberry Point, sensed the timing was right to sue the railroad for injury to its bivalves caused by the incessant pounding of the steam pile driver; it collected $1,500 for the trouble. Grim learned his lesson the hard way. By November 6, the *Marin County Journal* reported that the draw span had been reinstated and the bridge project was gaining speed. Charlie Gorrill's last diary entry indicated he paid off his men on December 16; the Strawberry Point Bridge was at last completed, just as the rainy season began.

Anxious to reverse the seemingly endless series of public relations disasters, Moore hired Howard Schuyler to replace Julius Smith. The recruitment was something of a plum. The much-heralded chief engineer of the Denver & Rio Grande was on the scene by May 15, 1873, the first prominent industry name to be connected with the project and the only one to list a major narrow gauge railroad in his résumé. Schuyler was as much a publicist as an engineer, and at twenty-nine years of age he was portrayed by the press as a dashing, young, energetic impresario. He took up residence at the fashionable Union Club in San Francisco, while Moore found ways to maneuver him into the Marin County limelight. He would cost Moore a pretty penny: Schuyler came to work at $416.33 a month, nearly a 30 percent hike over Smith's salary.[54]

Schuyler quickly found Marin audiences hostile. On July 31, in a heated meeting, the Marin County Board of Supervisors turned the railroad down cold on a last attempt to precipitate a new bond election. Throckmorton, still smarting from the drawbridge episode, was a principal speaker against the proposition. Many of Marin County's wealthy landholders united against the narrow gauge, especially property owners in San Rafael who were still in doubt if the railroad's mainline would even pass through the county seat.

The financial plight of the railroad would become public only the following March, when Schuyler admitted the narrow gauge was burning up $33,000 per mile in getting over White's Hill—a far cry indeed from the $13,500 per mile the Denver & Rio Grande had spent in its construction along the foothills of the Front Range in Colorado.[55] To company insiders, however, the numbers had grown worrisome by the fall of 1873. In a report to the board of directors dated September 30, Schuyler testified that $437,611 had been spent, and another $283,544 was obligated under contractual commitments with vendors, including a contract for $29,400 worth of rolling stock with the Kimball Manufacturing Co.[56]

Those obligations totaled $721,155. In the entire history of the company, only $600,000 had been raised. By Christmas, the treasury was dangerously close to empty.[57]

For the next five months, from the close of 1873 to June 1874, all forms of income—from stocks, bonds, bond hypothecates, or subsidies—ceased altogether. By the time Schuyler made his public remarks, the Richardson Bay bridge, a year after Carter's initial engineering work, was still unopened for traffic. If Schuyler's testimony was intended to instill public confidence, Marinites were confronted with strong evidence to the contrary.

Dark days haunted the railroad. With money running short, key managers were furloughed in anticipation of a long winter shutdown. In late October 1873, for example, the *Marin County Journal* reported that "Mr. Low, General Superintendent of the narrow gauge, has gone to Virginia City for the Winter." Contracts went unfilled; activity in the railroad's financial ledger entered hibernation by January 1874. There followed two months— April and May—when the only journal entries of any kind were Schuyler's salary vouchers.[58]

On October 2, Austin Moore buried his two-year-old daughter, a victim of scarlet fever.

Perhaps to get his mind off his troubles, Schuyler advised Moore to try fundraising in Europe that winter. Schuyler had sold stock for the Rio Grande in Germany and no doubt gave Moore names to contact. Austin departed by ship in November 1873, with the work in mothballs except for the subterranean, round-the-clock blasting in White's Hill tunnel.

The railroad, observed local humorists, was digging its own grave.

The North Pacific Coast contract seemed perfect for Kimball. A local Bay Area railroad would showcase Kimball's craftsmanship, giving the car builder credibility on its own turf. In turn, the contract would cement a key relationship for the railroad, a connection between the NPC and Ralston's Bank of California. The connection could be established through Maurice Dore, a Ralston investment partner and also the treasurer of the Saucelito Land and Ferry Co. If Moore needed Ralston's backing for the railroad (by

Early photographs of Kimball rolling stock on the North Pacific Coast are scarce, but the view at left, taken near San Rafael on Apr. 17, 1882, shows an unscheduled encounter between NPC number 9 and a bull, and provides a fine broadside view of Kimball coach 4 in the process. [Left, Bancroft Library; below, Department of Special Collections and University Archives, Green Library, Stanford University]

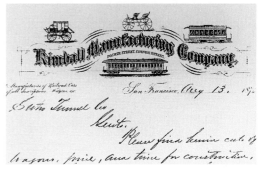

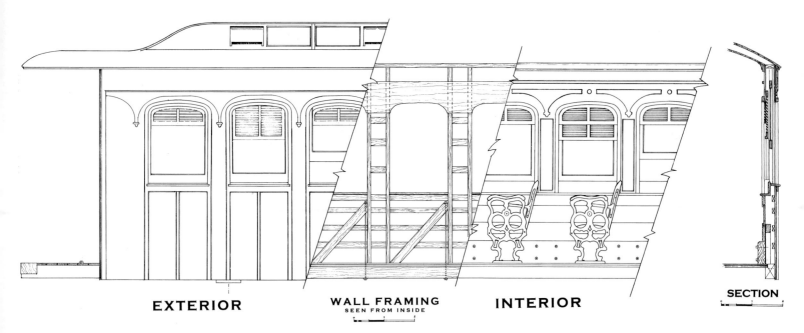

EXTERIOR

WALL FRAMING
SEEN FROM INSIDE

INTERIOR

SECTION

Architect's composite drawing of early Kimball car design for the North Pacific Coast, ca. 1874: interior and wall framing details from extant car body at Huckleberry Museum; exterior from 1882 photograph of Kimball car involved in wreck of number 9 near San Rafael. Numerous design elements appear to have been inspired by contemporary car decoration from the Wason Mfg. Co., in Springfield, Mass. [Boone Morrison, with research by Kevin Hassing]

late 1873, Moore was desperate for any backing), the purchase of Kimball products was a good way to encourage a relationship.

The Kimball contract (probably signed in September 1873) emphasized "high end" car work, consisting of twelve passenger cars equipped with fully equalized passenger trucks and clerestory roofs.[59] The 35' long, 7'6" wide coaches included at least one feature that earlier Kimball coaches, built for the Virginia & Truckee, did not. Miller hook "safety" couplers and platforms established the cars as being state-of-the-art.

The *Marin County Journal* reported the coaches retailing at $3,600 each, $900 less than the standard gauge Virginia & Truckee coaches 3 and 4 delivered by Kimball in August 1872.[60] The workmanship was probably quite similar. Both interior and exterior architectural details resembled Wason Mfg. Co. designs: duckbill roof, finial window detail, and an oval name plate. Richly lacquered interiors were mirror finished in California laurel, redwood, and maple—expressions of the car builder's art at its finest.

To a public unfamiliar with the narrow gauge concept, there were novelties in Kimball's car designs. Seating in the coaches, for example, was arranged "one by two," pairing a double-width seat with a single-width seat for half the length of the car, then reversing the order of the seats down the remaining half to balance the load.[61] There is evidence, however, that the structural design of the cars was a throwback to more primitive industry standards. By this time, six-frame sills had become common eastern practice in passenger car construction; the Kimball coaches were built with only four frame sills.[62]

There were strong reasons for the North Pacific Coast to delay this purchase as long as it could. As Schuyler publicly admitted, by March 1874 the NPC had already spent $600,000. The minimum rolling stock to equip the first fifty miles of line—eight engines, ten coaches, two baggage cars, and about two hundred freight cars—would cost $250,000 more.[63] The money simply didn't exist. Cables from Moore, reported in the *Marin County Jour-*

nal on April 1, 1874, described a lukewarm reception among European investors. Moore had little choice except to delay big capital purchases as long as he could. However, if the order wasn't placed until July 1874, five months before the projected opening of NPC passenger service, Kimball barely had time to complete the cars.[64] Roughly eight weeks were required for the painting process alone, to allow adequate drying time between each of eight coats of primer, paint, and lacquer. The long lead time required commitment. A contract balance of $29,400, noted in Schuyler's September 1873 report, was enough to cover the construction of at least eight passenger cars.

But freight car orders could not wait. Critical to construction, flatcars would have to be on hand when trains first crossed the Strawberry Point Bridge, opening up Collins Summit, Ross Valley, and White's Hill to delivery of stockpiled materials. Virtually overlooked by historians of the NPC, the first units of rolling stock to arrive on the North Pacific Coast were a pair of Kimball flatcars, delivered at Saucelito on or just before August 19, 1873.[65] At least two additional Kimball flatcars were delivered in September, and there is evidence that ten Kimball flats in all were on hand by the end of 1873.[66] Following standard Kimball practice, the wheel castings had been poured by Risdon Iron in San Francisco and fitted into Kimball-fabricated trucks. Few details of the cars have come to light, but clearly here is evidence that, even at the height of its money problems, the NPC intended Kimball to have the contract for all its rolling stock, both freight and passenger cars. At least $5,323.10, according to the railroad's financial summary as of June 1874, had already been paid to Kimball, apparently on its freight car balance.

Kimball was in sore need of the business. On February 19, 1873, the board of directors of the Bank of California met behind closed doors to review the bank's loan portfolio and reluctantly agreed that the loan to Kimball, $578,580.46, was "non-performing."[67] There were consequences. The bank directors demanded more equity in the property and quickly got it. The origi-

Eastern narrow gauge car design of the late 1870s was typified by the coach *Eureka*, built for the Eureka & Palisade Railroad by Billmeyer and Small in 1875; note offset seating in the interior view (above), intended to balance the narrow, light car body. B&S may have vended trucks similar to the *Eureka*'s to Carter Brothers for use on the Monterey & Salinas Valley in 1874, or the basic design elements may have simply been copied. [Both views, Smithsonian Institution]

nal loan had gone into the factory and tooling at Fourth and Townsend streets. The deed to these properties was held by Kimball's partner, Richard Ogden. On August 7, 1873, Ogden mortgaged his share of the deed for $45,000, and on October 17 signed the deed over to William Ralston for the nominal sum of $500. Estimates of the value of the physical plant and its tooling varied, but the R. G. Dun credit reports for the period quoted a figure of $230,000, less than half the value of the original loan. "This transaction," wrote the Dun credit reporter, "strengthens the belief that [George] Kimball has no interest in the concern and that Ogden is merely the representative of capitalists connected with the Bank of California."[68]

The public knew little of Kimball's debt problems with the Bank of California, but as the recession deepened in the early 1870s the search to "fill the plant" with work was a frequent focus of San Francisco Call and Bulletin articles.[69] Agricultural implements, circus wagons, scow schooners, tug boats, wagons, carriages, horsecars, scrapers, furniture, and even rickshaws for China were all markets that Kimball explored, but none of them were large enough to exert leverage on its enormous debt.

Following the Ogden mortgage, Ralston began to personally involve himself in a plan to salvage the Kimball investment. He began to move his own investments into businesses that would in turn buoy the struggling carriage shop.

One such tactic was designed to use Kimball's tooling to build six hundred sets of tables, chairs, and beds, enough to furnish Ralston's Palace Hotel, under construction in 1874 on Market Street. A portion of Kimball's Fourth and Bryant factory would therefore become the West Coast Furniture Co., whose sole customer was the Palace Hotel. To make high-volume lumber shipments to West Coast Furniture, Ralston would expand Kimball to a branch works on a slough in Mission Bay, set up for wholesale planing of lumber.

In August 1874, just about the time work was getting started on the North Pacific Coast contract, Ralston personally negotiated a prime Mission Bay site next to the main shipping channel.[70] In a new mill, built atop "made" land at today's Sixth and Berry streets, a Kimball branch would be set up to do rough planing and sorting of lumber for its various product lines. Ralston rented additional acreage on the block next door as storage for a consignment of mahogany logs, raw material for Palace Hotel stairways and furniture.

With its business strategy growing more diverse, and perhaps more overextended, Kimball's railroad work suffered from a loss of direction and focus. Kimball continued the demonstration car marketing strategy through early 1872, still trying to interest the Central Pacific and Southern Pacific in its products by creating an entire train of standard gauge passenger cars: baggage cars; coaches; and even an elegant compartment sleeper, named the *Siempre Viva*.[71] The sixty-foot sleeping car was a cabinet maker's triumph. Six sleeping compartments were arranged along the length of the car, each equipped with both single and double berths, water closets, tables, and closets. Thirty kinds of native wood decorated the interior, including California laurel, Mexican rose, coa wood, maple, and coral wood. Riding on six-wheel trucks, the *Siempre Viva* neared completion in May

1871 and was scheduled to begin a tour of the United States in a somewhat brazen attempt to infiltrate a market monopolized by the Pullman Corp.

The tour, and the entire marketing campaign, ended in disaster when the *Siempre Viva* burned in the Chicago Fire of October 8–10, 1871, a loss estimated at $26,000.[72]

When the rest of the completed demonstration train first left the Kimball plant about six months later, on January 17, 1872, it remained unsold and was placed on loan to the Japanese embassy to boost a marketing foray into Yokohama, where Kimball was selling streetcars.[73] The Central and Southern Pacific railroads were not, and would not, become Kimball clients.

Kimball's railroad designs lacked reliable field testing. Trucks delivered with Virginia & Truckee cabooses 9 and 10 were identified as the cause of several derailments on the v&t's tight mainline curves; they were replaced with trucks of the v&t's own design and manufacture in March 1873.[74]

Kimball struggled with low-quality materials. In a letter to the Virginia & Truckee on February 3, 1873, Richard Ogden admitted they were having trouble with flawed wheel castings and asked for the railroad's patience: "We have had to reject quite a number of wheels and have had some animated talk with the Risdon people about the quality of some of their *recent* wheels. Should any prove defective, let us know and we will replace at their expense."[75]

The problem continued to reflect substandard metallurgy from West Coast iron manufacturers, attributed to shipment of inferior iron stock from eastern suppliers and inability on Kimball's part to manage the quality of its suppliers.

Managing its suppliers, in fact, became a measure of Kimball's overall performance as a business. Since the construction of the huge plant in 1868, Kimball had assembled the critical pieces of a manufacturing "value chain" dedicated to high-volume manufacture of railroad cars.

The concept of a value chain is like an assembly line in which a portion of the net value of a product is added one step at a time. The choice of which component parts to make, and which to purchase from a supplier, depended on a firm grasp of the industry's core skills. For Kimball, carpentry, joinery, and cabinetry were competencies that had won them recognition over the entire lifetime of the company. Kimball's portion of the value chain—literally defined to be the percentage of a product's total dollar value derived from its own workmanship—was closely identified with such woodworking skills. Within those core skills, a manufacturer was wise to focus its own engineering, innovation, and capital spending—factors that would help it stand out from the competition. Outside the core skills, a manufacturer was well advised to outsource.

The manufacture of wheel sets, for example, was an extremely specialized process, which Kimball vended to Risdon Iron. Cut glass panels for clerestory windows were also vended, coming from the San Francisco glass shop of John Malloy.[76] Outsourcing specialized parts was a routine part of high-volume manufacturing, intended as a cost-effective alternative to buying specialized tooling.

But Kimball began to blur the boundary between core skills and outsourcing. Handles, window latches, deadbolts, and doorstops were cast by out-

---

The Field Notebook: High-Volume Versus Craftsman Build

As a manufacturer, Kimball may have been trying to transition between the craftsman-build process and something resembling what we think of today as modern high-volume manufacturing.

High-volume production focuses on assembly line organization, in which the manufactured item moves through multiple assembly steps. In this process, workmen perform only one specialized step at a time. In a craftsman build, however, a small team of highly skilled workmen perform all the steps in the manufacturing process together, as a team.

More than just a difference in the physical organization of the assembly process, the two types of build have divergent philosophies toward the role of the assembly worker. In high-volume production, a worker would repeat the same step over and over, as with drilling the same set of holes in hundreds of duplicate parts. In a craftsman build, however, the small team of workers would understand and execute all of the steps required to completely assemble the car. They would start on the frame and continue to add parts until the roof was in place. Though slower than high-volume production, a craftsman build encouraged broad skills in its participating workmen, better understanding of the entire manufacturing process, and the ability (especially in prototype work) to troubleshoot or solve problems. A small car shop like Carter's would have leaned heavily toward the craftsman-build process; the giant Kimball works, on the other hand, probably began to explore the economies of high-volume production.

side vendors but brought inside the Fourth and Bryant factory for plating, finishing, and assembly. The Empire Foundry, for example, manufactured light, ornamental iron castings for Kimball, which Kimball finished by nickel-plating in its own specialty plating shop. Pacific Rolling Mills forged heavy bar and round stock for truss rods and truck frames—purchased in rough form and finished in Kimball's own extensive hammer shops. Kimball thus risked a trade: by acquiring skills and tooling across a wider spectrum of the assembly process, it attempted to control a larger proportion of the product's value chain.

The justification for this approach could only be high-volume production, passing along to the customer a lower overall price in exchange for a high volume of work that used the capacity of its plant, including specialty shops, to maximum advantage. In essence, Kimball was trying to compete with its suppliers. As often as not, those suppliers could manufacture the same parts more cheaply than Kimball. Nearby Pacific Rolling Mills, for example, was the largest hammer shop on the coast in the early 1870s, yet Kimball still purchased power hammers and tooling and hired skilled mechanics to operate them, to perform the same tasks that Pacific Rolling Mills considered its core skills.

Little wonder that insolvency loomed. By the spring of 1874, Kimball's finances had endured nearly six years of high-interest loans and mortgages. Yet there was reason to hold out. Kimball had positioned itself to be sole source for what should have become more than $100,000 worth of North Pacific Coast car orders, including 12 passenger cars and approximately 165 freight cars the narrow gauge would need to handle anticipated lumber traffic from Dutch Bill.

The market value of the rolling stock was estimated in Howard Schuyler's September 1873 Chief Engineer's Report, estimates that probably came from Kimball itself.[77] More orders, Kimball assumed, would follow.

Moore wrote disappointedly, in February 1874, that no large sources of capital had yet been secured from the European stock markets. He returned to the States in late April, the newspapers noting only token success at fundraising. The railroad's ledger books noted no success whatsoever. No monies from bond or stock sales, simply, were reported.

The Marin County Journal continued to suggest paralysis. Good weather came, and still the project stalled. During Moore's absence, only the White's Hill tunnel was pushed forward with any energy (on Saturday, March 7, thirty-two simultaneous powder charges blew open a continuous passage through the 1,250-foot bore).

By the date of Moore's return, Milton Latham clearly was burdened with most of the financial risk in the project, loans totaling nearly half a million dollars, divided between the London and San Francisco Bank and the British Columbia Savings and Loan. Moore must have been blunt when he described the railroad's plight: Latham would have to invest more money to protect his original investment. All alternatives were exhausted. The project would die for lack of funds if he did not.

So Latham did invest, but this time on his terms. The evidence is compelling that in June 1874, he quietly began to take control of the entire project. Latham was equally blunt when he dictated his terms back to Moore. He would no longer buy bonds or bond hypothecates, but stock. With the stock, he would actively take over control of the railroad. On June 5, 1874, Journal no. 1 reported 3,000 shares of stock purchased in Latham's name, at $100 a share. The number of shares Latham purchased was calculated to move his equity position nearly equal to that of the largest stockholder. A. K. Grim, who had received half of his contract commission in stock, owned 3,210 shares at the time, making him the largest stock owner of record. But on August 31, Latham purchased an additional 250 shares, squeezing Grim into a minority position.[78]

Latham squeezed Grim even harder. On June 17, the Journal reported Grim's construction contract canceled, the railroad's obligation to continue to pay him in stock abruptly terminated. Milton Latham would quickly become—and remain—the company's majority stockholder.

No formal announcement of Latham's takeover would leak to the press until that December, and when it did, the irony of the takeover escaped most observers. Latham had used the money he made off the old San Francisco & North Pacific bond deal to buy control of its narrow gauge competitor. He had changed iron horses in midstream, leaping to a new mount currently stumbling toward the northern redwood belt. With Latham at the reins, the North Pacific Coast would soon gallop.

On July 2, 1874, the R. G. Dun credit summary verified that Latham had purchased a majority interest in the stock and gave the enterprise a clean credit report: "M.S. Latham, President of the London and San Francisco Bank (limited) states that he owns 3/4 of this concern and is himself furnishing the money to construct and equip the road; also that the company is clear of debt and has money at [10 percent] and is not seeking any credit."[79]

Soon Latham would buy control of the North Pacific Coast's timber resources. A year later, on September 9, 1875, a Latham partnership would secure the deed for four thousand acres of Moore's original Rancho Bodega holding, the first of a series of purchases of timber lands in the Dutch Bill Creek area.[80] Even before narrow gauge track reached the Russian River, Latham would control its primary revenue target.[81]

These deals were done out of the public eye. After the Cal P scandal, Latham grew shy about public exposure (he would not attend the NPC's opening in January 1875), and Austin Moore no longer needed to win public elections to raise money. Latham had another, more compelling reason to lower his profile. By February 1874, the London and San Francisco Bank had invested $400,000 in a wheat brokerage house named E. E. Morgan and Sons, about which more will be heard in Chapter Four. Both of these investments depended on completion of narrow gauge railroads. Together, $700,000 of the London and San Francisco Bank's money—about a third of its working capital—was now risked on controversial schemes involving narrow gauge railroad construction, an exposure that in the long run would bring the bank, and Latham, to the edge of failure.

In the short run, the money injected new life into the struggling North Pacific Coast. The railroad began to adopt a new public persona. There were no more humiliating defeats over bond measures, and no more apologies for contradictory surveys. Instead, the North Pacific Coast began to move purposefully into the difficult terrain of Marin and Sonoma counties, advancing on the redwood basin of Dutch Bill that Moore and now Latham regarded as the real motive for their investments. Passenger traffic into these nether regions would be scarce. Instead, the North Pacific Coast was beginning to shape a transportation network designed primarily to move millions of board feet of lumber.

Overnight, the railroad seemed to startle itself awake. On June 4, an article appeared in the *Marin County Journal* announcing that "NPC commences heavy work this week." The same day, the *Journal* noted four hundred workers leaving Saucelito en masse to repair washouts in the grade along Paper Mill Creek. Supply wagons followed them, laden with rice, tea, sugar, shovels, and picks. The line's first locomotive, the Baldwin *Saucelito*, was finally unloaded at its namesake town on June 16, 1874, fired up on the wharf, and run under its own power one mile to the completed Easterby Street shops. The twenty-ton 2-6-0 carried a builder's badge date of 1873 (Baldwin had written its specifications on August 18), mute testimony to the time that had gone by since its order. The railroad had been dormant nearly six months, and the moan of a locomotive's whistle on foggy nights might have been mistaken for a grounded ferryboat by the customers of Zingara's bar in Turney Valley, the area where the shops were located.

Absent from the project for more than a year, Thomas Carter became a regular at Zingara's sometime during June 1874, chain smoking hand-rolled cigarettes and talking quietly with men he knew. As word of the railroad's awakening spread, the bar began to resemble a gold rush saloon. Hopeful of getting even small grading or track-laying jobs, contractors began to ferret out scraps of information about the shake-up in the railroad's administration, feed off rumors about A. K. Grim, or start new ones. Carter quickly reestablished old contacts and talked his way into an introduction to Howard Schuyler as the "bridge man."

With Grim out of the picture, Moore had to quickly find enough new contractors to lay fifty miles of rail before the end of the season. But Latham also insisted on keeping the contracts small and circumscribed to single jobs. There would be no more stock deals, and no confusion about who was in control. White and Bugbee (the contractors responsible for White's Hill work) would continue with grading and tunneling projects. A new contractor—A. P. Wood—would follow White and Bugbee northward, laying rail on the fresh earthworks.[82] All these contractors would be paid from accounts in the journal, reporting directly to Schuyler. Tom Carter, using two foremen named Meigs and Dysant, got a small contract for supporting A. P. Wood with blacksmith work, tooling, and repairs.

Wanting more control over the work, Latham had to accept its consequence: more bookkeeping. Journal no. 1, normally reserved for stock and bond transactions, began to report a bewildering assortment of track-laying supplies, tools, and provisions—matériel that Grim had kept account of in his own books. Beginning in August, the railroad's accountant was keeping track of Wood's mess kits and tents just a few linear journal inches away from $250,000 bond hypothecate accounts. A sample of Wood's outfitting bill, from August 31, 1874, filed under account 60:

1 large tent	$70.75
1 Wall tent	$18.75
1 Sibley tent	$20.50
1 stove & Fixtures	$65.00
Asst. Cooking outfit	$30.00
5 pinch bars	$20.00
3 track guages [sic]	$16.50
5 lining bars	$10.00
8 spike mauls	$20.80
2 iron tongs	$4.00
6 picks	$7.00
2 iron cars	$220.00
2 padlocks & chains	$2.25

Carter's new journal entries also grew like a laundry list. Although assigned to "laying and surfacing track" by the company's bookkeeper, account 45 called out a variety of support services, including "house forge work," machine work on a lathe, and planing and sawing lumber; the jobs were largely in support of others. In short, Carter appears to have become a contract shop service, charging hourly labor for every type of tooling and repair required to keep construction contractors in the field. He was probably the only shop force in the embryo railroad (a situation that would not last for long), and the first contractor to occupy and use the two new shop buildings at Saucelito, ready since November 1873. It was a niche Carter would steadily widen.

Account 45 was soon showing considerable payout: $5,568.91 in July, $11,621.03 in August, $14,282.14 in October, and $12,619.98 in December.

Activity under account 45 may have given Carter a small toehold when Milton Latham banished the next contractor from Austin Moore's old list of cronies. Sometime in June, the Kimball Co. was informed that they would no longer be building freight cars for the North Pacific Coast. Latham's housecleaning may have been driven by a simple business reality. Kimball was owned by the Bank of California, a direct competitor to Latham's London and San Francisco Bank. Why, Latham concluded, should he line William Ralston's pockets with his own money? Kimball would hold onto the passenger car work, some of which was already started. But a far larger contract—initially for some $51,000 worth of freight cars—would, like track work, be reassigned to contractors who did not threaten Latham's sense of control. Such contractors would accept deals that he, not they, dictated. None would involve stock. With no single contractor clearly in a dominant position, those doing similar kinds of work would ultimately compete, acting as a check on their own prices and productivity, and making them easy to dismiss, if the need arose.

In this shakeup, Thomas Carter's contract repair shop was suddenly thrust into the shoes that Kimball had vacated. On July 9, the *Marin County Journal* announced that Carter—virtually inexperienced as an independent car contractor—had gotten the entire freight car contract for the North Pacific Coast.

Virtually no paper trail exists to explain these surprising developments, except this: beginning in December 1871, a leatherbound series of accounting records began to document in detail the financial activity of the North Pacific Coast. The records eventually spanned the full length of Carter's engagement (from 1873 until 1876) but are fragmented between three completely separate railroad accounting tools—journals, ledgers, and cash books.

No single accounting tool is a complete record. There is only one Journal, for example, number 1, covering account activity in the period December 1871 to December 1874. General Ledgers 1 and 3 are missing, the extant Ledger 2 covering just 1875. Cash books, on the other hand, begin in January 1875 and run unbroken until the end of the North Pacific Coast as a corporate entity in 1902.

Although they vary considerably in format and level of detail, the three tools work in conjunction with each other, and together they correlate in remarkable detail the fragments of the business that was rapidly becoming Carter Brothers. The one available journal provides chronological activity summaries by account. Individual credits or debits in the cash books roll up into major account headings (or "folios") posted in the journals and ledgers. The ledgers also cover activity by account, broken down under major account names (Thomas Carter, Baldwin Locomotive Works, Mason Machine Works, Renton Smith, and so on).[83] Journals, ledgers, and cash books therefore provide detail at different levels. They also offer a way of sorting the railroad's accelerating financial activity—and along with it, Carter's.

Carter's path through these volumes changes course a number of times. The day before Christmas 1874, account 45—Carter's contract shop activity—was closed in the pages of the railroad's Journal no. 1. Its final balance, $1,860.07, was due Carter as a note payable in ninety days. With one minor exception, account 45 contained no reference to car work.[84] In Ledger no. 2, two new Carter accounts subsequently appear to track a distinctly new business activity. These accounts assumed their numbers from the pages (or folios) where they first appeared in the ledgers. Account 561, for example, first appeared on February 27, 1875, on the ledger page of the same number, and grew one line at a time until its line items filled the page. Then, on July 31,

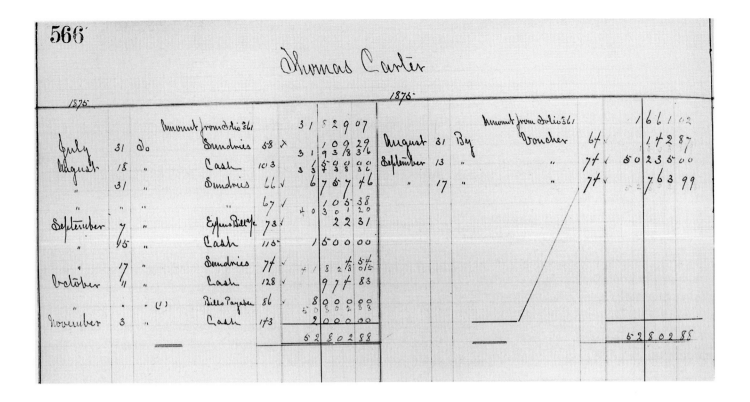

North Pacific Coast financial ledger, summary account page for Thomas Carter, 1875 and 1876, also identified as the new-car account, or folio 566. [California State Railroad Museum]

1875, the North Pacific Coast's bookkeeper transferred 561's balance over to account 566, beginning a new page, and a new account.[85] The railroad's bookkeeper referred to either folio 561 or 566 as the "new car account." Because the balances under these two accounts appear to roll forward, new-car account numbers missing with the 1874 ledger may simply be earlier subtotals of the 1875 total represented by account 566.

Primarily because Carter was not paid what was owed him until the contract was very nearly completed, the total value of his car building activity can be reconstructed even though the 1874 ledger is missing. On November 3, 1875, when the North Pacific Coast's accountant closed account 566, its balance totaled $52,802.88. If this number indeed reflects all of Carter's rolling stock construction activity during five months of 1874 and nearly all of 1875, it also reflects the total value of the original contract.

The ledger does not itemize the cars purchased under the scope of the account, but there is supporting evidence that 120 flatcars, 30 boxcars, and 2 "express cars" were placed on the roster before the account was closed.[86] Ten of the flatcars were probably Kimball products, already stored at the Easterby Street shop when Carter began work there in July 1874.

Therefore about 142 cars—30 boxcars, 110 flatcars, and 2 express cars—we believe were built new by Carter, for which the North Pacific Coast paid slightly less than the total account value, since an estimated $1,500 of the folio value went for repairs or alterations to existing rolling stock. In round numbers, therefore, the value of the Carter car work was about $51,000.

It is possible to then estimate the retail value of the cars that Carter produced under the contract: about $342 for a flatcar and about $438 for a boxcar.[87] Recall the retail prices Schuyler had been quoted (probably by Kimball) in 1873: $425 for a flatcar and $500 for a boxcar. If indeed these were

The materials and parts that went into an 1874 Carter car were nearly all obtained on the West Coast—with the exception of wheel-axle sets, which were imported from an East Coast vendor. Douglas fir, for example, coming out of Puget Sound, had just undergone a price hike from $30 to $42.50 per thousand board feet. A narrow gauge flatcar consumed just about a thousand board feet of Douglas fir, or "Oregon pine" as it was commonly known at the time. Four wheel-axle sets, procured in San Francisco, would have retailed at about $117. Odd castings from gray iron—including washers, truck center plates, journal boxes, and truss rod saddles—priced out at about three cents per pound, totaling about $22 per car. Bolts were priced at $15. Oak, to fabricate draw bar timbers, cost $3. Arch bars for trucks cost $20, forged truss rods $22; brasses cost about $5, draft springs $3; truck springs, $5; miscellaneous and shipping, $10; and $2 worth of mineral red paint would finish the cars.

Total raw material cost: about $266. Carter's retail price to NPC: about $342. If labor is factored in at roughly $34 per car, that left Carter with a calculated profit of about 12 percent. However, unanticipated variations in cost, and higher labor charges, probably drove Carter's profit margin closer to 10 percent (see endnote 91 for sources of prices).

Kimball's prices, it is not hard to understand how Carter beat the competition on price. Carter was put in the position of being awarded the contract only if he was willing to set his prices very near the bone. As we explain in the next chapter, a few weeks before the NPC deal was cut Carter sold his first flatcars to the Monterey & Salinas Valley for $490 apiece, and his first boxcars for $575 apiece, almost 30 percent higher than the marginally profitable returns he managed to eke out of the North Pacific Coast work. The Monterey prices, in fact, proved to be far closer to the prevailing market rate. Carter submitted flatcar bids of $450 to the Carson & Colorado in 1880, a 27 percent increase over the bargain prices charged to the NPC.[88] Clearly, Thomas had sharpened his pencil to get the NPC work, perhaps to the point of poor business sense.

Why did he undercut his own pricing, very nearly to the breakeven point? It was clear from the start that Carter had little working capital to bring to the job. Instead, the North Pacific Coast cut Carter a deal, in effect capitalizing his contract by using its own accounts with suppliers to pay for raw materials, and charging Carter's account interest for the loan. Here, the detailed transactions documented in the cash books are a valuable clue about the terms of the original contract.

For example, on April 13, 1875, the cash book noted "Thomas Carter; paid his draft as dated February 12, 1875 at sixty days favor Renton Holmes and Company: $1252.39." Similar "account balancing" exists for castings purchased for Carter on railroad credit from McCormick and Lewis. Loans for wheel-axle sets have not yet been found explicitly in the cash books, but a *Vallejo Chronicle* article of March 10, 1875, noted that wheel-axle sets were being delivered from the East Coast in conjunction with Carter car parts coming from the Vallejo Foundry of McCormick and Lewis, suggesting wheels may have been purchased through the foundry account. The railroad, in turn, fronted the money for Carter's foundry bills.

As long as it postponed paying him what amounted to his profit, the North Pacific Coast could maintain the Carter car accounts at close to zero balance, while Carter himself had only to meet his own payroll and pay for incidentals to deliver what he had contracted to deliver. Even though almost half of that obligation was delivered before January 1, 1875, it was not until April 17 that the first cash installment was paid on Carter's outstanding balance.[89] Then, once each month for the next eight months, ending on November 3, a payment was made on account 566, the amounts varying from a low of $670.76 to a high of $2,000. The monthly payments continued, uninterrupted; by November 3, a total of $10,581.15 had been paid. On this final payment, the bookkeeper noted "Thomas Carter paid balance of account in full this date."

This balance is extremely close to a settlement of 10 percent profit plus 10 percent labor, or 20 percent of the $51,000 total value of the work—in other words, a little more than $10,000.

Carter's profit can be estimated another way, by adding up the contemporary costs of raw materials and labor and then subtracting them from the retail car price mentioned earlier (see the Field Notebook: Pricing a Flatcar). Using this approach, the total raw material cost for a Carter 1874 flatcar can be estimated at about $266. Labor accounted for about 10 percent of the retail price of the car (dramatically less than the percentage labor represents in most manufactured goods today).[90] Together, labor, lumber, castings, and wrought iron work added up to about $300 per flatcar, or 88 percent of the estimated retail price of $342.[91] More than $30,000 in raw material costs were therefore required to supply the entire contract lot of 110 flatcars—a considerable balance, carried by the North Pacific Coast. This arithmetic also suggests that Carter cleared between 10 and 12 percent profit.

But even if the North Pacific Coast indeed bankrolled his capital expenses, Carter took a considerable risk in exchange for modest gains. From the perspective of July 1874, he was put in the position of being awarded the contract only if he was willing to accept long delays in payment. For a period of nearly eight months, from July 1874 until April 1875, little or none of the monetary value of his work came back to him. In fact, little cash of any kind flowed in his direction, since raw materials were being capitalized by the railroad. In the short run, labor directly charged to new car construction came out of Carter's own pocket, in addition to tooling, travel, and incidentals.

As a result, cash flow certainly became a problem. Evidence from the *Monterey Herald* suggests that there were months in the summer of 1874 when Carter could not meet his payroll.

The NPC financial volumes, the only known record of the structure and pricing of Carter's early business, may also offer a clue to his motives for accepting the onerous terms of the contract. They prove that Latham was willing to continue the contract-shop agreement that Carter provided under account 45. A separate folio or account, 269, was opened in January 1875 to keep track of the same kind of work.[92] Under this account, Carter's crew continued as a jack-of-all trades, doing a range of machine work, carpentry, and woodworking for the new railroad. The cash books over the next two years would demonstrate the variety and flexibility of Carter's skills. As 1875 wore on, Tom Carter's name appeared next to ferry boat and barge repairs, passenger and freight car maintenance, shop tool maintenance, water tank repair, track work, signage, and even locomotive cab construction, giving him and his men badly needed cash flow.

But the difficulty with such "bonus work" was that unlike the uncomplicated days of account 45, there was now an internal railroad car department operating within the North Pacific Coast, not to mention other small contractors with skills much like Carter's. The existence of a separate Saucelito shop record book, with accounts beginning in June 1875, is proof that the railroad, not Carter, was now running the shops.[93]

Numerous entries in the Saucelito shop book cite "materials supplied to car shop," "freight car repair," "water tank construction," and other carpentry projects, without mentioning Thomas Carter.[94] Other small contractors interleave the two in providing related services, such as painting of rolling stock, contracted to J. S. Cameron or Hoffis and Sons; car cleaning, contracted to F. W. Smith; dormitory bunks for the temporary housing of track workers, A. P. Wood. Osgood Stetson did tinsmithing, occasionally repairing locomotive headlights.

The relationship between Carter and the railroad therefore may not have been symbiotic, but rather parasitic. Carter often competed with the railroad's own car shop (and with other private contractors), relinquishing work

Early references to Carter's use of the
North Pacific Coast "machine shop"
came from an article in the *Marin
County Journal* on August 20, 1874;
the building was one of four shop
structures completed the previous
November: "carshop" (150' × 54'),
"machine shop" (100' × 42'), "engine
house" (20' × 22'), and "blacksmith
shop" (22' × 32'). The car shop may
have been used to store finished Kimball cars; the neighboring machine
shop drew power from a stationary
engine in the engine house and was a
logical site for mass production of
wood cars on the scale of the Carter
contract. As long as the Carters were
in Saucelito, there would be records
of their use of power and shop equipment, suggesting they may never have
left the machine shop.

In the summer of 1875, however,
the Shop record book reported
construction of an additional "car
shed." The third large shop building
to be built in the complex, this shed
may correspond to a 32' × 120' two-
track-wide building that first appears
on an 1883 map of the yards and
may be an alternate location of Carter activity at Saucelito. No known
document links Carter to this third
large building. However, a tradition
started by the late Roy Graves, who
worked at the shops shortly after the
turn of the century, suggested that
this building was remembered by
crews as the "Carter shop," a common usage that some of them may
have recalled firsthand from the
start-up of the railroad nearly thirty
years before. In fact, Carter could
have used all these buildings at different times.

when the NPC car shop was busy, working under pressured deadlines when
the car shop had no men to spare, and being put in a poor bargaining position in either event.

The net effect was that the operations of Carter Brothers and the railroad became deeply entwined. There was no separate factory building.
Carter simply moved into what the papers described as the machine shop,
one of two large railroad-owned buildings first erected in the Easterby
Street complex. It was the same building that housed the heavy locomotive
repair machinery and a stationary steam engine. By midsummer 1875, a
third building, identified by the shop record book as a "car shed," was constructed in the complex and could logically have been used by Carter's small
force, or for that matter by the railroad's in-house car shop, or even by A. P.
Wood. We know not which.

At first, the NPC charged Carter no rent (the very attractive terms would
change in 1876). Ledger number 2 documents other dollar-stretching practices that probably dated back to the beginning of the contract. Carter was
able to use the NPC's power tools at no cost; Carter employees (including
Martin Carter and John Carroll) appeared from time to time as NPC employees, working on railroad projects other than new car construction.

What Carter negotiated was a way to gather together and hold onto some
of the best car builders on the West Coast. When Carroll's name first appears in North Pacific Coast Journal no. 1 on September 30, 1874, it favored
him with $7.25 in labor charged not against car construction but on the rail-
road's grading account. We can only imagine what Carroll was doing: perhaps repairing Fresno scrapers for Wood? It didn't matter. He was on the payroll, and close at hand.

Thomas Carter was quietly putting together a team of master car builders under a borrowed roof.

The North Pacific Coast start-up occurred less than eight weeks after the
signing of another, similar Carter contract: to equip the Monterey & Salinas Valley Railroad with rolling stock. The two jobs were planned and executed so closely together that talking about them separately may actually
hide the critical importance of the coincidence. Undertaking one job at a
time, Carter could have continued to see his role as shop manager, contract
car builder, and craftsman. Forced to consider the two jobs together, Carter
had little choice but to see himself as a manufacturer.

The nearly simultaneous contracts strengthened Carter's belief in the
venture growth of California narrow gauge. With new work spontaneously
combusting around him, he perceived the opportunity for what it was: two
customers interested in much the same product, from which he could leverage one job into the other and both into a position of market leadership.
But he also may have mistaken it for what it wasn't: a repeatable and sustainable business model that could, in better economic conditions, grow
apace with California's pressing need for better transportation. The evidence
for such growth appeared to be all around him. If good, cheap narrow gauge
railroads could be built in hard times, they would thrive in good times.

Tom Carter saw the whole as greater than the sum of its parts, and he proceeded to plan for the whole.

Our understanding of this critical eight-week startup period has been slow to come to terms with the order in which these events occurred. The Carter "field factory" at Monterey (a topic to be taken up in Chapter Four) has always been understood as a satellite of an older, larger, better-equipped factory at Saucelito. But this scenario may have simplified the real challenge, and the real opportunity, Carter faced in the spring and summer of 1874.

Instead, consider the idea that Thomas Carter synthesized a flexible and extensible business model from the requirements of two customers who, served separately, might have required considerably less attention to how the work was accomplished. The manufacturing strategy—the how, rather than the what—was the unique problem that Carter had to solve. It was a strategy based on decentralized points of supply and remote field factories, and although it required balancing resources it was nothing really new or revolutionary. Since 1872, Pacific Bridge had been using basically the same strategy, a constantly changing bill of fixed factory locations, migrating field assembly sites, and suppliers scattered somewhere in between. Carter may have been influenced by early contact with the Gorrill brothers on the Strawberry Point work and was quick to adapt their tactics for field manufacture of wood and iron structures. It was, however, a radically different approach to manufacturing than Kimball's.

At the start of the worst recession to hit California since statehood, Carter tried to combine efficiency and cost savings with what would today be called a scalable manufacturing strategy. Thomas Carter committed to keeping two production shops, one hundred miles apart, fully staffed and supplied, mindful that both the parts he produced and the processes he used could be quickly and cheaply ported to new manufacturing sites in the region. Beginning in May 1874, Carter shuttled back and forth between San Francisco and Monterey on a Goodall, Perkins coastal steamer. For the fourteen hours of the one-way voyage, he chain-smoked in the pounding cabin of the steamers *Santa Cruz* or *Ancon*, thinking through the three complex stages of a regional manufacturing strategy.

Stage one was design. Wide separation of factory sites required engineering drawings that doubled as clear, concise, and valid assembly instructions, capable of communicating the same assembly process to craftsmen working a hundred miles away from each other. The men most likely associated with creating these drawings—John Carroll, Thomas Carter himself, and brother Martin—were based in Saucelito, leaving the success or failure of the Monterey shop dependent on their ability to communicate technical detail through drafting. None of these documents are known to have survived. But we do know that cars of virtually the same design, requiring the same raw materials and parts, came out of both sites during the same six months of 1874, hence from compatible production processes sustained by two completely different teams. The link between these activities, Carter understood, was better documentation than would have been required by a single assembly site. The earliest known surviving Carter drawings, drawn with india ink on linen, show such completeness, accuracy, and readability.[95]

These drawings were created in a remarkably short period. In less than

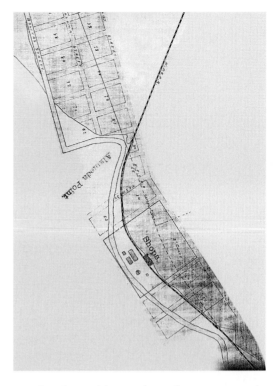

Saucelito shops of the North Pacific Coast, mapped in 1883 in a railroad survey of the Corte Madera cutoff. [California State Archives]

eight weeks, Carter's team of craftsmen came up with not only car assembly drawings but also drawings of component castings and parts. How do we know Carter designed his own castings? Over time, uniformly made castings show up again and again in Carter's products, including journal boxes, truss rod washers, lateral truss rod washers, ogee washers, brake wheels, brake heads, brake shoes, brake hangers, truss rod saddles, drawbars, cheek blocks, spring saddles (top and bottom), body center plates, and truck center plates. All were functionally the same part that might have come from Kimball or Billmeyer and Small, but with signature design elements that show up repeatedly on Carter products throughout their thirty-year lifetime. Roughly twenty-five separate castings were required to fabricate the freight cars that Carter built in 1874, yet all the parts we have examples of—from the simplest (a truss rod saddle) to the most complex (the journal box)—show consistent design elements: unmistakable brevity, lack of embellishment or decoration, minimization of form within function. The Carter "family" of castings would grow over the succeeding quarter century as his product line expanded.

Why was the simplicity of a casting so important to Carter's strategy? Designing his own parts and documenting the designs helped ensure their interchangeability as new suppliers, spread throughout northern California, were identified. To avoid shipping heavy castings a long distance, Carter looked for an iron foundry located as close to each factory site as he could find. We know about two during this time period: Amner Morton in Santa Cruz, which served the Monterey factory; and the Vallejo Foundry, serving Saucelito. But since foundries varied in their approach to mold making for a given part, a craftsman knew in advance that a design for a casting had to be "foundry-independent," making the same part interchangeable between foundries with slightly different casting processes. Simplicity in the original design was a key factor in interchangeable finished parts. Symmetry, avoidance of sharp curves or angles, and deliberate "draft angles" (allowing easy removal of patterns from the mold) all helped suppliers develop consistent, accurate casting processes. Carter casting drawings from later periods survive and are drawn full scale to act as templates for the pattern maker, thus adapting documentation to the needs of the external supplier.[96] We believe similar documentation was created in common for the requirements of the Monterey and Saucelito projects.

Stage two is prototyping. At some point, trial parts, milled lumber, and skilled craftsmen converged on the first assembly of the product. This point of convergence is traditionally called a prototype; it is the designer's first (and in this case, final) check on the integrity of a design before production began. Carter's first prototype, in this case a flatcar, was assembled in Monterey a few days prior to July 4, 1874, the first time a Carter-designed narrow gauge car ever came together. The event was noteworthy to the local press (the *Monterey Herald*) and was described accurately as a specialized step in a much larger manufacturing process: "One flat car has been put together in order to ascertain if the castings are correct, but it is not their intention to put up any more until the timbers are cut and prepared and ready for them all, when they will go up with a rush."

We've always understood this citation as if it applied to the Monterey work alone. But in reality, the event may have been the validation—of designs, suppliers, and assembly processes—for both the Monterey and Saucelito factories and the beginning of high-volume production for both. The *Herald*'s article was published just five days earlier than the *Marin County Journal*'s announcement that Carter had received the contract for North Pacific Coast rolling stock. The timing of these events suggests that the resources of Monterey Bay, in particular the small foundry that Carter had tapped in nearby Santa Cruz, did the prototype work for not only the M&SV contract but the North Pacific Coast as well.

Stage three is "ramping." With a successful prototype and a supply of parts and materials ensured, volume production could begin. But it didn't begin all at once. Instead, an experienced foundry "ramped" the process, deliberately increasing its production volume a little at a time until it could adequately control crucial variables in the molding and casting processes.

A foundry therefore traveled up its own unique ramp to produce castings, from low volume to high volume, as its control of the casting process improved. This supplier's ramp preceded and shaped Carter's entire manufacturing plan. The beginning of accurate pattern work required detailed part drawings, as well as a clear understanding of their assembly into the wooden car frame. The designs for all the parts in the car had to be substantially completed by late May 1874, to allow a foundry—in this case Amner Morton in Santa Cruz—to begin pattern work with enough lead time to meet its own ramp deadline. Again, the eight-week design window becomes the key to understanding the timing of both the Monterey and Saucelito projects, since Carter could not have signed the Monterey contract prior to late March.[97] That would leave April and May for design work, June for the foundry ramp, and early July for the assembly of a prototype, before beginning the first real production of cars in Monterey during the last three weeks of July. Even by today's high-tech manufacturing standards, Carter's timeline was compressed.

Carter's final challenge, to transplant the manufacturing processes to Saucelito, was a direct result of the ramp taking place in Monterey. Patterns (very likely owned by Carter) were shipped from Santa Cruz to the Vallejo Foundry of McCormick and Lewis. Again, Carter could have learned from the Gorrills, since Pacific Bridge faced a nearly identical problem as they moved bridge work up and down the coast. Henry Gorrill noted in his diary on April 17, 1874, that castings for bridge work in Oregon "all made at Palmer, Knox & Co. for 6 cts (per pound), and patterns are ours, without further charge."

Equipped with patterns, the Vallejo Foundry then faced its own ramp, starting with low volume until the foundry could adapt their own mold-making process and improve production through trial and error. Proof of the design, however, had been accomplished in Monterey. It remained for McCormick and Lewis to replicate the process and accelerate it in time to achieve the volume production required to support the Saucelito manufacturing ramp, which probably began in late July.

The timing of this complex set of events, today collectively referred to as a supply chain, would literally dictate Carter's success or failure.

Trucks were designed to transmit the load carried by a railroad car to the track. In almost all truck designs, the load passed through springs that filtered out unwanted vertical vibration created by the up-and-down motion of the load. Another kind of vibration, *lateral,* could not be filtered out this way. This vibration came from forces acting side to side on the car, caused by variations in track alignment or uneven wear on railheads. Swing motion was designed to cushion the car against such lateral forces. Patented in 1841, *swing motion trucks* were designed to cradle the car in a suspension system much like a front porch swing, allowing the entire car to rock side to side in response to lateral forces.

Extra hardware required to make a swing motion truck was expensive, complex, and potentially dangerous. The car sat on a *swing bolster,* suspended within the truck frame, allowing the car to pendulum back and forth about an inch in relation to the wheels and arch bars. The load of the car therefore passed through the iron *swing hangers,* U-shaped straps that cradled the truck bolster, which could and sometimes did snap under the strain, dropping the entire mechanism onto the tracks. Such a failure could lead to derailment. Even in normal operation, the swing motion system required extra maintenance, and its added value—thought to improve wheel and rail wear—remained in debate for as long as the truck was popular on American railroads, roughly from the 1850s to the 1890s.

Because of the added commitment of contract shop work, Carter chose to concentrate his most experienced craftsmen in Saucelito. The "brain trust" of the new start-up, many of the craftsmen who began at Saucelito, would remain with Carter Brothers for the next two decades.

Five were listed as "carbuilders" in the Great Register of Marin County[98]: John Carroll, by this time fifty years old and apparently in and out of work with the Southern Pacific car shop in San Francisco; brother Martin, twenty-nine, quitting the Langland partnership in Sacramento; Joseph Bartlett, age forty; Henry Aiken, twenty-three; and John Nelson, twenty-one. Too young to vote, Carroll's oldest son, Frank, then fifteen, began an apprenticeship under his father when the car work began. Martin, in turn, brought two of his best men from Langland: Bartolemew Essig, forty-five, was listed in the Great Register as a pattern maker; and Martin's father-in-law, John Larkin, age unknown, was listed as a carpenter. There were three other carpenters in the Great Register who were Carter men at a later date and who probably were affiliated with Carter in Saucelito: Alexander Finn, thirty-seven, who would remain with the Newark works until it closed in 1902; Henry Barth, age unknown; and John Armand, age unknown. A German painter, George Gibbon, age twenty-five, would be listed as a Carter employee when the Newark shops opened in 1877 and also appeared as a registered voter in Saucelito in 1875.

Except for the early mention of John Carroll in North Pacific Coast Journal no. 1, the names of Carter's craftsmen appeared first in the Great Register of Marin County, added between 1875 and 1877 as the craftsmen registered to vote.

John Carroll was probably Carter's most important team member, his closest personal friend, and the most experienced of the craftsmen. For the next two years, Carroll would remain the most experienced car builder at the Saucelito operation, setting up the production facility and very likely playing a key role in design work. With Carroll in charge of the production floor, at least ten men and probably more were able to start work at the Easterby Street shop in July 1874. For the next two years, brother Martin apprenticed to Carroll, as Thomas had at Folsom years earlier, adding production strategy and cost control to his knowledge of the car trade.

In contrast, the Monterey work featured new players, few of whom would have a long history with Carter. Francis "Frank" Geiser was assigned the foreman's job, a name not associated with Folsom or Portland projects. At the time, Geiser was a lead carpenter in the Southern Pacific's San Francisco shops (where Carroll may have recruited him) and in a lull period went moonlighting for Tom Carter. Twenty additional carpenters were hired from nearby Santa Cruz (a story continued in Chapter Four).

The stakes were high. As mentioned, the Saucelito contract included 140 freight cars, worth about $50,000. The Monterey work covered 2 passenger cars and 48 freight cars, valued at about $30,000.[99] Together, the contracts aggregated over $80,000 in retail value. Both projects were pitted against a deadline tied to the opening date for each railroad. Before Carter finished the M&SV contract, a high percentage of the Salinas Valley grain crop had been stored in warehouses near the unfinished railroad, awaiting its completion for shipment to the Monterey harbor.[100] The ships to deliver the wheat to Liverpool were already consigned.

Carter's total payroll reflected the pressure of deadlines, and the growing size of his risk. In the early summer months of 1874, the names mentioned earlier suggest that a core dozen were responsible for the startup phase of the car contract. But by the middle of July, perhaps forty craftsmen were drawing wages from Carter Brothers, representing a cash flow in the neighborhood of $5,000 per month.

Carter could ill afford a miscalculation. At that rate of expenditure, just six weeks of additional labor would have wiped out every cent of profit he expected to make from both jobs, combined.

—————

With only eight weeks to produce the drawings that would become his products, where did Carter get the car designs in the first place? The question lies at the heart of explaining the nearly overnight rise of Carter's business, but the term *design* may be misleading. Instead, Carroll and Carter *adapted*. The basic engineering concepts that they worked from, such as car framing, truck design, and brake layout, had been around for thirty years by the time Carter began early production work at Saucelito. But now there was the new, unique environment of West Coast narrow gauge in which to apply traditional mechanical parts and structures. The designs now had to work in a smaller and lighter car, work successfully on poorly built track, and be manufactured cheaply enough to fit narrow gauge budgets.

Under severe time pressure in the spring and summer of 1874, Carter and Carroll responded to these demands by simplifying and commoditizing designs that already existed. Original Carter documentation of these cars has not survived. What we know about the products comes from later drawings, a handful of contemporary photographs, and one extant car body, a boxcar built for the Monterey & Salinas Valley Railroad during the summer of 1874 (see the Field Notebook: Footprint Archeology).

In general appearance, Carter's 1874 car designs followed the emerging narrow gauge standard defined by Billmeyer and Small when it built the first batch of eight-wheel cars for the new Denver & Rio Grande railroad[101]:

24' long over sills, 7' wide
Four frame sills, hence the term "four stick car"
Two four-wheel trucks
Capacity of about eight tons
Tare weight of slightly over four tons

The design approximated, in overall dimensions and weight, the products Howard Schuyler had purchased for the Denver & Rio Grande, cars built in late 1871 and 1872 by Billmeyer and Small.[102] In Schuyler's mind, lightweight design was the key to narrow gauge economy. These basic design parameters were still in favor in October 1878, when the National Narrow Gauge Convention met and discussed mechanical standards in Cincinnati, a continuing example of the conservative nature of railway engineering.[103]

The Field Notebook: Footprint Archeology

There is strong evidence that the single extant Monterey & Salinas Valley boxcar was rebuilt, perhaps several times, during sixty-five years of service. The only reason the car survived at all (as Nevada Central boxcar 253) was a final rebuilding in 1896, a date consistent with 1922 and 1923 graffiti penciled on interior wall plates visible today. In the dry Nevada desert, the boxcar saw light service and relatively little deterioration until the 1938 abandonment of the railroad.

There is thus a good chance that many of the car's extant parts are not original. But the car body, preserved at Ardenwood Park in Fremont, California, may still represent the "footprint" of the original 1874 Carter car. As rolling stock aged, parts or assemblies were not all replaced at the same time. If a wall was rebuilt, the side sill (the foundation for the wall) might remain untouched, in good condition. Since the sill contained the mortices and holes that anchored the structure of the wall above it, a new wall would be erected in the footprint of the old wall, replicating its essential structure and dimensions.

At a later time, a rotted original side sill might be replaced with a new one. But the wall above it would provide the footprint for the new side sill, conforming within perhaps a fraction of an inch to its original measurements, which were replicated in the footprint of the wall parts.

In this way, an aging car body reproduced its basic dimensions even as individual parts wore out and were replaced. A Robert Schlechter drawing of the original Carter eight-ton boxcar (reproduced in Chapter Four) is based on the assumption that the remaining relic is virtually the same car as it was 126 years ago.

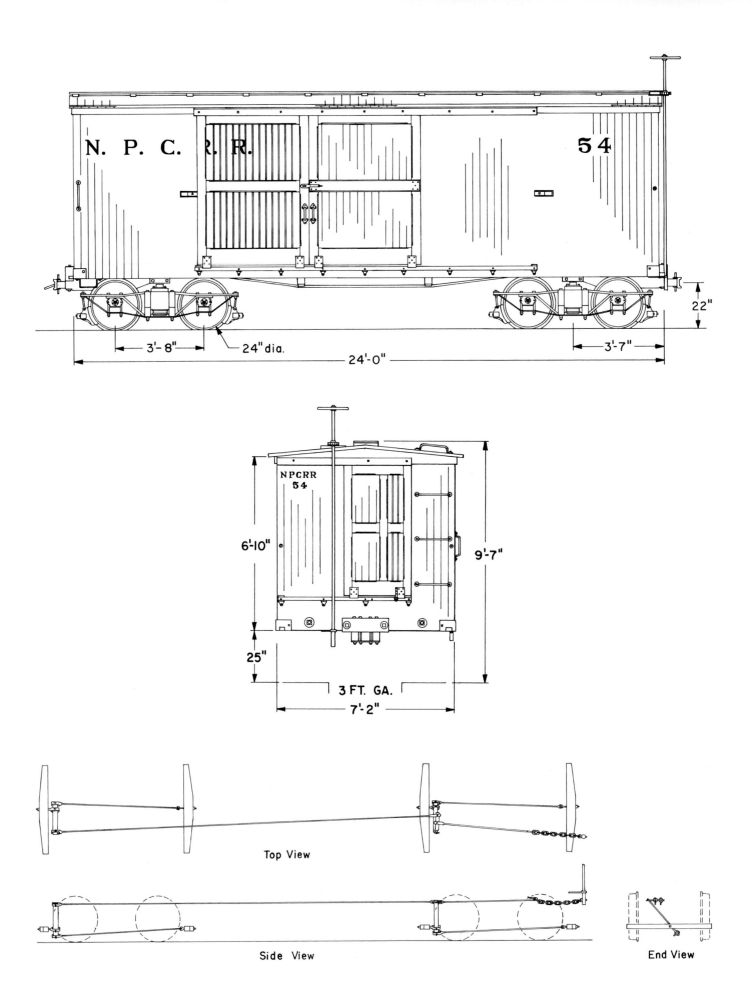

N. P. C. R. R.   54

22"

3'-8"   24"dia.   3'-7"

24'-0"

NPCRR
54

6'-10"   9'-7"

25"

3 FT. GA.

7'-2"

Top View

Side View

End View

But Carter, beginning the design work for the Monterey & Salinas Valley in April 1874, may have been less influenced by Schuyler and more influenced by the experience he and Carroll had gained on the Central Pacific. If we accept Billmeyer and Small's narrow gauge frame design as industry standard, the basic Carter framework was sturdier. Of ten structural parts compared between 1874 Billmeyer and Small boxcars and Carter boxcars, five Carter parts had a larger cross section, while only three Billmeyer and Small parts were larger, an overt attempt on Carter's part to beef up the product.[104]

In other ways, the 1874 Carter designs simplified and cheapened industry standards. Frills were eliminated. Billmeyer's patented platform buffer, a rubber spring-cushioned draft system built into the end platform, was never used on a Carter car. Carter's standard coupling system was a miniature replica of the Central Pacific's standard design.[105]

Billmeyer and Small brake systems of the period had six levers, whose function was to equalize pressure on each of the car's eight brake shoes. The 1874 Carter brake system had just two levers, a radical concession to simplicity and cost savings, but a solution that yielded poor mechanical advantage and no equalization of pressure on the car's eight brake shoes.

Most dramatic, however, was Carter's departure from the Billmeyer truck

Opposite: Herman Darr's reconstruction of the twenty-four-foot Carter combination boxcar, eight-ton capacity, first built for the North Pacific Coast in 1874 (not reproduced to scale). Details of the primitive two-lever brake system appear at the bottom of the drawing. Above: scene at Fallon Creamery, on the North Pacific Coast, showing the end view of combination boxcar and approaching northbound passenger train, with locomotive number 8, *Bully Boy* on the point. [Above, Robert Moulton collection; opposite, Herman Darr]

Computer reconstruction of mechanism in Carter Brothers fifteen-ton swing-motion truck. [Curtis Ferrington]

design. The most mechanically critical assembly in the car, the trucks had to carry the weight of the entire load in an extremely high-vibration, high-impact environment. The tight curvature of the North Pacific Coast mainline (250' minimum radius) only exaggerated these harsh environmental conditions. Clearly, unsuccessful designs caused derailments, as in the case of Kimball's Virginia & Truckee cabooses mentioned earlier.

American truck designers, in the 1870s, met these challenges through two functionally distinct approaches. Both used arch bars to form the basic framework for four journal boxes, two axles, and four wheels. The Billmeyer approach, however, kept this framework laterally rigid in relation to the car itself (hence the term "rigid arch bar truck").

The alternative approach allowed the car to swing laterally about one inch (at right angles to the track) in order to absorb side-to-side vibrations, hence the name "swing motion" (see page 118). This design was engineered into the truck by allowing the car to pivot on a "swing bolster." This was cradled between two heavy beams (called transom beams) that were rigidly bolted to the truck's arch bars.[106] The "spring plank" was hung from a pair of forged iron stirrups mounted to the transom beams, free to rotate on cast iron bearings—much like the suspension in an old front porch swing. Springs supported the swing bolster on either end of the spring plank. In this way, the spring plank—and the attached car body—could swing like a pendulum, set into gentle side-to-side motion by irregularities in track alignment.

Swing motion had gained a following with a number of broad gauge freight and passenger car manufacturers during the 1870s; though expensive to build and more intricate to maintain than a rigid arch bar truck, it had a loyal following among master car builders who swore it was easier riding, had less resistance to curves, and racked up less wear and tear both on itself and on the track. This argument raged on among American car builders for a quarter century and was never fully resolved. Versions of both kinds of truck can be found in use today.

Billmeyer and Small, in claiming a premier role in American narrow gauge car building, staunchly defended the concept of the rigid arch bar freight truck. Their reasoning was based on stability. If an already narrow car body were allowed the freedom to oscillate side to side, Billmeyer and Small argued that the chance of tipping over was increased. Swing bolster trucks, an advertisement claimed, "are best adapted where there is little or no curvature, but we think dangerous on short curves on account of the swing and overhang of heavy loads on such small base as three feet gauge, and besides are much more expensive in repairs."[107]

Thus the first generation Billmeyer narrow gauge freight truck was a 3'2" wheelbase rigid arch bar, devoid of swing motion. This is the truck that Schuyler purchased for the Denver & Rio Grande, three years before Carter went to work for Schuyler on the North Pacific Coast.

John Carroll, however, was schooled with the opposition. Davenport and Bridges held the 1841 patent on swing motion, and Carroll, if he worked for Davenport as we now believe, saw the technology applied to the Sacramento Valley's kit-built freight cars. Carter, working for the Central Pacific both at Sacramento in 1870 and at Donahue Landing in 1871, very likely witnessed the Central Pacific's transition to a swing motion design called

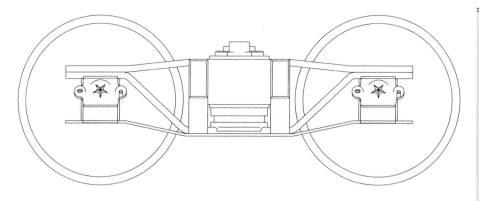

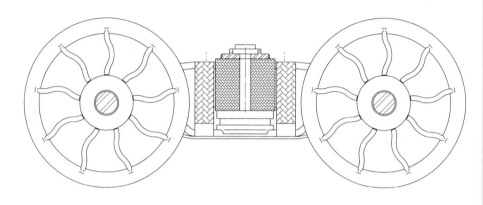

SECTION A-A

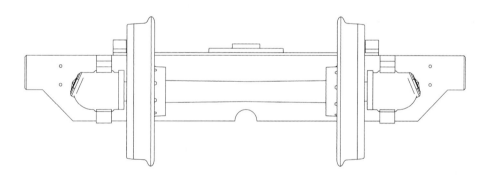

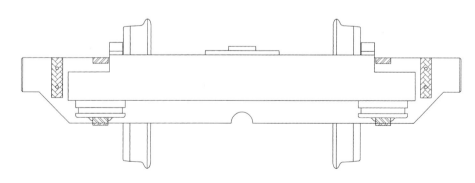

SECTION E-E

The Field Notebook: First-Generation Carter Eight-Ton Truck

The truck was light and simple. It had a 3'8" wheelbase, 24" single-plate wheels each weighing about 275 pounds, a pair of rubber springs, 3" axles, and approximately 2⁵/₈" × 5³/₄" bearings. All of its major wooden components were Douglas fir (with the possible exception of oak used to fabricate the truck bolster). Although designed to allow swing motion to be installed, the truck lacked a swing bolster and swing axles, making it difficult to classify as either swing motion or rigid arch bar.

In comparison, a Billmeyer and Small 1871 Rio Grande truck had a 3'2" wheelbase, four 20" diameter single-plate wheels also weighing 275 pounds each, 3" axles, and 2¹/₂" × 5" bearings. It was designed to be a rigid truck, with no upgrade path to swing motion. It was also sprung with two cylindrical rubber springs. Its wooden parts—truck bolster and spring plank—were probably oak.

The slight differences in bearing size were not enough to dissuade either builder from rating its cars identically at eight tons' capacity, a figure that—at least in Carter's case—was acknowledged by customers. A Jan. 1, 1878, local freight tariff from the Monterey & Salinas Valley Railroad, for example, listed a typical carload at sixteen thousand pounds, thus practicing what the builder preached.

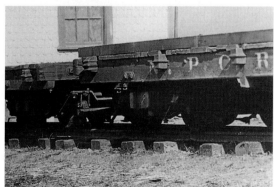

[Drawings: Curtis Ferrington]

the Allen patent, sometime in the early 1870s.[108] This truck was in part a response to the track conditions that Mark Hopkins described to Collis Huntington in his letter of May 31, 1865, notably, poor track surface through constantly reversing mountain curves. Early on, the Central Pacific realized that these conditions demanded extreme flexibility in the car body and especially the truck. Because of its popularity on the Central Pacific, the Allen patent truck became regionally known as the California truck, and we believe it was the basis of Carter's narrow gauge design.

The intent behind Carter's adaptation seems obvious. He attempted to simplify and cheapen a truck design that had been considered successful for thirty years. The essential transom beams of the swing motion truck were clearly present in the 1874 Carter truck, making the trucks appear in photographs to have true swing motion. But the guts of the swing motion were missing. The suspension system, including swing axles and bearings, was eliminated, in the process obviating the need for a number of specialized castings and forgings, which saved weight and expense. The result was a strange hybrid of the two truck types, motivated not only by cost savings but also by the extremely short lead time available to complete design and pattern work.

A look at the 1874 Carter truck from the underside (a rare perspective afforded by an 1893 photograph of a wreck on the Nevada County Narrow Gauge) reveals a truck bolster floating atop two cylindrical blocks of natural rubber. Doing away with most of the components of traditional swing motion hardware, Carter and Carroll had innovated a crude but inexpensive substitute. The rubber blocks acted vertically like a spring while shearing sideways like Jell-O, offering a "no moving parts" version of swing motion. Because of the Jell-O-like qualities of the rubber spring suspension, this earliest version of Carter's truck has been referred to as a "squirm" motion design, and its riding qualities probably left a lot to be desired.

The primitive Carter eight-ton truck appeared under virtually every known freight car associated with its 1874 and 1875 contract work, including cars on the North Pacific Coast, Monterey & Salinas Valley, and the Nevada County Narrow Gauge. Small variations were introduced to suit individual customers. For example, on the NPC and the NCNG, brake beams were hung from the trucks themselves, making it easier to keep the brake shoes in line with the wheels on a mainline curve as tight as a 250-foot radius—the NPC's worst. On the M&SV, however, the minimum mainline curvature was 579 feet, and body-hung brakes were standard on all cars.[109]

The design may have also included a deliberate migration path to future improvements. In 1874, the truck's Spartan features were dictated by reduction of the number of parts, light car weight, simplicity of design and construction, and ultimately low cost. But upgrading the design would also require little modification. By 1876, the so-called Carter ten-ton truck would accept a swing bolster into essentially the eight-ton truck frame, add slightly heavier axles and journals, and reuse many of the parts of the eight-ton truck. In the meantime, under the pressured startup conditions of the summer of 1874, Carter would overcome a design bottleneck with the expedient of squirm motion.

Before judging Carter's 1874 design work as penurious, we have to keep in mind that a wooden railroad car was built and purchased as a disposable product.[110] Its life expectancy was intended to be less than ten years, and even though the general trend was toward high-capacity cars, improvement in strength and life expectancy occurred in small, cautious steps. Carter's products, in particular, simplified traditional car-building practice into a low-cost adaptation better suited for low-speed, poor-track conditions, exactly the state of affairs on the North Pacific Coast. With thirty-five-pound rail, 250-foot-radius mainline curves, and four-ton tare weight on its flatcars, the NPC qualified as a textbook example of "lightly built."

As a result, there was no intellectual property protection in the 1874 Carter designs—no innovation that another manufacturer had not already adopted. He designed his early freight equipment as a commodity. Almost twenty years later, Tom Carter would create designs involving patent protection,[111] but in 1874 his leverage points on the market were primarily low cost and availability. By producing rolling stock on site, he saved the NPC large shipping fees from East Coast manufacturers (as much as $158 per flatcar or $197 for a boxcar, f.o.b. Chicago[112]).

In less than four months from design work to fabrication, the basic Carter eight-ton-capacity freight car became the builder's standard car architecture. With walls framed like a Howe truss (a framing design common to bridges of the era), the same structural design elements were adapted to create boxcars.[113] On the Monterey & Salinas Valley, the eight Carter boxcars were all of standard twenty-four-foot design, featuring a single side door. On the North Pacific Coast, however, Carter included ten double-door "ventilator" style cars in the fleet of thirty boxcars, featuring double side doors, which allowed shipment of livestock, fruits, vegetables, or berries.[114] Built in November 1874, the first NPC ventilator boxcars were early prototypes of one of Carter's most salable products, and a departure from commoditization.

Thus Carter filled a car order tailored to the revenue demands of the first segment of the North Pacific Coast, the agricultural midlands of Marin County. The car fleet was built to handle milk and cheese, newsprint from Sam Taylor's mill, "Bodega spuds" from Tomales, and firewood from the redwood belt around San Geronimo. The line's first revenue shipment—8,863 pounds of hardware moving from Saucelito to Sam Taylor's paper mill—probably traveled aboard a Carter car on October 15, 1874.[115]

The original 1874 North Pacific Coast contract covered fewer than 150 cars. But a future order, tailored to meet the needs of the extension to Dutch Bill and the Russian River, was projected to more than double the car roster, providing more than 300 additional cars for handling the lumber traffic from four new sawmills in the Dutch Bill watershed. The aggressive estimates for additional rolling stock were published in local papers in October 1875, but Carter should have understood the potential for additional work virtually from the start.[116]

The North Pacific Coast project might therefore have appeared to Carter as six times the size and value of the small Monterey & Salinas Valley job.

For the next six months, the North Pacific Coast machine shop came alive with the sounds of flapping leather belts, the scream of planer blades eating into thick wood beams, and the clock escapement of heavy car jacks, lifting frames off the floor one click at a time. Bartolemew Essig, the pattern maker, glued sticks of maple and rosewood together to create new patterns, rapidly expanding the Carter catalogue of parts. In April 1875, McCormick and Lewis's foundry moved from Vallejo to San Francisco, taking Carter's foundry work with it.[117] Living in San Francisco, Thomas occasionally commuted back and forth to Saucelito with an assortment of patterns tucked under his arm, all destined for McCormick and Lewis's new Industrial Foundry in Tar Flat.

Because of the cramped working conditions in the machine shop, cars were assembled using the build-in-place system. Two tracks entered the 80' × 125' building, allowing at least four and perhaps six cars to be sited on the floor at any one time. Raw materials were delivered to a staging area for each car, and all facets of the erection process—framing, ironing, installation of trucks, and finally painting—were carried out at the same spot. Instead of an assembly-line approach, the same small crew performed a craftsman's build, doing all the carpentry and ironing as a team, maximizing each car builder's understanding of the entire ensemble.

The handicaps inherent in the site were numerous. Large-scale car manufactories learned early on to partition erection and painting activities to minimize the amount of airborne sawdust deposited on freshly painted siding. Carter, housed in a single building, didn't have such a luxury. Worse, the machine shop was also the only locomotive repair facility on the railroad. Through Christmas 1874, only two engines were on the roster, placing little demand on the machine shop's intended use as a repair facility. In its early phases, the railroad jobbed out at least some of its locomotive repair needs to San Francisco machine works such as H. J. Booth and Co. (a story to be told in Chapter Five). However, as the North Pacific Coast added locomotives, and as wrecks became a more frequent occurrence, it was clear that Carter's days in the machine shop were numbered.

Space, in any event, must have been at a premium. Ricks of freshly milled Douglas fir sills, at least one hundred pairs of wheel-axle sets (occupying 360 lineal feet of outdoor track), stacks of forged truss rods, honeycombs of journal box castings and brake shoes, crates of bolts, barrels of cut nails, and gallons of linseed oil were repeatedly stored, moved, drawn upon, and stored again at various stages of the manufacturing process. Keeping track of this flow of material was by itself a consuming part of the work. No wholesale supply houses waited close by to make up a few lost or miscounted fasteners, and no junked car bodies moldered out in the yards from a previous generation of equipment, ready to be cannibalized for parts.

In the early phases of the project, Carter workers may have had trouble finding lodging close to the job. Saucelito hotels, noted the *San Francisco Bulletin*, were so crowded with tourists that by mid-July 1874 there was no room left in the local inns. The workers could have boarded at the Princess House, or the Green Hotel, or at Schultze's Railroad House, or at the new hotel Schultze built in late 1873 at Alameda Point, near the shop itself. There were seven hotels or resorts in town, but only these four remained open year-round, after the tourists had retreated back to the City for the winter months. Residence listings for Carter's men, appearing in San Francisco city directories, simply said "Saucelito," giving no other address, suggesting their mail went to general delivery as they moved among available boarding houses.

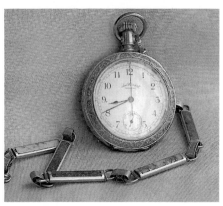

North Pacific Coast artifacts, including trainman's watch and switch key, from Sausalito Historical Society. [Bruce MacGregor]

In the late fall of 1874, as the weather got cooler, the huge interior volume of the machine shop dissolved the heat of wood stoves, and workers would take a break to drink hot coffee and warm their fingers before returning to the frigid handle of a wrench.

On the lee side of Mt. Tamalpais, out of the strong bay winds that chilled San Francisco during the winter of 1874, the village barely stirred from its prerailroad slumber. Except for twenty small summer cottages erected along the waterfront, most of the twelve hundred lots available from the Saucelito Land and Ferry Co. remained unsold and undeveloped.

There were two restaurants open year-round, Rety's and the Railroad Free Lunch, located on the wharf. J. S. Bellrude was still the only merchant in town, and he ran the general store, the livery, a lumber yard, and the meat market, as well as a branch store in Tomales (which was soon to be handily connected by rail to the mother store). Bellrude's was also the outfit station for John Wade and E. Y. Buchanan, field engineers who continued to probe the wilds of Dutch Bill Canyon for an outlet to the Russian River. The North Pacific Coast's facilities were Spartan. When the line opened, freight would not be transshipped at Saucelito. The railroad's freight cars were simply loaded directly onto 45' × 170' barges, destined for off-loading on the East Street wharves in San Francisco. Carter's crew, in their spare time, worked on the barges, named *Transfer 1* and *Transfer 2*.

Tucked into a cove in San Francisco Bay's inner approach to the Golden Gate, Saucelito lived inside the gray fringe of coastal weather fronts. In a driving rainstorm, through sooted glass windows, Martin's crew would watch construction trains leave the spit of land at Alameda Point, appearing to head out to sea on the catwalk of the Richardson Bay bridge, disappearing north by northeast into the storms that blew off the flanks of Tamalpais.

At night, in the dimly lit interior of the machine shop, the isolation and the cold must have caught up with Tom Carter, who was perhaps delaying returning to the City to walk among the unfinished skeletons of cars and take stock of the parts, or the workmanship, or the accelerating cash flow, the stump of his leg beginning to ache in the cold.

Yet the Carters intended to stay. In either late 1874 or early 1875, Martin bought a lot on Easterby Street, just up the hill from the shops. On it he built a house for Mary, who was expecting their second child. With a breathtaking view of San Francisco Bay at their feet, the Martin Carter family set up housekeeping.

Three years later, when the Marin County tax assessor inventoried Martin Carter's holdings, he noted that Martin and Mary owned a $300 lot, a $250 dwelling (which Martin probably built himself), $150 worth of household furniture, a $25 sewing machine, two American cows valued at $40, a half-breed horse worth $75, and a wagon, valued at $75.[118]

The cows, of course, were for Thomas Newton, who the family nicknamed Newt, and the new arrival, Francis Martin, who they called Frank.

In the fireplace, Martin would warm his family by burning loads of scrap lumber from the shop trim pile.

Returning late from the shop, walking uphill through the dark, cold night, Thomas would have taken shelter again at his brother's hearth.

NORTH PACIFIC COAST RAILROAD

MOST DIRECT ROUTE

TO

All Points on the North Coast

Stages leave Ingrams daily (Sundays excepted) for Stewart's Point, Gualala, Point Arena, Cuffey's Cove, Navarro, Mendocino City, Caspar, Noyo, Kibesillah, Westport, and all points on the North Coast.

The Only Route to the Redwood Forests on the Russian River, where Hunting and Fishing can be found, to the full enjoyment of the most devoted sportsman.

Thirty-day Excursion Tickets sold at a reduction of 25 per cent. on the regular single fare tariff rates. Excursion Round Trip Tickets sold on Fridays, Saturdays and Sundays, good to return on following Monday. To

| Camp Taylor | $1 75 | Tomales | $3 00 |
| Point Reyes | 2 00 | Ingrams | 4 00 |

Excursion Round Trip Tickets sold on Sundays:

| Camp Taylor | 1 50 | Tomales | 2 50 |
| Point Reyes | 1 75 | Ingrams | 3 00 |

Tourists visiting this State cannot find a more beautiful and diversified trip. The steamers leave the ferry slip at the foot of Market street for Saucelito, the only seaside Resort where good bathing, boating and fishing can be found. The route from here runs along Richardson's Bay to the base of Mount Tamalpais, one of the features surrounding the Bay of San Francisco. Stopping at the station named after the mountain, the traveler will find teams ready to take him up to the top of this giant, from which a magnificent view of the Farallone Islands and the Pacific Ocean can be had. Three and a half miles from this station are the far-famed Fairfax Picnic Grounds; thence in three quarters of an hour Camp Taylor is reached, where all facilities, including Dancing Hall and Bowling Alley for Camping and Picnic Parties, can be found. From this point to Point Reyes Station, a distance of eight miles, splendid trout streams abound, on whose banks most beautiful spots for private camps can be found. The route then skirts for a distance of sixteen miles the Bay of Tomales, which is covered with all kinds of wild fowl. The hills surrounding this town (Tomales) are one vast potato field, until nearly reaching Valley Ford, which town is situated in the grain district of the county; thence to Freestone, which is the beginning of the great Redwood Forests; thence along to Howard's Station, from which is shipped an immense quantity of bark and wood; thence along Russian River to Duncan's Mills; thence to Ingrams, which is the present terminus of the road, and one of the loveliest spots in the State, the climate being as soft and mild as that of southern France.

The Hotels and cottages are kept by old experienced hotelkeepers, thereby assuring every comfort and attention to the traveler.

| Ticket Office, | - - - - | Saucelito Ferry, Market Street. |
| General Office, | - - - - | 327 Pine Street, San Francisco. |

[Robert C. Moulton collection]

Well beyond the age of obsoles-
cence, the North Pacific Coast's
passenger operations depended on
locomotives, cars, and facilities
dating from its construction period; witness the twenty-five-year-
old Kimball coach (above left),
photographed at the Sausalito terminal at the turn of the century.
The car shed itself remained a
landmark from the 1870s (in the
painting below); by 1886, the
building had been cut in two parts
and spliced back together at right
angles, as shown in the Frank
Rodolph photograph at the upper
right. [Top, left and right, Bancroft
Library; bottom, Sausalito Historical Society]

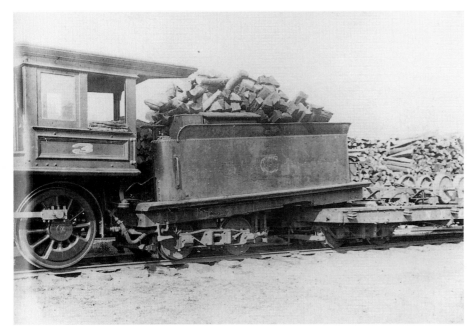

By 1895, when the picnic cars shown at the bottom of this page were under construction, the car shop once used by Thomas Carter was still the source of much of the line's new rolling stock. In the panorama below, the car shop is seen as the three-stall building closest to the water, on the left side of the complex. In the car shops and associated machine shops, the North Pacific Coast's aging car and locomotive fleet was maintained for nearly a half century. [Top, Jack Farley collection; middle, Robert Moulton collection; bottom, collection of Ray Roix, from Harold A. Lapham]

Saucelito: The Kimball Skirmish   129

The congested portal to the Saucelito pier funneled both freight and passenger trains into a narrow approach to the railroad's ferry slips. [Above, San Francisco Maritime National Historical Park; below, California Historical Society]

The Birth of California Narrow Gauge

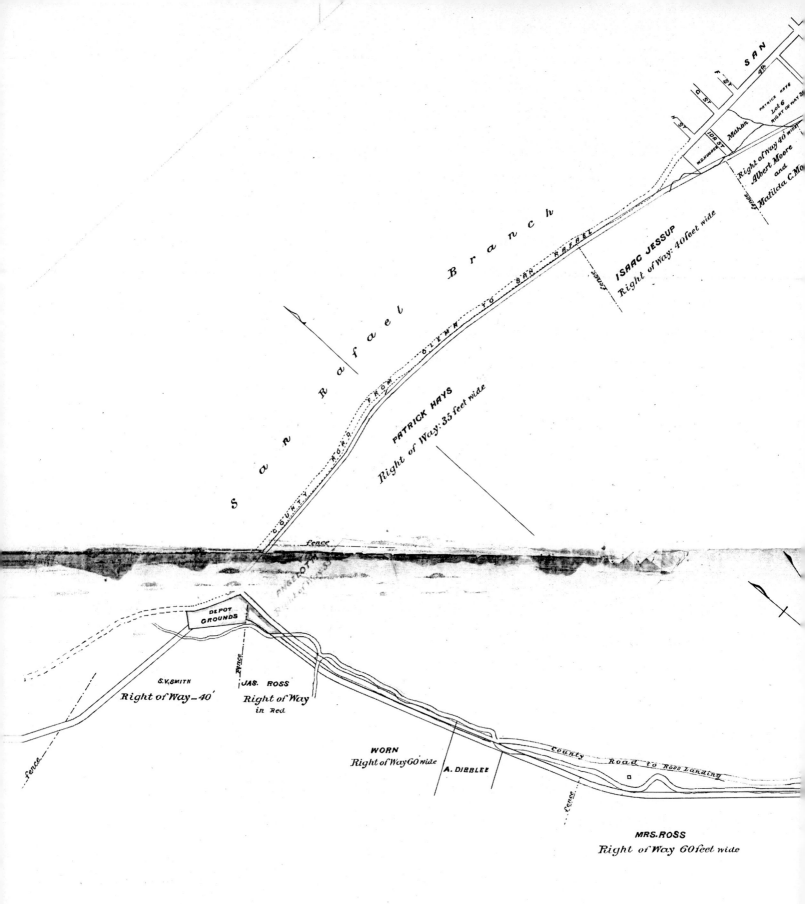

SAN

ISAAC JESSUP
Right of Way: 40 feet wide

PATRICK HAYS
Right of Way: 35 feet wide

DEPOT
GROUNDS

S.V. SMITH
Right of Way – 40'

JAS. ROSS
Right of Way
in Red

WORN
Right of Way 60 wide

A. DIBBLEE

County Road to Ross Landing

MRS. ROSS
Right of Way 60 feet wide

3

Both the right-of-way map and the remarkable photograph above portray the Junction, later known as San Anselmo station, in 1875; magnification helps identify a Radley and Hunter stack on the distant locomotive, as well as a Carter Brothers twenty-four-foot boxcar barely visible to the left of the locomotive—both, at the time of the photograph, just a year old. This and subsequent John Wade right-of-way maps (on several pages from here through page 147) run retrograde; that is, Saucelito is to the right side of each map and the railroad extends north to the left. [Map: California State Archives; this page, California Historical Society]

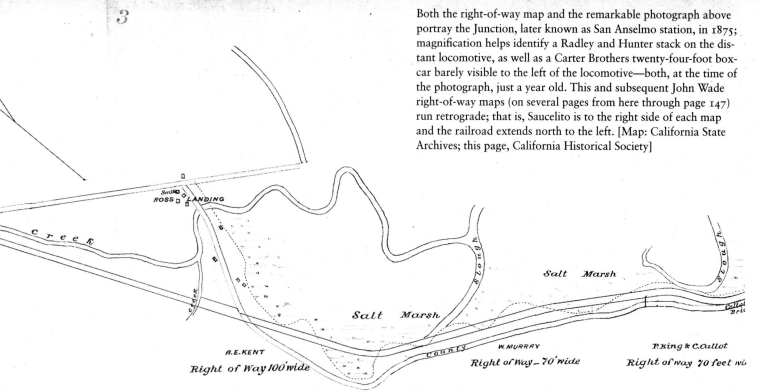

Twenty years separate the 1889 view of San Anselmo station (above) from the 1912-era view (opposite, below). Between times, the station anchored the northernmost end of the North Pacific Coast's high-density commuter corridor. Ferry-bound commute trains, seen below, behind the Mason 0-4-4 *San Rafael*, and picnic trains (opposite, above) terminated their normal routes in Fairfax, just north of San Anselmo. Beyond Fairfax, the steep climb over White's Hill acted as a barrier to the spread of Marin County demographics and as a thinning-out point for North Pacific Coast traffic. [This page, top, Marin County Free Library, Anne Kent California Room; middle, Robert Moulton collection; bottom, California Historical Society; opposite, top, Donald Duke collection; bottom, Society of California Pioneers]

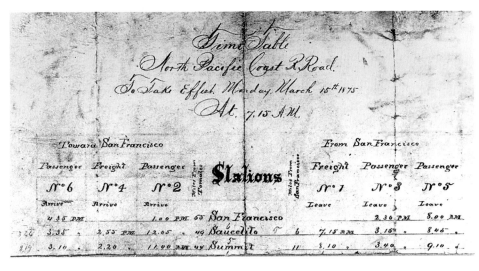

Time Table
North Pacific Coast R Road.
To Take Effect, Monday, March 15th 1875
At 7.15 A.M.

Toward San Francisco				Stations		From San Francisco		
Passenger	Freight	Passenger	Miles From Tomales		Miles From San Francisco	Freight	Passenger	Passenger
N° 6	N° 4	N° 2				N° 1	N° 3	N° 5
Arrive	Arrive	Arrive				Leave	Leave	Leave
4.55 P.M.		1.00 P.M.	55	San Francisco			2.30 P.M.	8.00 A.M.
3.35	2.55 P.M.	12.05	49	Saucelito	6	7.15 A.M.	3.15	8.45
3.10	2.20	11.40 A.M.	44	Summit	11	8.10	3.40	9.10

1872 engineering studies on White's Hill (middle) located a 400-foot tunnel near the bottom of the grade and a 1,650-foot tunnel near the top. In between, six large trestles were required to carry the line through the serpentine landscape, illustrated in the 1889 photograph to the right. At bottom, the 1875 Wade map of White's Hill is oriented toward Saucelito on the right. [Above, Marin County Free Library, Anne Kent California Room; below, Northwestern Pacific Railroad Historical Society]

Trestle N. P. C. R. R.

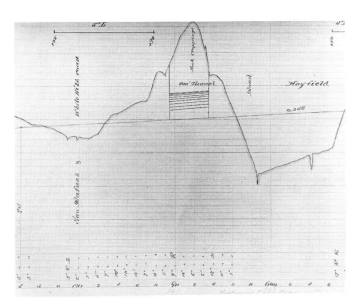

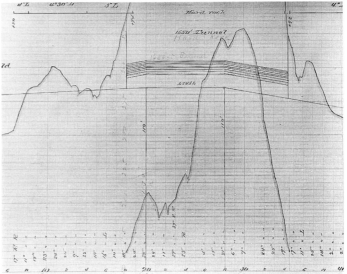

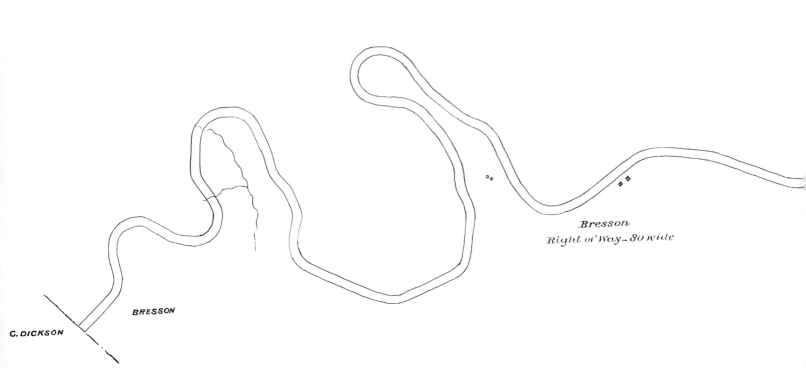

C. DICKSON

BRESSON

Bresson
Right of Way—80 wide

Doubleheading appeared to be the rule on the southern ascent of White's Hill, witnessed by this remarkable action view (above) photographed from a moving train in 1902 by A. Sheldon Pennoyer. On the point, number 8, *Bully Boy*, leads number 3, *Tomales*, both 1870s machines. Equally remarkable is an 1889 view of a long singleheaded passenger train doing battle with the same grades and curves, reproduced on the overleaf. [Left, Robert Moulton collection; overleaf, Marin County Free Library, Anne Kent California Room]

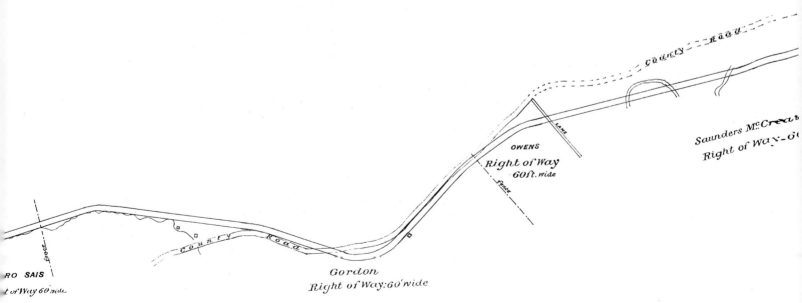

The North Pacific Coast San Geronimo depot portrayed in the late 1880s; by 2001, the San Geronimo depot, still looking much as it does in these photographs, is the last surviving example of a first-generation North Pacific Coast station. [Joseph Trinidad Silva, photographer, research by Frank Sternad, Sonoma County Historical Society]

The Gremke painting titled "Camp Teller" has been previously published as a Santa Cruz County view, as in *South Pacific Coast* (MacGregor, Howell North Books, 1968). Views ca. 1885 from the camera of Frank Rodolf, however (shown above and below), give evidence that the location was San Geronimo tank, on the North Pacific Coast. The 1875 Wade map of the right-of-way through San Geronimo Creek (today's Paper Mill Creek), at the bottom of the page, is oriented toward Saucelito on the right. [Above left, Oakland Museum; others, this page, Bancroft Library]

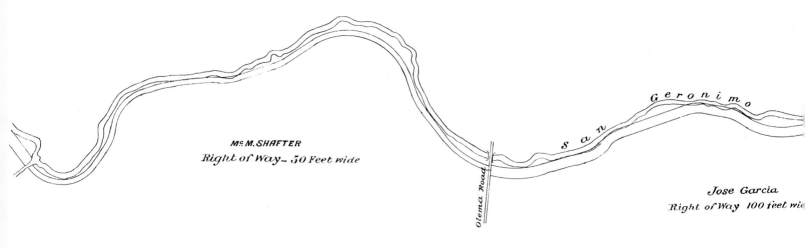

Mrs. M. SHAFTER
Right of Way — 50 Feet wide

Olema Road

San Geronimo

Jose Garcia
Right of Way 100 feet wide

The title of the Gremke painting on the opposite page may be a misattribution of "Camp Taylor," the resort and picnic grounds that developed around the original S. P. Taylor paper mill (above), today the site of Samuel P. Taylor State Park. [Bancroft Library]

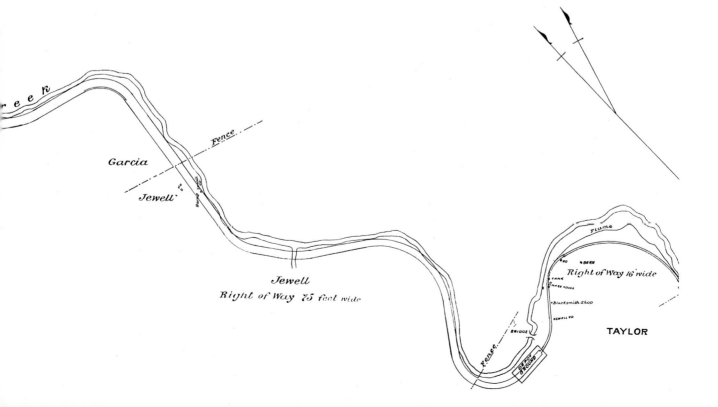

When the North Pacific Coast reached the area known today as Point Reyes Station, the nearest town was Olema; the rail head, first called Olema Station, developed as a stage connection to the older hamlet. The 1875 Wade right-of-way map (below) shows the Olema Station grounds (on the opposite page), and is oriented to Saucelito on the right. [Above, Robert Moulton collection; below, Marin County Free Library, Anne Kent California Room]

Line bet. Ross & Miller's Land.

Fence

ROSS
Right of Way 75'wide

A Y

TIDE FLAT

MURPHY'S P

The water tank at Point Reyes Station became a backdrop for numerous portraits taken by narrow gauge travelers; circumstantial evidence suggests this style of tank was one of the products Carter Brothers offered in their portfolio of services as general railroad contractors, a design that was reproduced on the South Pacific Coast and Nevada County Narrow Gauge lines as well as the North Pacific Coast. [Above, DeGolyer Library, Southern Methodist University; below left, Dewey Livingston Collection; below right, Ted Wurm collection]

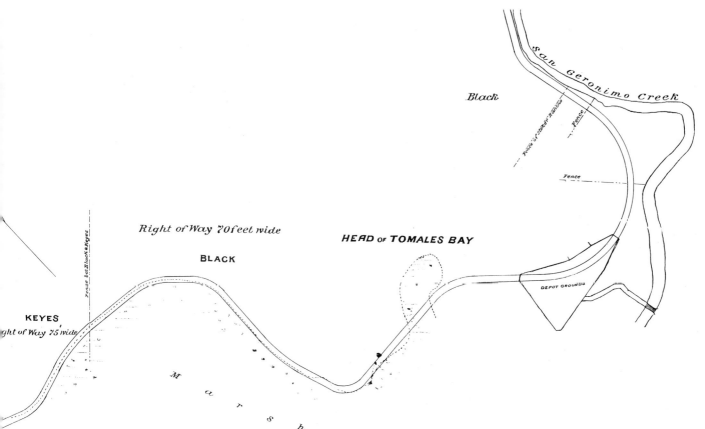

TOMALES

W. DUTTON
Right of way 60 wide

fence

Keyes

Buchanan

KEYES
Right of Way: 75 wide

Road from Tomales

BUCHANAN
Right of Way: 60 wide

Graveyard

Magnetic

fence

W. DUTTON
RIGHT OF WAY 60 WIDE

GRAHAM
RIGHT OF WAY
75 wide

Jos. Jacinthe
Right of Way 75 wide

Keyes Creek

ROWLAND
RIGHT OF WAY 75 WIDE

Franzen
Right of way 60 wide

Green gulch

or

Denman & Hill
Right of Way: 60 feet wid

Tomales, reached by North Pacific Coast passenger trains in January 1875, became the line's temporary northern terminal for nearly two years as the narrow gauge struggled to extend its track into the Russian River Basin. At the northern end of Tomales Bay (shown below in 1904), the railroad yards of Tomales were photographed from the roof of a giant produce warehouse (on the opposite page), built to cache the region's bumper crops of "Bodega spuds." At the bottom of the page, the 1875 Wade right-of-way map is oriented to Saucelito on the right and concludes with the Tomales Station grounds on the left. [Above, Arnold Menke collection; opposite, left, Charlie Siebenthal collection; opposite, right, Robert Moulton collection]

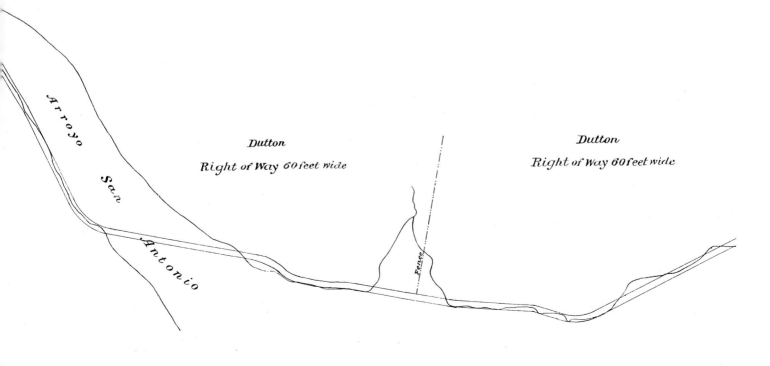

Arroyo San Antonio

Dutton

Right of Way 60 feet wide

Dutton

Right of Way 60 feet wide

Fence

C.W.J. Johnson's view of Monterey from the Presidio, showing the Monterey & Salinas Valley's second roundhouse (above the cannon barrel), depot, and remains of the original pier. The landscape dates from about 1885, after the Southern Pacific had standard-gauged the M&SV. The old cannon, long a landmark at the Presidio, was pressed into service to celebrate the opening of the narrow gauge in 1874. A broken drill bit, embedded in the touch hole, prevented the cannon from being fired. [Pat Hathaway photo collection, Monterey]

Monterey: The Field Factory

John Flint Kidder began work on the Monterey & Salinas Valley Railroad with a certain vengeance.

In 1868, he had worked *for* Stanford's organization, surveying its main-line across the California border and into Nevada territory. In 1874, he was working *against* it, caught up in a rising grassroots revolt against the growing Central Pacific monopoly.

Kidder's anger was, perhaps, personal. In 1873, he had been hired as chief engineer on what would likely have become the state's first narrow gauge common carrier. The California Central Narrow Gauge Railroad began construction on the Sacramento River at Benicia, grading its line east up the river toward Vacaville, Woodland, Marysville, and Red Bluff, charting a course through the heart of California's wheat belt.

The CCNG blossomed during the early phases of the Grange movement, when the first organized agrarian interest groups in the state began to form small, regional fraternities called farmer's clubs.[1] The values espoused by the clubs, including condemnation of wheat cartels and those who profited from price fixing, galvanized support for the proposed narrow gauge feeder.

Backed by Cornelius Cole (a Republican who had been a U.S. senator), the California Central Narrow Gauge planned to crisscross the valley with numerous branch lines, draining wheat traffic from the northern half of the state and funneling it to shipping on San Francisco Bay. There the wheat would be loaded aboard oceangoing ships for export to Liverpool, a remarkable circuit of fourteen thousand miles and five months made profitable by the high commercial quality of California's wheat and by the cartel's tight control over the cost of its shipping.

Cole played convincingly to the sympathies of the farmer's club movement by confronting the largest cartel on its home turf. The brokerage house of Isaac Friedlander, who was popularly known as the "Grain King," routinely chartered enough oceangoing vessels to reduce the total price of delivered wheat to a par with other wheat-growing regions of the world, notably Russia. But in the process, Friedlander also influenced the price farmers were paid for their wheat on the California market, raising accusations of price control and monopolistic profit. The claims were justified. Friedlander entered into cartel-like agreements over shipping rates with the Central Pacific, and he was frequently seen in the company of the railroad's management, scouting

Until Collis Huntington's death in 1900, political cartoons often portrayed him and the railroad monopoly he represented as the nemesis of California agriculture.

"WHAT WILL THE HARVEST BE?"

California wheat depots for intelligence on the size of each coming harvest.[2] With this information, Friedlander bought up as much as three-quarters of California's annual exported wheat tonnage during the early 1870s and cornered the shipping required to transport it.[3]

Thirty years later, Frank Norris's novel *The Octopus* was written as a fictional exposé of the California wheat cartels of the 1870s. Because of the novel's popularity, Norris became known as a "muckraker," and his book helped awaken the public to the need for governmental regulation of large corporations. But Norris also used the novel to project a personal view of the forces behind social change. Inherent in economic or social systems, Norris argued, were vagaries in human nature that, like the weather, could cloud the simplest of moral intentions. Good guy and bad guy, Norris argued, often colluded to trade hats.

The real Grange movement offered substantial proof of Norris's thesis. By using the CCNG as a funnel, Cole planned to leverage enough of the state's crop to a competing brokerage house to wage economic war against the notorious Grain King. Numerous brokers, among them Falkner and Bell or E. E. Morgan and Sons, were eager to play the role Cole described, which entailed chartering an independent wheat fleet. Showing solidarity, the farmer's clubs donated depot and warehouse lands to the CCNG in Benicia; they were determined to level the playing field against Isaac Friedlander.

Taking advantage of public sympathy for the embattled agrarian movement, Cole ceremonially broke ground in Benicia on May 1, 1873. He made speeches while his superintendent of construction, John Flint Kidder, got his hands dirty. Kidder was forty-three years old when he began work on the CCNG, and something of a legend among western civil engineers. He had surveyed the first (unbuilt) Virginia & Truckee Railroad in 1861, confirmed the disputed eastern boundary of California in 1863, assisted in the survey of the Sacramento & Placerville in 1864 (where he had probably met Tom Carter for the first time), located the Central Pacific from the Sierra summit to Reno in 1867, completed a location for the northern part of the Virginia & Truckee in 1868, superintended construction of the first ten miles of the Oregon Central and the first division of the Northern Pacific Railroad between 1870 and 1872, and—before he returned to California—led the demolition project to blow up sunken rocks at John Day Rapids on the Columbia River.[4] The dynamiting acted out Kidder's enormous force of character on the landscapes he challenged. He appeared in a portrait of the 1870s wearing a holstered revolver on his right side and a sheathed hunting knife on his left, perhaps trademarks he carried on the job. Balding, bearded, with riveting eyes, Kidder was a distillate of plain talk and enormous stamina who could drive men and capital in the same direction.

But in August 1873, under Kidder's watch, the CCNG's construction camp was ransacked by a gang of "roughs, hoodlums and shoulder-hitters."[5] Blood was spilled. Terrified, the Chinese graders scattered to the winds. The press showed little hesitation in attaching blame for the violence to "the lower purlieus of the Central Pacific," although no legal recourse was taken.[6] No doubt Kidder construed the bloodshed to be a personal attack on him, and soon was in an even bigger rage against Cole, who chose to halt construction in the face of so formidable an enemy.

But the enemy, it became clear, lay within. Hamstrung by lack of funds, Kidder had probably graded fewer than ten miles of line at the time of the attack. No rail was laid, and there were no newspaper accounts of rolling stock deliveries.[7] For the previous six months, Cole had begged money from investors anxious about the shortcomings of the farmer's clubs. In April 1873, for example, the clubs met and voted to boycott the sack cartels, attempting to force a lower price on quantities of burlap. The meetings were conducted in public and the scheme quickly leaked to the cartels, triggering higher burlap prices in retaliation. At the time, there were fewer than twenty clubs operating in the state, with a combined membership of less than eight hundred.[8] Hurt by the fiasco, the clubs learned the lesson of secrecy and began to reorganize.

Out of work by the fall of 1873, Kidder learned the critical importance of horizontal business integration. He always considered himself to be just a railroad engineer, but throughout the summer of 1873 he watched the Central Pacific construct the largest wheat port in the world at Vallejo, just three miles downriver from the CCNG's embattled camp. There, Stanford covered acres with grain warehouses. Friedlander co-located the state's first grain elevators. Looking like a small city, nearly a mile of continuous wheat storage fronted the river. That same summer, Stanford's heavy investment in the California Pacific would finally connect the Vallejo port to more than a thousand miles of Central Pacific and Southern Pacific track, consolidating the cartel's grip on the state's wheat trade.[9]

Kidder got the picture. Railroad, warehousing, and wharves formed three critical components of a delivery system essential to the cartel's operation. In economic terms, the wheat trade favored standardization, integration, and economies of scale, all attributes of a system designed to reduce the cost of bringing a commodity like wheat to market.

After the CCNG debacle, Kidder understood that he no longer could think of himself as just a railroad engineer. To fight the cartels for the wheat trade, he would have to engineer and build all three parts of the system.

He would soon rejoin the battle against the cartels by building exactly such a system, but on a Lilliputian scale. The Monterey & Salinas Valley Railroad would consist of a 1,208-foot wharf, two warehouses, and an 18.5-mile narrow gauge short line. Kidder would build all three.

The farmer's clubs quickly regrouped.

By April 1873, most of its members had been persuaded to join the national Patrons of Husbandry, also known as the Grange. The movement had won victories from cartels in the Midwest, and its membership was growing. They based their success on secret meetings and pooling resources with independent wheat brokers. By October 1873, there were 231 California Grange chapters, primarily in the northern half of the state, with a membership of more than thirteen thousand.[10]

The surge in membership attracted the services of an independent wheat broker. In July 1873, the new State Grange organization engaged E. E. Morgan and Sons to collectivize and market their wheat to Liverpool buyers, charter ships, and directly compete against the Friedlander cartel. Certain safety devices were installed in the business relationship, one being placement of a Grange accountant in Morgan's office, who was instructed to audit transactions and monitor "reduced brokerage fees."[11]

In turn, the presence of Morgan and Sons attracted badly needed financial backing to the struggling Grange. Milton Latham's London and San Francisco Bank began extending Morgan large loans in the closing months of 1873, reaching and exceeding $400,000 in credit by February 1874. These loans began just prior to Latham's heavy investments in the North Pacific Coast, and the large amounts involved gave some indication of the strategy, and risk, involved in what was becoming known popularly as the Grange movement. Finally in control of both the financing and the organizational savvy they lacked as farmer's clubs, the Grange movement unilaterally asked its members to use Morgan and Sons to sell the wheat crop of 1874. It was to be the year of the climactic battle with Isaac Friedlander.

———————————————————————————

Somewhere along the coast, Kidder could make the strategy work: put a significant quantity of wheat onto oceangoing ships *without* the influence of Friedlander or the Central Pacific. But where? Coastal ships, thousand-ton steamships such as the *Santa Cruz*, the *Golden Gate*, and the *Kosta Sacramento*, had little trouble putting into the Monterey Bay piers at Capitola, or Moss Landing, or the old Spanish presidio of Monterey itself. But the wheat carriers, oceangoing sailing vessels classed at sixteen hundred tons, two thousand tons, twenty-two hundred tons, and up, drew too much water to dock at the old facilities. In 1874, the architects of the Grange movement had to face, and solve, the problem of not only moving a huge volume of wheat to the coast but creating adequate port facilities to transship the wheat to an international market. That problem included covered storage, a critical insurance policy for preserving the value of the delivered crop.

John Kidder took responsibility for such a system when he became chief engineer of the Monterey & Salinas Valley Railroad in March 1874. Instead of engineering just a railroad, he designed and proceeded to build a seamless delivery network that would leave no gap wide enough for a cartel to crawl through. His passion for all phases of the project soon captivated the Monterey press:

> Mr. Kidder, the Superintendent, Constructionist, engineer and overseer of the Monterey & Salinas Valley Railroad, is one of the most energetic, live and enterprising men for which this age is remarkable. Although he has to oversee the whole work now in progress, from the building of the wharf, keeping time, laying out the road, and attending to every minute detail he has proved himself equal to the emergency. Under his skillful management the road is progressing systematically and rapidly, and as he says, he will give us a ride over the road at a speed of 40 mph within 4 months or less from this date, and we are convinced that he will do so. He is a man who always accomplishes every undertaking.[12]

John Kidder was very nearly a one-man solution to the Grangers' problems. The railroad he proposed to build had just two direct contractors: Thomas Carter, who would build the rolling stock; and R. C. Wrones, proprietor of Charley's Restaurant in Salinas, who held the contract to feed the construction workers. Kidder did the rest. He hired graders and track layers and directly oversaw their work. He (not Carter) designed the line's bridges—the biggest one, the straining beam over the Salinas River, spanned three hundred feet of channel—and oversaw their construction. He designed and built the 1,208-foot pile wharf at Monterey, a wharf that would give oceangoing ships the moorage they needed to dock and load safely.

In addition, he would build two huge grain warehouses to cache the harvests, and he would build depots and shops. Only in the specialized venue of rolling stock did Kidder let a contractor take up a major piece of the project, and then only a contractor he had worked with before and learned to trust. For the rest, John Flint Kidder managed the overlapping demands of railroad design and construction himself, saving the company time and money, two resources it had little of.

Nearby, the narrow gauge Santa Cruz Rail Road had eighteen contractors working on its grade, some on sections as short as a single cut.[13] Three additional contractors were involved in Santa Cruz Rail Road freight and passenger car manufacture, and two more contractors were retained for bridge work, one to do the engineering and one to build the bridges. Management of such a troupe proved troublesome. Kidder, by contrast, had to manage only himself, Tom Carter, and the caterer from Charley's Restaurant.

Kidder personally guaranteed the close control of money and schedule. The M&SV's backers pooled $260,000 to build the entire railroad, about $14,000 per mile.[14] Kidder could not do what the North Pacific Coast attempted to do with its shadowy financing, about which he must have heard horror stories from Carter. Instead, capital was raised up front. Seventy-three stockholders pledged and paid $241,000, and an additional $16,000 in floating debt came from smaller lenders, such as the Salinas City Bank. There were no bonds, and no sinking funds. "We consider," noted the 1876 M&SV financial statement to the State Board of Commissioners of Transportation, "everything invested in the road sunk."[15] The unfortunate language would come back to haunt the little carrier. But in the beginning, bills were paid on demand.

In the meantime, Kidder would manage the construction schedule to the same tight tolerance with which he managed the money. The valley's barley crop would begin to mature in early June, the wheat just two weeks after that. If he proposed to transport this year's crop before the first rains, fulfilling the Grange promise to Morgan and Sons, he would have to lay 18.5 miles of track in the twenty-four weeks he had construction forces on the ground.

On March 10, Kidder and a party of four civil engineers disembarked from the steamer *Santa Cruz* at the old Monterey wharf. By March 15, Kidder had a team of engineers in the field. Just two weeks later, on April 1, he hosted David Jacks, Carlisle Abbott, and Robert Gonzales aboard a spring wagon, driving north through sand dunes "to see the line of survey of said road."[16] The results of the reconnaissance confirmed Kidder's belief that the work would present few serious obstacles. Kidder infected the railroad's backers with his optimism.

Kidder brought his wife, Sarah, to Monterey in late April 1874, to take up residence until the project was completed.[17]

He held an ace in the hole. Six years earlier, in 1868, Kidder had done railroad location work on the Monterey Peninsula. By his own account, the early work was undertaken for Holliday and Brenham,[18] the shipping and staging company whose principal, Ben Holliday, would hire him for the Oregon Central work in 1870. Other accounts suggest the survey was done for one of two precursor railroad schemes, the Monterey & Salinas Railroad or the

Monterey & Natividad Railroad, both intent on laying track from the heartland of the Salinas Valley to a port on the Salinas River.

All of these schemes predated the California Grange movement and suggested that politically and demographically Kidder picked a county that was considerably ahead of its time in organizing resistance to the wheat cartels. The Minute Book of the Monterey & Salinas Railroad survives and reports its board of directors ordered the hiring of a surveyor on May 17, 1868.[19] It could easily have been John Kidder; the name is not explicitly mentioned. Any or all of the interested parties—the Monterey & Salinas, Monterey & Natividad, and Holliday and Brenham—might, sometime in 1869 or 1870, have been acting in concert to put railroad track into the well-worn ruts of the county's wagon roads.

The commerce they pursued, coastal wheat traffic, was well established long before Stanford and the cartels entered the county from the north. Stanford didn't make his appearance in the Salinas Valley until December 1871, basing a railhead in the town of Salinas City and demanding $5.50 a ton to transport wheat to the San Francisco Bay Area.[20]

Ironically, in 1873, nearly two years after the Southern Pacific opened up its rail link, a majority of Salinas Valley wheat was still transported out of the county not by rail but by coastal shipping, hauled in lumbering wagons down the same roads to Moss Landing that Kidder had assessed as a railroad route in 1868.[21]

The reason, clearly, was sticker shock. When it came on the scene, the Southern Pacific set prices that were perceived as a barrier to most of the valley's growers. A bumper crop of fifty thousand tons was in the offing for the 1874 season, a crop so large that existing Salinas Valley warehousing, located at Natividad, Pajaro, Castroville, Gonzales, Chular, Salinas City, Monterey, and Moss Landing, could hold only half its estimated tonnage. Fast, covered shipment was critical to keeping the value of the wheat high on the Liverpool market. In secret Grange hall meetings across the county, the bumper crop became an economic battering ram to use against Friedlander and Stanford. With high prices and an abundant crop, couldn't the valley's Grange members decide as a whole who would get to transport the wheat, and at what price?

The subscription book of the Monterey & Salinas Railroad suggests that a strong home-rule initiative had started in the valley long before Stanford's arrival. Between 1868 and 1871, the Minute Book of the Monterey & Salinas recorded more than three thousand subscriptions from growers all over Monterey County, most contributing just a few dollars.[22] In a county of just nine thousand people, this was evidence of widespread endorsement of local control of the wheat route down the Salinas River to Monterey Bay.

Two names stood out as major contributors in the subscription book: landowners David Jacks and Carlisle Abbott. On one hand, Jacks owned one hundred thousand acres of Monterey farmland; he was the largest landowner in the county, and probably the most hated, having acquired much of his holdings by foreclosing on local ranchers' mortgages. After Jacks lost an attempted court eviction against squatters on his Chular Ranch property in 1872, he received an anonymous letter that he kept, perhaps sentimentally, as an example of public regard:

Now . . . if you don't make good that amount of damage to each and every one of those settlers which you sued, as well as a reasonable amount for compensation to each of those settlers—if you don't do this inside of ten days you son of a bitch—we shall suspend your animation between daylight and hell.

By Order of the Executive
Committee of the Squatters
League of Monterey County[23]

Carlisle Abbott owned a modest sixteen thousand acres of wheat land, ran a hotel in Salinas named the Abbott House, and was popular enough to be elected to the state legislature in 1876. Jacks, by contrast, was disliked enough for him to admit the fear of arson to his far-flung properties.

Still, Abbott and Jacks appeared to have acted in concert on the Monterey & Salinas Railroad project, and they were its largest individual contributors. On November 19, 1870, Abbott signed the minute book for a subscription of $1,864.61; on November 20, 1871, Jacks signed for $1,594.35. The last entry in the book is by Abbott again, for an additional $1,787.72.[24]

Three years later, on February 26, 1874, Jacks and Abbott were clearly in control of a secret meeting that convened in the Salinas Grange Hall. The landowners in the room wrote new incorporation papers for the Monterey & Salinas *Valley* Railroad, taking pains to distinguish its name from the predecessor company. Many of those present had signed the subscription books for the Monterey & Salinas Railroad. Perhaps the change in name and organization mimed the reorganization of the farmer's clubs and allowed for new stakeholders and new methods. But the goals and leadership of the new project remained much the same: Abbott became president, Jacks treasurer. Of the $300,000 in capital stock issued at the February 26 meeting, $25,000 was subscribed and collected that day.[25] The Articles of Incorporation projected the railroad's length at twenty-five miles, a route designed to serve Castroville at an intermediate point between the terminals named in the company's title.

The bumper harvest would begin in June. With Abbott and Jacks driving the project forward, and both having enormous grain crops of their own to harvest and transport, smaller farmers were willing to hold off committing to Central Pacific transportation until Jacks and Abbott made their move. Move they did: Kidder was hired at the February incorporation meeting. On March 15, less than three weeks later, Kidder led a survey team into the field.

Just three weeks after that, on April 7, Kidder reported on final location of the line's first 12.5 miles, from Monterey to the Salinas River.[26] And just eleven days after that, on April 18, a hundred Chinese laborers arrived on the steamer *Pacific*, hired through the contract labor cooperatives of the San Francisco Chinese Six Companies.[27] Kidder met them at the wharf, organized them into rank-and-file formation, and (perhaps displaying revolver and knife) personally marched the procession toward the construction camp at the Salt Lagoon, three miles north of Monterey.

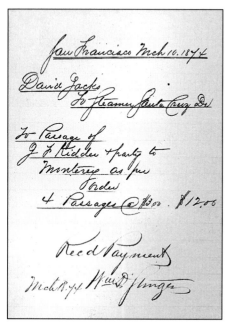

David Jacks's receipt for steamer tickets, covering passage for John Kidder and his surveying crew, March 1874. [Huntington Library, David Jacks collection]

The ledgers and cash books of David Jacks survive, covering the period of the Monterey & Salinas Valley's construction. Perhaps more than any other contemporary document, the cash books give an idea of Jacks's day-by-day involvement in the novel enterprise. The cash books give the impression that Jacks considered the M&SV not only as a grassroots initiative whose goal was reform of the cartel's rates and practices but also as a means of enhancing the value of his own businesses and properties in Monterey County.

Many of Jacks's entries were strategic to the railroad's legal incorporation, funding, or procurement. For example:

– On March 30, 1874, Jacks queried attorneys Williams & Thornton for legal advise about subscription and incorporation papers for the railroad. Fee: $10.10.[28]
– On March 30, Jacks wired an English agent about the price of rail. Wire fee: $20.00.[29]
– On February 23, 1875, Jacks traveled to San Francisco to secure a $65,000 loan from Henry Cowell for repairs to the Salinas River bridge, washed out the previous month. Fare for travel: $17.25.[30]

Many items suggest an interleaving of Jacks's personal businesses with the railroad he held office in. For example:

– On October 10, Jacks sold the M&SV 121 cords of oak wood "from near small lagoon"; and would continue to sell the railroad cord wood from his numerous properties. Price: $151.00.
– On November 16, 1875, Jacks paid to R. C. Wrones, food concessionaire for the M&SV construction crews, $100 for fuel wood and (in addition) for "oysters and ice cream furnished to David Jacks in 1874–1875."[31]

And some of the entries suggest the mind of Bartleby the Scrivener, hard at work:

– Entry in Jacks's hand, undated, 1874: "Paid Kidder's order favor of T. McNiel for 3 ¼ days, $5.68, deduct board $2.75. Deduct use of blanket, 25 cents."[32]

This was the time of the doldrums in the finances of the North Pacific Coast, a time—as far as we know—in which Carter's activity in Saucelito entered deep hibernation. Rumors of Milton Latham's takeover would not be on the horizon until June, and in the meantime Carter was actively looking for work.

In March, he picked up a bridge design project for the Santa Cruz Rail Road, which was just beginning construction between Watsonville and Santa Cruz. In April 1874, Carter was noted in the Santa Cruz press as both "the Architect of the Road" and its "Master Mechanic," exaggerated references to a contractual agreement to design four large Howe truss spans the railroad would need to cross the San Lorenzo and Soquel rivers and the Valencia and Aptos creeks.[33] He gambled that the bridge contract would lead to rolling stock work, but in fact the scope of the project, as of April 11, 1874, was confined to designing bridges alone. Carter set up an engineering field office in downtown Santa Cruz, and from late March until at least late April he kept a draftsman busy turning out the elevations of large Howe truss spans.

The timing of this work played a critical role in Carter's Monterey involvement. Santa Cruz County, in 1874, was an isolated but remarkably prolific manufacturing center (a topic to be explored in Chapter Six). The lumber industry was its obvious mainstay, boasting twenty-two saw mills, four shingle mills, several millwright shops, and retail and wholesale lumber outlets. But by 1874 a powder plant, a fuse factory, five lime works, a sugar beet mill, three flouring mills, eight tanneries, a glue factory, and a soap factory—not to mention the Philadelphia Brewery—also thrived on the cheap source of raw materials and power. Critical support businesses, including two foundries and at least two machine shops, kept the larger industries running.[34] After San Francisco, Santa Clara, and Sacramento counties, Santa Cruz County ranked a surprisingly precocious fourth in industrial capitalization among California's counties.[35]

In plain view of Carter's temporary office was a nearly complete set of industrial resources for building railroads. In March, for example, the Santa Cruz Rail Road was moving earth in a small fleet of locally built dump cars, so constructed that at very slight expense they can be changed to four wheel platform cars to be used for carrying lumber, gravel, stone, etc.[36] These products were objects of considerable local pride. The cars were made of castings poured at W. H. Martin's New Foundry and lumber cut, milled, and assembled at the Allen and Rennie planing mill.[37] At least four such cars were in service when Carter was in town, and more were under construction. Allen and Rennie had found a source of fir up the San Lorenzo River, "a very strong, elastic and hard wood, useful for car building and all kinds of mill and agricultural machinery and implements." With fir for structural members and a seemingly inexhaustible supply of local redwood for siding and roofing, a number of Santa Cruz planing mills began to enter the car-building trade, making it difficult for Carter to bid successfully on car work that Santa Cruz businesses thought of as their own.

Santa Cruz foundries were hardly operating on the scale of the Golden State or Union Iron Works of San Francisco, but they would soon be turning out technically demanding railroad castings, including chilled car wheels and axle boxes—and turning them out in quantity. Pattern making was done within the foundries, and in the case of Martin's New Foundry it was free to the customer if bundled with the purchase of castings.

The availability of local supplies of lumber and iron castings had an immediate impact on the economics of Carter's bridge projects. Like the North Pacific Coast Strawberry Point Bridge, Carter's designs were let out for bid, and by early May 1874 the Pacific Bridge Co. was under contract to do the work on the San Lorenzo River truss. By July, Pacific Bridge was advertising for local lumber men to supply ninety thousand board feet of material required to construct the enormous structure.[38] Observing the provisioning, Carter began to develop a strategy for supporting a car construction business in the Monterey Bay area. Ironically, he would first apply the strategy in Monterey, not in Santa Cruz.

Chapter Six ("Santa Cruz Supply Chain") focuses on the two narrow gauge lines that the well-equipped Santa Cruz industrial setting eventually created. But from Tom Carter's perspective, in the spring of 1874 the concentration of Santa Cruz foundries, planing mills, and smith shops, and the skilled labor that supported them, became the key ingredient in the contract work starting thirty miles south in the very nonindustrial setting of Monterey, which ranked near the bottom (at thirty-fourth place) in the industrial capitalization of California's counties.[39]

The Monterey work was probably planned in March 1874, when there was still no car work on the horizon in Saucelito. The M&SV contract required that fifty pieces of rolling stock be delivered in barely three and a half months. To fill the order quickly, the Monterey factory was conceived as a stand-alone facility. Not until June would Carter see the opportunity to leverage designs, pattern work, and procurement between Monterey and Saucelito. Carter may have been a little stymied by the demands of creating a production facility in an isolated and industrially undeveloped corner of the state. It was an expensive, logistically demanding strategy. New tooling would have to be rented or purchased. A car shop would have to be built and additional fabrication space located in downtown Monterey. Carter faced an acute shortage of labor. As far as we know, only one local craftsman found employment on the car contract, a Monterey tinsmith named W. W. James. Carpenters and painters would all have to be brought in from the outside, and boarded. Carter did not use John Carroll or brother Martin as foreman—a role they would play in Saucelito later that summer— which forced him to look further afield for leadership.[40]

The cost of the Monterey work, in terms of plant and labor, was probably the highest Carter ever incurred. Far from having an existing base of supply, instead importing many of the resources he needed, the facility that resulted might be called a "field factory." It was designed to operate as a complete but temporary production facility, set up to do all the steps of car construction and then—three and a half months later—be dismantled. Thus the neigh-

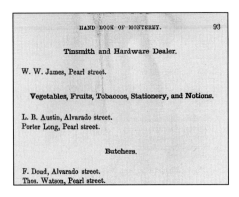

HAND BOOK OF MONTEREY.   93

Tinsmith and Hardware Dealer.

W. W. James, Pearl street.

Vegetables, Fruits, Tobaccos, Stationery, and Notions.

L. B. Austin, Alvarado street.
Porter Long, Pearl street.

Butchers.

F. Doud, Alvarado street.
Thos. Watson, Pearl street.

With the exception of a local tinsmith, most of the skilled craftsmen Thomas Carter required to construct rolling stock in Monterey had to come from nearby Santa Cruz. [Top, *Santa Cruz Sentinel*, July 4, 1874; bottom, Monterey City Library]

boring Santa Cruz County resources were critical to establishing a supply chain to support the work, and to keeping the supply chain as short as possible.

Consequently, Santa Cruz suppliers show up early in the project. By May 16, Tom Amner's foundry was shipping iron castings to the Monterey & Salinas Valley, presumably to Tom Carter. On July 4, Carter appealed directly to Santa Cruz for skilled labor by running an ad in the classified section of the *Santa Cruz Sentinel*, asking for twenty-five carpenters "to work on car building at Monterey." The Santa Cruz industrial base would thus provide the majority of his shop force. These resources became even more critical by June, when it was clear that Carter would have to start a much larger project at Saucelito and support the two projects in the same time period. At Saucelito, however, he would have the railroad's shop building and tooling to count on, plus supplies of raw materials the railroad had already procured. Tapping the nearby Southern Pacific San Francisco car shop for labor, Carter had a ready-made temp pool to staff the North Pacific Coast job.

Even so, Carter seemed to be pulling the Monterey factory out of thin air.

Apparently Kidder was able to take advantage of his 1868 survey work. The *Monterey Democrat* reported that Kidder's civil engineers

will get through quickly, doubtless, for the reason that the pegs formerly planted by Kidder are not likely to have been disturbed. The point at which to cross the river, that as we understand, was selected by Kidder, is just below what is known as the Estrada Crossing. The approaches to it from the Monterey side require little cutting; just there the [ocean] tide and [river] current meet, causing still water and so reducing danger to the bridge. Besides, being at the foot of the valley, abreast of Castroville, in the course of the road thence to Salinas City all the agricultural lands of the valley will have use of it.[41]

The newspaper's conjecture of a "sweet spot" where tide and river current canceled each other's effects, minimizing the strain on the bridge, was far-fetched. The winters had been mild since the first Kidder survey, and the Salinas River had behaved itself, but those were conditions that would change.

Kidder first located the 12.5 miles of line from Monterey to the river, leaving his options open for the remaining route to Salinas.[42] The location of the river crossing required balancing several engineering factors, only one of which included the reach of the tide. The topology surrounding the bridge also played a role. Along Kidder's route, the river meandered next to the western edge of the inland valley, bedded in the rich farmland of David Jacks's El Tucho Ranch. But the river's western bank rose abruptly up a steep scarp, delineating a coastal upland that separated the valley from Monterey Bay. To surmount the upland, a gain in elevation of some one hundred feet, Kidder had to create the most gradual inclined plane he could. By choosing a low spot in the scarp near the Estrada Crossing, at Cooper's Mill, he managed to keep the grade to just seventy-nine feet to the mile, persisting for twenty-nine hundred feet between the summit at Bardin's Ranch and the river crossing itself. Minimizing the grade, not the river, may have been the key factor in choosing the location of the bridge.

The company budgeted just $12,000 for the bridge and concentrated the money in five sixty-foot straining beam segments crossing the main channel. In reality, the riverbed was not three hundred but fifteen hundred feet wide at that location, most of it a sandy bottom dotted with young cottonwoods that had grown since the last high water. The cottonwoods should have been a clue; they marked active underground channels, flowing unseen below beds of quicksand. A series of relatively mild winters had left their growth undisturbed. To reach the main channel, Kidder's location crossed the long, sandy bottom with twelve hundred feet of light, inexpensive trestle work before reaching the main channel, and the sections of straining beam.

The first 12.5 miles of line contained virtually all the curvature and gradients on the entire Monterey & Salinas Valley Railroad. Both were minimal, compared for example to the North Pacific Coast. The M&SV could boast of a 1.5 percent maximum grade, and curves of 579-foot minimum radius. East of the bridge, the line descended to the level of the Salinas Valley itself. One gentle, right-hand curve at the Cooper Road, a half mile east of the bridge, brought the line into a six-mile tangent that led directly to Salinas. From Salinas City to the projected pier at Monterey, the entire route was just 18.5 miles long. With 12.5 miles of detailed location finished by the first of April, Kidder ordered materials and prepared to begin work.

On Monday, April 20, ground was broken for the project in the sand dunes three miles north of Monterey. A parade of buggies left Monterey about ten in the morning to see Carlisle Abbott turn the first spade of earth. Speeches were expected; the press had been alerted. That night, the celebration would expand to include a barbecue and a ballroom dance at the Washington Hotel. Living with the wheat cartels and their new, home-grown challenger, Monterey had bottled up a strange combination of frustration and euphoria. The town needed badly to pull the cork.

But there was no ceremony. The disappointed crowd arrived at the work site to witness a crew of seventy Chinese and fifty white laborers guiding scrapers back and forth across the sand dunes. Carr Abbott was nowhere to be seen. The impatient president had flatly refused to pay his men to sit and wait for an audience. Later the same day, Abbott explained his convictions to a reporter: "I haven't got the time for such demonstrations!" he blustered. "I am a workist and mean business!"

It was crystal clear that Abbott and Kidder would get along famously.

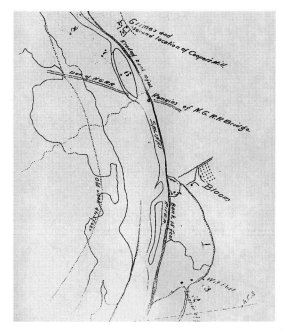

By the time of this undated map, illustrating the area around "Cooper's second mill," the Salinas River crossing of the M&SV could be located only by its ruins. [California State Archives]

It also became crystal clear that Jacks and Abbott would not get along at all. Sometime in the late spring, perhaps in May, the president and treasurer were locked in an argument over procurement. The penurious Jacks and board member Robert McKee tried to buy surplus North Pacific Coast rail; failing to find an adequate supply, they recommended that equivalent rail be bought from an eastern or European supplier. Abbott angrily objected. To wait for rail shipments around Cape Horn would cost the company its schedule. It could not possibly open in time to move the fall harvest. Abbott pointed out that the more expedient alternative, purchasing rail from the Pacific Rolling Mills in San Francisco, could be accomplished before the harvest but would cost the company extra cash—about $30,000 more than it had intended to spend.[43]

Abbott's logic won the board's approval, and the M&SV incurred its first cost overrun. Jacks and Abbott incurred a serious rift in their relationship.

Tom Carter's presence in Monterey was first noted on May 23, when the *Monterey Herald* reported "a gang of workmen are now engaged in clearing out the old Pacific Hotel on Main Street. The building is to be used as a work shop in the construction of cars, a contract having been let for the building of 42 flat cars, 8 box cars and 2 passenger cars."[44]

The renovation of the "Pacific Hotel," two weeks in advance of actual car-building activity, has remained something of a mystery. By early June, a car shop located at the foot of Washington Street, in the middle of the railroad yard, became the headquarters for Carter's project, and all references to car work in the Pacific Hotel vanished from the papers. What was the Pacific Hotel the *Herald* referred to? What part did it play in Carter's embryonic manufacturing strategy? Office space, drafting room, parts stores,

The Spanish adobe called the Pacific Hotel (below) was photographed near the Custom House in Monterey about 1876, two years after its conjectured use as a light carpentry shop by the itinerant craftsmen of Carter Brothers. [Monterey City Library]

light assembly, or even machining are all possibilities, although the awkward size and shape of car sills seems a poor match for a former rooming house.

At the time, indoor facilities for the new railroad project were clearly in short supply in the decrepit Spanish presidio. The M&SV rented space in at least two downtown Monterey buildings. Leese's building on Alvarado Street, for example, was refitted as a bunkhouse for workers in late May.[45] Additional dormitory space was found in an unused building near the Custom House.

Which building, exactly, did Carter use? The *Herald*'s reference to a Pacific Hotel on Main Street could refer to at least two known structures. One was the Pacific Ocean House, located on Monterey's *Calle Principal*. (The Spanish street name was commonly anglicized to "Main Street" in Monterey newspapers of the time.[46]) Judging from contemporary photographs, the Pacific Ocean House was one of the downtown commercial buildings closest to the new railroad yards, standing about four blocks due west from the open marshland on which the yards were being built. Two stories high and with a verandah, the hotel was about sixty feet long and perhaps thirty feet deep. However, the name Pacific Ocean House appears to have been in use in the late 1880s, which was after the period of the M&SV. In the seventies, the same building was known as the "Zinc House" or the "Hampton House."

A more likely candidate seems to be the Pacific Building, a far larger and older adobe structure that still exists on the Monterey Plaza, which was (and remains today) a westward continuation of *Calle Principal* toward the bay and the famous Custom House. At the time of California's statehood, the Pacific Building served as a hotel, but over the next twenty years its use and ownership changed several times.

Between 1868 and 1880, through the period of the M&SV, the Pacific Building's legal title was in the name of Matthew C. Ireland. But a letter written by David Jacks on February 22, 1868, makes the building's true ownership clear. It should be remembered that, at the time, Jacks was a shoe-in for the most despised man in Monterey County: "As I keep the hay for my horses in the Pacific [building] and it might easily be set on fire, I do not think it advisable to take the deed in my own name. And with Ireland's permission I will prefer to have it made out to him."[47]

Fearing reprisal, Jacks disguised the ownership of the building from the town but was clearly in control of the property at the time of Monterey & Salinas Valley construction. In use as a hay barn and in a state of poor upkeep, it was not hard to adapt the Pacific Building to the demands of a light carpentry shop.

As unlikely a car shop as it seems, it is possible to imagine how space in the Pacific might have accommodated the needs of a small manufactory. The closest machine shop was the Brown Brothers works in Salinas, at the opposite end of the unfinished railroad. If Carter intended to create a small machine shop in Monterey, the architecture of the Pacific Hotel was right for it, with heavy, open ceiling joists perfectly suited for supporting bearings for overhead shafting. The shafting in turn provided power through belt drives for machine tools—perhaps a planer, drill press, and table saw. Using a portable steam engine, Carter could have installed a battery of light woodworking power tools on the street level of the Pacific Hotel. The production shop would have supplied the main shop with finished parts, using a dray to shuttle back and forth along unimproved Washington Street.

Confined by small rooms and doors, the Pacific Hotel may have afforded Carter tooling and staging for wall posts, carlines, and bolsters for freight cars; and clerestory posts, rafters, carlines, wall posts, and window framing for the passenger cars that followed later in the summer. All these parts, with the exception of car sills, could have easily moved in and out of the Pacific Hotel's cramped quarters.

We have to speculate about the Pacific Hotel and its use, but we know that when the main car shop was put up near the wharf, it appeared to be too small to accommodate both car bodies under construction and a separate tooling bay. This primary car shop was built during the week of June 6 and was intended as Carter's main erection hall: "The carpenters have been busy this week putting up a workshop. This building stands on the beach a little east of the line of Washington Street, and is 35 by 63 feet in size. In this building the cars are to be built, the contractor already having arrived and the lumber for their construction is expected this week."[48]

Near this building, car wheels and castings were first stockpiled during the week of June 13, and on Thursday, June 25, the steamer *Solano* docked at the still-incomplete railroad wharf with car lumber. This shipment triggered the first construction of rolling stock, one day later. Tom Carter himself suggested to the *Herald* reporter, on June 27, that ten flatcars would be ready in fifteen or sixteen days; it was his only appearance, by name, in the local paper.

The *Herald* noted on July 4 that "at the car factory, all is activity. One flat car has been put together in order to ascertain if the castings are correct, but it is not their intention to put up any more until the timbers are cut and prepared and ready for them all, when they will go up with a rush."

We've already speculated on one of two significant conclusions that can be drawn from this citation: it represents the first prototype for Carter production car work that would soon be occurring in both Monterey and Saucelito. A second conclusion follows: that planing, morticing, and drilling of car sills was accomplished on site.

In the cramped main car shop, the dressed car sills were sorted into four designated build-in-place sites, each long enough for a twenty-four-foot flatcar or boxcar. Four cars could be built at once, two abreast. Little additional space existed, and when the passenger car projects began in July, requiring forty-three feet of clear track space for each car, there weren't enough lineal feet in the shop to handle both passenger cars and freight cars. Carter corrected the problem at the end of June; a twenty-foot addition to the west end of the building during the week of June 30 made it eighty-three feet long, able to accommodate two passenger cars and three freight cars at a time. Still, little room was left for machine tooling once the bays were filled with rolling stock, which was another reason the Pacific Hotel may have been critical to the production strategy.

The field factory adapted quickly to the lack of local suppliers. During the same week, a blacksmith shop was constructed on the south side of the main car shop, adding forging and tool-sharpening to the railroad's mix of locally available crafts. From the July 4 *Herald* article, it was not clear if the blacksmith shop belonged to Carter or to the railroad. It may simply have been shared.

Following a July 4 *Sentinel* ad for extra carpenters, Carter remained in Monterey to interview applicants. But he clearly relied on a straw boss to take the lead. Carter recruited "Frank" Geiser from the Southern Pacific shops in San Francisco. In periods of slack, the Southern Pacific furloughed craftsmen to a labor pool from which Carter could draw both skilled and unskilled workers. Geiser was listed as a machinist in the 1873 San Francisco city directory and as a carpenter for Southern Pacific in 1874; he could have joined Carter in Monterey in the time in between. He played the same crucial role as John Carroll: foreman, overseer of all production details, and ultimately manager of schedule and budget. In all these roles, Geiser would earn his salary.

By July 20, Carter's classified notice in the *Sentinel* had attracted twenty new carpenters to the project, and an additional eight or ten carpenters in the week following. Included in the roster is the recent discovery of Herman J. O. Prinz, a German emigrant to the United States who had trained as a cabinet maker in France and worked in a car manufactory in Milwaukee between 1868 and 1874, arriving in Monterey on July 22.[49] Apparently responding to the *Sentinel* ad, Prinz brought the car shop force to nearly forty men. By Carter's standards, the Monterey contingent was a large force. The Saucelito shop force, in contrast, is estimated at fifteen men or perhaps twenty. When the Newark factory was in its peak production years (1879 to 1880), Carter retained an average of twenty-five employees.[50]

As with other facets of an embryonic manufacturing strategy, Carter experimented with staffing levels. To meet an unusually short delivery schedule, as well as to hedge against a general shortage of skilled workmen in the Monterey Bay area, Carter was anxious to attract and keep skilled help. The unusually large force at Monterey is further evidence that it operated, for a short period of time, as a complete production facility.

But there was a downside. One problem was the relatively low experience level of this workforce as car builders, a factor in what would later be described as "quality issues" in the cars produced at Monterey during the summer of 1874. Another was the high demand for cash flow during the time Carter maintained a high staffing level; payroll accelerated to an alarming aggregate of $120 a day at Monterey alone. If by his own reckoning Carter could produce two-thirds of a flatcar in a single working day and the flatcar had a retail value of $490, it followed that labor accounted for a staggering 30 percent of the total price of his product—three times the normal business rate for the times. Carter was keenly aware that such costs could bankrupt him, and they nearly did.

Yet with this small army, possibly the largest crew he would ever have working for him at a single time, Carter kept his promise. By August 1, twenty flatcars were finished, all nearly identical to the eight-ton-capacity flats being assembled for the North Pacific Coast. Even without a locomotive, Kidder could use the flatcars to begin laying track.

With a crew now schooled in assembling flatcars, Geiser could take a few of his best men, Herman Prinz probably among them, and concentrate on the passenger cars. As August came, the frames of these cars could be seen rising in the shop building, presenting a complex lattice of compression posts, free-spanning clerestory ribs, and a hint of decoration in the quartered corner posts, turned on a lathe to capture the stateliness of columns.

———————————

Sometime during the week of June 13, Kidder resolved the last of the line's survey issues: location of the final six miles of its mainline and siting of its Salinas depot. It was a remarkable solution indeed. The line would not pass through Castroville but make a connection at Castroville crossing, shortening the mainline from 25 miles to 18.5 miles in length. The narrow gauge depot in Salinas would be located on the western outskirts of town, almost a mile away from the Central Pacific depot. There would be no proximate connection between the two companies. Much the opposite, Kidder had erected a barrier between the narrow gauge and its enemy. Any transshipped freight would have to be loaded into wagons and hauled nearly a mile through town to reach the standard gauge railhead. Passengers would have to take a stage or hotel hack the same distance to make the connection between standard gauge trains to San Francisco and narrow gauge trains to Monterey.

Salinas newspapers were incensed at Kidder's obstacle to commerce. Like a giant check valve, no wheat loaded by the narrow gauge could easily flow east to the Central Pacific; it could only go west, to the company's own wharf at Monterey. Kidder had dug a moat around his castle.

———————————

While the eastern end of the line grew shorter, the western end grew longer. Kidder's original cost estimates for the new wharf were based on a one-thousand-foot structure, but the depth of the bay at its extremity was only twenty feet at high tide. The big wheat clippers, fully loaded, drew about twenty-four feet. In a letter to the M&SV, Morgan and Sons warned against trying to moor its contract vessels in anything less than twenty-two feet of water, and then only in calm seas.[51] With the piling out only two hundred feet from shore, Kidder reassessed his first design.

In early June, he added another 208 feet to the pier's total length, pushing out toward shoal water plumbed to twenty-six feet at high tide. The extension was barely adequate to berth the *H. L. Richardson,* finally chartered by Morgan and Sons sometime in August to take on the railroad's first export wheat.[52] Even at the pier's new extremity, the *Richardson* would settle into the mud as it reached full tonnage during a low tide. But "it will be seen," assured the *Herald,* "that by working with the tide a vessel of its size can be easily loaded."

Kidder knew the solution was marginal. Even more draft would be required as the railroad struggled to increase the capacity of the pier. Early signs of an abundant harvest were becoming clear when the first barley was cut during the week of June 11. The *Salinas City Index* warned that mature wheat would not be far off, and that its harvest would "commence on a large scale" within two weeks.

Kidder began track laying on the new pier. About noon on Thursday, June 18, 1874, he personally spiked the first rail to its planking.

The premature harvest brought fresh headaches to the Monterey & Salinas Valley. Farmers who volunteered scrapers and teams were issued script in lieu of pay. The script became credit against charges for hauling their wheat after the railroad was finished; it was considered one way in which railroad and Grange would cooperate. A local source of labor saved Jacks and Abbott scarce construction dollars. In turn, if the railroad was completed before the peak of the harvest, the *Monterey Democrat* estimated it would save the valley $150,000 in excess shipping fees charged by the cartels.

The collaboration seemed to be working. By June 27, 1874, the Southern Pacific had voluntarily dropped its wheat rates from $5.50 a ton to $4.25 a ton from Salinas to San Francisco. About the same time, the M&SV published freight rates of $1.25 per ton from Salinas to Monterey; the rate included loading aboard ship.[53] "In fact," the *Democrat* summed up, "this little joker, the narrow gauge, actually, in the savings to the county, pays for itself the first year."

At the time of the early harvest, at the beginning of a hot and dry July, almost one hundred farmers were engaged in "script labor" for the railroad. But the harvest demanded their teams, equipment, and presence. By the second week in July, the same labor that Kidder needed to complete the railroad had changed roles, moving into the fields to load the sacks that would become the railroad's first cargo.

By August 1, Frank Geiser faced a mutiny in the car shop. The *Herald* of that date reported the growing unrest: "We have heard a great deal of complaint among the workmen and we should think it would be to the interest of all concerned if Mr. Geiser was not interfered with in his management of the men. The car department is in no condition for a strike just now. A word to the wise should be sufficient."

The *Herald* offered no details of the dispute but clearly was aware of several adverse conditions now coming home to roost for Tom Carter. There were numerous drains on his scarce cash: the demand for setup money for both Monterey and Saucelito shops, the need to capitalize raw materials for the Monterey job, an unusually large labor force in Monterey, and a new labor pool on tap in Saucelito. In sum, as of early August Carter was running short on cash and couldn't meet payroll. For two weeks, the survival of both projects hung in the balance.

We know when the troubles surfaced and we know when they ended, almost two weeks later, on Wednesday, August 12, when the *Herald* made a point of noting that the hands in the car shop had been paid up.[54] Somehow, Tom Carter had found the cash. In the meantime, Frank Geiser must have used every trick he could think of to keep his men from walking. He was, apparently, a good leader, liked and respected by his men, and he was often mentioned by the *Herald*. But personal credibility alone could buy him only a skeptical shrug from a large, unpaid workforce. While frantic telegrams went out to Carter, Geiser filled the time with the best distraction he could think of: hard work. Between August 1 and 12, the *Herald* noted, ten new flatcars were rolled out, nearly one per working day, beating Tom Carter's promised delivery schedule and nearly completing the shop's quota of thirty-eight flatcars.

Frank Geiser may have single-handedly saved the day. No record survives, but delivery of the flatcars might have been enough to trigger partial payment on the contract from Jacks and Abbott, letting Carter meet his payroll on August 12.

Kidder's second-in-charge was Henry Foy, commander of the "Knights of the Jack Plane," the railroad's own cadre of carpenters. Foy's men laid out and dressed the heavy timbers required for turntables, depots, culverts, trestle work, bridge work over the Salinas River, water tanks, and windmills. They performed the carpentry support work; construction of tool sheds, pile drivers, scaffolding, and the Carter car shop; and possibly the remodel work on the Pacific Hotel and even a scow for floating the pile driver in Monterey Bay.

While Kidder directly oversaw the track layers, Foy and his crew worked behind the scenes to keep dressed timbers flowing to the work sites. Even though the grading had not yet reached the Salinas River by the first of July, Foy used the Monterey yards as a staging area for laying out timbers for framing the Salinas depot. When the bridge was completed, the materials would be shipped to Salinas and assembled somewhat like a modern prefab building.

Foy's crews were efficient. Work began on a turntable on Monday, July 6, and the framework was completed (its parts stockpiled as an unassembled kit) by Saturday, July 11.[55] On August 1, Foy directed his men to begin framing the giant warehouses that would go up at both Salinas and Monterey—fifty- by four-hundred-foot structures that would be the railroad's first defense against the coming rains. Next, Salinas River bridge timbers were hauled on flatcars to the Salt Lagoon by horses and then painfully and slowly pushed by laborers uphill to Bardin's Ranch, where they were stored close to the bridge site.

The project continued to lose momentum as farmers left with their teams to attend to harvest. On July 27, the *Herald* reported:

> This week has been one of disappointment. Had the entire force remained at work and the Chinese that were expected come down at the proper time, you could have chronicled the completion of the grading to the river. But harvest has commenced and many farmers have been obliged to withdraw their teams, while others left because they can earn more in the harvest field, and only 22 out of the large number of Chinese that were expected have arrived. To check this desertion the Company have raised wages.

Slowly, as harvests were concluded in early August, grading teams returned to work on the Salinas side of the river, falling into drill formation on the long six-mile tangent that stretched from the river to Salinas City. Alongside the fresh grade, devoid of rail and ties, valley farmers heaped bags of freshly thrashed wheat, believing the railroad would magically appear to take them away.

Kidder and the rail gangs were right behind the graders, reaching the river about September 5 and opening up the pipeline for timber to flow from the Bardin's Ranch stockpile to the bridge work site. Without a locomotive, the movement of materials became an increasing bottleneck the further east the railroad got, and Kidder began to fear for timely completion of the project.

Mishaps began to occur more frequently as the period of good weather grew shorter. On August 1, Carr Abbott tied his team up in a thicket of willows to watch the pile driver at work in the Salinas River; after witnessing a couple of noisy thwacks, he turned to see his panicked horses tumbling down the twelve-foot bank, dragging his carriage behind them. The only damage, miraculously, was a broken carriage pole.

On August 15, a workman named John Sullivan got his left foot caught under a pile of rail he was helping to load. As the rail shifted, Sullivan suffered two crushed toes. Monterey's Dr. Wells amputated the damaged appendages while Sullivan was rendered unconscious with a new drug called ether. This was probably the first time the novel anesthetic was used in Monterey, and it would soon become a staple (like whiskey) in the battle to finish the railroad before the rains.

On August 21, the scow that carriaged the pile driver began to take on water in the Salt Lagoon, slowly listed, and finally rolled over and sank.

On September 19, Henry Foy was coupling flatcars together in the Monterey yards, assembling a train of timbers to be sent to the front, when his foot slipped. Both hands instinctively shot out to break the fall, and he grabbed the shank of the coupler exactly at the instant the two cars came together. Foy's thumb was crushed.

The accident gave Dr. Wells the next opportunity to demonstrate the wonders of ether.

––––––––––––

Frank Geiser started work on the two passenger cars during the week of July 4. Tom Carter was still in town, by day interviewing carpenters who had come in response to the *Sentinel* ad, and by night working on the endless details of two small combination cars, the first passenger cars he would build as an independent contractor.

More than any other artifact of the new railroad, the passenger cars would be identified with Monterey's coming status as a transportation hub. Sensitive to the criticism that narrow gauge railroads were not as comfortable, well-appointed, or safe as their broad gauge counterparts, the *Herald* was alert for any way in which the public could be led to imagine the M&SV as a real railroad. When the question came up, the two small passenger cars were invariably mentioned.

The passenger cars took shape in the midst of continuing, routine pro-

The Field Notebook: Restoring the Oldest Carter Passenger Car

Not long after the surviving M&SV combine entered the California State Railroad Museum restoration facility in Sacramento in 1977, the decision was reached to restore its original appearance, as built, in 1874. As a source of data for future research, this was good news for students of the M&SV (as well as for this book), but in practice the resulting research uncovered numerous reasons the target restoration date would be difficult to address with credibility. In the intervening 103 years since the car was built, the combine had been through enough modifications to throw the most dedicated researcher off track. A partial list of these changes: 1875, car repainted, with interior modifications including addition of a saloon; 1879, sold to the Nevada Central Railroad and repainted; 1881, apparently scorched in a fire near Austin, Nevada, and repaired; 1886, modified from nine to seven windows; 1892, derailed south of Battle Mountain and then repaired; 1895, probably repaired—with extensive truck work—and repainted; 1904, automatic couplers and airbrakes installed; 1915, possibly derailed, and repaired; 1917, coach house blew over at Battle Mountain in high wind, car repaired; 1927, coach house burns in Battle Mountain, car repaired.

Some of the car, certainly, was original when CSRM began its restoration study in 1977. Much of the description in this text comes from the resulting restoration report (1979), which was based on examination of original parts and materials. But after spending $125,000 and nearly two years on the project, as little as 5 percent of the original car was conserved in the final restoration on display when the museum opened in 1980.

Restoration of the surviving Monterey &
Salinas Valley combine, by the California
State Railroad Museum, 1977–78; more
than 90 percent of the wooden parts in the
restoration were new material, copied
from deteriorated original parts. [Bruce
MacGregor]

duction of freight cars. They were not as critical as flatcars, required immediately to move rail, ties, and timber. Still, it was important to start the cars,
since they were the most technically challenging and complex part of the
contract. Carter had brought the plans with him—drawn perhaps by himself or John Carroll—but he would not stay to see them completed. Sometime during the week of July 11, Carter caught a steamer for San Francisco,
anxious to be back in Saucelito, which left Geiser to manage the project.

With growing interest, the *Herald* followed construction of the combines
over the roughly ten weeks it took Geiser to manufacture and paint them.
The paper took pains to report, on June 27, that "the seats in the passenger
cars will be placed in the usual form, and will be forty inches in length"—
standard gauge format, if not exactly standard gauge dimensions. If two
adults agreed to the uncomfortable intimacy of occupying a single seat, each
car would hold thirty-four of Monterey County's proud citizenry.

On October 17, 1874, the *Salinas Index* echoed the *Herald*'s strong belief
in the substance of their new railroad: "in a little while, we suppose, the passenger cars will be put on. They are very beautifully fitted up, with rows of
double seats, just as with the broad gauge. In fact, so far as this class of accommodation is concerned, the NG will compare with any road."

Sensitive to the consumer appeal of the cars, Carter was careful about
creating the look and feel of mainline equipment they would inevitably be
compared to. The proportions of the cars, the style of trucks, the seating, the
finish, and the striping and ornamentation were all important features in
signifying the cars to be commercial vehicles. So was price. If money alone
is a guide, the $3,000 contract price of each car compared favorably with the
$3,600 cost of a new North Pacific Coast Kimball coach (a benchmark for
premium or high-end narrow gauge work on the West Coast).[56] In contrast,
one year later Carter would be offering two lower-priced passenger cars for
the short line market, one called a "first class" coach and priced at $2,300, the
second called a "second class" coach and priced at a bargain $1,600.[57] These
cars are described in Chapter Six; they simplified and cheapened the product Carter created at Monterey.

Throughout Carter's thirty-year history, the brothers would build for all
segments of the narrow gauge railroad market—low, median, and high. But
from the perspective of 1874, the Carter entry into the passenger car trade
was made with a product that, at least cosmetically, was positioned closer to
high-end Kimball products than to the low-end coaches that would begin to
appear with regularity in the Carter product line. First impressions were important. New or repeat work would be generated on the goodwill of Carter's
first products.[58]

The Monterey passenger cars included features that were to be identified
with Carter's mainline passenger equipment for the next six or seven years:
overall body dimensions of thirty-six feet, clerestory roof with duckbill ends;
seventy-six-inch spacing between wall plate and sill; ten-inch-high letterboards; deafening floor to muffle noise and vibration; "breadbox" style tin
ventilator boxes; two shallow truss rods; a modest catalogue of decoration,
including interior stenciling and ceiling cloth; and an exterior finish in what
would today be called Colonial Revival yellow, a common color from railroad supply catalogues of the time.[59] Proportionally, Carter designs may have

appeared slightly more diminutive than the narrow gauge work of Kimball or Billmeyer and Small, in part due to a lower clerestory roof and a lower center of gravity in the car as a whole. The duckbill roof was a universal style for American passenger cars built during the 1870s. Kimball was using it in 1874, although the "bill" portion of the roof was longer in Kimball's coach than in Carter's, and the Kimball clerestory was higher, which helps to distinguish one builder's roof from the other.

Other features appeared to be unique to the Monterey cars but died out with little or no follow-on in the Carter products of later years. Board-and-batten siding, as well as the truck design (see Field Notebook: The Passenger Truck Controversy) appear to fall into this category.[60]

There is no single roadmap to the provenance of Carter's design. Kimball's North Pacific Coast coaches were on the erection floor at Fourth and Bryant streets during the same weeks the Monterey cars were under construction and conceivably could have been a source for design ideas. But Kimball's framing—a signature of the designer—was different: Carter built its first cars on a foundation of six sills, using tiny $3^3/4" \times 4^3/4"$ fir beams (see Field Notebook: Design Flaws). These beams had nearly 40 percent less cross section than the side sills Carter would employ on its coaches built during the early 1880s, but they still aspired to standard eastern practice of six car sills.[61] Kimball, however, constructed its NPC coaches on just four sills, each measuring $4" \times 6"$, a throwback to an earlier era of car construction.[62]

The lack of photographic documentation of the cars in service on the Monterey & Salinas Valley has fueled an ongoing debate about their design. Passenger car trucks were the most technical part of a car's engineering, and a test of a builder's sophistication. What does Carter's choice of trucks for the Monterey cars tell us about the builder?

Judging from price alone, the combination cars were probably sold with "high end," compound-sprung passenger trucks. The key differentiator in type of truck was suspension. Freight trucks used just a single set of springs between the source of vibration and the car body. Compound-sprung passenger trucks placed two types of spring in series between track and car, each spring intended to filter out a different frequency of vibration. Most compound passenger truck designs also included swing motion. The added complexity of this design produced a far smoother ride, but at a considerable increase in cost. Again, judging just from the $3,000 retail price, the Carter combination cars probably came equipped with compound-sprung trucks. Further confirmation is provided by their healthy resale price to the Nevada Central Railroad in 1879: $2,850.[63]

But whose trucks were used? Did Carter contribute substantially to their design, or adapt them from his observation of industry practice? Or did he simply buy them, off the shelf, from another manufacturer? Again, these questions bear on Carter's stature as an emerging leader in the California railroad supply market. But evaluating these three alternatives is made difficult by the lack of direct photographic evidence. We simply don't know with certainty what the trucks looked like when they operated on the M&SV between 1874 and 1879.

Photographs, however, do exist of the cars taken just a few months after they left the M&SV, and they appear to demonstrate two things. First, the

**The Field Notebook:
The Passenger Truck Controversy**

During the 1977 CSRM restoration, twenty-one layers of paint were identified on the body of the M&SV combination car, but only seventeen layers were found on the extant trucks. CSRM researchers at first concluded from this finding that the trucks were not original. Mismatched hardware, for instance extant Carter pedestals dated 1897, seemed to support this conclusion. But the controversy deepened when the marks of a U-shaped pedestal were uncovered on the remaining wooden wheel pieces, closely matching the truck's configuration in the oldest known photographs. This evidence seemed to suggest that the original 1874 trucks may have been purchased from a car builder like Billmeyer and Small, known for truck designs featuring U-pedestals. Based on this evidence, CSRM restored the trucks to closely match their appearance in the oldest known photo.

Since the time of the restoration, the truck's originality has been supported by better dating of the oldest photograph, suggesting that it was taken four months or less, after the arrival of the cars from the M&SV in late 1879. Circumstantial evidence, including the $3000 price of the original cars, also strengthened the conclusion that the surviving trucks (in their U-pedestal form) were probably original.

Until conclusive evidence is found (such as photographs from 1874), it appears that the CSRM restoration may be a close approximation to the original truck. Carter may simply have bought the trucks from an eastern vendor to save time and expense.

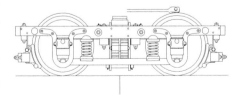

trucks show many of the features of a popular passenger truck manufactured by eastern builders, notably Billmeyer and Small. Second, the same trucks, although modified during the 1890s, were preserved and used by the Nevada Central and are the trucks that form the basis for the car's modern restoration.[64]

If these conclusions are true, it seems arguable that the cars' original trucks came equipped with high-end features—compound springing and swing motion—that remain visible on the restored car today.

It is difficult to say with certainty who built the trucks. One line of reasoning suggests that Monterey passenger car hardware was sourced the same way as freight car hardware. If Carter's casting work was coming from Santa Cruz, this thinking suggests, then passenger truck parts could have been procured the same way. But even though descriptive lists of these castings were published in the *Santa Cruz Sentinel*, nowhere is any part specifically called out for passenger cars or their trucks.[65]

A second explanation, advanced by the California State Railroad Museum research staff in 1979, suggested that the trucks were built in the East by Jackson and Sharp or Billmeyer and Small and sold to Carter for the Monterey work.[66] The distinctive U-shaped pedestal provides an obvious link between the extant relic and early narrow gauge designs of both prominent eastern builders. The trucks still in existence are also a close dimensional match to Billmeyer and Small trucks of the 1870s, although certain details do not match. This explanation is bolstered by Carter's maturing relationship with Howard Schuyler, who could easily have recommended the same vendor to Carter he had successfully used on the Denver & Rio Grande.

There is scant evidence to draw any conclusion except Carter's intention to equip the Monterey cars with fully sprung and equalized passenger trucks, comparable to industry practice at the time, and not to spend an enormous amount of his own time doing it. He had little enough to spare on freight car work. Within three years, Carter Brothers would invest design energy into a high-end passenger truck of its own, following the steady, industrywide evolution of this important assembly. This uniquely "Carter style" passenger truck, with a longer wheelbase than the Monterey truck and a stronger cast pedestal, substantially improved the 1874 design. But vended passenger trucks very likely got Carter through the tight deadlines of the Monterey contract.

Since John Carroll and Tom Carter were engaged in starting up the Saucelito shop at the time the combination cars were under construction, it is perplexing to consider that for such an important prototype neither appears to have had ongoing contact with the work. The Monterey shop crew were strangers to Carter when they were hired. Unlike Carroll, they were largely inexperienced with car-building practice. They suffered through late payrolls and talked of mutiny behind Geiser's back. Workmanship suffered. There are examples of lapsed quality to be found in the original car roof, where oversize, square-head tenpenny nails were intended to hold the tapered ends of the clerestory carlines in place but split them instead.[67] Other defects have been noted, as well; see the Field Notebook: Design Flaws.

The context of the work plays an important part in understanding its limitations. The fact that Carter attempted to enter the high-end passenger car market under field conditions, without his most skilled shop crew to perform the work, implies again that he was at least as interested in developing a manufacturing strategy as he was in developing products. The field factory was his first attempt at finding a solution, and at Monterey his methods revealed their shortcomings.

Still, the *Monterey Herald* tracked progress on the two cars with keen interest. It usually referred to them as "the passenger cars," although they were formally defined as "combination cars," or "combines" for short, referring to their provision for hauling baggage as well as passengers.

On August 1, the paper noted completion of one of the car frames, probably referring to six structural sills that made up the car's foundation. On August 8, the *Herald* noted accelerating progress when it reported that "the two passenger cars are assuming shape," a clue to the appearance of walls and roof members. Car sills, wall frame, floor, and roof were cut from Douglas fir. Redwood was used for roofing and baggage interior siding, and for board-and-batten siding as well.[68] The board-and-batten siding would first reveal the cars' design flaws, in the form of irregular drying and checking in panel boards, leading to visual scarring of the car's finish. Just a year after the car's completion, the *Herald* reported a complete repainting, a clue to the premature appearance of checks or cracks in the exterior skin.[69] The cars' next owner, the Nevada Central Railroad, would replace the board and battens with 2^1/$_2$" tongue and groove redwood. Over the next fifteen years, they would also make structural changes to the car bodies and trucks, including sistering the car sills as mentioned earlier.

On August 22, Monterey's resident tinsmith, W. W. James, was commissioned to assemble more than one hundred tin squares to create a watertight roof, soldering the squares together along lap seams. The car bodies must have been finished by September 5, when the *Herald* reported that both had already received "two coats of paint, and will soon receive their furniture." A week later, the reporter returned to the car shop to find the "ornamental painter at work," indicating at least a week of drying time had passed for the body's exterior coat before striping and lettering began.

The finished livery was striking. The bodies were painted a color approximating Colonial Revival yellow, a muted, slightly earth-toned custard.[70] The baggage door lintels, letterboards, and window trim (both main and clerestory) were finished in a faux mahogany wood grain created by overlaying a dark colored varnish on top of an orange base. On the letterboards, yellow striping probably created brackets for the sans serif block yellow lettering, boldly spelling out "Monterey & Salinas Valley."

Inside, wall paneling was finished in a soft gray with a slight bluish tint. Interior end paneling and window lintels were decorated with polychrome stencils that terminated the interior striping in a fountain-shaped gradation of neutral violet, Mars violet, and finally cadmium red,[71] blended together to create a spectrum. Rolled out into the summer sun, surely the combines seemed to glow.

One hundred three years later, researchers found, under layers of more modern leather seat covering, evidence of plush velvet fabric that might have been the first covering of the car's original seventeen seats when they were finally installed at Monterey during the week of September 12, 1874. Small

The Field Notebook: Design Flaws

During the 1979 restoration of a Monterey combine at the California State Railroad Museum, evidence of structural shortcomings in the body of the car was discovered. Most dramatic were six car sills, each of which was a sistered combination of two smaller sills. Discoloration indicated that one of each pair of sills was much older than the other half. If only half the "sisters" were present at construction in 1874, they were flimsy car sills indeed; the sistered side sills measured just 3^3/$_4$" × 4^3/$_4$", instead of 4^1/$_2$" × 6^1/$_4$" as used on later Carter cars.

It was not difficult to discover other design shortfalls. Only two carlines were used in the clerestory roof, not the normal three applied to later Carter coaches. A deep gain cut in the wall posts at the bottom of the windows (where moisture would collect) resulted in an ideal niche for dry rot and the point of structural failure by the time of the car's eventual restoration in 1979.

The clerestory, although apparently not original, may have been reconstructed in the footprints of the Carter clerestory and had vertical side walls, which tended to collect rather than shed rainwater. In later cars, the same assembly would be sloped at five degrees, leading one restorer to joke that Carter Brothers still hadn't discovered rain at the time of the 1874 Monterey work.

The original exterior of the Monterey cars—board-and-batten siding with panels approximately twelve inches wide—suffered from cracking and checking as the wood dried, creating ugly gaps in its otherwise lovely yellow finish. The car's new owner, the Nevada Central Railroad, would replace the boards with 2^1/$_2$" siding during the 1880s.

Gaining field experience, Carter itself would change strategy in all the structural areas mentioned.

fragments of two colors of material were found, one red plush and the other green plush. We do not know which was the original.

We also do not know for certain (but we can surmise from fragments of ceiling cloth found trapped under the top of the saloon wall) that the combines were built without toilets and ran for more than a year before this serious affront to Monterey's civic pride was corrected.[72]

On September 12, 1874, the *Monterey Herald* posed a whimsical question to its readers: "Why is a beautiful girl like the locomotive *C. S. Abbott*? Give it up? Because she draws a train, scatters the sparks, transports the males, and says to the tender, 'pine not.'"

The *Abbott*, a twenty-ton Baldwin, had arrived on the steamer *Golden Gate* at midnight four days earlier. It took the next day and a half to unload the tender and three working days to unload the engine off the undulating boat. But by dark on Friday, the *Abbott* was sitting on the wharf under a harvest moon. The paper correctly recognized the symbolism: Monterey's love affair with its railroad at last had a leading lady.

Kidder paid $10,000 in cash for the Baldwin, $2,000 of which went to transportation by rail from New York to San Francisco. The wood-burning machine was the ninth locomotive built in its Baldwin class, 8-18 D. It was a Mogul, or 2-6-0 type, identical in classification and just two serial numbers higher than the first narrow gauge Baldwin in California, the North Pacific Coast number 1, *Saucelito*. Both were freight engines, designed by Baldwin to drag five or six hundred tons along level track at eight miles per hour.

These were the first narrow gauge Baldwins to operate in California, and they entered the state as something of an experiment in market readiness. Though bearing nearly identical mechanical specifications, the *C. S. Abbott* and *Saucelito* were soon tested in dramatically different operating environments. The *Abbott* would operate on modest grades and curves, establishing a baseline for understanding the performance of the *Saucelito*, which was soon tasked with the heavy gradients and curvature of White's Hill. Within a year's time, drastic differences in performance and wear would be reflected in changes that both railroads made to their 8-18 Ds. For the M&SV, the changes were minor, but for the NPC the revisions were draconian (and will be explored in Chapter Five).

The *Abbott*'s paint scheme was called out in the original Baldwin specification sheet as "wine color, style 1," a combination of red, yellow, and white striping on a crimson base color of tender, cab, cylinders, headlight, and domes.[73] In Baldwin's extensive catalogue of colors, the engine's livery was considered plain. Her name was gold-leafed on the ash panel under the cab window, and M.&.S.V.R.R. appeared in larger lettering on the tender. Expectations for her performance were high. According to the Baldwin catalogue, the locomotive was capable of hauling about sixty cars on level track, one-third more cars than the M&SV owned.[74]

Over the next six weeks, minor adjustments to the *Abbott*'s hardware would become routine. On October 28, for example, David Jacks noted the

---

The Field Notebook: Revisions at Baldwin

Five months separated the order of the two M&SV locomotives at Baldwin: no. 1, the *C. S. Abbott*, was ordered in mid-June, and no. 2, the *Monterey*, was ordered in late November 1874. The two machines were different types, the *Abbott* being a 2-6-0 class 8-18 D and the *Monterey* a 4-4-0, class 8-18 C. But in that brief period, the M&SV mechanical department used the experience with the *Abbott* to enhance the configuration of its second engine. For example, a wooden pilot, used on the *Abbott*, may have gotten bad press when the engine smashed into the Monterey warehouse door on Dec. 5, 1874, splintering the pilot and prompting a change order to Baldwin to equip the *Monterey* with an iron web pilot. A special front drawbar was ordered for the *Monterey*, designed to the M&SV's specifications, perhaps to be built in duplicate for the damaged *Abbott*. The strength of tender springs was increased on the second engine, to go along with two hundred extra gallons of water capacity. There were no engine brakes on either locomotive, but the *Monterey*'s tender truck was equipped with adjustable brake shoes; the *Abbott*'s was not. The size of the lead truck "box cellars," or oil reservoirs, was increased, apparently to reduce the demand for servicing. A higher-quality steel was called out for the *Monterey*'s driver tires—fine German steel made by Krupp.

But the most curious change was apparently in the design of the whistle. For all its novelty, it wasn't easy to hear the *Abbott* coming. On the *Monterey*'s specification sheet, Baldwin simply noted a whistle "to be loud, and worked by lever."

purchase of "6 springs for engine tender" in his own cash books, a foreshadowing of heavier tender springs deliberately requested when the second locomotive was ordered from Baldwin.

Although the *Herald* waxed poetic about the aesthetics of the town's colorful leading lady, Kidder had designs on the lady's muscles. Up to that point, he had been forced to move ties, rail, and heavy bridge timber by an awkward combination of horse teams and men—the horses pulling flatcars as far as the Salt Lagoon, where the firmly packed sand ballast ended. Chinese labor then shouldered the cars uphill, over exposed ties, as far as end-of-track. The *Abbott*'s first assignment would be to retire the sweating supply chain.

Kidder's mechanic got steam up for the first time on Saturday, September 12, blew the *Abbott*'s whistle at three in the afternoon, and watched the crowds gather around the locomotive. Among them was Carr Abbott himself. In spite of his professed contempt for ceremony, the president stood gazing at the compact machine, allowing himself to be publicly complimented on his namesake. Pride may have swelled his thinking. He had never operated a steam locomotive in his life, but that afternoon, he reasoned, would be a propitious moment to learn. The few flatcars coupled to the *Abbott* were quickly packed. With rudiments of throttle and Johnson bar barely understood, the president of the railroad piloted his namesake Baldwin over the sand hills to end-of-track, about four miles to the southern edge of Bardin's Ranch—at which point the *C. S. Abbott* ran out of boiler water.[75]

At which point, John Flint Kidder calmly assumed command. He gave the order to kill the engine's fire. He explained to the confused crowd the basics of the sweating supply chain: the cars would simply be uncoupled from the spent locomotive and pushed southward over the unballasted track, across the open trestle work at Salt Lagoon, where horses would be hitched on for the pull back to town.

Somehow, the town's people came to the conclusion that it was all part of the celebration. Wives, waving merrily from the flatcars, cheered their hyperventilating husbands as they struggled to push the cars. Children wanted to pet the horses. The *Herald*'s resident humorist composed a satirical account of the event in her head as she walked the four sandy miles back to town, declining to add to the horses' burden.[76] Carr Abbott, walking the distance with the rest, smiled the smile of the emperor with no clothes.

Teams and wagons reached the stranded leading lady the next morning with every bucket, barrel, and laundry tub that would hold water.

Evidence of a record harvest was everywhere to be seen. Jack Preston ran a separator cooperative in Castroville, and by late September he had ten thrashing machines and their companion stationary steam engines working in rotation around the valley. On September 26, the *Herald* reported the loss of Preston's best thrasher, a "Little Red," in a fire: "its loss comes hard on the people of the valley, as there is more grain than can be threshed before the rains commence, even with the nine other machines constantly at work."

As late as September 19, the railroad was still in no position to deliver the valley's enormous harvest, but wheat prices were depressed, and the Salinas Valley Grangers were reluctant to make consignments to brokers like Morgan and Son while prices continued low. The presence of the nearly finished railroad and its warehouses, seemed to give the Grangers the luxury of time. They willingly stacked their wheat in the cavernous Salinas warehouse (an indoor spur allowed flatcars to be loaded or unloaded out of the elements), along the long tangent section of grade through the El Tucho Ranch, and at the location of the Bardin's Ranch siding—all locations without rail anywhere to be seen. When the Salinas warehouse was full, sacks were heaped in great piles outdoors.

As the drama neared its climax, an agent of Morgan and Sons wrote David Jacks from San Francisco on August 6, trying to kindle interest in selling wheat: "Liverpool advices today are quoted strong prices unaltered [although] local market continues dull."[77]

Other brokerage houses competed for the Grangers' attention. In the August 13 *Herald*, Falkner and Bell offered the lowest shipping rates the paper had yet seen: $18.12 per ton as opposed to the current rate of $20.57 per ton, plus 2.5 percent commission, delivered to Liverpool. Whether Morgan and Sons rebid Falkner's price sometime in September 1874 remains unknown, but the first "commission ship" to dock at Monterey would be a Morgan charter, suggesting that for the eight weeks preceding the harvest there was fierce competition for the valley's bumper crop.

On September 19, the *Herald* noted that the Southern Pacific had begun heavy wheat shipments in parts of the valley, estimating that fourteen hundred tons had already moved by extra freight trains toward the port at San Francisco. Apparently this movement was evidence of a mass selling at the prevailing price, but the paper confessed that "Whether the most of this 2,800,000 pounds of cereals are sold, or only shipped for storage, we don't know."

The news raised the specter that the narrow gauge would arrive a day late and a dollar short. The *Herald* expressed remorse that if the railroad had been finished six weeks earlier, the amount of grain it would ultimately carry might have doubled.[78] True or not, by September 19 the M&SV's Monterey warehouse, still under construction, was projected to be filled to capacity with wheat stockpiled along the uncompleted railroad. That amounted to four or five thousand tons, the equivalent of two Liverpool shiploads. The capacity of Kidder's "system" would clearly be taxed, if not overwhelmed.

But at least rolling stock would not be the cause of the bottleneck. By the last week in September, Geiser's shop crew was mopping up the loose ends of the car contract. Thirty-eight flatcars, the critical link in moving grain, were finished and could be pressed into revenue service the minute they were no longer needed for moving rails, ties, and ballast. In the last week of September, eight boxcars were going up in the car shop, along with two pump cars. The same week, Geiser expected the arrival of passenger car "furniture," walkover (reversible) style seats upholstered in plush velvet. Appetites whetted by the adventure aboard the flatcars, the public began to imagine a grand opening excursion aboard the yellow combination cars.

Carr Abbott, the old workist, imagined income.

David Jacks didn't have to imagine. Once the *C. S. Abbott* was under steam, he began to pocket several hundred dollars a month from the sale of cord wood to the railroad, which made him the only member of its stockholders to enjoy revenue from the operation of construction trains.[79]

By late September, John Kidder was committing his entire carpentry force, including Henry Foy and his crew, to the unfinished Salinas River bridge, which held up track laying on the final six-mile tangent from the river into Salinas City. In turn, reassigning carpenters held up framing the Monterey warehouse, thus increasing the chance that even if the railroad delivered the wheat to the port it could not protect it from rain.

By September 24, rail was laid to the river, allowing the *C. S. Abbott* to deliver bridge materials, but there were still problems with material shortages, and the *Herald*, hoping for completion of the line by October 1, had to admit the delays might add up to a week, perhaps more. So far, heavy rains had held off, but with thousands of sacks of wheat exposed to the elements, each passing day increased the possibility of disaster. Smaller farmers grew nervous, consigning their crops to the Southern Pacific or to coastal shipping at Moss Landing, unwilling to prolong the risk.

The breakthrough at the river finally occurred on October 3. "Today," wrote the *Herald*'s correspondent,

> I may say the bridge is done, and as it stands, is one of the best of its kind on the coast. It is called a "strut" or "strain beam" bridge, and when painted will present a fine appearance. There are five 60-foot spans, resting on piers consisting of 13 piles each, which are planked diagonally on each side with three inch plank, each pier presenting a cut water to the stream. On the top of the piles rests a cap, on which is placed the bolsters that support the cords or the main timbers of the structure, these timbers are 12 × 14 inches, and are supported between the piers by an upper cord and strain-beams, with braces between, all drawn tight by iron bolts. Resting on the cords are stringers on which are laid the ties. Altogether this is a piece of work of which the stockholders may justly be proud, being ornamental as well as substantial and durable. The lower timbers are four feet above extreme high water mark, thereby affording ample room for the passage of drift wood.

Next to the bridge, a temporary water tank was erected to supply construction trains, to reduce the number of trips the *Abbott* had to make back to Monterey.

No sooner had the bridge been opened than a tally of ready rail came up short. Kidder knew, by October 3, that track layers could not reach Salinas with the available supply. He sent an urgent cable to Pacific Rolling Mills in San Francisco, ordering more. Abbott's patronage of the San Francisco rolling mill paid off. Just four days later, on Wednesday, October 7, the rail was alongside the wharf aboard the ship *Santa Cruz*.

Kidder's luck was barely holding. The weather had turned threatening. There could be no further delay. Kidder threw all his forces at the front. In two days, the remaining six miles of rail went down on the east side of the river. On Friday, October 9, the *Abbott* steamed into Salinas City for the first time. Carr Abbott could listen to his namesake's whistle from the verandah of his own hotel.

[Monterey City Library]

Rain fell lightly that same day, wetting the exposed burlap grain sacks, but not seeping deep enough to injure the wheat. The *Herald* estimated that at the time, twenty-five thousand sacks of wheat were stockpiled along the line.[80] The elements had fired a warning shot; Kidder gave an ultimatum. No passenger trains would operate until the track was completely ballasted, and the *Abbott* would not be available for ballast duty until all the wheat was moved from track side to the Monterey yards. Kidder released men from the front to double back to the unfinished Monterey warehouse. By October 10, the fifty- by four-hundred-foot warehouse frame was erected, but it would take at least two additional weeks to complete siding and canvas roofing. As much as ten thousand tons of grain might have been stacked outdoors the first week of October, still in harm's way. As the skies darkened with storm clouds, tempers grew short in Grange hall meetings.

But chance seemed to favor the miraculous. On October 7, a workman named Robbins tried to swing onto a moving flatcar, slipped, and fell under the wheels. Both wheels of the forward truck passed over his legs, but incredibly, all he sustained were bruises. Dr. Wells's ether bottle remained stoppered and on the shelf.

Chance even favored the obvious. An unexpected source of covered warehouse space arrived in Monterey on October 15, when the grain ship *H. L. Richardson* tied up at the Monterey wharf. Under contract by Morgan and Sons, the twenty-two-hundred-ton vessel could take aboard wheat equivalent to half the available volume in the Monterey warehouse. Kidder probably was first to see the possibility; the ship itself would become a warehouse. He diverted men from warehouse construction to load the ship with wheat stockpiled on the depot grounds outside. When Kidder started to move wheat from the outlying ranches by rail on October 24, the cavernous holds of the *Richardson* were still unfilled.

The longer the *Richardson* remained in port, the better were Kidder's chances of successfully transporting the harvest. Its captain cooperated. As the weather worsened in the northern hemisphere, it got better in the southern, and the longer the ship waited in Monterey the easier its passage would be around Cape Horn. For nearly an entire month, the *Abbott* and its crew worked day shifts and night shifts to shuttle the wheat to Monterey. When the warehouse was declared "almost finished" on Halloween, there were already twenty thousand sacks of grain stored inside.

The ship remained in port through the middle of November. The *Richardson*'s crew had time not only to procure ship's stores, including fresh vegetables, but also to start new careers. I. J. Skerritt, a steward on the *Richardson*, opened a restaurant in the Robinson's Building on November 22; he would remain in Monterey after the ship departed.

The arrival of the *Richardson* bought Kidder time, but little closure. As long as the wheat was moving and the warehouse uncompleted, he would not spare engine, cars, or men on ceremony. He continued to pursue unfinished details—turntables; side tracks; extra ballast where track had subsided; doors on the Monterey warehouse; extra piles placed as fenders around the wharf; and finally, on Friday, October 23, a shakedown run for the first of the combines to be completed—with just the railroad crew aboard. On October 24, the *Herald* described the cars as "models of beauty and an honor to their builder." But no one, including the press, had yet been invited for a ride.

Monterey seized on the arrival of the *Richardson* to improvise closure of its own. On Thursday, October 15, the townsfolk took matters of celebration into their own hands when "a goodly quantity of powder was collected and after trying to drill the spiked cannon at the old fort and failing, the small cannon belonging to Gonzales was brought out and made to do good service, and though some did remark that "there was more smoke than bomb to the thing," it performed its part very credibly."[81]

Proclaiming success, the Salinas Valley Grangers were about to ship their first wheat directly to Liverpool.

One by one they packed their tools and left. John Flint Kidder departed Monterey on November 10, handing over California's first operating narrow gauge railroad to John Nesbitt, the new general superintendent of the Monterey & Salinas Valley. Kidder inspired loyalty. On November 7, fourteen of his employees published a card in the *Herald*, giving testimony of "their admiration of the indomitable energy and thorough knowledge displayed by you in the construction of said road—of their esteem for yourself, personally, for the gentlemanly manner in which you have borne yourself towards them."

Kidder took a surveying contract in nearby Hollister, beginning work on a proposed narrow gauge connection between the M&SV and the grain shipping region around San Juan Bautista, a market directly served by the Southern Pacific and for the Grange revolt a natural thrust deeper into enemy territory.[82] The connection, unfortunately, would never be built.

It was Frank Geiser, not Tom Carter, who was celebrated at the end of the Monterey contract. Geiser and his wife were treated to a surprise party on Saturday, October 17, before he returned to the Southern Pacific car shop in San Francisco. The *Herald* confessed that even after his short residence in Monterey, the popular car shop foreman would be missed. Geiser would moonlight again for Carter, a year later, when he took the foreman's position on the Santa Clara Valley Railroad at Dumbarton Point, the first of Carter's sojourning craftsmen and the one who probably traveled furthest.

The giant Monterey warehouse, painted light brown, stood nearly completed on the beach, filled with twenty thousand sacks of grain in addition to the eighteen thousand sacks already stashed aboard the *Richardson*. Most of Henry Foy's carpenters were discharged from the job on Monday, November 15. Foy could give his mangled hand a badly needed rest.

The next day, Monday, November 16, the Monterey & Salinas Valley Railroad finally held its inaugural celebration. Three hundred Salinas residents took the morning train, accompanied by the Castroville Brass Band. The Carter combines got their first public outing and, loaded to the seams, operated with no reported troubles. Their arrival in Monterey was chronicled by the *Herald*'s humorist:

> The train stopped; the whistle said "pough!" while from beneath innumerable handkerchiefs went up a universal response of "pough!" Joe

Watson, chancing to draw a full breath through his big horn, was knocked insensible. Things were coming to an alarming crisis when the President of the railroad, with his accustomed promptness, mounted a box car and in a graceful little speech informed the Salinas foreigners that it was nothing but a whale the Company had secured for the occasion. "Its breath is rather loud," he said, "but that is only because it had garlic for breakfast."

Downwind of the local whale rendering plant, the celebrants soon entertained themselves with the sights, sounds, and (it would appear) smells of the small coastal harbor. Furloughed workmen mingled with the excursionists, and the crowds strolled the wharf, inspected the wheat aboard the *Richardson*, and in the evening, tripped the light fantastic in the warehouse to the melodies of the Castroville Brass Band. Joe Watson, we assume, had recovered consciousness and was back on the big horn.

The dance in the grain warehouse, literally on top of the valley's cornucopia of wheat, would have been a triumph for the Granger movement except for the dark irony of the failure of Morgan and Sons. Two weeks earlier, on Halloween, the *Herald* announced that the contents of the Monterey warehouse had been bought by Isaac Friedlander.[83] The Grain King wasted no time after Morgan and Sons announced bankruptcy, buying the *H. L. Richardson*'s contract before the ship set sail from Monterey. The Salinas Valley Grange movement was now forced to do business within the cartel it had struggled to escape.

In late October, Latham's London and San Francisco Bank foreclosed on Morgan and Sons for $165,000, reportedly just half of what the broker owed them. The sizable loss of capital reserves provoked demands for the resignation of Milton Latham, embarrassing the financier at the moment he was struggling to open the North Pacific Coast to Tomales (a narrative that continues in Chapter Five).[84]

There were even darker ironies, recalling Frank Norris's discourse on human character in *The Octopus*. A receipt for 16,169 sacks of wheat, issued by Friedlander, was found among the David Jacks papers at the Huntington Library. Dated November 18, 1874, the receipt was evidence that much of Jacks's own personal crop had been consigned to the Friedlander ship *Eldorado*, loaded out of San Francisco during the first full month the Monterey & Salinas Valley Railroad operated in commercial service.

The total shipping charges to Jacks ($19,303.36) included $5,120 for rail shipment of the wheat from Salinas to San Francisco by the Southern Pacific Railroad—a transgression against the Grangers and the narrow gauge that would more than justify Jacks's fear of arson in the old Pacific Hotel.[85]

The sweet spot in the Salinas River turned into a "bloody chasm" that January when storms nearly filled the thousand-foot-wide riverbed with dark

Walking the original M&SV grade on the site of Bardin's Ranch, now within the City of Marina; distant line of trees marks the course of the Salinas River. [Bruce MacGregor]

brown water and then took out four hundred feet of trestle, cutting the narrow gauge in two. It took two months to replace the span with even temporary timbers. To his credit, Jacks bought new timber to help repair the bridge, the amount being listed in his cash books as $37.50, accounting for the purchase of fifteen new piles.[86]

Each winter for the next three years, the bridge would wash out. The Monterey & Salinas Valley's track boss grew so familiar with the habits of the raging Salinas River that he knew exactly where to pick up bridge timbers that washed downstream to the sandbars at Moss Landing, loading them up to put them back into the recycled structure when the water subsided.

During the long, dreary winter months when the bridge was out, Reuben "Reub" Morey leased the two Carter pump cars, placed one on each side of the bloody chasm, and, with a rowboat to make the dangerous ferry connection across the Salinas River, ran daily rail service for fish, mail, and Montereyans brave enough, or desperate enough, to travel to Salinas by "Morey's Express."[87]

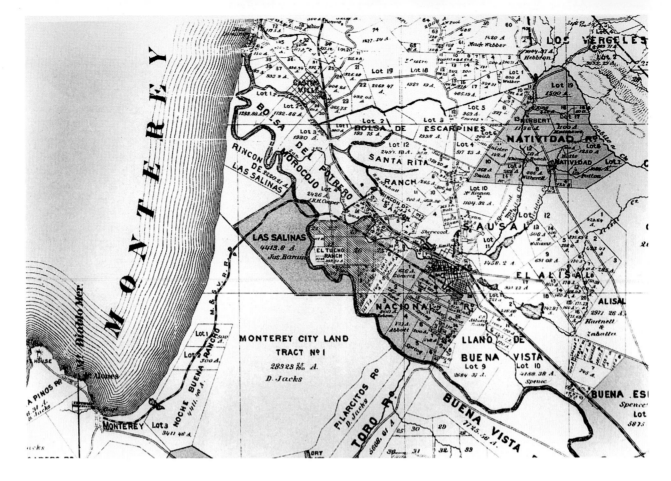

The Birth of California Narrow Gauge

Only three photographic images are known to show the Monterey & Salinas Valley during its brief lifetime (1874–1879). All three images come from the stereopticon camera of Charles Wallace Jacob Johnson, a Watsonville commercial photographer during much of the period of the M&SV's existence. Two are reproduced as a panorama below, photographed sometime before July 1875 (the month the railroad's passenger depot was built, missing from the image on the left). Taken from the roof of the railroad's grain warehouse looking south, the combined view shows the original car shop at the far left, first occupied by Carter Brothers in June 1874. Following the Monterey landscape toward the beach on the right, we see a cow grazing on the abandoned southern leg of a wye. Above the cow, across an expanse of open estuary and beach, is the Pacific Hotel, the possible site of a Carter carpentry shop; at the extreme right, tracks converge on the M&SV pier. [Below, Pat Hathaway collection; opposite, above, Monterey City Library]

Battle Mountain Station, Nevada

Details of Carter's early M&SV equipment can be gleaned from views of the Nevada Central Railroad—for example, the cabinet card of a mixed train at Battle Mountain (above), including a Carter boxcar, a combine, and the locomotive *Sonoma* from the North Pacific Coast. The image can be dated prior to April 1880, which is when the Central Pacific freight house (shown in the background) burned to the ground. The Nevada Central used ex-M&SV flatcars for cordwood service out of Austin (right). [Above, Guy Dunscomb collection; right, De-Golyer Library, Southern Methodist University]

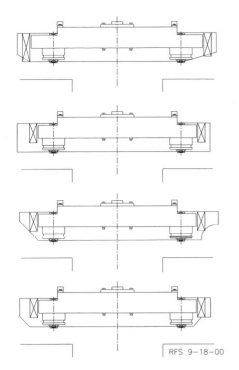

RFS 9-18-00

VARIOUS CONFIGURATIONS TO TRANSOM BEAM ENDS

DRAWN BY: ROBERT F. SCHLECHTER
Copyright 2000 Robert F. Schlechter "All Rights Reserved"

NOTES:

TRUCK BOLSTER WILL VARY IN HEIGHT ACCORDING
TO BODY BOLSTER ON CAR, WHEEL DIAMETER AND
COUPLER HEIGHT REQUIREMENT.

LENGTHS OF TRANSOM BEAMS AND SPACER BLOCK
LOCATIONS AND SIZES WILL VARY ACCORDING TO
THE VARIOUS PROTOTYPES.

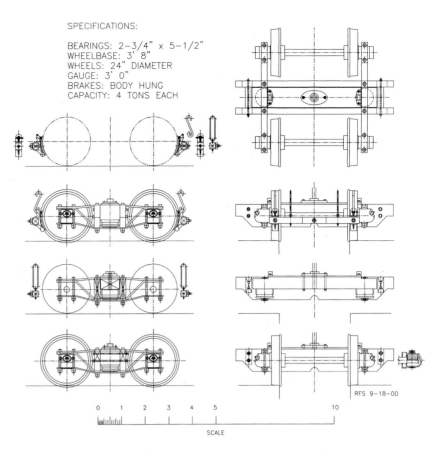

SPECIFICATIONS:

BEARINGS: 2-3/4" x 5-1/2"
WHEELBASE: 3' 8"
WHEELS: 24" DIAMETER
GAUGE: 3' 0"
BRAKES: BODY HUNG
CAPACITY: 4 TONS EACH

RFS 9-18-00

0 1 2 3 4 5   10
SCALE

DRAWN BY: ROBERT F. SCHLECHTER   Copyright 2000 Robert F. Schlechter "All Rights Reserved"

CARTER BROS., 8 TON FREIGHT TRUCK, ca 1874
Body Hung Brake Version

This page and overleaf: reconstructed twenty-four-foot Carter boxcar of the Monterey & Salinas Valley, as built and with variations on truck details (above) as the cars were modified in service. [All, Robert Schlechter]

CARTER BROS., 8 TON BOX CAR
ca 1874
MONTEREY & SALINAS VALLEY RAILROAD, No. 4

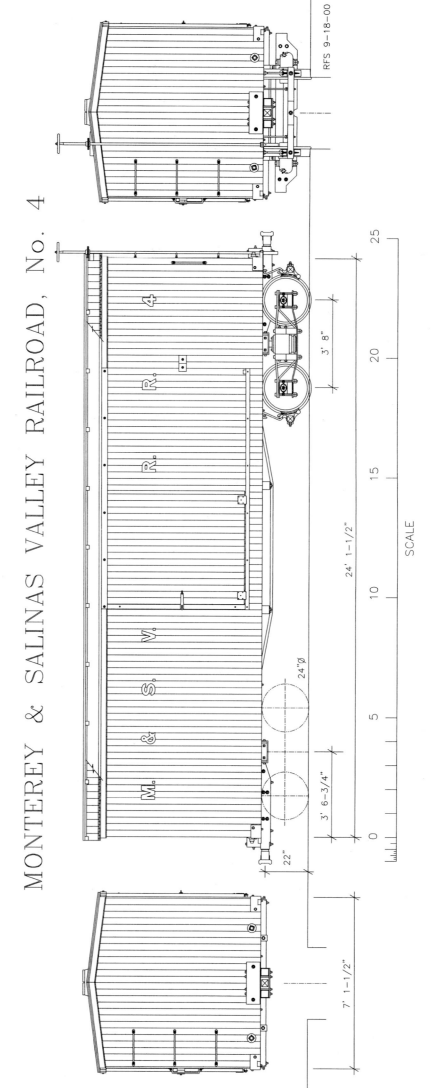

RFS 9-18-00

SCALE

0   5   10   15   20   25

24' 1-1/2"

3' 8"

3' 6-3/4"

24"ø

22"

7' 1-1/2"

4 · R. R.   V. S. & M.

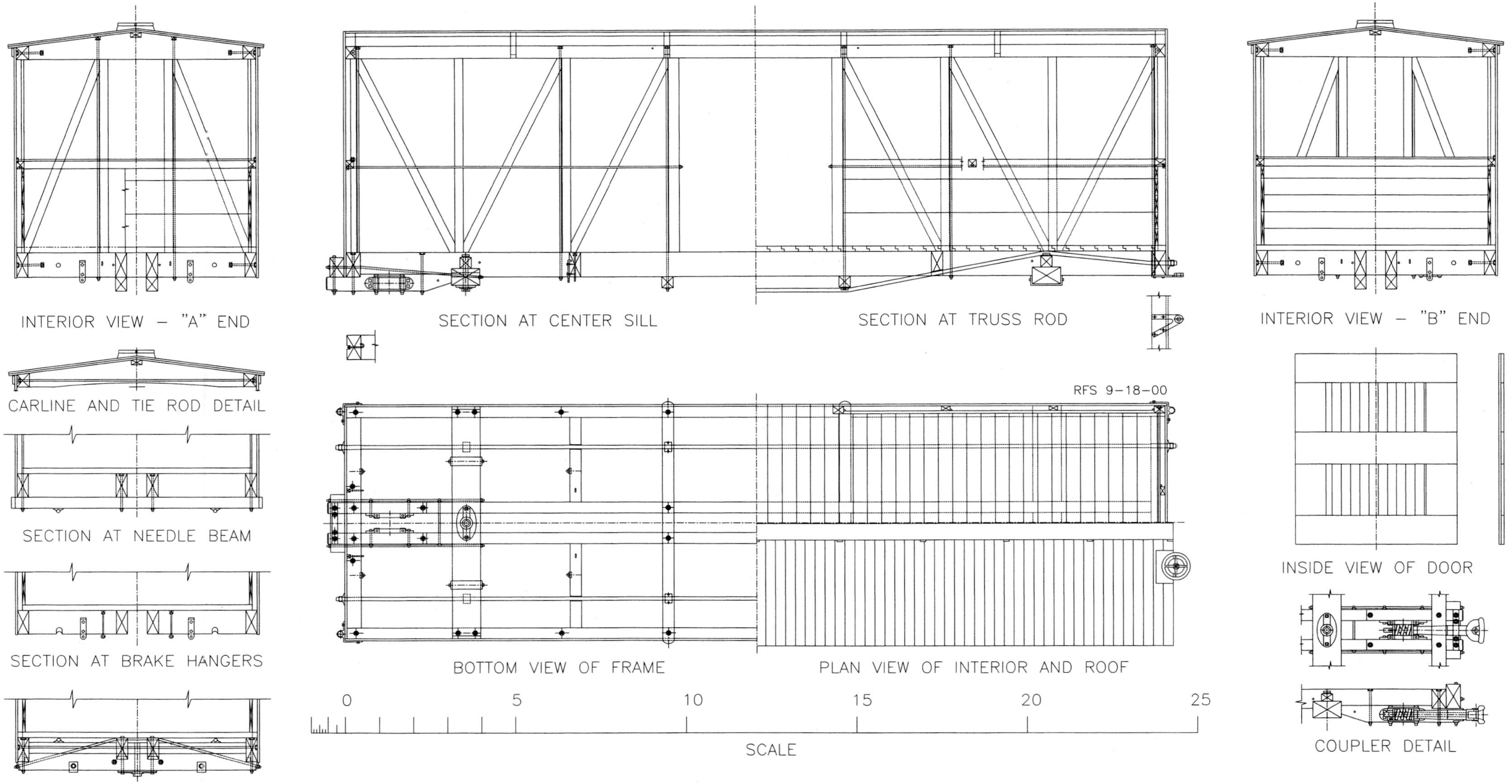

INTERIOR VIEW – "B" END

INSIDE VIEW OF DOOR

COUPLER DETAIL

SHEET 2 of 2

SECTION AT TRUSS ROD

RFS 9-18-00

SECTION AT CENTER SILL

PLAN VIEW OF INTERIOR AND ROOF

BOTTOM VIEW OF FRAME

SCALE

25   20   15   10   5   0

DRAWN BY: ROBERT F. SCHLECHTER   Copyright 2000 Robert F. Schlechter "All Rights Reserved"

INTERIOR VIEW – "A" END

CARLINE AND TIE ROD DETAIL

SECTION AT NEEDLE BEAM

SECTION AT BRAKE HANGERS

SECTION AT BODY BOLSTER

Photographs taken on the Nevada Central after the turn of the century reflect a rebuilding of the original M&SV Carter combines in 1897 (right), including cast replacement truck pedestals (middle); photographs taken in the late 1880s (such as the 1887 excursion below, taken at Ledlie by James Crockwell) show the combines with U-shaped pedestal trucks, thought to be the 1874 originals. [Above, Guy Dunscomb collection; below, John Schmale collection]

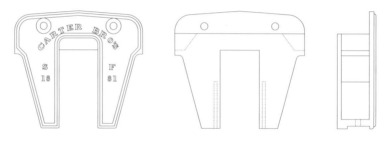

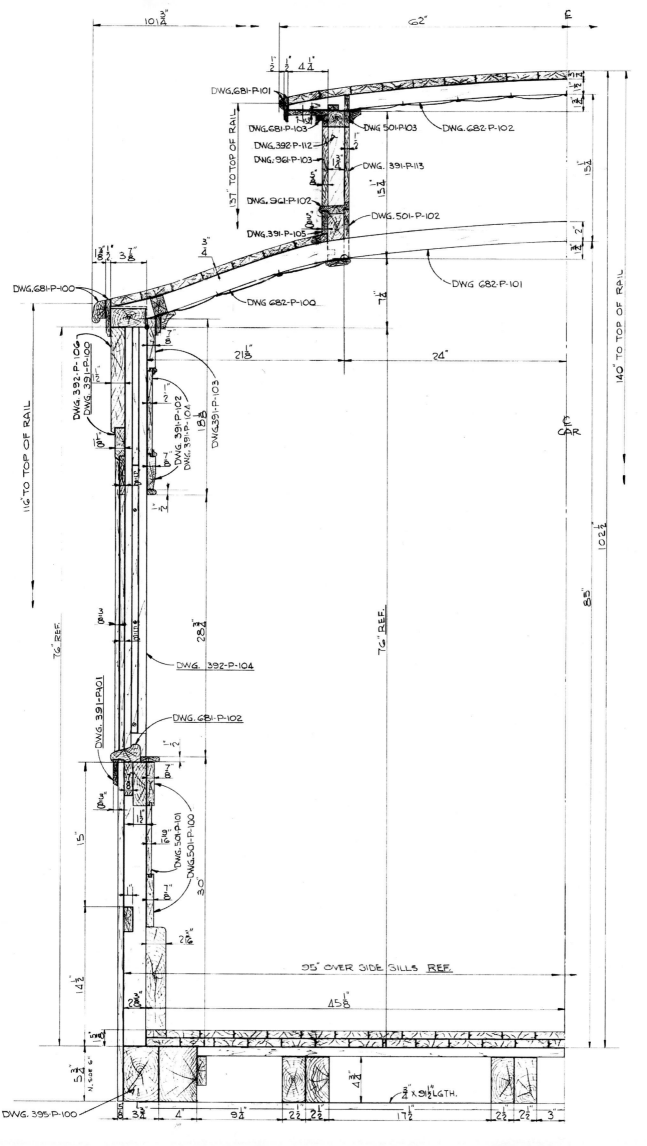

On this page, a section drawing made just before the 1977 CSRM restoration shows several of the M&SV combine's hidden flaws, including sistered sills and deep gain cuts in the wall posts. Overleaf: Michael Collins has drawn the combine as it probably appeared in 1874, in a seventeen-seat configuration, at the time of its construction. [This page, California State Railroad Museum]

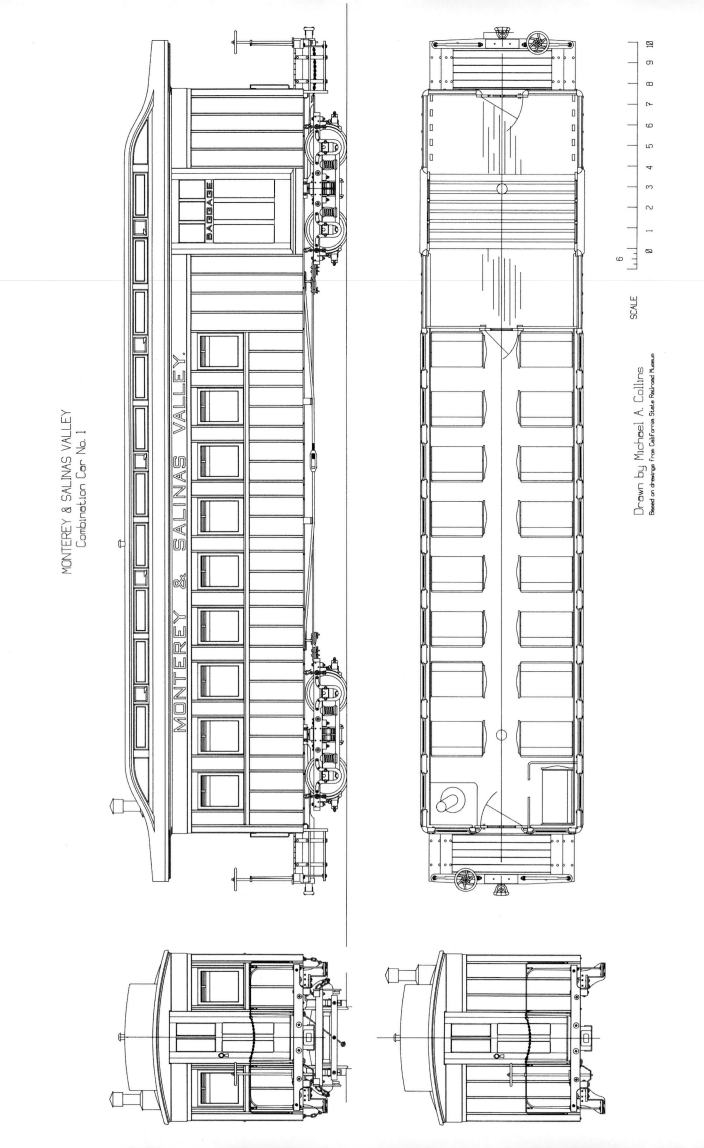

MONTEREY & SALINAS VALLEY
Combination Car No. 1

BAGGAGE.

MONTEREY & SALINAS VALLEY.

Drawn by Michael A. Collins
Based on drawings from California State Railroad Museum

SCALE

0 1 2 3 4 5 6 7 8 9 10

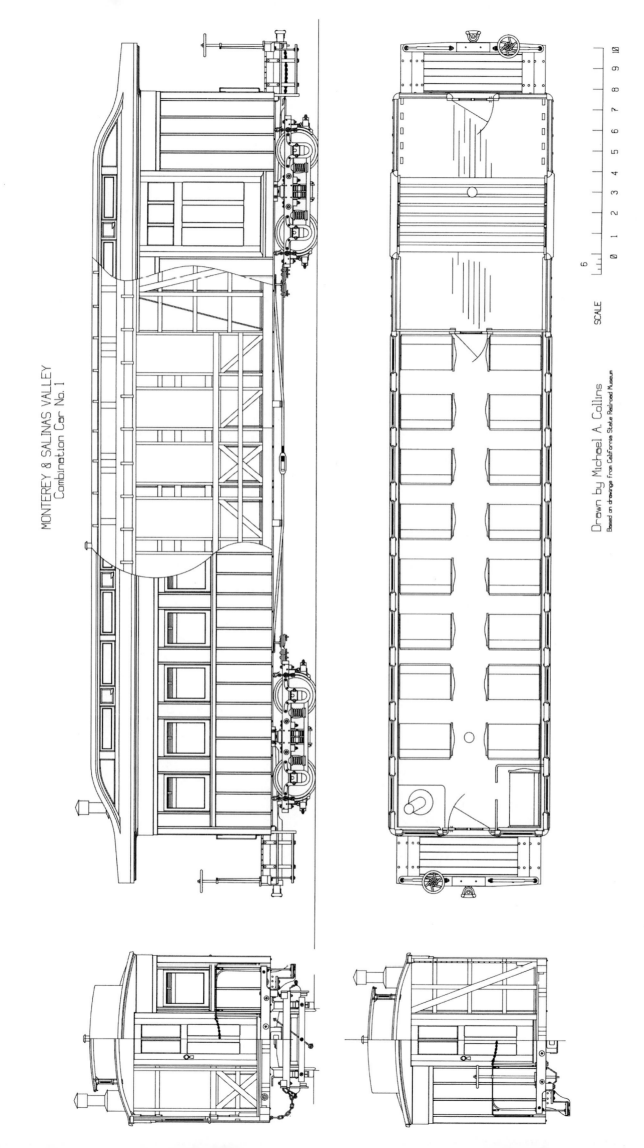

MONTEREY & SALINAS VALLEY
Combination Car No. 1

Drawn by Michael A. Collins
Based on drawings from California State Railroad Museum

SCALE

0 1 2 3 4 5 6 7 8 9 10

The Birth of California Narrow Gauge

An artist named Leon Trousett captured
the M&SV on November 1, 1875, in a remarkably detailed landscape of Monterey (above)
that shows the original narrow gauge roundhouse, warehouse, and pier; a Carleton Watkins panorama (below) shows much the same
landscape as it appeared ten years later, after
the M&SV was purchased by Southern Pacific
and standard-gauged. Artifacts of the narrow
gauge remained in the later view, such as
the small freight and passenger depots constructed by the narrow gauge. The small passenger annex was constructed in July 1875,
nine months after the narrow gauge opened.
[Above, Amon Carter Museum; below, Pat
Hathaway photo collection, Monterey]

The Birth of California Narrow Gauge

In the 1890s, California expatriates (opposite, above) were still in fine repair on the Nevada Central, including the North Pacific Coast's locomotive number 12, *Sonoma,* and cars from the Monterey & Salinas Valley. By the time of William Darrough's walk through the Battle Mountain yards in 1938 (opposite, below and above), the Nevada Central had become a museum of narrow gauge rolling stock from the 1870s and 1880s, most of it on the verge of being scrapped. Carter boxcar 253 was an exception, now preserved at Ardenwood Park in Fremont, California. [Opposite, above, Guy Dunscomb collection; opposite, below and above, William Darrough photographs, Jack Darrough collection; left, Bruce MacGregor]

The Birth of California Narrow Gauge

By the late 1880s (in the panorama above), the old cannon at the
Monterey Presidio was slumping into the earth, and signs of the short-lived
M&SV, like the few remaining pilings from its pier (visible above the cannon
barrel) were fast disappearing in the bay beyond. Faintly visible in the left
background is the Del Monte Hotel bathhouse (shown in detail at top left),
a symbol of the emerging presence of the Southern Pacific. By 1938, the remains of the last surviving M&SV locomotive, the Baldwin *Monterey*, were
rusting in Battle Mountain, Nevada (opposite, below). Western railroad
historian Gilbert Kneiss (shown at the right with the Nevada Central's last
manager John Hiskey) would be instrumental in saving one of the small
Carter combination cars still on the property. The hulk of the *Monterey*,
however, was scrapped the same year the photograph was taken. [Above,
Monterey City Library; opposite, above, Bill Wissel collection; opposite,
below, Guy Dunscomb collection]

North Pacific Coast number 9, the *Milton Latham*, photographed at Elim Grove near Cazadero
in the late 1880s. The locomotive still carries its stainless steel boiler jacket and dome casings,
extra-order appointments at the time the engine was delivered in 1875. [Jack Farley collection]

Saucelito Scale-Up

When the Monterey work ended in November 1874, Carter's base of operation remained in Saucelito, where he was roughly half finished with the North Pacific Coast contract. Winter had started. Construction activity on other narrow gauge lines in the state, some in the planning stages, some barely started, slowed to the tempo of the weather.

Tom Carter continued to live in San Francisco, probably at 19 Powell Street, his residence listing in the 1873 city directory. Settling into the Easterby Street homestead with Mary, Martin ran the day-to-day activity at Saucelito. The November payment for the Monterey work may have helped Martin's family move from Sacramento, as well as supplement the meager cash flow from the North Pacific Coast work. Carter's take-away from the M&SV contract was close to $5,000, a fortune for a man who made $1,000 a year when he worked as a shop foreman in Folsom in 1863.

Approaching the lowest ebb of the national recession, Christmas 1874 was a season of blessings for the Carters.

Blessings came to the struggling North Pacific Coast. On December 17, the *Marin County Journal* reported that the Hon. Milton S. Latham had ordered a luxury narrow gauge passenger car for his personal use. Its rumored price, $5,000, must have seemed immodest. No builder was named, but in October 1875, cash book number two recorded a single payment of $7,309.94 to the Kimball Co., more than double the cost of an ordinary coach. This was just one month after the first known newspaper account describing the arrival of what the paper called the "Director's Car."[1]

The evidence in the cash book may be misleading. Car account line items seldom mentioned which cars were being paid for, and the October 1875 line item is no exception. With eight other Kimball cars already on the NPC's roster by that date, and four additional cars nearing delivery, Kimball maintained a large outstanding balance in the cash books. But Kimball and Carter are the only car accounts in the cash books at this time, and Carter's work was restricted to freight equipment, which removes it as a candidate. Railroad records made almost forty years later finally yielded written evidence that the Director's Car was built by Kimball (see Field Notebook: Reversal of Fortune—Tracking the M.S.L.).

The earliest known photo of the M.S.L., Milton Latham's private car bearing his initials in place of a name or number, is the view below, taken at Mill Valley sometime in the 1890s after the car had been renamed *Millwood*. This photograph, and the oblique view above taken at Point Reyes Station about 1903, show the car's solarium-style end platform, offset end door, and cabinet-finish exterior paneling. Believed to have been built by Kimball, the car went into service on the North Pacific Coast in 1875. [Below, Ted Wurm collection; right, John Schmale collection]

Thought to be Kimball's last luxury railroad car, the Director's Car brought ostentation to the dog-poor North Pacific Coast. The earliest known mention of the delivered car dates to the September 16, 1875, *Marin County Journal*, and coincided with its earliest listing in a Saucelito shop record book, on September 30:

> The Director's car was in town last week, drawn by the new engine, No 9. Both the engine and car bear the letters "M.S.L." in monogram, without other name. The car is superbly finished, and is partitioned into four divisions. The first is a complete culinary department, supplied with every essential for setting forth a feast, and so arranged that by a turn of the wrist it can be thrown into four rooms, with a card table for each, where men of long purses may "pass the edge" or "go it blind." Next is the sleeping room, which is flanked by a princely reception salon, and in the rear end, an open observatory where, if you sit to windward of Mr. Euphrosyne, you can send the wreaths from your Gilroy up into the tall trees, while both enjoy the gorgeous and varied scenery afforded by the route. The car is finished in rare woods, paneled, and inlaid, damask curtains, and carpeted throughout, has two plush sofas, and several easy chairs, of various patterns. It is fifty feet long, being fourteen feet longer than the cars in use on the line. Mr. Campbell went up to Tomales on it Tuesday.

Compared to the Kimball day coaches already on the property, the Director's Car was a yacht. It measured 25 percent longer than the standard issue coach. It weighed nearly 20 percent more, rolled on six-foot-wheelbase trucks instead of the standard issue five-foot, and employed twenty-six-inch wheels instead of twenty-four-inch. When the car first appeared in the Saucelito shops, it dwarfed every other car in the yard. It came with its own wiper, a concessionaire named F. W. Smith, who cleaned and serviced the car between Latham's excursions.[2]

For Kimball, the Director's Car proclaimed entitlement to an emerging narrow gauge market Kimball thought it would easily dominate.

The locomotive mentioned by the *Journal* was the aesthetic sequel of the car it pulled. A standard Baldwin 4-4-0, class 8-18 C, the engine was special-ordered with a solid mahogany cab, and dome casings, bell, and trim fabricated in solid German silver, the predecessor alloy of modern nickel silver. Locomotive and Director's Car bore the matching monograms M.S.L., for Milton Slocum Latham. The monogram was affixed to the locomotive's cab on a round German silver frame. Baldwin sold the engine to the North Pacific Coast for $7,375, although for the fancy detail work (identified as "C5" in its catalogue of finishes) it charged an additional $523.96. Baldwin records document its first trial steam-up in Philadelphia on June 28, 1875.[3]

Latham was quickly becoming Moore and Tillinghast's not-so-silent partner. His money didn't just talk, it filibustered. Latham loaded canvases from his personal art collection, his Chinese cook Wan Sin, a four-poster bed, and a red marble commode aboard the M.S.L. and began to take over management of the North Pacific Coast.[4]

At the new year, when the North Pacific Coast finally opened its first fifty-two miles of mainline from Saucelito to Tomales, it looked like *his* achieve-

---

The Field Notebook: Reversal of Fortune — Tracking the *M.S.L.*

Much of what we know about the "Director's Car," named the M.S.L. after Milton Slocum Latham, comes from a bookkeeping error made by the Northwestern Pacific Railroad sometime between 1910 and 1919. In the official 1910 rolling stock inventory, the Director's Car is numbered 02 and is noted as built in 1874, with the builder unnamed. But by the 1919 inventory, the car became confused with a smaller, newer business car numbered 01. The two cars were in effect swapped at birth by the bookkeeping error: 01 is listed as built in 1874 and the 02 is listed as being built in 1892 (subsequent records identified the 1892 car as a Pullman product).

Although photographs clearly identified the 02 as the larger car, easily correlated to the extreme fifty-foot length of the M.S.L., the error was repeated through much of the modern literature on the North Pacific Coast, including Fred Stindt's *The Northwestern Pacific Railroad* (1964), in effect labeling the Director's Car as Pullman-built 01.

A 1916 ICC Valuation Report repeated the error but added a critical missing piece: 01 was listed as being built in 1874 and the 02 in 1892. But this time the records listed a builder for both cars: Pullman for the 02, and Kimball for the 01. If the original error was simply reversed by reversing the construction dates — and the names of the builders — the ICC report becomes the first and only written evidence of the Kimball parentage of the Director's Car.

ment, even though it wasn't. Latham had accomplished an overnight public relations victory for the struggling Moore. No longer known as the railroad that didn't know how to get out of Marin County, newspapers now talked proudly of the NPC dominating the entire coastal timber market, blasting through Sonoma County, north through Mendocino and Humboldt counties, and on to the Oregon border. From Freestone to Humboldt County and beyond stretched an unbroken timber belt, ten miles wide and almost two hundred miles long, through which the narrow gauge would pass.[5]

On January 7, 1875, two locomotives hauled six yellow coaches and two baggage cars up the pitching curves on White's Hill and along the shore of Tomales Bay, formally opening the southern half of the railroad as far as the village of Tomales. "Tomales Jubilates and Does the Handsome," the *Marin County Journal* trumpeted on January 14. Warren Dutton, the NPC's board member from Tomales, threw open the doors of the great railroad warehouse to the three hundred guests and welcomed them to a "groaning board," a savory collation of turkey, chicken, pork, lamb, and beef, and mountains of mashed Bodega spuds, steaming in thick crockery.

Speeches were also on the menu. A Mr. Peebles represented the London and San Francisco Bank, but Latham himself was not present. The directors were encouraged to paint him (and his resources) into the picture. "There is more money in this road," exaggerated John Shafter, "than has been put into any road west of the Rocky Mountains, more than in the Central Pacific or the Union Pacific . . . railroads are the greatest christianizers and civilizers in the world. Have you nothing to do but rejoice in these things?"

The guests rejoiced in more mashed potatoes and braced for the next speaker.

In back of the façade, the money *did* flow, not only from Latham's own London and San Francisco Bank but from banks at which he had arranged bond hypothecate accounts, examples being the Bank of British Columbia and the French Savings and Loan Society. These loans totaled $816,000 by April 1875.[6] By June 30, Latham had also lent the railroad personal funds totaling $248,733.20. Virtually all of the money, well over a million dollars in new liquidity, had been spent getting the tracks to the temporary terminal at Tomales.[7]

Wiped down to a lacquered shine, Latham's private car soon became the mirror of the railroad's new public image, perhaps both slightly out of place among the dairy herds of Marin County. The *M.S.L.* appeared on sidings of Olema Station and Tomales, the sole charge of the garish and equally wiped Baldwin locomotive of the same name. Together, they looked like a pair of monogrammed cufflinks. Moore, Tillinghast, and Latham could be glimpsed smoking cigars in the Director's Car's lounge, speculating about what the daily car loadings of lumber would tally once the narrow gauge reached Dutch Bill.

Moore soon learned to let Latham do the talking. Even though Moore still retained the authority of day-to-day management, at the annual stockholder's meeting of February 1876 the roles of the principals were switched. Moore became director-at-large, and Latham was the North Pacific Coast's president.

Beginning on New Year's Day 1875, the ledgers and cash books chronicled the second and climactic phase of the North Pacific Coast's construction. It was marked by increasingly subordinate roles for Moore, Dutton, and Howard Schuyler, and the increasing influence of officers handpicked by Milton Latham, among them John Wade, the new chief engineer, and Joseph Campbell, the line's new general superintendent.

In spite of his reputation, Schuyler accomplished neither of the two major engineering features on the railroad. George Black had laid out the White's Hill grade back in 1872. Sometime in the summer of 1875, Schuyler's replacement, Wade, located the big loop and high bridges that would be required to top the divide above Salmon Creek, giving the railroad access to the timber on the watershed of the Russian River, without which the enormous investment made no sense at all. The date of Schuyler's official separation remains unknown, but Wade was serving as chief engineer as early as August 5, 1875, when the *Marin County Journal* reported him at work on the "Northern Extension." By that time, Wade had been running experimental lines in the Dutch Bill country for the preceding thirty-one months.[8] By December 1875, at least two alternative routes had been confirmed over the Dutch Bill divide. Latham, returning from a trip east, would make the final decision about which route to adopt. Wade (not Schuyler) pared Latham's choice down to its lowest common denominator: money. Between July 1875 and April 1877, the railroad would spend $553,628 on grade, track, and bridges required to span just twenty-three miles between Tomales and Moscow—a cost of more than $24,000 per mile of completed track.[9]

The enormous expenditure counted no money for new rolling stock. Until rails reached the mill sites along Dutch Bill Creek (which would not happen until November 1876), additional flatcars were not required for revenue service. The daily scheduled passenger train from Saucelito to Tomales served a region with so little population that additional coaches, above and beyond the original six provided by Kimball, weren't added until November 1875, when Kimball delivered its last four coaches to the roster.[10]

At the date of the line's opening to Tomales, Carter had finished seventy-five of the required freight cars. But under the conditions of the contract, he had not been paid for them. Carter was obligated to finish another fifty cars to complete the contract before settlement would begin on the "new car account."[11] Compared to the heady pace of production set in the summer of 1874, the work was unhurried. It may not have been until May 10, 1875, the date of the first payment to Carter, that the last cars were delivered. If so, Carter's rate of production averaged about one completed car every two working days, half speed compared to the performance on the Monterey job the previous August. From the railroad's perspective, there was no need to work faster. Many of the new cars sat on sidings at the Saucelito shops, unused until the Russian River lumber traffic began more than a year later.

After the pressures of the summer of 1874, Tom Carter struggled with doldrums. He struggled with cash flow. He struggled with keeping his core craftsmen together. He struggled to find outside work (no record exists of any until June 1875, when the Santa Cruz & Felton Railroad ordered flatcars).[12] In the first six months of 1875, Carter resorted to contract shop work, paid under North Pacific Coast account 269, to keep the business alive.

In that time period, the North Pacific Coast cash books record an assortment of odd jobs Carter and his men undertook, none directly related to new car construction and none for a large sum of money. Examples include station repair ($2.09 on July 31), repair of roadbed and track ($2.10 on July 31), repair of passenger cars ($25.90 on July 31), repair of freight cars ($30.87 on July 31), repair of locomotives ($63.00 on July 31), repairs to shop machinery and tools ($141.75 on December 31), and repairs to the car float *Transfer* ($2.10 on July 31). On April 17, $409.97 was credited to Carter's new car account for converting flatcars to picnic cars.

Throughout this period, the North Pacific Coast actively maintained (and charged work to) its own car shop, as well as a number of independent contractors engaged in carpentry, painting, and car work. One of the NPC's shop foremen in particular may have been responsible for funneling work to Carter. Henry Foy, chief carpenter on the M&SV and now chief carpenter for the NPC, extended a three-fingered hand when he greeted Carter at Saucelito sometime in December 1874. They could share a drink after work and compare scars from the previous jobs they had worked.

Bad luck continued to follow Foy. On April 5, 1875, he suffered internal injuries when a coach he was riding in, swaying badly in a high wind, was blown off the rails near Collins Summit. Recuperating, Foy needed Carter to run woodworking projects, including the repair of the rolling stock damaged in the same wreck that injured him.[13] The names that the cash book subsequently records as direct labor to the railroad are those of Carter's best men: John Carroll earned $41.00 from the NPC in April, then $152.83 as "unclaimed wages" on May 19; Carroll's son Frank (now old enough to apprentice) received $53.73 on the same date; Martin Carter earned $5.75 under one account on June 14, and $2.62 under another account on the same date; Frank Carroll earned $42.52 on June 19.

The small and irregular payments suggest that even for Tom Carter's most valuable craftsmen no steady contract work existed during the first six months of 1875. Instead, Carroll, Martin Carter, and others were farmed out to the railroad, given piecework on general carpentry and repair jobs as the Tomales division gradually reached operating trim. In the interim, between jobs, Martin may have moonlighted for Langland and Cameron; Carroll might have worked part time for the Southern Pacific car shop in San Francisco. Thomas beat the bushes for any work that would justify bringing his small family of craftsmen back together.

What is clear from the cash books is that the piecework was largely confined to the first half of 1875, coinciding with the winter months when railroad construction and demand for rolling stock were held at bay by the weather. The lean period comes to an end that summer with the arrival of the first Carter contract work for the Santa Cruz & Felton. Additional outside work would follow, and Tom Carter was lucky to have found a way to keep the core of his original crew together during the protracted dry spell. For its part, the North Pacific Coast got a ready source of skilled labor, retained on a stand-by basis, much like temp labor pools today.

In return, Tom Carter got bits of intelligence on the railroad's procurement plans, and a favored position among its outside contractors. Eventually, when it finally reached Dutch Bill, the railroad would need to double its rolling stock to handle the timber traffic from the Russian River mills. At least six months prior to opening the new division, Latham would make a decision about who he wanted to build the cars. Tom Carter already had the inside track. When the time was right, the new contract should justifiably be his.

The long wait for additional contracts, meanwhile, would not have been possible without the day-rate shop work the North Pacific Coast provided. Carter Brothers ceased to be a factory and became instead a repair facility, maintaining cars that were, by the summer of 1875, already a year old.

John Carroll, by now fifty years old, must have come and gone from this scene like a migrant laborer, his dream of owning his own railroad contracting firm now circumscribed inside of Carter's struggling venture. Still, Carroll would not get so far away from the project that he couldn't come back.

What is hard to understand, given Latham's resources, given his taste for cultural display, given his obsession with control, was the North Pacific Coast's painfully long delay in pushing north into Dutch Bill.

By New Year's Day 1875, the railroad had come fifty-two miles to reach Tomales, a division that included the labyrinth of track over White's Hill. Only twenty-four miles remained to reach Moscow on the Russian River, the last ten of which would deliver the biggest sources of revenue on the railroad. Yet it would take Latham almost two years more to bridge the gap to this critical source of income.

During the winter of 1875, the cash books picture the North Pacific Coast as much like a bivouacked army, more concerned about lines of supply than advancing its position. On opening day, its track was saturated from rains and still "settling in the bed," making operation dangerous. On January 21, mud slides closed the line. On February 9, the slides had been cleared and the first trains got through. But on February 25, a cave-in at the short tunnel on White's Hill shut the line down again; it was not to reopen until the week of March 4. Two Chinese crews, one under a contractor named Ah Yung, the other under Ah Yan, worked through the winter to terrace the cuts, fill in the sags, and clean up an unending barrage of rock slides.

But even with the coming of good weather, little activity took place north of the unfinished Tomales tunnel. The tunnel itself was frequently worked from a single heading, the company apparently in no great haste to open it. The longest tunnel on the railroad, it would not be holed through until May 1876.

As a field general, Latham appeared indecisive. On March 26, 1875, the *Marin County Journal* announced the resumption of work on the Northern Extension. It appeared to be a false start. Latham became seriously ill that April, and another three months passed before the press announced again, on July 15, the resumption of work on the north end. Just two months later, on September 16 — far too early for winter — the *Journal* announced

North Pacific Coast right-of-way north of Tomales, near Clark Summit. [Don Marenzi collection]

North Pacific Coast passenger train, photographed at speed, north of Camp Meeker. [Collection of George F. Ward, D.D.S., from Harold A. Lapham]

the suspension of work, with the exception of excavation in the Tomales tunnel. No reason was given.

According to the *Journal*, John Wade didn't begin detailed location work on the most difficult parts of the Northern Extension until August 1875. Cuts got deeper and longer, like the Clark Summit cut, a gash twenty-seven feet deep and a thousand feet long through rolling pastureland near Fallon.[14] Bridges got more numerous. The Tomales tunnel—1,706 feet in length—would have to be breached before any of the Northern Extension sites could be reached with rail.[15]

North of Freestone, the broad dales of the Marin uplands began to narrow down into the wooded, shadowy bottleneck of Salmon Creek Canyon, a transition to the steep flank of the Dutch Bill divide. Just above the headwaters of Salmon Creek, Wade would face a hillside so steep that a horseshoe loop had to be constructed to gain enough altitude to crest the ridge above. The extreme grade took the railroad so far above the bed of Brown's Creek that just a mile before reaching the top a 137-foot-high truss bridge would leap the chasm to reach the summit at the hamlet known variously

Descending the Salmon Creek watershed, on Horseshoe Bend, ca. 1890. [Collection of Ruby Todd Mann, from Harold A. Lapham]

as Dutch Bill's, Howard's, or Occidental. In the winter of 1875–76, when contractor Martin and Wood erected the Brown's Canyon structure, it was the highest bridge on the Pacific Coast.

On the other side of the divide, Wade had to ease the mainline down another 121 feet to the mile grade in Dutch Bill Creek Canyon, then through the solid rock Tyrone tunnel to reach the mill sites.

Compared to the fifty-two-mile Tomales division, the engineering challenges of the Northern Extension—less than half as long—were considerably more numerous. There were three tunnels on the south end, totaling 1,718 feet. There were two tunnels on the Northern Extension, totaling 2,133 feet. Howe truss bridges stood in greatest contrast: there were five on the south, spanning 530 feet; but thirteen on the north, spanning 2,112 feet —nearly half a mile.[16] Wade clearly had his work cut out for him.

At the same time, the railroad's engineering standards got more stringent. Severe twenty-four-degree curves, used to navigate White's Hill, were prohibited north of Tomales; rail weight increased from thirty-five to fifty-five pounds per yard, and the newfangled "anglebar joint" was adopted, replac-

The earliest known photo of the Brown's Canyon Bridge (above) may date from the end of its construction in November 1876. Falsework is still in place under the massive Howe truss spans as a three-car passenger train crosses the chasm to reach Occidental. By the time of the photograph, the older Kimball coaches (middle car) have been upstaged by newer Barney and Smith cars, recognizable by more modern bullnose roof ends. The photograph is thought to have been taken by Muybridge, who was retained by the railroad to photograph its new right-of-way. His photographs were then converted to line drawings for the July 1877 edition of *Resources of California*. Ironically, the line drawing of the Brown's Canyon view never appeared in the magazine. [Mike Meyer collection, from Harold A. Lapham].

ing flat-bar joints, which were notorious for "crimping" on curves.[17] The new standards would toughen the railroad's physical plant for the lumber traffic soon to well up from Dutch Bill Canyon. When this work was finally complete, Wade would double back on the Tomales division, and bring its plant up to the new standard.[18] New plant standards would only accelerate the rate of Latham's spending, eating into strained cash reserves.

More cash was diverted into increasing Latham's control of the railroad's revenue targets. On September 2, 1875, the *Marin County Journal* announced the organization of the Russian River Land and Lumber Co., a new partnership among Latham, Moore, and Tillinghast. In a sense, Latham was able to use Austin Moore's original investment as a security deposit on his own long-term investment strategy. Moore first risked buying the timber land without the railroad to work it, but Latham bought a majority interest in the timber after the railroad was within striking distance. Then, and only then, did Latham invest in the timber, buying a substantial piece of Moore's original sixteen thousand acre holding.[19] With Moore's tract as a beachhead, Latham continued the strategy. On April 9, 1877, Latham was one of the original incorporators of the Sonoma Lumber Co., adding what would

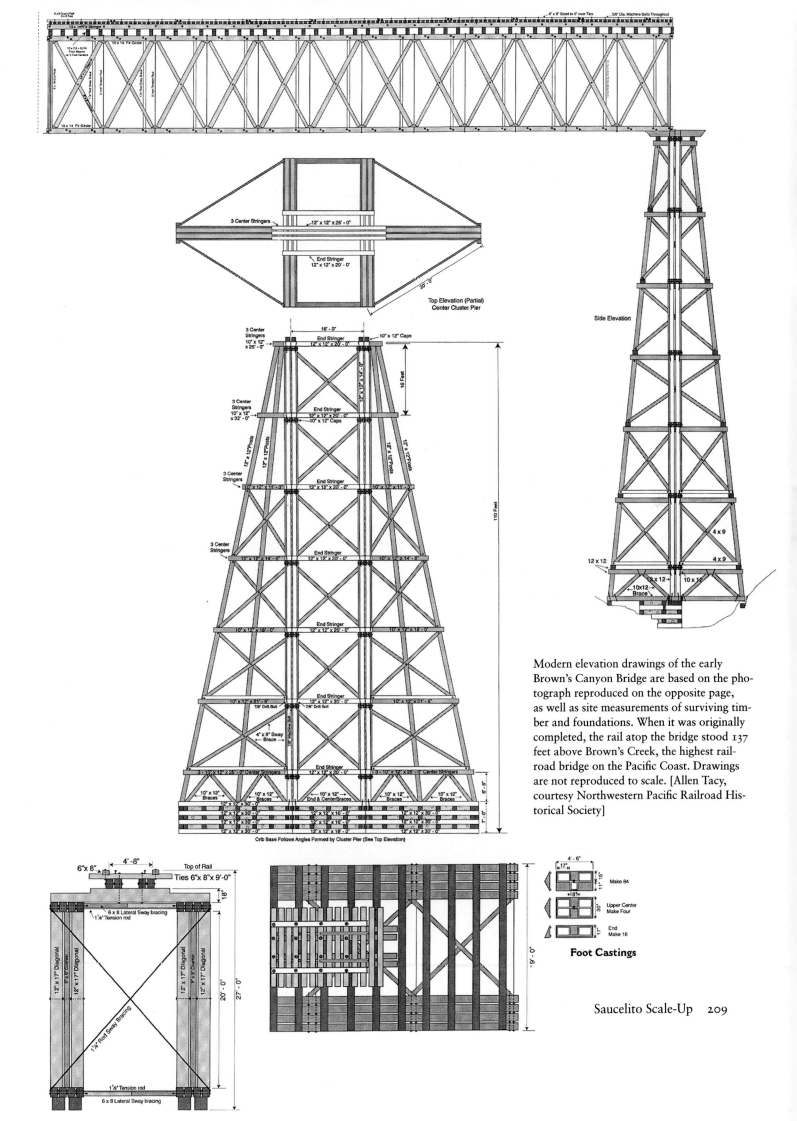

6 x 8 Guard Rail
6 x 8 Ties

8" x 8" Sized to 5" over Ties
5/8" Dia. Machine Bolts Throughout

10 x 14 Fir Stringer

10 x 14 Fir Girder

12 x [12 + 6] Fir
Floor Beams
on 5 Foot Centers

10 x 14 Fir Girder

Top Elevation (Partial)
Center Cluster Pier

3 Center Stringers

12" x 12" x 26' - 0"

End Stringer
12" x 12" x 20' - 0"

30' - 0"

Side Elevation

4 x 9

4 x 9

12 x 12

12 x 12   10 x 12

10x12
Brace

3 Center
Stringers
10" x 12"
x 25' - 0"

16' - 0"

End Stringer
12" x 12" x 20' - 0"

10" x 12" Caps

16 Feet

3 Center
Stringers
10" x 12"
x 32' - 0"

End Stringer
12" x 12" x 20' - 0"
10" x 12" Caps

12" x 12" Posts

12" x 12" Posts

110 Feet

3 Center
Stringers

10" x 12" x 11' - 3"

End Stringer
12" x 12" x 20' - 0"

10" x 12" x 11' - 3"

3 Center
Stringers

10" x 12" x 14' - 6"

End Stringer
12" x 12" x 20' - 0"

10" x 12" x 14' - 6"

End Stringer
12" x 12" x 20' - 0"

10" x 12" x 18' - 0"

10" x 12" x 18' - 0"

End Stringer
12" x 12" x 20' - 0"

10" x 12" x 21' - 6"
7/8" Drift Bolt
7/8" Drift Bolt

10" x 12" x 21' - 6"

4" x 9" Sway
Brace

3 - 10" x 12" x 25' - 0" Center Stringers

End Stringer
12" x 12" x 20' - 0"

3 - 10" x 12" x 25' - 0" Center Stringers

10" x 12"
Braces

10" x 12"
Braces

10" x 12"
End & CenterBraces

10" x 12"
Braces

10" x 12"
Braces

12" x 12" x 30' - 0"
12" x 12" x 30' - 0"
12" x 12" x 30' - 0"
12" x 12" x 30' - 0"

12" x 12" x 16' - 0"

12" x 12" x 30' - 0"
12" x 12" x 30' - 0"
12" x 12" x 30' - 0"

6' - 6"

7' - 0"

Crib Base Follows Angles Formed by Cluster Pier (See Top Elevation)

Modern elevation drawings of the early
Brown's Canyon Bridge are based on the photograph reproduced on the opposite page,
as well as site measurements of surviving timber and foundations. When it was originally
completed, the rail atop the bridge stood 137
feet above Brown's Creek, the highest railroad bridge on the Pacific Coast. Drawings
are not reproduced to scale. [Allen Tacy,
courtesy Northwestern Pacific Railroad Historical Society]

6"x 8"
4' -8"

Top of Rail
Ties 6"x 8"x 9'-0"

18"

6 x 8 Lateral Sway bracing
1 1/8" Tension rod

12 x 17" Diagonal

8"x 8" Counter

12 x 17" Diagonal

1 1/8" Rod Sway Bracing

12 x 17" Diagonal

8"x 8" Counter

12 x 17" Diagonal

20' - 0"

27' - 0"

1 1/8" Tension rod
6 x 8 Lateral Sway bracing

4' - 6"
1'7"
11' 15"

81"

Make 84

Upper Center
Make Four

End
Make 16

9' - 0"

Foot Castings

Remains of center cluster pier, Brown's Canyon Bridge, 1997. [Bruce MacGregor]

[John Schmale collection]

become Streeten's Mill to his growing list of timber holdings in the Dutch Bill reserve.[20] All of these investments had the effect of increasing Latham's equity in the narrow gauge.

But until the beginning of 1877, the revenue and the means to deliver it remained disconnected. Throughout the two years required to build the Northern Extension, there were constant rumors of Latham's insolvency. In December 1874, the *San Francisco Bulletin* speculated about the damage done by the failure of E. E. Morgan and Sons, the Granger credit house that would, if it had survived, have forwarded the grain shipments of the Monterey & Salinas Valley Railroad to Liverpool. Latham's London and San Francisco Bank held a worthless $355,000 note from the bankruptcy, and the *Bulletin* predicted that Latham would take the blame for the loss by resigning his position.[21] The bank claimed a total capital asset of $3 million.[22] If the figure is accurate, then the combination of Granger loans and loans to the North Pacific Coast encumbered almost 40 percent of the bank's total capital. Somehow, Latham avoided disaster. He remained president of the London and San Francisco Bank, and the bank remained open.

But the North Pacific Coast's cash books suggested hidden cancers in the railroad's financing. By June 1875, the loans from the London and San Francisco Bank, the Bank of British Columbia, and the French Savings and Loan Society—totaling $816,666—cost the North Pacific Coast $6,806 in interest per month.[23] When Latham leased the San Rafael & San Quentin Railroad in March 1875, a six-mile standard gauge connection between the county seat and a ferry terminal at the site of the state prison, he also incurred interest payments to the SF&SQ's bond holder, bringing the total debt service to about $7,000 a month. Operating expenses during the summer of 1875 averaged $12,000 per month, bringing the railroad's cash liability to an average of $19,000 per month.[24]

The R. G. Dun credit reporters would certainly have liked to know that NPC's interest payments were not made regularly. Between January 1, 1875, and November 1, 1877, the cash books reported only a single payment of

			WEIGHT.	RATE CTS.	FREIGHT.	CHARGES.	TOTAL.
2464 ft Lumber			9851	16	15 78		15 78
							13 84
							11 35
							11 80
							11 25
							5 70

FORM 10—A. 8-75.

Mr. _____ Station, Apl 19 187 ___

To NORTH PACIFIC COAST RAILROAD COMPANY, Dr.

For Transportation from San Fran _____ Way-Bill 605 Car 165

Received Payment, _____ 187 ___ J Bosley, Agent. $69.56

interest to the three lending banks, a total of $17,916.66, covering just three months' interest. Poor's Manual reported in June 1877 that of a total of over $250,000 in accrued interest, the North Pacific Coast had paid less than $74,000. Latham may have reasoned the new revenues from the Russian River mills would make up the difference in double payments. But first, he had to get there.

Meanwhile, revenues from the Tomales division were clearly not going to offset the combination of operating expenses and monthly interest. The dairy business was a good example. In spite of Marin County's population of twenty-one thousand milk cows, not all of them were conveniently located near the NPC mainline. A small forwarding company called Bernard's Express acted as a collecting point for dairy products and rented space in the line's baggage cars to fast-forward butter, cheese, and milk to San Francisco. Bernard's Express ran daily. But its traffic totaled 383 cases of produce between March 1 and March 12, 1875, worth $191.50 to the railroad, suggesting a monthly total revenue of less than $500.

The rental of the bar and restaurant concession on the ferry *Clinton* began in January 1875; it added $100 to the monthly cash flow. The "privilege for sale of papers" began on the through train to Tomales in February and brought the railroad $10.68 for a like time period.

Samuel P. Taylor's paper mill was producing about fifty thousand pounds of newsprint per month in the fall of 1875, good for perhaps six narrow gauge boxcar loads, bound for the pressrooms of the *Alta*, the *Call*, the *Bulletin*, and the *German Democrat*.[25] As through freight, the monthly revenue was about $7.33 per car, or $44 for the lot.[26]

The canyons surrounding the paper mill represented a timber reserve of nearly twelve thousand acres, mostly hardwoods such as laurel and madrone; it was owned by John Shafter, a director of the railroad. In late 1875, the reserve was opened up with the construction of the Shafter wood spur off the main line at Lagunitas. Mr. A. Malliard added a three-mile tram to the complex in April 1876, running horse-powered twenty-inch-gauge tram cars out of the Lagunitas Creek basin to a reload point on the Shafter wood spur. By June, Malliard was supplying the state prison at San Quentin with a few carloads of firewood each month. Billed as local freight, the revenue was about $15 per car, local freight rates being considerably higher than through rates.[27]

The NPC barge *Transfer* was soon riding low in the water with flatcar loads of laurel firewood, ready to discharge at San Francisco's Green Street pier. Billed as through freight to San Francisco, the railroad's rate on cord wood was scaled down to about $7 per car.

Picnics, on the other hand, showed considerably more promise. The first picnic train to appear in the cash book was a special for the Union Guards, on April 4, 1875. Two thousand fifty-one passengers rode from Saucelito to Fairfax, booking the trip at sixty cents a head, earning the railroad a handsome $1,230. The same month, the North Pacific Coast rented the Fairfax picnic grounds, owned by William Coleman, and began booking it for groups from all over the Bay Area. That same month, Carter was completing the conversion of flatcars to picnic cars mentioned earlier.

All totaled, the railroad's income for the relatively prosperous months of

The NPC number 1, *Saucelito*, in service on the L. E. White operation at Elk Creek, ca. 1897. Printed from the original glass plate by a photographer named Carpenter, this view shows the 4-4-0 doubleheaded with the diminutive *Tie-Coon*, an 1876 Baldwin locomotive L. E. White purchased from the Mendocino Railroad. [Robert J. Lee collection]

July, August, and September 1875 was $19,305.17, $17,423.49, and $17,252.54 respectively.[28] In short, with the exception of just one single month of the three, Latham was not making back the total of operating expenses plus interest liabilities. And he had not yet hit bottom. In January 1876, revenue would sink to a low of just $11,024.77.

As 1876 drew to a close, Latham's financial quandary became clearer. To put the situation into perspective, the total cost of twenty-four miles of right-of-way for the Northern Extension was $553,627, including the cost of bridges, tunnels, and grading incurred between January 1, 1875, and April 1, 1877.[29] That amount added almost $5,000 per month to the railroad's interest payments, equivalent to one week's net cash liability from operating the entire 52 miles of track between Saucelito and Tomales.

"The question can very soon be tested," posed the *Journal* on December 7, 1876, "whether the lumber business will justify the extension of the road."

Factory Notes on a Baldwin 8-18 C.4

Between January 1874 and September 1919, the Baldwin Locomotive Works produced 104 units of a truly classic locomotive design, the 8-18 C. In Baldwin's cryptic notation, "8" stood for the total number of wheels, "18" was a code based on subtracting three from the engine's cylinder diameter and then multiplying by two, and "C" stood for four driving wheels. These sparse engineering specifications—although important to the performance and success of the class—were almost the only common characteristics of the 104 engines that left the Philadelphia factory bearing the 8-18 C classification. Variety, instead, prevailed. There were seven gauges represented in the class, fourteen driver diameters, six boiler diameters, two distinctly different types of frame (inside and outside), ten rigid wheelbases, and seventeen boiler architectures—all of which bore the 8-18 C classification and offered proof of the engine's versatility and adaptability. The purchasers definitely represented an international market, coming from Guatemala, Mexico, Brazil, Norway, Australia, Argentina, and a widely distributed customer base in the United States. Baldwin kept track of the variations in the 8-18 C by referring to separate "drawing numbers" (from one to seventeen) that packaged the variations into distinct sets of engineering specifications. Drawing four machines, for example, were popular on the West Coast, while drawing nine machines found a steady market in Colorado. Producing these locomotives may have been a close match to the modern concept of mass customization—a manufacturing strategy based on offering variety within the economies and technical limitations of mass production.

The American narrow gauge movement in general, and narrow gauge lines in the Pacific states in particular, were quick to adopt the 8-18 C for its adaptability to poor track, and for its unique ability to function well as both a freight and a passenger locomotive. The first American sale of the class was a drawing four machine (denoted by classification 8-18 C.4) sold to the North Pacific Coast as number 4, the *Olema*, in August 1874. From the date of that sale until 1880, Baldwin shipped a total of eighteen locomotives of the class built to drawing four, outselling its closest competitor in the class, the drawing nine machine (of which just twelve locomotives were sold). Among the eighteen drawing four engines, sixteen were sold to Pacific Coast narrow gauge lines, and of sixteen, fourteen were sold to lines in California. The North Pacific Coast, South Pacific Coast, Monterey & Salinas Valley, and Santa Cruz Rail Road were all early adopters of the design and managed to move a significant fraction of their total tonnage behind the light (twenty-ton) but powerful eight wheelers.

Three class 8-18 C narrow gauge Baldwins survive in the United States today, and it may be fitting that all of them are drawing four machines. One of the survivors, NPC number 12 (the *Sonoma*), became an apt example of the engineering features that made the locomotive successful in the early environment of startup California narrow gauge railroading. The *Sonoma* was delivered to the North Pacific Coast in March 1876. Folklore persisted that the engine saw little service on the NPC, but recently uncovered records show that between January and August 1878, the *Sonoma* logged mileage on a par with other NPC locomotives. A downturn in lumber business, however, surplused the engine to the Nevada Central in 1879, where it lived out its commercial life until 1938.

Restored by the California State Railroad Museum in 1978,

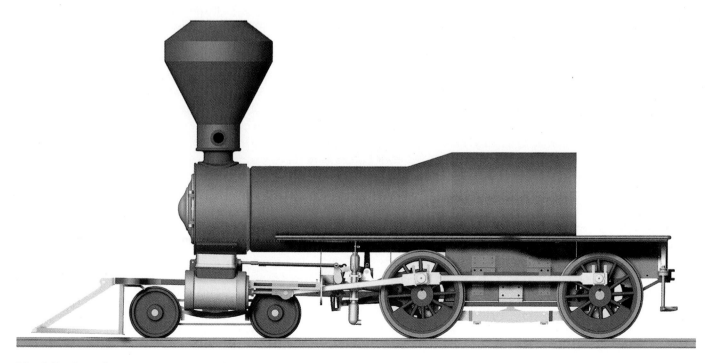

[Curtis Ferrington]

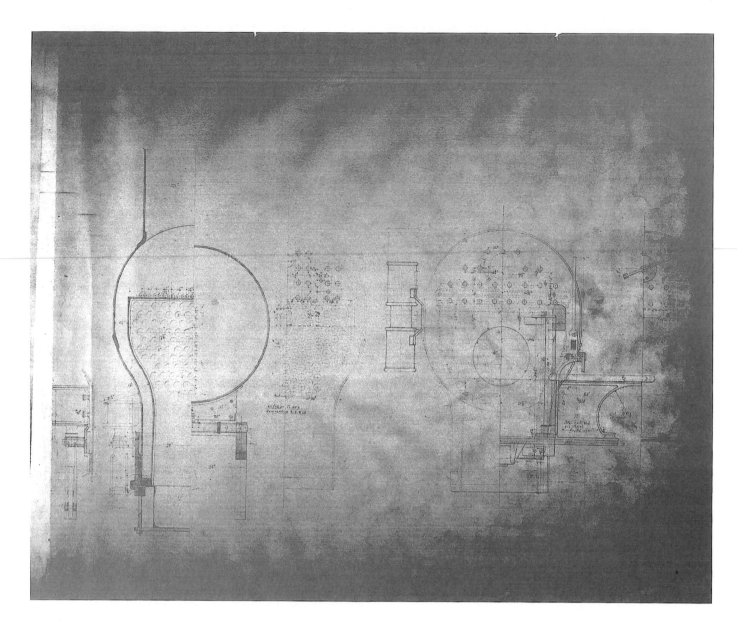

the *Sonoma* was salvaged as a mechanical artifact; the project also amassed hundreds of original Baldwin prints and drawings, many specific to drawing four machines. They formed the basis of a project to render the *Sonoma*, part by part, in a three-dimensional computer-aided drafting (CAD) application called SolidWorks 2001. What follows is the result: a digital *Sonoma*, created by graphic artist Curtis Ferrington. The objective of the project is to illustrate the assembly of the locomotive as we might have witnessed construction of the *Sonoma* on the erection floor at Baldwin in 1876. But the computer offers advantages that even direct observation cannot: the ability to simplify complex assemblies, render parts transparent, add color, or slice through a part at a section to reveal the structure and mechanism within. The computer is even capable of "lighting" the locomotive, using a complex optical simulation called "ray tracing" to bounce light off the engine into the "camera" of the eye. Ray tracing permits nearly photographic realism. Careful inspection of the graphic drawings reveals the reflection of parts of the engine in shiny metal surfaces. Every part and assembly in the three-dimensional CAD drawings is created in this way except for two: the name on the locomotive cab was photographed at the California State Railroad

Museum with a digital camera and inserted into the CAD program; a steam gauge was inserted in the same way.

The goal of this exercise is to recreate not simply the parts and subassemblies of the *Sonoma* but also the process that created her, what might be called "engineering intent" in modern manufacturing terminology. Like a storyboard, the following pages trace assembly of the locomotive through stages, illustrating (through both 3D CAD as well as original two-dimensional drawings from Baldwin) the philosophy behind the design. Keep in mind that the colors in the 3D CAD images do not imply the realistic colors of the original; they are used instead to clarify how complex mechanisms are put together. Also keep in mind that some details have been omitted from the engine, sometimes for simplicity but also (where drawings do not exist) for lack of data. Of some 5,000 parts on the original locomotive, the digital *Sonoma* has been created from only two-thirds of the total. For further reading on the restoration of the real *Sonoma*, see the California State Railroad Museum paper "A Restoration Report on Nevada Central Ry. Locomotive No. 5," by Richard M. Katz, Feb. 5, 1978. (Two-dimensional drawings in this section not reproduced to scale.)

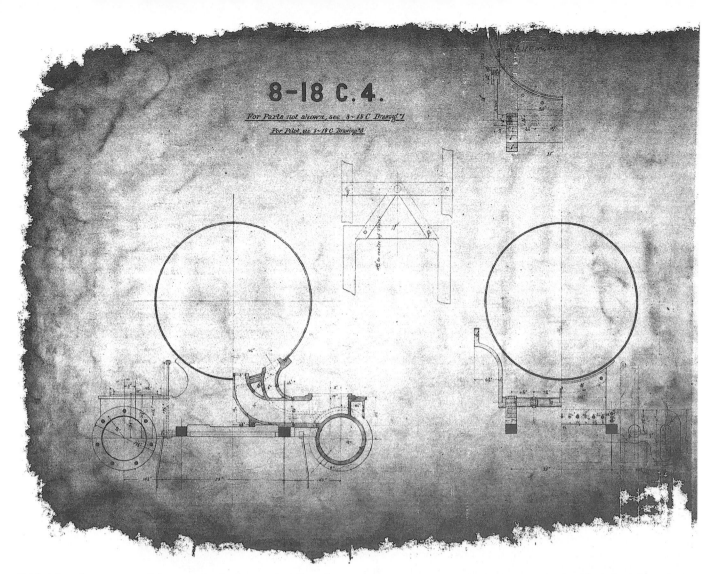

8-18 C.4.

For Parts not shown, see 8~18 C Drawing ⁴1

For Pilot, see 8~18 C Drawing ⁴8

Baldwin's unique process of documenting its locomotives flowed from the generic to the particular. The section drawings above are thought to be copies of the original Drawing 4 for class 8-18 C engines, and together with an elevation of Drawing 1 (not shown), were loaned to the California State Railroad Museum in 1977 by Eric Thompson. The drawings became key artifacts in the restoration of *Sonoma*. Although Baldwin referred to *Sonoma* as a Drawing 4 machine, the two drawings cross-referenced each other, and were apparently combined to produce *Sonoma*. Each drawing shows multiple features that might have represented options in actually manufacturing an engine (including optional injector, optional air brakes and compressor, optional boiler type, and an option for modified stroke). Drawing 1 and 4 may therefore have acted like a catalog of features, only some of which (those called out by the customer on an Order Sheet) were transferred to working drawings from which a single locomotive would be built. Supplemental drawings from a Baldwin standard practice manual (called the *Law and General Information Ledger*, shown at the right) applied to all classes of locomotives and were used to enforce general design features, such as the construction of wood-burning grates; still other types of documents, shown later in this section, provided detailed dimensional breakdowns of assemblies and parts.

Some time after the restoration work on *Sonoma* was complete, Thompson's original drawings were lost, leaving only copies behind. Because of their antiquity and link to the earliest 8-18 C machines, Drawings 1 and 4 became known to historians as the *Shroud of Sonoma*. [Above, Doug MacLeod Collection; right, Stanford University Special Collections]

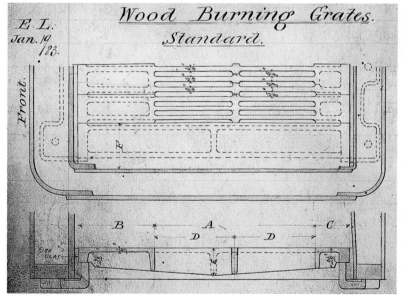

III

On this page: frame, driving axle box (with bronze bearing), and lead truck form components of the 4-4-0's flexible three point suspension. Designed to keep all driving wheels adhering to the rail, even on poorly surfaced track, *Sonoma*'s suspension system included a pilot truck with swing motion, below, that operated much like a swing motion truck in a freight car. By allowing the center bearing to move side-to-side, swing motion effectively shortened the engine's wheel base, allowing it to address tighter curves.

Opposite, bottom: with cylinders, driving axle boxes and equalizer beams mounted to the frame rails, the 3D CAD *Sonoma* begins to take shape. At the top, in the computer simulation, the valve cover has been removed from the cylinders, showing the D style slide valve riding on top of steam admission and exhaust ports. To its left, a page from *The Law and General Information Ledger* (also referred to as the "Old Man Book") defined dimensional guidelines applicable to any Baldwin 12" cylinder, while to its right a single color panel from the Painting Samples book documents cylinder striping and painting details for style 1—called out for *Sonoma* on its Order Sheet. [*Law and General Information Ledger* and Painting Samples illustration, Stanford University Special Collections; all others, Curtis Ferrington]

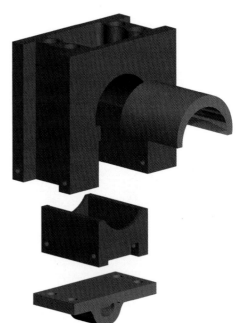

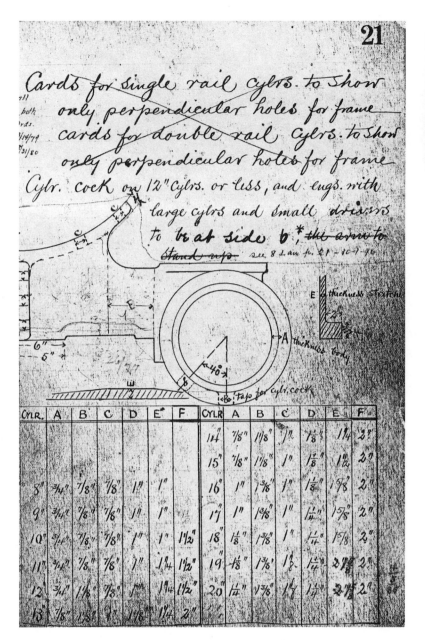

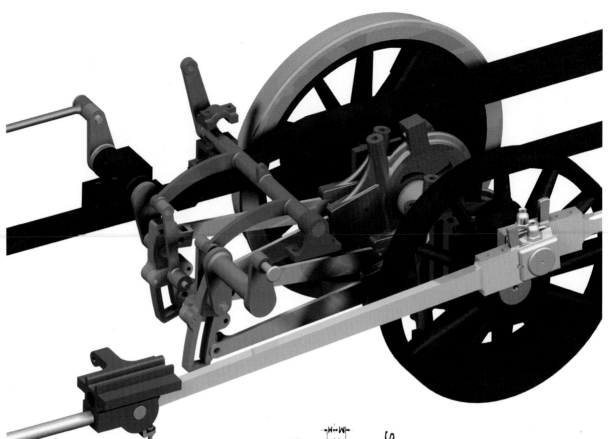

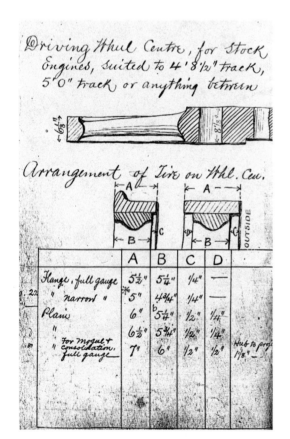

Driving Whl Centre, for Stock
Engines, Suited to 4' 8½" track,
5' 0" track or anything between

Arrangement of Tire on Whl. Cen.

	A	B	C	D	
Flange, full gauge	5½"	5¼"	¼"	—	
" narrow "	5"	4¾"	¼"	—	
Plain	6"	5¼"	½"	¼"	
"	6½"	5¾"	½"	¼"	
" For Mogul + Consolidation full gauge	7"	6"	½"	½"	Hub to proj. 1/8" —

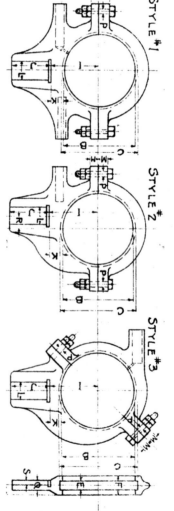

STYLE #1

STYLE #2

STYLE #3

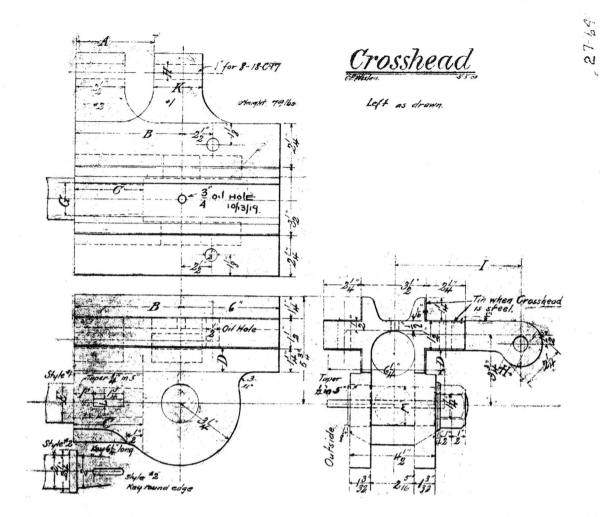

The most complex assembly in the entire locomotive, its Stephenson link valve gear, is simulated in the view opposite, top. Eccentrics (red) converted the rotary motion of the driving wheel into the reciprocating motion of the eccentric blades and links (green), which in turn pushed and pulled the rocker arms (gray) that actuated the valve stems. As lifter arms (blue) raised or lowered the links, the valve stems traveled shorter or longer distances, altering the duration of steam entry into the cylinders. For a given speed, steam admission could be long or short, helping to determine power and fuel efficiency.

The working drawings for eccentric straps (opposite, below right) and crossheads (above) supplied precise part and assembly specifications that would apply uniquely to the particular 8-18 C under construction. One additional drawing was required, since working drawings were created with unspecified dimensions ("A," "B," "C," etc.) that would only be filled in when they were matched with the correct "card," a small lacquered part or assembly drawing intended for use by the shop craftsmen. The complex scheme of drawings distilled thirty years of successful Baldwin practice as a manufacturer. In other views, general driver features are described in Baldwin documents such as the "Old Man Book" (opposite, below left) and the Painting Samples book (right). [Opposite left and this page right, Stanford University Special Collections; opposite right and this page above, California State Railroad Museum; others, Curtis Ferrington]

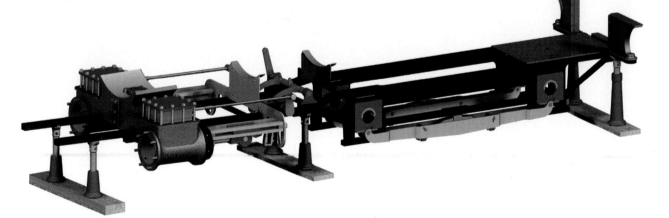

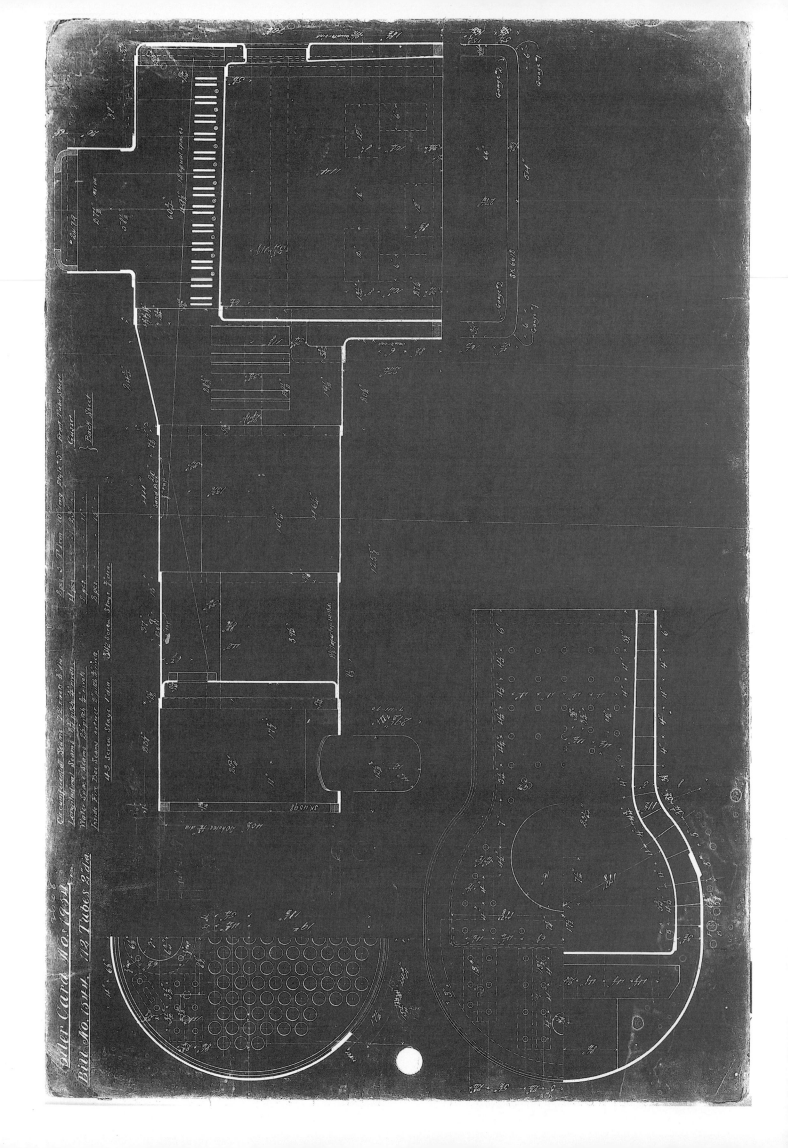

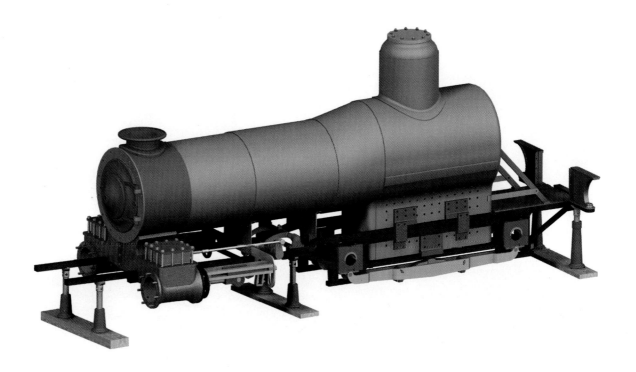

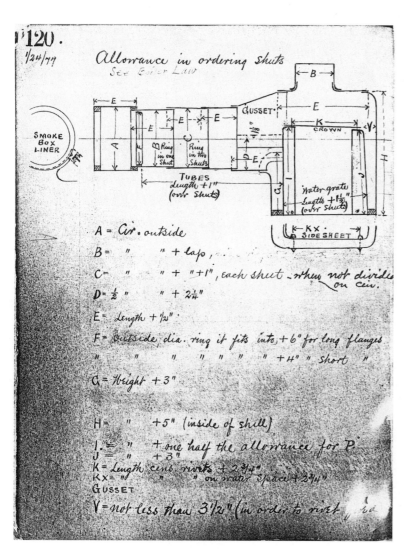

The *Sonoma*'s boiler was a traditional lap-seam, wagon-top design. The wagon top itself provided a reservoir of steam in the hottest part of the boiler, directly above the firebox. Pages from the *Law and General Information Book*, on this page, show standardized boiler features, while the boiler bill 1544, opposite, provided working drawings. The boiler was attached to the frame (above) by bolting it rigidly to the cylinder block. Because its length expanded by nearly two inches when the engine was hot, the boiler was supported at the rear of the frame by six brackets sliding freely on the top and bottom frame rails. [Top, Curtis Ferrington; others, this page, Stanford University Special Collections; opposite, California State Railroad Museum]

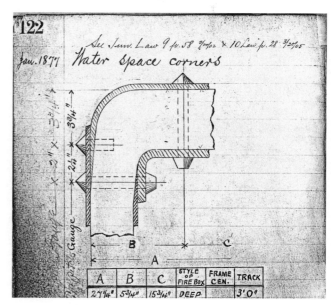

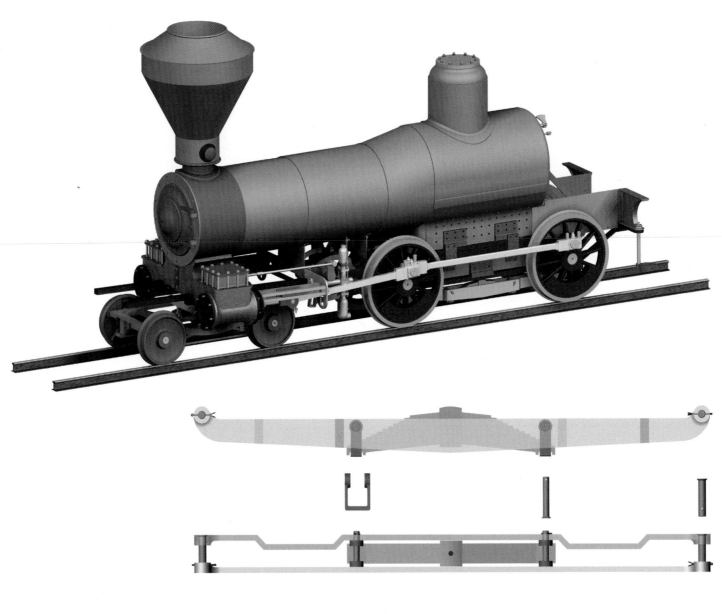

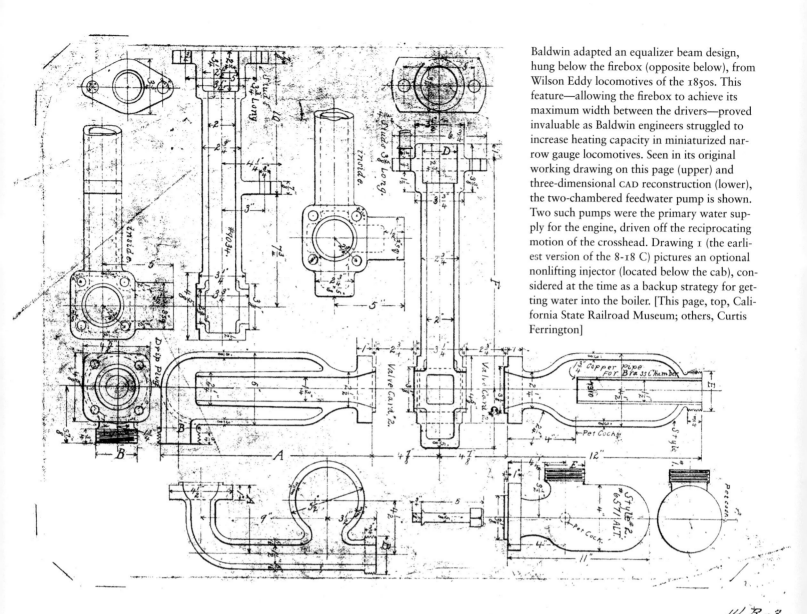

Baldwin adapted an equalizer beam design, hung below the firebox (opposite below), from Wilson Eddy locomotives of the 1850s. This feature—allowing the firebox to achieve its maximum width between the drivers—proved invaluable as Baldwin engineers struggled to increase heating capacity in miniaturized narrow gauge locomotives. Seen in its original working drawing on this page (upper) and three-dimensional CAD reconstruction (lower), the two-chambered feedwater pump is shown. Two such pumps were the primary water supply for the engine, driven off the reciprocating motion of the crosshead. Drawing 1 (the earliest version of the 8-18 C) pictures an optional nonlifting injector (located below the cab), considered at the time as a backup strategy for getting water into the boiler. [This page, top, California State Railroad Museum; others, Curtis Ferrington]

$21\frac{1}{2}''$ Sand Box.

P.G. Binder 11-4-09

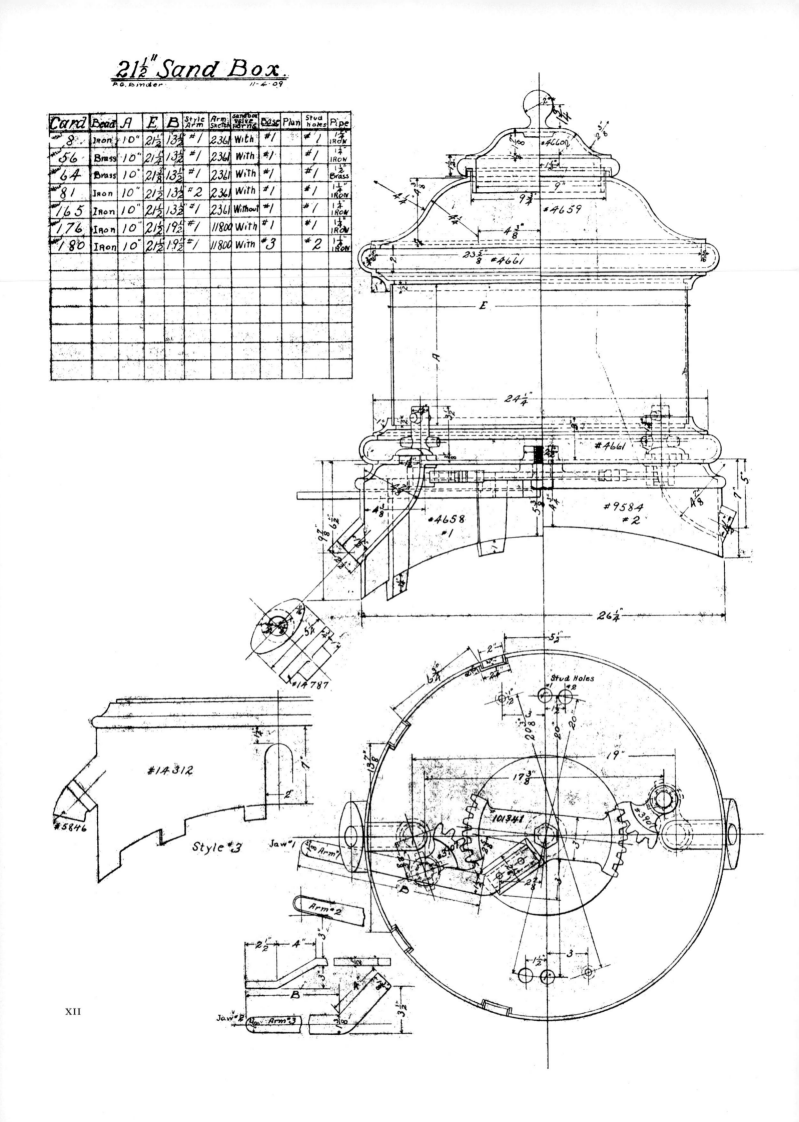

Card	Bead	A	E	B	Style Arm	Arm Sketch	sandbox valve horns	Base	Plan	Stud holes	Pipe
8	Iron	10"	$21\frac{1}{2}$"	$13\frac{1}{2}$"	#1	2361	With	#1		#1	$1\frac{1}{4}$" Iron
56	Brass	10"	$21\frac{1}{4}$"	$13\frac{1}{2}$"	#1	2361	With	#1		#1	$1\frac{1}{4}$" Iron
64	Brass	10"	$21\frac{3}{8}$"	$13\frac{1}{2}$"	#1	2361	With	#1		#1	$1\frac{1}{2}$" Brass
81	Iron	10"	$21\frac{1}{2}$"	$13\frac{1}{2}$"	#2	2361	With	#1		#1	$1\frac{1}{4}$" Iron
165	Iron	10"	$21\frac{1}{2}$"	$13\frac{1}{2}$"	#1	2361	Without	#1		#1	$1\frac{1}{4}$" Iron
176	Iron	10"	$21\frac{1}{2}$"	$19\frac{1}{2}$"	#1	11800	With	#1		#1	$1\frac{1}{4}$" Iron
180	Iron	10"	$21\frac{1}{2}$"	$19\frac{1}{2}$"	#1	11800	With	#3		#2	$1\frac{1}{4}$" Iron

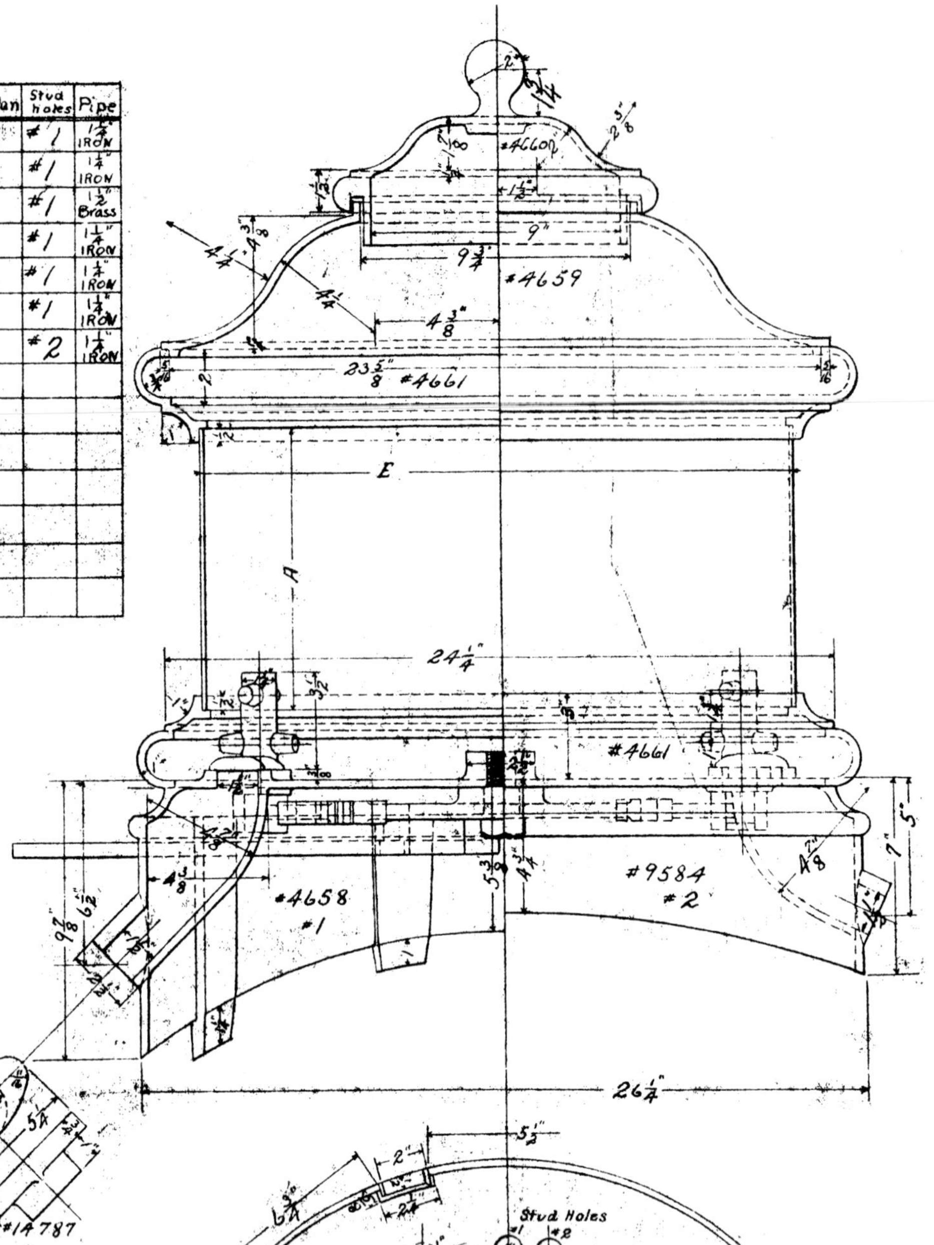

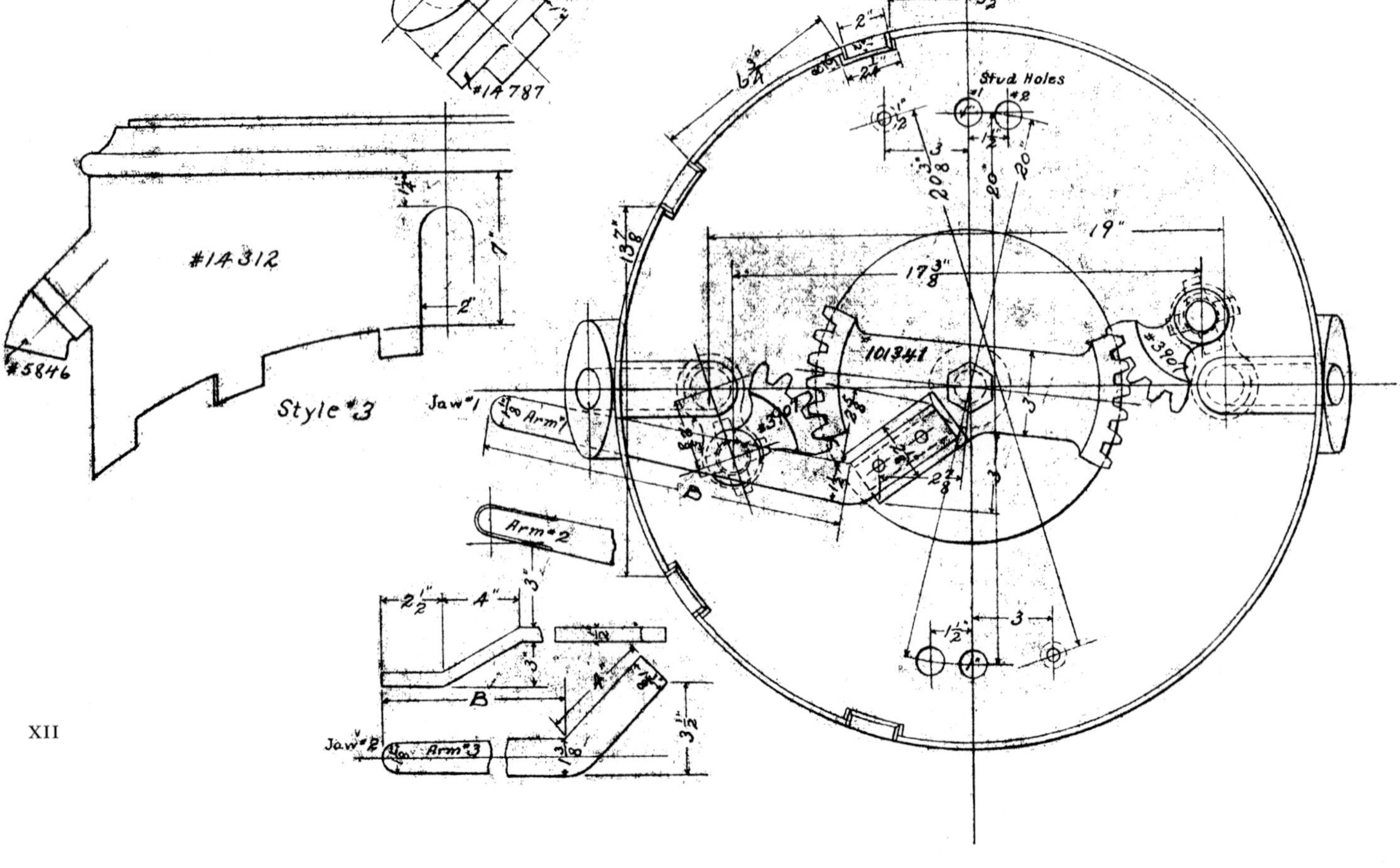

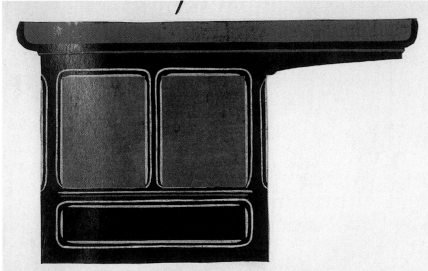

Baldwin's working drawings were based on tables, where various "card numbers" called out dimensionally different versions of the same assembly (for example, the sand dome, opposite). In this case, card 8 represents the specific card used for *Sonoma*. Lacquered to protect it from grime and oil on the shop floor, Card 8 it-self would be used by mechanics and craftsmen to construct the assembly. On this page, above, Baldwin's Painting Samples book documents the elaborate striping for completing the sand dome and cab. In the computer reconstruction at the top of the page, the locomotive has been equipped with major appliances, including pilot, stack, cab, and running boards. [Top, Curtis Ferrington; below, Stanford University Special Collections; opposite, California State Railroad Museum]

Stacks

MALLEY & C°   6-18-00

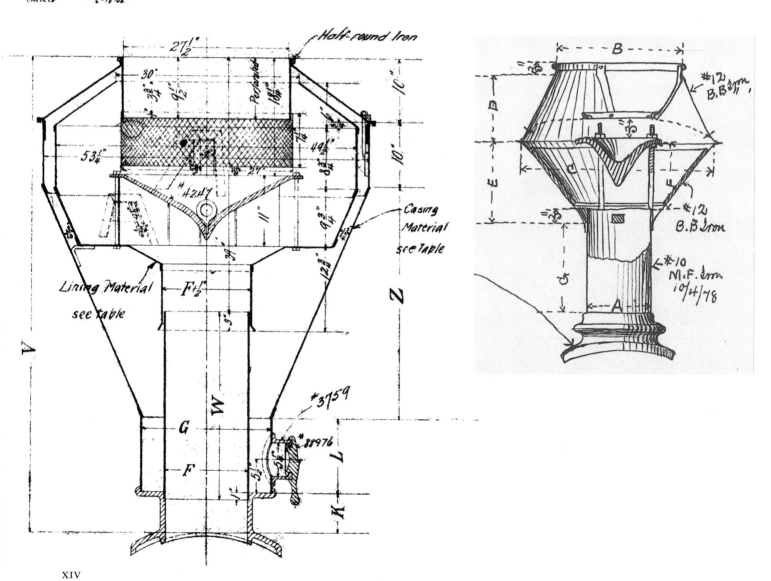

Half-round Iron

27½"

30"

3¾"

9½"

53¼"

Perforated
18½

10"

10"

44½"

8¼"

#4247

11"

9¾"

12¼"

Casing
Material
see Table

Lining Material
see table

F½"

3"

Z

V

W

G

F

#3759

#88976

L

K

B

#12
B.B Iron

#12
B.B Iron

#10
M.F. Iron
10/4/78

E

C

A

XIV

The nearly completed *Sonoma* appears at the top of these two pages, much as she would have looked on the floor of Baldwin's factory in the spring of 1876. Opposite, below, working drawings for the engine's Radley & Hunter style stack are shown at the left, while the "Old Man Book" (*Law and General Information Book*) shows a generic design for a diamond stack on the right. The digital *Sonoma* is shown with a simulated Russia iron boiler jacket, a planished surface that may have taken its delicate blue color from the reflection of the sky. In a neutral background, Russia iron appeared a glossy gray. In this computer simulation, reflective metal surfaces can be seen to mirror nearby objects, for example a corner of the cab glimpsed in the steam dome. [Top, both pages, Curtis Ferrington; opposite, right and this page, middle, Stanford University Special Collection; others, California State Railroad Museum]

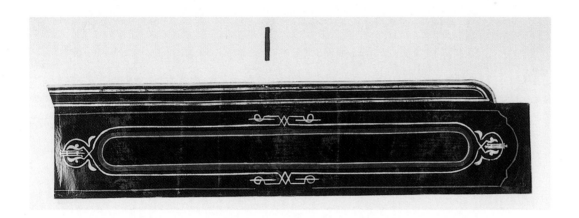

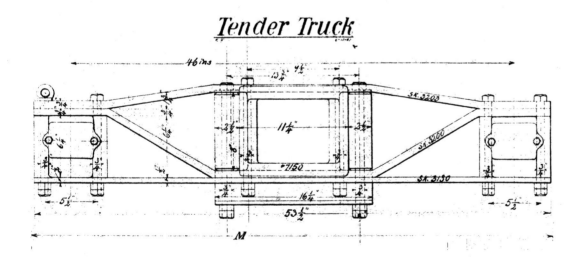

Tender Truck

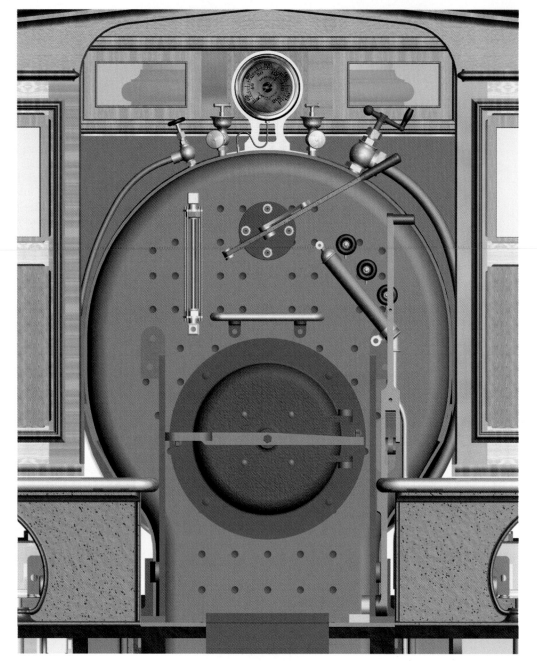

Most of the appliances pictured on *Sonoma*'s backhead (right) were authenticated from its January 15, 1876 order sheet or related Baldwin working drawings, including a pair of primitive steam-fed oil cups (appearing on either side of the steam gauge) and the engineer's injector starter valve, near the throttle handle. To maintain the consistency of construction-era hardware, a brass-faced Ashcroft steam gauge was digitally photographed from an 1877 original, and inserted into the computer-generated image. [Right, Curtis Ferrington; others, California State Railroad Museum; original steam gauge from the collection of William Wulf]

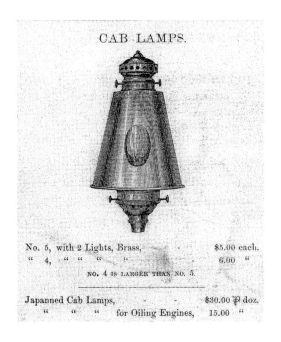

CAB LAMPS.

No. 5, with 2 Lights, Brass, - - $5.00 each.
" 4, " " " " - - 6.00 "

NO. 4 IS LARGER THAN NO. 5.

Japanned Cab Lamps, - - $30.00 ℗ doz.
" " " for Oiling Engines, 15.00 "

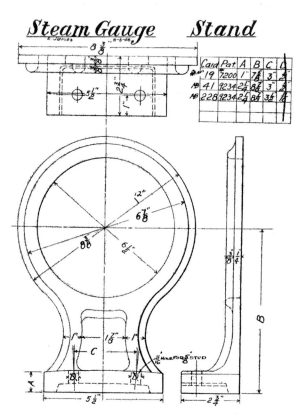

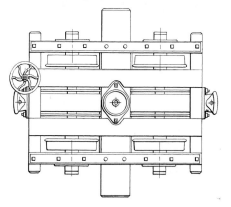

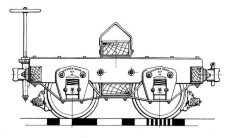

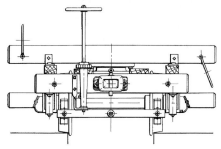

The question of whether the North Pacific Coast's meager locomotive fleet could haul such traffic was also about to be tested.

By 1875, salesmen began to circle, smelling a unique opportunity. Heavier, more expensive locomotives would become a critical component of management's strategy to open up and sustain high-volume lumber traffic from Dutch Bill.

But although Baldwin considered its standard narrow gauge products versatile enough to meet any kind of operating environment, the North Pacific Coast acquired a reputation early on as a test bed for experimental, nonstandard locomotive practice. Stories about the Frankensteinian conversion of the Baldwin-built one spot, nee *Saucelito*, have persisted in the literature for years.[30] The basis of the legend was apparently true. At some point in the *Saucelito*'s career—a date only recently documented—the Baldwin-issue 2-6-0, class 8-18 D, was converted to a home-engineered 4-4-0, altering her basic wheel arrangement. The conversion was usually attributed to the engine's eventual sale to the L. E. White Lumber Co. at Salmon Creek, occurring in January 1882, and explained by the lumber company's concern for its poor track.[31] But the reality is that seven years before it was sold to L. E. White, in the summer of 1875, the North Pacific Coast performed surgery on the locomotive in response to needs of its own.

The comparatively recent discovery of an 1875 Saucelito shop record book may provide the first known written account of the engine's metamorphosis, and an accountant's perspective on an engineering anomaly that still resists simple explanation.[32] The ledger recorded shop expenditures from June through December 1875. It routinely listed, month-by-month, maintenance expenses for locomotives, including the cost category "oil, tallow, and waste," consumables that were routinely charged to the same shop account and that gave a rough indication of locomotive usage.

In June, for example, locomotive number 1 drew $9.20 in oil, tallow, and waste charges—modest consumption compared to the $21.47 that NPC num-

California logging lines not only inherited secondhand locomotives from early narrow gauge common carriers, such as the NPC's *Saucelito* (shown in detail, top, left), but were also a market for new, specialized Carter Brothers logging equipment, such as the disconnect trucks shown top right, in use by the Sanger Lumber Co., ca. 1897. Three mechanical drawings show the Carter disconnect truck as it was built for West Side Lumber in 1898, but Carter's manufacture of similar disconnects can be traced to the early 1880s. [Top left, Robert J. Lee collection; top right, John Labbe collection; bottom three drawings, Russ Simpson]

ber 3 accrued for the same month. In July, number 1 drew $9.58, but in August the amount dropped to just $1.06, and the following series of repair expenses (and a credit) were noted for the month[33]:

> August 11, 1875:
> Turning tyres for No. 1
> Prescott, Scott & Co. $85.00
>
> August 31, 1875:
> Engine No. 1
> materials furnished in August $253.89
>
> To Locomotive No. 1
> old material returned in August (credit) $386.45
>
> Painting No. 1
> to J. S. Cameron (bill, August 31) $82.00

The entries appear to be consistent with a major shopping, including use of the considerable machining and foundry capabilities of Prescott, Scott, the 1875 owners of the Union Iron Works in San Francisco, which was previously owned by Peter Donahue and later by H. J. Booth.[34] The line item "old material returned in August" could logically have applied to a surplused forward driver pair, removed to make room for the lead truck of an American-style 4-4-0.

On September 3, the cash books noted a correction of $375.22 for "error in freight on returned locomotive," suggesting that number 1 had been returned from San Francisco after the work of Prescott, Scott was completed. Tom Carter may have even gotten in the act when he billed $63.00 to "repairs of locomotives" on July 31, 1875, possibly work on number 1's wooden cab. The timing is just about right.

The rebuilding program appeared to end, convincingly, in September, when number 1's oil, tallow, and waste bill jumped to $19.76, indicative of a locomotive returned to service.

The shop records fail to explain the reasons for the work, but they offer one intriguing clue: the earliest repair line item is for the "turning of tyres," suggesting premature wear on a locomotive that had been in service just a year. Unexpected wear might have triggered first the grinding and contouring of her driver flanges, and second a radical revision of wheel arrangement to shorten the engine's rigid wheelbase. The rigid wheelbase on the original 2-6-0 configuration was eleven feet eight inches; the revised rigid wheelbase was seven feet six inches.[35]

Central Pacific's experience with the 2-6-0 locomotive type offers support for this theory. A. J. Stevens, CP's master mechanic, noted excessive driver wear with two-wheel lead trucks, a reason CP favored four-wheel lead trucks in its locomotives as late as 1887.[36]

In this new configuration, number 1 operated in nearly complete anonymity until 1882, when the sale to L. E. White took place. A segment of locomotive operating records for 1878, included in the Saucelito shop book, substantiates the engine's routine operation for at least eight months of 1878. Photographs taken in the late 1890s on the L. E. White operation at Elk, California, show the engine as the *Ajax,* a 4-4-0, but still equipped with a

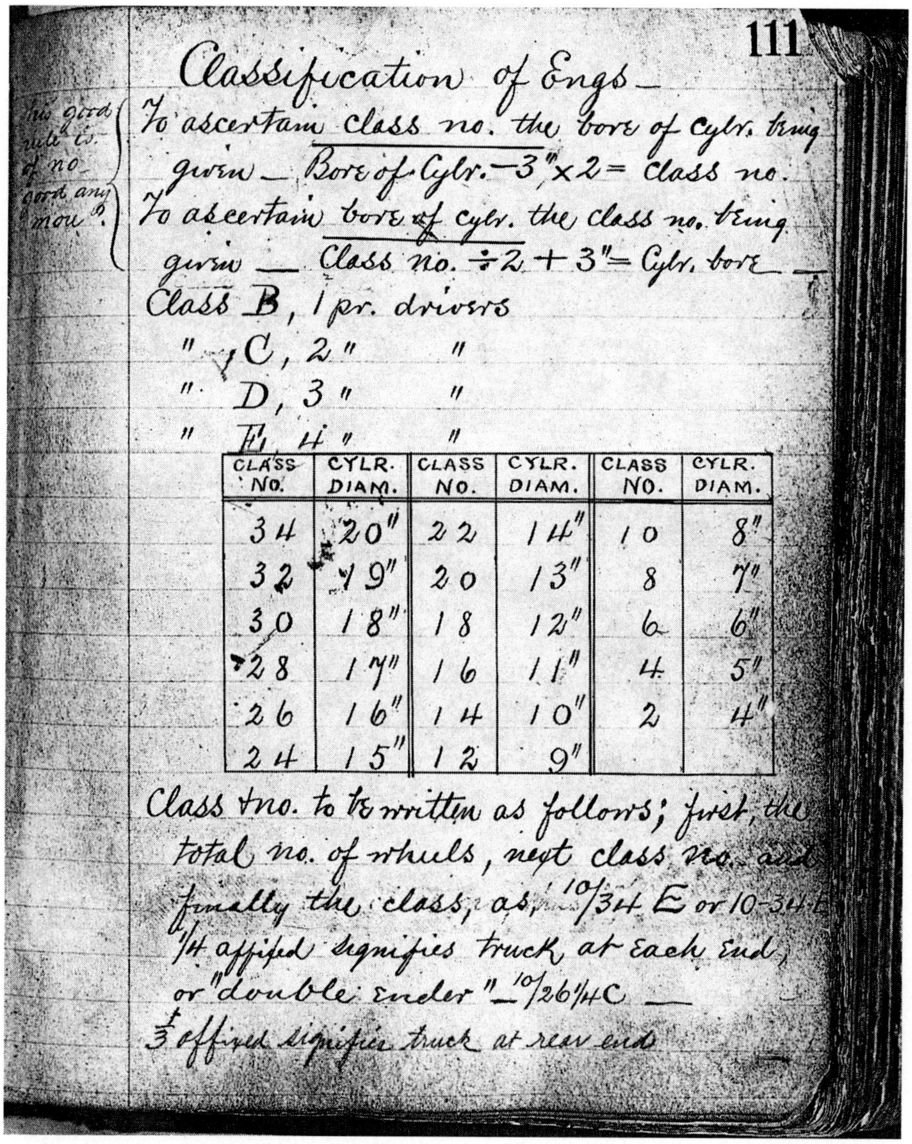
111

Classification of Engs—

(This good rule is of no good any more.)

To ascertain class no. the bore of cylr. being given — Bore of Cylr.—3" x 2 = class no.

To ascertain bore of cylr. the class no. being given — Class no. ÷ 2 + 3" = Cylr. bore —

Class B, 1 pr. drivers

" C, 2 " "

" D, 3 " "

" E, 4 " "

CLASS NO.	CYLR. DIAM.	CLASS NO.	CYLR. DIAM.	CLASS NO.	CYLR. DIAM.
34	20"	22	14"	10	8"
32	19"	20	13"	8	7"
30	18"	18	12"	6	6"
28	17"	16	11"	4	5"
26	16"	14	10"	2	4"
24	15"	12	9"		

Class no. to be written as follows; first, the total no. of wheels, next class no. and finally the class, as 10/34 E or 10-34 E

1/4 affixed signifies truck at each end, or "double ender" — 10/26 1/4 C —

t/3 affixed signifies truck at rear end

[Calculation of Baldwin class number, from *Law and General Information: Baldwin Locomotive Works*, Stanford University Special Collections]

crosshead, center-boilered steam dome, and other distinctive features characteristic of a Baldwin class 8-18 D, vestigial organs left over from the engine's first configuration.[37]

If the Saucelito shop book indeed recorded the conversion of number 1, the date affirms an early and precocious disposition of the North Pacific Coast toward experimenting with motive power. The story also helps to explain why all but one of the railroad's next six locomotive purchases were Baldwin class 8-18 Cs, the versatile narrow gauge 4-4-0 whose rigid wheelbase was identical to that of the reborn one spot. We do not know who was responsible for the conversion; nor can we fully appreciate the railroad's assessment of its outcome. But it was just the first of a series of adventures and misadventures the North Pacific Coast would have with the rapidly evolving engineering of commercial narrow gauge locomotives.

Abundantly diverse in topography and operating conditions, the NPC

Photographed a short time after its delivery in September 1874, the appearance of NPC's number 2, the Mason Machine Works product *San Rafael*, still included original cab, bell, headlamp, and other ornamental hardware unique to the builder. The original smokestack, however, was probably a Fontaine design, like the stack shown on the Mason *Bully Boy* at the time of its construction, opposite page. [Jack Farley collection]

became a proving ground for narrow gauge locomotive manufacturers, and a lightning rod for their salesmen. The scope of interest in the railroad's motive power was international. As late as September 2, 1874, the *San Francisco Bulletin* noted that part of the North Pacific Coast's locomotive fleet "will be made in England, and the others, as mentioned, in Philadelphia."

This statement may well have come from Howard Schuyler, who was keenly aware of the British-built "Fairlie double-ender"–style locomotive and helped import the first one into the United States. The engine combined two independent articulated power units underneath two separate boilers. The design was intended to blend high tractive force with agility on tight curves. The Denver & Rio Grande had ordered its first and only Fairlie patent while Schuyler was still working as its chief engineer, a British-manufactured double-boilered 0-4-4-0 named the *Mountaineer*. By late 1874, with Schuyler on the West Coast, the jury was still out on the *Mountaineer*'s performance. But Schuyler apparently brought the concept of the Fairlie to the West Coast and advocated its use on the NPC.

Perhaps Moore was less committed to the Fairlie than Schuyler was, though equally unsure about sole-sourcing the railroad's motive power with Baldwin. At the time of the *Bulletin*'s article, the NPC was only two weeks away from delivery of a Fairlie equivalent, built by the Mason Machine Works of Taunton, Massachusetts. Number 2, the *San Rafael*, was delivered to the North Pacific Coast on September 14, 1874.[38] Simplifying the Fairlie design to a single boiler, Mason retained the articulated power truck, accommodating the engine to narrow gauge lines with severe curvature and steep grades. In the American idiom, this version of the Fairlie became known as a Mason "bogie."

Fairlie, Baldwin, Mason, and Porter products were all competing for the new West Coast narrow gauge market, and their salesmen frequently jousted for the attention of startup railroads. F. G. Shalling, West Coast agent for Mason, offered a glimpse of the emerging marketplace when he wrote the North Pacific Coast on May 30, 1875, not long after the successful sale of the *San Rafael*, exploring the sale of a smaller Mason bogie:

Mr. Wm. H. Bent, Tr.,
Mason Machine Works
Taunton, Mass.

Dear Sir:

Yours dated the 17th and signed by Wm. Mason was received in due time. Mr. Moore has not seen it, have spoken to Mr. Campbell about it, he says he wants the engine (10 × 16) and Mr. Moore ought to take it. Mr. Campbell has more influence with Mr. Moore now more than anyone else, therefore I want him to see about it, before I see Mr. Moore. I am here to see what I can do with the Stockton & Ione people, the engine and me have the inside track with the Sup't and Chief Engineer but am afraid Mr. Williams from the Baldwin Works (who has been in Cali-

Delivered to the North Pacific Coast in June 1877, the *Bully Boy* is shown below in a builder's photograph at the Mason plant in Taunton, Mass. The powerful Mason bogie type locomotive was chosen to contend with the railroad's steep Salmon Creek and Dutch Bill grades on its new extension into the Russian River Basin. Historians have speculated that its rear pilot, visible at the left, may have indicated an intention to operate the engine backwards—a means of guiding the engine through curves, thus reducing wear on its driving wheels. Photographs of the engine in service indicate it was operated in both directions. [Robert Dockery collection]

fornia for three weeks or more) has much influence with the parties that furnish the money to build the road, shall know in a few days. . . .

. . . The San Rafael [NPC number 2] ran during the month of April 2205 miles, hauled 18500 passengers each passenger riding an average six miles, is in use from 6:30 A.M. until 7:30 P.M. used 46 Quarts of Lard Oil 16 Quarts of Machine Oil, 10 Quarts of Coal Oil and 20 lbs. of Waste, burned 30-$\frac{1}{2}$ cords of wood, the engine runs seven days in the week and has not lost a trip for more than two months but will soon have to because the cylinders must be fastened. The cylinders getting loose has been an argument against this kind of engine.

A short time since [I] saw parties interested in building a road in Mexico, was told Mr. Williams had been in, and in less than fifteen minutes afterwards they told me it was doubtful whether machinery could be held firm in its place on a movable frame, believing that this man would not of himself bring up such an objection, I was forced to believe that someone else had put the words in his mouth.

I hope you will see that the bolts in the lower part of the frame are put in solid and the nut screwed on, and not put the bolts in loose enough that they can be turned by the head and screwed into the nut. Please forward the reports I asked for as soon as you get them.

Yours respectfully,
F. G. Shalling (signed).

Clearly, Mason was actively marketing the bogie by claiming superiority over narrow gauge Baldwin products. For example, one advantage was easier steaming. The *San Rafael* had about 25 percent more grate area in its firebox than the twenty-two-ton Baldwin class 8-18 C. On the short but steep grind over White's Hill, Baldwins and Masons quickly differentiated themselves in their ability to maintain a head of steam; the Baldwins were at a disadvantage.

But the North Pacific Coast was making other kinds of comparison. Mason priced their products significantly higher than Baldwin. In a voucher dated April 2, 1875, NPC's cash book reported number 2's cost at $8,104.87. A contemporary Baldwin 4-4-0, class 8-18 C, cost the North Pacific Coast $7,430.50.[39]

There were additional drawbacks to Mason products besides price. Most were related to the swivel power truck. For example, without a rigid connection between the boiler and the running gear, the power truck did not have enough mass to resist the constant imbalance of forces caused by the oscillation of drivers, rods, counterweights, and pistons. As a result, as Shalling correctly noted, the oscillations loosened bolts connecting the cylinder block to the chassis.

Designed to pivot around curves, in practice the power truck rotated stiffly.[40] The weight of the bogie's boiler sat heavily on the center pivot, making it difficult for the engine to go around tight curves without great pressure on driver flanges. This effect showed up as excessive tire wear, exaggerated by the lack of a lead, or pilot truck in the early bogie designs. The *San Rafael* lacked such a pilot truck, an invitation to the kind of driver wear that may have triggered the problems with Baldwin number 1. Additionally, the flex-

ible steam coupling in a Mason bogie, connecting boiler with cylinders, often leaked.

The defects didn't phase Mason's salesmen. With the sale of the *San Rafael*, Shalling had closed the deal on the first North Pacific Coast Mason and soon pursued additional sales. His letter referred to a 10" × 16" Mason bogie, the same size engine Mason was selling to the Stockton & Ione Railroad. Howard Schuyler's brother, James, was chief engineer for the S&I, and to Shalling the personal connection must have proven irresistible. The North Pacific Coast, however, declined the smaller engine.

If smaller engines didn't sell, Shalling set his sights on bigger engines. He too was keenly aware of the scale-up in motive power that would have to take place to move the NPC's target traffic out of Dutch Bill Creek. He may also have been aware of the *Saucelito*'s troubles. He was close to convincing the NPC that it could solve its problem with a radical bogie design. Mason was so eager to make the North Pacific Coast a proving ground for its heaviest narrow gauge bogies that, apparently on speculation, they fabricated a 15" × 20" monster bogie and lettered it North Pacific Coast number 3, the first *Tomales*. A builder's photograph documents the appearance and lettering of the engine as manufactured. What we believe is the engine's factory specification sheet reported more than double the firebox grate area of a Baldwin class 8-18 C, and nearly 35 percent more water capacity than the *San Rafael*, implying a hefty increase in total engine weight.[41]

But the fifty-two miles of the Tomales division, complete by the time Shalling wrote his letter, was lightly built. The mainline was laid in thirty-five-

Mason's Locomotive Specification Ledger of 1874 suggests the reason the first *Tomales* was never delivered to the NPC. Loaded onto a standard gauge flatcar at Taunton, Massachusetts, the engine was too heavy for bridges on the Boston & Albany Railroad, trapping her at the factory. Her name and number were later assigned to a smaller, lighter Baldwin product, one of the first 8-18 C class engines built to a Baldwin specification called "drawing 4." [Robert C. Moulton collection]

pound rail, and although the track north of Tomales was being constructed with fifty-five-pound iron, the south end still had not been upgraded to the standards of the north. The heavy 15" × 20" bogie may have terrified the railroad's chief mechanical officer with the threat of broken rails and collapsed trestles. Still, Shalling continued to passionately promote the Mason bogie type locomotive on western narrow gauge railroads, suggesting variations of the design to Moore and Campbell.

The railroad's management, on the other hand, seemed to struggle for a consistent motive-power strategy. Endless permutations of locomotive weight, cylinder size, tractive force, turning radius, fuel economy, and price proved a confusing match with constantly changing civil engineering demands on the expanding railroad. Gradients, clearance, weight restriction on bridges, rail weight, curvature, and track surface were all evolving rapidly to meet the changing requirements of the railroad. No single NPC locomotive, by 1876, had enough in-service time to constitute a benchmark for understanding performance against these multiple demands.

Delivery dates of early NPC engines seem to suggest an ongoing debate over choice of builders, and perhaps off stage a heated battle among salesmen. Finally rejected as unmanageably heavy, the giant Mason bogie gave up her name and road number to a Baldwin machine. The new *Tomales*, second number 3 on the railroad, was delivered in October 1874. However, the delayed arrival of the Baldwin number 3 actually followed delivery of Baldwin number 4, the *Olema*, which arrived in mid-September along with the Mason *San Rafael*.[42] This reversed sequence suggests that Baldwin had regained a toehold in NPC's procurement planning even before Mason tried to sell the railroad the monster 15" × 20" bogie. The next three locomotives following the *Olema*—the *Bodega*, *Valley Ford*, and *Tamalpais*—were all Baldwin class 8-18 Cs, conventional 4-4-0's. With the interminable delay in the completion of the Northern Extension, these machines served the flat, lightly trafficked middle of the uncompleted railroad. Billed by Baldwin as passenger engines, they adapted easily to the NPC's demands for "general service."

Even after completion of the Northern Extension, it appeared that the North Pacific Coast would become a Baldwin stronghold. Three additional Baldwins were ordered on May 14, 1877, specifically to work the Dutch Bill lumber traffic: the *Moscow*, *Madrona*, and *Freestone*.[43] But the erection process for these engines took four to six months, during which business conditions began to fluctuate. Sometime between May 14 and October 23, a cancellation order was sent to Baldwin to stop delivery on all three engines. Baldwin redirected the *Moscow* to the Delphos & Kokomo Railroad and shipped the engine from its Philadelphia plant to the new customer. The *Madrona* and the *Freestone*, however, were redirected to an unspecified Cuban railroad. Still unfinished, the two remaining engines sat in the Philadelphia plant while the paperwork was shuffled.

Experiencing an autumn upswing in traffic, the North Pacific Coast sent Baldwin a reinstatement order on the *Madrona* and *Freestone* on October 23, 1877. Baldwin complied, canceling the redirect order from its books and committing the engines once again to California. Freight traffic then took its predictable winter downturn. In the early months of 1878, a second and final cancellation order was sent to Baldwin. This time the *Madrona* and *Free-stone* were redirected to the Chicago & Tomah Railroad, and this time they were shipped.

Mason salesmen smelled an opening.

The delivery of the Mason bogie named *Bully Boy*, designated North Pacific Coast number 8, occurred in June 1877, just before the first cancellation of the *Madrona* and *Freestone*.[44] Whatever internal squabbles were raging inside the company over selection of new engines, newspapers were clear about the reason the Mason was purchased. On July 12, 1877, the *Marin County Journal* reported the railroad's claim that "it would serve on the steep grade between Tyrone and Power with 10 cars, up from 5."[45]

Purchased to serve on the Salmon Creek and Dutch Bill Creek grades, the *Bully Boy* was a down-scaled version of the original *Tomales*. The implication that the Mason bogie could double normal pulling capacity was the semantic equivalent of canceling two Baldwins if one Mason could take their place; this is an argument that sounds as if it came from Shalling.

But the engine's specifications told another story. The *Bully Boy*'s operating weight was twenty-one tons, its tractive force seventy-six hundred pounds; a twenty-two-ton Baldwin 8-18 C carried a tractive force of about seven thousand pounds.[46] True, the Mason did gain a small advantage in pulling capacity by carrying more of its total engine weight on more drivers. But the difference in tractive force suggests a 10 percent improvement in tonnage rating, which is hardly double. Yet the testimonial was repeated, and exaggerated, a year later in a letter from Eliot Sparks to William Mason:

San Francisco, Cal. Dec. 7, 1878

Wm. Mason, Esq.
Dear Sir:

I have seen the N.P.C.R.R. and its shops together with your two engines and some of Baldwin's. The road itself is in excellent condition, principally of 55# rail, and good solid ballasting. Their sharpest curve is of 24°; the steepest grade is 135 ft. to the mile, which is on a curve of 15°. The Baldwin engines are of 12" × 16" cylinders, 42" drivers and of 22 tons weight in working order. These engines pull six cars of 12 tons each, including load, up the 135 ft. grade. The engineer of one I particularly examined informed me that she averaged 27 miles to a pint of oil; also that she had been running a year without turning off her tyres, which were in fair condition—those of the back drivers being worse than those of the forward, since on the short piece of road she was running on they do not turn the engines round but run them backward in going one way. The bogie engine of the same cylinders [*San Rafael*] and driving wheels but of only 19 ton weight in running order, will take ten loaded cars up the 135 ft. grade. Her engineer told me that she had run one hundred and twenty thousand miles without being off her wheels or center; he also said that she ran 50 miles to a pint of oil, 100 miles to 3/4 cord of wood and had frequently run her 3 1/2 miles in as many minutes, she running as easily as a car. Her tyres were still in excellent order,—better than any other engine I saw there whose tyres had not been turned off. Her brasses and wedges were in perfect order and her steam chests have never been taken off in the four years she has been running, her valves still being tight. The 13" × 16" bogie with six 36" drivers and of 21 tons weight [*Bully Boy*], is used for the heaviest freight traffic. She will take 14 loaded freight cars up the 135 ft. grade. Her tyres were in fair condition and have never been turned off.

The engines appear to be doing excellent work. I am informed that they steam beautifully and their steam joints continued tight, requiring little attention.

I remain, Sir,
Very Sincerely Yours,
Eliot Sparks (signed)

One year after the *Bully Boy* was delivered, Mason sold its first bogie to the Denver, South Park & Pacific Railroad for service in Colorado. Experience gained on the North Pacific Coast was valuable input for the design of next-generation engines. The first DSP&P bogie *Oro City* was apparently retrofitted with a pilot truck in November, 1878, converting it to a 2-6-6. With better tracking from a lead truck, the lateral play in the driving truck was better controlled and wear on the driving wheel flanges reduced. The *Oro City* retrofit was supervised by Mason factory mechanics, her engineering doubtless influenced by the builder's experience on the NPC.

The North Pacific Coast's uncertainty in motive-power strategy mirrored a deeper uncertainty about the business climate that greeted its arrival in Dutch Bill Canyon. Waiting for a boom lumber market to justify the motive power it had purchased, the North Pacific Coast instead found itself in market conditions characterized by rapidly declining lumber prices and unpredictable

NPC number 8, *Bully Boy*, much changed in appearance when photographed in the 1890s at San Anselmo, with fireman John Blaney. [Collection of Andrew J. Blaney, from Harold A. Lapham]

demand. The last Baldwin to arrive on the roster before the Russian River extension was opened (number 12, the *Sonoma*) was delivered in November 1876.[47] It should have been the vanguard of a flood of new traffic pouring over White's Hill and onto the Saucelito dock. Instead, stories have long persisted that the engine sat on a shop track, virtually unused.[48]

Little is known of the *Sonoma*'s short history on the North Pacific Coast. However, the Saucelito shop book recorded routine servicing of the engine for eight of the twelve calendar months of 1878, a brief period in which lumber traffic remained strong. During that time, the *Sonoma*'s consumption of oil, tallow, and waste hovered close to the average for the twelve locomotives in service. In July, for example, *Sonoma*'s expenses were $14.30, compared to the average service charge of $13.93 during the month.[49]

But in September 1878, the *Sonoma*'s recorded maintenance expenses vanished from the Saucelito shop book and did not reappear for the remainder of the year. The sudden omission suggests the newest locomotive on the roster was out of service, and also that the lumber traffic out of Dutch Bill Canyon had begun to dwindle.

If there was a single event to mark the low point in California's recession, it was the failure of the West's largest bank. The Bank of California suspended payments on all accounts on August 26, 1875. Two days later, its president, William Ralston, was dead, an apparent suicide.

The failure of one large bank triggered the failure of many smaller businesses. In just the first quarter of 1875, fifty-two bankruptcies were reported in California, totaling an aggregate value of $1.2 million. In the first quarter of 1876, the numbers rose to sixty-one failures aggregating $676,000.[50] The "weeding out of the weak horses," commented the *San Francisco Bulletin*, "will have a tendency to impart additional strength to those who survive." Nationally, in the same quarter of 1875, more than two thousand firms failed.

The truth about the Kimball Co. became public knowledge shortly after the bank's failure. For years, Kimball had been propped up by Ralston's personal support. The loans the bank made to Kimball, more than half a million dollars, were arranged by Ralston in the conflicted roles of Kimball board member and officer of the bank. Ralston covered up the conflict of interest. In failing to make payments, Kimball helped bring down the Bank of California. Now Ralston's failure would nearly destroy Kimball.

It took less than a month for the first assessment of Kimball's troubles to reach the public. On September 4, the *San Francisco Bulletin* noted:

> The Company have reduced their force to about one-half, and shortened up on their time to about eight hours, until they can get their affairs straightened out, the late events making it necessary that they should close up their old business and segregate interests. They are virtually going into liquidation and having a general settlement. They desire to give notice to all their customers to square up with them in order that they may in like manner settle with their creditors. It being Satur-

day noon, their usual time for paying off the men, we found them engaged in "calling the roll" and paying each one in full. They have paid their men regularly, and have met all their obligations so far, and will probably continue the business without material change. The company proposes to "go slow" until their business is all settled up.

The last known commercial ad for Kimball ran in the October 16, 1875, *San Francisco Newsletter*. With the delivery of the last four North Pacific Coast coaches the previous spring, production of railroad cars came to a standstill. From this point forward, Kimball would no longer be a major player in the accelerating California narrow gauge market.

Ironically, the same month that Kimball ran its last ad, the North Pacific Coast finally announced plans to more than double the size of its car fleet. The announcement had long been expected, the result of the railroad's initiative to reach the Dutch Bill mills and in the process tap its largest revenue source. In fact, the first press reports called out new car orders that would nearly triple the size of the freight car fleet, and double the size of its passenger car roster. The timing of Kimball's retrenchment must have seemed ironic to business observers such as R. G. Dun. Latham would acquire these cars without Kimball's help.

But Latham would also acquire the new rolling stock without Carter. The *San Francisco Bulletin* reported, on October 29:

> The Company are now getting ready for the increased business to be opened by the [Russian River] extension. They expect to run six through freight trains per day, and have already ordered from the East 250 flat cars, 60 box cars, 4 passenger coaches, and 6 engines, which will arrive early in the Spring. The rolling stock will then consist of 15 engines, 12 coaches, 100 box and 400 flat cars.[51]

It is unclear how long Tom Carter had known about the loss of the second, and largest, North Pacific Coast rolling stock contract, but the news must have come as a shock. The North Pacific Coast was his largest contract; it also gave Carter ties to an extended professional family, in which Carter and his crew cultivated long-term relationships with the railroad's entire mechanical department. Carter's first reaction may have been betrayal. Once on good terms with Moore, cultivating a place in Moore's organization through menial repair work paid at hourly rates, Carter might have cast about with suspicion and anger, trying to piece together an explanation.

The explanation remains elusive. Latham's vanity could have been a factor, fattened on shopping trips among large, established eastern car builders much as he did for locomotives or ferry boats (he would order two new luxury ferry boats from Lawrence and Foulkes's shipyard in Green Point, New York, in late 1876). Eastern suppliers were clearly making inroads into the railroad's procurement. Ramapo Wheel and Foundry in New York, Diamond State Iron Co. in Delaware, Bethlehem Iron Co., and Goodyear Rubber Co. all represented permanent accounts in the NPC cash books. All represented the influence of the established eastern railroad supply industry that had enjoyed, since the 1869 completion of the transcontinental railroad, direct access to California markets.

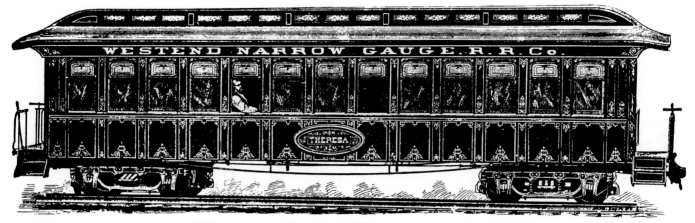

Narrow Gauge Passenger Car,

BUILT BY BARNEY & SMITH MANUFACTURING CO.,

DAYTON, OHIO.

35 ft. over sills, double seat each side of aisle, seats 46 Passengers, leaving room for stove and saloon. Weight 9¼ tons. Special notice asked to height of opening in window, giving ample room for Passengers to look out, and giving unusual opportunity for free ventilation through the large opening. All sash in deck made to open, a most important feature in so small a car with so great a carrying capacity.

Kimball's decline might have been a catalyst, leaving the railroad without a local source of new passenger equipment but somehow provoking deeper concerns about the stability of West Coast manufacturing in general, which was further encouragement to return to traditional marketplaces.

Possibly, Carter himself triggered the shift by demanding price equity with his Monterey work, and with successful contracts negotiated with the Santa Cruz & Felton during the summer of 1875. These new contract prices would have represented an increase of 30 percent above Carter's original batch of NPC freight cars, an increase Latham would likely have perceived as highway robbery.

Whether Tom Carter liked it or not, Barney and Smith, with nearly a thousand employees at its Dayton, Ohio, plant, got the new car work. It was considerably larger than Carter's original 1874 contract. North Pacific Coast Ledger no. 2 recorded the Barney and Smith account under folio 361. Its balance, on August 21, 1876, was $61,577.98.[52]

Under this contract, about 150 flatcars and 7 passenger cars were added to the roster, substantially fewer than suggested by the press but still doubling the railroad's freight cars and a 50 percent increase in its passenger equipment. Clearly, Barney and Smith had given Latham a deal. If, for example, Latham paid the original 1874 prices charged by Kimball and Carter ($3,600 for a coach and $350 per flatcar, respectively), the Barney and Smith order would have retailed at $74,100.

But the picture is not yet accurately drawn. Other charges were to be added to the total Barney and Smith balance. Labor, for example, jacked up the price of the freight equipment, since it was shipped west in the form of kits. These assembly costs added $35 per flatcar, or $5,250 total, raising Latham's out-of-pocket cost to $66,827.98. Transportation also had to be factored in, probably reflected in a $1,999.98 invoice from the Central

Pedestal detail (above) and elevation of the first Barney and Smith narrow gauge coach model, delivered to the North Pacific Coast as numbers 15, 16, and 17 in September 1876; the newer bullnose roof end style became a popular replacement for the older duckbill style as the 1870s came to a close. [Top, from Howard Fleming's *Narrow Gauge Railroads in America*, Kyle Wyatt collection; bottom, Bruce MacGregor]

By the mid-1870s, four large eastern car manufacturers (Jackson and Sharp, Billmeyer and Small, Ohio Falls, and Barney and Smith) offered comparable narrow gauge designs and products. All sought market share in the expanding western narrow gauge movement. On this page, Ohio Falls passenger trucks and first-class coach designs were illustrated in the *National Car Builder*, 1875. Of the four builders, Barney and Smith and Jackson and Sharp captured the largest western market share. [Smithsonian Institution]

Fig. 1.

Fig. 5.

Pacific Railroad to the North Pacific Coast dated May 28, 1877. The effective contract price, then, would have totaled $68,827.96.

But even with the extra charges, there was still a net savings to Latham, a difference of $5,273 between the total cost of completed Barney and Smith cars and the total cost that Kimball and Carter would have charged at their original 1874 prices. For Carter, the price squeeze was paralyzing, especially in the face of rising costs. By November 1875, he was paying rent and machine shop expenses to the North Pacific Coast, which bumped up his entire cost structure.

Hence the last and most likely explanation presented itself. The national recession gave Latham one of its few positive benefits, a dramatic price reduction from large eastern manufacturers intent on selling product at cost (perhaps even at a loss) to keep their factories in production. In the recessional economics of 1875, Latham could have made Barney and Smith a simple proposal. If they could beat current California prices, they would get all the rolling stock work for the Northern Extension. Latham, in turn, would get eastern-quality goods from an established master car builder.

Contemporary styling was included at no additional cost. The Barney and Smith coaches were more in vogue than Kimball designs. They sported newer bullnose ends on the clerestory roof, instead of the older duckbill style. Decorator glass was impaneled above the window sash. Their clerestory roof lines were lower and sleeker than Kimball's. Part of the order consisted of twelve-window cars, but the remainder of the cars were longer, featuring thirteen windows on a side instead of Kimball's twelve, adding seating ca-

pacity. Like the Kimball cars, the new Barney and Smith coaches were all equipped with Westinghouse air brakes and Miller automatic couplers.[53]

The coaches arrived assembled, probably in two batches—the first in September 1876, the second in May 1877.[54] The delivery of the first coaches preceded the opening of the extension by a comfortable margin of two months. Latham would not have to steal commute cars off the San Quentin train to open through passenger service to the Russian River.

The decision to ship the Barney and Smith freight cars as kits saved Latham money on transportation costs. Knocked down to sills and tightly bundled, several narrow gauge cars could ride west aboard one standard gauge flatcar.

How do we know the freight cars came as kits? On December 6, 1876, NPC's accountant made this entry on page 362 of cash book no. 2: "Our note dated November 22, 1876 favor Thomas Carter due and payable May 1, 1877 in payment for building 75 flat cars @ 35.00 as per voucher 423: $2625."

Tom Carter, willing to cut any deal with the North Pacific Coast that brought in revenue, had been reduced to doing the piecework of assembling another builder's product.

By 1893, the North Pacific Coast was ordering its first passenger equipment from Pullman, as is evident from the builder's photograph of coach 36, taken at the Pullman plant (top). An interior medallion (below) from the same coach was rescued from the badly decomposed car body of number 36 at Duncan's Mills in the 1980s, where the car had last served as a trackside residence. [Top, DeGolyer Library, Southern Methodist University; below, Bruce MacGregor]

In November 1876, the North Pacific Coast's steel gangs finally crossed the Brown's Canyon bridge, topped the divide at Howard's and descended Dutch Bill Creek into the heart of the timber holdings of the Russian River

Land and Lumber Co. The same month, Streeten's Mill was reached by rail and brought online. One by one, the other mills of the "big four" followed: Tyrone Mill, Madrona Mill, then Moscow Mills on the Russian River itself. The Tyrone and Moscow mills were both owned by Russian River Land and Lumber, the new Moore partnership that now included Latham. Streeten's Mill was also a Latham partnership, and both corporate entities operated separate wholesale lumber yards in Saucelito as an outlet for their Russian River operations. Only the Madrona Mill lay outside the fold of the Latham organization.

Each of these mill sites was laid out as a company town. Streeten's Mill was the example the *Marin County Journal* explored a few days before Christmas 1876:

> About five and a half months ago the first brush was cut away and the first tree felled in this virgin forest. Now there stands . . . a solid, substantial, model mill, with the best machinery. The mill was built on contract, by Mr. Brown, now its superintendent, and is an honor not alone to him, but also to its owner and projector . . . all of the 153 hands are

picked men. The Mills are surrounded with 25 dwelling houses—or
cottages, of various sizes, most of which would be an ornament to any
city. . . . They contain from three to four rooms, with kitchen, according to the size of the family. They are ceiled on the inside with tongued
and grooved 4-inch red and pine boards, alternately; outside rustic, oil
painted; height of room 10 feet, in the principle rooms; fireplace of
brick (burned on the place). . . . There is one very large house, with dining hall, kitchen, pantry, and rooms for the cook and his family; another house, with office and neat store, well stocked, with the exception
of liquor—where men and their families can buy everything at cost
price . . . blacksmith shop in another house, and so on.

   Now considering that six months ago this was a perfect wilderness,
and that all this thriving place has been built . . . all the lumber for the
whole having been manufactured there, and, with that on hand, is more
than three-quarters of a million feet, besides over three-quarters of a
million feet delivered to the railroad company—isn't that pushing
things?[55]

Latham, throwing money down a deep hole for two years, was desperate to "push things." No longer was the North Pacific Coast operating in a competitive vacuum. Peter Donahue had nearly succeeded in shadowing the North Pacific Coast's entire route. On the south end, Donahue's San Francisco & North Pacific was extending its track southward from Donahue's Landing, intent on breaching the Puerto Suello Ridge by tunnel and directly tapping the North Pacific Coast's business center in San Rafael.[56] On the north, Donahue's tracks had already reached the Russian River and slowly crept their way west, downstream toward Moscow Mills, until the San Francisco & North Pacific, by mid-1877, was less than four and a half miles from NPC's terminal at Moscow.

To fortify his position, Latham ordered the Russian River bridged at Moscow in December 1876. Spanned by a $24,000 Howe truss built by contractor Martin, the river crossing gained Latham access to a fifth large mill.[57] After promises of stock and other incentives from the railroad in July 1873, Alexander Duncan moved his operation inland from its original location at Jenner, on the mouth of the Russian River. By June 1877, Duncan was loading finished lumber onto North Pacific Coast flatcars. He also began promoting a business entity called Duncan's Mills Land and Lumber Co. First called "Duncanville," the resulting real estate development soon became known as Duncan's Mills.

On a wide flood plain of the Russian River, Duncan's Mills Land and Lumber laid out its town and mill yard. From an elevation on the north canyon wall, photographers could capture a view of Duncan's Mills in the foreground and Moscow Mills across the river, a landscape that soon included the imposing white mansion of Alexander Duncan himself. Perhaps there would be no more compelling a tableau to Moore and Latham's vision than this sweep of mills, narrow gauge track, and company town. But the same scene, viewed in winter, would often lie under three feet of brown Russian River flood water.

Now twenty-five miles from the nearest engine terminal at Tomales, Henry Foy's carpenters put up a turntable and two-stall roundhouse to serve not only mainline locomotives working the Dutch Bill divide but also the mill switch engine *Tyrone*, an 0-4-0 ordered from Baldwin to handle local mill switching. Piles of split stuff, as high as a locomotive tender, lined the turntable lead with fuel wood. The two-story, verandahed Julian's Hotel opened sixty rooms across from the depot, and was "full as a tick" by mid-June when tourists sniffed their way north, curious about the country the railroad had opened up.

The railroad came alive that summer. Doubleheaders squealed around the twenty-four-degree curves on White's Hill with a thousand members of the iron molders union, headed for the moss-carpeted picnic ground on Paper Mill Creek. The combined production of lumber from all five mills was estimated at 175,000 board feet a day.[58] Two freight trains ran south from the mills each week day, bringing fifty carloads of lumber to Moore's yard or Streeten's yard in Saucelito. Even with help from the Mason *Bully Boy*, delivered in July to help ease the bottleneck, the railroad still complained publicly about not having enough motive power to move the traffic: "Two freight trains [a day] now running are unable to do the business of the road. Extra trains are frequently put on and still the business crowds. A gentleman tells us that he thinks the freight business from above Tomales will exceed $500 per day this summer."[59]

The new revenue reached flood tide that same summer: $33,324.70 in July, $37,716.07 in August, and then a thrilling $41,254.62 in September.[60] Operating expenses for September, in comparison, were $23,462.99. Even with adjustment for the onerous interest payments (which the railroad seldom made), the North Pacific Coast was at last operating in the black.

For the few remaining months of 1877, twenty-car lumber trains crept across the twin Howe trusses at Brown's Canyon, shrouded in a faint blue haze from overheating brake shoes. Like sailors high up in ship's rigging, the acrobatic brakemen rode the top of the lumber loads nearly 150 feet above the creek. They soon learned to keep a tight eye on the bridge's water barrels as the train crawled across the top of the truss. "Surf in the barrels" was a sure sign of resonance in the enormous wooden structure and a sign that the bridge was in danger of shaking itself apart under the vibration of moving trains. Train crews would alert bridge gangs to ease up the tension rods, thus detuning the huge structure to a safe, enharmonic rattle.

Further south, the lumber loads went down the tortuous loops at White's Hill with handbrakes set by straining brakemen, to the signal of short blasts from the engine's whistle, often at night, and often in the dripping moisture of thick Bay fog that had crept inland from the Golden Gate.

Nightmares came with the heavy traffic. The *Marin County Journal* told the story of a brakeman sitting bolt upright in bed in the middle of the night, both hands gripping his screaming wife's head like the brake wheels he trusted his life to, while he dreamt of running away down the White's Hill grade.[61]

On June 26, 1877, the North Pacific Coast cash books recorded the payment of $1,750 to the monthly periodical *Resources of California*. Heavily slanted toward the interests of the Central Pacific Railroad and its nearly universal theme of economic development in the state, the publication was a showcase for capitalists willing to pay its vanity prices.

Latham orchestrated an elaborate four-part testimonial to begin with the June edition and conclude with September, timed to coincide with what was estimated to be the completion of track to the Russian River. He took advantage of the publication's large format (roughly 18" × 24" page size) to reproduce six engravings of the railroad's scenic landmarks, lumber mills, and bridges. The line drawings were based on work of the celebrated photographer Eadweard Muybridge, apparently commissioned by Latham for the series. None of the original photographs are extant, leaving the engravings as the earliest realistic documentation of the North Pacific Coast at the time of its completion.[62] The engravings, and the companion articles, portrayed the narrow gauge as evidence of a new prosperity spreading through California.

The *San Francisco Wasp*, on the other hand, took a surprisingly bellicose view of the completed North Pacific Coast. In its October 27, 1877, issue, the *Wasp* remarked at how rapidly the NPC would be able to denude the coastal redwood belt of native forest—a strangely modern, environmentally conscious perspective on the social and economic value that underlay the railroad. With the price of redwood declining rapidly in the recession economy, the *Wasp* understood the poor trade that the railroad offered the state. In the end, the irreplaceable timber would represent little or no actual monetary gain for the economy. In 1874, Thomas Carter paid $30 per thousand board feet for sawn redwood used in constructing North Pacific Coast boxcars.[63] Three years later, the price had plummeted to $12 per thousand board feet in the retail market, which, the *Wasp* concluded, "is just about the cost of its production and transportation. The object, apparently, is to create freight for the railroad, but it should be recollected that this freight cannot last much longer."

What kept Carter in Saucelito was not the piecework on the Barney and Smith flats but new contract work from outside. We know of at least four such contracts in 1875 and 1876, all relatively small lots of cars that Carter needed to supplement the increasingly meager work trickled down from the North Pacific Coast. The contracts were scattered across roughly twelve months, occurring toward the end of Carter's Saucelito tenure: ten freight cars for the Santa Cruz & Felton in June and another thirty in November 1875; thirty cars for the Nevada County Narrow Gauge in July 1875; twenty freight cars and four passenger cars for the Santa Clara Valley Railroad in November, although Carter didn't deliver the cars until early spring 1876, to the SCV's successor, the South Pacific Coast; and finally, in June 1876, two relatively inexpensive passenger cars for the Santa Cruz & Felton.

To support this work, Carter's kit strategy arose largely as a cost savings measure, using Saucelito shop capacity in lieu of expensive field factories. Again, John Carroll's experience with Davenport and Bridges gave him early experience in the kit strategy, and a model for Carter's adaptation. It was a hybrid approach to manufacturing, combining the advantages of both field factories and those in a fixed location. A permanent factory allowed mass production of mortices, tenons, gains, drill-outs, and moldings, doing the most technical, repetitive part of the job with skilled craftsmen based at a permanent site. Shipment of kits (not assembled cars) allowed dense packing of parts for delivery by rail or water, and also use of lower-cost labor as assemblers at the final destination.

The modularity of freight car construction (as opposed to passenger car construction) permitted easy, bolt-together assembly at the destination, relying on a large number of mortices and gains to interlock the pieces in a relatively foolproof assembly process. Kits also gave the purchasing railroad the option of buying and stockpiling the cars they would eventually need, but delaying assembly of a portion of them until they were actually required in revenue service, thus saving the railroad labor costs.

For the next two years, Carter relied on kit building for all of its contract freight car orders. The first Carter kits were probably manufactured in May and June 1875, for the Santa Cruz & Felton, a year before the first Barney and Smith kits arrived in Saucelito.

Few details of Carter's kits survive, but the idea was to package the pre-cut and predrilled sills, bolsters, decking, siding and roofing, castings, and bolts and fasteners necessary to put the parts together. In all, between June 1875 and the following June, roughly fifty-nine flats and thirty-one boxcars were kitted and shipped to customers other than the North Pacific Coast, along with six assembled passenger cars.

Only a portion of these kits may have been constructed in Saucelito. There is strong evidence that Carter operated a small San Francisco factory during at least part of this period, an attempt to control their own production environment and bring to closure a partnership with the North Pacific Coast that had, by the summer of 1875, reached the end of its usefulness. Chapter Nine explores the San Francisco operation under the title of "The Lost Factory," but it was clear, by the first of 1876, that Carter had found the motive to strike out on his own.

Because of Carter's shift to external customers, in December 1875, the North Pacific Coast began to charge him rent on the car shop, amounting to $50 a month plus additional charges for power, fuel, and materials; this was proof that the NPC's steam-powered woodworking tools were being used by Carter to produce cars for customers other than the North Pacific Coast. The amount of these charges varied from a low of $9.05 in July 1876 to a high of $256.11 in December 1875 (which coincided with the peak month of combined SC&F and SCV kit work).

To put these numbers into perspective, the shop's monthly expense for cord wood in December 1882 would total $87.50, during a period in which little new car building activity was taking place.[64] In the dimly remembered month of December 1875, Carter burned nearly three times as much cord wood in what may have been the most productive month in its entire history.

During the same period when rent and shop charges began, the shop books recorded little Carter activity around car repair, or woodcraft work for the North Pacific Coast itself, an indication that the railroad might have begun relying on its own car department for these services, and that the relationship between Carter and the NPC's management, once personal, was beginning to dissolve.

On paper, the retrenchment was at least orderly. There was still money to be made off the eroding commitment between Carter and the NPC. During the same period, from December 1875 until the close-out of all Carter activity in November 1876, the North Pacific Coast cash books reported payments to Carter of $12,508.62. The dates of payment fall completely outside the "new car contract" that covered the initial order of about 140 freight cars and are probably the least understood in Carter's four-year tenure with the NPC. Few payments were identified by the kind of product or service Carter provided. Of the total, $2,625 is accounted for by assembly of seventy-five known Barney and Smith flatcars. With a total of three hundred freight cars on the roster by July 31, 1877, at least seventy-five additional flatcars, allegedly sold as kits by Barney and Smith, were probably assembled by Carter and charged at a piecework rate. The cash books simply do not call them out by name.

Even the largest payment to Carter during this period, $5,320 in February 1876, was still small potatoes compared to the disbursements made to Barney and Smith—for example, $46,374.35 paid on January 11, 1877. Tom Carter must have watched the incursion of the eastern manufacturer with bitterness. For a time, he had let customers become partners. The relationship he established with the railroad's managers and crews was unusually, perhaps artificially, close. Believing he was one of them, a trusted member of the railroad's inner circle, Carter had to accept the fact that he was now an outsider. The NPC's startup phase had ended, and with it the business conditions that brought Tom Carter to Saucelito in the first place. It was not clear that those business conditions could be replicated again in recession-weary California.

Rent and shop charges stopped on November 1, 1876, the date of the final recorded Carter activity in cash book no. 2 and the likely date of Carter's exodus from the North Pacific Coast facilities at Saucelito.

Martin and his family stayed at the Easterby Street address throughout the spring of 1877, but the rest of the crew, or those who can be traced— John Carroll, Henry Barth, Alexander Finn, and John Larkin—began to gravitate to rented apartments at 608 Sixth Street in San Francisco.

Carroll's checkered involvement with the North Pacific Coast probably lasted until nearly the end. On January 11, 1877, the cash book credited $2.50 to Carroll as "unclaimed wages"; it was perhaps the company's last debt to the old railroadist.

———————

In January 1878, the press reported Milton Latham again ill, departing California for rest and recuperation in the East. There were rumors he would soon die, and there were also rumors he was searching for sources of badly needed cash to stave off impending bankruptcy. The three initial bank loans remained unserviced, remnants of the original bond hypothecate accounts set up in 1873. An embarrassing new loan, $350,000 borrowed at a hefty 10 percent interest from the Nevada Bank on January 20, 1877, may have been taken out from Milton's old adversary to manage payments on the first three loans.[65] Latham took the hiatus seriously enough to relinquish the leadership of the railroad. In his absence, a close personal friend, Joseph Eastland, was named president of the North Pacific Coast. The cash books contain proof that Eastland bought his way into a limited partnership, taking over a portion of a note that Austin Moore owed the railroad. The transaction was dated February 25, 1878.[66]

On April 8, Eastland was touring the line in the M.S.L., the Kimball Director's Car, attached to the end of the regular south-bound train. His wife and his infant daughter, Ethel, were aboard, along with the railroad's superintendent, John Doherty, and a party of officers, making a group of eight.

They could have been discussing the new business climate. The mills along Dutch Bill Creek had closed after a drop in lumber prices, and although the national recession was showing signs of easing, a dark cloud seemed to hover over the fortunes of the narrow gauge. Little interest had been paid on the $2 million indebtedness Latham had incurred since 1875, and creditors were becoming vocal.[67] Along with the presidency of the narrow gauge, Latham had resigned his position with the London and San Francisco Bank, making it more difficult for the railroad to negotiate any extension on loans.

Doherty was concerned about surplus motive power and had recommended cost-cutting measures, beginning with sale of the newest engine, *Sonoma*.

Suddenly the car shuddered violently. In a heavily wooded section of line at Tocoloma Station just north of the paper mill, the Director's Car derailed, whiplashed to the left, then to the right, wagging like a tail behind the moving train. Its Miller hook coupler was wrenched away from the coach ahead, letting the car roll to the edge of the creek, pitch over on its side, and slide roof-first toward the water. Part way down, its fall was broken by a bay tree that penetrated the clerestory roof, ripping the tree out by the roots and cushioning the descent.

Twenty-six-inch-diameter chilled iron car wheel, A. Whitney and Sons, manufacturers, ca. 1888. [Bruce MacGregor]

When the car settled sixty feet below the right-of-way, nearly upside down, its plush velvet furniture lay in a heap against the ceiling, trapping its passengers. Eastland lay unconscious. Doherty was bleeding from scratches on his face. Eastland's daughter sustained internal injuries, which would claim her life two days later.

The Marin County Journal reported what it knew at the end of the week: "No blame attaches to the railroad men, as the accident was one which could not have been foreseen. The car is on the track again, and not much is damaged. It [is] not yet known what caused the accident, but as the track was found all right, it must have been some break about the car."[68]

In subsequent reports, the cause was isolated to the car's trucks.[69] Apparently wheels or axles failed while the train was in motion, a strangely familiar echo of the troubles Kimball had suffered from the iron castings manufactured in local foundries, in particular Risdon, back in 1873. Risdon's culpability in the wreck of the M.S.L. is speculative, but the issue raised by the wreck persisted as the California railroad supply industry grew. Would the primitive technologies that had launched the narrow gauge movement in the seventies sustain it as traffic demand increased in the eighties?

Over time, California wheel manufacturing became an example of retrenchment. Carter Brothers would, during the 1880s and 1890s, routinely order wheels from Asa Whitney and Sons in Philadelphia, or Bass and Co. from the Midwest, an indication that large-scale eastern suppliers could produce specialized parts more cheaply, and more reliably, than their western counterparts.[70] The exception, of course, was the Southern Pacific Sacramento shop, its own supplier of chilled car wheels. The topic of Carter's supply chain of the eighties is explored in Chapter Eleven.

Coincidentally, just three months after the wreck of the M.S.L. George Kimball's creditors brought suit against him in federal bankruptcy court. The creditors included the California Wire Works, the Nevada Bank, Waterhouse and Lester, the Occidental Foundry, and the Goodyear Rubber Co., not to mention Kimball's one-time partner, Richard Ogden. Tottering on the brink of extinction, Kimball actually mounted a successful defense. Some of the key claims were dismissed by the court as unprovable; the others were too small to force Kimball to liquidate its assets. The bankruptcy suit was dismissed on March 31, 1879.[71]

The Kimball Carriage and Car Co. had become a legally owned subsidiary of the Ralston estate. Under its umbrella, now free from legal challenge, George Kimball would continue to build wagons and carriages in a small Fourth and Silver Street factory. But his days of producing mainline rolling stock were over. The unlucky M.S.L., later renamed *Millwood* by the North Pacific Coast, was one of the last railroad cars Kimball ever built.

Tom Carter, at least, could count himself the sole survivor. Looking for a home, cast out of the biggest narrow gauge railroad in the state by pressure from eastern manufacturers, in 1877 Carter was virtually alone in the West Coast car manufacturing trade.

Streeten's Mill, located in narrow Dutch Bill Creek Canyon some three miles north of Occidental, was the first of five large Russian River lumber mills to feed traffic into the North Pacific Coast when it opened in November 1876. Judging by the Radley and Hunter stack on the Baldwin 4-4-0 above, this photograph was taken shortly after the mill opened. By the following June, four additional mills—Tyrone, Madrona, Moscow, and Duncan's—would come on line with a combined capacity of nearly 175,000 board feet a day. Photographs by J. G. Smith. [This page, California State Library]

The ridge-top village of Occidental (below) became the gathering point for cars of finished lumber, hauled from the Russian River Land and Lumber Co.'s mills in Dutch Bill Canyon by the small Baldwin tank engine *Tyrone* (above) and assembled at the top of the grade. From Occidental, long strings of loaded flatcars would descend the Salmon Creek Canyon grade to the south. [Below, collection of George Taylor Hanson, from Harold A. Lapham; above, collection of Andrew J. Blaney, from Harold A. Lapham]

In November 1877, Occidental became a railhead on the North Pacific Coast, where local viniculture could be loaded aboard Carter twenty-four-foot boxcars parked in front of the Union Hotel (top of page). Seasonal marketing of Christmas trees became a local cottage industry. After harvesting the trees in early December, an entire family would accompany carloads of trees to San Francisco (lower right), operating their own Christmas tree lot until the cash crop was sold. [Top, collection of Sonoma County Historical Society, from Harold A. Lapham]

SONOMA Cⁿ   THE RUSSIAN RIVER R.R. BRIDGE .

Contractors Martin and Wood were awarded the $34,000 Russian River bridge project in March 1877. Once finished, the North Pacific Coast used the spindly Howe truss to gain access to the river's north bank and the newly completed mill of Alexander Duncan (below). First named Duncanville, the railhead quickly became known as Duncan's Mills. There, Julian's Hotel (right) offered the road-weary traveler sixty rooms and the best cuisine in town. [Top, California State Library; right, Jack Farley collection; below, California Historical Society]

By 1878, Duncan's Mills (below) had become the northern terminal of the railroad, with a turntable and cord wood pile marking the site of a small engine facility that would stable both road locomotives and the *Tyrone*, the mill switch engine. Most of the features of the small community are visible at this early date: from the right, the depot, Duncan's Mills Land and Lumber Co. office (directly above the depot), Julian's Hotel, Duncan's sawmill (directly above the turntable), and (on the extreme left) the mansion of Alexander Duncan, under construction. In the panorama reproduced on the overleaf, taken by Frank Randolph in 1886, a two-stall engine house has been added, evidence of substantial traffic originating from Duncan's sawmill itself and from Moscow Mills, visible across the river. Handicapped by the slowing economies of the lumber industry, the terminal gradually became a living museum. By the turn of the century (right), one of the line's original Carter boxcars remained in service, its primitive eight-ton wood beam trucks little changed over the past two decades. [Below, collection of Silvio De Carlie, from Harold A. Lapham; right, Bancroft Library; overleaf, California Historical Society]

R. R. Bridge Bayou.

Santa Cruz Supply Chain

Seven days before Christmas 1873, Howard Schuyler shook hands with Frederick Hihn in the knife-edged winds blowing across the Santa Cruz pier. Hihn, the state assemblyman from Santa Cruz County, greeted Schuyler at the California Powder Co.'s wharf as the twenty-nine-year-old engineer disembarked from a coastal steamer. News of the celebrated engineer's visit had already traveled by word of mouth around Monterey Bay, and the handshake exchanged on the pier earned Hihn the kind of politically crafted moment that a mayor might reap from a visit of the governor, or perhaps a U.S. senator: "He came here on the invitation of F. A. Hihn, esq., and with the latter gentleman took a drive on Thursday over a portion of the proposed railroad to Watsonville. Mr. Schuyler is a young man of acknowledged ability in his profession. He made many friends while here and was charmed by the climate and scenery of Santa Cruz."[1]

Schuyler may well have come looking for work. In the heavy rains that pelted Marin County earlier that month, grading on Schuyler's North Pacific Coast had completely shut down. Austin Moore had just departed for Europe on a dubious fundraising mission, leaving Schuyler with instructions to go slow. In response, Schuyler furloughed his field engineers for the winter. With little guarantee of new funding, Schuyler may have visited Santa Cruz to cultivate professional options.

Hihn and Schuyler dressed in mud boots and linen dusters and squeezed together on a buggy seat. Storms had soaked the Monterey Bay area as well. As their team grew leggings of gray adobe, Hihn drove Schuyler around the project, searching for an opening. The local press had grown to understand Hihn's guileless measurement of strangers: "though a cool, dispassionate, quiet appearing man, [Hihn sees] a person through-and-through at a glance. His eyes suggested the adage 'still waters run deep.' He is evidently a good man for a friend, but an undesirable enemy. His active physique is backed by a brain that is rarely excelled."[2]

Hihn could easily have patronized Schuyler's sense of self-importance to "the movement." Under Schuyler's stewardship, the vision of a coastal narrow gauge trunk line had first been rendered visible to the public by the work going on in Marin County. Now Hihn would reveal himself taking the next step: construction of a narrow gauge link between San Francisco and Monterey Bay, more than one hundred miles of narrow gauge every bit as techni-

Opposite: Soquel Creek Bridge at Camp Capitola, ca. 1876, in a R. E. Wood photograph. [Dan Matthews collection]

cally challenging as the North Pacific Coast. Hihn may have made his point by gesturing at the muddy wound of open earthworks at Woods Lagoon or Soquel Creek. The bulwark of a coastal trunk line would begin like this, small segments of inexpensive, locally financed short line, by happenstance lined up on the map like a serration of stitches. Given enough time and pluck, Hihn concluded, the seam created by such stitches would begin to hold tight against the expanding Stanford monopoly.

As they rode together, Schuyler and Hihn sized each other up—two generous egos crowded into a buggy seat. A national voice for an admittedly unproven technology, Howard Schuyler had begun to influence the state's thinking toward a narrow gauge movement that had taken root primarily in Colorado, the South, and the Midwest.[3] He was a spokesman for its technical, not its political, foundations. In the two years since his seminal work with the Denver & Rio Grande, Schuyler could point to rapid gains in the popularity of narrow gauge, measured, for example, by the sale of new locomotives. Baldwin Locomotive Works, in 1873, was experiencing a surge in orders for narrow gauge locomotives that would, in the following year, account for more than 25 percent of its revenue.[4] Schuyler was in a position to influence Baldwin's designs, and sales.

Hihn was in a position to influence the funding to buy such machines. Adroit at politics, he had slowly and painfully pieced together a local railroad initiative. Elected a state legislator in 1869, for two years Hihn championed public funding in a county that considered itself too poor to afford standard gauge railroads. So in 1872 he changed tactics, and gauge. A bond issue, finally brought to vote in a public election in September 1872, specified that the county would aid in constructing a railroad "of not less than three foot gauge," scaling the project to the county's purse and encouraging a plurality.

But by 1874 Hihn found himself in the position of the emperor without clothes, bringing money, resources, political influence, and (in his own mind) leadership to bear on a project he had few technical qualifications to lead. At forty-five the richest man in Santa Cruz County (if one didn't count outsiders Claus Spreckels or Henry Cowell), Hihn had never managed the practical, day-to-day details of building a railroad. He needed Schuyler—ironically not as a chief engineer, which Hihn imagined himself to be—but as an expert witness to the technology slowly transforming California's coastal transportation. After much of the railroad had been planned, surveyed, graded, and specified, Hihn turned to Schuyler for a badly needed reality check. Howard Schuyler's visit therefore offered the kind of risk Frederick Hihn routinely assumed as a politician: the possibility of his unmasking on the one hand, and his best alibi on the other.

Hihn undoubtedly turned to Schuyler for referrals to other professionals whose services would soon become critical. He needed to know, for example, the name of a good bridge contractor. Who could Schuyler recommend? What were their qualifications? Perhaps they stopped to look out over the long, shallow Soquel Creek arroyo that would soon cradle the longest bridge on the railroad. The arroyo would consume the stock of several large retail lumber yards before the spindly rails could cross to the bluffs on the far side.

That day, Hihn probably heard Tom Carter's name—and in the same breath the name of Pacific Bridge—for the first time. Carter's Strawberry Point drawbridge design had been finished in April, the bridge itself completed barely a month before Schuyler's visit to Santa Cruz. Yes, Schuyler knew a local bridge engineer, a man younger than himself, whose work he had personally witnessed. The contractor that executed his designs, Pacific Bridge Co., was already doing wagon bridge work in Santa Cruz County, some of it close to Hihn's right-of-way. Hihn could see examples of their work already completed within the county.

Eager to secure the services of the contractors, Hihn would not spend a cent on Schuyler himself. Instead, Hihn wasted little time getting in touch with Thomas Carter. Hihn was in San Francisco buying rail in early March 1874, and the trip offered an opportunity to meet Carter and close an engineering contract.[5] Carter had been living at 19 Powell Street in the City, listed in Langley's Directory as a draftsman. But in the intervening nine months since the Strawberry Point bridge work, he held no known jobs. Hihn didn't have to plead. Carter took up rented rooms in Santa Cruz less than three weeks after Hihn's visit to San Francisco and began laying out the first of five large Howe truss spans the Santa Cruz Rail Road would need to reach the Monterey County line.[6]

What Hihn and Schuyler actually witnessed that muddy December day was a piecemeal attack on the first, and most difficult, five miles of the Santa Cruz Rail Road's grade. That month, the work stretched from Santa Cruz south nearly to Aptos and combined the efforts of at least nine independent contractors, some who held contracts on sections as short as six hundred feet. Only one, Castle and Crofton, had prior experience in heavy railroad construction. John McLaughlin was a county road contractor and livery stable owner who lived locally in Corralitos. Seth Blanchard was a part-time tutor, well-digger, and sexton at the local Evergreen cemetery. The remainder, Jake Durm, John Woods, M. O. Boyle, James Corcoran, and Thomas Daniel Sargent, were farmers or laborers who owned teams, moonlighting to supplement their income.[7]

Michael O. Boyle, for example, patiently attacked a twenty-foot-deep, thousand-foot-long cut at the edge of Woods Lagoon, today's Santa Cruz small craft harbor. Boyle, a stone mason by trade, was credited with making the first cut on the railroad.[8] His contract made provision for himself, his sons, three laborers, and a single four-wheeled dump car, on loan from the railroad company. Boyle and his crew pushed the dump car back and forth on portable track that slowly, a few feet each day, descended into the deepening maw of the cut.

By April 1874, the size and complexity of this human ant hill had doubled. Excavations had been pushed out twelve miles from Santa Cruz to the edge of the San Andreas Ranch, in the hills that rimmed the Pajaro Valley and the proposed terminal of Pajaro. By this time, eighteen contractors were engaged. The biggest, Mead's job located south of Tannery Gulch, employed eighty Chinese laborers, twenty white laborers, and fourteen teams and scrapers. The smallest, under the stewardship of Mr. Steel, employed just six wheelbarrows.

Professional contractors, smelling an opportunity, quickly ran up against Hihn's fierce sense of local patronage. When a railroad contractor named Dennison showed up in early February and suggested he could solve all of Hihn's problems by combining the contracts into one, providing engineering services for the entire railroad, the *Santa Cruz Sentinel* gave the proposal rave reviews.[9] Frederick Hihn threw Dennison scraps: "a small job that can be done in two weeks."[10]

The message to Dennison was the same as the message to Howard Schuyler. Hihn would build the Santa Cruz Rail Road his way, which was to say, without the involvement of freelance industry professionals—and in particular, without the involvement of an outside chief engineer.

In August 1874, Hihn invited the stockholders of the railroad on a picnic to view the grade (still without rail). An attending reporter from the *Sentinel* may have captured a glimpse into Hihn's feelings toward Howard Schuyler: "No fancy salaries have been paid to ornamental engineers or to superintendents of construction. A cheaper road has never been constructed in California."[11]

The fact remained generally unchallenged that except for contract surveyors and bridge builders, no "ornamental engineers" were ever hired into a permanent position on the Santa Cruz Rail Road. Two local men were solely responsible for the management of the work: Frederick Hihn and Titus Hale. They had known each other since the days of the California gold rush, when Hale sold nuts and Hihn sold candy on the dirt streets of Sacramento.[12] Nearly twenty-five years later, they bounced over the muddy roads of Santa Cruz County together in a buckboard, stopping to direct scraper teams and shovelmen, managing the smallest details of the work. The *Sentinel* usually referred to the old friends simply as Hale and Hihn—intoned like the oath "hale and hearty," a condition of improving health in the prosperity of the project and the region.

In Hihn's own exaggerated assessment, based on court testimony given in 1878, his role covered virtually every facet of the railroad's civil engineering:

> I know pretty well all about the road. I superintended, assisted in the location of the road, and in fixing grades; that is to say, the ascents and descents, and making the calculation as to the quantities of dirt to be filled and to be excavated, and as to the location of bridges, and the length of bridges, and manner of construction of bridges and culverts, and everything else appertaining to it.[13]

Unlike Kidder's Monterey & Salinas Valley (by April 1874, well into its final location work), and unlike Schuyler's North Pacific Coast, Hale and Hihn managed largely local resources to accomplish what other startup narrow gauge lines were hiring from outside contractors. Their bias toward local control and local resources soon became an obsession. Early in the project, the *Sentinel* gave evidence that the Santa Cruz Rail Road, at $15,129 per mile, was indeed the most cheaply built narrow gauge in California at the time of its completion in 1876.[14]

The *Sentinel* told the truth, though it failed to grasp a corollary: it was also the most time-consuming narrow gauge, per mile, to be built in the state. It took three years to complete twenty-one miles of railroad. At that rate, it would have taken the Santa Cruz Rail Road more than a decade to reach San Francisco.

If Hihn believed the county was capable of building its own railroad, the county was more than ready to prove him right.

There was an ethic at work in Santa Cruz County that has been described as Yankee ingenuity, a manufacturing tradition having roots in the early California shipbuilding trade that predated statehood and persisted in the county, although on a small scale, through the 1870s. In a crude clapboard building tucked under a Santa Cruz landmark called Mission Hill, a blacksmith named Elihu Anthony set up one of the first foundries on the Pacific Coast in 1848, making ship irons in the same building where Tom Amner, in the 1870s, would begin to cast railroad parts.[15] Crossing the boundaries of any one business or industry, cottage manufacturing succeeded as an ex-

Bird's-eye view of Santa Cruz, ca. 1873, before the inception of the Santa Cruz Rail Road (or the Santa Cruz & Felton); from a lithograph by Gifford. [Museum of Art and History, Santa Cruz]

SANTA CRUZ, CAL.

Bird's-eye view of Santa Cruz, ca. 1880, after completion of the South Pacific Coast Railroad. [University of California, Santa Cruz, Special Collections]

pression of the region's character, a mind-set built on the vernacular genius of local tradesmen. Anthony, blacksmith, founder, merchant, town water concessionaire, and eventually state legislator, set an early example.

Somehow, even in the middle of the recession of the 1870s, these virtues shaped the character of not just the capitalists of Santa Cruz County but the wage earner, the small businessman, the one-man shopkeeper, the three-man factory—all in their own estimation connected to a larger share of the future success of their region than their counterparts in San Francisco or Sacramento.

The county's commercial renaissance had its poet, although his images were cast on photographic wet plates rather than paper. Romanes Erastus Wood, a thirty-five-year-old machinist, photographer, and inventor, and the owner of the 160-acre Troutdale Farm at the headwaters of the San Lorenzo River, was an embodiment of the cultural and industrial revolution going on around him. Wood's nascent ventures included watch repair and the manufacture of brooms, matches, potato knives, wisps, brushes, and dusters, as well as the "Wood Patented Gopher Trap," along with a photography studio that accounted for most of his living.[16] By 1875, Wood was in the early planning stages of a photographic exhibit at the American Centennial Exhibition in Philadelphia, where he would display a graphic testimonial to the entrepreneurialism and energy of Santa Cruz County. Working largely in stereo format, Wood captured his neighbors literally inventing a new economic basis for their lives. Many of the themes and locations he photographed were Hihn developments, and many views were closely connected with work on the Santa Cruz Rail Road, or its rival, the Santa Cruz & Felton.

Wood began depicting a period of rapid commercial integration in Santa

Cruz County. Like the house that Jack built, a number of the county's many small production units began to rearrange themselves into discrete steps of longer, more complex manufacturing processes. Similar businesses that normally competed began to specialize, each adapting to new demand that paid them to distinguish their products from those of their competitor, while both remained in the service of a larger, more technically complex industry. Described by Nathan Rosenberg as a "compulsive technological sequence," such rapid transformation of adjacent industries and markets tended to take shape in the press of a single, new integrating technology.

Examples of such a sequence began to appear in Santa Cruz County in 1873. Hihn's grading contractors, for one, encouraged integration and expansion in local foundries. To increase earth-moving capacity at his Porter's field and Ord's farm locations, John McLaughlin designed a mechanical excavator and was procuring castings and parts for a prototype at W. H. Martin's New Foundry in November 1873.[17] Thomas Amner was Martin's competitor at the Santa Cruz Foundry (also referred to as the "old foundry") on nearby River Street. Both firms supplied castings for heavy industrial applications: sawmill boilers and engines; pumps; parts for reapers, mowers, threshing machines, plows, stove castings, wagon hardware; and specialized castings for the powder mill. Both works had complete tooling if castings needed to be machined. But Amner would soon understand that by allowing Martin to specialize in one kind of railroad work, it could win other kinds, allowing each to specialize, and allowing each to profit. Soon, McLaughlin's finished prototype would be at work on Santa Cruz Rail Road cuts, nicknamed "Chinee mechanique."

Charles Wellington Davis encouraged diversification in the local lumber industry, which until this point in time was dominated by production of coastal redwood. Davis envisioned increased local production of a raw material basic to railroad construction: Oregon pine, commonly known today as Douglas fir. Mixed in with stands of redwood along the summit of the Coast Range, Douglas fir remained one of the least used of the county's forest products.

Before coming to Santa Cruz County, Davis had worked as master car builder for the Market Street Railway in San Francisco and later as car builder for the Southern Pacific. He came to Santa Cruz as an architect primarily in Hihn's employ, developing his commercial properties and in 1873 completing his Santa Cruz residence. When Davis gave an interview to the *Sentinel* in 1872, railroads, not homes, were the focal point of his search for commercial potential. He emphasized the unique role that the county's stands of fir might play in manufacturing railroad rolling stock. He mentioned the success of the wood in crafting ceiling joists in Hihn's Pacific Avenue store. Fir could play a similar role in railroad car sills. "It is a superior material," the *Sentinel* paraphrased Davis, "for building truck platform[s] and passenger cars. It is superior in point of strength, elasticity, hardness and durability. We hope railroad and car builders will make a note of this."[18] Indeed, they did.

Frederick Hihn encouraged the synthesis of lumber and foundry industries in the manufacture of railroad rolling stock. Sometime in the late fall of 1873, after finishing the drawings for Hihn's Santa Cruz home and the

R. E. Wood's commercial photography logo (top) and portrait (bottom). [Bottom, Special Collections, Meriam Library, California State University, Chico; top, Dan Matthews collection]

Pacific Avenue store, Charles Davis got Hihn's contract for designing and building some of the cars for the Santa Cruz Rail Road. It may have been Davis, in fact, who encouraged individual Santa Cruz suppliers to assign themselves a new role in the local supply chain. Within a geographical radius of one mile, in a city of less than four thousand people, Davis pieced together sources of raw materials, tooling, and labor for an emerging railroad supply business.

Davis himself did mechanical engineering and working drawings; George Treat cut commercial grades of local timber; George Gragg's planing mill (and Allen and Rennie's mill) surfaced and molded the lumber; the blacksmith shop of Evan Lukens forged iron hardware out of bar stock; the New Foundry and the old foundry both supplied castings and machine work; Davis's son Calvin (joined by a carpenter named Charles Kaye) provided contract car construction. Soon Kaye and Davis were working as a partnership. Two lead carpenters, Houston Logan and Charles Painter, went to work for the railroad, or perhaps indirectly for Kaye and Davis (the *Sentinel* often failing to make a distinction between partners, business entities, and their suppliers). A sign painter named B. C. Gadsby did finish work and ornamental painting on car bodies, and occasionally did tin work, as on passenger car roofing. For the first time, an ensemble of small Santa Cruz businesses created a product that no one business could have produced on its own.

By December 1873, when Schuyler first saw the Santa Cruz Rail Road taking shape, a surprisingly complete railroad supply chain had emerged within Santa Cruz County. The most technical components of a manufacturing process, the transformation of raw materials into specialized parts and assemblies, were all to be found within city limits. Capital flowed into the top of the chain. Manufactured goods, parts, and support services, flowed from the bottom.

The supply chain supported development not just of the railroad, but also of each component business. The various skills represented in the mix of railroad-related operations in turn began to reinforce and focus each other. Rather than compete, the two foundries in town, for example, rapidly differentiated their work. Martin's New Foundry developed expertise in chilled ring casting, a technology aimed at production of railroad wheels, while Amner's Santa Cruz Foundry emphasized smaller castings produced by simple sand molding. Both foundries would flourish over the next three years.

The same small businessmen and contractors who contributed to the supply chain also invested in the railroad itself. John McLaughlin, B. C. Gadsby, Charles Davis, George Treat, Ben Nichols, George Gragg, Charles Kaye, Evan Lukens, the partners Amner and Morton of the Santa Cruz Foundry, and W. H. Martin of the New Foundry—nearly every individual contributor to the supply chain and a hundred others, almost all of them small, local businesses—bought stock in the Santa Cruz Rail Road.[19] Most of the shares were purchased in the summer of 1873, before construction work had started and before there was tangible evidence that the railroad would succeed. The risks taken were proportionally small. All of the stock subscriptions except one were in lots of one to five shares, subscribed at 10 percent of the share price. The exception, George Treat, agreed to pay 10 percent of the face value of his two hundred shares in cash, but the remainder would be paid in "redwood and fir lumber, at the current market rates, delivered at Santa Cruz, as may be and when required by the company."[20] But the end result was symbiotic. The supply chain would own a piece of what it supplied.

In the midst of a deepening national recession, still without a connecting railroad to the outside world, this small reservoir of self-interest would inspire the editor of the *Santa Cruz Sentinel* to declare the county the "narrow-gauge centre of the world."[21]

The manufacturing renaissance of 1873 is perhaps even more surprising since Santa Cruz County was (and still is) the second smallest county in California by geographical area. It is contained within a coastal shelf about fifty miles long, extending back into forested hills ten to twenty miles deep. Much of its depth is cast into the steep hillsides of the Coast Range and unusable for commercial or urban development. The county was and is handicapped by remoteness, cut off from the San Francisco Bay Area by a continuous barrier of hills perforated—like scar tissue—by the cleft of the San Andreas Fault.

High above the seascape, the mountains form a nearly continuous summit, effectively walling off Santa Cruz County from the population centers of nearby San Francisco Bay. Only one river penetrates the ridge from the interior; the Pajaro drains the lower Santa Clara Valley through a canyon at Aromas, emptying into Monterey Bay and, in the process, forming the extreme southern boundary of the county.

Prior to 1860, to reach Santa Cruz from San Francisco required a twelve-hour journey by bay steamer to Alviso, a day's ride by stage and mud wagon to San Juan Bautista, followed by a traverse of the Pajaro River Canyon to Watsonville, where overnight lodging put the exhausted traveler within a half-day's stage ride of home. The county's export goods did not travel the same route. Bulk Santa Cruz County products—primarily redwood, lime, and tanned hides—took at least a day by coastal steamer to reach distribution centers in San Francisco, a risky commerce when the piers at Santa Cruz, Moss Landing, or Monterey were wracked by winter storms.

Still, Santa Cruz was, behind San Francisco, the second busiest port in California. By 1870, in spite of a population of just eight thousand people, it was the fourth largest manufacturing center of any county in the state.[22] Lime, blasting powder, finished and rough lumber (redwood, pine, and fir), shingles, posts, pickets, piles, cord wood, rolled leather, butter, apples, fuse, live fowl, wine, cheese, glue, soap, and machined or manufactured goods constituted a tidy million dollars worth of export by the year 1875, largely delivered to ships from the California Powder Co. wharf in the city of Santa Cruz.[23] Most of the lumber traveled to the Salinas and Santa Clara valleys.[24] Davis and Cowell lime, produced from quarries on today's site of the University of California, was a key component of cement, used by customers such as the California state prison system. Isaac Davis and Henry Cowell were San Francisco capitalists who virtually monopolized the lime industry, which was the largest and most profitable one in Santa Cruz County.

Sixteen Davis and Cowell ships, including the schooners *Pride-of-the-West*, *Queen-of-the-West*, and *Adrianna*, shuttled back and forth between the company's private wharf at Santa Cruz and Bay Area markets, transporting some ten thousand barrels of lime a month.[25]

Much of the county's flourishing manufacturing was cheaply and reliably powered by the very hills that imprisoned it. Water power, literally created by the drop of rivers and streams over the fall line of the coastal hills, was the historical energy source of the county's first industries. The powder mill and paper mill, for example, operated off weirs in the San Lorenzo River as early as the 1850s. When an October 1865 earthquake shuffled the water levels in numerous creeks across the county, the *Sentinel* was quick to report not property damage but a change in the dollar value of the altered flow rates.[26] The combined waterpower of the San Lorenzo, Blackburn Creek, Soquel Creek, and Laguna Creek, the *Sentinel* estimated, would equal four times the energy available to the famous mills of Lowell, Massachusetts, if it could all be put to use.[27]

Manufacturing, population, and wealth were concentrated primarily in the north part of the county, in and around Santa Cruz itself, while the south end of the county, including Watsonville, remained primarily agricultural. A little like the Northern and Southern United States before the Civil War, differences in wealth, population, culture, and ethnicity brought tension between north and south Santa Cruz County.

Hihn had long since grown disillusioned about the sectionalism. The surrounding mountain range contained an estimated three billion board feet of timber, much of it too remote to be logged until some kind of mechanization could move it cheaply either to coastal shipping or over the steep summit ridges to the Santa Clara Valley.[28] Owning more than fifteen thousand acres of northern county timberland (most of it in a tract called the Soquel Augmentation Rancho), Hihn repeatedly attacked the problem of transporting finished lumber from his lands by proposing railroads developed with public funds.[29] He repeatedly failed to convince the divided county of the value of any of the schemes, even though they all promised to put an end to the county's painful isolation.

As early as 1868, for example, the county surveyor, Thomas Wilson Wright, had done location work on a Hihn proposal to cross the mountains with a railroad up the San Lorenzo River Canyon. The river did not completely cross the range, but from its headwaters, upstream from the modern location of Boulder Creek, Wright located a long tunnel that could join Santa Cruz and Santa Clara counties with a railroad of moderate grades and curves. Wright meticulously worked and reworked maps to find the cheapest route. But his lowest figure, $600,000, managed only to infuriate both ends of the county's divided electorate.[30]

Instead of public bonds, Hihn turned to private funding to gain a toehold in the mountains. Incorporating the project as the San Lorenzo Rail Road, Hihn would extend its tracks into the lower San Lorenzo River Canyon only as far as Felton. An 1869 engineering prospectus on the project called out forty-pound rail and curves "too sharp for use, excepting with horses and the shortest geared cars," suggesting that the line would be narrow gauge.[31] In the spring of 1868, Hihn began grading the San Lorenzo Rail Road in the canyon near Felton, acquiring right-of-way by condemning land, primarily from the vast holdings of Davis and Cowell.

Hihn soon realized the resolve of his enemy. Davis and Cowell had virtually fortified the San Lorenzo Canyon with land titles, cordoning off commercial access to the mother lode of limestone deposits. The full extent of the limestone deposit ran from Davenport to Felton, with Davis and Cowell's quarries roughly in the middle. But at several locations near Felton— primarily along Bull and Bennett creeks—small, independent lime producers had purchased commercially viable outcroppings at the southern end of the deposit. Davis and Cowell moved aggressively to stop a rail link before such competition got a foothold in the marketplace.

On July 27, 1868, Davis and Cowell's attorneys filed a court injunction to stop work on the San Lorenzo Rail Road. Subsequent court actions and appeals, continuing over the next six years, brought work on the San Lorenzo Rail Road to a standstill. Just two miles of line had been graded when work was suspended.[32] Aroused by fear of monopoly, the political sympathies of the north county began to swing back to Frederick Hihn. The *Santa Cruz Sentinel* reminded the community of the threat Davis and Cowell posed not just to Hihn but to commercial development of the entire county. Of the lawsuits, the paper commented, "was not the objection raised to protect a lime monopoly, and every advantage of the law's delay, crook and turn, pettyfogging, resorted to?"[33]

Now pitted against Davis and Cowell, Hihn's sudden popularity in the county swung the tide in an election year. Hihn won a seat in the state legislature in 1869 and began a new campaign for railroad development. He returned with renewed vigor to the idea of public subsidy, writing funding bills for a railroad whose main trunk would link Santa Cruz with Watsonville and Gilroy, but whose branch lines included a spur up Soquel Creek— a corridor for reaching Soquel Augmentation lumber without interference from Davis and Cowell. But in the judgment of the *Watsonville Pajaronian*, Hihn's self-interest was the glue that held the bill together: "O! for a Representative who had neither purse nor scrip: neither lands in Watsonville, nor lands in Soquel, nor lands in Santa Cruz; yea, who had no wealth of moneys nor lands in any place but who, to make up for the lack of filthy lucre, was possessed of an earnest desire for the welfare of the county at large."[34]

Hihn's reputation in southern Santa Cruz County was ironically not much better than Davis and Cowell's in the north. Which part of the county was he representing? Who would Hihn tax for the money to develop his own commercial interests? Hihn's legislation appeared only to divide the county further. An anonymous correspondent, signing his name "Seyante," began to publish letters in the *Santa Cruz Sentinel* that attacked whatever public stance Hihn seemed to take on railroad construction. Historian Stan Stevens, emphasizing Hihn's embattled position at the end of the 1860s, conjectured that Hihn himself was "Seyante," a fictional character who would at least debate the railroad issue openly and honestly.[35]

One year later, it appeared Hihn would not fight the battle alone. The "Five Percent Act," introduced in the state legislature of 1870, would vest the power to raise money for railroad development at the county level. The act would allow county governments to grant public railroad bonds up to

5 percent of the assessed valuation of the county—a boon to counties all over the state that could not hope to attract a large railroad corporation.

Ideally suited to the needs of Santa Cruz County, the act contained a fatal loophole. The Southern Pacific manipulated the Five Percent Act to extract money from counties it wanted to enter. The worst abuse was against Los Angeles County, which was forced to hand over $610,000 in public bonds to the Southern Pacific to guarantee rails would be laid into the county's namesake town. Los Angeles, at the time, had a population of barely six thousand people, just a thousand larger than Santa Cruz.[36]

Anger toward the Five Percent Act signaled growing public frustration with the excesses of the Southern Pacific. Just one year after the Five Percent Act became law, Hihn watched, demoralized, as public pressure mounted to kill the legislation. In 1874, the same year California elected Newton Booth as its first antirailroad governor, the legislature repealed the Five Percent Act, leaving Santa Cruz and other remote California counties without the legal means to raise money for local railroad development.[37]

Frustrated by his attempts to break out of the county on the northern or southern flank, Hihn next tried to find a way through its mountainous middle. On July 29, 1871, the *Sentinel* published an engineering study by William J. Lewis, retained to survey a railroad between San Jose and Santa Cruz over Taylor's Pass—about six miles southeast of the modern summit of Highway 17. The survey took advantage of the Soquel Creek Canyon to provide an unbroken watercourse from modern-day Capitola almost to the summit ridge. Sensitive to public perception of costs, Lewis clearly identified the survey as narrow gauge, quoting numerous statistics on the cost and carrying capacity of rolling stock then being employed on the Denver & Rio Grande. Grades on the survey reached a maximum of 2.5 percent, and curves a minimum radius of 130 feet; these were track standards that would only be practical with narrow gauge locomotives and cars. Hihn (apparently sharing expenses for the survey with San Jose investors) personally assisted Lewis; in his final report, Lewis gave Hihn credit for carrying and using one of the party's aneroid barometers to measure altitude—early training for Hihn's enthusiastic tutelage as a rod-and-chain man on the Santa Cruz Rail Road.

Seven years later, Lewis's survey would become the proximate route the South Pacific Coast used to breach the wall between San Jose and Santa Cruz County. It would cost some $2 million to build the mountain segment alone, four times what surveyor Wright had estimated it would take to cross the range. A prophet with few subscribers, Hihn continued to fight against nearly overwhelming odds that any of his surveys would actually be built. In 1874, the California Supreme Court awarded Davis and Cowell damages for loss of timber in the wake of the San Lorenzo Rail Road's voracious grading crews. Still lacking public funding, the San Lorenzo Rail Road was bled dry by legal fees. Hihn's lumber holdings on the Soquel Augmentation Rancho remained landlocked until he could find a way to outflank Davis and Cowell.[38]

"If talking would build a railroad," the *San Francisco Bulletin* grimly noted, "Santa Cruz would have emerged sometime ago from its present isolated condition. Its principle [sic] hotel would not now be closed, and there would be fewer complaints of dull times."[39]

The talk ended in 1871. The Southern Pacific arrived in the town of Pajaro, just across the river from Watsonville, on November 26. Santa Cruz County would not have to pay the Five Percent Act subsidy—money that Watsonville would have considered blackmail—because Southern Pacific's rails entered the outskirts of Watsonville entirely on the south side of the county line. To Watsonville, the event appeared to be an unconditional victory over the debt-prone railroad schemes of Frederick Hihn. With its crops assured of reliable transportation to city markets, Watsonville couldn't have cared less what Santa Cruz, or Frederick Hihn, thought of its good fortune.

The south county's hubris remained engorged for just two weeks. On December 11, 1871, Frederick Hihn entered Watsonville's victory celebration like a thief through a second-story window. He successfully lobbied the County Board of Supervisors to hold a December election for new county railroad bonds. A county subsidy of just $6,000 per mile, his ballot measure proposed, would partially fund a standard gauge rail link between the new railhead at Pajaro and the orphaned north county.

The politics suddenly flip-flopped. Motivated by envy, representing roughly four times the population as its rival south county, north county supervisors saw $120,000 of bonded indebtedness as a cheap down payment on a twenty-one-mile connection to an existing railroad. Hihn finally got the politics right. Only when he concentrated on the populated coastal shelf, and only when the coastal towns of Santa Cruz, Aptos, and Soquel could see a working railroad virtually at their front door, would the county's voters finally think of a railroad as a public project.

Ironically faced with paying for a railroad it didn't need, the city of Watsonville voted 343 against, 25 in favor of the bonds. Sensing the answer to most of their problems, the city of Santa Cruz voted 694 in favor to 22 against, with Soquel, Davenport, Aptos, and Felton sustaining similar majorities, easily forcing the passage of the subsidy.[40]

The election nearly polarized the north and south parts of the county. The editor of the *Pajaronian* had to think long and hard to come up with a new name to describe the villainy, but he rose to the occasion. The election earned Frederick Hihn the memorable title of the Great Santa Cruz Railroad "blo-viator,"[41] and the status of *persona non gratis* in the south county.

South county tempers smoldered. In Watsonville saloons, an oft-told joke about voting the city of Santa Cruz out of Santa Cruz County was repeated with fresh indignation. But Watsonville, of course, lacked the votes.

The heavy bond majority gave Hihn unexpected bargaining power. First, in exchange for the subsidy, came an exploratory offer from the embryo Atlantic & Pacific Railroad to build track up the coast from Los Angeles to

San Francisco. If the subsidy were delivered, Santa Cruz would be included in its route. In April 1872, when the first proposals were made, the A&P scheme appeared to Hihn as little more than bait, floated inside Stanford's perimeter to test the waters for competition. The chum soon attracted Stanford.

As early as April 4, 1872, Hihn made personal visits to Stanford in San Francisco, dangling the implied threat of the Atlantic & Pacific, compensating with the promise of the county bond subsidy to help Stanford grasp the alternative: a Southern Pacific branch line from Pajaro to Santa Cruz.[42] Hihn offered other incentives. Redwood ties, for instance, critical to Southern Pacific's expansion to Los Angeles, could be had by the hundreds of thousands from the upper San Lorenzo basin, at twenty-five cents apiece, if the branch were built to haul them out.

At first, Stanford's interest appeared to be genuine. In December 1872, the Southern Pacific assigned a surveying crew to run a preliminary line. Just before Christmas, a crew of Southern Pacific civil engineers went to work on the hilly divide between Watsonville and Santa Cruz, along the contour of the stage road. To clear a line of sight for their transits, they set fire to a marshy area near the summit, "destroying numerous snakes and bullfrogs."[43] Like a primitive signal fire, the dark smoke could be seen for miles, marking the progress of the work.

Stanford's surveyors never reached Santa Cruz. Hihn grew to distrust such displays as a stalling tactic. As early as March 1873, the County Board of Supervisors, openly skeptical of Stanford's intentions, publicly invited proposals for a narrow gauge railroad between the two ends of the county, hoping to encourage some sort of independent action. Hihn was more than prepared to call Stanford's bluff. At an April 5 board meeting, Hihn eagerly paraded the Railroad Executive Committee in front of the supervisors. Titus Hale, Amasa Pray, Lucien Healy, C. Cappelmann, and B. P. Kooser all would enthusiastically support a home rule initiative. But Hihn's proposal was far more than a spur track to the Pajaro railhead. Some harmonic, deep inside Frederick Hihn, began to vibrate in the tightening economics. A change came over the way he related to the project. He became its manager, not its agent. At this meeting, Hihn made it obvious that he had begun to take ownership for the contradictory reality they were becoming a part of. If he got his wish —if one of his railroad proposals could escape the mountain prison—it would have to compete effectively with Stanford's growing empire. Therefore Hihn's starched linen maps portrayed a narrow gauge railroad connecting Pajaro not only with Santa Cruz but also with San Francisco. Hihn argued that the county would have to achieve a virtually autonomous transportation link to California markets if it were going to survive the double threat of difficult times as well as the enmity of the Southern Pacific.[44]

Signs of deepening economic troubles were obvious. Business in Santa Cruz itself had slumped, emptying foundries and planing mills of work. By early March 1873, Southern Pacific's surveying crews had vanished from the Soquel uplands. Frogs and snakes returned safely to the blackened marsh near the summit of the stage road. Smoke from a larger, more distant fire could be glimpsed in reports of feverish "stock-jobbing" in New York markets. A pyramid of leveraged railroad bonds began to collapse under its own weight, first undermining banks on the East Coast and then spreading slowly but surely west, shrinking credit, dragging down the bonds of healthy railroads, and forcing a temporary halt to Southern Pacific's southward expansion to Los Angeles. The domino effect would result in the collapse of the Fisk Banking House in September 1873, the beginning of an international financial panic. It was the same financial reverse that had forced Stanford to sell the San Francisco & North Pacific back to Peter Donahue, a temporary remission in the unchecked spread of Southern Pacific's influence across the state.

Santa Cruz Rail Road embossed seal. [Frederick Hihn Archives, University of California, Santa Cruz, Special Collections]

To fund such a scheme, the Railroad Executive Committee of Santa Cruz County began aggressive promotional activity, all of it local. "Get your cash ready," the *Sentinel* extolled the county on May 31, "as the road will commence [the grading] on or before the 1st of August." Through the Executive Committee, Hihn began to convince the county of the need for local control, and local financing, for the entire project. Clearly, Hihn had been working on a detailed business plan. The committee concluded, on May 24, 1873, that for $300,000 an operating railroad could be built between Santa Cruz and Pajaro. Of the total, $120,000 would come from the county subsidy, $150,000 from local stock subscriptions, and just $50,000 from floating debt. The modest capital investment would buy a twenty-one-mile narrow gauge railroad, two British Fairlie locomotives (a choice that Howard Schuyler may have influenced), three passenger cars, ten boxcars, and twenty-five flatcars.[45]

On June 3, 1873, the Railroad Executive Committee voted to incorporate as the Santa Cruz Rail Road Co. On August 4, the county's supervisors voted to award a construction contract to the company for the purpose of laying track from Watsonville, through Santa Cruz and on to New Year's Point, the northern county line and just fifty miles short of San Francisco, as far as the taxpayer's money could legally go. Since county bond liability would more than double with the added distance, safeguards were quickly added to the contract. At least $90,000 of the county bonds, for example, would have to be spent building railroad track *south* of the San Lorenzo River, thus guaranteeing that Santa Cruz and Pajaro would be linked with rail before Hihn set off up the unpopulated, rugged north coast for San Francisco. Other safeguards ensured that no bond money would be paid before five miles of railroad were finished—proof of Hihn's solvency and performance.

Outgunned on the 1871 subsidy vote, the supervisors from Watsonville were reduced to haggling over checks and balances in the contract's fine print. Painfully recalling Hihn's proclivities for maneuvering publicly subsidized railroads toward his own properties, they argued for impartial oversight in addition to the contract. Outside professionals—"railroadists," the *Sentinel* called them—had to be hired to monitor both Hihn and the survey he would create. Hihn, not to be given free rein with Watsonville money, was placed in the position of working under the surveillance of whomever the board chose.

Andrew Jackson Binney appeared as the designated watchdog in late August 1873, a year after he quit as chief engineer of the North Pacific Coast. Although he had served as a contractor on the California Northern Railroad between Marysville and Oroville, supervising civil engineering, grading, track laying, and subsequent operation of the pioneer company, Binney joined the project with less than three months of experience as a chief engineer.[46] For the next six months, Binney, leading "his efficient corps of Topographical Engineers," was contractually in charge of the location of the Santa Cruz Rail Road. Watsonville expected Binney to keep Frederick Hihn under a short leash.

Titus Hale and Frederick Hihn, however, quickly found a way to keep a leash on Andrew Jackson Binney.

While Binney got the title of chief engineer, Hihn's close friend, county surveyor Thomas Wilson Wright, was inducted into the project as Binney's assistant—along with two unskilled but enthusiastic field hands: Hale and Hihn.

Wright hardly needed Binney's help in laying out a railroad through Santa Cruz County. With the exception of a period of eight years, Wright held the job of county surveyor continuously between 1850 and 1890. The job gave him unusually detailed knowledge of county topography, geology, mineral, timber, and water resources. He plotted roads, surveyed the Soquel Augmentation Rancho (Hihn's largest timber holding), laid out street gradients, designed a sewer system, and mapped flood and overflow channels for the city of Santa Cruz.[47]

For the previous twenty years, Hihn had relied on Wright for technical support in most of his early industrial and railroad proposals, and for honest advice about promoting them. Through long, protracted battles over unpopular causes, Hihn regarded Wright as something of a war horse. Like Hihn, Wright was quick to join a fight and slow to leave. For example, Wright performed his public service as a staunch Democrat in a decidedly Republican county. Fond of debating politics over strong drink, Wright was well known for bloodying the noses of political opponents.[48] From the start, Andrew Binney must have felt like the butt of a local joke.

In the hot month of August 1873, the awkward foursome went looking for a passage along the rugged coastline of the southern county. The original Southern Pacific survey did not seem to influence this second, more careful reconnoiter, and the *Sentinel* noted the party doubling back and forth across the ridges, exploring new contours.[49] By August 16, they had zeroed in on a location that hugged the rugged coast, ignoring the high saddle where the stage road crossed at the tule marsh. The highest point on the new survey was 183 feet above sea level; the highest location on the SP survey was over 400 feet in elevation.

In exchange for gentler grades, the surveyors would have to work lower down on the coastal shelf, forcing the route to cross the wide mouths of arroyos and rivers where they emptied into the ocean. The Soquel Creek crossing was a good example. Little more than a brook where the stage road crossed it near the town of Soquel, the water course would require a nine-hundred-foot-long bridge to span its outlet at what today is Capitola beach. The San Lorenzo River, Woods Lagoon, Leonard's Gulch, and Mc-Kamish Gulch all presented similar obstacles where they widened out at the ocean.

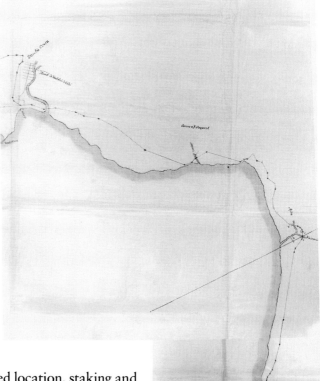

In September 1873, Binney got to work on a detailed location, staking and leveling a route that should have hugged the coastal bench for nearly eight uninterrupted miles, from a point at the Soquel wharf south to McKamish Gulch. But in October, the *Sentinel* became aware of segments of work—for example, the Soquel and Aptos creek crossings—that stubbornly remained incomplete, a cloak of secrecy drawn over the location between the two water courses. In the second week of October, Binney's location suddenly detoured inland; his transits seemed to swing toward the nearly magnetic attraction of Claus Spreckels's Aptos villa, a mile from the coast. The new Spreckels sugar mill, in which Hihn had invested, was in the early phases of construction not far from the Soquel Landing wharf. The press had little trouble interpreting the change in direction. Hihn would enhance the value of the Spreckels developments by adding the proximity of the railroad, and he expected likewise in return.

Strange bedfellows turned back the sheets. Without bond money (none would be forthcoming until five miles of railroad were finished), Hihn would have to turn to private financing through stock subscriptions. At the time of Binney's survey, Hihn had collected almost $100,000 in cash from such subscriptions.[50] But out of 137 subscribers, 2 individuals—Frederick Hihn and Claus Spreckels—contributed almost half the money. Spreckels, "a noble specimen of the middle aged German, well preserved and large-souled," had matched Hihn's $20,000 subscription with one of like amount. The two German immigrants became uneasy partners.

On holiday from the rigors of running an international sugar refining syndicate, in 1873 Spreckels had just moved into a 2,390-acre villa at Aptos, purchased as a vacation home. Before the year was out, he was building a resort hotel on the grounds, and getting to know Hihn, who was thinking about developing a camping site at nearby Soquel Landing, soon to be renamed Capitola. Hihn and Spreckels began a kind of mutual aid pact. In

Map filed in the civil court case of *Santa Cruz Rail Road* v. *Patrick Tracy, et al.,* showing route of SCRR from Pajaro to San Mateo County line. Only 21 miles from Pajaro to Santa Cruz is shown; india ink on polished fabric, 24" × 53" original. No scale; first filed Sept. 29, 1874. [Museum of Art and History, Santa Cruz; map documentation by Harold Brockman]

Early renderings of the Aptos Hotel include a sketch by Steinbuhler, 1879 (top), and a general view of the grounds (below), from W. W. Elliott's *Santa Cruz County Illustrations,* 1879. [Top, Capitola Museum; bottom, University of California, Santa Cruz, Special Collections]

1873, Spreckels purchased a parity stock subscription in the railroad. In 1874, Hihn invested $22,000 in a local sugar mill, developed by the Spreckels syndicate. The mill would provide sugar beet traffic for the railroad; the railroad would reciprocate with low-cost bulk hauling of refined sugar for the mill.

But a pattern of quid pro quo soon escalated into a rivalry. Hihn's next stock purchase consisted of two hundred more shares in the railroad on January 11, 1875; seven days later, Spreckels purchased two hundred eleven additional shares. And so it went. Hihn knew Spreckels was buying his way into a position of influence in the railroad, and he nervously considered sharing a certain amount of control over the project in exchange for backing, as long as backing did not become fronting. In either event, Hihn needed the money.

Andrew Jackson Binney became a pawn in a game of local hegemony. Sometime in early October, Hihn persuaded Binney (or Hihn persuaded Wright, who persuaded Binney) to resolve the surveying dilemmas by locating the Santa Cruz Rail Road close to both of the Spreckels projects, even if the relocation had to be paid for with public money.

By mid-October 1873, the politicking surveyors finally agreed to a revision of the original line, at the cost of one additional bridge over Valencia Creek. Now five truss bridges—over the San Lorenzo, the Soquel, the Aptos, Valencia, and the Pajaro River at Watsonville—would be required to finish the railroad. If Spreckels's villa had not been circumnavigated, there would have been only four. In terms of hard cash, the difference between the two plans came close to $16,000—enough to convince the Watsonville cynics that Hihn had indeed slipped his bridle.[51]

At the end of the location work, Wright and Binney certainly knew, even if Hihn did not, that a professional bridge man would be indispensable to the project.

So would the services of Charles Wellington Davis.

The Santa Cruz supply chain came alive in a *Sentinel* feature article dated December 20, 1873:

S.C.R.R. No. 1.

A Triumph for Santa Cruz

The First Car for the Railroad Completed

Designed and Constructed in Santa Cruz

The first rail for the Santa Cruz Railroad Company was laid yesterday. The first car was also placed on the track yesterday at Woods Lagoon. Every bolt, plate and piece of frame work used in the construction of this car was made in Santa Cruz. The car was designed by Mr. C. W. Davis, the construction engineer of the road and one of the most talented architects on the Pacific Coast. It is known as

A Dump Car

And will be employed in carrying the dirt, sand, and gravel requisite for grading the road. The platform, by a peculiar device, is made to swing down to the right or left, the sills opening like an apron, at the same time, thus allowing the load to roll out. The dimensions of the car are five feet wide and nine feet long. It is thirty inches from the bed of the car to the ground. The wheels are eighteen inches in diameter, and almost concealed from view. The car will hold two cubic yards of dirt. The workmanship is thorough throughout and reflects great credit on Messrs. Amner, Morton & Co., the proprietors of the Santa Cruz Foundry, the builders of the car. It is painted dark red and on the side is inscribed the following:

. . . .
S.C.R.R. No. 1.
. . . .

The car was on view Thursday at the Foundry and many citizens called to see it. Mr. Davis, the designer, and the foundrymen came in for a large share of the compliments. The construction of the car shows that our foundries are capable of turning out superior work. All the castings and wheels were made in Santa Cruz, and this is something for the community to feel a just pride in. Mr. Davis' fame as an architect is widespread. He drew the plans for some of the best buildings in San Francisco, including Tucker's Jewelry store, and the late Rev. Dr. Star King's church. For the Santa Cruz Railroad Company he has designed plans for the construction of passenger, and baggage cars on novel principles. These cars will all be built in Santa Cruz, under his supervision and their construction will give employment to a large number of mechanics and machinists.

Although a modest achievement from the perspective of even the smallest West Coast car manufacturer, the Davis dump car was a little like the construction of a small, crude nuclear weapon by a Third World country; perhaps it proved that the Santa Cruz supply chain at last had clout.

Thus Thomas Carter came to Santa Cruz in March 1874, without the home team advantage. He arrived in town as dump car number four was completed by Charles Davis's son, Calvin.[52] The younger Davis and his partner, Charles Kaye, had set up shop in Allen and Rennie's planing mill near the beach and there tooled up to produce railroad cars. They called themselves "Kaye and Davis" and were the first car manufacturing partnership in Santa Cruz. Carter undoubtedly had a chance to view their products, and their small manufactory, in detail.

As they were completed, the dump cars were assigned to the larger grading contractors at work on the first five miles of line. Drays flexing with heavy timbers, Chinese crews with their traps bundled on their backs, supply wagons, and occasionally a spring wagon with Hale and Hihn aboard passed south, following the work. George Treat's promised lumber was being delivered to a staging area on the beach near Leibbrandt's bath house. Carpenters were in demand.

Carter decamped at an unspecified hotel in town under fair spring skies, prepared to make his mark on the busy scene. For the previous nine months, since the engineering of the Strawberry Point Bridge, he had held no known contract work. Suddenly, he not only had a signed contract for designing one or more Howe truss bridges for Hihn but at the same time faced developing a supply base for the Monterey & Salinas Valley car contract (a logistical challenge described in Chapter Four). Calling on foundries for competitive prices, he renewed contact with the Gorrill brothers of Pacific Bridge, who would certainly bid on the results of his bridge design work. Hungry for opportunity, Carter watched the booming activity, keen to corner as much engineering work as he could.

His expectations, evidenced by articles in the local *Sentinel*, may have been high. In two separate articles, the first on March 28, the *Sentinel* introduced Carter first as the "Master Mechanic" and next, on April 11, as the "Architect of the Road," taking pains to use initial capitals in each title. With Binney and Howard Schuyler both long gone from the scene, the paper appeared to assign the thirty-four-year-old itinerant engineer a surprisingly central role in the Santa Cruz Rail Road[53]: "The drawings, plans and specifications of the [San Lorenzo River] Trestle work and Bridge are now being made by Mr. Carter, who is the Architect of the road, and has had a lifetime experience in constructing Railroad Bridges. He has recently been in charge of the same kind of work on the Saucelito road."

Crafting his own job titles, Carter managed to turn a squib into a résumé, suggesting he might have been cultivating a larger role in the Santa Cruz Rail Road organization. Beginning a bidding cycle on rolling stock in Monterey, courting local suppliers such as Amner, Morton, he would certainly make a similar bid for Santa Cruz car work. If there were no other professionals on the job to argue the point, Carter's small exaggerations would simply become credentials.

Bestowing such titles on an outsider in turn added credence to the paper's endorsement of the project, letting it appear to support the local supply chain on the one hand and to credit Hihn for seeking the advice of outside professionals on the other; it was a treatment equivalent, as Schuyler and Binney had exemplified, to an injection of antibiotics. Thomas Carter and Frederick Hihn's untested professionalism, in other words, helped bid each other up in the marketplace of public opinion.

But instead of a public relations victory, Carter may have succeeded in creating the biggest professional malaprop of his career. He polished the wrong job title. To Hihn, Carter's choice of titles could have sounded arrogant, a little too reminiscent of the "ornamental engineers" he had struggled to cleanse from the project. In spite of the self-appointment as master mechanic, Carter's role appears to have lasted less than two months and been circumscribed only to bridge work.

The earliest newspaper description of Carter's role, on March 28, credits him with drawing "the plans and specifications for the various bridges required," that being bridges plural—perhaps as many as four (over the San Lorenzo, Soquel, Aptos Creek, and Valencia Creek). Two of the bridges in question were significantly larger and more complicated than the structure he designed for the North Pacific Coast. The San Lorenzo truss in particular would measure 150 feet in length, an imposing, complex design project that justified the *Sentinel*'s testimonial. Whether or not Carter designed the line's other large bridges, as the paper suggests, remains one of the unresolved mysteries of his Santa Cruz tenure. The three weeks between the *Sentinel* articles of March 28 and April 11, 1874, mark the only period of time that Carter's presence in Santa Cruz can be proven, offering at least circumstantial evidence that he might not have had time to design more than one bridge (singular) over the San Lorenzo River. Follow-on newspaper reports were infrequent. A short *Sentinel* item dated April 17 indicated that the drawings of the San Lorenzo River bridge were nearing completion following two weeks' work on the part of an unnamed draftsman, presumably Tom Carter:

> The plan of the railroad bridge across the San Lorenzo river near the home of Mr. Bliss[54] is thoroughly prepared, and on paper looks like an imposing structure. The draughtsman was two weeks maturing and perfecting the plan. The bridge proper will contain something over 90,000 feet of lumber. There are two other bridges of greater length than this: the one over the Soquel, the other over the Pajaro River.[55]

But Carter may have tried to showcase his talent on the wrong bridge. The *Sentinel*'s immodest praise for Carter's work (which we assume was fully commissioned by Hihn) still managed to ignore the fact that his drawings would not soon see construction.[56] The terms of the August 4, 1873, county contract were specific: five miles of line, built in a southerly direction from the San Lorenzo River, had to be completed before Hihn could claim a cent of bond money. Furthermore, the contract stated explicitly that the San Lorenzo bridge could not be started until $90,000 in bond money had been paid. Why (one wonders of Hihn) order the design of the San Lorenzo River bridge seven months before it would be built? Why, knowing that rail would not reach the city of Santa Cruz until the spring of 1875, would he raise the expectations of Santa Cruz residents when he really needed their forbearance and fortitude in the grim fight to build five miles of track completely outside of city limits?

Why (one wonders of Carter) would he seek acclamation for a project that was, at that moment, irrelevant to the five-mile subsidy claim, when designing and completing the Soquel bridge (critical to the subsidy claim) would have easily made him a hero? There are no documented answers to these questions, only the suspicion that Frederick Hihn and Thomas Carter were not, professionally or personally, in synch on the political as well as technical overtones of the bridge work. In spite of the fact that Henry Gorrill sketched the San Lorenzo bridge in his diary on May 18, just three weeks after Carter allegedly finished the engineering drawings, nothing further was done on the construction of the bridge until November 1874. Practical logistics in supplying the construction of the other bridge projects—Soquel Creek, Aptos, and Valencia Creek—quickly drew Gorrill's time and attention, but nowhere in the remainder of Gorrill's diary (which doesn't end until September 1874) is Carter's name mentioned.

When the North Danville, Vermont, paper *North Star* published notice of the death of Fowler Pope in November 1897, it included a biographical sketch of a little-known episode in the engineer's life: "In [Santa Cruz] County he was the first engineer of the construction train in the building of the road between Santa Cruz and Felton, and brought the first engine, the *Betsy Jane*, from Watsonville to Santa Cruz."

Although much is known about Pope's role on the Santa Cruz & Felton, little is known of his employ by Hihn's Santa Cruz Rail Road. If the story in the *North Star* is true, it means that Pope helped set up the tiny 0-4-0 at the temporary Woods Lagoon engine house and operated it not from Santa Cruz to Watsonville but over the available five miles of rail between Woods Lagoon and the unfinished bridge over Aptos Creek.

The story would help explain how Pope got an offer from Lucien B. Healy, on May 23, 1875, to inspect and set up the Porter, Bell locomotive *Santa Cruz* for the SC&F.

The story would also help explain the naming of the *Betsy Jane*. Pope's mother, who lived near her son in Santa Cruz, was Betsey Webster Pope; at the time of the arrival of the first locomotive in the county, she was a spry eighty-four-year-old widow.

Gearing up for the five-mile marathon, Hihn ordered construction of a temporary shop in Woods Field, just south of the San Lorenzo River, to store the line's first locomotive until the San Lorenzo bridge was finished. Then, in the spring of 1875, the railroad's permanent shop and terminal facilities would be located near the center of downtown Santa Cruz. In the meantime, Hihn would concentrate all his resources on the five miles between Woods Lagoon and Aptos. By the third week in May, public focus would shift squarely to the critical Soquel bridge—the obvious bottleneck in the five-mile subsidy battle.

That week, Pacific Bridge Co. was named as the general contractor for the Soquel Creek, Aptos Creek, and Valencia Creek spans. The earliest recorded newspaper record of work on the Soquel bridge was a *Sentinel* article on May 30. Henry Gorrill's earliest record of work on the same bridge identifies his foreman (Anderson) heading for Santa Cruz just four days before the newspaper story. Bridge materials began to move into the Soquel wharf in early June. In the battle to construct five miles of track, the drawings in which the *Sentinel* took such pride would play no further role. Perhaps neither did Tom Carter. A short note appeared in the *Sentinel* on July 19, 1874, indicating that because work on the Aptos Creek bridge was about to begin, "the [bridge] architect and foreman are in town and have engaged rooms for the season." But this time the reference was probably to the Pacific Bridge Co.'s foreman Anderson, and the title "architect" was no longer capitalized.

The same summer that the Monterey and Saucelito projects were launching Tom Carter as the fastest-growing car builder on the coast, Carter appeared to cede one of the most dramatic California narrow gauge markets to the embryo car manufactories of Tom Amner, the Davis family, and Charles Kaye.

But Carter would soon reenter Hihn's supply chain, through the back door.

The closer the Santa Cruz Rail Road got to Watsonville, the stronger grew the smell of dead rat. The arrival of the *Betsy Jane*, a six-ton construction engine purchased in San Francisco for $4,200, brought derision from the October 22, 1874, *Watsonville Pajaronian*[57]:

> On Friday morning last, two wagons came from the depot, and passed through town on route to Santa Cruz. On one of the wagons was a diminutive locomotive and on the other the tender, all for use on the Santa Cruz & San Andreas [sic] Railroad. As the wagons passed along the street, the people flocked out of their business places to gaze on the machinery. Some thought that Al Brown, the skillful dentist, possessed greater drawing capacity than the engine; a discussion arose as to whether four men could lift it upon the wagon but George Wright settled the matter by saying that five men were required. One man— but he lives in the country—thought the tender was a patented bathtub and the engine, the heating apparatus. As far as its hauling capacity is concerned, it seems to go along all right when we saw it on the wagon.

Watsonville photographer Albert Webster Fell took at least two images of the pioneer engine *Betsy Jane* on Jan. 11, 1884, in Watsonville, as the engine was being shipped to an unknown buyer. One image has been often reproduced; the lesser known view, shown here, was in the collection of engineer Fowler Pope and offers circumstantial evidence that Pope may have helped set up the locomotive when it was delivered to the Santa Cruz Rail Road in October 1874. Other evidence comes from credit given in his obituary, published in the *North Star* paper of Danville, Vt., in November 1897. Pope may even have been responsible for naming the small engine; according to the *North Star,* his mother's maiden name was Betsey Webster. [Norris Pope collection]

In order to enable the Stockhold-ers and their families to view the Railroad a train will be run from the engine house in Woods' field to the present terminus on the Aptos Ranche, on Friday, Dec. 18th 1874. Train will start at o'clock and return at o'clock.
Santa Cruz R. R. Co.

When stockholders were invited to tour the SCRR in December 1874, the tracks went no further south from Santa Cruz than the small village of Aptos. [Vernon Sappers collection]

In order to make a show of hauling a heavy load, the driver had the brake on, but he took it off when he got out of town. The Struggling Flea would be an appropriate name for it. One good thing about it is that if it should break down, a mule could be put in its place and do just as well. The narrow gauge ought to be fenced on both sides to keep cattle from crowding the locomotive off the track.

Sequestered in the temporary shops at Woods Field, the *Betsy Jane* would remain out of the public eye until Frederick Hihn decided to use her in modest celebration of the first bond requisition, an event precipitated by completion of the first five miles of track on December 7, 1874.[58]

Photographed in 1999, this view of the only known surviving example of a Pacific Bridge Co. Smith Patent truss (bottom) depicts the modern restoration of the California Powder Works Bridge over the San Lorenzo River, near Santa Cruz; the original bridge was built in 1872, under the supervision of Henry Gorrill. Top, restored builder's stencil on the truss plate. [Bruce MacGregor]

Still suffering from the debilitating effects of tuberculosis, Henry Gorrill was enjoying surprising success in the third year of his new business venture. In the summer of 1874, he had wagon bridge projects running on the McKenzie and Santiam rivers in Oregon; another in Alameda, California; and a cluster of bridge projects at various stages of completion in Santa Cruz County.

The county, especially, represented a source of repeat business. In May 1872, Pacific Bridge completed a 168-foot-long covered wagon bridge at the Santa Cruz Powder Works, which was based on the patented Smith high truss. In November 1873, the county signed a contract with Pacific for two highway bridges: one over Valencia and one over Aptos Creek, both Smith patents, foreshadowing the railroad bridge work near the same sites. A third public highway bridge would go up over the San Lorenzo in September 1874. In December, a fourth new highway bridge would be erected over the Pajaro River at the south edge of the county. The highway bridges brought contract prices between $6,000 and $15,000.[59]

Santa Cruz County was quickly becoming a bridge builder's dreamscape. In 1874, the Santa Cruz Rail Road would add four large truss bridges, and a number of pile trestles, to Gorrill's already crowded bookings. The bridge projects, in turn, would inject new business back into the county. Gorrill was already identifying a few local suppliers, including Ben Nichols's sawmill near Soquel, that could cut fir planking and redwood siding.[60] At first Gorrill fabricated fir bridge timbers at his San Francisco erection yard on Berry Street, shipping them to the county on schooners; but with abundant first-growth fir available within a fifteen-mile radius of the jobs, local raw materials and craftsmen could be brought together at the work site. As Santa Cruz County projects multiplied, the Gorrills looked for additional sources of local lumber, fittings, and castings. By May 18, Huntington and Comstock, a Soquel timber retailer, was supplying beams for the Soquel Creek railroad bridge.[61]

To support work on these numerous fronts, Henry's younger brothers, Charles and Winfield (or "Winnie"), began to play a larger role in Santa Cruz County projects, giving Henry badly needed breathing room. On February 20, 1874, Addie gave birth to twin boys in Oakland, a fact that Henry noted proudly in his diary.

Distracted by the birth of the twins, Gorrill still had to deal with the complex logistics of supplying distant projects with material, laborers, and management. By early May, he had taken up weekly rooming in Santa Cruz to watch over procurement. On May 30, the *Sentinel* noted castings arriving at Soquel wharf on the steamer *Santa Cruz*, coming from foundries in San Francisco. But on June 3, Henry signed a contract with W. H. Martin for local manufacture of castings from the New Foundry, saving transportation costs from the City. By July 7, he had opened a bank account in Santa Cruz to make payment of local subcontractors such as Martin easier.

Work on the Soquel bridge commenced with dispatching foreman Anderson to the job site on May 27. Anderson wasted little time getting started, telegraphing Henry the next day to send a contract pile driver with its own foreman, a man named Howden. By June 20, Pacific Bridge was expanding its active construction sites to include the big trestles over Rodeo Gulch and

Arana Gulch at Woods Lagoon. Carter's drawings and bills of material were the basis for ordering timber, castings, and bolts that the Gorrills required at each job site, but they were little guarantee that the materials, once procured, would do the job they were designed for. Charlie wrote to Henry—for example, on August 20—that piles ordered for the Woods Lagoon trestle were too short. Unlike a similar incident on the Strawberry Point Bridge project, Gorrill's frustrated foreman refused to delay the project to wait for new material. Instead, he came up with work-arounds: "The mud at Wood's gulch is 60 feet deep and the piles all have to be spliced. Howden will be through there by the end of the week, he has been much bothered."

With Charlie's help, Henry was able to keep material flowing to at least five active construction sites, expanding the scope of the work. By July 19, Pacific started the Aptos Creek bridge, and work on Valencia Creek commenced a few weeks later. Three large Howe trusses, and at least two large pile trestles, were under way at the same time. It is interesting that two of the bridges—Aptos and Valencia—lay outside the boundaries of Hihn's five-mile increment, which indicates Hihn's strong belief in his ability to finish the increment while advancing construction beyond it.

The San Lorenzo bridge was finally started in November 1874, in part because of the Gorrills's ability to meet deadlines and in part because of Hihn's near certainty of finishing the first five miles of line by early December. The Gorrills had helped increase the odds in Hihn's favor by relying increasingly on parts and raw materials purchased from the local supply chain. Timber for the San Lorenzo bridge—sills, plates, and diagonals—was purchased from Huntington and Comstock and fabricated on level beach sand near Leibbrandt's Santa Cruz bath house. The open air work was reminiscent of Carter's field factory at Monterey, but with even less overhead. There were no buildings involved, and no rent to pay.

Before his brother Charlie took up full-time residency in the county, Henry battled the daunting logistics of setting up and running these multiple jobs by himself. He worried incessantly about delivery of lumber. On June 27, he wrote "just no timber delivered at all" to the Soquel site; as a result, the work was at a temporary standstill. He worried about supporting men at remote locations. On July 16, he took a horse and buggy to the southern extremities of the work, beyond the unfinished Valencia Creek bridge, in order to size up the next construction site. He concluded "we will have to camp at Rodeo Gulch" if they were to keep to the construction schedule.

He worried about getting good help. Suffering from a recurring cough, Henry wrote to Addie from the Soquel site on July 24:

I have been out here today where [the pile driver] engine was expected. It came on time, Driver as drunk as a fool. He upset so nearly that another man had to be put on to drive. We then backed engine down the hill, and it not going fast enough we hitched a span of mules on behind to haul it down. It started and went with a (. . .). Struck a mule, and made it scamper, and grunt wonderfully. We now hope to get to work shortly, and shove things some.

In following letters, Henry complained to Addie of continuing "sick headaches" that often became so painful he would seek out the warm sand of the Santa Cruz beach, and spend hours sleeping in the sun, trying to recover enough of his strength to sustain the enormous task in front of him.

The county's contract was clear, concise, and legally binding: Hihn could apply to the supervisors for the first $30,000 of bond money once a construction train had run over the first five miles of completed track, and not before. Hihn claimed the prize on December 7, 1874, when the *Betsy Jane* steamed over five miles of completed railroad between Woods Lagoon and the uncompleted Aptos Creek bridge. $30,000 in county bonds, Hihn demanded in writing the next day, were due the railroad.

With cold premeditation, the south county picked exactly that moment to exact revenge. On December 12, 1874, the *Sentinel* reported that a Watsonville attorney named William H. Patterson, and a political aspirant named Dr. Charles Ford, won a restraining order in Superior Court against the county payment of railroad bonds. Their motives appeared to be transparent. Patterson had been an attorney in court actions against Hihn's San Lorenzo Rail Road. Ford was a partner in the Snodgrass, Ford, and Sanborn stage line that connected Watsonville and Santa Cruz, eventually to come under competitive pressure from the railroad. Patterson and Ford argued that the state's Five Percent Act, having been repealed in 1874, no longer gave county government the right to collect public taxes to subsidize railroad construction. The Superior Court agreed. Payment of bonds was denied the Santa Cruz Rail Road. For fourteen months, the court injunction embargoed not just the five-mile subsidy but increments of new bonds Hihn won as track laying continued, until the entire $120,000 in bonds, nearly a third of Hihn's entire construction budget, was held hostage by the courts.

Even Hihn's old adversaries expressed dismay over the court action. The County Board of Supervisors (including its member from Watsonville) and the Watsonville City Council (which had granted Hihn a charter to lay rail into the city) roundly condemned the vindictive politics. Ford and Patterson, the *Sentinel* angrily claimed, were inciting a taxpayer's revolt in which a quarter of the county's population held the remaining three-quarters hostage. It remained unproven, in the absence of a subsidy law, that counties did *not* have such power. The only thing that was clear, the paper argued, was that Ford was out to win a seat in the state legislature by keeping Santa Cruz squarely under Watsonville's thumb.[62] "Failing in that," Hihn later testified, "it left us to finish rather in bad shape, and we did not know what to do."[63]

Fearing another protracted legal battle like the one that paralyzed the San Lorenzo Rail Road, Hihn limped southward on luck and barter. The first ship bearing rail around Cape Horn, the *John Bright*, sank in a storm off the coast of Brazil. Insurance on her contents, bought at 10 percent more than its value, provided windfall cash that Hihn converted to rail at the Pacific Mills in San Francisco—enough to reach from Aptos to Leonard's Gulch.

But insult piled atop injury. Completion of the narrow gauge to Aptos, on May 22, 1875, perhaps something of a miracle in virtual financing, was bannered in four decks of *Sentinel* headlines as "The Great Event of the Season." The *Betsy Jane* was given credit for dragging four flatcars of celebrants the full six route miles of completed line to an all-night ball and dinner thrown by Claus Spreckels at the Aptos Hotel. Thanks to the host's influence, and certainly thanks to his infusion of cash into the railroad, Governor Romualdo Pacheco attended and returned the favor by proposing long, felicitous toasts to the health of Claus Spreckels. The governor unfortunately omitted any reference to Frederick Hihn, his railroad, or their connection to the future economic health of the county. The *Sentinel* wasn't much smarter. Of fifty prominent citizens named as sponsors of the railroad, Hihn's name appeared forty-third in the *Sentinel*'s roster. Titus Hale came in forty-fourth, perhaps some indication of the public humiliation that accompanied the Watsonville injunction.

The Santa Cruz Rail Road was cast in the role of a connecting hack between downtown Santa Cruz and a political rally for the governor.

The severe budget restrictions that followed Patterson and Ford's injunction had the effect of accelerating cost-cutting measures that Hihn began during the summer of 1874, bringing new economic pressures to bear on the embryo supply chain.

In July 1874, in preparation for construction of the San Lorenzo River wagon bridge, the Pacific Bridge Co. advertised in the *Santa Cruz Sentinel* for local bids on piles, shakes, redwood, and pine timber.[64] The implication was that Pacific Bridge ran the bid process, including the acceptability of prices, terms, and conditions.

Two months later, Hihn took over control of the bid process for Santa Cruz Rail Road bridge work. Evidence appeared in the *Sentinel* on September 12, 1874, at the height of the bridge-building activity:

> **WANTED**
> Lumber,
> > Hewed Timber,
> > > Piles,
>
> > > For Bridges
> > > --AT--
>
> Santa Cruz
> > Aptos,
> > > Leonard Gulch,
> > > > Pajaro Slough
> > > > > Pajaro River
>
> > For further particulars, inquire of the
> > Santa Cruz Railroad Co.

Clearly, Hihn wanted control of the suppliers' suppliers. Now he could keep a tight rein on prices, terms, and conditions by acting as procurer for Pacific Bridge's raw materials. The ad was evidence of Hihn's motive for supporting a local supply chain in the first place: control of costs. But it was also evidence that the Santa Cruz supply chain was reaching a level of maturity at which bridge manufacturing, once the domain of San Francisco–based industry, was not impossible for local firms. Hence the second explanation: the Santa Cruz Rail Road had begun to build its own bridges.

Bridge construction at the Pajaro River would not begin until November 1875, when the effects of the Patterson and Ford injunction had starved Hihn's already meager budget well past the point where he was desperate for additional money. Nowhere in the *Sentinel*'s reporting of the work was Pacific Bridge Co. mentioned.[65] Nearly every facet of the Pajaro railroad bridge —labor, management, timber, iron castings, a pile driver, even paint created from lime burned in the kilns of Felton—had been locally supplied by Santa Cruz County. It makes sense that Hihn supplied the general contractor services as well: "The bridge timbers and trestles are all the same size and build as those of the Central Pacific Road, and have a similar appearance, except the latter are painted brown while all the former are white. This whitewash is made of lime and oil, a composition which is fireproof and protects the timber from rot, and the iron from rust, to some extent."[66]

Put together with a cookbook of local recipes, Hihn's work on the Pajaro bridge marked the heyday of the Santa Cruz supply chain.

Sometime in April 1874, Tom Carter realized that the point of being in Santa Cruz had little to do with the Santa Cruz Rail Road. Instead, the two foundries in town were the closest and cheapest source of castings Carter would need to fill the new Monterey contract. If he couldn't break into the car-building business for Hihn's Santa Cruz Rail Road, Carter could at least borrow the critical elements of its supply chain. Celebrated in the local press as Hihn's "Master Mechanic," Tom Carter moved about the Santa Cruz industrial district with a ready-made letter of introduction, and—assuming Hihn had snubbed him—a new purpose. No longer would such credentials be useful to seek status, or to counterfeit himself as a local business leader. Instead, during April and May, Tom Carter began to piece together the infrastructure of a virtual manufacturing organization extending beyond the borders of Santa Cruz County.

Here Carter first faced the technical and logistical demands described in Chapter Three. A manufacturing process-within-a-process, the foundry work required the longest lead time, and the most technical know-how, of any stage of car manufacturing. In a time period of about eight weeks, beginning with the signing of a contract with the Monterey & Salinas Valley, Carter's drawings had to be translated to patterns, patterns to molds, and molds to castings. The castings, finally, had to match the drawings that began the process, enabling the prototype work that would take place in Monterey in July.

Used to seeing the foundry process played out on the scale of the Tar Flat industries in San Francisco, Carter was probably disheartened by his first look at the ramshackle Santa Cruz Foundry. But appearances were deceiving. Tom Amner maintained a complete pattern-making service in the loft above his foundry and offered patterns free for the lot price of the castings.

Amner's mastery of the pattern-making process was critical to the success of the foundry work. Given Carter's drawings, Amner had to engineer location of parting lines in the patterns and location of pour spouts and vents. All these placements were essential to determining not only the quality of the finished castings but ultimately the speed and cost of their manufacture. Trial molds followed completion of patterns. Out of the molds came "first articles," the earliest examples of parts that would let Carter confirm critical dimensions, matched to specifications in the original drawings. There were approximately eighteen castings required to build a Carter eight-ton-capacity flatcar (an additional five to seven were required for a boxcar). Most of the castings were characterized by one or more critical dimensions—for example, displacement between holes—that had to be maintained accurately in the production run of finished parts. In the two months we believe Carter was in Santa Cruz, he had his first and only chance to confirm that Amner's castings would work in a design that existed only on paper. If they didn't, Carter faced the time-consuming task of changing the design, modifying the pattern, recasting, and finally inspecting a new round of first articles.

Sometime in April, Carter began to work through these risky and expensive steps. To get Amner to commit, Carter had to guarantee him the full lot of Monterey castings—more than twenty-five tons of gray iron—covering all car parts except wheels. Amner, in turn, had to prove he could produce accurate first articles. As Amner increased his production volume in May, flaws became more noticeable, their cause easier to isolate and correct. Amner continuously revised both patterns and process until the finished parts could be duplicated quickly, easily, and accurately—and most important, cheaply.

Thus by June 20, 1874, Amner's molding room was flooded with production car parts. The *Sentinel*, on that date, described a foundry substantially "up the ramp" to full-scale production: "Amner, Morton & Co., of the Santa Cruz Foundry, are now busy making a large amount of castings for the Monterey and Salinas city Narrow Gauge Railroad. About twenty five tons of Axle-boxes, rockers, Bumpers and Couplings, Break-Irons & c. sufficient for fifty platform and box-cars, constitute a part of the order. The car wheels are cast in the city."

By early July, it was clear that the development work taking place at the Santa Cruz Foundry would be doing double duty. The patterns would soon be shipped to Vallejo to support the North Pacific Coast contract. But by that time, Amner was near the top of the Monterey ramp, his production operating at peak efficiency, his confidence high.

If Carter left Santa Cruz at the end of May, as we suspect, he trusted Tom Amner completely to oversee the production work and ship it to Monterey on time. By early July, Amner was at maximum production. On July 25, the *Sentinel* noted that Amner had cast enough parts for thirty-five of the forty-eight required M&SV cars.[67] At that rate, it would have taken the Santa Cruz Foundry until mid-August to finish the order—just two weeks short of Carter's September 1 deadline for completion of the Monterey & Salinas Valley's rolling stock.

Perhaps an understanding came to Tom Carter, sometime before he left Santa Cruz, that relationships with foundrymen like Amner counted more than his exaggerations to the press, that after a failure to bluff his way into a position of authority in an organization that considered him an outsider, he would have to build a business, and a reputation, one foundryman at a time. Success meant partnering with a team of craftsmen who, in reality, would themselves hold claim to being the architects and master mechanics (lowercase) of the railroads Carter was accountable to. Thus Tom Carter underwent much the same transition that Santa Cruz was going through as a manufacturing center. In developing a close-knit team of technical and manufacturing interests, Carter began to put his own ego into perspective. If he couldn't influence politics with Frederick Hihn, he could earnestly talk nuts and bolts with Tom Amner.

The team delivered. For the twelve weeks that Amner held the contract, Tom Carter virtually owned the railroad hardware production resources of the Santa Cruz Foundry. Ironically, Frederick Hihn's Santa Cruz Rail Road, priding itself on locally manufactured hardware, would not need the same parts until nearly a year later.

In January 1874, the San Lorenzo Rail Road lost its final court battle with Isaac Davis and Henry Cowell. On an appeal from the District Court of San Francisco, the Supreme Court of California acted to deny the San Lorenzo Rail Road the right to unlimited use of timber and other resources during the six years in which the railroad had condemnation suits pending against Davis and Cowell.

The result was precedent-setting. Supreme Court case number 1828 effectively altered the constitutionality of railroad condemnation suits, and in the process it made the San Lorenzo Rail Road liable for "despoiling the estate of Davis & Cowell" during a time in which it held no long-term tenure on its land. The decision marked the death of the San Lorenzo Rail Road and the end of Hihn's incursions into the San Lorenzo watershed. In a broader sense, the decision marked the sway that California's growing antirailroad bias held on its court system.

A bitter pill for Hihn to swallow, the long-protracted courtroom drama was symptomatic of society's changing attitude about railroads in general. The public had grown wary of paying for railroads that could in turn pillage both public and private property. Only two of the six narrow gauge railroads described in this book were built using public bonds or subsidies: the North Pacific Coast and the Santa Cruz Rail Road. The remaining four were financed from stock subscriptions, mortgages, and loans. As the decade reached midpoint and the recession deepened, what financing could be found for short-line railroads came largely from banks. Santa Cruz County followed the trend. In 1874, private investment—not public subsidy—finally opened a rail corridor into the San Lorenzo Canyon.

Tom Carter undoubtedly heard rumors during his stay in Santa Cruz. Principals of the Farmer's National Gold Bank in San Jose had stayed at the St. Charles Hotel in Santa Cruz the previous September. Together, they had taken day trips up the San Lorenzo to investigate routes for a lumber flume.[68] An indenture, signed earlier, on June 3, 1873, provided easements for a portion of the flume's right-of-way from land owners in the upper San Lorenzo, among them John West, Samuel Brimblecorn, J. W. Peery, and Francis Nalty.[69] Not surprisingly, the names Davis and Cowell were conspicuously absent from the list.

Charles Silent (president of the Farmer's Bank), brothers Charles and Lucien Healy, and a small group of potential investors had taken day trips by horseback very nearly to the headwaters of the river. Lucien Healy, the county surveyor of Santa Clara, knew the up-river country by heart. The San Lorenzo reached deeper into the range and drained a larger timbered watershed than any stream in the county. The timber it reached was easily the county's largest uncut lumber reserve. Silent's plan was to construct a flume from a mill site called Crediford's at the headwaters to the beach at Santa Cruz, using it as a conveyor belt to port lumber to coastal shipping. The industrial design of the flume was tailored to the demands of moving lumber in high volume: "The flume will be triangular, forty inches across the top, thus providing against the possibility of a 'jam', for if anything lodges in a bend, it immediately 'backs up' the water, which floats the obstruction to a wider part of the flume and clears the passage."[70]

Even when the lower eight miles of the flume were reengineered to a three foot gauge railroad, a change publicly announced in October 1874, the resulting system was still conceptualized as an industrial tram, not a common carrier. The flume was designed to penetrate much of the distance from coast to summit, but the newspapers revived none of Hihn's transmountain visions of a public highway. The flume and its captive railroad would simply fill a gap in a rugged stretch of the San Lorenzo River Canyon where it was prohibitively expensive to operate lumber wagons in summer and impossible in winter. Since water only flowed downhill, there was little chance that a single flume would ever cross the range to San Jose.

While predicting a rate reduction of 50 percent over the wagon drayage of cordwood, the *Sentinel* treated the flume project more coolly than the Santa Cruz or San Lorenzo railroads. The paper's coverage of the "Silent project" indeed remained silent throughout 1874. Especially after the California Supreme Court decision of January, an unspoken belief that Davis and Cowell monopolized the canyon and its commerce—although an exaggeration—may have created deep cynicism about Silent's future.

During the winter of 1874, Charles Silent and the Healy brothers struggled with many of the same problems that had confronted Frederick Hihn and Thomas Wright on the aborted San Lorenzo Rail Road, and gradually they came to the conclusion that the flume by itself could not span the entire distance from mill to coast. They took into account four factors. First, the huge amount of lumber and cord wood transported, up to thirty thousand board feet a day, would have to be sorted and stored for commercial drying.[71] Land for a sorting yard was prohibitively expensive in Santa Cruz but cheaper in the hamlet of Felton, eight miles upstream.

Second, the supply of water required to operate the flume came from side streams pouring into the upper San Lorenzo: Bear Creek, Boulder Creek, Newell Creek, Two Bar, and Kings Creek. Below Felton, few feeder creeks entered the steep San Lorenzo River Gorge. Sustaining an adequate water level in the lower parts of the San Lorenzo Canyon would be difficult, especially in late summer.

Third, a vertical granite formation in the middle of the canyon, known as the Hogback, had created obstacles for both the San Lorenzo Rail Road and the powder mill water supply. Intruding like a molar in the canyon, rising hundreds of feet from river level up the western flank, the Hogback forced both projects into tunnels close to the level of the river—in the case of the powder company, a nine-hundred-foot diversion tunnel through the solid granite formation itself. Since the lumber flume would have to maintain a constant elevation drop, like the San Lorenzo Rail Road and the powder company's tunnel, it occurred to the Healy brothers that it too might be forced into a long, expensive tunnel if the railroad attempted to pass the Hogback at river level.

Reasons one through three paled in comparison to reason number four: the insurmountable barrier of Davis and Cowell. For over a year, from October 1873 until February 1875, the public knew nothing of the negotiations taking place between Charles Silent, Isaac Davis, and Henry Cowell. But it was aware of a changing competitive environment in the Felton lime business. IXL Lime (read "I Excel") began operating kilns near Felton in 1874, using the 1868 county toll road to dray the product to Santa Cruz. IXL was the third independent producer to go head-to-head with Davis and Cowell, and though small it was able to deliver cord wood to the kilns and product to the Santa Cruz wharf and still compete with the conglomerate. A monopoly no more, Davis and Cowell changed tactics. As the 1870s matured, they realized they would have to compete by cutting costs, thus launching a war of attrition against independents like IXL.

The biggest cost factor in producing lime was to supply the firewood demanded by the monstrous appetite of the kilns for fuel. In spite of the obvious fact that the Santa Cruz & Felton would haul competitors' lime out of the canyon, Davis and Cowell gambled that the competitive advantage of dramatically cheaper fuel would give them back control of the Santa Cruz County lime industry.

Silent would soon have what Davis and Cowell needed most: an unlimited, cheap supply of cord wood to feed the hungry fires of their lime kilns. The kilns were located close to limestone quarries on today's site of the University of California campus (long since despoiled of burnable timber). Porting firewood to the site was circuitous and expensive until, in 1862, Davis and then-partner Jordan bought a sawmill and moved it to a high plateau atop the Hogback, using it to cut firewood from thinning stands of timber in the San Lorenzo Canyon. The plateau was isolated. The toll road between Santa Cruz and Felton wouldn't be built for another six years, leaving Davis and Jordan's road the only access. To port the firewood to the kilns, Davis and Jordan cut a three-mile shuttle road from the plateau, lying flat against the contours of the western wall of the canyon and running directly to the lime kilns. Twelve years later, by the time of the Santa Cruz & Felton proposal, the old sawmill was in ruins, but the shuttle road remained. All the Healys had to do was bring the narrow gauge survey onto the high plateau (the site destined to be renamed Rincon), which would allow flatcar loads of cord wood to be reloaded from the railroad onto Davis and Cowell's rejuvenated three-mile shuttle road.

All Charles Silent and the board of the Santa Cruz & Felton had to do was grant Cowell and Davis transportation of the wood at a low, fixed rate in order to negotiate in their turn the critical right-of-way through the entire canyon. The deal was recorded in detail in the Santa Cruz County Book of Deeds on February 23, 1875.[72] Davis and Cowell would give the Santa Cruz & Felton Railroad right-of-way through the canyon at no cost, in exchange for shipping fire wood to "saw mill flat" for $1.25 a cord from any point on the flume, or 50 cents a cord from any point on the railroad. "If rates are charged to other customers at a lower rate," the deed added, "then the rates to Davis & Cowell are to be reduced accordingly." The deed provided for a three-hundred-foot spur at Sawmill Flat for offloading the wood, as well as fixed rates on other kinds of lumber shipment. Such a deal would have been impossible for the San Lorenzo Rail Road. Locked into a route that never left the river, it passed seven hundred vertical feet below Sawmill Flat, missing entirely the connection with the three-mile shuttle road.

With Sawmill Flat acting like a fulcrum for their planning, Lucien and Charles Healy reengineered the entire project. Before the winter of 1874, the brothers Healy thought up an intermodal system to replace the flume. It consisted of the original flume running fourteen miles from mill to Felton; a sorting yard at Felton to size, store, and transship the various cuts of lumber; and a narrow gauge railroad running the last eight miles to Santa Cruz down the steep, narrow San Lorenzo Gorge.

The railroad in turn allowed gradients in the canyon that would be required to reach Sawmill Flat. Instead of confronting the Hogback and a nine-hundred-foot tunnel located near river level, the Healys deliberately inclined the railroad to run up the side of the Hogback to a location where only a two-hundred-foot tunnel was required to penetrate the nape of the granite tooth. The 1868 toll road had pioneered this new approach, avoiding a tunnel altogether by incurring a steep climb to the plateau. Long considered by historians to have been motivated only by cost savings, the steep route up the canyon wall was in fact the strategy that finally brought Davis and Cowell to the negotiating table.

Charles Silent quickly divided the intermodal delivery system into two separate business entities, the San Lorenzo Flume and Transportation Co. and the Santa Cruz & Felton Railroad Co., apparently to distinguish the enhanced commercial possibilities of the railroad. But the combined system was still an industrial tram. The Healy brothers designed the railroad with curvature unheard of on Hihn's Santa Cruz Rail Road. Hihn's tightest mainline curve was 574 feet in radius. Fifteen of the SC&F's curves had radii of 188 feet; two curves dropped to 155 feet, and a temporary curve around a rock slide dropped again to a contortionist 146.6 feet. But the curve at the St. Charles Hotel in Santa Cruz, required to get the track from River Street onto Mission Avenue en route to the pier, set the record, at 118-foot radius. Around this curve, even the line's ten-ton Porter, Bell steam locomotives did not routinely pass.[73]

R. E. Wood view of the flume yard at Felton. Photographs of the Santa Cruz & Felton can sometimes be dated by the presence of the line's Carter passenger cars, which arrived in July 1876. [California State Library]

Capturing high ground on top of the plateau obviated the need for a long tunnel through the Hogback, but it forced a brutal gradient of 137 feet to the mile in order to descend from Sawmill Flat (now referred to as "Summit") to Santa Cruz. Grades on the Santa Cruz Rail Road did not exceed 105 feet to the mile. Silent selected rail weight close to the lightest practical size for three-foot-gauge equipment. Hihn used thirty-pound rail on the Santa Cruz Rail Road; the Santa Cruz & Felton would, in contrast, make do with twenty-pound rail, substandard for narrow gauge common carriers operating in California at the time and lighter than the manufacturer's recommended rail weight required to support the Porter, Bell engines.[74]

All these engineering specifications reinforced the characterization that the line was an industrial logging tram, not a common carrier. In designing the SC&F, the Healy brothers did not think early on to provide for flexible operation of passenger and freight trains. No siding, for example, was installed at Treat's lumber mill near Felton; flatcars were simply spotted on the mainline for loading at night. The notorious curve at the St. Charles Hotel was a bottleneck in operating trains to the beach and pier area. Politics added another bottleneck. On January 9, 1875, the city of Santa Cruz granted the SC&F a charter to use Pacific Avenue to reach the site of the railroad's pier but decreed that the trains be pulled by horses on the intervening mile of city street track, thus virtually killing the chances for through passenger train operation between Felton and the beach.

To comply with the city charter, the SC&F constructed its first engine house on the north side of the St. Charles Hotel curve, regimenting its steam operations outside the downtown area. On River Street, by the front door of Amner's foundry, the line's Porter, Bell locomotives would uncouple from loaded flatcars. Horses would be hitched up for the long, hard pull through the St. Charles Hotel curve, onto Pacific Avenue, and down the mile of business thoroughfare to the pier.

However, primitive engineering standards resulted in faster construction. It took thirty-six months for Frederick Hihn to complete twenty-one miles of narrow gauge track between Santa Cruz and Watsonville; it took Charles Silent nine months to complete eight miles of track between Santa Cruz and Felton in the far more adverse topography of the San Lorenzo River Gorge. Heavy construction had already started in January 1875, when a break in the weather allowed bridge gangs to begin placing footings—like a climber's pitons—in the rocky cairns of the gorge. Five frame bridges and nineteen smaller trestles were required to cross steep gullies that creased the San Lorenzo Canyon on its flanks. Charles Silent appointed Benjamin Franklin Williams, just twenty-three years old, to superintend construction of the railroad. Little is known of Williams or his background, but he was to remain with the project until its completion.[75]

With so little emphasis placed on public conveyance, Silent ordered flatcars in the spring of 1875 but declined to order passenger cars. The public, encouraged to think of the Santa Cruz & Felton as a conveyor belt to the timber regions of the county, was welcome to ride on the lumber.

The Field Notebook: The SC&F's Porters

All three Monterey Bay narrow gauge lines—the M&SV, SCRR, and SC&F—purchased two road engines apiece, and all three railroads were quick to apply the lessons learned from the first engine to the second. Case in point: SC&F's number 1, the *Santa Cruz*, was shipped to San Francisco from Porter, Bell on May 14, 1875. Bearing serial number 218, it was a ten-ton 0-6-0 Class C with 9.5" × 14" cylinders. There were few other notations on its specification card. One year later, Porter diverted a second 0-6-0 to the SC&F from another order. Designated serial number 236, also a 9.5" × 14" machine, the engine became SC&F number 2, the *Felton*. But number 2 also came with numerous design changes, all noted on its spec card. They included extra play in the thirty-inch drivers; more rivets in the attachment of the cross equalizer brace to the frame; one extra leaf in the forward driver springs; the "escape pipe" raised so live steam wouldn't accidentally enter the cab; a notation of "special care of stack and ash screen" to prevent escape of sparks; and finally, "extra pains painting and lettering gilt stripes and letters" and a "glass name plate in cab panel." Many of these changes were motivated by the experiences of Fowler Pope, who ran the *Santa Cruz* for her first year in service and who wrote about the mechanical problems of daily operation in his diary. Pope's diary, reproduced in the next chapter, can be scanned for clues to the origins of the changes that appeared in Porter, Bell no. 236.

By mid-March 1874, two hundred men were at work on the first units of the flume.[76] They finished a fully functional sawmill first, using it to feed an unending supply of lumber into the intestine of the rapidly advancing flume. The first quarter-mile section of flume (in operation by March 20) replicated itself once every week, as preassembled sections of flume box floated down from the mill for installation by a moving carpentry shop, advancing down the river on the conveyance it was building:

> The engineer lays off the route, the bushwhacker follows with his axe and clears the way, the trestle-makers put up their work, it having a fall of an inch and one fourth to each sixteen feet. Much of the trestlework is thirty feet high, and some of it will be fifty, the upper part having to cross the river about every mile. The V framework is nailed together at the mill, (made of 2 × 6 scantling,) and the box, or V section, is also put together here. A board is nailed over the upper end for the water to push against, its own braces (three for each length) placed in it, and the whole set afloat. Arrived at its destination, four men are ready to place the V braces on the trestle-work, the section is brought to place and firmly nailed, by which time another has arrived for the same operation. So rapidly is this done that these men will place from forty to fifty sections in a day.[77]

On Sunday, May 5, 1875, Romanes Wood photographed the five-hundred-pound camp wood stove, the camp cook, and her provisions floating down the flume on their way to the next camp site. The stereopticon photographs would become a centerpiece of his Philadelphia exhibit, a tableau to the dramatic technological achievement taking place in near-wilderness. Wood returned often to photograph the flume construction project, and its narrow gauge partner, as the Centennial year approached.

Wood captured on silver halide emulsion an entrepreneurial spirit gripping the entire San Lorenzo River basin. Two miles south of the mill site at Crediford's, the town of Lorenzo was booming as a base of operations for the flume crews. Henry Saxtorph opened the Lorenzo Hotel "with new towels," noted the paper, while Frank Newell started a new blacksmith shop in the same village. At the other end of the flume, Felton was anxiously watching construction of a hotel called the Big Trees House, and a bar called the Snug. Romanes Wood took stereopticon photographs of both.

Very much like Hihn's early support of Santa Cruz foundries and planing mills, the Farmer's National Gold Bank put together its own supply chain for the Santa Cruz & Felton. They owned the land on which grew the trees, cut the trees to build the flume, and built the flume to transport the trees from the land they owned—the tightly fitting pieces of a house that Jack built.

The bank's partners were largely capitalists, not tradesmen, but they too brought critical skills and experience, not just money, to the project. Charles Silent had been a developer of the early San Jose street railway system and could claim experience in operating horse railroads on the Alameda in San Jose. His experience would come in handy on the mile of Santa Cruz street trackage. By July 31, 1875, the line's thirty-five stockholders included Charlie and Winfield "Winny" Gorrill of Pacific Bridge Co., suppliers who broad-

Original San Lorenzo Flume and Transportation Co. mill on the San Lorenzo, the flume head for the Santa Cruz & Felton. [Dan Matthews collection]

ened their interest in the project to include a share in its ownership, and eventually, for Charlie, the presidency of the railroad.[78]

The Gorrills quickly provided the Santa Cruz & Felton with the same heavy timber fabrication services they had sold virtually everywhere else in the county, including a contract for a $16,322.85 pier to port the flumed lumber to coastal ships. In April 1875, Pacific Bridge got to work driving piles in the surf at Santa Cruz, locating the new wharf midway between the Davis and Cowell wharf and the powder company wharf:

> The wharf contract was let to the Pacific Bridge Company, of San Francisco, work to be completed on or before June 15, 1875. The wharf will be 1278 feet long, and will be extended as soon as the company can bring their own piles and lumber on the road and flume.
>
> It is to be the most complete and substantial structure of the kind ever erected outside of San Francisco. The tops of the piles are to be mortised and dovetailed, in addition to the usual bolt, the whole thoroughly braced.[79]

The wharf became a living example of the leverage effect of the Santa Cruz supply chain. At first, the wharf would be used to land railroad iron from the steamers *Tokio* and *Arizona*, coming up the coast from early winter crossings of Cape Horn. Later, on its broad stage, Tom Carter would build the railroad's rolling stock. Then, for nearly five years after its completion, the Gorrills would witness most of the manufactured goods of Santa Cruz County exported from the commercially strategic wharf.

Romanes Wood photographed the pier for the Philadelphia exhibit.

―――――――――――

Having two railroad construction projects in town made for heady times. The *Santa Cruz Sentinel* speculated that the convergence of rail lines in the community would soon boost circulation to the point where the owners would consider changing the masthead from the *Weekly* to the *Daily Sentinel*.[80]

The paper also speculated that ongoing excavations on Beach Hill, which were required to put both lines in direct touch with wharf facilities, would eventually remove the large natural obstacle from the town's view of the ocean, raising property values.

Before the big bridge was finished, property values also began to go up at Soquel Landing. Hihn's tenant, Samuel Hall, raised barley and hogs on the bottom land under the trestle, but soon, watching the bridge timbers rise, he came to regard use of the land differently. In the summer of 1874, he took out a modest classified in the *Sentinel,* advertising a limited ten-day camping season beginning on the Fourth of July. Response was modestly encouraging. Members of the San Jose Silver Cornet Band were the first tourists to pitch canvas tents in Hall's barley field, celebrating with a clambake and dancing in a small open-sided pavilion that Hall constructed near the beach, close to the mouth of Soquel Creek. Hall charged a dollar per day for adult campers and fifty cents for children, but he made most of his money by boarding their horses on the barley crops he harvested. The next season, he

Cook moving on San Lorenzo Flume, S. C. Co., Cal.

Flume construction workers, ca. 1875 (upper); below, moving the cook and stove, heralded by the cook's dinner horn, to a new construction camp on Sunday, May 2, 1875; both images, R. E. Wood, photographer. [Upper, Dan Matthews collection; lower, Peter Palmquist collection]

Hotel (top) and store (bottom) in the village of Lorenzo, the seed of modern Boulder Creek. Photographs by R. E. Wood, ca. 1875. [Dan Matthews collection]

enclosed the pavilion and created a dining room where "all who wish can have hotel fare."[81] Hihn's completed railroad, whenever it was finished, would swell Mr. Hall's registration book. Hall's resort, called Camp Capitola, soon became a new local industry, and the subject of several Wood stereographs.

By the spring of 1875, work for both railroads had back-ordered the two foundries and two planing mills in town. Without permanent quarters, Kaye and Davis adopted the blacksmith shop of Evan Lukens as a temporary erection bay, handily adjacent to the Amner, Morton foundry, and started to build dump cars for the Santa Cruz & Felton.[82] Both foundries anticipated orders for new rolling stock for the Santa Cruz Rail Road soon to follow.

The issue of permanent space for the town's fledgling railroad manufactories may have reached a crisis point in early 1875. Lukens's blacksmith shop was barely adequate for erecting dump cars (each was a compact nine feet long and five feet wide), but a shift to production of full-sized rolling stock required space adapted uniquely to the manufacturing need. Batches of twenty-four-foot flatcars would ideally have to be built in groups of four or six, adjacent to the railroad, to achieve economies of scale. Such space did not exist in town during 1874 and the first half of 1875.

Even without larger facilities, Hihn ordered construction of the first SCRR rolling stock in March 1875, using one of the two planing mills, or possibly the Lukens location, as a temporary erection site. Evidence was soon forthcoming that the Santa Cruz foundries were gearing up to produce the most technically demanding part in a railroad car, chilled cast wheels: "The two foundries and two planing mills in Santa Cruz are busy turning out machinery and doing work for the two railroads now being constructed into town. A large number of cold-chilled car wheels has been cast, and the bridge irons are completed by Martin & Co. Amner, Morton & Co. are at work on car boxes and other small castings."[83]

Difficult to make reliably (even for San Francisco foundries), chilled iron car wheels represented a higher threshold of technical capability for the new Santa Cruz supply chain. As noted earlier, Tom Carter ordered chilled iron wheels for the Monterey project from San Francisco, while relying on Amner for all other casting requirements. But as its largest customer, Hihn strongly influenced local capability with his own procurement decisions. Would he outsource these high-end parts from the established railroad industry (as Carter had with the Monterey work), or gamble that the local supply chain could successfully manufacture them in quantity? Hihn equivocated. At first, as early as February 1875, he developed outside sources for wheels when the line's first passenger car, under construction at Lukens's shop, sat "nearly finished, and will be on the track as soon as the trucks, now on the way, are received."[84]

But by June, local suppliers had convinced Hihn that they were capable of handling the pouring of chilled car wheels. In the June 19, 1875, edition, a *Sentinel* reporter noted twenty pairs of brand new, dull gray, chilled car wheels stacked outside the New Foundry at the same time the Santa Cruz

Rail Road was beginning to build flatcars—proof of Hihn's willingness to commit to local vendors for wheel stocks. With this critical component at hand, the most active phase of Santa Cruz Rail Road rolling stock assembly began. Between June and December 1875, fourteen flatcars and one boxcar were added to the equipment roster, all apparently fashioned from locally supplied parts and materials (including wheels), and all assembled in town.[85]

Increasingly concerned with managing the supply chain he depended on, Hihn tightened his span of control around the ensemble of tradesmen, suppliers, and assemblers. In early February 1875, he hired a local carpenter named Houston Wallace Logan as car shop foreman. Twenty-nine years old, one of only two county residents listed in the Great Register of Voters as a "Car Builder," Logan bore primary responsibility for Hihn's car work over the next two years.[86]

As Hihn's confidence in Logan's ability increased, the scope of his effort shifted to more visible, high-end passenger car construction, marketing the value of his investment directly to the tastes and fashion of the traveling public. On May 8, 1875, Logan and an ornamental painter named B. C. Gadsby got credit in the *Sentinel* for completing "a passenger car tastefully finished in Bird's eye Maple and Rosewood grain. . . . The two styles of grain form a beautiful and harmonious contrast, giving the work the appearance of a first-class car."[87]

Begun in rented space at Lukens's shop, the arch-roofed car was completed at the railroad's new Rincon Street depot that month.[88] The event also signaled the long-delayed opening of the San Lorenzo River Bridge (actually on April 17), finally linking the operating railroad to downtown Santa Cruz and the railroad's permanent shops. From that time forward, Logan would use the Rincon Street facility as the principal car shop for the railroad. The range of car designs supported by this small shop is remarkable. Soon he crowded additional high-end car projects into the two-track covered "car house."[89] Along with the freight cars already noted, Hihn needed horsecars to span a short extension of the mainline between the Rincon Street depot and the Lower Plaza, the center of downtown, just three blocks away. Versatile enough to craft any type of railroad car body, Logan completed the first horsecar (with seating capacity for fourteen passengers) in mid-August.[90] The horsecar was soon the subject of a Romanes Wood stereograph, illustrating its elegant pagoda-style roof. Two more Logan-manufactured horsecars would follow.

Houston Logan's talents as a car builder appear to have come out of the blue. Younger brother to the county's prominent and well-liked district attorney, James Harvey Logan, Houston had no known background in railroad work. But the family was inventive and resourceful; James Logan carried on experiments in horticulture. Before the incorporation of the Santa Cruz Rail Road, the younger Logan apprenticed as both a blacksmith and a carpenter. He may have returned to his previous trade in 1877, when the *Sentinel* noted Logan building homes in Santa Cruz as a private contractor.[91]

But the car-building trade could not be learned from books. Logan's apprenticeship as a car builder may have taken place in the only local trade school offering car building in its curriculum, Tom Carter's 1874 Monterey shop. The evidence is circumstantial. Twenty Santa Cruz County carpenters responded to Carter's ad for carpenters, placed in the *Sentinel* on July 4. Most, apparently, were hired onto the Monterey project. If one of them was Houston Logan, he would have quickly been in a position to understudy the details of narrow gauge flatcars, boxcars, and even passenger cars during their manufacture for John Kidder. Apprenticing under Francis Geiser, Logan might have quickly realized the value of his blacksmithing and carpentry skills in the new, technical environment of car building.

If Houston Logan in fact worked for Carter, it might help to explain why Carter-like designs began to appear in Santa Cruz Rail Road rolling stock. A single extant photograph, taken in Santa Cruz County in 1882, shows a flatcar illuminated by late afternoon sunlight, posed on Aptos Creek with the locomotive *Betsy Jane*. The low light shows off many details of the car that would be lost in shadow under midday sun, including a Carter-style eight-ton-capacity freight truck, and elements of car hardware virtually identical to Carter's eight-ton designs, including shallow needle beams, truss rods mounted directly to the needle beams with cast pads, and a double-nut washer casting designed to tension nuts directly in line with the angle of the car's lateral truss rods.[92]

The details appear to add up: Carter's contract work with Tom Amner, completed in the summer of 1874, equipped the Santa Cruz Foundry with drawings for individual castings as well as concepts and designs for whole cars. This resource came with no intellectual property protection. Carter held no patents on the truck or its components. We can speculate that under these

Some of the original Santa Cruz Rail Road rolling stock was sold to the Loma Prieta Lumber Co. in 1882; this view in Aptos Creek Canyon shows the *Betsy Jane* and an SCRR flatcar built by Houston Logan (the line's master car builder), possibly from Carter-designed parts. Photographer thought to be Gilfillan and Co., from their series *Building the Loma Prieta Railroad—1882.* [Morgan North collection]

circumstances, Amner was free to reuse drawings to recreate the original pattern set, an option that Houston Logan may have exercised in 1875 when he was asked to produce, from local materials at the lowest possible cost, a fleet of cars for the Santa Cruz Rail Road.

When inventory was taken of the Santa Cruz Rail Road in April 1881, thirteen car patterns were listed among the contents of the Rincon Street car shop office. The patterns were not individually identified, but the count represents three-quarters of the patterns required to build a complete Carter-style eight-ton flatcar. Clearly, Houston Logan was able to use the patterns to recreate as complete a car manufactory as that developed by the Carters.[93]

Like strands of DNA, the patterns represented the genetic material of a design that no longer belonged to Carter (if it ever had) but was now adapted into new commercial markets by the same manufacturers who had produced the design for Carter. That DNA was, in the spring of 1875, identifiable inside the Santa Cruz supply chain.

Logan was then able to duplicate Carter's product while beating his price. The California Board of Commissioners of Transportation reported the cost of Santa Cruz Rail Road boxcars at $583 each. A comparable Carter boxcar (sold to the neighboring Santa Cruz & Felton just six months prior) cost $651. Flatcars evidenced similar differences in price: $461 for a Logan car versus $475 for a Carter.[94] The savings reinforced Hihn's belief in the value of a locally controlled and locally sustained supply chain.

We referred earlier to "compulsive technological sequences," in which a new technology succeeds by redirecting traditional manufacturing to alter and integrate its processes, thereby transforming and aligning supporting industries. By 1875, the elements of such a sequence were all present in Santa Cruz County. Houston Logan, we believe, understudied Carter's designs and assembly methods. Local foundries gave Logan the infrastructure he needed to obtain not just raw materials but finished parts and subassemblies as well, from which Logan could assemble entire cars. For local industry, differentiation, not competition, allowed a business to specialize, pushing its technical capabilities to a level where a higher percentage of component parts could be made locally, consequently increasing the overall profitability of the ensemble. The best examples, of course, were locally made chilled cast iron wheels.

Producing cast wheels in Santa Cruz in turn minimized shipping costs. Frederick Hihn translated this unique alignment into a low-cost production facility that then enabled low-cost construction of the Santa Cruz Rail Road. Politics, social dictates, and economic readiness were briefly in harmony. For a period of nearly three years, Santa Cruz County appeared to be capable of sustaining many of the technical and commercial resources that other startup narrow gauge railroads were forced to procure from the East Coast.

But there were hidden costs associated with such technological gallop. The metallurgical risks inherent in cast iron wheels were well known, and the Santa Cruz Rail Road did not escape their annoying habit of shattering along unseen crystalline flaw lines buried deep inside the casting. Casting flaws on wheels from the New Foundry, used on all of Logan's cars, were apparently the cause of a broken wheel under a moving train in December

From *The Wasp*, Aug. 4, 1877. [California State Library]

1876.[95] No one was hurt in the incident, but it was a sobering reminder of the risks entailed in any rapid technological development.

Tom Carter, too, might have first counted the Santa Cruz experience as a bitter lesson in the realities of startup business. Having sold Hihn no rolling stock, and instead seeing his design work wind up in local knockoffs, Carter might have had good reason to give up on Santa Cruz County. Virtually the opposite happened. At the same time Logan was entering production work on Santa Cruz Rail Road cars, Carter returned to the Santa Cruz supply chain, where, like a cache of ammunition, he would use Amner's foundry to reload for a second volley.

Let's speculate further: Carter gifted the Santa Cruz supply chain with more than just car designs. He hired twenty of the city's carpenters to work on the first prototypes of his own product line, and in the summer of 1874 he schooled them in the practice and art of car building. Recruited in Santa Cruz, the carpenters showed up in Monterey in late July, worked on M&SV rolling stock, and presumably returned to Santa Cruz by late October or early November.[96]

Then winter came, slowing work on the county's narrow gauge railroads. But by spring 1875, contractors looking for skilled labor were in a unique position. Carter's small pool of Monterey apprentices, noted the *Sentinel* on July 10, 1875, made available journeymen to assemble Santa Cruz & Felton cars:

> The Felton Railroad Company has within the last week constructed ten new cars for the purpose of carrying freight, although at present some of them will be used as passenger cars. They are what are termed flat cars, being 24 × 7 feet, and they are built of strong timber, which with the fine iron work make them durable and altogether as neat a lot of cars as we have seen. They were made at Saucelito, and are being put up by Mr. Cutter. As soon as the locomotive arrives, which will probably be in a few days, it will again dawn on the people that another railroad is a matter of fact and not a phantom of the future. Mr. Cutter has also drawn up specifications of passenger cars, which have been handed to the Board of Directors, but their answer has not been received.

Was "Cutter" in fact Tom Carter? The only Cutter listed in a contemporary Santa Cruz business directory is James Cutter, a pharmacist who had invested in a few shares of Santa Cruz Rail Road stock back in 1873. A commercial druggist, however, would make an unlikely candidate for a car construction foreman.[97] It seems much more likely that the paper interviewed Tom Carter himself, confusing his name with the local pharmacist. Whomever the paper was referring to, a Saucelito car manufactory was clearly selling its product in Santa Cruz County. Carter Brothers was the only such business in Saucelito.

Eight months after completion of the Monterey work, Carter was able to hire back at least part of his old crew. Unskilled in car work a year before, the same carpenters now quickly swung into action on the Santa Cruz & Felton assemblies, handling familiar tools to assemble familiar parts.

The cars were assembled where the material landed, in fresh ocean air on the SC&F's Santa Cruz pier. The July 10 *Sentinel* article documented the first of two lots of Carter flatcars delivered to the Santa Cruz & Felton. Material for this lot arrived by ship in late May or early June 1875.[98] The next lot, at least twenty cars delivered in December, brought the total to twenty-four flatcars, worth a retail value of $6,776.47, and six boxcars, worth $3,907.30.[99]

The project was about half the size of the Monterey job and provisioned largely from Saucelito, where Carter's permanent crew created the components for kits, precut and predrilled car sills, bundling them tightly for shipment aboard coastal schooners. The July 1875 Santa Cruz consignment is the earliest known example of Carter-manufactured kits. It represents a significant shift from the field factory strategy of Monterey, toward a new and flexible kind of manufacture whose primary aim was reduction in cost. Small lots of cars, built for a remote short line, didn't justify moving an entire factory, or even a field factory, to such a location. At least three new customers would receive kits in 1875: the Santa Cruz & Felton, the Nevada County Narrow Gauge, and the Santa Clara Valley Railroad. But the total production for all three railroads barely added up to half the volume of cars Carter produced for the North Pacific Coast. In a year of diminishing demand, reflecting a rapidly spreading recession, Carter turned to kit work as a means to attract and keep smaller customers who would not justify the expense of on-site manufacturing.

A key part of the kit strategy sought to identify a local source of comparatively unskilled labor to assemble parts that had been manufactured by a more skilled labor pool at the factory, leaving the factory labor pool free to manufacture more kits. In Santa Cruz, Carter began the Santa Cruz & Felton work with a real advantage: a list of experienced craftsmen who could guarantee accurate, rapid assembly of flatcars and boxcars. The paper never attached names to the project, but a few likely candidates can be identified from Santa Cruz directories and voter registration records: Alanson Burgess (who would become the lead carpenter for the SC&F), Charles Painter (associated with the Santa Cruz Rail Road car shops), and Houston Logan may well have been recruited from the original M&SV labor pool to play a role, eight months later, in assembling the first known Carter Brothers freight car kits.

Add to this list the name of John Nelson. What little we know of him suggests a link between the earliest and latest phases of Carter's career, and something of a sojourner through its far-ranging geographies. The first known record of Nelson occurs in the Great Register of Marin County, where he registered to vote, in Saucelito, on August 20, 1875. Just twenty-two years old, he listed his occupation as a car builder the same summer that Carter was packaging kits in Saucelito for the Santa Cruz & Felton. Nelson certainly worked for Carter.

Just six weeks later, on October 7, Nelson registered to vote in Santa Cruz County; this preceded Carter's second shipment of SC&F kits, which would begin in November. He again listed his occupation as car builder, giving the impression that he was an experienced carpenter or a even a field boss, perhaps sent by Carter to run the job. Along with Houston Logan, his is one of just two entries in the Santa Cruz register referring to the occupation of car builder.

Nelson remained in Santa Cruz County after the rolling stock was assembled. We believe he appears in the diary of an SC&F engineer named Fowler Pope, coming to Pope's home for dinner in early June 1876, serving as Pope's conductor on Friday, July 28, and again on Friday, October 13, 1876. A month later, "downsizing" reduced the number of employees on the SC&F. As a result, Nelson left Santa Cruz County (his voting records are removed to Mono County on August 27, 1879); he vanishes from the record for twenty years. But he surfaces again, briefly, in Carter's time rolls for June 1899, working at the Newark shop during the last three-year period of Carter's commercial existence.[100]

It's not difficult to imagine Nelson's career path extending backward in time to its logical first step: an apprenticeship with Carter in Monterey in 1874, at the age of just twenty-one. Proof, unfortunately, is lacking.

Still, Nelson's patchwork biography may be the longest running example of the part-time labor that Carter relied on to meet the swells and troughs of his business. John Nelson grew old in Carter's employ. Nearly fifty years old by the time Carter Brothers closed its doors, he wove deep loyalties from the loose thread of venture capital, emerging technologies, and home-schooled mechanical skills, the whole cloth of the Santa Cruz supply chain.

There is no speculation about the source of Carter's SC&F iron work. He came back to the same suppliers he had helped create. On June 18, 1875, a paper called the *Santa Cruz Local Item* noted that SC&F wheel sets were delivered by ship from San Francisco, while smaller castings were being provided by the Amner, Morton and W. H. Martin foundries.[101]

Amner's black-market parts may not have been as competitively damaging as it would at first seem. Having used Carter-based patterns for car work on the Santa Cruz Rail Road, local foundries maintained practice in the work, so they were already part way up the ramp of volume production. In effect, Santa Cruz suppliers continuously manufactured Carter parts to Carter specifications, keeping their foundry process tuned and ready. When Carter needed the suppliers again, the Santa Cruz foundries had men and tooling qualified to run the job.

In the process, Tom Carter was learning the value of long-term business relationships. It is likely that he owed the success of the Santa Cruz & Felton car work to his affiliation with the Gorrill brothers, which was now entering its third year. With 8 percent of the Santa Cruz & Felton's stock in his family's portfolio, Charles Gorrill could have been the crucial link in getting Tom Carter exclusive rolling stock contracts for the SC&F. Affiliated in bridge work, both men were at a crossroads in their careers. Gorrill was moving up in the administration of the SC&F and acutely aware of the need to rapidly furnish the line with rolling stock. Both would look like heroes if Carter could provide cars quickly, at the right price.

Restoration of the *Jupiter*, a Baldwin class 8-18 C of 1876, on display at the Smithsonian Institution, 1992. [Bruce MacGregor]

The uncomplicated delivery and efficient erection of Carter cars probably bolstered Gorrill's position in the Santa Cruz & Felton. By September 1876, Charlie Gorrill had replaced Charles Silent as the SC&F's president and taken up residency in the Branciforte district, just east of Santa Cruz.

The evolution of the Santa Cruz supply chain had reached maturity. In the case of the Pacific Bridge Co., a key part of the supply chain was now managing the railroad it supplied.

For the remainder of 1875, until Hihn could get his hands on the money to buy something better, *Betsy Jane* and her crew struggled heroically with the task of moving rail and timber to the front. A reporter's first-hand account from November 8, 1875, gives some idea of *Betsy*'s burdens: "a carload of fence lumber, three carloads of ties, one carload of rail [estimated overloaded at nine tons], plus 'some empty cars running in the sugar beet interest from Soquel.'"[102]

By doubling the worst grades (taking only half her train to the top at a time), the six-ton *Betsy Jane* horsed this ponderous load to the edge of the Pajaro Valley, nearly the whole length of the railroad.

By the time the railroad neared Watsonville, Hihn was running out of luck, as well as money. The road's pile driver and donkey engine, assigned to

Exactly like the SC&F's Porter, Bell 0-6-0s, the first Baldwin engine delivered to the Santa Cruz Rail Road was the basis for modifications to the second locomotive, built to the identical class. In the eleven months between delivery of the 8-18 C class *Pacific* and the *Jupiter*, the Santa Cruz Rail Road formulated numerous changes to the basic design. Here are the highlights from Baldwin spec sheets: *Jupiter*'s stroke was increased to eighteen inches from *Pacific*'s sixteen (a change that should have resulted in alteration of the engine's classification from 8-18 C to 8-18½ C but inexplicably did not); the half-inch driver play on *Pacific* was widened to five-eighths inch on *Jupiter* after excessive flange wear was experienced; *Pacific* had all her drivers flanged; *Jupiter* received blind forward drivers; her boiler feed pipes were copper, improved from iron feed pipes on the *Pacific*; stay bolts were attached in an improved way; two safety valves were installed instead of one; and air brakes were installed on *Jupiter*'s tender trucks and (says the Baldwin spec sheet) drivers, although the driver brakes do not appear in known photographs of the engine.

All the changes were not necessarily improvements: the *Pacific*'s swing bolster lead truck was replaced by a rigid truck on *Jupiter*, and *Pacific*'s lovely Russia iron boiler jacket was replaced with a plain American iron jacket.

foundation work on the new Pajaro River Bridge, were washed downstream in the flood of December 1875, and for a time lost.

A badly needed loan from Spreckels, worth exactly the $125,000 of hostage county bond money, began to turn the situation around in September 1875.[103] But to Hihn, the loan was humiliating evidence that years of frugality and financial caretaking, not to mention his political influence in the county, were being eclipsed by opportunism from Claus Spreckels. Hihn repaid the loan, but he privately feared losing control of the railroad to Spreckels.

Quietly, over the next four years, Hihn purchased an additional 1,522 shares of Santa Cruz Rail Road stock and transferred its ownership to his sister Emma, living in Switzerland, thus reinforcing his narrow majority. When he itemized a final accounting of the railroad's stock on October 1, 1881, Hihn penned a short, revealing explanation into his day books: "to the above should be added cost and interest of 1,522 shares of S.C.R.R. stock, purchased to prevent S. obtaining control."[104]

Struggling to complete the railroad to Watsonville, desperate for a full-sized locomotive, Hihn pushed *Betsy Jane* past the breaking point. She ran into trouble in March 1876, when a mechanical failure forced suspension of all construction trains for the remainder of the week.[105] Two weeks later, *Betsy* was back on line to move the railroad's first revenue freight (two carloads of potatoes) on April 1, 1876.

Hihn placed the order for a full-sized Baldwin in July 1875 but delayed delivery for ten months, which suggests that he was unwilling to risk more debt until Watsonville's injunction was settled and the bond money finally secured. *Pacific*, the railroad's first full-sized locomotive, was finally delivered on May 9, 1876, just over two months after the injunction was finally lifted in the Santa Cruz District Court.[106] A second engine, the *Jupiter*, would not be delivered until nearly a year later.

The six-ton "patented bathtub and heating apparatus," as the Watsonville paper once described the *Betsy Jane*, built the railroad and opened it to revenue traffic before the Baldwins arrived.

There were places in the San Lorenzo River Gorge where the railroad and the wagon road clung to the mountainside like strands of cooked spaghetti sticking to a wall.

In the steepest part of the gorge, the Santa Cruz & Felton occupied the lower position in the delicately balanced trapeze act. To carve a path along the wall, the line was forced to remove portions of what precious little mountain existed above it to support the highway. Any attempt to improve the hold of one usually succeeded in weakening the foundation of the other. The river, indiscriminately, undermined both.

The winter of 1876 attacked all three.

The remarkable diary of Fowler Pope, much of which is reproduced in Chapter Seven, begins with the attempt to open the Santa Cruz & Felton Railroad at the start of one of the worst winters in the county's memory. The engineer of the line's first locomotive, *Santa Cruz*, Pope began the Centennial year by trying to move an enormous backlog of flumed lumber out of the mountains to the wharf, but he wound up instead in near-combat conditions with rockslides and uprooted redwood trees.

Pope comes across in the diary as a sober, serious man, but in the midst of the dangers he faced each day he managed to fashion a wry sort of humor from the uneven contest between the San Lorenzo River Gorge and the narrow gauge railroad that challenged it. He wrote disparagingly of the flickering yellow light cast by his engine's headlamp on night runs through the canyon. Both the manufacturer's headlight and a locally supplied replacement failed to give Pope the light he needed to safely run through the treacherous canyon. On January 19, a new headlight arrived, and Pope noted sarcastically that "a new head lamp came for our engine and is not a very good one."

As the winter drew on and slides worsened, sarcasm turned to anxiety:

Friday, February 25, 1876
Run *Santa Cruz* all day. Tucker fireman.

Made two trips to Felton doubling up the hill both times and having to wait in Felton both trips to load. The last trip we waited until dark before we started & came through the canion in the dark, so dark I could not have seen obstruction of any kind had their been any on the track & was risky & dangerous work, but we got home safe, a little before 8 o'clock P.M. I feel almost sick.

Had rain.

If the track was open, Pope brought the commercial loads down from Felton in daylight. If slides blocked his way, he used the engine to snag enormous redwood trees off the easily kinked twenty-pound rails. By night, he brought gravel trains into the canyon to shore up the right-of-way behind massive cribs of 2" × 12" planking. He worked seven day weeks, days that began at six in the morning and seldom ended until eight at night. Pope and his wife normally attended the Santa Cruz Congregational Church. But in the seven months between March and October 1876, he worked every single Sunday. An estimated quarter of Fowler Pope's time was spent maintaining the *Santa Cruz*. To keep the locomotive's downtime at a minimum, Pope did almost all the mechanical work on her at night, or during periods of foul weather.

Through his diary, we glimpse what could be thought of as the last phase of the Santa Cruz railroad supply chain. In the daily battle to maintain the engine, Pope routinely counted on many of the businesses that Hihn had helped gain prominence as local railroad suppliers. The blacksmith shop of Evan Lukens, for example, performed work on the smokestack netting to stop it from bleeding sparks; Amner, Morton (handily located on the SC&F at the point where horses took over for steam engines) installed new oilers on the cylinder chests and helped babbitt main and side rod bearings; Frank Waterman's plumbing supply house sold the SC&F piping and valves; painter and decorator B. C. Gadsby worked on the engine's troublesome headlight; William England, a machinist and gunsmith, did light drilling and tapping on parts, including installation of the engine's clock, as well as babbitting of journals.

Fowler Pope often walked downtown in the evening after work, dropping off or picking up parts he would need to raise a head of steam the next morn-

ing. At night, exhausted, he penned a short summary of the day's events into the 3.5" × 6" black, leather-bound diary. Usually short and dispassionate, the entries still captured the very personal sense of commitment that the small commercial houses felt toward keeping the railroad running. The entry for Sunday, May 21, is a graphic example:

> Worked on *Santa Cruz* all day and all the Eve not having her fixed at 12 at night. Tucker worked all day on Engine. Blew off & washed out boiler & done other work. Mr. England came & helped me take down connections & took to his shop. Plain [sic] & drilled out & babbet with Garratt mettle. Then went to Engine house & worked on them until past midnight. I done a lot of drilling with a foot lathe which I found was hard work.

If it thought of itself as a railroad manufacturing center in the heady days of '74 and '75, the Santa Cruz supply chain soon had to stand aside and watch a more established, vastly larger industrial network beat down its door. The first intruder arrived in the aftermath of John McLaughlin's apparently unsuccessful grading machine, whose parts were cast at the New Foundry in 1873. The contraption vanished without a trace after a commercial grading machine arrived from G. G. Haslup and Bros. of Sidney, Ohio, in July 1874. "The cost of the [new] machine," noted the *Sentinel* on July 21, "was $400, and does the work of 7 men. The company are highly delighted with its working capacity. Go and see it work."

The public was more likely to have gone to see the new coach *Therese*, $4,000 worth of mirror-lacquered cabinetry manufactured by the Barney and Smith works in Dayton. Named for Hihn's wife, the coach first made its appearance on the Santa Cruz Rail Road on May 7, 1876, along with the new Baldwin engine *Pacific*. The expenditure seemed very much out of line with Hihn's frugal, minimalist investments in homemade rolling stock over the previous three years. But the coach celebrated (perhaps to excess) the release of county bonds through court action the preceding February.[107] *Therese*'s arrival signaled a dramatic change in how Hihn viewed local suppliers, an open shift toward courting popular taste through conspicuous spending on brand-name manufactured goods.

On September 9, the county watched *Therese*'s companion coach, *Stella*, arrive from the same builder, repeating the point for those who might have missed it. Color ads for Deising's Fredericksburg beer soon appeared, neatly framed, inside the two coaches.

Between the arrival of *Therese* and *Stella*, the Santa Cruz & Felton took delivery of two smaller coaches from Carter on July 1, 1876. Built to identical framing specifications, they were finished differently. One, described as a second-class coach (no sash or glass was installed in the windows), cost $1,600. Its companion, described as a first-class coach, cost $2,300.[108] Both were a far cry from the Barney and Smith cars but, in comparison to the flatcars that the public had been conditioned to ride on, a modest luxury. The *Sentinel* still played up the local angle: the car bodies had been built in Saucelito but the trucks were locally fabricated, a nod to Carter's old supplier Amner, Morton.

Even with side or bench-style seating, and even with al fresco ventilation, the cars helped shift the little SC&F's image from industrial tram to public carrier, a transformation that summer weather made easier to believe. "Two new passenger cars arrived this Eve over the s.c.r.r. for our road, and look very well," Fowler Pope noted in his diary on Saturday, July 1, 1876, just three days away from the nation's Centennial celebration.

With the arrival of the two Carter coaches and the Santa Cruz Rail Road 4-4-0 *Jupiter*, the two Santa Cruz short lines had virtually completed their lifetime equipage of rolling stock.

By 1876, the Santa Cruz County supply chain no longer existed for its own sake. Root-bound as much by economics as by geography, the short lines it had built grew to their practical limits. The Santa Cruz Rail Road was lucky to make payments on its debt, much less embark on the hundred-mile trek up the rugged coast to San Francisco, and the Santa Cruz & Felton was no longer in the market for new rolling stock. Tom Amner or William Martin's foundries poured few axle boxes or chilled car wheels after the mid-seventies. The nights when the old foundry floor glowed from the incandescent light of dozens of molds filled with narrow gauge parts were a memory that would fade with the untimely death of Tom Amner in 1882.

Houston Logan was seriously injured when a hot metal rod entered his eye socket in November 1876,[109] nearly costing him the vision in one eye. Apparently recovered from the accident, wearing "round optics" to help him see, he died in 1879, not long before Hihn sold the Santa Cruz Rail Road to the Southern Pacific and got out of the railroad business entirely. Houston's district attorney brother, James Harvey, kept the family name alive and dabbled with horticultural experiments in his back yard. In 1890, he crossed a wild blackberry and a tame variety, in the process inventing the Loganberry and ensuring the family name a lasting place in history.

Henry Gorrill succumbed to tuberculosis in September 1874, at the height of Pacific Bridge's Santa Cruz County operations. His diary entries described a trip to the mountains east of Marysville in mid-August, where he surveyed the site of a proposed lumber flume by horseback. By September 2, he had returned to the busy construction sites in Santa Cruz County, from which he penned the last diary entry on September 6, a note to send his wife the monthly household allotment of $29. He died six days later, at home in Oakland, leaving his brother, Charlie, to run the bridge business.

Some of Santa Cruz County's early narrow gauge pioneers graduated to projects in other parts of the state, becoming—like Binney, Schuyler, and Carter—railroadists. Benjamin Franklin Williams, who came on as the twenty-three-year-old superintendent of the Santa Cruz & Felton, left the short line in late October 1875 to become superintendent of construction of the Santa Clara Valley Railroad, the forerunner of the South Pacific Coast.[110]

Evan Lukens, the blacksmith responsible for early dump car work for

reek.

"Making Railroad ties"; R. E. Wood stereograph, taken near Boulder Creek, ca. 1876. [Dan Matthews collection]

the Santa Cruz Rail Road, perhaps survived longest of all in the local car-building trade, constructing horsecars for the East Santa Cruz Street Railway Company as late as 1890.[111]

Frederick Hihn's vision of a self-contained Santa Cruz railroad supply chain lasted just three brief years, from 1873 to 1876. Yet at its conclusion, a role in a new, larger supply chain was clearly beginning to emerge.

On July 22, 1876, the *Sentinel* reported the export of 5,388 broad gauge ties on the northbound schooner *Truckee*. Flumed from the headwaters of the San Lorenzo and taken to tidewater aboard the Santa Cruz & Felton, the ties were consigned to the narrow gauge South Pacific Coast Railroad at Dumbarton Point, twenty miles down the bay from San Francisco. The South Pacific Coast would use the ties to return to Santa Cruz County. Its narrow gauge mainline, built with broad gauge ties and rail nearly as heavy as the Central Pacific's, would reach south from Alameda through the spine of the Coast Range and enter Santa Cruz County just ten miles north of the Santa Cruz & Felton railhead. Charlie Gorrill quietly began to negotiate a sellout. The SPC would use the SC&F to reach Santa Cruz. In the process, the South Pacific Coast forged the longest and most expensive segment of the coastal narrow gauge link Frederick Hihn had envisioned in the sixties.

In the updraft of new dollars and new markets, the South Pacific Coast's president, Alfred Davis, ordered his surveyors to stake the rugged folds of the Santa Cruz Mountains as early as May 1876, looking for a way to tunnel into Santa Cruz from the San Jose side. Ironically, the tunnel would emerge in the upper Soquel Creek watershed of Frederick Hihn's Soquel Augmentation timber holdings, finally giving Hihn a way to commercially develop his timber holdings buried in the county's backwoods. Hihn, and many of his neighbors, got busy producing and shipping redwood ties to Davis. Some day, they told themselves with satisfaction, their children and grandchildren would be riding over them on their way to San Francisco.

Under the circumstances, photographer Romanes Erastus Wood, hiring Chinese crews to help harvest ties on his Troutdale ranch near Boulder Creek, canceled his trip to exhibit photographs at the Philadelphia Centennial exhibit.

View of portion of Santa Cruz, Santa Cruz Co., Cal.

Lower Plaza

Lower Plaza, Santa Cruz, showing the earliest days of the "Red Line" horsecar, which used the SCRR's tracks on Chestnut Street to reach the beach from the Lower Plaza, two miles distant. The horsecar is thought to have been built by Houston Logan; R. E. Wood stereo, later than August 1875. [Dan Matthews collection]

The new Ely's Block, Pacific Avenue, Santa Cruz; R. E. Wood stereo, ca. 1875. [Dan Matthews collection]

The Santa Cruz House, Front Street, Santa Cruz; R. E. Wood stereo, ca. 1875. [Dan Matthews collection]

Flume builder's camp, upper San Lorenzo River; R. E. Wood stereo, ca. 1875. [Dan Matthews collection]

Scenes on the Flume, Santa Cruz Co. Cal.

Scenes on flume, upper San Lorenzo River; R. E. Wood stereo, ca. 1875. [Dan Matthews collection]

Snug saloon, Felton; R. E. Wood stereo, ca. 1875. [Dan Matthews collection]

St. Charles Hotel, Santa Cruz, before the arrival of the Santa Cruz & Felton in the summer of 1875; the SC&F's mainline would exit River Street, to the right of the hotel, and navigate a 118-foot-radius curve onto Mission Street, roughly following the wagon tracks in the right foreground; this was the tightest curve on the railroad. Because of this curve, the line's steam locomotives would remain on the north side of the St. Charles Hotel and the flatcars were dragged through the curve by horses. R. E. Wood stereo. [Dan Matthews collection]

Often reproduced from copies, this extremely clear view of the Baldwin 8-18 C *Jupiter*, photographed on Chestnut Street near the line's Santa Cruz terminal, was made from the surviving original cabinet card. A lithograph from W. W. Elliott's *Santa Cruz County Illustrations* of 1879 helps fix the photograph's location as well as identify the owner of the residence appearing in the photograph above the locomotive's bell, Mr. W. P. Young. [Left, Randolph Brant collection, courtesy Emiliano Echeverria; above, Museum of Art and History, Santa Cruz]

To get building material to remote SCRR bridge sites, at first Pacific Bridge Co. had to land timbers and castings at the old Soquel wharf (right), where materials were stockpiled for construction of the Soquel Creek Bridge (opposite, above). When Pacific Bridge built the San Lorenzo Howe truss (below right), material could be landed at commercial Santa Cruz piers, less than a quarter mile away. An early sketch of the San Lorenzo River Bridge appeared in Henry Gorrill's notebook (below), dated May 18, 1874. The bridge appears at right angles to the page, labeled "160 feet." [Right and below right, Dan Matthews collection; below left and opposite, below, Center for Archival Collections, Bowling Green State University]

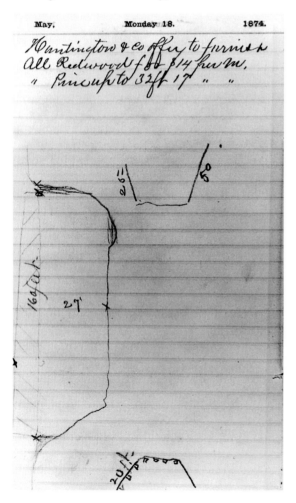

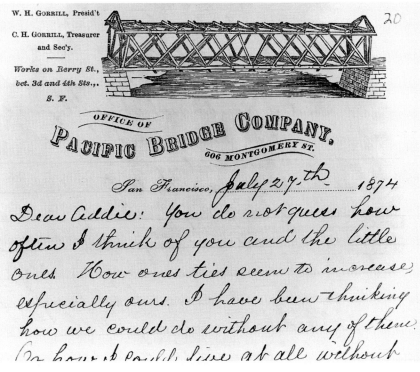

W. H. GORRILL, Presid't

C. H. GORRILL, Treasurer
and Sec'y.

Works on Berry St.,
bet. 3d and 4th Sts.,.
S. F.

20

OFFICE OF

PACIFIC BRIDGE COMPANY,

606 MONTGOMERY ST.

San Francisco, July 27th 1874

Dear Addie: You do not guess how
often I think of you and the little
ones. How ones ties seem to increase,
especially ours. I have been thinking
how we could do without any of them.
Or how I could live at all without

The Carleton Watkins panorama of the SCRR's Soquel Creek Bridge, at Camp Capitola, was taken sometime after 1876, when Watkins began the "New Boudoir Series" of photographs following sale of the old series negatives in a business failure. Arguably the most famous nineteenth-century western photographer, here Watkins captured the Baldwin *Pacific* stopped on the bridge with a northbound mixed train, including the Barney and Smith coach *Stella* or *Therese* at the end of the train. Visible at midtrain, the arch-roofed coach and boxcar were products of Houston Logan. On this page, Camp Capitola appears in an earlier stereo image from the camera of R. E. Wood; opposite, below, the SCRR trestle across Twin Lakes, today's Santa Cruz small craft harbor. [Right, William Wulf collection; below, Special Collections, Meriam Library, California State University, Chico; opposite, below, University of California, Santa Cruz, Special Collections]

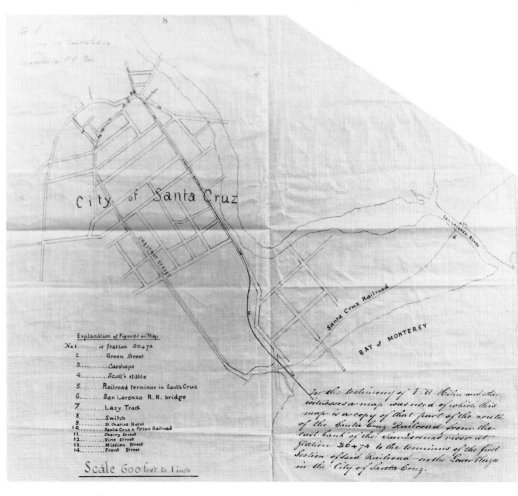

8

City of Santa Cruz

CHESTNUT STREET

San Lorenzo River

Santa Cruz Railroad

BAY OF MONTEREY

Explanation of Figures on Map

No 1 .... is Station 30+74
2 .... Green Street
3 .... Carshops
4 .... Scott's stable
5 .... Railroad terminus in Santa Cruz
6 .... San Lorenzo R.R. bridge
7 .... Lazy Track
8 .... Switch
9 .... St. Charles Hotel
10 .... Santa Cruz & Felton Railroad
11 .... Cherry Street
12 .... Vine Street
13 .... Mission Street
14 .... Front Street

Scale 600 feet to 1 inch

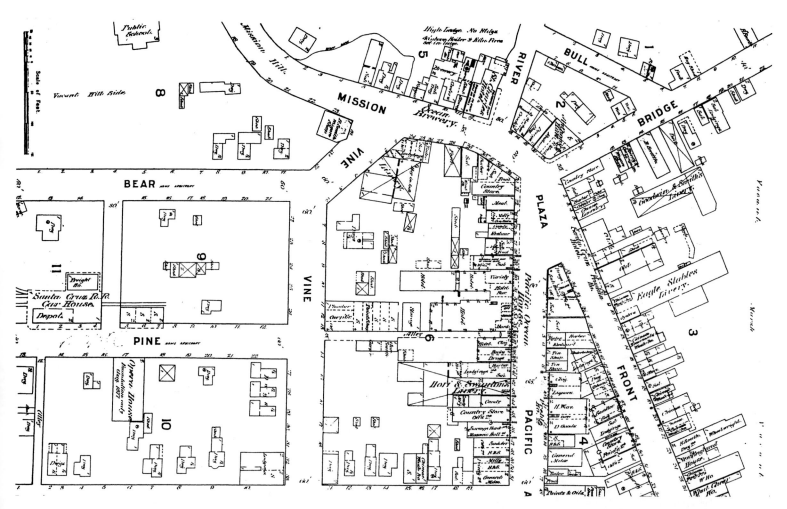

R. E. Wood photographed what is believed to be the 1876 Centennial Fourth of July celebration on Pacific Avenue, in Santa Cruz (opposite, above), not quite a year after the Santa Cruz & Felton's original tracks were placed in the street. The ink-on-linen map (opposite, below) was entered as evidence in the case of *County of Santa Cruz* v. *Santa Cruz Rail Road*; it portrayed narrow gauge street track ca. 1878, sometime after the Santa Cruz & Felton tunnel was drilled through Mission Hill. The oldest known Sanborn Fire Insurance map of Santa Cruz (above) gives details of the Lower Plaza area in 1877, while the same area appears in a photograph (below) looking up Mission Street from Lower Plaza, with the St. Charles Hotel on the right. [Opposite, above: Special Collections, Meriam Library, California State University, Chico; opposite, below, and this page, Museum of Art and History, Santa Cruz; this page, above, University of California, Santa Cruz, Special Collections]

F. A. Cook stereo image of the Felton flume yard, reproduced from the original 5" × 7" glass-plate negative, ca. 1878; this negative is numbered "1"; additional numbered Cook negatives, reproduced on subsequent pages, may have been taken on the same day. Locomotive "Santa Cruz" on the left; locomotive "Felton" on the right. [Nevada Historical Society, Elliott collection]

F. A. Cook stereo images of Santa Cruz & Felton, including the locomotive *Felton* with a long freight train (above left); the locomotive *Santa Cruz* with a single coach (above right), and one of the railroad's two Carter coaches (below), all photographed at the same location in the San Lorenzo River Gorge. Reproduced from 5" × 7" glass-plate negatives, numbered 5, 7, and 9, respectively. [All, Nevada Historical Society, Elliott collection]

F. A. Cook captured a moody, late afternoon view of a Santa Cruz & Felton train moving north-bound through the San Lorenzo River Gorge, an unnumbered image taken on the same day as the two numbered stereo views below (12 and 13, respectively). The monitor-type lime kiln in the stereo image on the right may have been photographed by Cook on a side trip from Felton to the Bull's lime kiln, located nearby up Bennett Creek. [All, Nevada Historical Society, Elliott collection]

Freight traffic on the Santa Cruz & Felton largely moved south-bound, to the Gharkey pier in Santa Cruz, the middle pier of three shown above in an F. A. Cook stereo image and (at left) in a W. W. Elliott lithograph of 1878. Also dated 1878, the ink-on-linen map (below) shows the Gharkey pier on the left, and the California Powder Works pier on the right. Photographs of the late 1870s show the S-shaped connecting pier built between them. [Above, Nevada Historical Society, Elliott collection; below and left, Museum of Art and History, Santa Cruz]

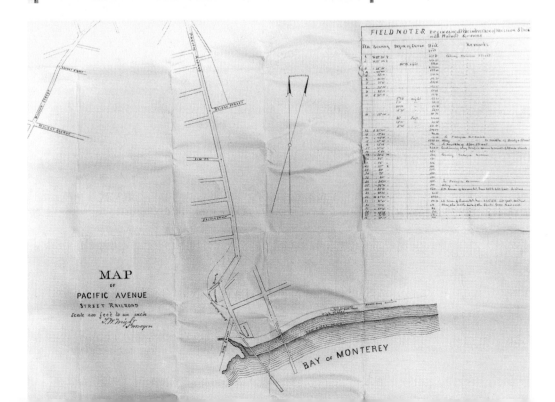

MAP
OF
PACIFIC AVENUE
STREET RAILROAD

BAY OF MONTEREY

View of Santa Cruz California, from Kittredge House.

Santa Cruz, California.

Emerging from a widespread recession, Santa Cruz experienced a local industrial revolution, celebrated by the opening of the Centennial Flour Mill in 1876, in the Perkins view, top. Adjacent to the yards of the Santa Cruz & Felton, as well as the wharves, the mill appears directly above the tip of the powder company's wharf (bottom) in a lithograph of 1877 published in Holland. The detailed bird's-eye view even includes a glimpse of the second Santa Cruz & Felton roundhouse, directly above the train posed on the Gharkey pier. [Above, California Historical Society; below, Bancroft Library]

Also a sign of economic recovery, in November, 1883, the first Southern Pacific standard gauge trains reached Santa Cruz over the original right-of-way of the Santa Cruz Rail Road (above), launching a fierce schedule war between the narrow gauge South Pacific Coast and its rival Southern Pacific. To accommodate heavier trains, the original narrow gauge San Lorenzo River bridge, shown in the Cook photograph at the left, had to be extensively rebuilt. [Above, Randolph Brant collection, courtesy Emiliano Echeverria; left, Nevada Historical Society, Elliott collection]

Fowler Pope's Diary: 1876

In the new connectedness of her narrow gauge railroads, Santa Cruz County watched the clocks speed up, the distance between cities shorten, and—in the Centennial year of American independence—the heartbeat of its commercial centers quicken.

It was to be a year of modest recovery for Santa Cruz County, in spite of the effects of the recession and despite signs of socioeconomic fallout that accompanied rapid industrial development. In 1876, Santa Cruz County seemed beset with much the same economic undertow that high technology brings with it today. Along with industrial acceleration came organizational cost-cutting, downsizing, and unemployment (a fate that was to befall Fowler Pope himself). Along with widespread unemployment came demonstrations of racism. In Santa Cruz County, ethnic friction first became visible in 1876, when a chapter of the Order of Caucasians began meeting in public; it was a symptom of a larger, more violent movement that would soon sweep California.[1]

Fowler W. Pope, whose diary for the Centennial year follows, simply called the year "eventful."

At the heart of the new optimism was a resurgence of railroad construction in the county, which Pope witnessed from the privileged role of first engineer on the "San Lorenzo road," the Santa Cruz & Felton Railroad. Forgoing the job security offered by the expanding Southern Pacific, he had quit his position as engineer on the SP's Hollister branch to deliver the SC&F's first engine, *Santa Cruz*, to its new owner on July 5, 1875.[2] Lucien Healy extended Pope an offer for permanent employment on the condition that he and his fireman, one James M. Tucker, perform routine maintenance work on the engine. Healy noted in his letter of May 23, 1875:

> Your brother Horace showed me a letter your [you] wrote to him in which you say you "did not understand whether or not he considered 30 days a month." I do not suppose he thought about the matter, and would be governed in that respect by what is customary. I know however he is opposed to working Sunday, unless it is absolutely necessary, and I do not think you will have the least trouble about your salary.[3]

For the generous sum of $125 a month, Fowler Pope could afford to be flexible about the demands the railroad would place on his Sundays.

Pope's decision to go to work for the short line was strongly motivated by

Opposite: Santa Cruz & Felton locomotive *Santa Cruz*, photographed as a stereograph at Felton, some time after July 1876, with engineer Bill Porter. [Society of California Pioneers]

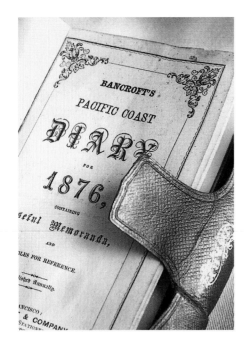

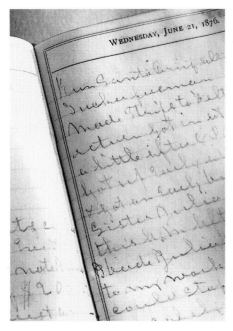

Fowler Pope's 1876 diary: cover (top) and interior (bottom), now in the collection of the Museum of Art and History, Santa Cruz. [Bruce MacGregor]

considerations of marriage and family. When the diary begins, he is forty-eight years old, newly married to Harriet, or "Hat," who is forty-three and expecting their first child. The risks of the late pregnancy may have focused Pope's attention on the domestic blessings of living and working in the same community. The diary commences with the reflection that life, at that moment, is "bringing with it many joys and much happiness to me, giving me a good, happy, pleasant and agreeable home, giving me a good situation on the railroad that runs into Santa Cruz my adopted home where my dear old mother and brothers live, where I can live in my own home with a good wife to take charge of it & [who] makes home pleasant & agreeable and happy."[4]

In turn, Pope was an attentive and caring husband. When his son, Norris, was born on March 27, Fowler hired, from of his own pocket, a substitute engineer, paid the man's stage fare from Watsonville to Santa Cruz, and laid himself off for three weeks to take care of Hat and his infant son.

Fowler Pope was optimistic about his family's future. Over the course of the year covered by his diary, Pope built new cabinetry for the kitchen. He added a new back "stoop" to the house. Apple trees bloomed in his yard, and he smoked his own hams in the barn. With loans from older brother Horace (who owned a resort hotel in town), he invested in property in Santa Cruz, which he began to subdivide and market through a local real estate agency named Hinds and Hoffman. Sales were good, which was further justification of his belief in economic recovery from the suffocating recession.

But the diary leaves little doubt that Pope's life revolved around his livelihood, the Santa Cruz & Felton Railroad. From a primitive engine house located in what was called the Mission Orchard, along today's River Street, Pope and Tucker struggled through a dark, rainy January to pilot construction trains through the dangerous San Lorenzo River Gorge.

It was life-threatening work. Entire mountainsides, vertical scabs of decomposed shale running up the canyon wall, turned to slurry in heavy rains and obliterated the railroad without warning. Redwood trees five feet in diameter avalanched onto the tracks at night and were impossible to see in the weak illumination of the engine's oil headlight. As work trains were replaced by sixteen-, seventeen-, and eighteen-car revenue freights (the limit was constantly being pushed upward), Pope battled five miles of 137-foot gradient going uphill and prayed the hand brakes would work going down. The ever-present dangers were seldom registered in the diary's short, matter-of-fact entries, which usually began simply "Run *Santa Cruz* all day. Tucker fireman."

In fact, there was only one death reported on the Santa Cruz & Felton in the Centennial year, and it occurred not on the railroad but on its companion flume. Mr. Thomas M. Lilly, the flume superintendent, apparently slipped on a wet catwalk ninety feet above the ground, and fell to his death. Pope had the sad duty of returning the body to Santa Cruz in a boxcar.

For nine months, Pope would pilot the *Santa Cruz* down to the River Street engine house with an enormous quantity of forest products in tow. One hundred and sixty thousand board feet of lumber, seven thousand freshly cut railroad ties, and five hundred barrels of lime were recorded on the railroad's waybills for the single week ending August 23, 1876.[5] Horses (according to the city charter) were required to portage the loads from the River Street terminal, through downtown, along Pacific Avenue to the wharf. This work was done at night, and it became such a bottleneck that by April 1876 the SC&F began digging a tunnel through Mission Hill to divert the traffic around downtown, through Chestnut Street, obviating the need for horse teams. Pope's diary records the first work on the tunnel.

Over the course of the next five months, Pope used the *Santa Cruz* to haul "chock rock" out of the deepening tunnel excavation and, on October 10, 1876, bring the first freight train through the new bore, down Chestnut Street to the new yard and terminal at the beach.

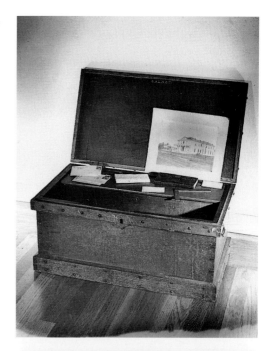

Miraculously, Fowler Pope did not get so much as a wheel off the track until that day, October 10, when the *Santa Cruz* thumped down on newly laid ties in the company's yard by the wharf. There were no injuries and no damage. Pope indignantly dismissed the blemish to his record with the assertion: "It was not my fault."

Until late July, the *Santa Cruz* was the only locomotive on the railroad, and Pope took enormous pride in his trusteeship as her engineer and maintainer. Pope and Jim Tucker were an inseparable team (Tucker was a frequent dinner guest at the Popes' home), and Pope was outspoken to management about increasing Tucker's meager wages. Pope loaned Tucker money and occasionally contrived to get him a few hours off engine duty to visit friends. Tucker, in turn, loaned Pope money and would occasionally drop him off at the St. Charles Hotel, the line's downtown depot, and put the *Santa Cruz* to bed himself while Pope visited his aging mother, Betsey.

Fowler Pope's trunk, with initials. [Norris Pope collection]

Pope took offense when anyone besides Tucker ran his engine. He especially resented William Porter, whom Pope regarded from the beginning of the diary as an adversary and nemesis. Normally a conductor, Porter was a substitute engineman when Pope laid off. Bill Porter is easy to spot in early photographs of the railroad, posed with arms akimbo and shoulders back, as if to call attention to himself in any group portrait. Ironically, it is Porter, not Pope, who appears in the photograph of the *Santa Cruz* at the beginning of this chapter. Pope hated the pretense and regarded Porter as a cad. He was quick to dig up the dirt on Porter's termination from an earlier job on the Santa Cruz Rail Road, and equally quick to pass judgment when Porter derailed the line's second locomotive, the *Felton*, on August 14. "A bad beginning for Engine and Engineer," the diary reports.

A continuing friendship with Charles Silent kept Pope on the favored side of the railroad's politics until Charlie Gorrill, president of the Pacific Bridge Co., took over the presidency of the SC&F in early September 1876. At the time, the company employed nearly one hundred men, and Gorrill apparently wasted little time in downsizing.[6] Ironically, major capital improvement programs were begun at the same time, including heavier rail, reinforcement to bridges, new warehouses in both Felton and Santa Cruz, and a new three-stall engine house located at the beach terminal.

Under the new regime, Pope and Tucker got their walking papers on November 6 and were told simply that Gorrill had ordered a reduction in force to a single engine crew. Bill Porter would get Pope's job, and his locomotive —a bitter pill for Pope to swallow. With growth and new construction so evident, Pope concluded Gorrill was not telling the truth. He took the news

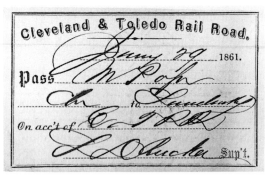

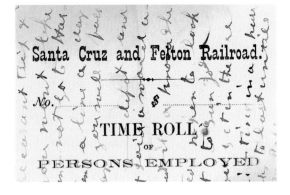

Company passes, exchange ticket, and time roll marking Fowler Pope's long career as a locomotive engineer; from the top: 1856, 1861, ca. 1864, and 1876. Pope would continue to run locomotives on the Mt. Diablo coal lines until the mid-1880s. [Norris Pope collection]

personally, concluding that Gorrill "did not want me, mi friends & wife any more."

But in fairness, Pope should have seen the layoff coming. The *Santa Cruz Sentinel* had noted three weeks earlier, on October 18, that "the running expenses of the Felton Railroad have been reduced to the lowest possible figures."

Obviously, not quite the lowest, as Pope discovered. For a few weeks, he "takes it easy" and seemed reflective. But he ended the year with a burst of activity on his real estate investments, personally remodeling a house he bought to rent. He clearly missed the railroad. He would sometimes take a long detour on his way to work on his rental, reaching the Santa Cruz Rail Road depot on Rincon Street in time to see the morning train leave for Watsonville with his friend Charles Garcelon at the throttle. A wave, and a sigh, were not recorded in the diary.

The loss of local employment forced difficult choices on the Pope family. Fowler returned for a time to an engineer's job on the Mt. Diablo coal railroads, a position he had apparently held before coming to Santa Cruz. He was rooming in a boarding house in Pittsburg Landing, in January 1883, and writing to Hat not to wear herself out trying to keep the back yard up, with its small orchard of apple trees. In the late 1880s, he found part-time work as an engineer on the logging railroads in the Loma Prieta basin, just south of Santa Cruz, which brought him closer to home.[7]

He continued to maintain a permanent residence in Santa Cruz, where he and Hat raised their son and developed real estate interests. These included, by 1878, nearly three acres of subdivided land that made up "F. W. Pope's Building Lots," a small real estate development off Soquel Avenue, on the east side of the San Lorenzo River.[8] He also helped his brother Horace establish Pope's Hotel, "the most modern of all the fashionable summer resorts in Santa Cruz. It is surrounded by ample grounds in which are numerous pretty cottages smothered in trees and flowers."[9] Located on Mission Street, with a view that extended over most of the city and on to the ocean, the property was still in family hands when Fowler died there on October 31, 1897, on his sixty-ninth birthday.

As a witness to his time and place, Fowler Pope forthrightly reported what he saw but was circumspect about what he thought or felt. He measured beauty and utility on the same scale. He took pride in the arrival of the two Carter coaches on July 1, 1876, noting they "look very well," but didn't take particular note of the flourishes in scroll work that Carter had incorporated into the finish, the only ornamentation on the railroad besides the paint jobs on the two Porter, Bell locomotives. It was enough that the new cars trailed in back of his train, sticking to the rails.

His diary is the only firsthand account we have of the daily realities of early Santa Cruz County railroading, and its central truth is the portrayal of the balance between routine and heroics that kept the pioneering narrow gauge lines operating. As a witness to daily events, Pope was truthful, but at times his memory could be selective. For example, on March 24, 1876, the *Santa Cruz Sentinel* reported a nearly disastrous mishap near the old River Street terminal:

Forgot to unhitch: a team used to haul the Felton RR Company's cars to and from the wharf was left standing hitched to several flats, the other morning, on Water St [sic], when the engine came up, coupled on the other end of the train, and started off. The horses kept backing until the cars got to going so fast they couldn't keep up, when they were thrown to the ground. At this juncture some of the foundry employees rushed out and informed the engineer of the facts of the case, when the poor brutes were released from their perilous position.

The engineer was Fowler Pope, who reported only this in his diary entry for the same date: "Run *Santa Cruz* all day. Tucker fireman."

Locomotive *Felton*'s reconstructed head-light, manufactured by Bausch and Lomb, in the collection of William Wulf. [Bruce Mac-Gregor]

The text of Fowler Pope's diary is presented here with some abbreviation of content. Grammar, spelling, and punctuation have been preserved from the original text, but corrections required to make the text clear, or readable, are made in square brackets [. . .].[10]

Saturday, January 1, 1876
[Inscribed at top of page around the date:] Happy New Year
Worked on *Santa Cruz* all day in house. Tucker fireman.[11]

We got raidy to go out on the road to work today but gave it up on account of the wet weather.

I took of[f] our cone[12] and took down to Frank Waterman's where I drilled a number of holes in it to prevent the netting stopping up.[13] Tucker helping me. I done other chores on the engine.

[Upside down starting from bottom of page:] The year 1875 has passed away having rolled smoothly & pleasantly along with me, bringing with it many joys and much happiness to me, giving me a good, happy, pleasant and agreeable home, giving me a good situation on the railroad that runs into Santa Cruz my adopted home where my dear old mother and brothers live, where I can live in my own home with a good wife to take charge of it & [who] makes home pleasant & agreeable and happy, which she has fully and nicely done & may she live long & happy & may she enjoy our happy home as I do. It being the year in which I first had a home of my own to live in and which first commensed to keep house on that year since which I have had a happy and apreciated home.

Sunday, January 2, 1876
After breakfast got ready & went to church with wife & sister Julia. We went to the Congregational Church where we heard a good sermon.

Monday, January 3, 1876
Worked all day on engine in shop. Billie Johnson helped me. Tucker was sick. We worked at fitting the bonnett down on the ring on top of the smoke stack making it much better. Had rain so the train did not run.[14]

Tuesday, January 4, 1876
Worked all day on engine in engine house, Billie Johnson helping me as

Tucker was sick. We worked at fitting the nitting [netting] on top of stack getting it so fire or sparks would not get out under the bonnett & made a good job of it.

Wednesday, January 5, 1876

Run *Santa Cruz* all day on construction. Tucker fireman. We ran up sight of Powder Mill where we worked near all day. J. M. Tucker fired up in AM & as he was not well he walked back home & let Fred Tucker fire for him.

Friday, January 7, 1876

Worked on *Santa Cruz* all day. Fred Tucker fireman in J. M. Tucker's place who is not well. Rained this AM so we did not go out. I blowed off boiler & took out plugs so to wash out mud, cleaning it all out. In PM took bonnett latch[15] down to blacksmith shop & got handle put on it, but when I put it up, it did not fit, but made do for the pressant.

Saturday, January 8, 1876

Worked on *Santa Cruz* all day in house. Tucker fireman. It looked like rain in the morning so we did not go out. I took the latch off the bonnett & took [it] down to blacksmith shop & had it made over. got back at about noon. After dinner put on latch to bonnett, oiled stack[,] boiler heads, and done a few other chores. I got a board of Gregg[16] for our sink. Got my boots from Baldwin's,[17] etc. Fred Tucker still in J. M. Tucker's place. Jim not feeling well yet. Fred cleaned up engine first rate. This AM I went down on our new wharf for the first time.

Monday, January 10, 1876

Run *Santa Cruz* all day on construction. Tucker fireman. Worked in cut near Powder Mill.[18] Weather cleared off, quite plesant. We left train in canion and ran down & boiled rain water before train got down.

Tuesday, January 11, 1876

Run *Santa Cruz* all day. Tucker fireman. Worked on construction from forks of Powder Mill road to bridge no. 15.[19] Two little girls Lena & Aggie came with us & rode down with us on engine. They brought me a few rags. We boiled rain water out of tank near engine house.[20] Was downtown in Eve & got 80 bbs [barrels] of beal [meal?]. Our blacksmith rode down with us in the evening.

Wednesday, January 12, 1876

Run *Santa Cruz* all day on construction. Tucker fireman. We worked in AM at upper end of long cut above sawmill flat.[21] In PM ran further up the line & before night we got up to the cribbing, put it in place of the long high bank wall that went out below the big slide.[22] In the Eve wife, Julia & I made short call at brother Horace's. When I got into yard in Eve with my engine I found Horace who had come around to see us come in. I took Horace down a green oak stick to make chips to smoke his hams with.

Thursday, January 13, 1876

Run *Santa Cruz* all day on construction. Tucker fireman. We worked in canion filling in the cribbing where the bank wall gave out a short distance below the big slide. Mr. Silent & friend came up & made a short stop with us at about 12:30 PM. They rode down with us on the engine in the eve. Fred Tucker came up in PM & stoped until night & rode down with us. I saw a tall fir tree fell in opposite direction to what it was leaning. It was done by sawing in & waging [wedging] over. It fell on the cribbing & broke some of the timbers. In the [Eve] wife, Julia and I went down to Doc Bailey's, but as he was gone we called in to Mr. Stewart's and spend the Eve & had a good time.

[On side of page:] We fitted in a new draw bar to front of engine. Washed out tank and filled with clean water.

[Upside down at top of page:] Cleaned out water tank up in canion.

[Upside down at bottom of page:] I was up to the big slide in the PM and looked around a little.

Saturday, January 15, 1876

Run *Santa Cruz* all day on construction. Tucker fireman. We drew durt into the cribbing. Worked late trying to get through to Felton. Got the track connected at about 5 PM so we could get around the cribbing & the big slide but thought best not to undertake it after dark. Mr. Silent came out with us in the morning and stoped with us all day. Cordell & Fred Tucker came up in AM & rode back with us in the Eve.

Sunday, January 16, 1876

Run *Santa Cruz* all day. Tucker fireman. We worked at cribbing until 2 PM filling in durt and ballasting up the track. A little after 3 PM we took all hands on board & started for Felton. Ran around first cribbing all right & reached Felton safe having no trouble on our way where we stoped for an hour & returned home, reaching Santa Cruz at about 6 PM. We had not been to Felton for a long time before. When I got home found Dan Moulton[23] & wife there. Was glad to see them.

Tuesday, January 18, 1876

Run *Santa Cruz* all day on construction. Tucker fireman. We drew ballast on the road in the canion cleaned out ditches etc., dumping some on to cribbing.

Thursday, January 20, 1876

Run *Santa Cruz* all day on construction. Tucker fireman. Made two trips to Felton and return. We took up 7 cars in the forenoon and took back 11 cars loaded with lumber, timber, etc. In PM took up 2 new boxcars and four or five new flats[24] with enough old flats to make ten cars which was a heavy train & more than we took up before & was first time we took any box cars over the road. We took down two cars loaded with wood and one empty flat. The train of lumber we took first was the longest ever over the road. Mr. Silent went with us all day.

We were late getting down in the PM. Went down the grade in the dark when we could not see anything and is wild [?]. Had rain and a little snow in Felton.

Friday, January 21, 1876

Run *Santa Cruz* all day. Tucker fireman. Made one trip to Felton loaded six box cars with lime sixty bbls [barrels] in each car. Five flat cars with posts & one car with timber, lumb[er], etc. making in all twelve cars we took down which was a heavy load for us sticking in the Butte cut with 100 pounds of steam. 120 however took them through.[25] Stopped again near the water tank when we ran to tank for water. We got in all right & with heaviest load yet over the road.

Saturday, January 22, 1876

Run and worked on engine all day. Tucker fireman. We did not run over the road but was out and done switching for an hour or two in the rain. Had hard showers of rain and hail and quite a little spurt of snow for an [?]. I done a few chores in PM on engine.

Sunday, January 23, 1876

Didn't turn out until after 8 o'clock. After breakfast I built a fire in our fireplace and soon after Porter[26] came in and said if it was pleasant Mr. Silent wanted me to run up to Felton in the P.M. I took up some empty cars but as it rained I did not go near the road. After dinner I went over to Jo's [Joseph Pope, Fowler's younger brother] finding them comfortable. The baby was better. Came home in the rain by Moulton and Farley's where I called. Found Mr. F and Mrs. M was not very well. Rained hard al[l] the while I was gone.

Tuesday, January 25, 1876

Worked on engine all day. Tucker sick. I took down both slides so to take off back cylinder casings & screw up the heads which were leaking. Found it to be an un pleasant and hard job. Mr. Silent was up to house some time. I find he is getting down on Tucker. Had showers of rain quite often all day.

Wednesday, January 26, 1876

Run *Santa Cruz* in AM & in PM until 7 o'clock when knocked off on account of the rain. We drew out on to dump chock [chalk] rock out of the tunnel.[27] In PM went downtown & saw head light. Got some wire, etc. In the PM I fixed up a slop [?] bucket and took home.

Thursday, January 27, 1876

Run *Santa Cruz* all day on construction. Tucker fireman. In PM ran up to dead man's cut and drew out some stumps with the engine. Took down a load of rock in the Eve. Mr. Silent was out on work most of the day with us. In the Eve went down to office for pay but did not get it. When I got home found Mr. Healy[28] at our house. Had a pleasant visit with him.

Friday, January 28, 1876

Run *Santa Cruz* all day on construction. Tucker fireman. Ran up to slide in AM with the men then down to Gharkeys fill with two cars of ballast then back to slide & got load of rock & took down town & done some switching. Shoved posts up on street. Lite dinner. Got wood & water & then ran back to slide and hitched engine to hall [haul] out some large stumps. I took down rock at night. In PM I put in to right hand oil cups and some new feeders. Was down to office in Eve.

Sunday, January 30, 1876

Run *Santa Cruz* all day on construction. Tucker fireman. Ran up to slide in AM with the men. In PM drew out some stumps with the engine. Went to engine house in PM at about 3 o'clock. I got wood and water left cars at slide for the men to come home on. Got home to supper at a little past 4.

Tuesday, February 1, 1876

Run *Santa Cruz* all day on construction. Tucker fireman. Ran up to Powder Mill slide in AM and stayed until after dinner when we ran down town. Turned engine, took wood and water. Done a little switching. Took on seven empty flats & ran back to slide & when there got the track finished around the slide. We took 7 cars & started for Felton & got as far as the slide above the ledge & found track blocked so we ran back home.

Thursday, February 3, 1876

Run *Santa Cruz* all day. Tucker fireman. Ran to upper slide in the AM with the men then back to town & switched out some empty cars & took up to slide & worked an hour or two pulling out stumps & when we got track clean we started at 9 o'clock PM for Felton where we loaded & took to town 8 cars of lumber and shoved up near the St. Charles Hotel.[29] I had a tusle [tussle] with a big old tomas cat which I laid out after a hard struggle breaking my lantern in the scrap but the old cat I carried off on the tines of a pitch fork.

Friday, February 4, 1876

Run *Santa Cruz* all day. Tucker fireman. We made two trips to Felton for lime and lumber. Had switching to do at both ends of road which took up much of our time.

Received a Fifty dollar check of SC&FRR Co. on account.

Sunday, February 6, 1876

Run *Santa Cruz* all day. Tucker fireman. Made one trip to Felton taking part of our train up the hill first then run back & taking up what we could draw up the grade & from there taking them all, 15 in number, to Felton. We brought down but open loaded cars.

We did not hurry up this morning but buy [?] in had until 8 o'clock lifted breakfast. Went down to enginehouse to blow off boiler but did not, as soon found we had to run up to Felton with empty cars. Jo rode up the hill & back with me. We had some passengers.

Monday, February 7, 1876

Run *Santa Cruz* all day. Tucker fireman. Made two trips to Felton. Brought down 20 loaded cars. Had a hard show of rain in the PM on the road. Had no rain in Santa Cruz.

Tuesday, February 8, 1876

Worked all day on *Santa Cruz*. Tucker worked all day with me. Rained hard and wind blew hard last night & today so we did not go out. We blew off boiler, took out plug, & washed out all the mud we could. I trimmed and cleaned headlight & done other chores on the engine. The San Lorenzo River is high this Eve. Received a letter from Wm. H. Minnie.

Wednesday, February 9, 1876
Worked on engine all day. Tucker worked all day. Raining this AM so we did not go out. I filed & lined up back end of right main rod, put shims in gides [guides] to front spring hanger so to raise front end,[30] sandpapered & painted smoke stack & done other chores on engine. Blacksmith put springs on tender to keep brakes from rubber [rubbing] on the wheels.

Friday, February 11, 1876
Worked on engine all day in shop. Tucker fireman. Rained all day so we did not go out on road. I had a spring made at Luckin's [blacksmith Evan Lukens], Is for ketch [catch] to reverse lever.[31] Took it to a gun smith & had it drilled & fastened on to the hand piece to ketch [catch] & have new holes drilled in pins to reverse lever & in one of the pins to throttle lever which I fixed a little. Gun smith charged $1.00 for his work. I had to work until past 7 PM to get the levers together.

Saturday, February 12, 1876
Tucker fireman. Worked in AM on *Santa Cruz* in house. In PM run out on road & worked all PM on construction. Rained in AM so did not go out. I finished and fixed parts of my reverse and throttle levers that I did not have time to do last PM. At noon I was called on to go out so we got up steam & run to a small slide below Porter's powder barn cape [?] & worked until night.

Monday, February 14, 1876
Run *Santa Cruz* all day on construction. Tucker fireman. Worked near all day cleaning out cut, new Powder barn cape [?]. Silent was on the work with us all day. We took down some green fir for wood in the Eve & a little green hard wood. Had a warm and pleasant day.

Thursday, February 17, 1876
Run *Santa Cruz* all day. Tucker fireman. Made two trips for lime, lumber, wood, etc. I feel almost sick with a cold.

Friday, February 18, 1876
Run *Santa Cruz* all day. Tucker fireman. Made two trips to Felton. Brought down lime, lumber & wood. Felt sick all day. Charlie Garcelon[32] rode up with me in the PM. He thought our little engine worked first rate. He said he would run for me next Sunday if I wished. We brought down [my?] redwood, lime in the Eve.

Saturday, February 19, 1876
Run *Santa Cruz* all day. Tucker fireman. We made three trips to Felton. Brought down [91?] cars [31?] cars of lime, 1800 bbls earning nearly $950

[or $350?]. I felt poorly all day. Was in to H's [probably brother Horace] a short time in the Eve.

Monday, February 21, 1876

Porter run engine all day. Tucker fireman. I was so poorly I did not go out with train. Was downtown a short time in PM. I done a few chores about home. Mother made us a call in the PM.

Tuesday, February 22,1876

I run *Santa Cruz* all day. Tucker fireman. Made two trips to Felton and return with excurtion train. Had quite a lot of passengers. Sister Julia, Eva, & another lady from H's went up first time on train & rode back on engine & seemed to enjoy the trip. Porter run Santa Cruz to Felton in the Eve to take up cars, so said to be, but in fact it was so to go to Felton to a bake. He doubled up the hill or went up with part of the train & came back after the ballunce [balance]. I don't like to have him run her.

Wednesday, February 23, 1876

Run *Santa Cruz* in PM. Tucker fireman. Porter did not get down from Felton until noon, so his night work did not amount to much. In PM I run with part of the cars to top of hill,[33] then came back. Took some more cars and run through to Felton & back making one trip. Feel poorly.

Friday, February 25, 1876

Run *Santa Cruz* all day. Tucker fireman. Made two trips to Felton doubling up the hill both times and having to wait in Felton both trips to load. The last trip we waited until dark before we started & came through the canion in the dark, so dark I could not have seen obstruction of any kind had there been any on the track & was risky & dangerous work, but we got home safe, a little before 8 o'clock PM. I feel almost sick. Had rain.

Sunday, February 27, 1876

Worked on *Santa Cruz* all day. Tucker worked with me. Fitted & lined up connection & side rods to engine. Packed injection [injector] & blower valves. Blowed off & rinsed out boiler & done all the chores on engine with Tucker's & Porter's help. Got home before dark. Had hard rain & lots of water running through my place & had to be looked after. Was up in Boston's lot & turned off some after the water that was running over into my lot.

Friday, March 3, 1876

Run *Santa Cruz* in the AM up to Crib and back. Then worked on hearth [?] rest of day. Tucker fireman. Had rain in last night and today. In the Eve I brought home some empty bble [barrels] from H's and rinsed out then set out to ketch rain water.

Saturday, March 4, 1876

Run *Santa Cruz* down to Amner's shop in AM. I had a new pair of lubricators put on her steam chests. Went home to dinner. I done a few chores about the house. Painted our sink and Jo came over after some of his corn [?]. I found the mis [mice] were destroying it so he picked it up from floor and put in ba—ils boxes.

Sunday, March 5, 1876

In AM run engine up to crib with men on 6 cars. Then run empty engine back to town and into house where I left her. I went home to dinner. After dinner went down to engine house. Got engine out. I took 4 cars to crib and waited and took men home at night. When went down in AM took down on tender a few redwood, lime, I cut some tin zinc for woo- [?]. Left them at Imus's crossing.

Monday, March 6, 1876

Worked on engine all day. Tucker fireman. Rained in AM and showers during the day so we did not go out on road, but stayed in and worked on our engine. I run engine down by Umner's[34] [Tom Amner's] shop and had him put on a new pair of lubricators onto our steamchest. We took off our old two inch ones and put on a pair of three inch.

Tuesday, March 7, 1876

Worked all day on engine. Tucker fireman. Rained in AM and was showery all day, so I did not go out but laid in and worked on engine all day. Jacked up and raised front end a little. Johnson and Nelson helping us abow[?]. I was down to Gadsby[35] to see about headlight and to Waterman's to see about fixing for my whistle.

Wednesday, March 8, 1876

Worked on engine all day. Tucker fireman. Rained in AM some. Laid in. I worked awhile on fixing to hold our whistle lever that Frank Waterman made for me. Had to take it down and git it upset. Done other chores on engine. Went over to Moulten's in AM. He came over to——me and got some window fasteners and took up to my house and put in windows and put up a shelf for us. I went home to dinner. Moulten put up one fastener he gave me when I was East. We little thought he would put it in my house here in Cal.

[Written upside down at the top of the page:] We got headlight——from Gadsby's and put up and cleaned reflector.

Sunday, March 12, 1876

Run *Santa Cruz* all day. Tucker fireman. Run out chock rock from tunnel in AM. In PM made a trip to Felton and got down 6 cars of powder, wood, and 4 open cars of lumber, timber.

Thursday, March 16, 1876

Run *Santa Cruz* all day. Tucker fireman. Made two trips to Felton. Run back from Felton empty, put way and worked on road until night. I took on tender some wood and threw off Pamases [Imus's[36]] Crossing with some I leave there.

Friday, March 17, 1876

Run *Santa Cruz* all day. Tucker fireman. Made two trips to Felton. The track and repairmen did not work it being St. Patrick's Day.

Saturday, March 18, 1876

Run *Santa Cruz* all day. Tucker fireman. Run out chock rock from tunnel until near noon, then made one trip to Felton and brought down one carload of lumber and two cars of wood. Then ran out chock rock on to curve on River St. and one load of ballast from it on curve above Gharkey's. Went to RR office in the Eve. Porter said he had to get out *Santa Cruz* to haul some cars off the street which I did not much like and wish he would let the engine alone and tend to his own business.

Monday, March 20, 1876

Run *Santa Cruz* all day. Tucker fireman. Made two trips to Felton. Last trip up had a light train. Run through to Felton in 40 minutes.

Tuesday, March 21, 1876

Run *Santa Cruz* all day. Tucker fireman. Made two trips to Felton. Brother Horace went up and back with me on engine. We learned in Felton that Mr. Lilly had not been seen since yesterday morning. When we got in to Santa Cruz the hand car from Felton overtook us with word that Mr. Lilly had been found ded [sic]. It was supposed he fell off the flume where it was over 90 feet high. In the PM we ran up with ties and brought back one box car containing the remains of Mr. Lilly and one flat car. He was taken to San Jose thie[?]—or started for there.

Monday, March 27, 1876

I went down to depot to go up graid but did not go as they were going through. Came home where I stoped most of the time with my poor sick wife who was a great sufferer, patiently bearing terrible pains until near 5 PM when she was somewhat relieved by giving birth to a Boy. We were all pleased to see her so well over her troubles and fine. She was out of danger and also to see such good prospects for the son which seems to be doing well.

[Upside down at bottom of page:] I was up all last night. so was Doc Baily, Mrs. Meng [Menz], Ann[37] and I.

Tuesday, March 28, 1876

Stoped by about home most of the day tinkering about. I trimed up a big rose bush a little & done other chores about the place. Was down town in the Eve & over to Jo's. I bought a clothes wringer of Bowman for $7.50. In the AM sent a——y our boy by Bootche [butcher] for 7 dls [?] per pound on foot. She weighed 920 [?]. Am pleased to know. Hat and hers are getting a long well. they are having lots of callers.

Wednesday, March 29, 1876

Fralks [?] smart, bright & improving. Hope they will continue to do so. I chored about house & burn most of all day. I fixed slupe [slope?] to barn doors, etc. Dan Moulten paid me $20 I had loaned him.

Friday, March 31, 1876

I done a few chores about our place. In the AM went down town to see Mr. Silent but found him busy. We are having great excitement in town to-day. A real railroad war. Our company commensed to lay track on the tunnel rout[e] to get the start of Heighn [Frederick Hihn] who was going to put in a side track to bother our folks, but they were too soon for him. He was terrible wanton [wanting] the fight, but it was no use for—we had too many men for him.[38]

Tuesday, April 4, 1876

I finished pruning apple trees in AM & done other work & chores about the place. Helped mother over to our house this PM & home again. Poor old lady is getting so lame she can hardly walk. Went down town in the Eve to look for a man to help me but found no one. Was down to Doc Baily's.

Friday, April 7, 1876

Rained this AM so the men I had engaged to work for me did not put in an appearance. I fixed up my smoking machine & put ham to smoking.

Sunday, April 9, 1876

After breakfast went over to see Mother where I made a short stay & went home & stoped until noon. Then went down to our engine house & made out a list of tools and supplies I have on hand for our engine belonging to co. Jo came in so I went home with him & got supper & looked over the place to see where our new streets and lots were coming, etc. Did not get home until after dark.

Friday, April 14, 1876

Chored about garden & yard triming & fixing vines, bushes, and trees, etc. In the Eve I got home from Horace's a lot of shavings. In the Eve Mike[39] came up & said Lee was sick so I went down to engine house to see him. He said he was not able to work & I would have to take the Engine tomorrow.

Saturday, April 15, 1876

Run *Santa Cruz* all day. Tucker fireman. Made 3 trips to Felton. Turned out at 4 AM & built fire and soon after ate breakfast & went to Engine house & got ready to start. In the Eve I paid 82.00 (to Lee) for working for me 19 [days] and his stage fare from & to Pajaro.

Sunday, April 16, 1876

Run *Santa Cruz* all day. Tucker fireman. Made 3 trips to Felton. Filed connection in the Eve.

Sunday, April 23, 1876

Worked on Engine all day. Tucker worked all day. We blew off & washed out boiler, packed the throttle. Ground & packed blower valve. Ground blow-off cock. Took down Excentric straps. Cleaned out oil holes & re-packed them & done other chores on Engine. Jo called in the shop to see me. Hinds & Hofman[40] were in to see about selling my lots over the river for me.

Monday, April 24, 1876

Run *Santa Cruz* all day. Tucker fireman. Made 3 trips to Felton. Cap. Garratt went up first trip. He is having a platform built at the Big Trees landing.[41] Carpenters working at it today.

Wednesday, April 26, 1876

Run *Santa Cruz* all day on Passenger or Picnic train. Tucker fireman. Made four trips up the grade. First trip we left at 8 AM with 6 cars & took to Big Tree Station & backed back from there I took 7 cars heavily loaded through to Felton I had a hard old pull to get them up the hill but done it without stalling which was doing a big thing for so little a machine I got much prais[e] for looking & doing so well & is well deserving of it all. Among others was the Odd Fellows from Watsonville. I made two other trips. Every one seemed to have a good time. Had no bad luck. All ended well.

Thursday, April 27, 1876

Run *Santa Cruz* all day. Tucker fireman. Made three trips for lumber, lime, etc. The Co. are burning brush along the tracks in the caniion this PM. Mr. Silent, Mr. Carter[42] & other directors came down on last train.

Saturday, April 29, 1876

Run *Santa Cruz* all day. Tucker fireman. Made 3 trips to Felton. Saw Jo in the Eve. He said our lots are going fast.

Monday, May 1, 1876

Run *Santa Cruz* all day. Tucker fireman. Made three trips to Felton. Brought down lime, lumber, passengers & two carloads of rock. Capt. Garratt went up first trip in AM & came back on Seckund [second] trip. Silent went up on 2nd trip & back on 2nd. Had some talk with Garratt about pay for fireman, etc. and find he is not willing to pay what is right. Circus in town this AM & Eve made out monthly report. New style this Eve.

Tuesday, May 2, 1876

Run *Santa Cruz* all day. Tucker fireman. Made three trips to Felton & return. Brought down lumber, timber, ties, wood & rock. Got in with last trip at about half past 7 PM. I went home from the Engine house round by Locus[t] St. Saw Mr. Silent at Hotel & gave him my time report from last month and the size on a pipe of our headlight chimney. I had a talk with him about fireman's wages & told him I thought he did not pay enough.

Sunday, May 7, 1876

Run *Santa Cruz* one trip to Felton & return in the AM. Tucker fireman. After we got in we blew water out of boiler, washed out mud, etc, & filed & lined up left hand syde rod brasses besides doing other chores on Engine.

Saturday, May 13, 1876

Run *Santa Cruz* all day. Tucker fireman.

Made 3 trips to Felton. I ran down to shingle mill & waited to load one car with shingle. Found George Copeland at my house when I got home in the Evening at about 8 o'clock. After supper, I went downtown with Copeland I looked for Trengrove [?]. Saw Capt. Garratt at Hotel. He said we would have to double the hill [?] and make one trip to Felton. Was in Hinds [and Hoffman's] & got two contracts.

Wednesday, May 17, 1876

Run *Santa Cruz* all day. Tucker fireman.

Made 4 trips to Felton & back. First trip we took our train to Felton & left it & returned to Santa Cruz with Engine alone. The other 3 trips we took down freight of diferant kinds. I took off injector pipe & sent downtown by Mr. Silent to be fixed. Was downtown in the Eve. & paid faire 25v [?] for Juten to Santocolm [Santa Cruz?]. Saw Judge Ireland [?] at Hotel.

[Written upside down at bottom of page:] Received a $150.00 note of Charles Steinmetz. Copeland rode up with us in AM.

Saturday, May 20, 1876

Run *Santa Cruz* all day. Tucker fireman.

Made 4 trips to Felton. In the Eve went downtown & down to the beach to Mr. England's[43] to get him to help me fix connections to Engine.

Sunday, May 21, 1876

Worked on *Santa Cruz* all day and all the Eve not having her fixed at 12 at night. Tucker worked all day on Engine. Blew off & washed out boiler & done other work. Mr. England came by & helped me take down connections & took to his shop. Plain & drilled out & bobbet [babbit] with Garratt mettle. Then we went to Engine house & worked on them until past midnight. I done a lot of drilling with a foot lathe which I found was hard work.

Monday, May 22, 1876

Run *Santa Cruz* all day. Tucker fireman.

Made 3 trips to Felton & one to top of hill. I did not get to bed until 2 o'clock this AM. Did not get our Engine fixed until near that time. We worked all day yesterday from 7 AM until near 2 o'clock this AM. Tucker helped us until past 1 this AM.

Saturday, May 27, 1876

Run *Santa Cruz* all day. Tucker fireman.

Made 4 trips to Felton & return with heavy trains & brought down in all 38 loaded cars which is the best day's work yet.[44] We drew up two car loads of heavy rails[45] and left at the Powder mill crossing.

Sunday, May 28, 1876

Tucker & I worked on *Santa Cruz* near all day. Blowed off boiler, took down left connecion, cleaned and oiled smoke stack & done other chores.

Had dinner at home at about [?] o'clock. Copeland was there & had dinner with us. After dinner Horace called in & made a short stay. Copeland & I went into & on top of H's new house. The scene from there is beautiful. Copeland & I went over the river to Jo's & stoped an hour. It was dark when I got home & then house chores to do.

Monday, June 5, 1876

Run *Santa Cruz* all day. Tucker fireman.

Made 4 trips to Felton. In AM took up train of empty cars & left it at Felton & run Engine down with out any cars. We took down three loaded trains. Mr. Doctor Blanchard of Derby, Vt. rode up & back with me on Engine in AM. Capt. Garratt went up last trip & was in a hurry to get back & wanted me to make it as quick as I could. I run down from Felton in 35 minutes & stopped twice. Once I took on two cars of rock.

Sunday, June 11, 1876

Worked on engine all day in the shop. Tucker worked all day with me. Blowed off & washed our boiler, filed and lined up side rod boxes & done many other chores on Engine. Went in to see mother in the Evening. Found her sick in bed.

Wednesday, June 14, 1876

Run *Santa Cruz* all day. Tucker fireman.

Made 3 trips to Felton and return. Had a picnic up to Big Tree[s] and two of the ladies rode up on Engine seeming to enjoy it much as they seemed happy & gay and made lots of noise. Called in to see Mother on my way home. She is quite feeble & poorly.

Saturday, June 17, 1876

Run *Santa Cruz* all day. Tucker fireman.

Made 3 trips to Felton.

Was downtown in the Eve where I saw Mr. Healy & had quite a chat with him about matters & things. Learned why Porter was discharged off the Santa Cruz road.[46] I was in to see Mother in the Eve. She is a little better.

Wednesday, June 21, 1876

Run *Santa Cruz* all day. Tucker fireman.

Made 3 trips to Felton and return. Got in at night a little after 8 PM. Got up early all of us & got an early breakfast as Sister Julia leaves for home this AM. After breakfast bade Julia good by[e] & went to my work wishing I could stop at home & see her safely off. Hope she will have a safe & pleasant trip & find our folks & friends all well when she gets home.

Thursday, June 22, 1876

Run *Santa Cruz* all day. Tucker fireman.

Made 3 trips to Felton & return. We took down lumber, wood, etc. Took powder wood for powder mill[47] & in Eve took down rock. It was after 8 o'clock when we got through which made a long day's work. Mr. Silent & some of his friends went up to Felton in PM. We took them down to Big Tree Station on Engine.

Sunday, June 25, 1876

Ran *Santa Cruz* to Felton & back to Big Tree[s] Station then to Felton & return to Santa Cruz. McFersons [McPhersons] of the Sentinal [*Sentinel*] rode up with us on Engine & back. Tucker fireman. Had a small lot of passengers. Had a good dinner at home and a pleasant hour or two in my own family. Stoped by a minute to see Mother in the AM & made her a short call in the Eve. Mr. Healy came up & took breakfast with us in the morning. Had a pleasant time.

Monday, June 26, 1876

Run *Santa Cruz* all day. Tucker fireman.

Made 2 trips to Felton & return. Dan Moulton called over to Engine house & rode up to Felton & back on Engine. Capt. Garratt rode up to Felton on Engine last trip. Mr. Mowbree[48] takes charge at Felton this AM in Taber's place. Went down town in the Eve. Signed more papers at Hofman & Hinds. Got hair cut, etc.

Friday, June 30, 1876

Run *Santa Cruz* all day. Tucker fireman.

Made two trips to Felton. Berger[49] was expected in with two new passenger cars for our road over the S.C.R.R. Was downtown this Eve. Saw Capt. Garratt at S.C. depot & had a talk with him about matters in general, etc.

Saturday, July 1, 1876

Run *Santa Cruz* all day. Made two trips to Felton & return. Tucker fireman.

Went down town in Eve. Deposited $725.00 seven hundred and twenty five dollars in Gold in Coxes bank[50] (see Rowland) for one year at 10 percent interest per annum. Some of the money was silver I took of Hinds & Hofman which I sold Mr. Cox at four percent discount. Sold him $467.30 of silver which amounted to $448.60 in gold. Two new passenger cars arrived this Eve over the S.C.R.R. for our road and look very well.[51]

Thursday, July 13, 1876

Run *Santa Cruz* all day. Johnson fireman.

Made two trips to Felton & return with Passengers & freight & one trip with empty cars to top of grade in AM & one load of chockrock. In AM Johnson was late so George Smith fired up grade for me. I went in to Hunter's to see Tucker and found him quite sick. In the AM Garratt & Healy went up on train to Felton. In the Eve I proped up fruit trees & done other chores.

Monday, July 17, 1876

Run *Santa Cruz* all day. Johnson fireman.

Made two trips in AM with chock rock, etc. Made two trips to Felton & return with Passengers and freight. Capt. Hom [?] started his sawmill this PM. Burges [Burgess[52]] went up to Felton with his men to put up a water tank for us. Went downtown to offices after pay but was too late. Saw Capt. Garratt in Biases.[53] I saw the two new Engineers of the Santa Cruz R.R.

Tuesday, July 18, 1876

Run *Santa Cruz* all day. Johnson fireman.

Made two trips to Felton & return with Pas[enger] & freight. Train run out chock rock in the morning. In the Eve I walked down Chestnut Street on our new track to the R.R. office & got my check for last month $125. Saw Mr. Garratt & Macky. From office I went up town & then home.

Monday, July 24, 1876

Run *Santa Cruz* all day. Johnson fireman.

Made 3 trips to Felton & return. In Eve ran a special to Felton after the Directors. Took one coach. Trengove called up to house to see about building a chicken yard for me. Late in the Eve I went over to Joe's to take over $100 to send to bank by him to San Francisco.

Tuesday, July 25, 1876

Run *Santa Cruz* all day. Johnson fireman.

Made two trips to Felton & run chock rock in the Eve. Mr. Tren Grove came up to house this AM to work for me build chicken yard, etc. Heard our new engine had arrived. Our new water tank at Felton works badly.

Wednesday, July 26, 1876

Run *Santa Cruz* all day. Tucker fireman.

Made two trips to Felton & return. In AM run Special to Felton to take up directors. On return trip we brought down a few carlodes with ties. Ran out 5 cars loaded with chock rock after arrival to SC. Made two trips on freight, etc. Brought down two carloads of rock for water works which we ran back to Gharkies [Gharkey's] in Eve. R. M. G. [Gorrill] went up on last trip. Had no fireman in AM so Mike Castello fired up. Tucker came back & went on work on second trip. Was bothered to get water all day. Tren-Grove worked on chicken yard all day.

Thursday, July 27, 1876

Run *Santa Cruz* all day. Tucker fireman.

Made four trips to Felton & return, two Specials with freight besides our two regular trips on Pas[senger] & freight. R. M.Gh. [Gorrill] went up & back on No. 1 & 2.[54] Burgess went up & fixed water tank. Tren Gove worked for me all day on chicken yard. I split a little wood in the Eve.

Saturday, July 29, 1876

Run *Santa Cruz* all day. Tucker fireman.

Made two trips to Felton & run chock rock. Porter not back [home with Engine] yet. He had to side track her as her excintricks [eccentrics] got hot. They should have been disconnected.

Sunday, July 30, 1876

Run *Santa Cruz* all day. Tucker fireman.

Made two trips to Felton & return with pas[enger] & freight. Charles Dorman rode up & back with me on last trip. Liked our road, engine, & town. We went home to supper with M. In the Eve went down town with him & looked around a little. We saw Charles Garcelin. We saw our new Engine come through the street & went & took a look at it. I don't like it as well as I do the *Santa Cruz*. I introduced Dorman to Capt. Garratt.

Monday, July 31, 1876

Run *Santa Cruz* all day. Tucker fireman.

Made two trips to Felton & return with pas[enger] & freight train besides run rock up to Gharkies for water works & run out chock rock in AM. Our new Engine runs rather rough.

Wednesday, August 9, 1876

Run *Santa Cruz* all day. Tucker fireman.

Made 3 trips to Felton & return with Pas[engers] & freight. Last trip was a special freight. Billie Johnson was taken off train to stay at Felton to take charge of Station. In AM toed [towed] new Engine into house so to put on stack, etc.

Friday, August 11, 1876

Run *Santa Cruz* all day. Tucker fireman.

Made 2 trips to Felton & an Extra to top of hill. After we got in with our last regular train, went back to Felton with an Extra with 16 cars & the new Engine *Felton* to help us up the grade. We had a hard pull & had to d[ouble] most of them as the new engine foamed[55] so she could not shove much but we got them through. Trengove called in to our house & spent the Eve.

Saturday, August 12, 1876

Run *Santa Cruz* all day. Tucker fireman.

Made two trips to Felton & return. The *Felton* ran through to Felton for the first time working well. Miss Adda Jewet went up with us on Engine to Big Tree[s] Station in PM & came back on train. Was downtown in the Eve & got a deed of lots from Hinds & Hofman & took up to Horace's & made him a presant of four building lots by giving him the deed.

Sunday, August 13, 1876

Run *Santa Cruz* all day. Tucker fireman.

Made 2 trips to Felton taking up empty cars bouth [both] trips, but no freight cars down. Had trouble in AM with pump gauge, etc. In the Eve went down to Engine house and cleaned out water gauge, gauge cock, packed throttle, & done a few chores on Engine.

Monday, August 14, 1876

Run *Santa Cruz* all day. Tucker fireman

Run out chock rock in AM. Made two trips to Felton with pass[engers] & ft [freight] train. The *Felton* made two trips to Felton & on last trip ran off the switch in Felton. (A bad beginning for Engine and Engineer).[56] We got in a little before dark.

Saturday, August 19, 1876

Run *Santa Cruz* all day. Tucker fireman.

Made two trips to Felton & return on pas[senger] and freight trains. *Felton* made one trip. Our tube to Water gauge broke this AM. I went downtown in the Eve, but didn't stop long. Run out chock rock in AM.

Monday, August 21, 1876

Run *Santa Cruz* all day. Tucker fireman.

Made two trips to Felton & return with Pas[enger] & ft[freight]. The *Felton* made two trips. In PM we left SC at 2:30 & Felton at 5:20. Had a man splitting my wood, etc. at home. Paid him $4.00 for work what he done.

Friday, August 25, 1876

Worked on *Santa Cruz* all day in shop. Tucker fireman.

In AM Blew off boiler & washed it out. Then got Lee to sit Engine in our house. Then I took off main connections & side rods, taking left but[t-]end connection box & side rod. Brasses to Armas [Amner] to get babbited. Got main rod b[abbitted] & fitted. Went down to office & got check for last month. Rode up & went in South [end of] tunnel.

Saturday, August 26, 1876

Worked on *Santa Cruz* all day in shop. Tucker fireman.

I got main rod box done & fitted. Side rod boxes not babbited until Eve. Went down town in the Eve. Went to bank & got my check for last month's work cashed. It was $125.00.

Sunday, August 27, 1876

Worked on Engine all day in Shop. Tucker fireman.

Worked on side rod boxes all day with Armas' [Amner's] man to help me. He had to plane out[57] & babbit two of them this AM, so he helped me fit them. Barnard FitzJereald [Fitzgerald?] & wife took dinner with us this AM. Got news that [first name unclear] Thompson had killed himself.

Monday, August 28, 1876

Worked all day on Engine in Shop. Tucker fireman. Worked fitting & finishing side rod boxes. Put them up & got ready to run when wanted. Called in to see Mother this Eve who is sick. Porter up to house in Eve.

Tuesday, August 29, 1876

Run *Santa Cruz* all day. Tucker fireman.

Made two trips to Felton & return on mixed train besides drawing chock rock in AM. Our connection boxes work first rate & do not heat or give any trouble. Capt. Garratt & Mr. Green of the S.P.R.R. rode up to Felton in AM with us. The *Felton* in shop to have her smoke stack fixed so not to throw so much fire.

Thursday, August 31, 1876

Run *Santa Cruz* all day. Tucker fireman.

Made 3 trips to Felton & return besides [?] chock rock a while in AM. After we returned with the Special, we ran out at 6 o'clock AM. Mr. Lee & Porter called at my house in the Eve. Soon after they left Tucker & two friends called. I done a little tinkering on chicken house in the Eve. Piled a little wood, etc.

Wednesday, September 6, 1876

Run *Santa Cruz* all day. Tucker fireman.

Made two trips to Felton & return on regular train of Pas[sengers] and freight. On last trip leaving Santa Cruz at 2:50 instead of 2 PM, we had 9 loaded box cars,[58] one empty box, five empty flats & one passenger car. A heavy load but we took them up first rate. The *Felton* made two trips to Felton & return.

[Written upside down at bottom of page:] in AM we backed two empty cars into tunnel (north end) with the *Santa Cruz*, it being the first time an Engine or cars were run into the tunnel.

Saturday, September 9, 1876

Run *Santa Cruz* all day. Tucker fireman.

Made two trips to Felton & return on regular mixed train. The *Felton* made one trip to Felton & return on special. In the Eve when we shoved up our last train to the St. Charles, I got off & went over to Dan Moulton's where I found Hat & baby and stoped to supper and stoped until near dark. Dan went over with us to town when we went home. Had a pleasant time. After we got home, I went down to Engine house & to town & to S.C.R.R. Depot when train came in.

Wednesday, September 13, 1876

Run *Santa Cruz* all day. Tucker fireman.

Made two trips to Felton & return waiting in Felton until PM on last trip. The *Felton* made 2 trips.

Sunday, September 17, 1876

Run *Santa Cruz* all day. Tucker fireman.

Made 2 trips to Felton & return. Had passenger train up with empty cars. Had only passengers down. We drew out chock rock. We had a good run of passengers.

Wednesday, September 20, 1876

Run *Santa Cruz* all day. Tucker fireman.

Made two trips to Felton & return on mixed train. In AM we took 10 cars into Felton. The *Felton* helped us up the hill. Some of the way up the hill we had 23 cars with 3 of them loaded. The [second trip] *Felton* did not come up. She is working on Gravel train. Went downtown in the Eve to Hinds & Hofman's with [?] papers who had made a payment there on and interest he paid $70. & $260 interest all of which was endorsed on the paper.

Saturday, September 23, 1876

Run *Santa Cruz* all day. Tucker fireman.

Made two trips to Felton & return on mixed train. The *Felton* run a Special passenger train to Felton in the Eve to a Denocrat meeting. I got our Engine out in the Eve & done a little switching. Then went downtown, etc.

Wednesday, September 27, 1876

Run *Santa Cruz* all day. Tucker fireman.

Made two trips to Felton & return on mixed train. The *Felton* working on construction. In PM she undertook to help me up grade with 13 cars in mi [my] train & hitched to them but conductor cut them off as they were not helping us any. I was drawing the whole of our train besides towing them, at least [we] were drawing some of their load.

Saturday, September 30, 1876

Run *Santa Cruz* all day. Tucker fireman.

Made two trips to Felton & return on mixed train. The *Felton* run working train. She helped us up the hill in PM & in the Eve she run a Special train of passengers to Felton to a republican meeting. Paid John $400 [$4.00?] for sawing wood.

Monday, October 2, 1876

Run *Santa Cruz* all day. Tucker fireman.

Made two trips to Felton & return. The *Felton* worked on construction in AM. In PM she lay in the house. The workmen in the Mission Hill tunnel blowed a hole through so a man can pass from one end to the other. Mr. Anderson was in to our house in the Eve to see about hiring some money. I piled up wood in the Eve.

Tuesday, October 3, 1876

Run *Santa Cruz* all day. Tucker fireman.

Made two trips to Felton on mixed train. The *Felton* made two trips on freight. We took out the chock rock. Got empty cars for chock rock, etc. I piled up some wood in the Eve.

Saturday, October 7, 1876

Run *Santa Cruz* all day. Tucker fireman.

Made two trips to Felton & return on mixed train. The *Felton* made three trips to Felton & back, two trips on freight & one on a special passenger to a political meeting & got off track in Felton, making 3 times for them. I drew $1000.00 out of bank this PM to loan Mr. Anderson. In the Eve I left it in the bank for safe keeping until next Monday. Was downtown in the Eve when Special went out to Felton.

[Written upside down at bottom of page:] One year ago today I run to Felton for the first time on our road & since then I have not had a wheel of our engine off or a break down.

Monday, October 9, 1876

Run *Santa Cruz* all day. Tucker fireman.

Made two trips to Felton & return on mixed train except last trip down which was ran without any freight. Borrowed $40.00, Forty dollars, of J. M. Tucker to make out a certain amount of money for Professor Anderson. I deeded him the lots I sold him & loned [loaned] him mone[y] & took a mortgage of the place, house, etc., for $2100. The construction Engine ran through the Mission hill tunnel this Eve. The *Felton* run on construction all day.

Tuesday, October 10, 1876

Run *Santa Cruz* all day. Tucker fireman.

Made two trips to Felton & return on mixed train. All but 2 o'clock train out of Santa Cruz we only had two passengers making the run to Felton in 25 minutes, the fastest time we made over this road.[59] We took down 20 cars of freight & the passenger car which was the largest train ever taken down with one Engine all at once, making the top of the hill in 20 minutes & mission orchard station in 40 minutes passing through Mission hill tunnel for the first time & taking through the first regular train & the first train down Chestnut Street and into yard & on Wharf.[60] In yard got four driving wheels off the switch, which was the first time ever had an engine wheel off. It was not my fault.

Wednesday, October 11, 1876

Run *Santa Cruz* all day. Tucker fireman.

Made two trips to Felton & return besides doing any amount of switching in yard & on wharf in the AM. before we went out & lots of it at noon & in the PM after we got in. We commensed to run regular from the yard at the wharf near the office. The *Felton* run on construction train.

Friday, October 13, 1876

Run *Santa Cruz* all day. Tucker fireman.

Made two trips to Felton & return on mixed train besides working in the yard at the wharf. The *Felton* helped us up on 10 o'clock train. *Felton* on construction. Lee was sick so Porter run *Felton* in AM. Lee all right in PM. Nelson was our conductor part of the day. In the Eve Horace came into our house, also Mary Barnes [Burns?] & Kate Blake.

Sunday, October 15, 1876

Run *Santa Cruz* all day. Tucker fireman.

Made two trips to Felton and return. Took up empty freight cars on both trips with passengers. In PM we took up both coaches.

Monday, October 16, 1876

Run *Santa Cruz* all day. Tucker fireman.

Made two trips to Felton & return on mixed train. The *Felton* on construction. In Eve we brought empty cars back to mission orchard.

Thursday, October 19, 1876

Santa Cruz laid up for a few days in the car house. Tucker & I going to lay off a few days. The *Felton* running the train. I went down to go out, but found Engine had no steam up. So I came home & helped Miller pick apples, pile up wood, etc. We cleaned pine wood, etc. out of yard & piled up in stable besides taking in considerable of my redwood kindlings, etc.

Friday, October 20, 1876

Worked about home most of the day. In AM went down to Gregg's plaining [planing] mill & got some slats for eve [eave?] spouts [drain spouts?] getting Daniel's[61] team to take up for me, going round by Engine house & taking some things home for me I had there. Miller cleaned out ditch up in the Boston lot to prevent water from flowing over mi [my] lot, besides cleaning out ditches in yard, etc., besides helping me fix up roof.

Sunday, October 22, 1876

Went to Church in AM with wife, the first time since last Spring, this being the first Sunday I spent at home or was off duty since last Spring. In the Eve I went down to R.R. office and got a check for last month's work—$125 —which I took to bank & got cashed. I received from Hinds & Hofman $100—less the amount they had charged to me, amounting to less than a dozen dollars, money they collected from Mr. Chapman for lot. Paid Horace $100—borrowed money.

[Written at top of page:] Miller & I laid a floor for a stoop on back side of house.

Thursday, October 26, 1876

Worked near all day at home patching up roof to house. Received 5 bbls of flour lacking one sack which we had previously had on trial from Centennial mill for which I paid $25.00. Had rain. I put up a conductor spout to take away from the eve spout on front of house the water. Was down to the R.R. new Engine house in the AM.[62]

Sunday, October 29, 1876

Stoped about home all day. Was not out of yard untill Eve, when I went down to Goodwin's & got a bucket of water for baby.

Monday, October 30, 1876

Run & worked on *Santa Cruz* all day. Got Engine out & got a flat car & picked up all our traps[63] in one little Engine house in Mission orchard & moved down to our new house in the Blackburn orchard. Picked up & packed a few things in PM.

Received $10.00 of J. M. Tucker.

Paid H. W. Pope $20.00.

Tuesday, October 31, 1876[64]

Run *Santa Cruz* all day. Tucker fireman.

Made two trips to Felton & return with a special freight & helped regular 10 o'clock train up the grade. We had 23 cars. We run up to tank & got water. Took down two cars of ballast. We run the special out at new [?] 1 o'clock PM. Was downtown in the Eve.

Thursday, November 2, 1876

Run and worked on *Santa Cruz* all day. Run around the yard awhile in AM, then went in house & commensed to get raidy to overhall and fix up our Engine.

Friday, November 3, 1876

Worked all day on *Santa Cruz* all day. Tucker fireman.

Took down side rods, filed & lined up one & commensed the other. Was feeling poorly, in fact was too sick to work. Had a headache and one sore hand with a boil on it & one on the other arm.

Saturday, November 4, 1876

Worked all day on *Santa Cruz*, Tucker with me. I felt poorly and did not go down to the shop untill the Santa Cruz train went out at 9 AM, riding down to our Engine house with Chas. Garcilinon [Garcelon] on his Engine. Saw Garratt at the S.C. Depot. I finished filing & lining [up] side rods. Took off pipes & got raidy [ready] to jack [it] up.

Monday, November 6, 1876

Went down to Engine house to jack up [the engine] and fix the *Santa Cruz* and when I got there I got word from President Gorrell that did not want me, mi friends, & wife any more. So tucker & I went to the office & got our checks & all the reason we could get for our being put off was that they was going to dedus [reduce] expenses & do with one Engine.[65] So I packed up my tools & traps & went up town to bank a [and to] claim my coin & went home.

Tuesday, November 7, 1876

I tinkered about home a little. Went down town & looked around a little passing the time pleasantly and taking things easy.

Wednesday, November 8, 1876

I took things easy all day. Got my trap home from Engine house. Saw Capt. Garratt at Depot who told me he new [knew] nothing about my being put off untill he got home from San Jose. I told him Gorrill said he left it all with him which is what he *did* tell me, so a *lie* is *between them*. I told Garrat[t] I thought I could stand it as well as they could & so I think *I can*.

Tuesday, November 14, 1876

Went down to S.C.R.R. depot after breakfast & as the train was about the start, Mr. Hieghn [Hihn] invited me over to go over the road to Pajaro as they were to cross the new bridge over the Pajaro River for the first time.[66] So I jumped aboard & started & had a pleasant ride. Saw the boys at the Depot. Got dinner at Pajaro at Hieghn's [Hihn's] expense & home again. Had a pleasant time & a good ride.

Friday, November 17, 1876

Moulton & I worked on house all day. I did not get to work untill near 9 AM. We were putting on rustic all day. I took dinner at Moulton's. I took home Mr. Cape's [Cope's?[67]] Jack Screen [?] this Eve when I came home. Saw Tucker this Eve on the street. Paid Horace $100—in full for borrowed money.

Monday, November 20, 1876

Moulton & I worked on house all day putting on rustic, fixing around the windows, etc. Got the rustic all on & had considerable more than we wanted. Norman Gos [?] & wife & a friend was at Moulton's to dinner. Harriet came down to Moulton's in PM bringing baby in his little buggy. Mrs. Finly [Finley?] came with her. Hat & I stoped to supper. I wheeled baby home. Went downtown in Eve.

Friday, December 1, 1876

Moulton & I worked on house all day. Getting raidy for the masons who are lathing. In the Eve Harriet & I went down to Burnhiem's [Bernheim's] hall to a Sociable or as it was called a Centennial tea party for the benefit of the Congregational church. Had a very pleasant & good time. Eva went with us. I saw Humbut—Gorrall [Gorrill] was there.

Wednesday, December 13, 1876

I packed our pork in AM & done other chores in PM. I helped Horace fix & rub his & our Hams & Shoulders. Was downtown in AM. Saw & had a talk with Mr. Silent. He don't seem to think much of the way Garrall [Gorrill] is managing things on the Felton road or for Garrall [Gorrill] either. Was down town in the Eve. saw Mr. Silent at Hinds and Hofman.

Sunday, December 24, 1876

Stoped about home nearly all day. In PM went over to see Mother. Found her quite well. Jo was at H's & come home with me and stoped an hour.

Monday, December 25, 1876

[At top of page:] Pleasant.

Merry Christmas once more.

Did not get up untill past 7 o'clock. Had a merry good breakfast, then called in to see Mother & wish her a merry Christmas. Then I went downtown to bootcher shop. Then to Gregg's [Gragg's] & ordered board for sink. Came home & scalded our pork brine, cleaned out water barrels, etc. Had a good supper of rost beef & went in again to Mother & had a short & pleasant visit. Went downtown again. Saw Moulton who came home with me. I paid him $40.00. Harriet went with baby over to H's to Christmas tea & brought home a lot of nice presants for herself & baby.

Saturday, December 30, 1876

Was downtown & in to Hofman's and Hinds' most of the day. A number of parties came in there to make payments on some of those building lots I sold over the river.[68] I was in to Court House & about town. Jo Paid me the payment due now on Mrs. Samuel's lot. Was in to Hofman's in the Eve.

Sunday, December 31, 1876

Turned out at 7 AM & soon after had a good & harty breakfast of good baked pork & beans. I read the papers & took things easy all day. Was in to see mother a little while in the AM. In PM went over to Jo's & went with him to see his new house. It will be a very comfortable one. Was downtown in the Eve to Hoffman's.

[Upside down at bottom of page:] This is the last of you old book & old centennial year of 1876. This closes this eventful year.

Factory notes on a Porter, Bell class C

Unlike the Baldwin Locomotive Works records for its 8-18 C class engines, too few Porter, Bell drawings survive to create a digital version of its narrow gauge class C, an 0-6-0 that found limited markets in the early California narrow gauge movement. In 1951, the Canadian Locomotive Works purchased the H. K. Porter Co. (successor to Porter, Bell) and moved its documents and records from Pittsburgh to Kingston, Ontario, while offering replacement parts to long-time Porter customers. But in the early 1960s, Canadian Locomotive Works closed, and by 1968 most of its documents, including the complete drawing collection of Porter, were being hauled to landfills. Several historians, including the curator of the Canadian Museum of Science and Technology, literally rescued what they could from dumpsters. Fewer than half of the Porter drawings were saved, among them some locomotive elevations and parts drawings. The elevations remained with the Canadian Museum; the parts drawings found their way into private hands, and eventually into the collection of George Thagard.

Of the drawings that survived, a small percentage are associated with the 9.5" × 14" cylinder class C, a machine of the same class that Porter, Bell sold to the Santa Cruz & Felton as serial numbers 218 (named *Santa Cruz*, shown below as built in 1875, and in later life, ca. 1913, opposite, below) and 236 (named *Felton*, not pictured). Specifications of boiler, chassis, and running gear were identical for the two engines. The *Felton* carried a larger smokestack, and a higher level of decoration than the *Santa Cruz*. Original Porter elevation drawings that survive are of later machines of the same cylinder size and basic running gear, but they differ in appliance configurations and overall appearance. Original parts drawings that survived from the class C series were often redrawn and modified at the factory over a period of twenty years, but the earliest of these drawings, created using ink on card stock and often saturated with shop oil and grime, bear dates from the early 1870s, when the design of the class C engines was being perfected. Like looking for traces of ancestral DNA in the drawings that remain, one can still find small pieces of the 1874 class C architecture in the examples here, including the elegant Porter, Bell builder's medallion, reproduced from the original elevation.

Porter marketed its class C as an engine ideally suited to the extremes in physical plant that narrow gauge railroads presented. The class C was just half the weight of a Baldwin 8-18 C. It was designed with a shorter wheelbase (7'3") covering three axles than the Baldwin 8-18 C machine covered with just two axles (7'6"). The Santa Cruz & Felton appeared to offer the extreme of extremes: with twenty-five-pound rail and 118-foot radius curves, it had the most restrictive mechanical standards of any of the railroads featured in this book. But Porter, Bell published testimonials of its engines operating on sixteen-pound rail and around curves as short as 80-foot radius. Here, then, were locomotives for the most primitive conditions of three-foot-gauge railroading, a perfect case of adaptive mechanical engineering. [Below, Vernon Sappers collection, from an R. E. Wood stereograph; opposite top, builder's medallion, George Thagard collection]

An elevation of Porter, Bell serial 501 (below) was drawn in 1882 but still shows the 1874 boiler profile of the *Santa Cruz*, serial 218. The *Santa Cruz* is shown at the bottom of the page, on the Nevada County Narrow Gauge, about 1913. [Below, Canadian Museum of Science and Technology; bottom, San Francisco Maritime National Historical Park, Livingston Collection]

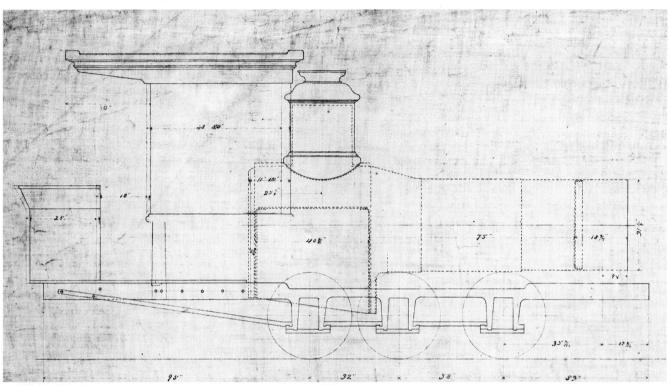

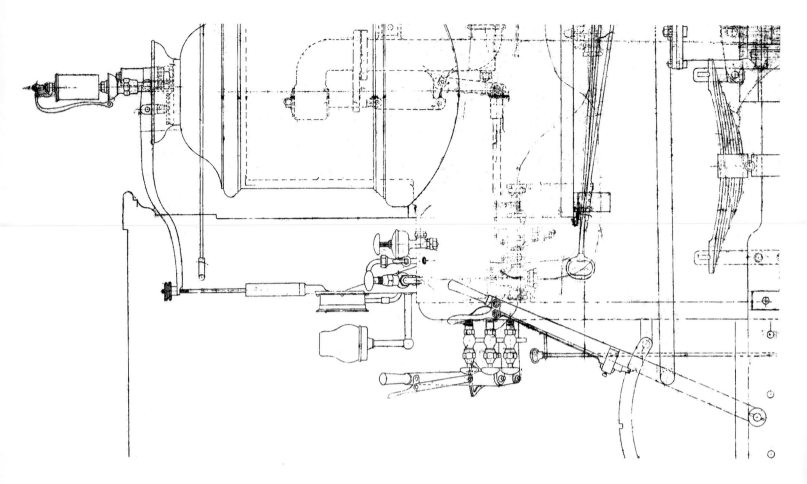

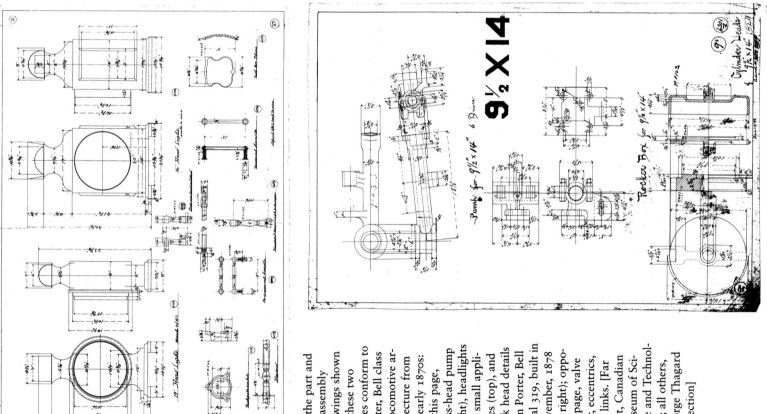

All the part and subassembly drawings shown on these two pages conform to Porter, Bell class C locomotive architecture from the early 1870s: on this page, cross-head pump (right), headlights and small appliances (top), and back head details from Porter, Bell serial 319, built in November, 1878 (far right); opposite page, valve gear, eccentrics, and links. [Far right, Canadian Museum of Science and Technology; all others, George Thagard collection]

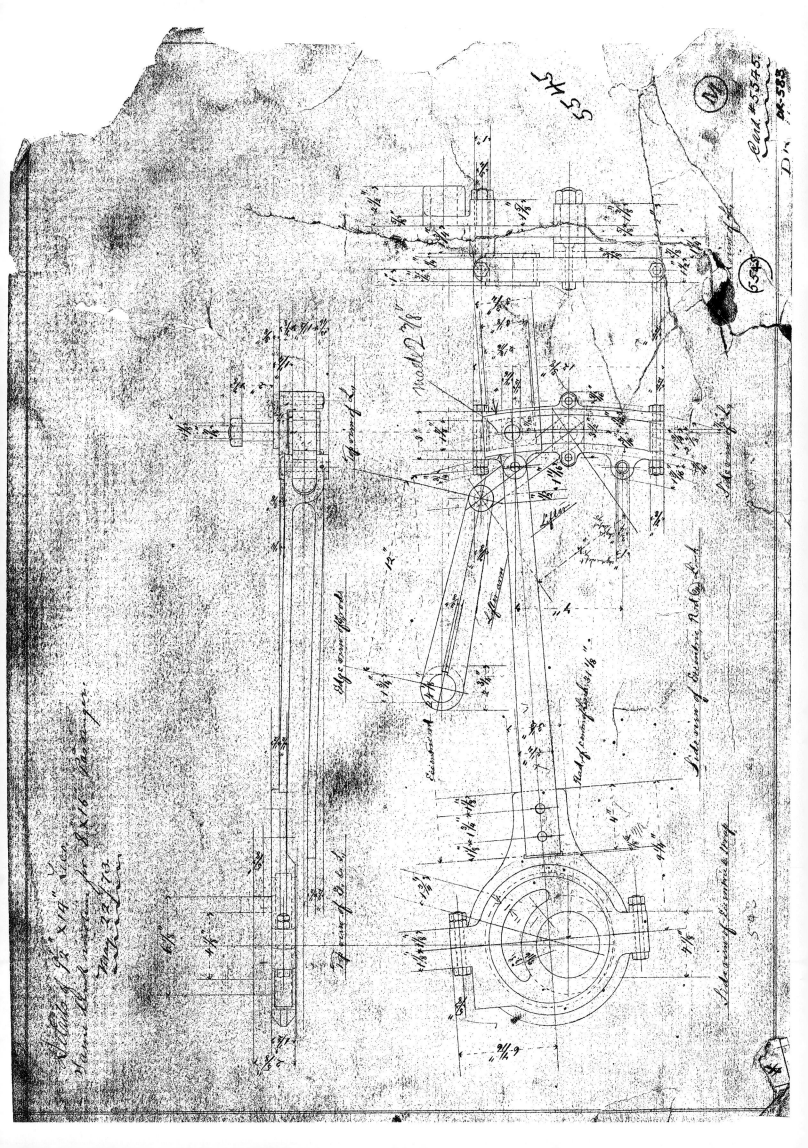

The Great Railroad Game in the Marsh

While tiny Santa Cruz County showed unusually precocious signs of transforming its railroad-related markets and industries, the larger industrial complex, located primarily in San Francisco, gave only weak indications of following the trend. Noticeably lacking was specialization. The fact that key businesses remained undifferentiated—that locomotive manufacturers and car manufacturers did not establish themselves separately from the larger mainstream of foundries, machine shops, and their suppliers—suggested that deeper forces were at work in the market, forces that would ultimately test the business model of isolated manufacturing start-ups in Santa Cruz County.

One of those forces was the volatile pattern of speculation in the Comstock Lode. So rampant was mining stock speculation in the early 1870s that capital available for new foundries and manufactories simply could not be raised in the public marketplace. At the same time, eastern manufacturers and suppliers gained direct access to the same market segments that California manufacturers were struggling to win. Established car builders such as Wason and Stephenson both maintained a presence in the West Coast railroad market, including (in Stephenson's case) what today would be called OEM-ing to California manufacturers—building generic or kit railroad cars that San Francisco builders such as Casebolt would finish and sell. But a third force, and by far the largest, was the market-killing presence of the Central Pacific and Southern Pacific railroads. Virtually an industry unto itself, the Central and Southern Pacific had become large enough, by 1873, to sustain their own car production and even their own locomotive manufacture.[1]

In the same time period when Santa Cruz County was fostering cottage car manufacturers such as Kaye and Davis, observers looked to Kimball in the belief that it was big enough to seed a West Coast railroad supply industry based on the fraction of remaining market share that the Central and Southern Pacific had not cornered—short lines, narrow gauge, and street railways. One of the most optimistic of those observers, Henry Fairfax Williams, was visionary enough to clearly see these emerging new markets, and practical enough to create a business plan around them. Williams was a broker of industrial properties in San Francisco, a planner of what might today be called a business "campus." He saw his role as a kind of business

Opposite: Santa Clara Valley Railroad first mortgage gold bond, issued by the Nevada Bank in January 1876. [John Schmale collection]

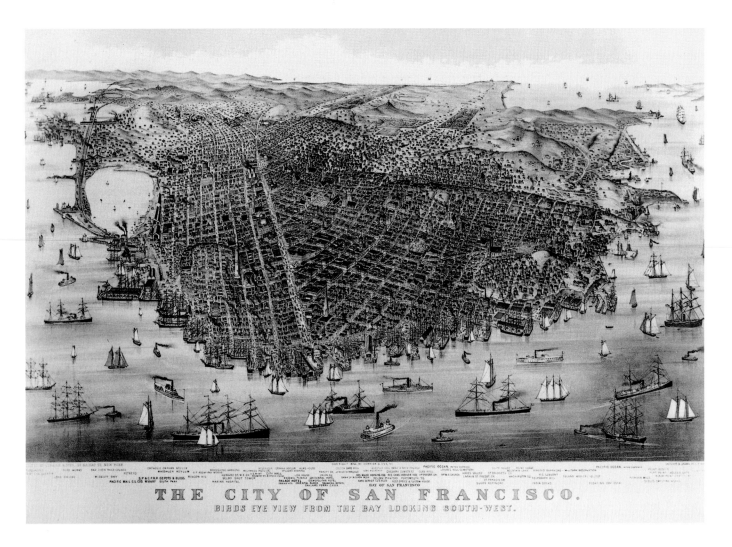

THE CITY OF SAN FRANCISCO.
BIRDS EYE VIEW FROM THE BAY LOOKING SOUTH-WEST.

In 1878, Mission Bay, appearing in the left side of the bird's-eye view of San Francisco (above), was ringed by landfill. The long warehouses and car shops of the Central Pacific, bordering the right edge of Mission Bay, mark the new industrial area near Sixth and Berry streets. [Bancroft Library]

match maker, bringing together pieces of a new industrial ensemble that could not only sustain itself but significantly affect California's entire economy. Railroad manufacturers and suppliers in general, and narrow gauge suppliers in particular, played a significant role in his thinking. But if this vision were to succeed as a commercial venture, to achieve the market force of a "disruptive technology," Williams also knew that the industrial infrastructure supporting a narrow gauge movement would have to be an order of magnitude larger than the cottage industries of Santa Cruz County. Foundries, machine shops, lumber retailers, and fabricators—and the manufactories that depended on them—would have to achieve regional presence, low prices, and (most important) independence from the Central and Southern Pacific railroads to have any real impact on the economy.

The basis of Williams's vision was a San Francisco real estate development called Mission Bay. In 1870, Mission Bay consisted of some five hundred acres of open water, with the Kimball Manufacturing Co. sprawling on its muddy northern shore.

"The Times," Williams paraphrased Shakespeare in his diary entry for April 29, 1871, "are very much out of joint."

Williams spoke from the strain of a wrenching personal decision he was about to make that would, given the wrong choice, plunge him into financial ruin: "My mind is now fully made up to curtail my operations and pay off my indebtedness as fast as I can sell property to do so, for it does not pay to hold on to property and be annoyed by debts overdue."[2]

Williams had borrowed heavily from the Bank of California to purchase tidal lands in San Francisco's Mission Bay area, and he was willing to incur the additional expense of filling and improving the lands to be able to offer them as building sites for new industry. His relationship to this project was complex, but the long-range gains he expected to make were clearly linked to the successful sale of the land for commercial and manufacturing development.

In the early 1870s, when Williams's involvement in Mission Bay was at its height, California's manufacturing was deeply troubled by high interest rates and aggressive competition from the East Coast. Williams could buy and develop industrial land relatively cheaply (an incentive that helps explain the size and complexity of the Mission Bay project). But he faced a battered, wary marketplace in attempting to sell it. Two years later, he wrote of the period: "Had a long business talk with Mr. Dore and we fully agreed that the signs of the times do not warrant a belief that the real estate market will revive in this city this year. Another year of depression stares us in the face."[3]

Sooner or later, the forces of basic economics would squeeze him between unpaid loans and unsold real estate lots. In Williams's case, the result would be bankruptcy in 1877.

Economic observers of the time explained the high interest rates by pointing to California's awkward relationship to currency. There were three money systems operating in California in the 1870s. All three—gold, silver, and script—were "legal tender," and all three in essence competed with each other. The state's production of gold, for example, was minted into negotiable coin that was more valuable as a commodity in the world's precious metal market than it was as legal tender in the state that produced it. This fact tended to make gold coin scarce in California, driving its price up in relation to silver or paper:

> It is worthy of special consideration that the circumstances of the people of the Atlantic States, their manufacturing and other industrial affairs are not in any way affected by this enormous drain of treasure. The cause of this immunity is, that the currency with which their business is conducted is of more value at home than it is abroad; while with us [in California] the export of an extra million of dollars, or even the probability of such a circumstance, causes a derangement of business, because our peculiar currency is of more value abroad than it is at home.[4]

The result was higher interest on money lent within the state itself. In 1872, the cost of money lent to manufacturers in California often reached a rate of 12–15 percent, compared to 4–5 percent in New York. The difference gave eastern manufacturers a large, sustainable advantage. In that same year, the value of imports into California exceeded $71,000,000, compared to $53,581,300 in exports.[5] The effect was like an imbalance of nearly

Viewed from the south in 1892, the open water of the original Mission Bay has grown smaller, its surface area filled to add "made land" to San Francisco's South of Market industrial development. [Bancroft Library]

$20,000,000 in trade between two nations, driving down the value of one's currency in relation to the other.

By 1875, this situation had changed little. For small manufacturers especially, the price of capital was a steep barrier to doing business. Carter Brothers, for example, would have been exposed to 12 percent interest on the outstanding balance owed to Renton, Holmes for car lumber or McCormick and Lewis for castings, if the North Pacific Coast had not agreed to cover Carter's materials on their own accounts with the two suppliers.[6] The fact that the railroad did agree to such terms may have been the reason Carter survived the contract at all.

In stark contrast, Henry Fairfax Williams seemed to be lending money to buyers at an interest rate between 5 percent and 8 percent to speed the sale of Mission Bay property.[7] Between 1869 and 1874, when Williams offered these attractive rates to potential customers, his diary recorded numerous real estate transactions, including buying, selling, leasing, and brokering activities, all focused on Mission Bay. Between 1869 and 1871, for example, Williams received installment payments from Kimball Manufacturing Co. for the purchase and development of the land for their main factory at Fourth and Bryant streets. On the edge of the original Mission Bay tide line, the site was one of the earliest Mission Bay land developments, and a benchmark for Williams's early optimism in the location.[8]

Williams's receipts from Kimball totaled nearly $25,000 in this period.[9] No interest rate is noted for the loan, but it represented one of the earliest Mission Bay developments and a strategic one, reinforcing Williams's belief that railroad activity and support services would be critical to the commercial success of the Mission Bay area as a whole. Like William Ralston, Williams believed that Kimball would soon market its products and services to the Central Pacific. The year Kimball acquired the Fourth and Bryant parcel (1868) was the same year the Central Pacific received its Mission Bay land grant. The two companies were neighbors by design.

By July 1874, Williams was selling Mission Bay land in parcels as large as three blocks at a time, priced at $150,000 per block; except for a $25,000 down payment, he was carrying all of the sale price as a five-year, 8 percent loan. By August, Williams concluded a smaller sale with a loan carried at just 5 percent.

But even with attractive interest rates, few buyers could afford Williams's prices. The Kimball Co. was a dramatic example: the $25,000 that Kimball paid Henry Fairfax Williams in loan service was, in turn, a minuscule part of a half million dollar loan that Kimball took from the Bank of California. By 1875, Kimball had virtually stopped payment on the larger loan.

The diaries of Henry Fairfax Williams begin in 1849 and continue to 1904, bearing witness to the first half century of California's statehood. In their pages, Williams would take credit for several of the most basic building blocks of San Francisco's early civic foundation, including the start-up of the city's first carpentry shop, and a contract to build its first post office.

Much like the personal, leather-bound journal of Fowler Pope (which the engineer addressed in the familiar "you old diary"), Williams kept one that he referred to as "my companion." Through it, he narrated daily rituals that extended to mind, body, and character—a centering of thoughts and feelings that helped him manage his life. "My companion" was written in legal-sized, bound business ledgers, but often, because of extended travel or simply the pace of business life, Williams would write of the day's events on any handy piece of paper, hotel stationery, foolscap, or a discarded ledger page, hoping to recopy the day's events in their rightful place on blank pages in the "companion." But he seldom found time. Like many of the projects he worked on, the refugee pages remained uncopied and scattered until brought together in the holdings of the Bancroft Library, long after his death.

The "companion" reflected Williams's boundless enthusiasm for what today would be called networking. To do business in San Francisco in the 1870s meant to make rounds like a postman on foot, meeting business partners in bars, on the streets, in their offices, on ferry boats, at christenings, or at funerals, never straying far from the constant flow of news that came down the sidewalks of Montgomery Street.

There was no e-mail to speed this process. To get access to Leland Stanford in a particularly busy time, Henry Fairfax Williams had to hastily embark on a riverboat the governor was catching to Sacramento, only to contend with Senator Nye and others for a share of Stanford's time. On another occasion, Williams unexpectedly enjoyed an hour of Stanford's company when his appointment with Mark Hopkins was canceled during a visit to the Central Pacific's new office building at Fourth and Townsend, a site marking the northern edge of Mission Bay. He was clearly on personal terms with Stanford and confided to the "companion" that Stanford "is truly a busy man and an overworked man, but his strong constitution enables him to stand up under what would kill most men."[10]

In turn, Stanford trusted him. Williams was given the delicate task of lobbying the state legislature for an extension of the timetable for filling in the Central Pacific's original core sixty acres in Mission Bay, a responsibility that became more critical as Stanford began to see the Mission Bay site as one of his last, best options for terminal lands in the Bay Area.[11] Williams's lobby successfully won Stanford the extra time and brought himself an extended timetable on his own Mission Bay projects.

In turn, a relationship with Stanford guaranteed Williams access to Central Pacific's middle management, men such as civil engineer Robert Gray, who offered valuable consulting on Mission Bay landfill issues.

In a time of growing suspicion of the Central Pacific's monopoly and its legendary ability to "buy the souls of men," Henry Fairfax Williams was a businessman of considerable integrity. He never lost a fundamental loyalty to the working men who moved mountains of dirt to develop the property he managed. When his contractor, James Graves, could not collect what was owed him by the landowners of block 21, Williams went swiftly into action: "I have spent a good portion of the day trying to collect for Graves a sufficient amount from his grading contract to pay his men tomorrow, but

I did not succeed . . . it is another illustration of the way wealthy men of this city act towards poor contractors who improve and enhance the value of their lands."[12]

Failing to collect from landowners he thought he could count on (for example, Peter Donahue and H. M. Newhall), he asked Ralston to lend Graves $2,500 and got the money the next day. Ralston, on this occasion and others, represented Williams's financial bedrock. As the Mission Bay project progressed, it was Ralston who emerged as the principal sponsor of Williams's work, and at times something of a father figure. The two businessmen achieved an easy confidence: as the companion noted in 1874, "Mr. Ralston talks very freely with me about men and things and frequently asks my opinion of men which I never fail to give in decided manner either for good or bad as I may happen to know the parties."[13]

Williams restlessly walked the streets of San Francisco, working the relationships he had built up and promoting a new kind of business foundation for the city, one based on manufacturing and transportation that would establish the city as one of the world's preeminent commercial centers. By April 7, 1874, Williams's belief in the Mission Bay development was so strong he elected to move his office from the Montgomery Street Financial District to Block 16, the corner of Fourth and Berry streets, on the muddy fringe of Mission Bay. Most work days, he wouldn't leave the office until midnight, riding the Potrero & Bay View horsecar to his South San Francisco home, and to his sleeping wife, Catherine, and (by 1874) their four children. When meetings or travel delayed his commute until after the Potrero & Bay View horsecar had shut down, Williams got a downtown room at the Occidental Hotel, following fourteen, sometimes sixteen, hours of constant work.

Only on Sundays did his regimen pause for morning service at San Francisco's Grace Church, where he served in the vestry along with Lloyd Tevis, J. B. Haggin, and Leland Stanford. On a rare Sunday afternoon, he would give himself the luxury of a Russian steambath at the establishment of Dr. Zeilies.

The Carters were still headquartered in Saucelito (although on shaky terms with their landlord) when Henry Fairfax Williams began to create what would become the next Carter factory site in Mission Bay. It is unlikely that at the time, the spring of 1875, Tom Carter and Henry Williams knew each other. Williams makes no mention of Carter in his diaries, yet their paths were clearly marked to cross in the small community of business leaders that they both knew—Peter Donahue, Milton Latham, Austin Moore, John Kidder, Ben Holliday, Charley Gorrill, and of course John Ambrose Carroll, whom both Carter and Williams, at different times, employed.

Henry Fairfax Williams thought of himself primarily as a property manager, although the term does not do him justice. He was the confidant and friend of the most influential men in California; he "closeted" himself in frequent private audiences with William Ralston, Peter Donahue, and Leland Stanford, often simply to assess the subtle signs of change, for better or worse, in the business climate. At other times, he received, and returned, their favors. Ralston and Donahue both lent him large sums of money in the early seventies, and he constantly looked for ways to be of service to them. He named his fifth child after one of the benefactors; William Ralston Williams was born on January 18, 1874.

With the exception of John Kidder and John Carroll, all of the industrial leaders just mentioned came to Williams in pursuit of land in the huge Mission Bay project. The project was viewed as a money pump working inside a sluggish local economy, slowly seeding growth around the Central Pacific's sixty core acres of unreclaimed tidal lands in the Mission Bay alcove just south of Market Street. To Williams and to other speculators, the sixty acres represented the terminal of the Central Pacific's entire transcontinental system, a platform from which its international traffic could be leveraged.

Stanford trusted Henry Fairfax Williams to be the chief instrument for development not just of land for this crucial facility but of an overlapping, interconnected community of partners, feeders, agents, distributors, forwarders, and dealers who would mesh the transcontinental system to its commercial customer base. The Mission Bay development would act as a gateway for Stanford's growing international empire. Into its spider web (still under water in 1872), smaller investors such as Donahue, Latham, Moore, Holliday, and Gorrill eagerly jumped.

Williams spun an intricate web. Shortly after the legislature granted Mission Bay land to the CP in 1868 (for a consideration of just $100 per acre[14]), Williams began to buy, in some cases lease, and in some cases broker, neighboring underwater lots. He was early on the scene, and he understood the need to enhance the value of the property if he were going to interest buyers. In 1868 he became the primary stockholder of the horse-powered Potrero & Bay View Railroad, which crossed the open nape of Mission Bay on a trestle called Long Bridge and united downtown San Francisco with the Potrero and Bay View districts, creating a conduit for developing submerged properties west of the trestle.

In 1867, the year before the horsecar line was completed, John Carroll went to work for the P&BV as its car builder. When the railroad opened for business on Friday, August 16, 1867, both Williams and Carroll were publicly thanked at the ceremonies.[15] They undoubtedly knew each other. The presence of the giant Kimball works, opened at the Fourth and Bryant terminal of the P&BV just a year later, suggested that the car building and railroad supply industries would continue to be a major business theme of the Mission Bay development.

Within the five hundred acre Mission Bay itself, a shallow, half-moon-shaped inlet stretching from Potrero Point on the south to the Kimball factory at Fourth and Bryant streets on the north, Williams acted as land developer not only for the Central Pacific but also for such industrialists as Peter Donahue, William Ralston, Maurice Dore, and H. M. Newhall. Dore and Newhall, in turn, were also real estate agents who brokered their land to others.

The economics of this activity involved more than simply buying and selling. Williams organized owners of underwater blocks into assessment districts, collected fees, and used the money to employ subcontractors to fill and grade lots, and finally pave the new streets that formed the properties into a grid. He maintained his own stable of horses, owning and leasing the teams that worked the grading. He held patents on the "Williams process" for street paving, an experimental system of tightly fitted redwood blocks with a covering of asphaltum, a ready (if untested) solution to paving not just Mission Bay streets but other San Francisco streets as well.

The recession made this process slow and painful. From photographs taken as late as 1877, it is clear that the majority of the original area of the bay remained open water, the development confined to its northern shore. Williams was frustrated by the pace of the work. In 1872, he noted in his diary that "the prospect is anything but encouraging, owing entirely to the want of financial aid from the moneyed men. Legitimate industries are entirely overlooked in the scramble for sudden gains in stock gambling."[16]

By "stock gambling," Williams referred to the sometimes chaotic, ruinous speculation in mining stocks that wreaked havoc on the fortunes of California investors throughout the early 1870s. He witnessed, for example, the steep ascent and subsequent freefall of Savage Mine stocks in June 1873 and refused to take the kind of risks that it represented. He had risks enough in his own portfolio.

The Mission Bay development was plagued with problems unique to a city running out of buildable land. Without modern compaction methods, the first Central Pacific warehouses erected at Fourth and Townsend streets settled a foot into the soft underbelly of mud. The structures had to be torn down and rebuilt. The settling would happen convulsively in an earthquake. Most of the recorded deaths in the 1906 quake occurred in wooden frame buildings collapsing on "made land," much of it in Mission Bay.

A new San Francisco sewer main, emptying sluggishly into Mission Bay just past the foot of Sixth Street, had a nasty habit of backing up at high tide, leaving the stagnant back bay around Sixth and Berry an open cesspool. At the edge of filled land around Eighth and Berry, an illegal but flourishing garbage dump further enhanced the perfumes of made land.

The seminal role of the Central Pacific in Mission Bay was viewed with suspicion and distrust. Wary San Francisco politicians created legal firewalls to prevent the railroad from gaining unlimited control of deep water wharves. New City laws prescribed a "guard band" of three hundred feet, separating the CP's terminal tracks from most points of encroachment to the bay. The grid of city streets created in Mission Bay contributed to the boxing and containment of Central Pacific activity. Except for deep water access at the Second Street wharf, the core sixty acres of railroad land was effectively landlocked.

Numerous members of the so-called Committee of One Hundred supported the guard-banding tactic, believing it would keep another Bulkhead scheme from monopolizing the waterfront. But many on the committee were also businessmen who stood to profit from the railroad terminal and feared, equally, the threat that Stanford would take his terminal business to Oakland, or Saucelito.

Williams, not personally a member of the committee, had mixed feelings about the ethics involved. In April 1872, he wrote:

> Gov. Stanford and his company have in my judgment far more cause to complain of the actions of the people of this city than they have of his

actions toward them. They [the city] have by their narrow and niggardly policy very effectually prevented his doing what would have resulted in lasting benefits to this city, and now they complain of him for not having done just what they themselves check and prevented.[17]

The Central Pacific, however, was not blameless. On January 27, 1872, Williams recorded that his grading contractor, James Graves, had encouraged his men to join the Central Pacific in roughing up squatters occupying railroad lands at Fourth and Townsend streets. Williams may have blamed him for the violent turn of events (noting in his diary that Graves drank too much) but could not bring himself to criticize Stanford for leading the corporation that had simply exercised its rights as a land owner.

Stanford could not afford to gamble in such a politically volatile environment. While the City struggled with consensus over the expanding influence of the Central Pacific, he quietly and methodically created alternative sites for the "great transcontinental hub," the catalyst of the Bay Area's terminal wars. One was at Saucelito (a plan, described in Chapter Two, that was more feint than commitment). By 1874, any thought of a Central Pacific terminal at Saucelito had been ceded to the North Pacific Coast and to Peter Donahue's San Francisco & North Pacific Railroad, a predecessor to the Northwestern Pacific.

But the Goat Island plan, in contrast, was slowly and systematically fortified. The more complex and difficult the Mission Bay plans became, the more urgently the Central Pacific advanced the Goat Island scheme, even if it too was, by 1872, a bureaucratic quagmire. A two-hundred-acre island halfway between Oakland and San Francisco, Goat Island was owned by the federal government and kept as a military preserve. Congressional action would be required to rescope its use as a railroad terminal. But the Central Pacific had already purchased shoal water north of the island and engineered, on paper, a vast complex of warehouses and piers, connected by causeway to a terminal at Oakland.

Eager to steal the transcontinental hub from San Francisco, the City of Oakland in 1868 donated 50 percent of its entire waterfront to the Central Pacific.[18] By 1873, Oakland was already acting as the Central Pacific's principal base of operation for its numerous Bay Area lines. The Central Pacific's largest railroad yard outside of Sacramento was located along the Oakland harbor, while at high tide the imagined Mission Bay facility still lay under twelve feet of salt water.

Throughout the terminal wars, Stanford played the role of misunderstood philanthropist. He asked for public empathy in condemning San Francisco's reticence to help the Central Pacific gain harbor access. Stanford questioned, almost rhetorically, the value that nearly free wharf privileges returned to other commercial shippers. The *San Francisco Bulletin* of January 21, 1873, labeled Stanford's comments "cunning evasion and equivocations." As early as 1872, the Committee of One Hundred had rallied San Francisco's hostility toward the Goat Island proposal. It was during the brief period that the committee courted other transcontinental railroads, like the Atlantic & Pacific, attempting to bluff Stanford into believing that San Francisco could command his presence.

In this pot-boiling environment, Henry Fairfax Williams may have been one of the few credible negotiators of a compromise, struck between the Committee of One Hundred and the Central Pacific in August 1872.[19] Williams appeared to be a confidant of both sides, walking a thin line between disinterest and heavy personal commitments already made in Mission Bay real estate.[20] On the one hand, he obviously saw the benefit of competition to the otherwise monopolistic practices of the Central Pacific; on the other, he had already invested considerable money in Mission Bay real estate on the premise that the Central Pacific would use it as its transcontinental hub. Williams wrote, just before the visit of a rival midwestern railroad contingent:

> The St. Louis Party consisting of the Mayor and a number of prominent railroad men are expected to arrive in this city this evening. I shall be pleased to see steps taken to secure an opposition railroad across the continent but do not wish to see any steps whatever taken to hamper the CPRR from getting all the accommodations which they need. They have now made a fair start to build up depot accommodations in this City and I say with all my heart God speed the work. So far as I am concerned I will not put a straw in their path.[21]

Williams's relationship with Stanford, his influence with state legislators, and an abiding belief in compromise may have helped achieve a settlement. A summary of the outcome, noted in his diary on March 22, included deliberate reference to the value of "several transcontinental railroads": "The San Francisco Committee [of One Hundred] and the Members of Board of Supervisors have been employed paving the way for such legislation as will transfer to the City full control of China and Central basins to be used for depot purposes for the several continental railroads when they reach the city."

The compromise allowed the Central Pacific to create deep-water piers in San Francisco, one at the foot of Second Street and another at the foot of King Street, as outlets for its Mission Bay terminal facilities. Williams watched with pride as the first grain shipment was loaded aboard the *Newcastle* of London on September 21, 1873, the first use of the CP wharf and the first San Francisco cargo loaded south of Canal Street. Still, the resulting facility was tiny compared to the sprawling Oakland harbor complex across the bay—even without its Goat Island annex.

Throughout the imbroglio, the public still believed there would be a single transcontinental terminal, chosen to benefit both the Central Pacific and the city lucky enough to border its real estate. But like an incomplete puzzle, all the various Central Pacific strongholds in and around San Francisco Bay still didn't add up to such a facility. As pressure from the federal government mounted to keep Goat Island out of the Central Pacific's hands, Stanford in turn pressured Williams to speed up the grading work in Mission Bay.[22]

At the same time, Stanford pressured his own engineering department to come up with faster rail access to the San Francisco Peninsula. If he couldn't forge a direct link to Mission Bay via Goat Island, he would have to create a flank attack at some less fortified bay crossing to the south.

The earliest mention of the "Ravenswood Proposal" occurred in Williams's diary on August 8, 1872, when a scheme became public to bridge San Francisco Bay at Ravenswood Point, twenty miles south of San Francisco, as a means to speed transcontinental rail access to Mission Bay. Until such a bridge became available, the Central Pacific's transcontinental trains had to continue south to San Jose before they could turn north, and then finally east, at Niles. The Committee of One Hundred endorsed the bridge and recommended to the San Francisco Board of Supervisors (in November) that the city float a $3 million bond issue to pay for it.

Speculators shadowed the Central Pacific's circumlocution. While the Ravenswood scheme was in vogue, Williams remained well-connected to a group of investors and land speculators who had purchased key tide lands in the East Bay opposite Ravenswood Point, wetlands that the Central Pacific would have to cross to reach the proposed Ravenswood bridge.

Williams's interest soon narrowed to a wind-scoured appendage of marshland called Dumbarton Point, named after the Scottish homeland of a British capital group called the California Land Investment Co., Ltd. The English company had recently purchased nearly twenty thousand acres of wetlands, including the point and its surrounding tidelands, as an experiment in a new kind of agriculture. They would attempt to reclaim the baylands, turning saltwater marsh into arable land. Small parcels of marsh, a

Early Western Pacific truss bridges across Alameda Creek (in modern Niles Canyon), ca. late 1860s. Part of the original transcontinental route from Sacramento to the Bay Area, the bridges and tight curves of Alameda Creek canyon were a bottleneck that promoted the search for alternate routes to an as yet undetermined "Pacific Terminal." Alameda Creek Canyon remained a viable route while the Ravenswood bridge scheme was in vogue; it lost favor with the emergence of the California Pacific route through Davis and Vallejo. [Left, Robert Dockery collection; below, Guy Dunscomb Collection]

At right, above, the Dumbarton Point area in 1878, showing the completed track of the South Pacific Coast; at left, an aerial view of the location today, looking west toward Dumbarton Point and the Bay. The twin pipes of the Hetch Hetchy water main closely follow the original location of the South Pacific Coast, and the Santa Clara Valley Railroad that preceded it. [Left, Bruce MacGregor]

few acres at a time, were diked to exclude the action of tides. Freshwater artesian wells were then sunk nearby and used to irrigate the enclosures.

Dumbarton Point apparently had one small pilot reclamation project under way in 1874, but most of California Land's vast holdings remained undeveloped. In these uninhabited fringes of the Bay, the caretaker of the "English company," as it was known locally, tamed the landscape by naming geographic features after his homeland. He apparently adapted the name Dumbarton from a town near Glasgow on the River Clyde, and he borrowed a companion name, Newark, from the ruins of a castle nearby. Dumbarton Point labeled the bay narrows at Ravenswood where the Central Pacific wanted to bridge the Bay; Newark labeled a town site about three miles east, envisioned as a kind of outpost and supply base for the giant land reclamation project that surrounded it.

Three smaller business entities clustered together, contained within the English company's reclamation project. They included a startup dairy called the Green Point Dairy and Transportation Co., a separately incorporated business entity that developed the town site, which was called the Newark Town and Land Association; and there was a salt company called Efford and Hall, operating on one hundred acres of land leased from the Green Point Dairy.[23]

Henry Fairfax Williams took an early interest in integrating these various schemes into a commercial unit something like Mission Bay. Many of the strategic ingredients of Mission Bay were present: a town, commercial developments, and their supporting transportation services, including direct access to deep-water shipping channels that Mission Bay lacked. Without being sure of the Central Pacific's Ravenswood plans, Williams may have tried to catalyze them. He proposed building a three-foot-gauge railroad from Dumbarton Point to neighboring communities on its uplands, linking various parts of the commercial development. Intended perhaps to whet Stanford's interest, Williams appeared to assume the mantle of narrow gauge promoter. For at least the first three miles, the route of Williams's railroad would lie virtually in the transit lines of the Central Pacific's approach to the Ravenswood bridge—securing, one argument went, the eventual interest of Leland Stanford in a partnership, or more likely a buyout.

Soon, Williams was a passenger aboard older riverboats such as the *Milton S. Latham,* bucking strong winds and tides on a number of voyages into the South Bay, exploring the site of the proposed narrow gauge project on Dumbarton Point.[24]

Out of this scenario, and perhaps conditional to its success, came a passion for narrow gauge railroad projects that seemed to deeply contradict Williams's peaceful coexistence with Leland Stanford.

With his investments concentrated at Mission Bay, the seedbed of a corporation that was rapidly on its way to controlling most of California's transportation industry, Williams began to take risks with his mentor and fellow vestryman. He became a backer of at least three narrow gauge schemes in the same time period the Mission Bay development was in its startup phase. He supported the projects openly and in full public view—and he supported them knowing they could all compete, if only within a limited range, with the Central Pacific.

Williams may have simply been trying to reinforce and diversify the economics of Mission Bay. He negotiated with Austin Moore, for example, for a retail lumber yard for the Russian River Land and Lumber Co., giving the North Pacific Coast a city outlet for its forest products. Moore was interested in siting the yard on Block 12 of Mission Bay, near Fourth and Channel streets, along with other area lumber retailers.[25] Grouping the lumber dealers made sense. It gave them access to a common shipping artery running, like a vein of salt water, through the middle of Mission Bay landfill. The lumber merchants of Channel Street would also be a centralized resource to another Williams project. Redwood from the North Pacific Coast was shipped to Williams's planing mill, where it was cut into short, square blocks for his street paving projects.[26]

Similar economic integration was in the planning stages. By June 1874, Charlie Gorrill was talking with Williams about space for a Pacific Bridge Co. yard on Block 21, further to the west near Sixth and Berry streets.[27] In 1874, two of the partners in the Dumbarton Point narrow gauge proposal, the English company and the Green Point Dairy and Transportation Co., talked to Williams about building wharves in Mission Bay as an outlet for their products and services. The same year, the Kimball Co., Ralston's shining industrial star and an early Williams client, was talking about expanding its works to a new Mission Bay site on Block 21.

But perhaps Williams had some larger venue in mind for the small businesses he patronized, sensing, if his diaries are taken as an indication, that the emerging narrow gauge movement was a critical balance wheel to the health and welfare of California business as a whole. When he toured the Central Pacific's Sacramento shops in February 1872, he reported witnessing a thousand men at work in the shops, "employed in building and repairing cars for the several roads now owned by CP Co. I was not alone pleased but astonished at the magnitude of the works, which it is evident are only now in their infancy."[28]

But in the same breath, Williams certainly had to realize that such a facility could be used to fight and win a war of attrition with Kimball. Home industry, in its infancy and a struggling infancy at that, would only succeed if a healthy, competitive business climate gave impetus to new capital and new startup businesses.

His narrow gauge promotional efforts therefore were not captive to the Mission Bay project. Williams worked as a "glue" factor in the early phases of the movement, seeking out its advocates, networking the names and resources he collected, culling and sharing sources with others of like mind. He probably met John Flint Kidder for the first time at the early meetings of the California Central Narrow Gauge Railroad Co. and struck up a friendship. They had a common friend. John Carroll worked for Williams's Potrero & Bay View in 1868, and for Kidder's Oregon Central in 1870. Perhaps Carroll was slated to do work for the CCNG once car building got started. There is no record of the company's tactical plans beyond the grading work that Kidder supervised.

Williams's first California Central Narrow Gauge meeting was noted in his diary on October 16, 1872. Soon, he was deeply involved with both the railroad and Kidder. He met frequently with U.S. Senator Cornelius Cole, CCNG's president, and recorded meetings with the railroad's directors and contractors as late as February 1874, when the contractor, unpaid, was forced to cease work. If Williams knew of the strong-arm tactics that the Central Pacific visited on Kidder's construction camp in August 1873, his diary makes no mention, but he continued diplomatic ties with both antagonists in spite of the increasing militancy of the Granger movement.

Long after the CCNG ceased construction, Williams kept in touch with Kidder. They met in Portland, Oregon, in April 1873, for an extended tour of the Northern Pacific, and Williams had ample opportunity to listen to Kidder's views on the vitality of narrow gauge technology. They had a chance to update each other on Carroll's whereabouts, and perhaps on the availability of Tom Carter, who had just taken his first independent contract for the design of the Strawberry Point Bridge in Saucelito. Kidder, Carroll, and Carter all knew each other. It is not difficult to imagine that Williams's network soon included Carter.

Stillborn, the CCNG served as a kind of clearinghouse for the growing California narrow gauge network, a source of contacts, resources, and best practices, without accomplishing the laying of a single rail. The California Central Narrow Gauge Railroad was insolvent by early 1874. But less than a year later, Williams was heavily involved in a new narrow gauge proposal, ironically named the California Narrow Gauge Railroad (not to be confused with the California *Central* Narrow Gauge Railroad), sitting astride the survey line Stanford would have to occupy to reach the Ravenswood Bridge, twenty miles south of San Francisco. The only apparent connection between the two like-named projects was the presence of Henry Fairfax Williams, self-appointed broker of the California narrow gauge movement. Through him, and perhaps because of him, the movement would begin to size up the resources required to survive a protracted conflict with Stanford's enormously powerful opposition.

By March 16, 1875, Williams was no longer just an observer of this flow of events. He filled a seat on the California Narrow Gauge Railroad board of directors.

<hr />

On May 5, 1874, Williams made a note in his diary that would grow to haunt him: "Attended auction sale of buildings on North East corner of Montgomery and Pine—few bidders—secure all but two small buildings for $1500.00, Mead House for $650.00 and Maurice Dore Auction House running clear back to California Market for $750.00 Plan to make a bundle."

Williams planned to act as a contractor to move or demolish the old buildings, and then clear and grade the land they stood on. On June 19, he reported that workers had "finished clearing lots for Flood & O'brien buildings." At which point, another contractor moved in to begin work on what would become the Nevada Block, a four-story ensemble of office suites clustered around a newly organized financial institution called the Nevada Bank of San Francisco.

Williams was probably more aware of the significance of the "Flood & O'brien" development than he let on in the diary. It was public knowledge, by the spring of 1874, that four Irish partners had unlocked a Comstock silver discovery that would fund the new bank and give it enormous leverage in California's money markets. James Flood, William O'Brien, John Mackay, and James Fair (the mine superintendent who had successfully mapped the ore body) were quickly being identified as the new financial elite in town. They were an unknown quantity to Williams. His diaries recorded no business dealing with any of them prior to house-moving work on the site of the Nevada Block. Most of the outside capital Williams counted on to develop the Mission Bay properties came from the Bank of California.

But in 1874, William Ralston's bank, already at risk from nonperforming loans from Kimball, lost more ground when Ophir mining stock, a dot com of its day, began to plunge with news that its ore boundaries did not include any part of the Flood and O'Brien discovery. The Nevada Bank was the clear heir of the wealth that would soon pour from the Consolidated Virginia Mine; to an astute financial observer like Williams, its sudden incursion should not have come entirely as a surprise.

But it seemed to. The growing influence of the Nevada Bank did not appear to weigh in to Williams's diary. He reported, during the summer of 1874, that Ralston appeared as optimistic as ever, including Williams in the early planning stages of a project that would cap his career as a San Francisco benefactor.

On August 28, 1874, Ralston asked Williams to secure Mission Bay storage for a large shipment of mahogany logs. The material would be used to build furniture and staircases in Ralston's elegant new Palace Hotel. From

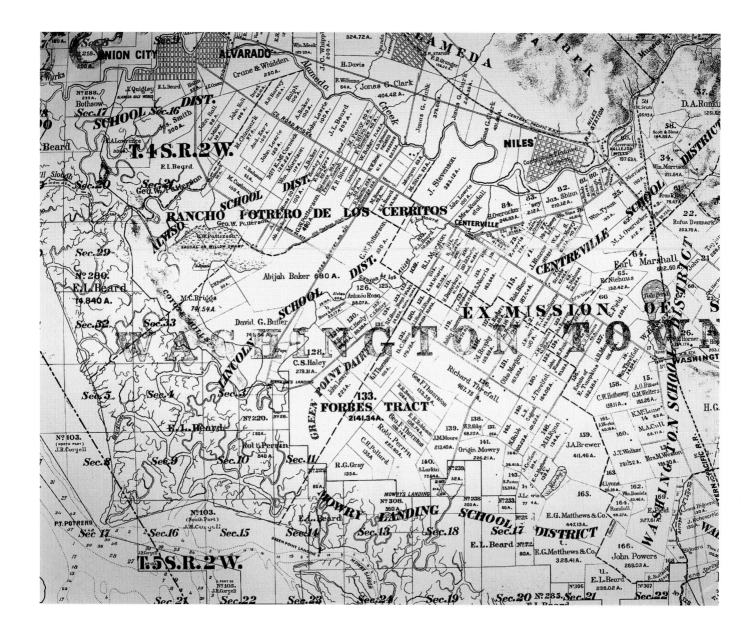

An 1874 Allerdt map of the Forbes Tract, the site of the Green Point Dairy and the future site of the town of Newark. [Robert Fisher collection]

Williams's perspective, Ralston appeared to be on the verge of turning the recession into new prosperity.

In the extreme southern waters of San Francisco Bay, two marshy promontories, called Dumbarton Point and Ravenswood Point, squeezed the navigable waters of the bay into a narrows. There, Stanford's engineers told him he could most easily build a drawbridge onto the San Francisco Peninsula, connecting the original Central Pacific mainline through Niles with its future terminal lands at Mission Bay.

The windswept wetlands were miles from the nearest settlement. Veined like a leaf with salt water sloughs, Dumbarton Point, flanking the east side of the Bay, was covered with spongy cord grass and an orange parasite called dodder. A colony of shy harbor seals had a pupping ground on the southern flank of the point, an indication that the area was still wilderness.[29]

One of the sloughs, the longest, was called Beard's Slough (or sometimes Mayhew's Slough) and was navigable nearly three miles inland to a landing where local ranchers loaded hay and grain. The captains of three-masted schooners, barks, and sloops would not hazard being trapped in the far reaches of the sloughs, even at high tide. The "creeks," as sloughs were known locally, were the province of flat-bottomed scows, a two-masted, square-nosed raft that was designed to navigate shallow water. Scows were the escape artists of the Bay. A pivoted centerboard folded into the hull on impact with a shallow bottom. Its topmost sail, called the "fisherman," unfurled from the highest mast to catch any breeze it could when the mainsail and foresail went slack in the lee of an embankment.

The scow trade into the landings of Dumbarton Point was brisk, serving the hay and grain ranches of the Mayhews, Mowrys, and Larkins much as quarter boats had done in the early days of the Spanish hide trades.

Williams's first contact with this nether region of the Bay seemed to have been through his relationship with Dr. Edward B. Perrin, perhaps as early as August 1870, when the two created a real estate package called Forbes Ranch. Perrin had practiced medicine as the chief surgeon of the Confederate Army and had come to California with his brother Robert to start a new career in real estate three years after the end of the Civil War.

Williams and Perrin seemed, in many ways, compatible. Perrin's fame in the War Between the States brought color to Williams's circle of commercial lenders and financiers. Williams helped Perrin gain access to San Francisco capital. A $31,500 loan from Lloyd Tevis "eased matters" on the Forbes deal in September 1870.[30] Perrin, in turn, required a wharf location somewhere on Mission Bay as a San Francisco outlet for the fresh milk and dairy products produced by the Green Point Dairy and Transportation Co. Tevis, along with a partner named Alfred Davis, would sell the dairy products at their booming California Market in San Francisco. Williams, of course, would benefit from the sale of wharf and warehouse lots in Mission Bay.

Williams and the Perrin brothers embraced each other's friends and associates. E. B. Perrin took on Tevis's clerk, Butler B. Minor, as a roommate in 1875. B. B. Minor, in turn, knew Tevis's partners and probably introduced Williams and Perrin to Alfred Davis, a wholesale butcher affectionately known by insiders at the California Market as "Hog" Davis.

It was the remarkable Williams glue at work again, beginning to bind layers of a complete, self-sustaining economic development plan. The Forbes tract, purchased by E. B. Perrin with Williams's help, lay just three miles inland from Dumbarton Point, surrounded by the twenty thousand acres of California Land Investment reclamation project. Dumbarton Point commanded the gateway to both the reclamation project and Stanford's Ravenswood Bridge. On December 22, 1873, Perrin incorporated the Green Point Dairy and Transportation Co. to introduce commercial dairy cows to the Forbes pasture land. Some fifteen hundred acres were involved. The corporation's name derived from a small wharf that Perrin built at Green Point, in the shallows just south of Dumbarton, not far from the colony of harbor seals. He contracted for a road from the landing to the site of the dairy on the uplands to the east.

The idea for a town may have come from the California Land Investment's overseer, J. Barr Robertson. The open, level pasture land of the Green Point Dairy became the town site of Newark. Robertson, Perrin, Williams, and a real estate broker named Charles Peters (whom Williams introduced to Perrin), were the principal organizers of a town site that would act as a nucleus for the land development projects around it. On February 27, 1875, Williams, Perrin, and Robertson walked the new town site and agreed on the direction and width of streets as well as the size of town blocks.[31] Surrounded by the herds of dairy cows, the three entrepreneurs had to watch where they stepped.

But unlike the imaginary, submerged streets of Mission Bay, Williams could touch and smell the ground he was developing at Newark. Plans sketched in dark, smoke-filled offices almost jumped off the linen maps onto the fertile ground under his feet. He visualized wide, tree-lined streets. He visualized a crescent-shaped city park, and a fish pond in a dammed section of slough. To Williams, the walk through new spring grass, with few manmade structures anywhere to be seen, was like parturition.

The same landscape made J. Barr Robertson homesick. Far from his native Scotland, coping with a sixty-day turnaround on communication with his home office in London, he was struggling with insecurities that seemed personal rather than professional. Robertson's letters capture a feeling of disorientation, bordering on helplessness, in a business context he did not completely understand.

Boarding at the Occidental Hotel in San Francisco[32] (where Williams occasionally stayed when returning late from a business trip), J. Barr Robertson probably concluded, early in their relationship, that Williams, although sympathetic, would not be a shoulder to cry on. Williams was a pragmatist with a secure place in community, family, and friends. Robertson, by himself, "left London rather hurriedly in the beginning of June [1874]," just two months after the venture capital firm was put together.[33] Unsure of his role, apparently poorly funded, he wrote letters back to the home office that vacillated between overoptimism and tantrum. But Robertson's letters make it clear that he needed Williams and Williams's important connections to the California railroad industry, if he were to survive.

Tentatively, Williams, Robertson, and Perrin began to piece together the elements of town, landing, and land reclamation project. On March 15, 1875, just two weeks after the three capitalists walked the Newark town survey, they met again in San Francisco and agreed that a narrow gauge railroad was essential to link the numerous pieces of the small, complex, muddy kingdom together.

It would grow more complex.

In just two years, 1875 and 1876, two separate land development projects, three town development projects, and three entire railroad schemes (not counting Central Pacific's Ravenswood survey) all competed for a niche on Dumbarton Point's suddenly congested uplands.

J. Barr Robertson's letter books, which are largely correspondence with his boss, J. M. Walker, in London, prove that he and Williams were the instigators of many of these overlapping business initiatives. They attended many of the same meetings, belonged to the same boards of directors, and tried to influence the same people. They appeared together, for example, at Leland Stanford's office to question him about the Central Pacific's Ravenswood Bridge campaign, the shadowy initiative that seemed to drive the smaller players in similar directions. With increasing urgency, their concerns became focused on the likelihood that Stanford would take the properties off their hands.

Stanford remained difficult to read. Williams noted a lengthy conversation with him on December 22, 1874, intended to reveal his thinking about the Ravenswood strategy but resulting only in a promise of discounted excursion tickets, which would be useful in attracting buyers to tour the Newark town site.

Still, Williams's relationship with Stanford was Robertson's best chance to leverage the investment. As 1874 drew to a close, Robertson appeared to track Stanford's whereabouts with keen interest[34]:

To J. M. Walker, London:

I observe that Stanford's name is down in the list of passengers that were to arrive by the overland train last evening, so I shall take an early opportunity of seeing him. I will place before him the [financials?] and information for his Company of building a [Central Pacific] branch from Washington Corners [today the Irvington District in Fremont] to Cariboo [an earlier name for Dumbarton Point].

Failing to induce Stanford to actually build a railroad to Dumbarton, Robertson instead began the subterfuge of creating a backfire. Perhaps, he reasoned, a perceived threat would force Stanford to protect the Central Pacific's interest from a small, irksome obstruction. Robertson needed something the right size and shape—a competing railroad scheme small enough to control, yet big enough to threaten. In a September 21, 1874, letter to Walker, he compared the usefulness of the Stockton & Ione narrow gauge with a local, Bay Area railroad proposal called the San Jose & Alviso, and concluded that "the proposed line from San Jose to Alviso and thence to Cariboo I fancy a much more [legitimate] opportunity for investment."

But instead of flame, Robertson got smolder. By the time he wrote the letter, the Stockton & Ione was insolvent. The San Jose & Alviso was the corpse of a railroad scheme dead and buried for nearly nine years. Prior to 1865, the quicksilver traffic from the New Almaden mines had commercialized a stage-steamboat connection at Alviso, just six miles north of San Jose. Alviso, the "city of sloughs," was predicted to become a sizable port and the terminal of a rail link to San Jose. As years passed, however, Alviso's sloughs breached their muddy bottoms at low tide, making the port inaccessible to larger vessels. Completion of the San Francisco & San Jose Railroad in 1865 siphoned off the quicksilver traffic and put the steamboats out of business entirely. An attempt to reorganize the railroad scheme as the Saratoga, Santa Clara & Alviso in 1868 ended with an expired charter, and a right-of-way without rail or ties.

By October 1874, however, Robertson was aware of an attempt to revive the Alviso railroad portal. By then, agribusiness had replaced quicksilver as the chief traffic along the route. Shallow-draft hay scows maneuvered up the sloughs to Alviso, offering low-cost shipping to San Francisco. San Jose's Grange movement fared poorly against cartel shipping prices for grain, hay, and seasonal fruits. But they had also watched the nearby Monterey & Salinas Valley Railroad mount an effective resistance with just eighteen miles of narrow gauge track. To respond in kind, the San Jose Grange would have to lay just six miles of track from Santa Clara to Alviso.

Robertson at last felt the heft of a potential weapon. Stanford had suffered a recent flesh wound from the M&SV, and would not be likely to underestimate the power of the Grange. Robertson was soon talking to San Jose & Alviso's leaders, including a strawberry grower named Carry Peebles.[35] He imagined Peebles would be easy to manipulate. Robertson could offer him a resource the old SJ&A lacked: a deep-water terminal at Dumbarton, if he considered extending the project twelve miles north of Alviso, passing through the Newark town site. Robertson wrote to Walker[36]: "Regarding the railway to Alviso, there are parties still talking about it, and I think really by next spring an effort will be made to have it constructed. The Dairy Co. [Perrin] offers $5000 as a bonus to the parties who are talking of it, and other [offers?] are expected. If this was decided to be constructed, we could be more independent in dealing with the Central Pacific Railroad."

Two pivotal letters, written before the close of 1874, seemed to demonstrate Robertson's guile in luring the San Jose & Alviso interests onto reclamation property. On November 25, Robertson wrote Walker to ask him for a donation of company land at Dumbarton as an inducement to third parties interested in using the point as a railroad terminal. On December 4, he notified Walker that he had taken a directorship on the Newark Town and Land Association board, the first of the town incorporations, arguing it would improve the value of their own lands.

But to Walker, viewing the increasing complexity and cost from London, the web of activity appeared fragmented, a distraction from the central thread of land reclamation. To Robertson and Williams, one part forced the next, leaving them little choice but to manage the ensemble.

But Robertson's backfire had yet to flame. Even though the prestidigitized railroad didn't need to actually lay track, or operate trains—or in any way, shape, or form become a real railroad—it had to *appear* real enough to threaten Stanford. By New Year's of 1875, Robertson's short list of potential partners had failed to commit to any of his offers. The San Jose growers continued to talk, with little action. Robertson grew impatient and thought of another subterfuge. To flame the backfire, he lit *another* backfire.

Facing similar inertia from Peters and the Newark Land Co., Robertson and Williams took matters into their own hands, incorporating the California Narrow Gauge Railroad and Transportation Co. on March 17, 1875. Its charter specifically called for construction from Dumbarton Point south to Alviso, "thence by the most practicable route to the City of Santa Clara . . . thence . . . San Jose, thence to New Almaden." Robertson may have launched the scheme simply to tweak San Jose's nose. Finally roused to action, the San Jose & Alviso would then be prodded to tweak Stanford's.

Railroad and town were quickly united. A dashed line representing the CNGRR (again, not to be confused with the CCNG) first appeared on a March–April 1875 map of the Newark town site, labeled simply "Newark and Dumbarton Railroad." It was three miles long, an umbilical between wharf and town site. The new presentation, augmenting the value of the town site with a direct rail link, attracted prestigious investors. Samuel Purdy, an ex-lieutenant governor of California, was on the board of directors, as well as Philip Caduc, financially successful president of the City Paving Co. of San Francisco. Both were, of course, friends of Williams.

On paper, the pieces came together like another compulsive sequence. The railroad and town were incorporated just one month apart (the Newark Town and Land Association on February 12, 1875; the California Narrow Gauge Railroad on March 17[37]). Only two directors overlapped between railroad and town: Williams and Robertson. But both boards of directors worked together, meeting, for example, in San Francisco on February 4, 1875, intent on advantaging one scheme from the other.

G. H. Thompson map, Newark, 1875; done for H. M. Newhall and Co., auctioneers, by the Newark Land Co. [Robert Fisher collection]

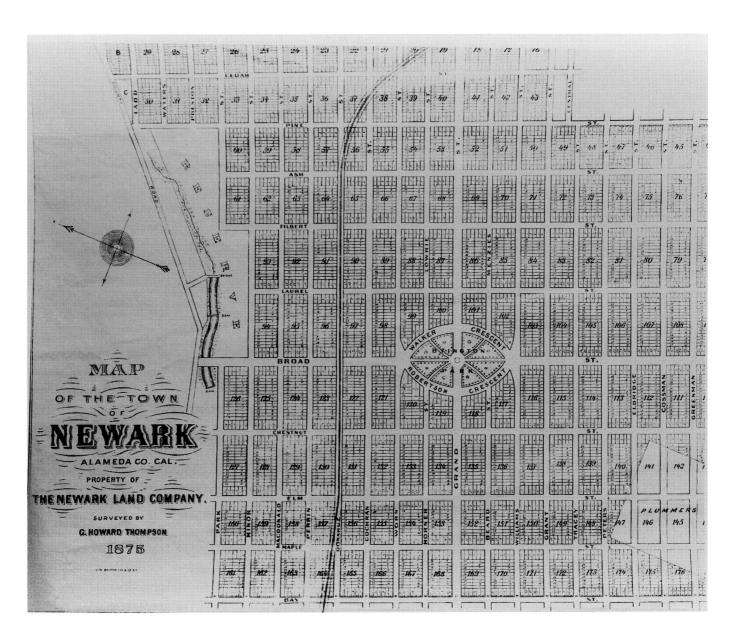

Newark Land Co. map of Newark,
March–April 1875. [Robert Fisher
collection]

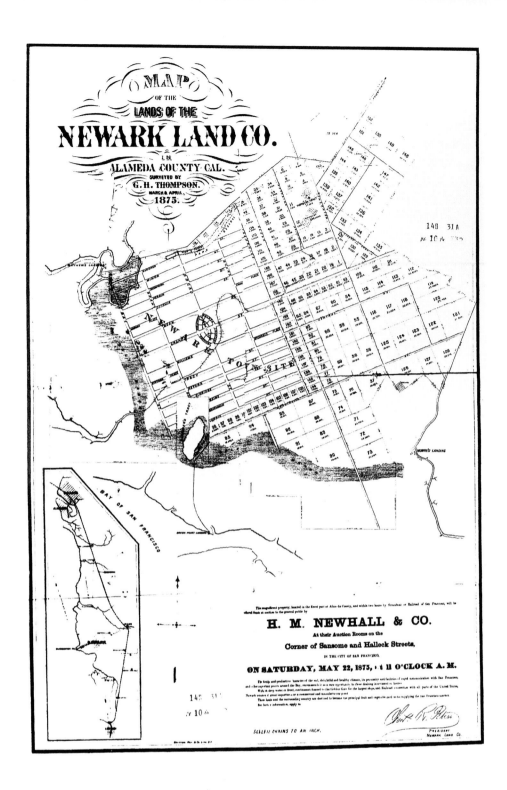

Williams invested small sums in the town site,[38] but he seems to have
grown wary of Robertson's paper railroads: "Met with Peters and Worn to
discuss Newark. Already talked to Robertson and Howland and got their
latest RR items. Want of concerted action seems likely to prevent the immediate building of RR which to my mind is all important to insure success of
Newark but Peters can not see it in that light."[39]

Williams, no rank amateur, was made to feel like one. For want of technical expertise, none of the interlocking business groups had any working

knowledge of railroads. A good example was its misguided motive power strategy, which appeared prominently in the California Narrow Gauge Railroad's incorporation papers. By specifying that the forty-mile-long railroad would be powered "in whole or part by means or horses" the board had bid to become a laughing stock.

From Walker's perspective, land reclamation and farming, the original focus of the English company, appeared to languish in favor of town and railroad developments. The previous fall, Robertson retained a contractor named Lillie and a small Chinese crew to complete levees and two artesian wells near Dumbarton Point, intended as a pilot reclamation project.[40] But after impounding twelve hundred acres, "all unnecessary" reclamation work was suspended in May, when Robertson appeared to concentrate his interest on lot sales at the Newark town site.

Town manager Charles Peters actively advertised public excursions to view the town site, but he drew criticism for sham and misrepresentation. In a March 5, 1875, advertisement in the *San Francisco Call,* for example, Peters promised he would soon haul a thousand people "by steamboat and railroad," which raised false expectations that a railroad would be in operation from Dumbarton Point. Even more disturbing were ads aimed at the investment potential of the Newark Town and Land Association, which, Peters claimed, for as little as $300 per share could "double your capital and no risk."[41]

Squabbles within the association multiplied Robertson's complaints to Walker. On July 9, 1875, Robertson wrote the London office that "I fear in my next I shall have to writ a short & simple tale of woe regarding Newark, altho' the clouds are clearing off . . . I hope within a week to inform you of a new plan of action involving I hope a change in the management."

Instead of slow, methodical progress on land reclamation, Robertson began to bend to pressure to turn a quick profit on real estate. While the association tried to muster the courage to fire Peters, the cost of the Newark development appeared to be rising out of control, resulting in an $1,827.60 assessment Robertson was obliged to pay himself. Half of the assessment he advanced in Walker's name—no doubt giving Walker new cause for apprehension.

The first public auction of Newark lands was held on May 22, 1875, by Williams's friend and occasional partner in Mission Bay land sales, H. M. Newhall. But the auction, according to Williams, "I regret to record was not so great a success as anticipated. About ⅓ of the property was bid off and then the sale was postponed till another day. All hands had to admit that the course pursued by Peters had been bad. His style of advertising had brought the enterprise into ridicule."

There was little of material value to show for the investment. The town site itself contained nothing but Perrin's dairy barns and the milker's dormitory (called the "cookhouse"). Under pressure from the board of directors, Peters constructed a large, permanent wharf at Dumbarton Point, where the narrow gauge, at least in theory, would reach deep water and a connection to boats faster than the *Milton S. Latham*. But except for the wharf, no trace of the California Narrow Gauge Railroad existed.

The new wharf was finished in the first or second week of June 1875.[42]

Its original dimensions are unknown, but it may have been built to its 1878 size of nearly two hundred feet on a side, a structure large enough to be a platform for a 50' × 200' warehouse and a small railroad yard, a facility that would be in operation by December 1875.[43] Early engineering work on the wharf, however, was hit and miss. Its artesian well, required by the *Latham* and other steamboats to replenish boiler water, had been incorrectly located by Lillie. Instead of drilling it at the mooring, he located it back on shore. Robertson whined to Walker on April 30: "At the Wharf it [the well] would have been the property of Newark [Land Association], where it is it will belong to us. However, the blunder cannot be remedied, and tho' very annoying now that we are daily waiting to have water at the shore so that steamers may get fresh water, & there is the well being sunk I fancy a quarter of a mile off."

Short on funds and becoming more desperate for results, Robertson wrote to the mayor of San Jose on August 10, 1875, and copied Walker:

> Hon: Mayor Murphy
> San Jose
>
> Sir,
> I observe from the San Jose papers that you are taking a leading interest in the project for a Narrow Gauge Railway from San Jose or a point further south to deep water on the Bay of San Francisco. As the representative here of the above Company owning 20,000 acres of marshland beginning on the eastern bank of Steamboat Slough in which Alviso is situated, & running eastward & then northward along the Bay, I desire to point out to you that there is no deep water point to which you can carry a Railway short of Dumbarton Point opposite Ravenswood, & called Potrero Point on the Coast Survey Map. An examination of the water of the Bay will show that for large steamers or seagoing vessels there is no safe navigation for more than two miles south of Dumbarton Point, whereas at this point there is ample depth of water for the largest vessels, and from this Point to San Francisco, there is an excellent & safe navigable channel superior to that between San Francisco & Vallejo. I hope therefore that you may be pleased to examine into the merits of this question of a Railway Terminus at Dumbarton Point where there is already a substantial Wharf, as I am satisfied that it [is] the most desirable place that can be found.

Mayor Murphy obligingly introduced Robertson to Major Henry Bartling, ex-president of the Kansas Pacific Railroad, retained by Carry Peebles and a citizens' committee to investigate revitalization of the old San Jose & Alviso project. On August 16, Robertson reported to Walker that he and Dr. Perrin had met Bartling and taken him for a tour around Dumbarton Point: "the effort now being made [by Bartling] looks more like business than anything that I have seen yet; and I think we shall see the construction [of the railroad] begin soon."

Robertson's secondary backfire, it appeared, had finally ignited the main backfire.

It quickly became clear that Major Bartling was in control of a railroad scheme that would span, north to south, the twenty thousand acres that J. Barr Robertson was haphazardly trying to promote. Bartling seemed to bring integration to the various plots and subplots that Robertson imagined. It was also clear, after a successful local fundraising meeting at Centerville on September 13, that Bartling was able to spread some of the financial responsibility for his promotion from the San Jose constituency to the farming and ranching communities upland from Dumbarton. The exchange for Bartling had therefore became parasitic: he would remove the old California Narrow Gauge Railroad as a competitive threat, while appropriating its financial backing, as well as its superior landing on Dumbarton Point.

Bartling's Santa Clara Valley Railroad Co., incorporated on October 4, 1875, took over the old San Jose & Alviso prospectus, claimed the options on rights-of-way, and extended the survey to Robertson's deep-water landing at Dumbarton. In addition, Bartling proposed an extension to Santa Cruz, an expensive piece of track that would not, Bartling added under his breath, be built until the fifteen-mile trunk line to Dumbarton was completed. Robertson hardly cared. The California Land Investment Co.'s interests would be protected in the first fifteen miles of track laid to the north of Santa Clara.

In exchange for resources primarily in land and right-of-way, Bartling promised the action that Robertson desperately needed, an operating railroad between Dumbarton and Newark, since it was the vital link to town lot sales. Railroad grading would begin first on Dumbarton Point and then extend south toward Alviso and San Jose. For the first fifteen miles of its route, the Santa Clara Valley Railroad would rim California Land Investment Co. property, enhancing the value of its land reclamation project.

But in spite of the real progress on the railroad, by the fall of 1875 Robertson was embarrassingly short of cash. He was moonlighting as a stock broker, acting as a commission agent for the Best and Belcher, the Ophir, and the California mines—for the most part, stocks on the decline. Even as the crucial railroad development seemed within reach (construction actually began on September 30), he grew preoccupied with the Comstock excitement, trying to raise capital to buy mining stocks from several London business partners.

Distracted by the mining speculation, Robertson wrote a truly incredible letter to Walker on August 27, 1875. He alleged that silver ore had been discovered in the Coyote Hills, bordering their company's lands just three miles from Dumbarton Point. He proposed to name the lode the "Glasgow Mining District." Three days later, a following letter reported assay tests that alleged two point three ounces of silver per ton of ore, bearing a commercial value of $3 per ton. If Robertson's claims were true, the Coyote Hills strike represented the only known commercial silver discovery in the San Francisco Bay Area. More than likely, it represented a hoax.

His letters to Walker grew stranger. On September 11, Robertson fabricated a connection between the silver, the Santa Clara Valley Railroad, and his own plans for the future:

> [I plan] to return thursday evening, by which time I expect to have all the hills immediately behind Dumbarton bonded. I think the Rly. people [Bartling] will want the Newark people to do more than they possibly can in the way of finding money, and there will be a temporary hitch in the negotiations. If so, it is my idea to change the name of Newark to Glasgow & incorporate the Dumbarton & Glasgow Junction Railway, then to let out my secret about the gold & silver ore (if on further examination after the bond is signed I find there is abundance of ore there) and insist on the Railway going on our embankment up Beard's Creek. . . . the Alameda [County] farmers have subscribed about $15,000 for the other project [the CNGRR], & if I find the mines there that I think there are, I will make a move to try to bond the shares in the Rly. they are prepared to take for a period of twelve months & by this & other means try to control the Railway. Fact is, I expect they will turn over their $15,000 to my project. The San Jose people can then have running powers over it down to the Point.

Briefly resuscitated, the vestige of the California Narrow Gauge Railroad gave Robertson the illusion of controlling the "San Jose people." A strong arm grip on the railway, in Robertson's thinking, would give him new leverage over the town project. On October 6, he wrote to Walker: "The Newark scheme is the only one into which I have really put any money since coming here, and it has cost me at least £1000 beyond my income to keep things going . . . the narrow gauge railway is getting up a party (with reporters) to go over and see the quartz ledge on Walker's property, and the field of rly. [railway] operations, before launching our new Newark scheme."

News of the alleged silver strike appeared in the *Oakland Tribune* on October 11: "Samples assayed and pronounced profitable for mining."

It was the first, and last, public notice to appear about Robertson's "Glasgow Mining District." Robertson never mentioned the mines again to Walker.

Major Henry Bartling, meanwhile, kept his promise. On the last day of September 1875, forty scraper teams and a hundred laborers began to mound a three-mile embankment between the new wharf at Dumbarton Point and "Dairy Ranch," the headquarters of the Green Point Dairy and Transportation Co. A pile foundation for a single drawbridge across Beard's Slough was begun. The wharf was probably extended to its built-out dimensions of two hundred feet on a side, and a substantial car house started, an imposing fifty by two hundred feet in outside dimensions. A 24' × 36' depot building was erected where the railroad grade intersected the Newark town site.[44]

By early November, two hundred Chinese were added to the work force. A pile driver, completing work on the Beard's Slough bridge, was floated into position on Warm Springs Slough to begin work on bridges that would

carry the line across its remotest location, the site of the future outpost of Drawbridge, and onto dry uplands at Alviso. From there, the survey called for just six additional miles of track, dead level and nearly straight, to reach Santa Clara.

In contrast to this energetic image of fast moving construction, there is evidence that in the earliest stages of the project the Santa Clara Valley practiced slipshod, perhaps intentionally impermanent, and even illegal construction methods. Efford and Hall's 160 acres of salt beds, leased from Perrin's Green Point Dairy, were the object of two years of legal action when its owners filed for injunction to stop the railroad from crossing, and damaging, its evaporating ponds. Affidavits were developed from Noah Efford, testifying about the intrusion of Santa Clara Valley Railroad graders into the salt works in October 1875:

> In said month of October, 1875, affiant Hall did receive a telegram
> from said Anderson, and said Hall thereupon went to said premises,
> and there stated to one Derby, the engineer of said company in charge
> of its men, that affiants had a lease of said lands, and that said com-
> pany must not enter thereon, and forbade him to enter thereon for any
> purpose; that, nevertheless, after the said Hall had returned [to San
> Francisco], the said company proceeded forcibly, wrongfully, illegally,
> and without the consent of affiants, to partially grade their roadbed
> across said land and works, which occupied but a few days, when
> withdrew from said premises.[45]

John Plummer's Crystal Salt Works, a pioneer solar evaporation plant, predated development of the town at Newark, whose town center and railroad depot would be located just a mile to the north. Crystal Salt Works was still in production in 1884 (above).

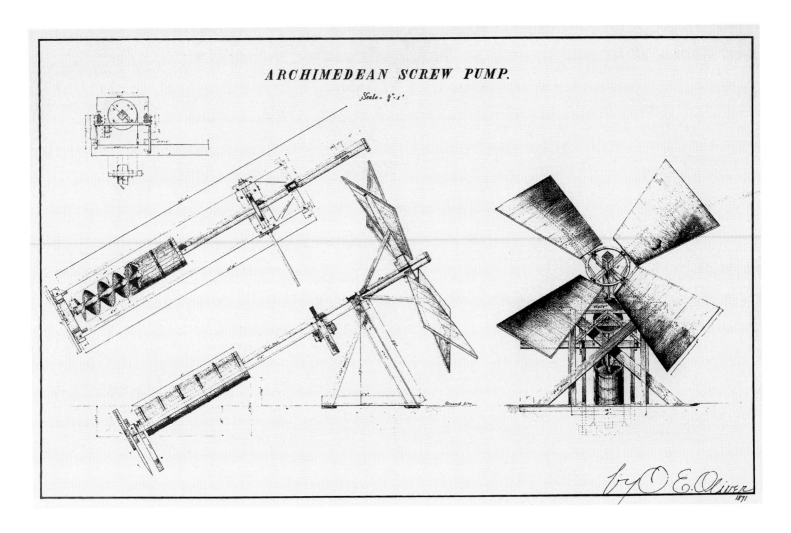

ARCHIMEDEAN SCREW PUMP.

Scale = ¾"·1'

by O. E. Oliver
1871

Power for the early San Francisco Bay salt industry was largely provided by wind. In the line drawing above, an 1895 design for a windmill pump was based on the principle of the Archimedes screw. Such pumps had been in use in the Bay Area since the 1860s. [Cargill Co.]

Countercharges were also introduced as affidavits, claiming that the salt company's manager, Anderson, had willingly lent shovels to the Santa Clara Valley workers to assist in the grading work. But the charges and countercharges did not call into question the railroad's crude methods, nor its unfinished work. The evidence supports the belief that the Santa Clara Valley Railroad grade on Dumbarton Point was, just a few weeks after the work started, unfinished, perhaps abandoned.

Henry Bartling was fighting similar battles just a few hundred yards to the west of the salt company. On December 17, 1875, the *San Francisco Bulletin* described a legal skirmish between the Santa Clara Valley and the owners of Mayhews Landing:

> This morning H. Bartling, President of the Santa Clara [Valley] Railroad Company, appeared before Judge Wheeler to show cause why he should not be fined for contempt of court. It appeared from the statement of counsels on either side, that President Bartling had control of a squad of workmen, overseers and a civil engineer who were engaged in building a bridge across Mayhew's [Beard's] Landing Creek, thirty-eight miles from this city. Complaint was made that the driving of piles and the building of a central or pivot pier, on which to swing the draw, obstructed the navigation of the stream, and the Court issued an order restraining the progress of the work for the time being. Counsel for the

complaining parties [Francis Jarvis] set forth that Mr. Bartling . . . had ordered his workmen to proceed after the order of the Court had been served upon him to suspend operations. On the other hand counsel for the Company maintained that no work tending to increase the obstruction had been ordered. . . . the court accepted the explanation, and purged Mr. Bartling of contempt.

Watching his budget drain away, encountering legal contests seemingly in every mile of track he built, Bartling may have resorted to hit-and-run tactics, hoping to build a more permanent right-of-way once the legal challenges were resolved and funds became available.

But to Bartling's credit, he also appeared to be actively negotiating for critical supplies the railroad would need once it could guarantee its right-of-way. In late October, the railroad signed a contract with Abraham Weaver of Santa Cruz for fifty-five thousand ties. The contract called for six-foot redwood ties, six inch face and five inches deep, delivered at Alviso on or before December 1.[46] A contract for rail was signed with Pacific Rolling Mills of San Francisco, the first lot slated for delivery on December 12.[47] The contract called for seven hundred tons of thirty-five-pound iron, enough to lay slightly more than eleven miles of track, which would easily span the distance from Dumbarton Point through Newark to the Warm Springs Slough.[48]

On November 6, the *San Francisco Bulletin* reported a car contract had been signed just as work on the Dumbarton Point wharf and car shed was completed: "The Santa Clara Valley Railroad Company closed a contract on November 2d with T. Carter, of San Francisco, for two first-class passenger cars, two baggage and express cars, ten box cars, ten platform cars, one hand car, and two iron cars. A portion of the above cars are to be delivered by December 20th."

Tom Carter was now enjoying referrals within the small, fraternal narrow gauge community. Young Benjamin Franklin Williams, quit from the Santa Cruz & Felton as its construction superintendent, took the same position with the Santa Clara Valley Railroad on or about November 1, 1875. Williams was in an unusually good position to recommend Carter to Henry Bartling. Terms would be similar to the Santa Cruz & Felton contract, its second batch of cars then under production and slated for delivery in December. Williams understood Carter's business strategy and convinced the scv's resident engineer, Ellis L. Derby, that the kit approach would be ideal for the Santa Clara Valley. It was one of the few parts of the project that were immune from the heavy rains that began that November. Car parts and workmen were landed by boat on Dumbarton Point. Their work continued under cover even when the marsh roads back to the Green Point dairy barns and "cookhouse" grew impassable. Supplies would continue to reach Dumbarton Point by boat.

By November 11, Frank Geiser, the Carter field boss experienced on the Monterey & Salinas Valley work, moved into the Dumbarton Point car shed; it was a sign that assembly of freight car kits was starting.[49] By the

The Field Notebook: The Search for the Santa Clara Valley

Two significant clues survive to suggest what kind of cars Carter built for the Santa Clara Valley Railroad. No known photographs exist of narrow gauge equipment lettered for the Santa Clara Valley. But ten boxcars, believed to have been built for the scv, show up in the South Pacific Coast roster of 1888, the first year spc cars were reported in the *Railway Equipment Register*. The boxcars carry even numbers 2–20. They are listed with dimensions of early Carter cars: 24' long and 7'11" wide, appearing to match the group of ten boxcars listed on the spc roster in June 1876, just after the takeover from the Santa Clara Valley. The 1892 *Railway Equipment Register* lists these as ten-ton capacity cars, probably upgraded from original eight-ton.

Evidence of passenger cars that Carter intended to deliver to the Santa Clara Valley is more difficult to substantiate. There is a single photograph of a six-window combination car numbered 1, derelict, in use as the Le Franc depot in 1913. Although it looks like an 1882 South Pacific Coast caboose (see caboose 47, Appendix B) the Le Franc car includes a number oval plate—a detail reserved for passenger cars, not cabooses—as well as small variations in its letterboard and roof design that suggest the car may be a throwback to an earlier Carter design period.

Together, these facts suggest Carter was, at least in part, building 1874 designs for the scvrr in 1875.

A forerunner of the Baldwin class 8-18 C, the South Pacific Coast's number 1 (above) was an earlier, lighter version that bore the class number 8-14 C. Its unusual cab roof, in what was called the omnibus style, was considered obsolete by Baldwin and discontinued after 1875. The Santa Clara Valley Railroad originally ordered the locomotive in November 1875, with money borrowed from several Newark area landowners. [Vernon Sappers collection]

time Geiser was in position to start work, the shed contained two parallel tracks each two hundred feet long, the biggest car shop a Carter project had ever occupied.

It is possible that the freight car kits were produced in a new San Francisco facility (a topic to be taken up in detail in the next chapter). But Carter's work on SCV passenger cars was staged in the still-occupied Saucelito shop. We know this because the following April the North Pacific Coast would lease the car float *Transfer* and its tugboat *Tiger* to bring the cars from Saucelito to Dumbarton. En route, the flotilla picked up the line's first locomotive at the dock in San Francisco and then transported a virtually complete passenger train almost forty-five miles through the choppy waters of the South Bay. The North Pacific Coast cash books recorded the date: April 30, 1876. The barge fee was a hefty $500. Clearly, the delivery was later than the Santa Clara Valley contract dates first stipulated.

Some bridge work may have been included in the first Carter contract. Carter might have been the design engineer for the Beard's Slough (also known as Mayhew's Slough) bridge, the project that nearly earned Henry

Bartling a contempt of court ruling. The earliest extant Carter mechanical drawing is for one of the three drawbridges in the first twelve miles of track —one over Beard's Slough and two at windswept Station Island just north of Alviso, all believed to be identical in design. The drawing, unfortunately, is labeled for the South Pacific Coast Railroad, not its predecessor, the Santa Clara Valley. It does not designate the location of the bridge, and it bears no date.

We do know that the Santa Clara Valley Railroad order helped swell Carter's December workload at Saucelito to what appears to be a high point for the year 1875. It probably included Nevada County Narrow Gauge and Santa Cruz & Felton kits, as well as assembly of Barney and Smith flatcar kits for the North Pacific Coast itself. The cash books recorded debits the NPC charged Carter for "power, materials and fuel" involved in outside contract manufacture, a crude indication of Carter's production volume. In December 1875, the month when most of the Santa Clara Valley work was likely to have been done, the debit was $256.11, roughly equivalent to burning seventy-three cords of wood in the shop's stationary engine; this is a good indication that the small Carter crew was working overtime on kits, including those for the Santa Clara Valley.[50]

But the Santa Clara Valley work also marked a danger point in the trends of Carter's business. Even though the month of December was the busiest production month for Carter at Saucelito, at least two of the three customers were so small that no follow-up orders for additional freight equipment were likely. The possibility for new or expanded work now rested solely on the Santa Clara Valley Railroad. The Santa Clara Valley, in turn, was probably not, at the time of the proposed deliveries, in a position to pay Carter for the work it had ordered. On January 29, 1876, the *Alameda Independent* reported grimly that "law suits against the Santa Clara Valley Railroad at Newark have resulted from lack of funds to pay for work." As a result, except for the assembled flatcar kits stranded on Dumbarton Point, Carter was forced to stop delivery on the Santa Clara Valley Railroad cars he had produced.

Consequently, production work at Saucelito nearly ground to a halt after New Year's 1876. Moving forward through the first three months of 1876, the succession of cash book debits billed to Carter as "power, materials and fuel" dropped dramatically. From the high of $256.11 in December, the debits dropped to $89.76 in January, $25.94 in February, and $22.94 in March. That winter was likely to have been remembered as the low point in the fortunes of the small startup manufactory.

Uncertain of the Santa Clara Valley's future, Thomas and Martin began the winter months by burning December's enormous pile of trimmings for heat.

Without the allure of a local silver mine, even without a locomotive, even without rail and ties, the frenetic pace of Bartling's activity convinced J. Barr Robertson, in late October 1875, that train service to the new town site of Newark was imminent. On October 20, he wrote Walker:

The Field Notebook:
The South Pacific Coast's One Spot

A forerunner of the popular and widespread Baldwin 8-18 C class American, the engine that became South Pacific Coast number 1 was an 8-14 C, a lighter version of the 8-18 C, built from a specification drawn up by Baldwin on Feb. 22, 1875. Built as the *Jefferson City* for the Missouri Central, the engine went undelivered until diverted to the "Newark & San Jose," to quote the Baldwin order sheet, in November 1875. Revisions were made to the original spec sheet on November 4: wood replaced soft coal, and a Radley and Hunter stack replaced the original diamond stack. In other areas of her design, she was a throwback to more primitive standards: crosshead pumps, with no backup injectors, required the engine to move to replace boiler water, and there were no engine brakes—only hand brakes on the tender. The engine's finish was exquisite, including a painted ash cab and a winecolored (crimson) finish in Baldwin's classic style number 1. But there were inconsistencies in the Baldwin spec sheet. The specified road name "Newark & San Jose" was not the corporation's true name (Santa Clara Valley Railroad), and its Missouri Central road name, *Jefferson City*, was now irrelevant, but not erased.

The engine went undelivered to her owners until April 1876, when the South Pacific Coast had her transported to Dumbarton Point on the North Pacific Coast barge *Transfer.*

I may state that the railway will be running from Dumbarton to Newark on November 20, and already we have had sufficient applications for land to cause us to put our MINIMUM price at $200 per acre. We can easily get $50–$100 per acre more now with the Railway than we could without, & our MAXIMUM price for town lots near the Railway is $100 or allowance being made for streets $600 per acre. This afternoon we are advertising for the first time, and I have not the slightest particle of doubt that before November 30, the time of our public sale we shall have sold land enough to make our minimum price of $250 or $300 per acre. . . .

Every acre at Newark will be sold at large profit. Believe me,

Yours very sincerely,

Squabbling, however, continued to unsettle the board meetings of the Newark Town and Land Association. On February 12, 1875, its board voluntarily reorganized, attempting, as Robertson hinted, to clean out the dirty laundry of internal disagreement. Reorganized as the Newark Land Co., the board next attempted to market Newark through the California Immigrant Union, a Central Pacific–sponsored referral agency for new settlers. Tacitly, the Newark town development was operating with the Central Pacific's blessing, a step Robertson had imagined leading to a lucrative buyout from Stanford. But acrimony seemed to persist inside the town association, frequently pitting the new president, C. Mitchell Grant, against the old one, Charles Peters, who was still on the board. Robertson, it is evident from his letters, disliked them both.

Agricultural experiments continued on reclaimed marsh. Robertson assessed methods of plowing the leached silt on company land at Alviso, while on Dumbarton Point, he reported to Walker on October 20, "I am going to try to have some sort of vegetables growing there by November 20 when the trains begin to run."

Just a week later, however, Robertson confessed to Walker that the land sale had been delayed by ten days. By the date of the sale, November 30, it had been raining nonstop for a week. By the middle of January, eleven inches of rain had fallen. Robertson's vegetable patch lay submerged in a fresh water lake impounded inside the company's own levees. Chinese grading crews huddled in shacks in Alviso, watching the hastily bladed right-of-way dissolve in the downpour. No ties had arrived and no rail had been laid. By December 1, Robertson noted in a letter to Walker that the land sale had been postponed until January 6.

Other cracks were developing in the plan, suggesting the railroad's cash flow problems began earlier than the press reports suggested. Sometime in November, Robertson received a visit from Ruben Coldren, a director of the Santa Clara Valley Railroad and an emissary from Henry Bartling. Coldren tried to talk enthusiastically of the coming land sale and the role the narrow gauge would play in making it a success, but in the process he also extorted money. As Robertson reconstructed the conversation in a letter to Bartling on December 27, it was the first clear proof that the Santa Clara Valley Railroad was in financial trouble: "Dr. Perrin and I [Robertson] bought the engine needed to complete the work on Mr. Coldren's representation that if it was obtained the cars would certainly be running on [January] 6th & we hope that there will be no such thing as failure seeing that so much depends on it."[51]

Overextended on grading, rolling stock, bridges, and buildings, Coldren argued that the SCV could not procure a locomotive in time for the Newark Land sale—unless, Coldren no doubt struck a note of hope—the officers of the Newark Land Co. were willing to pay for it. Bartling already had an engine on order, an 8-14 C class Baldwin 4-4-0 that had been sitting in the factory for nine months, unclaimed by its original buyer, the Missouri Central. Baldwin records show that the Santa Clara Valley Railroad's order had been received at the factory by November 4, 1875, when the builder went to work on a short list of modifications, including fuel conversion from coal to wood and the addition of a Radley and Hunter stack. The work, apparently, was ordered by Bartling.

To take delivery, however, Robertson and Perrin would have to pay a San Francisco agent a significant sum, probably in the vicinity of $7,500. To Robertson, already in debt over the Newark land scheme, the added burden was painful. But Ruben Coldren was persuasive. Everything now depended on the locomotive. Either in partnership with Perrin (as Robertson would later testify) or perhaps under the name of the "Newark & San Jose" Railroad (as the Baldwin order sheet testified), Robertson rescued the railroad's sole locomotive from hock. The heroics, however, would apparently fall short of the deadline. The first mention of the locomotive's arrival in San Francisco came on January 27, 1876, a full three weeks after the intended date of the land sale.[52] The miss was as good as a mile. By late January, there was still no rail to run on.

The railroad's troubles were not confined to locomotives. Carter, whose delivery of cars would not have been adversely affected by weather, had committed to deliver enough passenger equipment by the end of December to provide cars for the January 6 land sale. Unable to collect the price, however, Carter did not move the cars from Saucelito.

In a last-ditch effort to raise money, Bartling engineered a mortgage bond issue, underwritten by the newly chartered Nevada Bank. Five hundred fifty first mortgage bonds were to be issued on January 1, 1876, placing the bank in first position as mortgage holder over $400,000 of bonded indebtedness. The bonds themselves were printed but apparently never issued. Instead, the Nevada Bank would exercise its mortgage position by compelling Bartling to cede control of the railroad. The public, and J. Barr Robertson, apparently knew nothing of the Nevada Bank's first mortgage, or the power it would soon influence over the struggling Santa Clara Valley Railroad.

Sometime during the holidays, Robertson probably grasped the catastrophe that had befallen the Santa Clara Valley. In a December 27 letter to Bartling, he expressed belief that the January 6 land sale was possible and that the railroad would play a part. On December 31, however, he acknowledged to Walker that "the sale of the Newark property has not taken place yet; but we expect it to take place on the 6th proc. tho' the Railroad will not be completed for a week later."

On the last day of the year, he pretended that Walker would take pity,

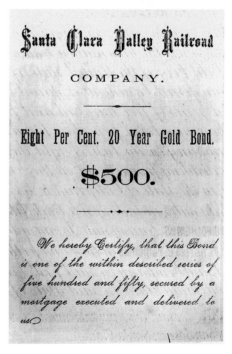

Details from Santa Clara Valley Railroad first mortgage gold bond. [John Schmale collection]

copying this letter to London into his letter book: "I am much obliged to you for the assistance you have rendered me personally & for your kindness in protecting my interests . . . and I may state in conclusion that tho' my connection with the California Land Investment Co. is likely to terminate disastrously for myself, I feel particularly assured that you & your friends will have every reason yet to congratulate yourselves on having made the investment."

Three weeks later, Robertson's connection to the Santa Clara Valley Railroad did indeed end disastrously when Major Bartling began selling off the railroad's assets. They included Robertson and Perrin's locomotive. Reaching his limit, Robertson wrote to Bartling on January 21:

> Dear Sir;
> I was very much surprised this morning to learn that you had given a
> Bill of Sale on the Engine belonging to Dr. Perrin and myself, an Engine
> for which we paid personally & which never was your property nor
> that of the Railroad Co.
>   I now beg to intimate to you that if I find in taking the necessary
> steps to ascertain the facts, that by your act the Engine belonging to
> Dr. Perrin & myself is detained by other parties, I shall place the matter
> in the hands of my lawyer so that he may deal with the whole question
> on its merits.
>   There are limits to our forbearance as you will probably find out,
> & it seems to me that the limit has been reached.

The "other parties" that Robertson refers to were agents of the Nevada Bank, moving quietly to consolidate their possession of anything they believed the Santa Clara Valley Railroad owned. Two weeks later, the press would know their names.

It continued to rain throughout most of February 1876, contributing to Robertson's melancholy.

———

Henry Fairfax Williams, meanwhile, appears to have withdrawn a safe distance from the troubles of the Santa Clara Valley Railroad and the Newark Land Co. He attended meetings of the land company fairly regularly, the last recorded meeting on February 7, 1876, which was deep into Robertson's troubled winter. The two businessmen grew further apart. The slow sales of Newark land at the May 1875 auction had not picked up substantially by fall, and Williams awaited completion of the Santa Clara Valley Railroad to "infuse new life into the locality," as he noted hopefully in his diary on September 3, 1875.

That summer, Williams was distracted by troubles of his own. Investments in Mission Bay continued to be disappointing. His planing mill on Fourth Street burned the night of May 9, 1875, with an estimated $25,000–30,000 loss, including the loss of the personal tools of his workmen. The next morning, Williams opened a line of credit at Resakrans, a local hardware store, allowing his men to buy new tools and return to work.

But Williams also noted, the same day, that "Ralston does not recommend rebuilding but to let [the] ground to lumber dealers"; it was an indication of constricting credit at the Bank of California and evidence that even for close friends, Ralston's deep pockets had zippers.

Some of Ralston's visions were becoming reality. Kimball, that September, was turning out carriages and coupes to equip the nearly completed Palace Hotel. Ralston's West Coast Furniture Manufacturing Co., occupying space in the original Kimball building, was turning the mahogany logs stored at Mission Bay into chairs "of the square pattern, massive and upholstered in blue and green velvet plush" and tables "marble topped and of neat and unique design, while the bedsteads are sufficiently massive to give assurance that they would not tumble down the first time they were slept on. There is an appearance of solidity about every article."[53]

But Ralston's fortunes were not so solid. The news had leaked to the press the previous January that a deep-running silver vein marbled through the heart of the Consolidated Virginia Mine, owned by Fair, Flood, Mackay, and O'Brien. There was no trace of the vein in Ralston's Ophir mine. The public was soon being treated to estimates that the Con Virginia strike might contain as much as half a billion dollars in a single ore body, an estimate that drove its stock prices to $800 a share.[54] As a result, Ophir stock plummeted.

Literally preparing the vaults to hold the Consolidated Virginia's treasure, Henry Fairfax Williams cleared land for the Nevada Bank that summer, and by the first of September 1875 he was watching the four-story office complex near completion. From news reports, he knew that its owners, Fair, Flood, Mackay, and O'Brien, planned on opening the bank the first of October.

With warning signs everywhere, Williams's diary gives almost no indication of the real trouble Ralston was in.

Openly critical of speculation in mining stock and its debilitating effects on California manufacturing, Williams himself turned to the darker side of the California economy. Unable to balance his own monthly cash flows on Mission Bay, he began to pin his hopes on reports of a silver strike that he imagined helping discover. On October 8, 1875, Williams noted, on loose-leaf pages, a meeting with a Professor Paraf in downtown San Francisco. He told Paraf an appealing story of self-discovery. While the Central Pacific Railroad was widening the old Potrero & Bay View horsecar cut at Potrero Point, Williams was acting as contractor, ensuring that rock loosened by blasting would wind up as fill in Mission Bay and in the bulkhead under construction along Channel Street. During the excavation, a foreman—perhaps James Graves—was attracted to a discoloration in rock samples from the cut. The samples had come to Williams, and Williams engaged Professor Paraf and his assistant, Engine Levy, in running assays. The tests, Williams at first quoted Paraf, "turn out quite satisfactorily."[55]

Soon Williams was gathering rock samples from the cut himself, delivering them to Paraf, and returning to the cut for more. Paraf encouraged him. The assays were reporting silver and gold in commercial concentrations. More tests, for which Paraf charged modest fees, would be required before the Potrero could be proven as a lode. Williams grew more animated about "the project," imagining a silver discovery virtually on the front door step of the Mission Bay development. Such a discovery, he wrote on loose-leaf on October 16, could make him wealthy and "do an immense amount of good."

On October 19, even before he told his wife, Williams noted that he had confided the discovery to his friend Leland Stanford. That day, the two spent all afternoon at Paraf's lab, the first of many long sessions the governor and his contractor would pass in staring, transfixed, at the white-hot interior of Paraf's assay oven. Stanford seemed captivated by the process and himself ground the sample to fine powder, added flux, and reduced the mixture in a ceramic crucible. He eagerly hefted the small metallic buttons remaining when the crucible cooled, and took pleasure in their authenticity.

With Paraf's help, both Williams and Stanford learned to run the tests themselves. The results were nearly all positive. On November 5, after an entire day of lab work, Williams described the results to his wife and noted in his diary that they "seem so big that I cannot yet myself realize whether they are genuine or fictitious." Riding home in a buggy with the governor on November 17, after nearly six weeks of testing, Stanford raised the issue that neither had been able to voice. He posed Williams a simple question: Would they be wise to conduct the tests alone, without Paraf in the lab?

Growing suspicious, Williams agreed. On November 20, Stanford and Williams sent the professor off to look for a new pyrometer with which to better control the temperature of the ovens, and then they ran tests all afternoon by themselves. All the tests failed. "My suspicions are now grossly aroused that a deception is being practiced upon us," Williams wrote at the end of the fateful day.

Under similar circumstances, more tests failed. In early December, Williams became debilitated with the piles and took to bed. Weakened, he dragged himself back to the lab on December 14, and confronted Engine Levy about "suspicious circumstances of some of the assays." Levy was tight-lipped.

Stanford, convinced of the hoax, returned to neglected duties at Fourth and Townsend. But Williams sought some sort of harder evidence, perhaps hoping against hope that the fortune he imagined was real. There were more tests in the lab on December 18, with positive results. But on December 21, 1875, admitting repeated failures, Williams finally, angrily, used a small sheet of loose-leaf to brand Paraf a fake and put the episode behind him.

Chastened, perhaps dealing for the first time with the grim economic reality that surrounded the Mission Bay development, he returned home to spend a long, rainy Christmas holiday with his wife and children.

The date was exactly two months and ten days after the "discovery" of silver in the Coyote Hills had been reported in the *Oakland Tribune*.

View of Dumbarton Point (distant right) and Bay & Coast Railroad mainline (distant left), which extended the South Pacific Coast Railroad from Newark to Alameda. This view is looking south, from an area near today's San Mateo Bridge toll plaza. [Thompson and West's *New Historical Atlas of Alameda Co. California Illustrated*, 1878]

Detail from panorama of Bear River Bridge, on the Nevada County Narrow Gauge, 1876. The photographer recorded the new Baldwin 2-6-0 *Nevada* as well as a string of Carter Brothers eight-ton-capacity flatcars, all less than a year old at the time of the photograph (by J. M. Jacobs). [California State Railroad Museum]

9

The Lost Factory

By January 1873, Kimball Carriage and Car Co. was showing signs of a dangerous cash shortage. Kimball's foreman, writing to the Virginia & Truckee Railroad on January 7, pressured the Nevada short line to pay its bills on work delivered the previous August (two day coaches and two baggage cars). He began with "the sharp stick question":

> Here us are again on the sharp stick question, all the time after you. We wouldn't trouble you if people didn't trouble us, but on the 10th our black Friday, all the town will call to pay their respects and request us to pay their bills.
>
> The Bank of Cal, will have to hold their doors until [we] can make a deposit before they know whether they can open. We are objects of great interest to others (one per cent a month) and we don't like to see Mr. Brown's troubled countenance glaring at us from his desk.[1]

At the bank, William Ralston in turn was putting the sharp-stick question to Kimball, pressuring them to make payments on a $600,000 note, desperately trying to offset some $3.5 million in nonperforming loans the bank directors had begun to view through grim expressions. On February 19, 1873, just five weeks after the sharp-stick letter to the Virginia & Truckee, the bank's directors met and demanded that Ralston assume personal responsibility for the Kimball loan.

Far more annoying to the Virginia & Truckee, however, was the fact that the new Kimball cars had to be extensively rebuilt less than two years after delivery. In November 1874, the *Territorial Enterprise* commented:

> These cars were purchased by the Virginia & Truckee Railroad Company some time since and were run on the road for a time, but they were of such shoddy manufacture that they soon began to shake to pieces: therefore they were placed in the company's shops at Carson to be overhauled. It was found necessary to almost wholly rebuild them. All the interior wood-work is new and is of the best white ash, oiled and varnished; new floors of Oregon pine were laid in all the cars.[2]

The structural failure of the cars could be accounted for by the drying out of poorly seasoned lumber in the arid Nevada climate, with subsequent loosening of the car frame. The experience sent the Virginia & Truckee recoiling to eastern car builders, purchasing its next passenger equipment from the Oxford Co-Operative Car Co. and from J. G. Brill in 1873.[3]

Other observers noted fiscal problems endemic to Kimball's size. The R. G. Dun and Co. credit report of October 6, 1873, suggested that Kimball's enormous capacity was generating inventory that simply could not be sold: "[They] are still working with a great accumulation of manufacturing stock for which at present there is but little demand. The concern is too large for this coast and in consequence the demand for their goods has never been equal to their capacity for production which is likely to be the case for many years to come."[4]

The contract for twelve North Pacific Coast passenger cars, noted in a July 1874 credit report, did little to convince R. G. Dun that demand had increased enough to justify the size of the company's enormous capital investment. On July 10, 1874, the credit reporter added: "[Kimball has] been for the past year running with a small force . . . are endeavoring to work off their manufacturing stock and have recently discharged more men and are giving out that they intend to convert their establishment to a furniture manufactory."[5]

An astute observer of Mission Bay business trends, Henry Fairfax Williams undoubtedly knew of Kimball's troubles and helplessly watched the benchmark industry drift closer and closer to insolvency. He may not have believed what he was reading when a message arrived from Ralston on August 25, 1874, containing surprising news. Ralston was proposing an apparent expansion of the Kimball operations:

> As we passed by the office I stopped to read my letters and found a message had been left by Mr. Ralston for me to call at the Bank to see him which I did at 11 o'clock and was pleased to find he wanted me to say that Kimball Manufacturing Co. wanted a location on Channel St. for a branch establishment where materials could be landed and sawed up in dimensions. Nothing had occurred in a long time to please me more and an appointment was made for him to meet me tomorrow morning to make the selection and state just what would be needed.[6]

The next day, Williams personally escorted Ralston, George Kimball, and his partner, Richard Ogden, on a tour of Mission Bay. Kimball and Ogden expressed interest in a site on block 22, the western extremity of the fill between Fifth and Sixth streets. Prime Mission Bay real estate, the site lay on the banks of "Channel Street," the navigable waterway that would serve as a direct connection to bay shipping.

But Ralston, Kimball, and Ogden did not share all the details of "the expansion" with Williams. A year before the tour of Mission Bay, Ralston responded to pressure from the bank by tightening the reins on Kimball. In partial repayment of their debt, Kimball and Ogden deeded the original factory at Fourth and Bryant over to Ralston on August 7, 1873, and agreed to divide the business into two smaller, more manageable units.[7] The carriage business would move across the street into leased quarters at Fourth and Silver, and the car works would remain in two long sheds at the old Fourth and Bryant location. The agricultural implement business would seek smaller quarters on Mission Bay, built and managed not by Kimball himself but by a new partner named Eugene Soule. Ralston would then convert most of the original brick building at Fourth and Bryant to a furniture manufactory (dedicated to producing more than six hundred room sets for the Palace Hotel). The remaining space would be leased to the Cornell Watch factory.[8] Kimball, in essence, was being downsized.

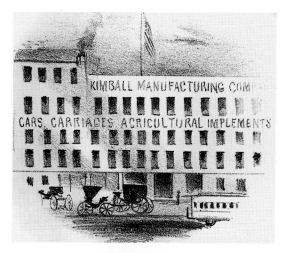

But viewed through Williams's optimistic perspective, proof of the "expansion" arrived on August 29 when Ralston's cargo of mahogany logs was stacked on empty land on block 21, adjacent to the proposed Kimball mill site, where the logs could be "worked into dimensioned lumber" for the Palace Hotel. Williams was in high spirits when he noted in his diary, on the same date, that "it already gives the block the appearance of a huge lumber yard."

Willing to sacrifice for the common good, Williams was able to make a clear distinction between his own self-interest and the success of a larger, regional economic recovery plan. His own Fourth Street planing mill could easily have turned out dimensioned lumber for the Palace Hotel, but he concentrated instead on the recovery of Kimball. What, he must have asked himself, would turn the struggling company around? If he helped Ralston, wouldn't Kimball's gains reflect in higher land values everywhere in Mission Bay?

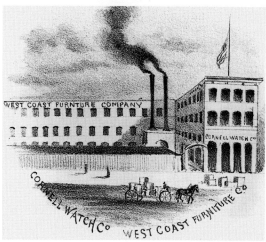

By 1875, at the time these sketches were made of the Kimball factory at Fourth and Bryant streets, it was occupied by new tenants, including the Cornell Watch Co. and the West Coast Furniture Co., an attempt to improve revenue from failing cash flows at Kimball. [California State Library]

Ralston apparently anticipated Williams's quandary and quickly provided him with an incentive. On February 10, he awarded the contract for all of the Palace Hotel doors to Williams's Fourth Street mill, at a handsome seven dollars each. There were, by Williams's estimate, three thousand doors in the Palace Hotel.[9] The work would tide him over while Kimball's fortunes were given time to recover.

Williams's optimism, however, was premature. Five months went by before development work actually started on the new Kimball facility. It was a long, anxiety-ridden time, during which Ralston tried to understand the impact of the silver discoveries in the Consolidated Virginia Mine—an ore body that did not, it slowly became clear, cross the dividing line into his own Ophir mining properties. Williams, usually unemotional about mining news, may have correctly read the handwriting on the wall in this diary entry, written on December 8, 1874: "The excitement on California Street consequent upon the fabulous ore developments in some of the mines on the Comstock lode is simply immense. Two thirds of the brokers and their patrons seem to be crazy."

Williams remained aloof from the excitement. He focused much of his energy on building the bulkhead along the length of Channel Street and developing the adjoining "campus" of lands, encouraging lumber dealers to locate wholesale distribution yards there. The Central Pacific had contracted to pay for the bulkhead, $75,000 in rock fill and wooden cribbing that was designed as a wharf for numerous commercial middlemen, wholesalers, and merchants who would help move goods to and from the transcontinental hub. Customers for this real estate would soon include Austin Moore of the North Pacific Coast Railroad, looking for an outlet for the Russian River Land and Lumber Co.[10] Pope and Talbot, the largest Douglas fir producer and distributor of Puget Sound, would site a yard on Channel and Fourth streets. Other bulk commodity dealers would follow suit, including hay merchants.

Kimball's plan seemed to be working, but in slow motion. It wasn't until January 15, 1875, that Williams signed a development contract for work on the new site. The delay brought revisions to the original plan. Kimball announced that the new factory would focus exclusively on its line of agriculture implements, plows, wagons, hay presses, and harvesters, a product line displaced from the Fourth and Bryant factory. The delay also brought about the re-siting of the new works from block 22 to block 21, moving the facility one block away from direct water access on Channel Street. The inland lot, located at the intersection of Sixth and Berry streets, was cheaper. But lacking frontage on the Channel Street bulkhead, its selection signaled a retreat from Williams's original campus plan. Drayage would be required to move bulk raw materials from the Channel Street wharf to the site.

In January 1875, Williams met Kimball's new partner. Eugene Soule signed the lease for the empty lot on the 15th for a consideration of $100 a month.[11] Raised in New York and apprenticed in the carriage trade, Soule was an acquaintance of Leland Stanford's. George Kimball may have thought him a good influence over future business with the governor, business that had thus far failed to materialize. Soule was apparently given broad latitude and control over development of the "branch" business, under an agreement that Soule later insisted gave him 25 percent ownership.[12] Williams was not privy to the details, but he watched Soule aggressively manage construction of the new building, installation of tooling, and purchase of raw materials.

By January 29, Williams had crews grading and leveling the site, a 60' × 120' lot located on the northeast corner of Sixth and Berry streets—the southwestern end of block 21.[13] The site was at the extremity of the Berry Street fill, a kind of no man's land, cratered with sink holes where the red rock fill had begun to settle into soft alluvial mud. The new factory sat just across King Street from the Central Pacific's car repair shop, the largest building erected up to that time at the western edge of the Mission Bay development and adjacent to the giant Central Pacific freight terminal.

Further west, on partly filled land still unrecovered from Mission Bay, an informal city garbage dump sprawled along the foot of Seventh Street. Squatters who gleaned materials from the dumps lived in shacks on the mudflats, which were soon nicknamed the Filth Hotels. Together with the smells from the sewer effluent, the scent of the dump combined in an easterly breeze blowing over the Mission Bay development, contributing to the corroding smell of the landscape.

On February 16, 1875, Williams noted in his diary that Eugene Soule had begun construction of the factory, acting as his own contractor. By mid-April, the work was nearing completion, and the *Mining and Scientific Press* published the most detailed description known of the new Kimball branch works:

Manufacture of Agricultural Implements

The Kimball Manufacturing Company are enlarging their sphere of enterprise by the addition of a branch establishment for the manufacture of agricultural implements. For the accommodation of this new indus-

try, a commodious building, 90 × 220 feet in its exterior dimensions, has been erected on the corner of Berry and Sixth streets.

It is proposed to manufacture every implement needed on a farm from a garden trowel to a lumber wagon. Heretofore our farmers have depended almost wholly on Eastern manufacturers for their implements and as a result a large sum has annually been sent away which could as well be retained to circulate in our own State.

The most approved machinery will be introduced by the Kimball company and they intend that their agricultural implement department shall be fully equal in reputation to their other manufacturing departments which is a sufficient guarantee of its excellence. The building is two stories in height. On the ground floor is the engine, of eighty-horse power, twelve forges, lathes and necessary machinery. The upper room is divided into a drying room, a painting room, wood workers' room and an office for the Superintendent, Mr. E. Soule. Between seventy five and one hundred hands will be employed when the manufactory is in operation, which is expected to be about May 1st. In time it is the intention of the company to add a foundry for the casting of such light work as is needed for their business.

This will form a valuable acquisition to the constantly increasing manufacturing enterprises of San Francisco. We feel that its success is assured.[14]

In spite of the advance press, San Francisco business directories were slow to list the new Kimball subsidiary. The 1875 Langley's directory still noted Eugene Soule in his former role as an independent blacksmith. The 1876 directory listed him as superintendent of Kimball's Fourth and Silver operation,

The famous twin Muybridge panoramas of San Francisco include the 1877 view of Mission Bay (reproduced as a detail, above) and a nearly identical view made a year later, shown at the top of the page in a segment containing about 15 percent of the 360 degree sweep of the complete panorama. Both views reveal detail in the area around Sixth and Berry streets, identified as a small cluster of one- and two-story industrial buildings rising on the muddy fringe of Mission Bay, directly above the sign "PHOTO-GRAPHS" at the bottom of the image. One of the buildings in the cluster is thought to be the Kimball/Carter factory at Sixth and Berry streets. [Top, Canadian Centre for Architecture; above, California State Library]

which was by this date the site of Kimball's downsized carriage operations.

Not until 1877 would Langley's directory report Soule in charge of the agricultural implement business at Sixth and Berry. But there is evidence that long before this date, the agricultural implement branch had declared bankruptcy. Because of the failure, Kimball may have suspended its operations at Sixth and Berry as early as February 1876, barely a year after the factory was completed.

In the first quarter of 1875, fifty-two businesses declared bankruptcy in California, their net worth aggregating $1.2 million. For the same period in 1876, sixty-one failures occurred, totaling $476,000.[15]

The South of Market industries of Tar Flat and Mission Bay were probably among those most affected by the severe economic downturn. In 1875, there were seventeen iron manufacturers in San Francisco, employing 1,705 men who together turned out $4.7 million worth of patterns, castings, and fabrications. A year later, fifteen iron industries remained, employing 1,200 men creating $3 million worth of product.[16]

The effect of this sharp decline in economic welfare must be understood against a backdrop of relative prosperity for the nearly twenty years California had been a state, the period from 1850 to 1869. San Francisco's wage structure was generally higher, and its cost of living no worse, than that of New York City during this time period.[17] This prosperity appeared to favor much of the city's diverse ethnicity, contributing to a sense of upward mobility shared by both blue-collar and white-collar populations and by the spectrum of the city's occupations. Hence the deepening recession of the 1870s appeared to be a nearly universal calamity, increasingly severe in its repercussions for all ethnicities and all walks of life.

Economic statistics thinly masked the human costs of the economic downturn. The diary of an Irish iron molder named Frank Roney survives as a testimony to the day-to-day subsistence of workers in the San Francisco of 1875. It evidenced a repeating cycle of layoffs, loans, repossessions, and the search for new work. At the end of 1875, Roney faced this situation with a wife, a child, and a baby on the way. Even brief extracts from his diary make his plight — and that of all iron workers in San Francisco — painfully clear:

> **April 1875** And, as the situation is about as disagreeable as it can be, and as my wife is in no condition to be on a continual move, I have decided to remain where I am, No. 37 Clementina St, San Francisco. . . .
> I began work on the 12th instant in the Pacific [Iron] Works, Ed. Jones [is] foreman. What my wages is, I don't yet know and may not for some 6 weeks yet. . . .

> **May 1875** Sunday is the molder's picnic. Would like to go but cannot for want of funds. . . .

> **June 1875** Business still continues to get dull, and but very little prospects of it being much better.

PACIFIC ROLLING MILLS.

On the 17th my wife was confined, and at 7:15 AM another boy was born. Everything turned out all right. Mrs. McDevitis evidently both skillful and considerate as midwife.

July 1875 Moved to another house, No. 225 Perry St, . . . rent $17. I got laid off at the Pacific and began work at the City Iron Works. During this month, my mind has been in an almost [constant] whirl of excitement. I feel the accumulations of responsibility without [having] the means readily or within view to meet them. And, to help [make] matters [worse], since C.B. came here . . . a great deal of beer has been consumed.

August 1875 Moved to No. 3 Margaret Place; rent $13 per month. Was laid off in [the] City foundry. I disliked the place all the time I was there. And, it seemed to me [that] the foreman appreciated my dislike and made it disagreeable for me.

October–November 1875 During these months, I have done little better than in the November, previous. Paid off indebtedness to the parties mentioned in 1875 the previous month . . . business dull and growing duller.

The Lost Factory   393

December 1875 The last month in the year! And so, time rolls on recording each hour and day and month and year with a precision and relentlessness in sad contrast to the vacillations of poor mortals who, either compulsorily or recklessly, idle the moments so mercilessly recorded beyond the power of recall.

. . . I began the year working at $2 a day, and the last and only work [I have] had during this month was at the same price. . . . And so, after all my expectations, I begin the year of grace 1876 in greater debt than the previous one and, too, after undergoing greater humiliation in my endeavory to keep level.

January 13, 14, 1876 No success so far. As usual, I have visited those shops where I might reasonably hope to get a job, but the ill fortune which has persistently followed me for 25 months still clings to me as tenaciously as ever. While I regret my circumstances, I am aware [that] others are a good deal worse off. I still keep house. Of course, in a poor fashion, but yet I manage to eat some and secure enough of warmth and sleep. But, my wife and children [are] pent up from week to week without a sufficiency of warmth or of warm clothing. They feel the effects of this mode [of] living, and it begins to tell upon them.

January 20 Began to work this day in the Union Iron works. I was afraid I was not going to begin work, but after a [little] while, the foreman came to me and told me [that] if I wanted to work for $3.50 a day, I could start. And, further, [he said] that he had orders to start no new men at any higher price. And so, I started. Worked the full day of 9 hours and all night and next day (21st) till quitting time.

February 10, 11, 12 Worked with five others on a walking beam for a compound pumping engine for Flood and O'Brien during these days, and cast it on the last day. Its length was 34' and its weight, 14 tons. . . .

February 28 Time, 10 hours. Job, plunger, 1,000 pounds. A.J. Phillips, formerly of the "Sheridan Hill" Smelting Works, called upon me today. Was dead broke. Took him home and gave him a bed and supper.

February 29 Time, 10 hours. Job, plunger, 1,000 pounds. P. had breakfast, and supper, and bed.

This records the second month of this Centennial Year of Grace 1876, during which I have earned $84.50 and produced 15 tons [of iron castings], averaging clear profit to the proprietors [of] $450.

I have not much to regret this month, thank god.[18]

The situation Frank Roney found himself in did not materially improve during the next two years. By 1877, he was a leader in a local political movement called the Workingmen's Party, and the social unrest Roney describes in his diary was taking on an undercurrent of violence.

Thomas Carter moved to a house at 224 Second Street sometime during the period of Frank Roney's diary. Like Roney, Carter was an Irish immigrant caught in the tightening grip of California's recession. Unlike Roney, Carter might have been in a position to purchase his house, according to one account written in 1878, by paying $20,000 outright.[19] But in spite of his upward mobility, the human landscape he lived and worked in differed little from Roney's world. A thick pall of smoke, with its throat-searing smell of coke, rose from Tar Flat just three city blocks away from Carter's address, marking the borders of the foundry district and creating a castle wall around the largest manufacturing center west of the Mississippi River. Inside the wall, Thomas Carter would settle down for the rest of his life.

Carter's new residence was not far from his brother's old flat on Howard Street, the place he had probably spent recuperating from his accident in 1868. Now almost a decade after losing a leg, Carter still walked with a cane, but he walked with more confidence, better adapted to his artificial leg, striding gracefully to cover distance.

His daily rounds took him to the same shops, foundries, and fabricators he had first discovered in 1868. He shook hands with many of the same owners and foremen, now friends, asking them about new projects. In the time it took to roll cigarette papers, Carter showed them new blueprints of his own for estimates. But since 1868, the railroad-related industries of Mission Bay had noticeably declined.

Such early South of Market car builders as Duncan McLean and Palmer Cox had simply vanished from the scene. Vulcan Iron, which had been home for Cox's small car building shop in 1868, returned to its original focus of general casting and fabrication. By 1873, Cox himself was a successful cartoonist—a surprising departure from car manufacturing.

Turning south on First Street, Carter would have noted changes in the foundry district itself. By June 1875, H. J. Booth and Co., the old Union Iron Works, had become Prescott, Scott, which, although doing modifications on the North Pacific Coast's one spot (a reengineering project Carter might have witnessed in the summer of 1875), was no longer manufacturing locomotives. Down the street, Risdon Iron Works would begin repair work on NPC's tugboat *Tiger* on Beale and Howard streets that November.

The Miner's Foundry had undergone a merger with the Golden State Foundry in 1870, emerging as the Golden State and Miner's Ironworks though still located on First Street and still operated as a cooperative, building an extremely diverse catalogue of products from the prolific (and often competing) work of its tenants. By 1875, Golden State's product lines included steam engines and fittings; boilers and boiler fittings; water wheels; food processing mills; saw mill equipment; dredging machines; presses for cider, oil, vermicelli, and cotton; pumps; furnaces; quartz processors; grinders and amalgamators; sugar mill equipment; oil refinery equipment; flour mills; hoisting machinery; and hydraulic machinery.

In March 1875, the GS&M Foundry was fabricating all-metal "grading cars" for the Los Angeles & Independence Railroad, further diversifying their work into railroad rolling stock.

Crossing the corner of Beale and Folsom streets, Carter took pride in seeing his old Vallejo Foundry supplier, Thomas McCormick, succeeding

San Francisco depot scene, in *The Wasp*, Dec. 16, 1876. [California State Library]

in a new partnership with Oscar Lewis, now called the Industrial Foundry and opened for business in early April 1875.[20] McCormick and Lewis advertised a specialty in architectural castings, but the foundry was clearly linked to much of the casting work for both the North Pacific Coast and for Carter Brothers during the remainder of 1875. The Vallejo headquarters of McCormick's expanding foundry business remained active throughout, and perhaps after, the opening of the location at Beale and Folsom streets.

Kimball railroad products were conspicuous by their absence from local trade shows. In 1874, Casebolt was the only exhibitor of railroad equipment at the San Francisco Mechanic's Fair, winning a prize for the much-lampooned "balloon street car," which turned on its own built-in turntable at the end of the line. A year later, Casebolt started designing and building revolutionary "grips," or cable cars, for the Sutter Street Railway.

Down Bryant Street to Fourth, Carter strolled along the original marshy border of Mission Bay, which was now solidly filled in as far south as Berry Street. Struggling with debt, the Kimball empire was undergoing fragmentation. The huge L-shaped brick factory building at Fourth and Bryant was still a landmark, but by mid-1875 most of its space was let to two other Ralston-sponsored industries, the Cornell Watch Co. and the California Furniture Co.[21] The main branch of Kimball's car and carriage firm relocated to smaller quarters on Fourth and Silver streets, raising speculation in the credit community that George Kimball himself was not in control of the concern.[22]

To save his leg, Carter could have boarded a Fourth Street horsecar by Kimball's old factory and ridden the two blocks from Bryant to Townsend. Recently reclaimed from the waters of Mission Bay, Fourth and Townsend was the new epicenter of the expanding Central Pacific Mission Bay terminal. By 1873, the Central and Southern Pacific railroads had spent a million dollars to bring the tracks of the San Francisco & San Jose from their original Market Street terminal, through the vast freight sheds of King Street, east to the passenger terminal itself at Fourth and Townsend, and on another two blocks to the massive freight slips and docks at the foot of Second Street. A large part of that investment went into Henry Fairfax Williams's contract filling work, reclaiming useful land from tidal mud.

This extension of the original SF&SJ penetrated the heart of the original sixty-four acres of Mission Bay land, deeded in 1868. It represented not only the symbolic center of the Central Pacific but its physical headquarters, where it had cost the railroad $200,000 to erect a "magnificent building of pressed brick and stone dressing" at the corner of Fourth and Townsend.

On the top floor of the headquarters building, in the company's thickly carpeted board room, the last tie in the transcontinental railroad, of polished California laurel wood, was placed on display as a trophy of the railroad's dominion over the West. Not far from the board room was Leland Stanford's private office. In 1876, his company would control four hundred new miles of track to Los Angeles under the once-independent business entity of the Southern Pacific. From Los Angeles, the Southern Pacific would begin construction of an entirely new transcontinental, laying track east toward New Orleans. A six-hundred-mile extension north to Portland, Oregon, was under construction through the upper Central Valley.

Changes to the railroad's physical plant clearly positioned San Francisco as the geographic hub of the expansion. A new roundhouse was added back-to-back with the original San Francisco & San Jose locomotive facility, and by 1870 repair shops and warehouses lined the tracks for nearly sixteen hundred lineal feet along King Street; it was infrastructure that began to shape and define Mission Bay as a staging ground for the Southern and Central Pacific railroads.

Henry Fairfax Williams strongly believed that free market conditions would attract, and cement, a large railroad supply industry to the growing Mission Bay complex. But he no longer had illusions about selling locally manufactured rolling stock to Stanford's expanding empire. In tight economic times, eastern car builders were eager to sell their products at or near cost, and western railroads found both quality and price at a variety of established eastern houses. The Virginia & Truckee, for example, purchased eastern-built baggage cars from the Oxford Co-Operative Car Co. at a bargain $2,000 each, to which would be added transportation costs in the neighborhood of approximately $200.[23] Locally manufactured Kimball baggage cars, of inferior construction, had cost $2,500 each. "High end" eastern or midwestern rolling stock was becoming a Central Pacific standard. In 1875, Barney and Smith built luxury drawing room sleepers and day coaches for the Central Pacific, appointed in Brussels carpet, Cerise plush seat coverings, damask curtains, and combined French and American walnut finish.[24]

By 1878, 54 percent of the nearly three hundred passenger cars in the Central Pacific fleet had been built by eastern or midwestern manufacturers, with the vast majority of the remaining 46 percent built by the Central Pacific's own shops in Sacramento.[25] The opening of the Southern Pacific mainline to Los Angeles gave new impetus to the Sacramento facility, which undertook construction of seven hundred new freight cars in January 1876 and employed almost two thousand men in the car shop alone.[26]

Walking through the maturing heart of Mission Bay, Carter could weigh the pros and cons of Williams's original vision. Simply locating an independent car works next to the Central Pacific was not simple at all. The family of Thomas Paizotti, a shop employee in Central Pacific's Sixth Street San Francisco car shop who occasionally moonlighted for Carter, passed down a story that portrays open antagonism between the CP and the fledgling Carter Brothers car business.[27] The story recounts Thomas Carter's difficult search for a new location for the firm, a search that, in the story, finally discovered Niles, a sleepy hamlet of two hundred souls within modern-day Fremont. Two Central Pacific lines merged at Niles, and with good shipping facilities and a low-cost, rural environment it seemed like the perfect location for a car manufacturing business. But Carter, the story concluded, soon met an icy reception from the Central Pacific. Both Niles real estate and access to Central Pacific spurs were controlled by the CP affiliate Contract and Finance Co., which allegedly rebuffed Carter with high prices and forbidding terms. The Paizotti story suggests the experience occurred at the end of Carter's Saucelito tenure, providing a motive for his move into

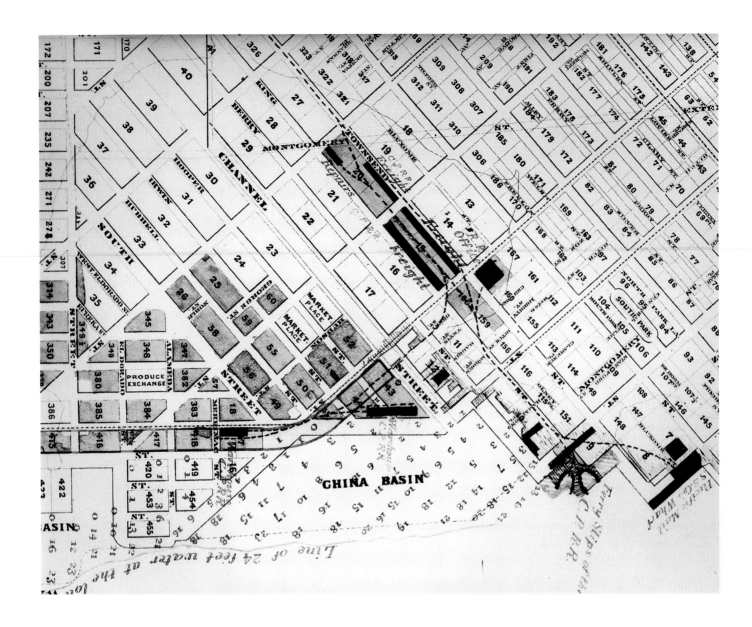

Detail from a map of the City and County of San Francisco published in 1870, showing the subdivided areas of Mission Bay, with Central Pacific lands or facilities indicated by shading. The Kimball agricultural implement building, thought to be the site of a short-lived Carter Brothers factory, was located in the lower-left corner of block 21, opposite the Central Pacific's car repair shop. Much of the lower-left-hand portion of the map was still under water in 1870, but as Mission Bay was slowly filled in, Channel Street became the only open water remaining from the former bay. Channel Street remains a landmark in San Francisco to this day, home to houseboats in the China Basin area. [California Historical Society]

Mission Bay. Thomas Paizotti went to work for Carter after the plant relocated to San Francisco.

But in truth, Carter's move was probably motivated more by his suppliers and less by his competitors. The motive was more likely an effort to shorten Carter's supply chain, bringing sources of lumber, castings, fasteners, and blacksmithing as close as possible to the fabrication and assembly process. The exigencies of kit manufacture may have brought these factors into sharp focus. For the kit business to be successful, a tight configuration of suppliers was critical, creating a way to shorten the rapid conversion of raw materials into kit parts and increase production capacity. Carter found such suppliers compressed into the space of eight city blocks, all in the neighborhood of Mission Bay.

South of Market, Carter walked by a supplier of virtually every part his business needed. Within Tar Flat lay the largest concentration of iron foundries and fabricators on the Pacific Coast. To the south, lumber suppliers were congregating in Williams's Mission Bay campus.

We picture Carter walking the last two blocks from Townsend to Berry Street, passing Henry Fairfax Williams's office at 740 Fourth and reaching the riprap of the Channel Street bulkhead. There, on the corner of Fourth and Channel, the Pope and Talbot lumber yard stretched for a full city block, a storage area for nearly three million board feet of Puget Sound Douglas fir. As Carter passed the corner of the yard, he could visualize the three thousand narrow gauge flatcars such a volume of lumber could construct.

The carnival of lumber dealers and lumber-related businesses continued along Berry Street, following the uncompleted course of the Channel bulkhead. Turning southwest onto Berry, Carter paused to get his bearings. The original 1868 waterline of Mission Bay had been filled a full block from Townsend back to Channel Street. Williams's diaries document the extension of the bulkhead between Fourth and Fifth streets as early as March 1874, extending the commercial envelope further and further to the southwest.[28] An 1877 Muybridge photograph shows stacked lumber covering much of block 21, bounded by Sixth, Fifth, and Berry streets.[29]

Along the new reach of Berry Street, wood product businesses began to fill in. Carter now walked past them, many built atop "made" land less than a year old. Boat builder Timothy Collins was located at 120 Berry, one of a handful of addresses on the street known to have a number. Beyond First, business locations on Berry were identified in Langley's directory with cryptic phrases such as "north side," "between," and "corner of"—the addresses of an industrial frontier. Shipsmith James Christy was simply located "between Third and Fourth"; Castner and Co., ship caulkers, lay "between Fifth and Sixth." Other wood-related industries filled in empty lots, most with a narrow twenty-two-foot street frontage. Jesse and Drew were stair builders located near Fourth, Cook Brothers were box makers between Third and Fourth, L. and E. Emanuel made furniture between Fourth and Fifth, and the San Francisco Furniture Factory turned out a similar product line between Third and Fourth.

Beyond Third, the Berry Street alignment became poorly surfaced, potted with depressions wherever fresh fill settled. Growing tired, Carter began to drag his leg along the empty, eight-hundred-foot length of block 21, graded smooth but filled only with stacks of timber and a few remnants of Ralston's exotic mahogany logs. By 1875, the Gorrill brothers were using part of block 21 to frame bridge timbers, apparently in the open air.[30] On the north side of Berry, between Third and Fourth streets, the lot was the staging ground for bridge timbers bound for Santa Cruz County. Perhaps Carter inspected, firsthand, his own Santa Cruz Rail Road bridge designs taking shape in the form of 8" × 12" truss sills.

In 1875, the bulkhead and fill along Channel Street did not extend as far west as Sixth Street but stopped halfway between Fifth and Sixth, marking the current end of the Mission Bay development. The sweeping landfill ended in the swampy delta of city sewers, where one isolated cluster of new factory buildings stood like an outpost at the intersection of Sixth and Berry. Pushing himself to the extremity of Mission Bay landfill, Carter would have finally come upon the large, framed, two-story Kimball agriculture works. Almost at the edge of the fill, it sat alone, just across King Street from the Central Pacific's giant car repair shop.

If Thomas Carter peered through the sawdust-coated windows, it is likely that he saw rows of silent, lifeless machinery.

———————————

Circumstantial evidence strongly points to November 1876 as the date when Carter Brothers intended to make a permanent move to San Francisco. It was the last month, according to the North Pacific Coast cash books, in which Carter paid rent at the Saucelito shop.

The exodus of Carter's key craftsmen from Saucelito seemed to occur in the same time period. John Carroll, Henry Barth, Alexander Finn, and John Larkin were listed for the first time in the same residence in Langley's 1877 San Francisco City Directory, at 608 Sixth Street, a rooming house called the Excelsior Hotel. A seedy South of Market apartment building that catered to Central Pacific shop employees, the Excelsior was located between Brannan and Townsend, just two blocks north of the new factory location at Sixth and Berry. Martin, with a growing family and a milk cow to take care of, apparently remained in Saucelito and became, at least in the first few months of 1877, a commuter.

Carroll, Barth, Finn, and Larkin all listed their occupations with exactly the same words in the city directory: "Carpenter, Carter Bros." The cutoff date for new additions to Langley's Directory was early January 1877, which suggests that for most of the men the move did indeed take place some time in the two months preceding January 6.[31]

Carter's move to the industrial center of California must have provoked nostalgia for the small community of Saucelito. Home to the Carter workmen for almost three years, the bayside neighborhood was still rural and undeveloped. Martin Carter and his family loved it. Indeed, the family cow and two horses would remain members of the Easterby Street homestead until at least 1878. But the rustic setting failed to attract any industrial infrastructure. In the entire time Carter was an on-site contractor, no foundry moved into Saucelito. Rather than becoming a distribution point for the NPC's lumber traffic, holding yards at the pier dispatched most of the board feet directly to San Francisco, a strategy Moore reinforced when he leased a distribution yard in Mission Bay. In cold, hard economic terms, the attraction of an industrial campus like Mission Bay can be explained in terms of a shortened inbound supply chain, lowering the cost of transporting raw materials to a plant site. One last time, perhaps in the early months of 1876, Carter struggled with a fundamental business decision: to become a manufacturer, or remain a captive, in-house shop support service to the North Pacific Coast. The answer, as the decade reached its midpoint and Carter's revenues declined, was aggressive and risky. He would move the business, change manufacturing tactics, and stand alone, without an organizational host.

No newspaper articles appear to mention the move. There are only two known photographs of the building at Sixth and Berry, and they were taken (like satellite reconnaissance photographs) from roughly two miles away atop Nob Hill.[32] The location of the two-story building in the photographs appears to match that described by Langley's Directory, the northeast corner of Sixth and Berry, exactly where the Kimball agricultural implement building was located in a previous directory. But the proportions of the building (which appears square in the photograph) do not seem to match the 90' × 220' rectangular shape described in the *Mining and Scientific Press* in April 1875.

Uncertainty about the physical appearance of the site is shadowed by uncertainties in the dates of use as a Carter facility. Shreds of evidence suggest, inconclusively, that Carter Brothers may have been using the facility much earlier than November 1876. Since the Saucelito shop was occupied by Carter prior to this date, a "two shop theory" has been suggested to account for the overlap. Although controversial, the theory helps explain two contrasting business strategies that Carter Brothers adopted: kit work and build-in-place work. The production and supply demands of each strategy suggest, in turn, that two different kinds of facility may have been needed to support them.

One piece of evidence for the two-shop theory focuses on Kimball's agricultural implement manager, Eugene Soule, who filed for personal bankruptcy in February 1876, claiming that he owned "an undivided 25%" of the Kimball agricultural implement business, for which he was not compensated. Whether the claim was true or not (Ogden swore it was not), the date of the bankruptcy suggests that the Sixth and Berry works may have suspended commercial operation shortly before Soule's petition. By May 1876, Kimball listed the agricultural implement business for sale.[33] It was not Carter's style to purchase facilities, but a lease at a reasonable rate could have occurred virtually anytime in the first ten months of 1876. Kimball undoubtedly would have welcomed the cash.

Even earlier evidence for the two-shop theory comes from three companion entries in the North Pacific Coast cash books. The first, dated June 7, 1875, charged Carter $29.93 for movement of "freight" from San Francisco to Saucelito on four dates in May (7, 10, 19, 28). The second, dated June 26, reported "amount of transfer on car material from Saucelito to San Francisco as per expense bills of E. W. Dysent" dated June 17 and 22, 1875. The bill was for $9.69. The third, dated June 30, reported transfer of car material going the opposite direction, from San Francisco to Saucelito; shipping costs totaled $90.21.

It is difficult to explain the transfers as simply delivery of castings from a San Francisco foundry to Saucelito, since the material appears to be moving in both directions. Instead, the billing might be accounted for by customers other than the NPC, for example kit work for the Santa Cruz & Felton, work that Carter may have routed through Kimball's Sixth and Berry streets works just after it was opened.

Why would Kimball divert floor space to Carter Brothers, a competitor? The reason behind Soule's bankruptcy may help explain the business conditions that Kimball faced in mid-1875, shortly after opening the Sixth and Berry works. In addition to the recession, a severe drought was playing havoc with California agriculture. Farmers were in no position to buy new ploughs and wagons. Kimball was paying $100 a month just for the lease of land the factory stood on. If Soule was desperate enough to fill unused shop capacity, a deal with Carter could have been one of the few sources of steady revenue in sight. That deal could begin simply as millwork—planing and working timbers Carter needed to fill contract work for the Santa Cruz & Felton.

From a car builder's perspective, the tooling and skills required for an agricultural implement business were an excellent starting point for a car shop. Whether for a wagon or a flatcar, mortices, tenons, let-ins, gains, and drill-outs all required similar manufacturing techniques. John White, writing in *The American Railroad Freight Car,* comments on the ease with which plough and farm implement makers retooled as railroad manufacturers.[34]

Keeping such contract work out of Saucelito perhaps simplified, at first, the increasingly awkward relationship Carter was experiencing with the North Pacific Coast. Displaced by Barney and Smith as the car builder of choice, Carter Brothers had been relegated to the role of odd jobs and kit assembly. Although newspapers made reference to Carter flatcars built at Saucelito for the Santa Cruz & Felton in July 1875, such work put Carter in the position of doing outside work without compensating the NPC for rent.

Why didn't the NPC charge Carter for rent, fuel, and materials for the earlier outside contract work? One strong possibility is the two-shop theory: the assertion that at least some of the 1875 kit work was not produced in Saucelito at all, but at Sixth and Berry in San Francisco.

What is clear is that Carter's outside contract work started six months earlier than its rent payment at Saucelito, which began in December 1875. During that time, Carter and Kimball could have cooperated on smaller lots of cars for the Santa Cruz & Felton as early as May or June 1875, and the Nevada County Narrow Gauge as early as July of that year. A division of labor between the two shops made sense; the Kimball works would get Carter's outside contract work and Saucelito the remaining North Pacific Coast work, some seventy-five freight cars that were the last remaining portion of its original 1874 new car contract.

Such evidence is circumstantial. But if the two-shop theory is true, it helps explain a San Francisco newspaper reference to Carter's production of cars for the NCNG, noted in the *San Francisco Newsletter* of September 11, 1875:

> Work was commensed in grading, etc., early in the Spring, and already much of the iron is laid on the track. The contract for everything, including rolling stock, is $450,000, and is entrusted to Mr. Thomas Furdlay [Findley]. He expects to have the line in running order early in November. *The freight and passenger cars are being constructed in this city* by Mr. Thomas Carter, the well-known builder of the Monterey and Salinas Valley Railroad and the North Pacific Coast railroad cars [emphasis added].

The article's accuracy is flawed by the fact that a midwestern builder, F. E. Canda and Co. of Chicago, built the passenger cars for the Nevada County Narrow Gauge. But Carter definitely built the freight equipment, and the *Newsletter* suggests that the Sixth and Berry factory was the manufacturing site.

But the real appeal of the two-shop theory lies in explaining Carter's unusual 1875 production strategy, a combination of build-in-place and kitting.

Three examples of kit work—Santa Cruz & Felton, the Nevada County Narrow Gauge, and the Santa Clara Valley Railroad (to name only the ones that are known)—all occurred between May and December 1875, when we believe the Sixth and Berry building was still leased and operated by Kimball and when the record of materials transferred to and from Saucelito occurred in the North Pacific Coast cash books.

The kit approach was unlike anything Carter had previously attempted. It differed dramatically from the build-in-place system used for the NPC work in Saucelito and was intended to reduce manufacturing costs once a design was successfully prototyped and marketed. The kit strategy required workmen to narrow their skill sets. One workman would learn the operation of one machine and repeat the same task (for example, morticing dozens of duplicate car sills). Other workmen would specialize on, say, drill-outs using a belt-driven drill press; others would cut the same gain, over and over, on a band saw.

The kit strategy was a means of clustering the most repetitive, machine-intensive processes of car construction within a high-capacity production facility. Once cut, shaped, drilled, and perhaps painted, the twenty-five-odd wood members of a flatcar would be bundled together and then shipped unassembled to a customer. At a field location, without skilled labor, without even a roof overhead, the parts would be rapidly assembled with no need for power machinery and at minimal labor cost. This strategy turned the factory into a high-capacity parts production house, able to turn out hundreds of duplicate parts for multiple jobs going on at distant locations.

Each manufacturing strategy, kitting or build-in-place, required its own kind of supply chain. The faster production rate in a kit-oriented factory required a higher volume of raw materials. Lumber, castings, and specialized parts had to be delivered in a narrower time frame to meet the deadline for bundling and shipping. Kit building required an individual factory worker to master production skills for only select parts of a car, but the strategy demanded closer management of overall parts flow, including ordering, inventory level, and cross-training of employees on critical machinery. Poorly adapted to passenger car construction (where a four-week drying period was required for finish painting), the kit strategy expedited flatcar and boxcar manufacture, where volume might be considerably increased and cost decreased in a kit-oriented process.

The Sixth and Berry works offered Carter exactly such a facility. Close to iron foundries and wholesale lumber dealers on Channel Street, raw materials were easily and quickly obtained. Eugene Soule originally designed the building for the induction of big beams through power machinery situated on the first floor—planing, shaping, and drilling the beams in a logical, linear sequence. In Carter's adaptation, the beams would simply continue on through the building, unassembled, emerging preshaped and predrilled for bundling and shipping. Even if Carter wanted to, there was apparently no easy way to assemble full-size cars at Sixth and Berry. Custom-built for the manufacture of agricultural hardware, the Kimball building apparently made no provision for twelve-foot-high doors, large enough to clear an assembled passenger car.

Who would have managed production work at Sixth and Berry (assuming Carter Brothers occupied the site before November 1876)? Carter never had a surplus of talented foremen. With Martin Carter and John Carroll both resident in Saucelito, the demands of maintaining two active production facilities must have taxed Carter's resources to the limit.

Two names come to mind. Consider the possibility of Thomas Paizotti, the car repairman for the Central Pacific. He was an example of the flexible labor pool from which Carter could draw at the Sixth and King Street CP car shop, his neighbor one block north. Paizotti was listed in Langley's between 1875 and 1877 as a CP car repairer (or sometimes as a car inspector); he moonlighted for Carter during the same time period. The fact that Paizotti was the source of the story about the purported Niles expansion suggests that he played a management role for Carter, rather than day labor.

Francis J. Geiser may offer an even more compelling résumé. "Frank" Geiser was Carter's shop lead at Monterey while employed by the Central Pacific at the Sixth and King Street repair facility. By November 1875, he was Carter's foreman on the Santa Clara Valley job at Dumbarton Point while maintaining his employment status with the Central Pacific.

Frank Geiser may well be the missing link in the two-shop theory. Experienced on both the factory and assembly ends of kit building, he could have run the Sixth and Berry factory while managing assembly of resulting kits at a field location, perhaps during furloughs from the Central Pacific repair shop. The absence of his name anywhere in the North Pacific Coast cash books makes it believable that until Carter's permanent move in November 1876 Geiser ran the most specialized and unique Carter facility of all, focusing wholly on producing car kits.

The business necessity for a kit strategy came from rapidly encroaching eastern competition.

Whatever went on at Sixth and Berry during the volatile months of 1875, it was clear that Carter was shifting his production strategy to support a new kind of customer: the short line railroad in a remote location that needed a relatively small lot of cars inexpensively and quickly. Geographically dispersed, the short lines that Carter served were too small to warrant opening a field factory like the one at Monterey. For at least eighteen months, from mid-1875 through the end of 1876 and perhaps later, this type of order appeared to sustain Carter's weakening sales.

Eastern car builders, too, were aware of the same trend and targeted the emerging short line market. The president of Carson & Tahoe Lumber and Fluming Co., H. M. Yerington, wrote to the Detroit Car Works on September 2, 1876, emphasizing the quality he expected in a small batch of new narrow gauge flatcars:

> Our business has increased so rapidly over our narrow gauge R.R. we are obliged to order ten (10) flat cars about which we had certain correspondence in June last. We think you can & will build cars to suit us both in regard to quality & price so we now make the order something on the basis of yours of June 15th. Dimension of cars as follows, viz.

Platforms of flats 7 × 22 feet. We think side sills should be 4 × 10 in. of oak and inside sills 4 × 8 in. These cars will be called on to carry from 8 to 10 tons & we want bodies as light as possible, yet strong & prefer to *pay extra* for A-1 Oak timber which *we expect* you to use in these cars. Wheels 24 in diam. bored 3 3/4 in axles 3 3/4 in of best rolled or hammered iron. Journals 3 in diam 5 1/2 in long. Height of 25 inch from top of rail to center of link—brake staffs made so they can be unshipped. 4 stake pockets on each side of car and 4 at each end 4 1/2 × 3 3/4 in and 5 inches deep.

As a general proposition we wish these cars to be put up, made & trussed very much in the style of the 50 flats you furnished the V&T only that the timber used must be of much better quality. Please make center plates strong, so in event of a car getting off the track it won't go straight to pieces. Rush them out as rapidly as possible for we want them right now. Give us an A-1 car & make price as low as possible, we pay cash as usual. Will write you again in reference to manner of shipment. . . .

P.S. paint cars yellow & number 21 to 30 inclusive.[35]

No prices were reported for the Detroit narrow gauge cars, but the Virginia & Truckee standard gauge flatcars mentioned in Yerington's letter were sold by Detroit for $477.96 apiece, exclusive of transportation, a few months before the Carson & Tahoe Lumber and Fluming Co. order was placed.[36] In spite of Yerington's critical comments, the V&T flatcars he mentions featured high-quality oak sills, offering high strength and long life.

Transportation, however, could add $150 or more to the delivered price of eastern cars. If the cost of transportation is factored out, the price point for eastern rolling stock was rapidly dropping to parity with Carter's prices. A sign of a maturing market, Carter's pricing was being forced inside the price points dictated by the competition. In such a market, the only way Carter could continue to make any profit was to dramatically reduce the cost of production; again, this is an important clue to the role that kit manufacturing was intended to play.

John Kidder's considered opinion of Carter was at least in part based on the thin edge of a price advantage. Kidder had moved on to the Nevada County Narrow Gauge Railroad by January 1875, and as the line's superintendent of construction he was again in a position of authority to choose vendors for the railroad's rolling stock.[37] Kidder ultimately paid Carter Brothers $600 for a flatcar and $706 for a boxcar, prices that almost certainly included transportation of kit materials.[38] Using the Detroit flatcars as a benchmark, it is clear that Carter prices were set just slightly below the total cost of the eastern equivalent—a sign of open competition and justification for an aggressive cost-reduction strategy on Carter's part.

John Kidder was an example of the emerging market Carter could ill afford to lose; he was a repeat customer. For Kidder, using Tom Carter meant familiar designs and materials, a return to eight-ton capacity cars that were operating successfully after a year's time on the M&SV and North Pacific Coast. It is telling that Kidder did not order additional passenger equipment from Carter, perhaps because he harbored a lingering doubt about the qual-

Colfax, ca. 1872, before the coming of the Nevada County Narrow Gauge; three years later, the Central Pacific yard would become an open-air assembly site for Carter Brothers. [Bancroft Library]

Most of what we know about Carter's eight-ton freight cars comes from the Nevada County Narrow Gauge. The original series of fifteen boxcars, delivered in 1875, appeared on the NCNG's October 1912 California Railroad Commission report. The cars were numbered 2–30, even numbers only; they measured an inside length of 23'10", an inside width of 6'7", and an inside height of 6'5". Still rated at eight-ton capacity, the trucks were listed with twenty-four-inch wheels and 2¾" × 5½" bearings with "swing beams." According to the inventory, the boxcars were rebuilt in 1902, which may account for modifications to the trucks that appear in photographs of the NCNG. At the time of the 1912 inventory, a boxcar held a "reproduction value" of $486.

The 1912 flatcar listing, on the other hand, shows evidence of extensive rebuilding. What probably was a stock twenty-four-foot flatcar in 1875 had been modified to 25'4" length; and of fifteen original flatcars in the odd number series 1–29, only seven cars, numbered 1 to 13, were still occupying the original number series, but these were rebuilt (probably extensively) in 1895. This rebuilding date is significant, coming two years after a photo of the 1893 "circus train wreck" yielded what is probably the most detailed photograph of a Carter eight-ton flatcar known. The rebuild date suggests that the 1893 photograph shows a nearly original NCNG Carter eight-ton flatcar.

Robert Schlechter's drawing of an NCNG eight-ton flatcar, reproduced elsewhere in this chapter, therefore represents a car little changed from the 1875 Carter original.

ity of the two Monterey & Salinas Valley combination cars. Instead, he chose F. E. Canda to deliver two coaches and two combination cars. For Carter, the repeat business was additional mileage on old work. Designs developed a year previous could now be reused. The kit strategy was a means to minimize cost and maximize profit.

The kit strategy offered Kidder additional cost savings. Rather than assemble all the cars at once, he had the option to put together only what he needed for the startup phase of the Nevada County Narrow Gauge, stockpiling other kits for future expansion and saving the initial cost of assembly until the cars were actually required. The price per assembled car was high, but as mentioned Kidder stockpiled unassembled kits and saved the cost of labor.

The June 30, 1876, California Board of Transportation inventory of Nevada County Narrow Gauge rolling stock offered a snapshot of how Kidder initially distributed dollars among various car classes:

Boxcar	15	$10,600
Flatcar	15	$9,000
Handcars	3	$600
Track laying	2	$700
All other rolling stock, extra material		$8,575.15

The "extra material" noted in the summary might have translated to as many as fourteen additional flatcars, stored as unassembled kits until the Nevada County Narrow Gauge began operation. New boxcars, built by the railroad a year later, probably contained Carter kit material delivered in 1875.[39]

The Nevada County Narrow Gauge work offered evidence that the kit strategy, by itself, was not likely to win Carter the sustained battle for the West Coast car market. Cash books, or even detailed newspaper accounts of the Carter work at Colfax are almost nonexistent, which draws a curtain over our understanding of the extent of Carter's involvement in the NCNG. But Carter probably offered Kidder an additional incentive, perhaps the key factor in winning his business. Carter reportedly sold Kidder turntables and water tanks, also unassembled when they arrived at Colfax in the fall of 1875.[40]

Between August and November, the ensemble of Carter carpenters required to support these woodworking projects gave Kidder the same kind of on-site shop services that the NPC had enjoyed. Conceivably, other carpentry projects, for example the shop buildings in Grass Valley, could have been scoped within Carter's contract. Carter's real advantage over eastern manufacturers was his ability to offer Kidder a complete solution to the Nevada County Narrow Gauge's woodcraft requirements—an edge no eastern manufacturer could hope to duplicate.

On the morning of August 26, 1875, thousands of shares of Ophir mine stock went on sale at the San Francisco Stock Exchange, forcing its price into a free fall. Speculation in the press suggested that Fair, Flood, O'Brien, and Mackay, whose Nevada Bank was scheduled to open six weeks later, had deliberately dumped the stock. Both James Flood and William Ralston denied the rumors.[41] Whatever the cause, the falling stock price precipitated a run on the Bank of California the same day. The collapse of smaller banks all over the state soon followed. The bank of Thomas Findley, holding Nevada County Narrow Gauge construction accounts, would fail on October 23, temporarily throwing Kidder's finances into paralysis and probably delaying payment to Carter Brothers for delivery of rolling stock. Although the Findley bank would resume payments, any interruption of Carter's cash flow only emphasized the severity of their growing business slump.

On August 27, one day after the closure of the Bank of California, Ralston placed a letter of resignation on his desk and left early for his customary swim at North Beach. A few minutes later, Henry Fairfax Williams stopped by the bank to visit. Williams immediately sensed something was wrong. An hour later, he heard news that Ralston's body had been found floating face down in the bay between two anchored ships; the death was attributed to drowning. Although the inquest (in which Henry Fairfax Williams took part) found the cause of death to be natural, the suspicion of suicide hung over the tragedy. Heartbroken, Williams was able to write nothing in his diary until August 31: "Business was on part resumed today, but a deep gloom hangs over the city and from almost every man you meet, you hear expressions of deep regret for the irreparable loss we have sustained as a community."

Williams did resume the ordinary motions of his business day (even setting up a meeting with Flood and Fair on October 7), but it was clear that one of the touchstones of his life had vanished. He appeared to withdraw from the Newark and Santa Clara Valley projects, although both were reaching dramatic conclusion in the land sales planned for the fall. He sought out Leland Stanford for closer personal contact, taking pleasure in visiting the governor's new Nob Hill mansion on September 21 and perhaps subconsciously trying to keep Ralston's fatherly presence alive in Stanford.

Ironically, Williams's troubles with the Central Pacific began to multiply not long after Ralston's death. Large sums of money owed him for development of the Channel Street bulkhead remained unpaid, and he appealed to all levels of the Central Pacific, including Stanford and Hopkins, to make good. By February 1877, cash flow was so critical that Williams took out a loan of $6,000 from Peter Donahue to pay off his grading crews.[42]

"The railroad people," Williams wrote on May 14, "are treating me very badly about my last assessment." Not a word of personal rebuke was aimed at Stanford in hundreds of pages of day books and loose-leaf notes kept by Williams during the period. He even asked Stanford for (and received) a personal petition to the board of supervisors to apply his "Williams patented street paving" to California Street between Powell and Leavenworth.[43]

The filling of Mission Bay, however, came to a virtual standstill.

By November 1876, when Carter Brothers finally settled into permanent residence at the Sixth and Berry Street location, the most active period of kit building had ended. Demand dropped for short line rolling stock delivered at remote sites. Irregular payments (for example, on the Nevada County Narrow Gauge and the Santa Clara Valley Railroad) further hampered steady cash flow.

Carter continued the kit strategy as the South Pacific Coast took over the Santa Clara Valley Railroad (a topic to be explored in detail in the next chapter). Between June 30, 1876, and one year later, the South Pacific Coast added fifty-seven additional Carter flatcars to the previous batch manufactured for the Santa Clara Valley, presumably built as kits at Sixth and Berry and assembled at Dumbarton Point.[44] These cars appear to be the entire known production of Carter Brothers for the year in question, and most if not all of the production from the Sixth and Berry site during the period of known Carter occupancy. These fifty-seven cars represent just half the volume of the sluggish period of 1875–76, when more than one hundred freight cars were kitted for the SC&F, the SCV, and the NCNG, not counting any deliveries to the North Pacific Coast. Measured in terms of cash flow, for Carter Brothers the recession had reached rock bottom.

The shift to a kit strategy, then, was primarily a cost-saving measure that would achieve economy under conditions of high-volume production. On the assumption that high-rent factory space could pay for itself if it were fully used, the kit strategy probably achieved little differential cost savings when volume dropped as low as it did in the twelve months between mid-1876 and mid-1877, especially if the Sixth and Berry site commanded higher rent. Little evidence exists of commercial kits from Carter after this time period.[45] More cost-effective business strategies were soon on the horizon.

The slump took its toll on the Carter regulars, encouraging them to moonlight. John Carroll, Carter's most senior foreman and the likely architect of the kit strategy, went to work for the Central Pacific's King Street repair shops long enough to record his occupation in Langley's 1877–78 Directory as "machinist, Central Pacific." Like Geiser and Paizotti, he crossed King Street to the Carter Brothers facility only when there was contract work.

It is possible that Martin Carter was finally put in the same position as Carroll. Vandall's 1877 Directory of San Francisco (a competitor of Langley's) lists "Carter _____, machinist, foot of Sixth Street," probably a reference to Martin and suggesting that in the lowest ebb of the recession he too was forced to find temporary employment with the Central Pacific. Although there are multiple entries for a Martin Carter in the city directories (as well as multiple entries for Thomas Carter), this particular Carter shows his residence as the Excelsior Hotel, which remained the address of choice for the itinerant Carter shop crew.[46]

In any event, the directory suggests that Martin took up temporary residence away from Saucelito. It was not the life that he and Mary had planned. Martin could not imagine moving his family into the Excelsior Hotel, with its stark landscape of Mission Bay and the toxic smells of Tar Flat and the Sixth Street sewer. Undoubtedly, Martin missed the green hills and fresh salt breezes of Marin County. He missed Mary and the boys, and his horses, and he considered the choices he would have to make if the struggling firm of Carter Brothers could no longer justify the space it rented, or the tiny crew it kept together on a standby basis.

We know that John Carroll was living a similar life, also rooming in the Excelsior Hotel for the remainder of 1877 and probably living by himself, walking two city blocks to the foot of Sixth Street to go to work each day. Carroll was fifty-three years old in 1877, and in a period of economic stagnation facing an uncertain future.

In another year, Carter Brothers would be expanding its business dramatically into new markets and new designs, but it is unclear what role, if any, Carroll played in the revival. The last known record of John Carroll is the withdrawal of his voter registration from Saucelito on September 5, 1877, which made it possible for him to vote in the San Francisco precinct for the election that November. By that time, Carter Brothers, as a business, had moved to Newark, California. The voter registration records suggest that Carroll did not go along. It was one of the lasting ironies of the long, bitter recession that at its conclusion, on the verge of a dramatic turnaround in the car business that John Carroll had helped found, he would not remain to share in its biggest success.

Sometime after November 1877, John Ambrose Carroll, self-proclaimed builder of the first railroad car in California and mentor to Thomas Carter for nearly fifteen years, vanished from the record.

For the tradesman, the shopkeeper, the laborer, and their families, the failure of the Bank of California meant a sudden and interminable disappearance of money. For six weeks after its closing, loans in any form—gold, silver, or currency—were simply unavailable, which drove the recession to a nadir.[47] Adding to the pall that hung over San Francisco, the Workingmen's riots erupted in July 1877, the culmination of four years of unemployment, economic stagnation, and growing social unrest. The troubles, variously interpreted as either political reform or anarchy, quickly led to bloodshed.

The Carter tradesmen who moonlighted at the Central Pacific shops were among the lucky few. For two years, California's unemployed had been pouring into San Francisco, looking for nonexistent jobs. Conservative estimates of San Francisco's unemployment rate averaged 15 percent of the work force in 1877, but the number swelled as summer weather encouraged transience from other parts of the state.[48] At first disorganized and nameless, the unemployed clotted around orators in empty city lots, shouting anti-Chinese slogans. But on the evening of July 23, they fused together in mob action, looting and burning a dozen Chinese laundries. In the lingering daylight of the summer evenings that followed, the mob ebbed and flowed through the streets, hunting for new targets.

The day after the attack on the laundries, influential San Francisco businessmen met to erect a line of defense around their businesses and property. William Coleman chaired the meeting. A merchant and real estate developer, he had earned a reputation for organizing vigilante movements in the 1850s; working outside the law, Coleman's "Committee of Vigilance" dealt with early San Francisco crime by trying and hanging the offenders. Twenty years later, something of a legend in the urbanized environment of San Francisco, Coleman's credibility remained high. In the face of the Work-

Graphic depiction of the 1877 San Francisco Workingmen's Riots, in *The Wasp*, Nov. 17, 1877. [California State Library]

ingmen's riots, federal authorities offered to issue government rifles to Coleman if he would use them to stiffen the city's resistance to mob rule.

Coleman showed leadership, but also restraint. The government rifles remained locked up in the Benicia arsenal, while Coleman opted to limit defensive weapons to hickory pick handles. On the afternoon of July 25, Coleman gave orders for nearly six thousand members of the "Pick Handle Brigade" to move into position at the foot of the Pacific Steamship docks. The docks symbolized two convenient scapegoats for the state's economic woes: large corporations in control of most of California's commercial interests, and the Chinese whom the corporations imported as a source of cheap labor. Twenty-two thousand Chinese had entered the state the previous year, most disembarking at the Pacific Steamship docks.[49] That night, the rioters again fused into a single unit, intent on burning the docks. But before they could reach their target, they faced the sobering sight of thousands of stout hardwood handles thumping into the open fists of Coleman's army. That night, Coleman's line of defense held tight. The mob did not reach the docks, and no lives were lost.

But the element of fear persisted. As cartoons in the *Wasp* bore witness, the city was gripped by the image of its own destruction. "Do [the rioters] not know," the *Wasp* decried, "that if Chinatown is burnt down the greater part of the city would be given to the flames, and a reign of terror inaugurated?"[50] Thanks to Coleman, the worst scenario was avoided.

But the cause of the riots smoldered long after the Pick Handle Brigade disbanded. A month later, one of Coleman's lieutenants, Dennis Kearney, adopted much of the mob's rhetoric in an effort to solidify a political response to the social ills that were still plaguing the California economy. Appealing directly to the same crowds he had helped to control, Kearney tapped the emotions of the displaced workers and channeled them into the Workingmen's Trade and Labor Union.[51] In empty sand lots scattered across San Francisco, Kearney delivered increasingly militant diatribes against the Chinese, the Central Pacific Railroad, and the men who profited from both. At the same time, he espoused a new political structure to cope with the perceived threat. Eastern papers were quick to label him "Kearney, the Kalifornia Kommunist." In California itself, the movement became known simply as the Workingmen.

In his own personality, Kearney seemed to embody the forces tearing at California's social fabric. On October 29, at the height of the tension, Kearney chose an empty sand lot on Nob Hill, near Stanford's mansion, to deliver a fiery attack against railroad monopolists. Only a thousand Workingmen gathered to listen, but Kearney magnified their frustration to the threshold of violence. Leland Stanford, fearing reprisals on his home, wrote a letter to the chief of police, asking for special protection for his family. City police responded by hiring 150 private officers to beef up patrols. The City of San Francisco passed ordinances forbidding public speakers to incite violence and invoked the ordinances to arrest Kearney, who, by then, had acquired a large and united following. The strong-arm tactics of the authorities only served to consolidate, rather than disperse, the movement.

As the Workingmen's movement grew in numbers, an unexpected source of support came from the California Grangers. Weakened by drought and high transportation costs, the Grangers recognized a strong common cause with the Workingmen: intense hatred of cartels and large corporations. In the next two years, the Granger movement and the Workingmen's Party would form a new and powerful coalition against the cartels, joining forces in 1879 to promote boycotts of Chinese business and to reform the state's constitution. Ironically, although the constitutional reforms promoted stronger legislative control over the railroads in the state, they encouraged even stronger Central Pacific hegemony into politics, influence peddling, and secrecy.

From the perspective of an average day laborer living in San Francisco in the summer of 1877, violence, not reform, was shaping the course of events. Kearney swore his supporters would stage a mass protest on Thanksgiving Day, even if they had to march "up to their knees in blood." The alleged provocation to violence got Kearney thrown into jail. Swearing he had used the word "mud," not "blood," witnesses quickly secured his release.[52] But the Chinese received the worst of the social venom when Kearney angrily condemned "the railroad robbers and the political cutthroats of [California] who have pooled their issues to import long-tailed lepers from Asia."[53] He frequently ended his speeches with the invective "The Chinese must go!"

Other ethnicities gained a measure of protection from the intense scrutiny Kearney focused on the Chinese. The Workingmen's movement protected the niche the Irish occupied in the community. Eight years before the Workingmen's troubles, the San Francisco Irish paper *Monitor* wrote: "Our Countrymen need not fear . . . that they will have to encounter the prejudices against their race or religion, that are such drawbacks to their settlement in many parts of the Eastern States. Irishmen have made themselves a position here fully equal to that of any other nationality in our cosmopolitan population, and newcomers of the same race need fear to find no prejudice to bar their advancement."[54]

Dennis Kearney, himself Irish, cloaked the Workingmen's movement in the ideology of Irish ascendancy. The Workingmen's Party was often accused of exploiting the dregs of Irish "hooliganism" and representing only the unskilled and unemployed, but in fact the movement built its popularity on the rising earning potential and new social stature of first- and second-generation Irish immigrants. Irish dominance of San Francisco politics was already widely recognized. San Francisco was the first major American city to elect an Irish mayor (Frank McCoppin, in 1867), preceding a national trend that soon continued in Boston (1884) and New York (1880).[55]

In 1879, 27 percent of the city's voters were Irish-born, the largest ethnic voter's group. From census records, it can be demonstrated that the ranks of skilled Irish blue-collar and white-collar jobs steadily increased from 1850 to 1880, while the percentage of unskilled Irish labor steadily shrank. White-collar Irish workers, for example, advanced from 15.4 percent to 19.9 percent of the population during this time period.[56] Frank Roney, the Irish molder who was hovering near the poverty line when he wrote his diary in the 1875–76 period, rose to prominence in the Workingmen's Party in 1877 and shared its leadership with Kearney.

While Dennis Kearney vilified Stanford, Huntington, Crocker, and Hopkins (and their holdings—the Central Pacific Railroad and the Pacific Steamship Co.), he avoided implicating the Irish owners of the Nevada Bank in any kind of moral or social culpability. Ironically, both groups of capitalists, directly or indirectly, supported widespread use of Chinese labor.

The San Francisco literary and satiric journal *Wasp* quickly exploited the racist themes running through the Workingmen's movement, cartooning a strong Irish presence among the Workingmen's power brokers but portraying the Chinese and Irish workers as linked in a common plight: exploitation by large corporations. Both San Francisco ethnicities were roughly equal in size in the 1870s.[57] But the Irish, in sharp contrast to the Chinese, could vote, and they had an established role in the social fabric of the community.

Henry Fairfax Williams described St. Patrick's Day, 1877, among the Irish laborers and graders working on Mission Bay. He accepted their society and customs as a permanent context, and he wrote matter-of-factly in his diary: "My laborers generally being Irish, they took a holiday, and my work was suspended."[58] The Chinese received no such quarter.

Nonpolitical by nature, Thomas Carter found himself part of a new, rising social strata. An insular man, he lived with a growing contradiction. Now part of what might be called the "Irish mainstream," he was also fast becoming an integral part of the corporations the Workingmen were struggling against. Like a lightning bolt, money from the Irish-owned Nevada Bank leapt across the bleakest year in the recession and kept Carter Brothers alive. In early 1876, Nevada Bank money paid off Carter's balance with the Santa Clara Valley Railroad. The car contract would continue (and expand) under the corporate umbrella of the South Pacific Coast Railroad, funded entirely by Fair and Flood's Comstock profits, which represented a steady (and perhaps only) source of income for Carter Brothers in the cash-starved Centennial year.

But the cultural shift taking place in San Francisco was about more than money. Carter moved into an elite circle of Nevada Bank investors and stock traders reforming the way investment dollars were spent. He was quickly becoming more than a contractor, offering business and technical consultation about where and how new capital could be invested. One of James Fair's most powerful lieutenants, Alfred Edward Davis, listened carefully to what Carter had to say and began to conceptualize a $3 million investment based substantially on Carter's advice. (The focus of the investment, the South Pacific Coast Railroad, is discussed in detail in Chapter Ten.)

In return, "Hog" Davis offered both Carters advice on personal investment. Thomas bought a house in San Francisco and began to bank considerable cash reserves while looking for other real estate to buy. Martin bought blocks in the Mission Bay development near the Sixth and Berry Street works. Over drinks with Davis in financial district saloons, Thomas could peer deep into the inner workings of a new economy, coached, as Henry Fairfax Williams had been, by the bankers in power on Montgomery Street.

But it is difficult to imagine Thomas Carter having a drink with Dennis Kearney. Virtually all of the railroads that bought Carter cars employed Chinese labor. A double standard was clearly at work, encouraging development of short lines that could remain independent of the Central Pacific on the one hand but condemning the almost universal employment of Chinese on the other. Seeking the economic benefits of development, the Workingmen condemned its instruments.

The "troubles," as they were known locally, made Thomas Carter's choice painfully clear. During the summer of 1877, the noise and shock of the Workingmen's riots invaded his sleep, cautioning him on the price of success. For the second time, he faced a clear and present need to retreat from the threat of hostility. Martin might have cast the deciding vote. Settled into country life in Saucelito, he would not move his family into the path of the troubles in San Francisco. The two brothers now talked more as equals. If Thomas at first defended the Sixth and Berry Street factory as a permanent seat for the family business, Martin could easily have spoken to the risk in doing so. No letters survive from either, but from the outcome it is clear that Martin became a conscience for the business, and a strong voice in making its decisions.

As early as July 1877, Carter Brothers was building passenger cars in the nascent town site of Newark, twenty-five miles south of San Francisco. The Martin Carter family moved to Newark along with the work. With the opening of the Newark shop, the kit strategy became irrelevant; the cars they produced were delivered to a customer whose mainline ran fifty feet away from the car shop. The process of closing the Sixth and Berry shops was probably completed by the time Dennis Kearney delivered his famous Nob Hill address in late October.

Thomas, however, would not leave the City. In the next two years, he would watch the Workingmen and the Bank of Nevada clash over their disjointed vision of a new California social structure.

Forced to take sides, Carter belonged to neither.

On August 28, 1875, one day after Ralston's death, R. G. Dun and Co.'s credit reporter expressed confusion about the true state of affairs in the Kimball Carriage and Car works:[59]

> It is impossible at present to give anything definitive as to the condition of the concern, but stray fears are entertained that it will not be able to sustain itself owing to the recent disastrous failure of the Bank of California and the death of W. C. Ralston who has from the start been the main support of this concern. Until further developments take place it will be only prudent not to extend them any credit without having the most ample security.

By January 1876, it was clear that the Kimball works would be included, under terms of court probate, in the holdings of Ralston's estate. Reduction of the company's considerable debt was begun, in part by turning over stock and inventory to creditors. Its two primary business sites, the carriage works at Fourth and Silver and the agricultural works at Sixth and Berry, remained the property of the Kimball Carriage and Car Co. George Kimball and Richard Ogden continued as managers, apparently concentrating production work at Fourth and Silver streets. Business continued at a much reduced scale. R. G. Dun's credit report, for January 21, 1876, continued:[60]

> Ogden & Kimball, who are the only partners, say that the property is worth in the vicinity of $104,000 and that the liabilities are from $30–$40,000. [They] are now taking an inventory and say that they will have a balance sheet in a few days, which they will exhibit to us . . . they intend to continue the business on a much smaller scale than heretofore, and claim that they have means enough to handle it.

In this time period, during the month of November 1875, Kimball delivered a small lot of three-foot-gauge cars to the San Luis Obispo & Santa Maria Valley Railroad, under construction on California's central coast. The prices for the rolling stock suggest the forces of Carter's competition at work: one second-class coach cost $2,000, two boxcars were priced at $560 each, and twenty-two flatcars cost $358 each.[61]

Such orders were becoming rare for Kimball. When the San Luis Obispo & Santa Maria Valley next ordered cars, as the Pacific Coast Railroad in 1881, a substantial order for freight cars would be placed with Carter Brothers. Reports of unsold Kimball cars can be found in the same time period, when three passenger cars, built for the California Pacific but undelivered, were finally sold to the Vacaville Extension Railroad in May 1875.[62]

Throughout 1876 and 1877, R. G. Dun's credit investigator continued to cast a jaundiced eye on the business. When Kimball and Ogden shared the results of their inventory, claiming surplus assets of nearly $245,000, the credit report coldly noted that Richard Ogden has "given us no proof whatever of the correctness of his statement and when told of the great discrepancy between it and the one made by his partner Kimball, he replied that when they two took inventory, things turned out better than they expected."[63]

The report further intimated that Ogden was trying to sell out his share, a separation accomplished in October 1876. It was also clear that by March 1876, a court battle was shaping up between Kimball and Eugene Soule, who still pressed his claim for 25 percent interest in the Sixth and Berry agricultural implement works. Also that March, R. G. Dun reported Kimball's intent to sell the agricultural branch of the business and cut its losses.

The date of the reported intent to sell is still eight months shy of what is generally accepted as the time of Carter's final move from Saucelito, November 1876. There certainly would have been ample time, and incentive, for Carter to occupy the Sixth and Berry facility as early as March of the Centennial year. Kimball, we suspect, would have made him a good deal on rent.

Embattled, operating under the court-administered Ralston trust, Kimball survived an attempt by its creditors to declare it bankrupt in July 1878. The list of plaintiffs read like a who's who of the coastal railroad supply industry: Occidental Foundry, Goodyear Rubber Co., California Wire Works, and N. S. Arnold were all selling parts and supplies for railroad manufacture; all sued Kimball for back debt. Among the plaintiffs were Richard Ogden, Kimball's former partner; and Eugene Soule, who was bringing court action on the alleged Sixth and Berry Street partnership. Even the Nevada Bank had a sizable loan, of $8,000, outstanding and unpaid.[64]

On March 31, 1879, the District Court rejected the plaintiffs' suit on the basis that most of the claims weren't provable; the decision allowed Kimball to remain in operation for another four years. Few, if any, commercial railroad cars are known to have been built by Kimball in this period. But stubbornly, the brand name that Kimball had started refused to die. So did Eugene Soule's persistent claims. In the October 1883 issue of the *National Car Builder,* Soule was named as successor to the railroad manufacturing business of the "Kimball Car Company." On his business card, which was probably printed the following year, Soule proclaimed himself manufacturer of "Cars, Wagons and Carriages, Plows, Agricultural Implements of all Description." His business address was listed as Fourth and Bryant, most likely in the cavernous old 1868 Kimball factory. If Soule produced any railroad rolling stock after this settlement, it has never been documented.

In his November 1877 entry, R. G. Dun's credit reporter wrote a kind of final assessment of George Kimball's pioneering role: "He is steady, a good mechanic and bears a good character, but appears inclined to undertake too much for his means and there is a lack of confidence in his ability as a manager and local houses have a disposition to restrict him to small lines."[65]

George Kimball died on August 23, 1884.

Eugene Soule held a partial interest in Kimball's agricultural implement business and sued Kimball in bankruptcy court after the closing of the business in 1875 or 1876. At the time his business card (above) was printed, Soule was leasing space in Kimball's old Fourth and Bryant works and continuing the carriage business. [California Historical Society]

Eastern car builders, of course, smelled an opening.

San Francisco railroad manufacturing was not, in the last half of the 1870s, a growth industry. Production figures for railroad cars made in the city suggest a business held captive by recession: 1875–76, forty cars; 1876–77, two hundred cars; 1877–78, fifty-five cars; and 1878–79, fifty cars.[66]

Except for an abrupt spike of activity in 1876–77 (caused, we can speculate, by Carter's kit business), most of the rolling stock represented by these statistics was probably street railway equipment built for San Francisco itself. Henry Casebolt carried on the manufacture of early cable cars for his Sutter Street Railway, experimental versions of the grip car that was undergoing tests in January 1877.[67]

The Central Pacific car shop in Sacramento was capable of at least five times the manufacturing capacity of the rest of California's car industry put together. This left only two marketing niches for independent contractors: street railways and narrow gauge.

By the late 1870s, the narrow gauge niche was a particularly attractive target for eastern and midwestern manufacturers. As Barney and Smith demonstrated with the North Pacific Coast, eastern builders too could kit and ship hundreds of narrow gauge cars in a single order. Their craftsmanship and materials were demonstrably superior to those used in West Coast products and normally would have commanded a premium price, exclusive of the added cost of shipping. The national financial crisis had the effect of dropping prices even further for eastern manufactured goods, promoting their importation into California. Hence, for the first time, agents based on the West Coast began to bundle ensembles of eastern products especially for the narrow gauge market. In 1877, Williams, Blanchard and Co., which had offices at 218 California Street, advertised "Narrow Gauge Railroad Supplies" that offered, emporium-style, rail from the Trenton Iron Works, loco-motives from Baldwin, and rolling stock from the Jackson and Sharp Co.

Like natural selection, difficult business conditions were eliminating weak competitors from the field. If Kimball's resources could not create and domi-nate a West Coast car market, one argument went, how could such manu-facturing survive in California in any form? Williams, Blanchard were bet-ting that when interest rates began to drop on the West Coast, promoting new capitalization, eastern manufacturers would virtually own the territory.

Sometime before the 1884 Coast Survey Map was published, the factory at Sixth and Berry streets vanished.[68]

Williams reported occasional fires among the lumber stockpiles along Channel Street, and the Kimball factory was surrounded by lumber deal-ers, making it especially vulnerable to conflagration. But subsidence was also a destructive force shaping the Mission Bay development. The relent-less settling and compaction of newly deposited soil into a marshy basement had already claimed one of the early Central Pacific warehouses on King Street. The Sixth and Berry building was two stories high, which brought considerable structural weight to bear on its mud sills and raised the pros-pects of racking and twisting.

The building's fate remains unknown. When the Coast Survey map was published in 1884, block 21 appears vacant. The Kimball agricultural works have simply gone.

In 1877, Langley's City Directory listed the Carter Brothers address as Sixth and Berry, in the industrial outback of the city. One year later, in 1878, Langley's reported Carter Brothers at suites 20–21 of the Nevada Block, in the heart of the city's financial district. The new Montgomery Street address, located inside the castlelike complex of offices and suites con-structed by Fair, Flood, Mackay, and O'Brien, was a pretentious move for the small builder.

Not only had Carter Brothers moved its offices uptown into the heart of the financial district, it was co-located with the headquarters of the South Pacific Coast Railroad—a visible and hegemonious extension of the Com-stock Lode fortunes into California investment. Completed in October 1875, like a nail in Ralston's coffin the Nevada Block was the new seat of finan-cial power for both the bank and the South Pacific Coast. Within a year, the Nevada Block would also serve as a nucleus for satellite firms such as the Bay and Coast Telegraph Co. and the Pacific Land Investment Co.

Propelled from obscurity, Carter had clearly joined the Nevada Bank's inner circle. The circumstances of his meteoric rise remain something of a mystery. It might have coincided with the exodus of Kimball from the Sixth and Berry Street works, and the assumption (on the part of the Nevada Bank) that Carter would take over most of Kimball's old venue. It could have fol-lowed the large Nevada Bank loan to the North Pacific Coast ($350,000, negotiated in late 1876), although by that time Carter was nearing the end of its tenure in Saucelito. But the new trappings of prestige and influence followed Thomas Carter's appointment to superintendency of the South Pacific Coast Railroad, which occurred in January 1876. Both of his new positions—superintendent of the railroad and partner in the outside contracting firm of Carter Brothers—had adjoining Nevada Block addresses: suites 20 and 21.

Business observers of the era were quick to point out that the railroad's office wasn't in the Nevada Block at all, but a few doors down Montgomery Street at the drinking establishment of Salvin and Silas Collins and James Wheeland, known simply as Collins Saloon. Captain John Leale, soon to take charge of the South Pacific Coast's new ferry boat, explained that "in those days, Collin's Saloon on Montgomery Street at California was in full blast and was headquarters for 'A.E.D.' Mr. Davis was an inveterate tobacco-chewer and the quarter circle of sawdust on the floor at the cigar stand was known to all as 'Davis Corner.' Many an important deal for the railroad was put through in this saloon."[69]

At the saloon, in the muffled reverberation of the conversation of stock brokers, insurance dealers, and real estate agents, Thomas Carter sat down to talk with Alfred Davis sometime in the rainy weeks just after New Year's Day, 1876. Unlike Frederick Hihn or Milton Latham, Hog Davis listened.

Judging by the lack of a headlight, the 2-6-0 *Nevada* had just been delivered when it posed on the Bear River Bridge in July 1875, in the stereographic image below; also new, in the detail view of the Bear River Bridge (top), a string of Carter twenty-four-foot flatcars, barely a year old, show features of the builder's early eight-ton-capacity trucks, including the heavy wooden transom beams that formed the truck's structural framework. [Top, California State Railroad Museum; below, Bill Wissel collection]

The original Bear River Bridge was a standard Howe truss completed by Martin and Co. in December 1875. Standing ninety-six feet above the river, it was the highest bridge in California until the same contractor finished the Brown's Canyon Bridge on the North Pacific Coast about a year later, breaking its own record with a span that towered 137 feet above the river. After the Bear River Bridge burned in 1896, it was replaced with a modified truss design, shown above. This view also shows the confluence of Greenhorn Creek, coming in from the left, and the Bear River itself, on the right. [Above, Searls Historical Library]

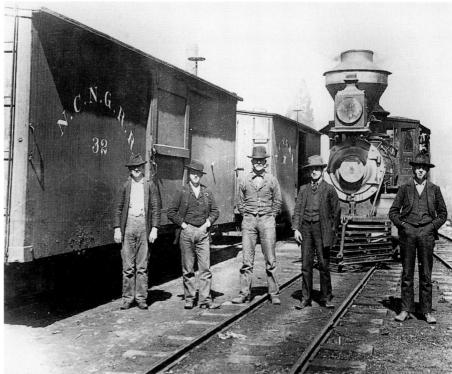

The influence of Carter Brothers on the early Nevada County Narrow Gauge may have extended to the design and construction of the railroad's water tanks. The example at the left above was located in the Grass Valley shops, seen below in an interior view from the turn of the century. Above right, the crew of NCNG number 1 poses with boxcar 32, the first car to follow Carter's series 2-30 in the original roster. Spare Carter kit material, surplused from original car construction in 1876, may have been the basis for car 32's construction in 1877. [Above, Doug MacLeod collection; left, Vernon Sappers collection; below, Rich Dunn collection]

The infamous circus train wreck of Sept. 6, 1893, was notable not only for releasing the wild animals of the Sells-Renfrow Circus but also for turning over Nevada County Narrow Gauge flatcar 7, revealing to the camera (below) more details of a Carter eight-ton freight truck than are available in any other known contemporary photograph. It is likely that this car was rebuilt at least once in the nearly twenty years it operated, but most of the features of the original car, including rubber block springs and a primitive two-lever brake system, remained intact at the time of the wreck. These photographs are the foundation of the mechanical drawings on the pages that follow. (The circus train wreck, however, convinced Sells-Renfrow never to return to Nevada City.) [Both photographs, Holt-Atherton Department of Special Collections, University of the Pacific Libraries]

CARTER BROS., 8 TON FLAT CAR, NEVADA COUNTY NARROW GAUGE RR

ca 1893

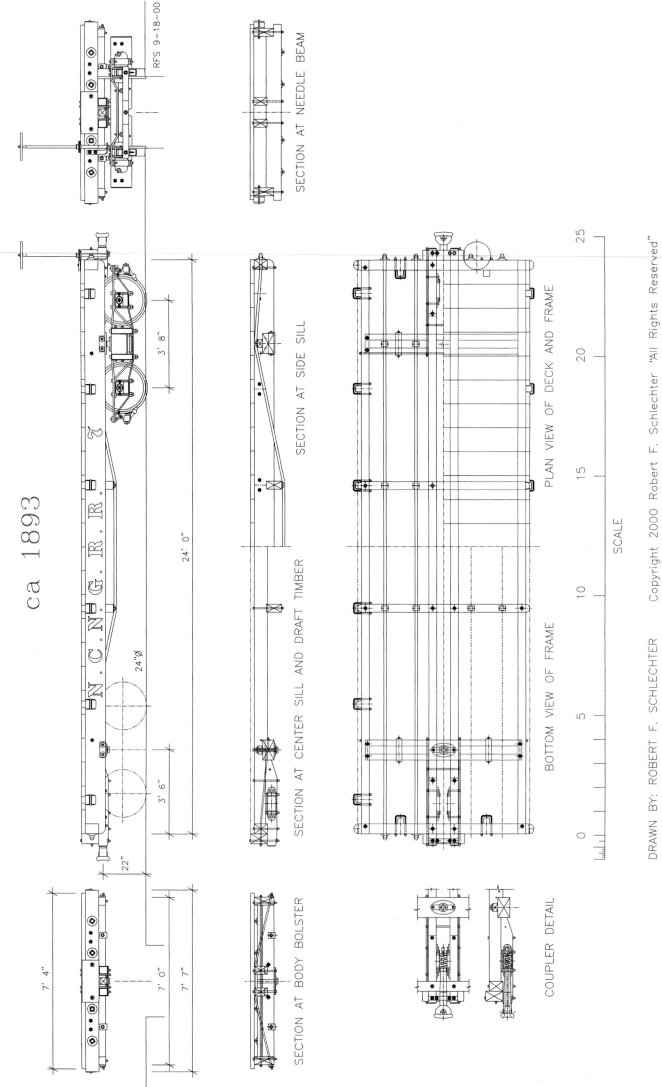

RFS 9-18-00

3' 8"

24' 0"

24" ∅

N. C. N. G. R. R. 7

22"

7' 4"

7' 0"

7' 7"

3' 6"

SECTION AT NEEDLE BEAM

SECTION AT SIDE SILL

SECTION AT CENTER SILL AND DRAFT TIMBER

SECTION AT BODY BOLSTER

PLAN VIEW OF DECK AND FRAME

BOTTOM VIEW OF FRAME

COUPLER DETAIL

SCALE

0   5   10   15   20   25

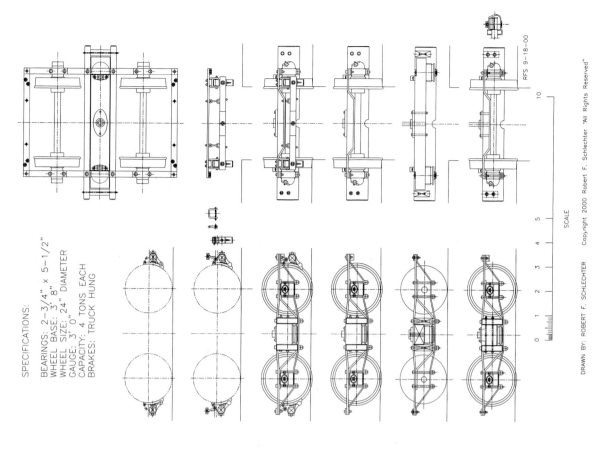

SPECIFICATIONS:

BEARINGS: 2-3/4" × 5-1/2"
WHEEL BASE: 3' 8"
WHEEL SIZE: 24" DIAMETER
GAUGE: 3' 0"
CAPACITY: 4 TONS EACH
BRAKES: TRUCK HUNG

SCALE

CARTER BROS., 8 TON FREIGHT TRUCK, ca 1893
Truck Hung Brake Version

Robert Schlechter's two-dimensional drawings of a Carter eight-ton-capacity flatcar, reproduced on these two pages, are based on the car's appearance and configuration in 1893. Small variations from its 1875 builder's appearance are apparent; for example, the contour of the ends of the transom beams has changed, suggesting a rebuilding of the trucks, but in general the car is almost unmodified since it appeared in an 1876 Nevada County Narrow Gauge photograph by Jacobs (above). [Drawings, Robert Schlechter]

Perhaps courting higher public esteem, John Kidder ordered eastern-manufactured cars, rather than Carter products, to complete the railroad's passenger roster. Examples of the F. E. Canda coaches and combines, manufactured in Chicago, appear at Colfax (above) in 1878 and on the Greenhorn bridge (right) at about the same time. [Above, Searls Historical Library; right, Bill Wissel collection]

Tom Mankel   Bill Mutton. Engineer   Eugene   Charles, conductor

Until 1900, the Nevada
County Narrow Gauge
maintained passenger service with just four original
F. E. Canda cars, built in
1875, usually operated in
pairs for mixed train service, as in the photograph
at Long Ravine Bridge
(below) taken in the mid-
1880s. Trains requiring
more capacity, such as the
Masonic special photo-
graphed at the Colfax
freight transfer shed
(above), used converted
flatcars to handle the
crowds. [Above, Stan
Kistler collection; below,
Guy Dunscomb collection]

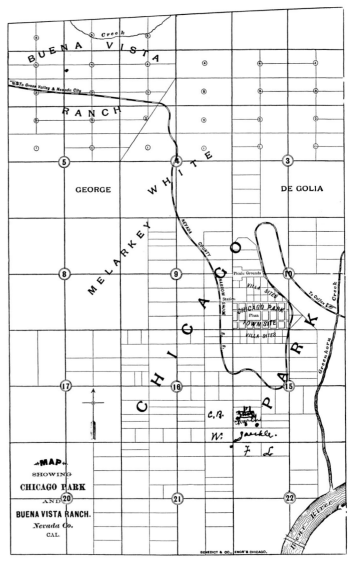

The high country around You Bet tunnel, photographed (below) in the winter of 1875–76, was still wilderness when the narrow gauge completed its crossing of the ridge that separated the Bear River from Greenhorn Creek. Slowly, development followed the railroad. Storms Ranch, on the west side of the divide, became the site of a large picnic grounds, a destination for trains of canvas-roofed flatcars during the summer season. In 1888, the Chicago Park Land and Development Co. bought three thousand acres near Storms Ranch (above) and attempted to sell subdivision-style lots. [Above left, Heritage Graphics; others, Searls Historical Library]

John Coleman's Mohawk Lumber Mill (right) was the early motive for his financial backing of the Nevada County Narrow Gauge, securing an outlet for the mill's timber production to local mines. Small contractors working out of You Bet Station (below) supplied cord wood for consumption by narrow gauge locomotives. [Below, Doug MacLeod collection; above, Earl Failla collection; right, Heritage Graphics]

Archeological investigation into early Carter designs usually begins with wrecks, fire, or other disaster, in this case the Grass Valley roundhouse fire of 1915 (opposite), which crippled all but two of the railroad's locomotives. Desperate to return damaged engines to service, the railroad concentrated on 2-6-0 number 5 (shown above), which had been stored outside the burning roundhouse. The engine itself was relatively unharmed, but fuel in its tender had caught fire, badly damaging the tender trucks. Working under pressure and on a shoestring budget, Master Mechanic Johnny Nolan rebuilt the tender's trucks with parts on hand, which may explain why number 5's tender was equipped with journal boxes allegedly recycled from discarded Carter eight-ton freight cars. If this explanation is true, the remains of number 5, on display today in Nevada City, may contain the only known surviving Carter eight-ton journal boxes.

Ironically, another California narrow gauge artifact from the 1870s, Santa Cruz & Felton's Porter, Bell locomotive *Santa Cruz*, was given a reprieve from the scrap line after the same fire. The engine had been sold to the Nevada & Oregon in 1881, then to lumber railroads around Lake Tahoe, and finally to the Nevada County Narrow Gauge in 1899. Visible at the left-hand edge in the view opposite below, the hulk of the small locomotive was quickly restored and pressed into operation—the last time the historic Porter would steam.

Overleaf: In the 1890s, Nevada County Narrow Gauge number 1 pauses with a mixed train on the Bear River Bridge. [Opposite, Searls Historical Library; this page, San Francisco Maritime National Historical Park, Livingston Collection; overleaf, California Historical Society]

South Pacific Coast number 16, manufactured by Baldwin in 1885, is shown (above)
on freight service in Los Gatos Canyon.
Based on the successful 4-4-0 wheel arrangement, the locomotive was an outgrowth
of the class 8-18 C, but almost 15 percent
heavier. In contrast with machines of the
1870s, number 16's streamlined domes and
boiler appliances testify to an evolutionary
change in Baldwin engineering. South Pacific
Coast crewmen coming into engine service
about the time the 16 was delivered, such as
Colby Lorenzen, would be among the first
to compare the performance of the two
types of locomotive. [Above, William Wulf
collection; right, Ken Lorenzen collection]

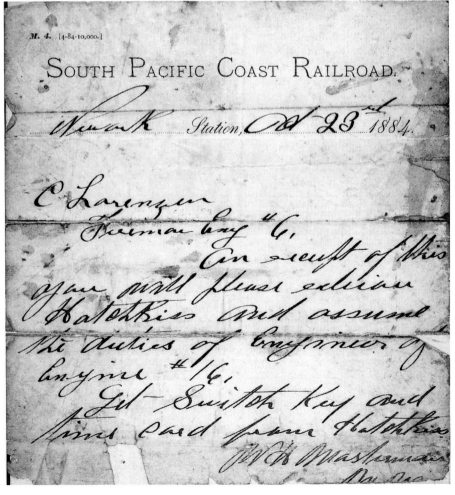

10

Reengineering: The South Pacific Coast

Alfred E. "Hog" Davis probably approached Thomas Carter in late December 1875 about the unpaid balance Carter was owed by the Santa Clara Valley Railroad. There is no evidence that the two had ever met, but Davis would have had little trouble winning Carter's attention with an offer to negotiate a settlement. Probably over drinks at a Montgomery Street saloon named Collins, Davis offered to pay off Carter's overdue invoices. It was Davis's style to pay in cash, a lump sum of approximately $5,000.[1] Already two months behind in cash flow on the Santa Clara Valley job, his factory virtually at a standstill, Carter quickly became the beneficiary of Davis's deep pockets. Davis, in turn, won a small negotiating advantage. It wasn't just the rolling stock that Davis wanted Carter to finish. It was the entire railroad.

The timing of this meeting is the key to understanding the relationship between Davis and Carter, for it could only have taken place in a window of opportunity so short that impulse, calculated or not, forced the course of action both would take. Just a few weeks after the abrupt cessation of Bartling's construction project in the torrential rains of December 1875, Thomas Carter would be propelled from third-party contractor to the highest level of management inside the new company. After assuming complete control over the Santa Clara Valley Railroad by February 4, and having invested as little as one month in active negotiation, Davis made up his mind that Tom Carter would manage the railroad's construction.

The business planning behind the South Pacific Coast, its capitalization, confirmation of Alfred Davis as its president, staffing of its key positions, and the crucial buyout of Bartling, Peebles, and Robertson—all must have happened in four weeks or less, in the same time period it took the Santa Clara Valley Railroad to show symptoms of insolvency. The last known date of a Santa Clara Valley business transaction was a day or two prior to January 6, 1876, when the scv ordered twenty thousand board feet of lumber for a construction camp Bartling intended to build in Santa Clara.[2] Lawsuits from local right-of-way grantors (for example, David Bane and John Lowrie) might have signaled the fiscal breakdown of Bartling's organization, no later than January 29.[3]

Even if Davis were warned in advance of internal financial troubles within the Santa Clara Valley Railroad, he had only a couple of weeks in which to put together the critical components of the plan that would become the South Pacific Coast Railroad. In Davis's mind, the driving force behind the plan was very likely not the railroad itself but real estate, some forty-five hundred acres represented by the Newark town site and adjoining lands held by the English Company's reclamation project. But the railroad was the key link between the real estate and Dumbarton Point, which was the nearest port of access. Both the Perrin brothers and J. Barr Robertson recognized that without the railroad their investments in local land projects would be worthless, a fact Davis turned into a negotiating tactic to use against them. Davis would first gain control of the Santa Clara Valley Railroad and then approach the Perrins and Robertson about buying land. With the Nevada Bank's first mortgage bonds, he controlled the railroad. With the railroad in operation, he controlled the real estate.

Davis still lacked one critical resource to put the pieces together: a working knowledge of railroads. Though a miner, capitalist, commercial agriculturist, distiller of spirits, and manager of a large fresh meat and vegetable outlet called the California Market, nowhere in Davis's twenty-five year business portfolio was there a single railroad property, nor a single partner who could claim such experience. Neither did the purchase of the Santa Clara Valley bring in leadership to administer the takeover. Major Bartling and J. Barr Robertson, listed initially on the South Pacific Coast board of directors, were both gone in less than six months, poor handmaidens for Davis's autocratic and authoritarian management style.

The greatest performance of Thomas Carter's entire life was to convince Davis he could fill the painfully obvious gap.

———————————

J. Barr Robertson, convinced the sky was falling, regarded Alfred Davis as a combination of Leland Stanford and the devil. Robertson may have been among the last of the original players to understand Davis's real intentions. Perhaps he was aware of Davis as early as January 21, 1876, when the sale of the line's sole locomotive "to a new buyer" aroused Robertson's suspicions of a takeover. But as late as February 11, Robertson could still have labored under the false assumption that the Santa Clara Valley Railroad was a viable enterprise, when he noted active litigation by Bartling's attorney on unsettled land sales.[4]

By March 6, however, the true picture was becoming painfully clear, when Robertson wrote to J. M. Walker:

My Dear Walker,

I have been extremely busy these last few days with the changes in the Railroad & Newark. The argument addressed to me to console me for my loss is that our Company's property will be more benefited by the capitalists taking over these enterprises, than any other property, and I must say that this is perfectly true, tho' while I sustain the loss, I shall under the most favourable circumstances, get only a fraction of the profit.

Incorporation papers have been drawn of the South Pacific Coast Railroad Company, but they have not been registered yet.

The Newark property has been sold subject to the Newark Land Association's bond which expires on April 1st.

The evidence is accumulating to show that Flood, O'Brien, MacKay [sic] and Fair the great mining firm, are in the circle that are taking up the Railway & Newark; and in the meantime I have to ask you to hold my shares for the present if at all possible until I can judge of the possible course of events. It is raining nearly every day.[5]

Unbeknown to Robertson, two days before this letter was written Davis quietly purchased the core sixteen hundred acres of Dairy Ranch, the center of the Newark town site, from E. B. Perrin and B. B. Minor, who still controlled ownership of the town through the Green Point Dairy and Transportation Co. Without arousing suspicion (especially Robertson's), Davis bought the choicest piece of real estate along the railroad for $160,000.[6]

Minor might have been the invisible link between Davis and Perrin, and possibly Davis's spy into the financial condition of the Santa Clara Valley Railroad. Davis had known Minor since 1867, when he was clerk for Haggin and Tevis in the California Market development; as a reward for smoothing the Newark deal, he installed him on the South Pacific Coast's board of directors (a seat entitled by a single share of stock). Davis continued to rely on Minor's intelligence for the purchase of twenty-nine hundred additional Green Point Dairy acres at a price of $140,000. The combined sale netted Davis forty-five hundred acres, placed under the ownership of the subsidiary Pacific Land Investment Co. on May 13, 1876.

The secret buyout caught Robertson by surprise. "My loss" (as he referred to the episode) included his direct investments in "two Newark companies and two Railway companies," an amount he estimated to Walker at $10,200 "exclusive of the $1400 subscription to the railway."[7] Stung by the reverses, Robertson thrashed about for compensation. In a letter to Walker on April 12, 1876, he gave the impression that his motives, and loyalties, were linked first and foremost to enhancing the value of the British company's stock: "You informed me some time ago that if the Railroad went through, you would be able to get an advance on my shares to a much larger extent, and I feel constrained to ask you do that but to hold over my shares until I can make a sale within a short time, as it may be that the whole property may become the subject of negotiation."

However, on March 23, more than two weeks before this letter was written, Robertson wrote a personal letter to Alfred Davis, offering to sell out his share of the property. Acting like an independent agent, Robertson offered to sell Davis, in his own name, 274 acres at the tip of Dumbarton Point for $15,000 in gold. "Dumbarton Island," as Robertson referred to the tract surrounding the Santa Clara Valley Railroad wharf, was arguably strategic ground. A competitor railroad could just as easily use it to gain deepwater access, so Robertson offered Davis a chance to own a nearly impregnable fortress around the Dumbarton Point wharf and terminal.

But Davis reacted cautiously. He probably knew that Dumbarton Point was embroiled in a legal technicality.[8] Attached to the shore of Alameda

County, it was bounded by a gerrymandering protrusion of San Mateo County, which crossed the open water of the Bay from Ravenswood Point to adjoin the tip of Dumbarton. A land attorney had warned Robertson that the California Land Investment Co.'s original deed, filed only in Alameda County, might therefore be invalid. At the time of Robertson's offer to Davis, the boundary line was being resurveyed. Aware of the contested boundary, Walker was never consulted on the offer to Davis; it was a symptom of growing distrust between Robertson and his London manager.

The distrust grew over the next two months. Pressured by Walker to repay cash for advances taken against his stock, Robertson changed tactics. He began to peddle California Land Investment Co. shares to Davis on May 5, offering him controlling interest in the company's twenty thousand wetland acres. By this time, Walker was telegraphing fire sale prices to Robertson, hinting the board of directors would support a sale at two pounds a share—half the value Robertson was convinced the property was worth.

Robertson did not hide his anger in a May 5 reply:

> To mention such a price [to Davis] . . . would be fatal, why[,] I feel certain I could borrow that amount at the Nevada Bank (Flood & O'briens), as Mr. Davis in a sly way hinted to me not long ago that they could advance to me if I transferred my shares to them. But this would be rather dangerous, at least in the face of a prospect for selling them. . . . I have been afraid for the last two months that Davis might learn in any way that Beard's[9] [twenty-one hundred] shares are for sale.

Davis, meanwhile, played Robertson like a fish. Loans were dangled in front of him, available at low interest if stock were put up as collateral. A seat on the board of the South Pacific Coast and a seat on its real estate subsidiary Pacific Land Investment Co. were offered Robertson, and accepted. But the leverage Robertson thought he exerted on Davis through these directorates proved to be an illusion. He complained to Walker on July 12 that "as Davis' friends are finding all the money, no meetings of Directors have been held since the statutory meetings to complete the incorporation. Davis does everything himself & the qualifying shares of the Directors were not issued at all, but simply endorsed by us in blank, that being their method of transfer here."

Robertson hunted in vain for a lifeboat. Davis made no firm offers for either stock or land but continued to hint of the potential value of the 274 acres surrounding Dumbarton Point. On June 12, Robertson admitted to Walker that "Davis is still hankering after Dumbarton Island, tho' he says London ideas [prices] are too high for him to make an offer. He thinks he can afford to wait, but in this he may find himself mistaken. The property is however more likely to sell with Dumbarton as part of it."

The last line is especially ironic, recalling Robertson's attempt to sell "Dumbarton Island" by itself just two months before.

Davis, however, had secured the pieces of land he really needed: the right-of-way Robertson's company originally donated to the Santa Clara Valley Railroad, and the key forty-five hundred acres of the Newark town site. From neither of these transactions had Robertson benefited one cent.

San Francisco ferry terminal, foot of Market Street, in *The Wasp*, Feb. 2, 1878. [California State Library]

In the process, Davis revealed the performance art of his own business style: stealth, the persuasive power of cash, and co-opting of potential adversaries. Also perhaps a knack for predicting the future. Two years later, in 1878, Davis would no longer need Dumbarton Point. After extending the railroad's mainline north to Alameda and creating a new ferry terminal on Alameda Point, just fifteen minutes away from San Francisco by fast boat, the sheds and pilings on Dumbarton Point slowly began to whiten under colonies of seagulls. By 1880, the rail connecting the point with Newark was pulled up, recycled to a commuter branch line being surveyed into Oakland.[10]

By the time Dumbarton Point was abandoned, Robertson still managed the original twenty thousand acres of marshland under the virtually paralyzed business entity of the California Land Investment Co., Ltd. Cord grass and dodder, the brilliant orange parasite of the salt marsh, slowly reclaimed the reclamation.

Alfred Edward Davis had acquired the nickname "Hog" in a short, bloody bidding war for a shipload of live pigs that arrived in San Francisco from the Sandwich Islands sometime in 1851 or 1852.

Commissioned for gold-on-delivery by Baron Steinberger, the town's reigning meat wholesaler, the cargo of live pork had no sooner docked than Steinberger and the ship's captain fell into a heated disagreement about price. Accustomed to buying rustled cattle, the baron reasoned that the captain would thank him for taking the pigs off his hands at little more than the price of ballast. Instead, the captain entertained a dark-horse offer from a South of Market potato merchant. Davis offered to buy the shipload of hogs for fifteen cents a pound if the captain would extend Davis credit on a handshake; the captain put Davis's hand in a vise grip. Davis quickly slaughtered the lot and sold the dressed meat to the city's retailers for eighty cents a pound. The captain was paid off in gold, Baron Steinberger was taught a valuable lesson about competition, and Alfred Edward Davis acquired a nickname that followed him for life.[11]

The nickname matched his character, not to mention his fullness of frame. Biographers noted "a certain bluntness in his manner" and a coarse, unpolished vernacular.[12] A fragment of the Davis idiom survived in an interview published in the *San Francisco Call* on March 26, 1895, when he recounted his early experience as a California forty-niner:

> "A man never knows when he has a good thing," said capitalist Alfred E. Davis to a Call reporter in the Lick House yesterday. "Now, to show you what I mean. In May, '49, I landed at San Francisco on the clipper *Gray Eagle*, having sailed around the Horn.
>
> "H'gh," said Mr. Davis, clearing his throat, as he frequently does when conversing.
>
> "Well, I had a partner named Thomas with me, and the first thing I did was to borrow a cart and harness and hire a mule from a man named Tom Kittleman. Hanged if I know whatever became of him.

CAPITALIST DAVIS, WHO BELIEVES IN KEEPING A GOOD THING.

[*Sketched from life for the "Call" by Nankivell.*]

Pen-and-ink sketch of Alfred E. "Hog" Davis, March 1895, in *San Francisco Call*.

H'gh. Anyhow, I agreed to feed the mule and give Tom half of the proceeds." "What did you do with the cart and mule?"

"Hauled anything and everything I could get my hands on. . . . H'gh. But together we cleaned up a good deal of money . . . hundred dollars a day for four weeks. Made it hand over fist. Got $5 for hauling a trunk across the street. Beat anything you ever saw. H'gh? Now to continue. My partner got it into his head that mining was the thing for us to get at, so we sold out the hauling business and took passage on the sloop *Carolina* for Sacramento with about $600 between us. Paid twenty five cents a pound for baggage, and the boat only moved when the wind blew. Hotter 'n blazes. Took seven days to make the trip. H'gh?"

"What camp were you heading for?"

"That's what I'm getting at. It was Coloma. After we got to Sacramento we paid some Spaniards five bits a pound to haul our baggage over there. Never saw such damnable roads in my life. Had to grab roots and limbs of trees to stay on the earth. Did you ever see that kind of road? H'gh? We didn't know a thing about mining, but we took up a claim and went to work. . . .

"Well, we were making a hundred dollars a day hauling trunks and other things in San Francisco, and in Coloma we found that we had scraped up a dollar between us for each day of the week we stayed there. Thomas was the most disgusted man I ever saw, and we finally sold out all the sugar, tea and flour we had for $2 a pound and started to walk back to Sacramento. We had been living on flapjacks made of flour and water fried in a little bacon grease. H'gh? Then the thought of that one hundred-dollar-a-day job we had abandoned was about all we could stand.

"Then I went back to San Francisco. Never should have left it. Don't ever leave a good thing. H'gh?"

Alfred Davis (identified as the full-figured gentleman in the Palace Hotel rotunda, bottom) grew to prominence through his management of San Francisco's celebrated California Market (top). [Above, Muybridge photograph, Bancroft Library; below, Watkins New Series view, California Historical Society]

For the next twenty years both mythology and fact layered onto Davis's growing reputation as a San Francisco capitalist, suggesting a homely genius for a wide assortment of business deals.

In the fifties, Davis farmed potatoes on a lot at Fifth and Mission, allegedly the first commercial vegetable crop grown in the City.[13] In the mid-1860s, Davis and his younger nephew, Samuel, ran Dow's Distillery on Mission Creek, overseeing the manufacture of "about three thousand gallons of whisky daily, . . . alcohol, pure spirits, and high wines."[14] A year later, with partners James Ben Ali Haggin and Lloyd Tevis (whose clerk, B. B. Minor, played the role of inside tipster to the Newark development of 1875), Davis created the California Market, contracting with sixty-six permanent vendors of fruit, vegetables, poultry, oysters, fish, dairy products, fresh meat, and game. It was the largest market in the city under one roof (measuring 75 by 275 feet), sited near the financial district at California and Pine streets—next door, by 1875, to the financial fortress of the Nevada Block.

In 1871, Davis and Haggin purchased 320 acres of swamp land in the San Joaquin River Delta with an eye to land reclamation and commercial agriculture. They incorporated two separate syndicates, the Jersey Island

Packing Co. and the California Asparagus Co., as holding companies for the project. In turn, the Jersey Island tract would help supply the California Market.

Mining ventures that ended disastrously in the early fifties turned to alchemy in the early sixties, when Alfred and nephew Samuel partnered on the Comstock Lode. Alfred was listed in the San Francisco directory as superintendent of the Ophir Mine from 1864 to 1865. In the same period, Samuel, then just eighteen years old, was listed simply as "miner." The profitability of the Ophir during Davis's tenure was among the highest of any mine on the Comstock Lode, but his superintendency was eclipsed by, and at times confused with, that of his successor, James Fair, who first appeared on the Comstock in 1865 and was managing the Ophir by 1866.[15] In fact, Davis continued as director of the Ophir until at least 1868, working at its San Francisco office in rooms at the U.S. Court Block on Montgomery and Jackson streets.

Although roles and accomplishments are not completely understood, the best guess is that Fair and Davis worked in partnership in the Ophir during a time of steady, profitable harvesting of its ore bodies and remembered each other as allies. Fair used the Ophir to gain a better understanding of the thousand yards of adjoining mining property that would become the Consolidated Virginia, the venue for the great bonanza of 1875. Davis moved on to another mining property, the Allison Ranch mine near Grass Valley, purchased by Davis in the late 1860s and operated while he was in residence in Grass Valley.[16] Legend quickly grew about Davis's management style at the Allison Ranch: "The tradition has been current in Grass Valley ever since the late '60's that the mine, which was still paying well, was allowed to fill up with water by A. E. Davis, the owner, in order to drown out a party of tributers who had a lease on a portion of the mine, with whom Mr. Davis had quarreled."[17]

The article in question continued, however, to clarify that James Flood and John Mackay soon partnered with Davis in the Allison Ranch, an important and early link between Davis and the "silver kings," in particular, between Davis and Fair.

Throughout the sixties and early seventies, Davis listed his primary residence as 331 Minna in San Francisco. By business standards of the day, he was successful, and happily married to Elisabeth Butterfield.[18] Alfred, age forty-five; "Lizzy," age thirty-six; their son, Clifford, age six; and daughter, Susan, age four, were all listed as resident at 331 Minna in the 1870 San Francisco census but were accidentally double-counted in the Grass Valley census, where Alfred maintained his Allison Ranch mine residence in a downtown hotel. The double census entries differ. For example, Alfred's net worth was listed as $125,000 in San Francisco but $150,000 in Grass Valley; his San Francisco residence worth $60,000 in the City entry and $100,000 in the Nevada County entry. Lizzy had probably answered the survey questions when the census taker called in San Francisco, while Alfred, away in Grass Valley, probably assumed it was up to him to answer the same questions in absentia. From either perspective, the family was well off.

In 1873, Davis's residential address migrated to the lower reaches of

Nob Hill at 605 Stockton, just a block away from Leland Stanford's mansion at Pine and Powell.

But after the Ophir excitement, after Allison Ranch, after the start-up of the California Market and the Jersey Island reclamation, Davis, nearing fifty, appeared to settle into less physically demanding roles, leveraging his money and the money of his partners through investment. Lizzy bore Alfred a second son, Willis, in 1871. Langley's Directory listed Davis's professional activity as real estate for the first time in 1873, a change in focus intended perhaps to keep Davis closer to home and, briefly, on the threshold of early retirement.

But the explosion of Consolidated Virginia profits in 1875 brought old friends to Davis's door, flush with money they never before imagined they would have, needing his old magic at investment management. By January 1875, Davis appeared reenergized, launching investments first into the Indian Queen Mining and Milling Co., with principal holdings in Eureka, Nevada. Co-investor Edward Barron, president of the Consolidated Virginia in 1876, continued Davis's connection to James Fair, who was still serving as the Con Virginia superintendent. Fair's "investment club" sprang into existence when Con Virginia's revenues first began to flow in late 1874 and continued, uninterrupted, for at least three years.

Davis brokered large chunks of his partner's new wealth into real estate. By May 1875, he was acting as treasurer of the Kern River Land and Canal Co., expanding his investment interests into Central Valley farm land, irrigation, and water rights.

Secondary investments of Consolidated Virginia profit helped launch the Nevada Bank, upsetting the Bank of California's historic dominance of West Coast capital. In turn, the secondary investment reinforced the primary investment. By November 1875, Davis—along with James Flood and William

The rise of the Nevada Bank is illustrated both by its imposing Montgomery Street façade (right) and by the richly embellished engraving on its exchange notes (above). [Above, Huntington Library; David Jacks collection; right, California Historical Society]

O'Brien—was a principal in the Pacific Wood, Lumber, and Flume Co., a scheme for supplying Comstock mines with timber from the Lake Tahoe basin and integrating support industries that supplied the Comstock mines with raw materials.

Little in this upwelling of new investment explains Davis's sudden move into the heavily monopolized California railroad industry. Instead, a kind of circumlocution seemed to take place. Focusing on real estate, conversations with Butler B. Minor helped Davis visualize the intertwining roles of railroad and town, woven through much of Minor's contact with the Green Point Dairy project. Davis understood, for the first time, that a cash-starved railroad held key rights-of-way and wharfing privileges that were the only viable access to the real estate development of Newark. Although no development work had occurred, Newark had all its legal boundaries and tenants in place, a year of marketing in its portfolio, and credible investors committed. Among them, Minor mentioned Henry Fairfax Williams's name. Although Minor could tell Davis horror stories, including Bartling's failure to pay off his creditors, the railroad and town by that point were nearly inseparable.

In short, to Davis the insolvent Santa Clara Valley Railroad was at first simply a means of reaching and controlling forty-five hundred extremely reasonably priced acres of an undeveloped rural town site called Newark.

Collins Saloon, haunt of Alfred Davis and unofficial office of the South Pacific Coast, was located in the Nevada Block between Pine and California streets.

The tail soon wagged the dog.

On February 5, 1876, the *Alameda County Independent* reported that Davis had concluded, in remarkably little time, negotiations for "property and rights" of the Santa Clara Valley Railroad, clearing the way—Davis kept his focus—for land purchases at the town site itself. The deal, probably leveraged through the defaulted Santa Clara Valley first mortgage bonds, got Davis the wharf and car shed on Dumbarton Point, a rain-eroded right-of-way stretching south some seventeen miles to Santa Clara, and a handful of structures, lumber stockpiles, and pilings. The paper identified a 24' × 36' "depot" at Newark as part of the Santa Clara Valley Railroad's original development, a station with no rails laid in front of it and no town to serve had there been any. More functional buildings were in short supply. The railroad made arrangements for boarding and feeding its crews at the old milker's dormitory at the Green Point Dairy, a building Davis soon owned with the purchase of the Perrin lands.

The deal also brought Davis the unpaid debts of the line's contractors. Sometime during the four weeks that bracketed the negotiation, Alfred Davis met Thomas Carter for the first time, probably at Collins Saloon, to settle the debts and obligations of the Santa Clara Valley Railroad to Carter Brothers for delivered and undelivered rolling stock.

At this meeting, Carter might have given Davis his first glimpse of a far more aggressive, far more expansive vision than a real estate development in the baylands. Beyond the muddy kingdom of Newark lay a shadow world on the far side of the Coast Range, where the crescent of Monterey Bay enclosed one of the largest concentrations of commercial timber on the coast.

It was Carter, not Davis, who knew of the ongoing attempts to bridge the Coast Range with rail, and probably Carter who first foresaw the nearly imaginary Santa Clara Valley Railroad extended southwesterly to become a fifty-five-mile link between San Francisco Bay and Monterey Bay. Carter probably described to Davis the conditions under which the Santa Clara Valley could compete head-to-head with the Stanford cartel for the business of the state's first, second, fourth, and eleventh most economically valuable counties.[19]

It is doubtful that Davis grasped at first what Carter tried to tell him. Methodically, Carter set about convincing Davis that he had helped shape every existing link in the chain—the Santa Cruz & Felton, the Santa Cruz Rail Road, and the Santa Clara Valley. The short lines Carter described had struggled to bond into a north-south network that—at least within the range of a one-hundred-mile radius from San Francisco—would be commercially superior to the network forged by the Stanford cartel if—and it was a mighty if—the chain could somehow breach the Santa Cruz Mountains at their summit. Like the subject and object of a new commercial grammar, Carter could match up the supply on the far side of the mountains with their demand in Bay Area markets: Hihn's Soquel Augmentation lumber, the flume traffic off the upper San Lorenzo River, and the cornucopia of wheat in the Salinas Valley. Central and Southern Pacific track reached these markets in roundabout contours that followed, at a safe distance, the edges of coastal mountains. Carter told Davis where the verb must go: Thomas Wright had located a tunnel at the summit of the Santa Cruz Mountains that would pierce the spine of the mountain, directly connecting supply and demand. Carter could accurately tell Davis the tunnel's location. It lay in a notch in the summit ridge some thirty-eight miles southwest of the Dumbarton Landing, most of the miles comparatively flat. About seventeen of the thirty-eight miles Davis now owned through the acquisition of Santa Clara Valley rights-of-way. Davis, Carter argued, was in a position to forge the missing link in the chain.

It was a meeting that turned the careers of both men. The two personalities, both defined by strong egos, suddenly fit together like upper and lower mandibles. Their roles would not compete. Unlike his pretentious relationship with Frederick Hihn, Carter had no need for Davis to patronize his tacit superiority as a leader. They were each what they appeared to be. Raised a Quaker, Davis had acquired a taste for social drinking and a kind of whimsical guile, as Robertson put it, the art of "hinting in a sly way." Davis would instinctively assume the risks, manage the politics, and, when the time came for a showdown, stare the cartel in the eye. Raised Irish Catholic, Carter had learned to hide his emotions with an outward rationality, a core protected by reason. Carter would systematize the risks, minimize them, and reengineer them into a solution. In this fashion, Carter and Davis would operate as a team for the next four years. At this meeting, probably taking place in the torrential rains of late December 1875, the two saw their differences as strengths and agreed for their own reasons that they had hit on the same extraordinary idea. That idea was the South Pacific Coast Railroad.

Of the several conventional explanations for Tom Carter's rise to solid status among the business consortium of Fair, Flood, Mackay, and O'Brien, most are based on circumstances that lay far beyond the venue of the December 1875 meeting. For example, James Flood, born in New York City in 1826, was the son of poor Irish immigrants and also an accomplished carriage maker when he came to San Francisco in 1849; he was thus a close match to Carter's background and trade.[20] Fair had an engineer's knowledge of mining machinery and managed, day-to-day, its application to pumps, hoisting works, skips, stamp mills, and amalgamation tables in the Consolidated Virginia and its affiliated mills. But there is no evidence that Carter knew Flood or Fair before the first meetings with Alfred Davis that December. Far more likely that Davis took Carter's case to Fair and gambled his own reputation that, in a few weeks, the critical elements of a business plan would be proof of Carter's credibility.

Just two months later, on March 24, Fair's approval was made clear in the legal incorporation papers Davis filed with the state. The South Pacific Coast was to build a fifty-five-mile (eventually eighty-mile) link between San Francisco Bay and Monterey Bay that would closely compete with the Stanford cartel for the business of San Francisco, Alameda, Santa Clara, and Santa Cruz counties[21]:

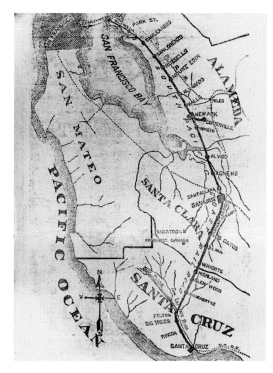

Maps of the South Pacific Coast drawn before 1885 usually show the original Santa Cruz & Felton flume (above), still in commercial service between Felton and Boulder Creek.

> Formed to construct, conduct and maintain a railroad for transportation of passengers and freight and to receive compensation and tolls therefore.
>
> The said railroad is intended to run from a point on the Bay of San Francisco at Potrero Point, otherwise called "Dumbarton Point" in San Mateo County, State of California, through the Counties of Alameda, San Mateo, Santa Clara and Santa Cruz on the most practical route to the town of Santa Cruz in said Santa Cruz County, State of California, with intermediate branch lines to Saratoga and New Almaden from such points as may be designated by the Board of Directors of said corporation. The estimated length of this railroad with its intermediate branches is about 55 miles.[22]

The incorporation read like a digest of Carter's life during the past two years. It was because of his knowledge of Monterey Bay narrow gauge development that Carter could convince Davis that the technology existed to breach the high wall of the Santa Cruz Mountains with a narrow gauge railroad. He had designed and built much of the rolling stock then in commercial operation on similar railroads in Santa Cruz and Monterey counties. He knew their management, their plans, and their business models. Carter reconstructed in detail William J. Lewis's survey over Taylor's Pass, and the Santa Cruz & Felton's surveys up the San Lorenzo. With the difficult summit link completed, Carter could convincingly argue that the South Pacific Coast could connect with the Santa Cruz Rail Road and the Monterey & Salinas Valley Railroad, completing a regional narrow gauge trunk line nearly 150 miles in length. Santa Cruz was then eight hours away from San Francisco, whether by Southern Pacific Railroad or coastal steamer. Even with the steep mountain barrier at Taylor's Pass, the distance Carter proposed to bridge between San Francisco and Monterey Bay would become the shortest of any of these routes, shrinking the travel time to something like four or five hours.[23] At a meeting we think took place in December

Improvements in rolling stock and track ultimately allowed the South Pacific Coast to win and keep a competitive advantage in express train schedules between San Francisco and Santa Cruz. The one-way run took three hours and forty-five minutes (above) and was routine by 1881; by 1884, the time had been shortened to three and a half hours, fifteen minutes faster than rival Southern Pacific. [William Wulf collection]

1875, Carter somehow convinced Davis that he could win, and hold, a significant competitive advantage against Leland Stanford within a region the Central Pacific considered its stronghold.

In return, all Davis had to convince Carter of was unlimited supplies of money. Stacks of gold double eagles, payment for the Santa Clara Valley car work, probably slid across the bar top at Collins Saloon as proof.

Davis reported, almost two years later, that the first work on the railroad began April 5, 1876.[24] By that date, Thomas Carter assumed responsibility as Davis's chief field operative and superintendent. He would manage four remarkably separate and distinct areas of the project, each usually the province of a single experienced professional: grading the first five miles of railroad (all the work the Santa Clara Valley did had to be redone); designing and constructing both trestles and large bridges; manufacturing all the line's rolling stock; and carrying out the duties of general superintendent, including the authority to hire and fire.

Before the month was out, Carter arranged transportation for completed rolling stock from his base of operations in Saucelito. On April 30, the North Pacific Coast's tug *Tiger,* and its car float *Transfer,* docked at Dumbarton Point with some of Carter's completed cars, as well as the purloined Green Point Dairy locomotive, which was taken aboard in San Francisco.[25] This was the first of two shipments of Carter cars by NPC barge (the second occurred in August 1876). But since each barge could only hold the equivalent of twelve narrow gauge freight cars, the single April 30 delivery alone cannot account for the twenty flats, three passenger cars, and one locomotive on hand at Dumbarton by May 13; this suggests that a portion of the flatcars were indeed leftovers from November and December kit building activity taking place on site at Dumbarton Point.[26]

By the time of *Tiger*'s delivery, both Davis and Carter were fully vested in the role each would play during the four long, expensive years required to complete the South Pacific Coast. The roles quickly usurped those of the men who worked for the Santa Clara Valley: Ellis L. Derby, the SCV's civil engineer, was gone from the project before February 26, 1876, taking a new contract for laying out a county road to the top of Mt. Hamilton.

The press was soon aware that Tom Carter held the high-profile duties of superintendent.[27] It is likely that he was in the lead position as of the March 24 incorporation. If so, Carter served from the start as his own contractor, taking over regrading of the first five miles of line, as well as completion of the drawbridge over Beard's Slough (and most likely the twin drawbridges at Station Island as well). Major Henry Bartling remained as president of the South Pacific Coast for less than a month, stripped of any real power by Davis's immediate assumption of the duties of treasurer, and he vanished from the board of directors by early March 1876.[28] From that date forward, Alfred Edward Davis served as the line's president.

The evidence quickly grew that the South Pacific Coast was not the same railroad Bartling and Derby had set out to build. Across the entire span of wetlands on Dumbarton Point, Carter raised the grade three to four feet higher than the original Santa Clara Valley line. Decomposed red rock was available at an outcropping of the Coyote Hills about two miles to the east, close to Mayhew's Landing. In addition to his other contractor duties, Carter would have run his own quarry operation and linked it to the work site by a combination of barges, wagons, and in the most isolated sections two-wheel carts, manhandled through the cord grass. However, without a rail spur into the quarry, it was expensive to haul Coyote Hills red rock. We know that when the work reached Station Island, ten miles south of Dumbarton, Carter set an entire mile of track atop trestlework, a strategy necessitated by the prohibitive price of ballast poured endlessly into deep, unstable mud.[29] The strategy would be repeated on the Alameda mudflats.

Heavier rail—massively heavier rail—was substituted for Bartling's original, undelivered thirty-five-pound iron.[30] Newspaper reports variously listed its weight as either fifty or fifty-two pounds per yard, quickly touted in the press as "nearly that of broad gauge." The claim was basically true. Average rail weight on the Central Pacific Railroad was listed as fifty-six pounds per yard in the California Board of Commissioners of Transportation report of June 30, 1877.[31]

It was also clear that the quantity of rail ordered, probably from the Pacific Rolling Mills of San Francisco, would extend the South Pacific Coast far past the Newark real estate development. The May 13 edition of the *Independent* noted 450 tons of rail on hand and another four thousand tons on order. At fifty pounds per yard, such quantity was adequate to lay fifty miles of single-track railroad. The size of the order is substantial evidence that Davis and Carter were intent, from the start, on routing the project past San Jose to Los Gatos, so as to position the railroad for the climb into the Santa Cruz Mountains.

Tom Carter hardly paused when the rails reached the Newark town site around the first of July. A week later, new track extended another five miles beyond to the northern bank of Warm Springs Slough, where the work halted to await completion of the drawbridges that acted as a portal to Station Island.

The old Green Point Dairy dormitory building offered bed and board for one hundred Anglo graders and track layers, and a base of command for Tom Carter as well. It was a long, two-story building that sat just south of the road connecting Mayhew's Landing with the Mission San Jose, about one-half mile north of the railroad grade. The building quickly became the base of field operations for the South Pacific Coast.[32]

Green Point Dairy was still in operation when Carter took charge of the grading work (Davis appointed his brother, Sam—not to be confused with his nephew, whose name, we have seen, was also Sam—to run it, probably to supply the California Market with dairy products). On cool, early spring mornings, well before dawn, Carter got up with the milkers, rolled a cigarette, and calculated the cubic yards of rock required for the day's work. At first light, his crews were working scraper teams back and forth across the new levels, raising the grade steadily out of reach of the tides.

Field conditions prevailed. Nearly three miles of new grade lay in the wetlands of Dumbarton Point. The tide crested twice a day, saturating the earth fill, flooding the cord grass with dark water, and disguising sink holes

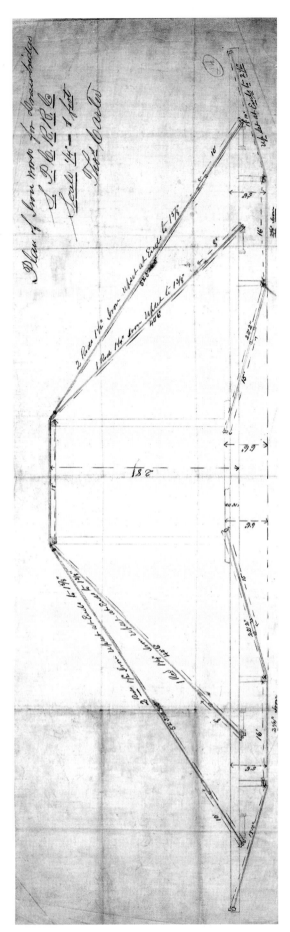

that waited for a misstep of man or horse. Without compaction, fresh fill would sag with each tidal flow, undergo new leveling during ebb, and then sag all over again as the cycle repeated. Prevailing winds from the northwest blew constantly across the marsh, frothing up an egg white foam called "globber's salt." The brass verniers of sight levels grew sticky from a coating of chemicals and mud. With the mud, tide, and brackish water came the rank smell of decaying detritus. Morale among the graders went steadily downhill.

Carter's crew soon took to strong drink. A story appeared in the November 10, 1877, edition of the *Santa Cruz Sentinel,* establishing a context for what had already become an all-Chinese work force as the South Pacific Coast project slowly migrated south. To set the stage, the *Sentinel* described the first units of work that Tom Carter had run on Dumbarton Point more than a year earlier. On any given Monday morning in the spring of 1876, the paper narrated, only a quarter of the track crew were fit for work. The rest, more than one hundred men, were either "drunk or sobering." "With the exception of just seven men," the article concluded, "the entire force was what is denominated as *tramps.*" Chinese, as a consequence, began to appear in Carter's grading gangs.

Like most California papers not directly owned or influenced by the Central Pacific, the *Sentinel* soon descended into the ethical morass of the anti-Chinese movement. Persuaded to openly revile the Chinese laborer at every available opportunity, the paper could not find a consistent frame of reference in which to condemn the railroad that employed the Chinese. Much of its rhetoric was intended to rationalize the moral force of new railroad construction, for example by mounting the argument that the economy could somehow achieve comparable results in no more time using white labor. But ironically, in the case of Carter's experience in the spring of 1876, even the *Sentinel* had to agree that it was difficult for him to remain aloof from the moil. Carter, we assume, fired all but the seven abstemious laborers in his charge and was soon assigning South Pacific Coast grading contracts to agents representing the Six Companies of San Francisco, supplying the railroad with Chinese gangs as large as five hundred men at a time.

For a short time, Carter fulfilled virtually every management responsibility on the project. He procured rail, ties, spikes, and angle bars. He acted as both specifier and contractor for new rolling stock. He designed the trestlework as well as the bridges over Mud Slough and Coyote Slough (or the "creeks," as the newspapers referred to the early site of Drawbridge) and saw to their construction.[33] Carter's original drawing of the ironwork for these bridges survives, undated, although newspapers make it clear that crews were at work on the twin drawbridges by early July 1876, making the document a candidate for the earliest known original Carter Brothers' drawing.[34]

The motive for building twin drawbridges across closely paralleling waterways, a century and a quarter later, still isn't clear. Warm Springs Slough and Coyote Slough were separated by just half a mile at the point the railroad crossed between them, and they then converged, completely ringing a barren wetland called Station Island before continuing an eastward course towards Warm Springs Landing.

It's unclear who built the bridges. A fabrication yard was set up mid-island, and throughout July and August the bridges Carter designed were fitted out, perhaps by the Pacific Bridge Co., although no record of the contractor's name survives. What does survive is the provenance of the iron-work used in the drawbridges, massive 1.5" diameter truss rods embedded in a timber structure that looked like a gallows turntable. Carter's drawing, simply labeled "Plan of Iron Work for Drawbridge, s.p.c.r.r.c[o.]," was part of a set of Carter drawings found in the Graham Hardy collection, now in the archives of the California State Railroad Museum. Included in the set are drawings of car parts, trucks, turntables, and other metal assemblies identified as coming from Carter and delivered to several California short lines. The drawings span a period from 1876 to 1889. Several of the parts or assemblies can be independently identified as products of the Golden State and Miner's Ironworks in San Francisco, suggesting that the entire portfolio found its way into the Hardy collection from the same foundry.[35]

Carter, we conclude from these drawings, changed foundries, pulling his work out of McCormick and Lewis and, by 1876, adopting the larger, higher-capacity Golden State and Miner's foundry. The arrangement would, if dates on the drawings are any indication, be in effect from the beginning of the South Pacific Coast until some five years after the James Graham Foundry moved to Newark, in proximity to the new Carter car shop. The choice of Golden State was surely an early indication of higher demand from Carter's supply chain, a need for increased capacity (and lower prices) in casting and fabrication services, and the first clear sign of the magnitude of the South Pacific Coast manufacturing work to follow. It was a clue that Carter was planning for the added capacity required to deliver the same rolling stock and bridges he would procure—a testament to his new authority.

The completed sixty-two-foot, hand-operated drawbridges went into service in early September 1876. The four remaining miles of right-of-way to Alviso were spanned with rail a few days later.

Skylarking out of Alviso in small sailboats, pranksters soon learned to hornpipe the Coyote Slough bridge open on the south end, slip quietly through Connection Slough, around the backside of Station Island, and then repeat the hornpipe on the reverse tack down Warm Springs Slough, forcing the infuriated bridge tender to jog one and a half times the distance across Station Island to service the same boat. On the cold, rainy winter days that followed, the bridge tender sat alone in his shed at mid-island, wishing the pranksters would come back.

Thus was born the town of Drawbridge, the loneliest outpost on the railroad.

Davis's prime commercial target, the town site of Newark, was meanwhile getting off to a slow start. The land sales that Robertson had struggled to hold in January 1876 never took place. For six months there was little or

The "Plan of Iron Work for Drawbridge," signed by Thomas Carter, probably represents engineering drawings of one of the two Station Island turnstile bridges built for the South Pacific Coast in 1876 (opposite). It is the earliest surviving Carter drawing. The completed drawbridges at Station Island are portrayed in the 1890s (above), by this time named Drawbridge. [Opposite, California State Railroad Museum; this page, top, San Francisco Bay National Wildlife Refuge; bottom, Mrs. John Massera collection]

Like the 1876 wooden bridges of Draw-bridge, the 1904 steel replacement could still be manually opened by capstan in 1983. [Bruce MacGregor]

no publicity about the town or its development—a result, perhaps, of Davis's preoccupation with the railroad, but also the result of a painstaking revision of the original town development plan.

Davis had the town site completely resurveyed. The original street grid was realigned, possibly to conform to the newly located railroad track. The second survey, conducted by T. P. Wilson, was interpreted in early newspaper articles as a "relocation" of the original Newark Land Association town site. The *Alameda County Independent* noted, on June 24, 1876:

> The Narrow Gauge Railroad Company have removed the site of Newark from its old location to a higher spot, nearer the Dairy Rancho, where there is better ground and plenty of water. Their blacksmith and machine-mending shop will be there, also their first station and R.R. depot, and the dwellings of some of their workmen, and after a while probably different manufacturing industries suitable for the place. The new town has been surveyed off into lots and blocks, streets and squares, and places left, we suppose, for schools, churches and other buildings of a public nature. The new site is a decided improvement over the old. May it flourish.

Street names were coined anew. On the north-south grid, Thompson arrayed names of local landowners as well as railroad partners, individuals who would figure into the early growth and expansion of the narrow gauge. Carter's name is among them, confirming his early rise to prominence in the affairs of the railroad a full year before the Carter car shop would be located adjacent to the same street.

East to west, Newark's streets were all assigned the names of trees: Birch, Cherry, Sycamore, Locust, Spruce, Chestnut, and Alder, although the tree that would soon landscape most of the town, the Australian blue gum eucalyptus, was conspicuously absent.

In spite of the improvements, bad press continued to dog the town project. The early exaggerations of developer Charles Peters continued to snare trusting emigrants, perhaps nonnative English speakers traveling to California on the promise of ads Peters had written in 1875. On August 5, 1876, the *Independent* dredged up evidence of fraud and suggested Davis was also to blame:

> One of the evils of Peter's management of the [Newark Land Association] is seen in the communication of a newly-arrived immigrant last week in the S.F. *Post*. He came here relying upon the glowing accounts sent East in circulars, maps and newspaper articles concerning the great natural advantages of the lands of this association. What was his astonishment to find these advantages almost wholly a myth! He and others find themselves deceived and wronged in this way, yet without means to obtain redress or even a certainty as to who is liable in damages. At all events, he very justly concludes, great injury is caused by transactions of this sort. Who is to blame? Is it Charley Peters alone?

Charley Peters had been gone from the Newark town development since March 1876, and by May 13 the town site was administered by a Davis-owned subsidiary called the Pacific Land Investment Co. But even as late as

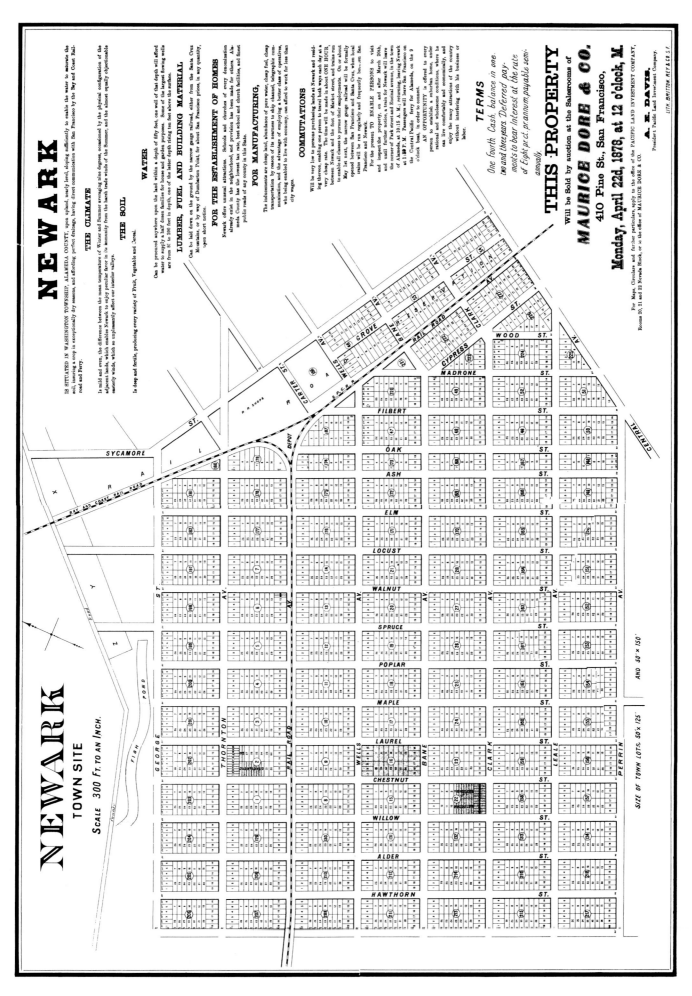

Town site map of Newark and description of commercial real estate offering, drawn by T. P. Wilson for the Pacific Land Investment Co., 1878; note the reference to Dumbarton Point as a freight terminal for the developing town, a wharf that would be obsolete before the year was out, replaced by the new narrow gauge terminal at Alameda.

September 1876, Davis was taking deliberate steps to correct one of Peters's most obvious shortfalls, the failure to connect Dumbarton and San Francisco by fast boat. That month, Davis announced plans to build a 300-foot ferryboat, the *Newark,* at Collier's shipyard in the Potrero district of San Francisco, launching her the following spring as a commute boat.[36] In Davis's mind, even the first stages of real estate promotion couldn't begin without such a boat, perhaps the most important reason the Newark land project incurred long delays. For most of the Centennial year, there was little visible development on the town site itself, and memories of "the immortal Charley Peters" seemed to churn through the skeptical press.

Until the month of December 1876, what actually greeted a visitor to Newark was the sight of Perrin's original herd of 250 milk cows grazing peacefully in the fields where suburban neighborhoods and manicured city parks were indicated on Thompson's site maps. Except for the milk barns, the "headquarters" building, the 24' × 36' depot, and the mainline of the South Pacific Coast, no structures graced the metropolis of Newark. As late as September 1876 (and likely through the following July), new locomotives and cars were set up in the big shed on the windswept tip of Dumbarton Point.[37]

Newark simply did not yet exist.

In three short years, Tom Carter cultivated a network of professionals who, like himself, followed the unpredictable trail of work through the startup phase of California narrow gauge and gambled that a job for one might become a career for another. The formula worked for John Kidder, who was promoted to superintendent of the Nevada County Narrow Gauge at nearly the same time Carter became superintendent of the South Pacific Coast. But there were few guarantees of Kidder's roadmap for success. Carter had worked for Julius Smith on the North Pacific Coast in 1873; three years later, Smith was working for Carter on the South Pacific Coast.

Smith and E. H. Mix, both NPC locating engineers, and Charles Silent, president of the Santa Cruz & Felton, are the three Carter cronies who have been identified during the construction of the SPC. By October 1876, Smith was on board the SPC as its chief engineer. Mix followed in the same position perhaps a year later. Silent was hired as the railroad's property attorney and chief litigant in its first year of construction. Their presence was a sign that Davis was serious about moving the project forward and that Carter needed practical civil engineers to do it, men he knew and trusted.

Smith's name first appeared in the press just a month after Carter completed the twin drawbridges at the Creeks, as rail was reaching the outskirts of Santa Clara.[38] Smith's arrival probably coincided with the furthest southerly extension of the Santa Clara Valley's legally acquired right-of-way, bringing the railroad to the edge of its location maps. New survey work, new property purchases, and new condemnations would be required to push the track south into San Jose and on to Los Gatos.

Smith would get help from another Carter relationship. Carter had gotten to know Silent, attorney and ex-president of the Santa Cruz & Felton, during the rolling stock contracts of the summer of 1875, and he was retained as the railroad's right-of-way attorney. Not counting the owners of lots or blocks within the city limits of Alviso, Santa Clara, San Jose, and Los Gatos, forty-one individual landowners had to be persuaded to sell their land for right-of-way between the first and last towns named, and not all were willing.[39] A total of $61,000 was spent in acquiring land between Santa Clara and San Jose alone, including purchase of an operating lumber yard and settlement of condemnation suits.[40]

Julius Smith's name began to show up frequently in the *San Jose Mercury* and the *Santa Cruz Sentinel*, as speculation grew about the location of the Coast Range crossing. Smith was charged to do a preliminary survey, developing just enough engineering detail about alternative routes to allow Davis to compare their costs. But Smith's work was also something of a political litmus test, gauging public reaction to alternative routes before hard dollars were spent on construction. A complex set of choices, including engineering tradeoffs, revenue sources, likelihood of condemnation suits for right-of-way, and ultimately operational efficiency, all became clearer through Smith's calculated leaks to the press.

Smith was indeed vocal about his field work. On October 28, 1876, probably less than a month after he was hired, he described to the press a route from Los Gatos over Morrell Pass (the route of the Los Gatos–Santa Cruz stage), down Bean Creek and finally to Felton, in general terms the twenty-mile mountain crossing that was finally adopted, although he failed to predict to the press that two and a half of those miles would have to be tunneled. Instead, Smith showboated, confusing largesse with sound civil engineering practice. "The Company," the reporter quoted Smith, "has directed [me] to locate where the best time can be made, regardless of expense." Alfred Davis would respond to media questions about the final selection of route by insisting that all options were being studied; this was a foil for letting Smith's work seek its own level in the marketplace of public opinion. Frederick Hihn's untapped timber resources in the Soquel Augmentation tract, for example, lay close enough to one of Smith's routes to encourage speculation that Hihn would negotiate free access to the railroad. Davis, in the meantime, kept his own options open.

Unlike Julius Smith, Tom Carter was publicly tight-lipped, often giving the impression that his role was somehow overshadowed by those he hired. It was probably a reclusive Tom Carter who was interviewed by a reporter from the *Alameda County Independent* on July 7, 1877: "I went down to Newark to gather what news I could in regard to the new railroad. I saw the leading man there, who said he had not given any news to any paper, and he did not wish the affairs of the road to appear in print, but he said he would give me a few items of interest for your paper."

Behind the scenes, however, Carter was beginning to behave like a bureaucrat in a rapidly growing, increasingly specialized organization. What had started out as a drunken track gang in the muddy winter of 1876 quickly became a family tree of departments organized under managers who in turn reported to Carter—dispatcher, roadmaster, road foreman of engines, master mechanic—and who in turn managed foremen who daily managed carpenters, mechanics, track gangs, bridge crews, and contractors with third-party relationships to the railroad. By 1878, when the South Pacific Coast opened for business between Alameda and Los Gatos, Carter ran an organization of some 250 permanent employees.[41] At the same time, in the process of growing the organization, the subtle contours of authority, influence, and proxy grew sharper and more edgelike. Factions became visible within the company. With factions came animosity.

In his autobiographical *Life Story*, George Colegrove narrated the events of meeting "old man Davis" aboard the public stage he operated, a small business that, by April 1879, was "jumping" shorter and shorter distances between the advancing SPC railhead and the city of Santa Cruz. First the stage connected twenty-nine miles from San Jose, then twenty-four miles from Los Gatos, and finally twenty-two miles from Lexington as the railroad advanced up Los Gatos Canyon, shortening the distance Colegrove had to jump. As a business venture, the stage line had a short future. Once the long summit tunnel opened and the mountain barrier was finally breached, Colegrove was out of work.

Davis occasionally hired Colegrove to drive him over the mountain in a private buggy, developed trust in the driver's skill and judgment, and encouraged him to ask Carter about a permanent job on the railroad. In telling the story, Colegrove added without explanation that Davis asked him "not to use my name" when speaking to the superintendent. Colegrove's first meeting with Carter took place in Santa Cruz in August 1879. Colegrove recounted the results of the meeting the next time he saw Davis:

> When I got back the next night into Santa Cruz Davis was there in front of the Ocean House. He was very interested. "Well, did you see Carter?" "Yes. I asked him [about a job]. He didn't give me much encouragement. He said he would see what he could do."
>
> Well, [Davis] just went out of his head and he said, "Well, he didn't give you any encouragement. Well when you get ready to go to work you let me know. I will show Carter that I am boss."[42]

Colegrove's story suggests that the relationship between Carter and Davis had chilled by 1879, leaving Colegrove caught in the middle of a widening gap between the two authority figures. Davis indeed showed Carter he was boss. But rather than confront his superintendent, Davis went behind his back. In the summer of 1879, he quietly arranged a brakeman's position for Colegrove on the Santa Cruz & Felton, which was by this time a subsidiary company still physically unconnected to operating South Pacific Coast track and still outside of Tom Carter's administrative control. The episode surely did not endear Carter to Davis, but it did make visible the reach of Carter's authority, and his autocratic style. The story, transcribed from an oral history Colegrove completed in the 1930s, may have captured the last fleeting memories of the resentment Carter felt toward Colegrove.

The strain on Carter and Colegrove's relationship was a pretext for the "Powder Mill wreck" (explored in Chapter Twelve). Buried in the reconstructed dialogue of Colegrove's *Life Story* is the only direct testimony that hard feelings from Colegrove's hiring directly or indirectly caused the deaths of fifteen people about nine months after Colegrove was hired. Carter's version of the tragedy, if it ever existed, does not survive, leaving George Colegrove the only witness.

But Carter should have been on firm ground in rebuffing Colegrove's original petition. By the time Colegrove approached him, Carter had already hired managers whose job it was to hire train crew. Would Carter have so carelessly bypassed the upper management structure that he himself had put in place? Colegrove's own testimony suggests a business formality and structure that Davis—not Carter—was struggling to manage from the perspective of an absentee landlord. As the South Pacific Coast organization reached fighting trim, Carter's personal authority—defined by the number and positions of the men who owed him their jobs—reached a point where his day-to-day influence on the company equaled or exceeded that of Alfred Davis. The Colegrove story, in effect, may be an artifact of increasing tension between the two leaders, a signal of a struggle for power that mirrored the company's growing success as a competitor in the marketplace.

The peak of Carter's authority probably came in the summer of 1877, when he hired his brother Martin into the dual job titles of master mechanic and master car builder for the railroad. Martin held both positions simultaneously as the new backshops opened in Newark that July. In addition, Martin ran Carter Brothers, which opened in new quarters next to the railroad shops, thus virtually assured of getting the contracts for South Pacific Coast rolling stock.

The Carter brothers, in effect, were now the power behind the throne.

If the argument can be made that the South Pacific Coast was designed as a single mechanical system—that most of its critical components, track, cars, and locomotives were either chosen or designed to fit into a physical plant capable of heavier loads, denser traffic, and higher speeds than any of the West Coast narrow gauge lines that had come before it—then the argument can also be made that the Carter brothers were its designers.

The emphasis here should be on the word *system*. The improvements that were made in designing track and right-of-way were shadowed by improvements in designing rolling stock, and the resulting system as a whole was tuned to higher speeds and heavier loads than other California narrow gauge railroads built up to that time.

At least five months before Julius Smith's arrival, most of the standards that distinguished the South Pacific Coast's physical plant were all obvious to a curious press. Rail weighing fifty-two pounds per yard, manufactured by the Pacific Rolling Mills in San Francisco, was adopted as the standard rail weight everywhere on the mainline, virtually indistinguishable from the standard gauge Central Pacific. Mainline ties, hewn from first-growth Santa Cruz County redwood, were cut to standard gauge length (eight feet). The ties were spaced twenty inches apart, aggregating thirty-eight hundred to the mile and laid on a bed of coarse gravel. Maximum curvature was limited to a gentle eight degrees, about 750 feet in radius, on the mainline between Dumbarton Point and Los Gatos.

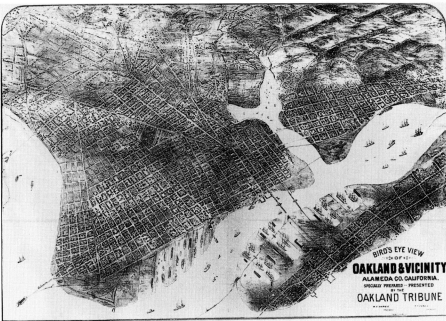

BIRD'S EYE VIEW
:OF:
OAKLAND & VICINITY
ALAMEDA CO. CALIFORNIA.
SPECIALLY PREPARED · PRESENTED
BY THE
OAKLAND TRIBUNE

Alameda Point was the hub of South Pacific Coast's northern terminal, where both freight and passenger trains converged on ferry slips and terminal buildings along the Alameda Estuary, or "Creek," as it is still known today. In the early bird's-eye view at the right, the Oakland branch diverges from Alameda Point and crosses several small drawbridges on its way to the Webster Street crossing into Oakland, while the larger Central Pacific standard gauge Oakland terminal parallels the narrow gauge on the opposite side of the Creek; ca. early 1880s. [Left, San Francisco Maritime National Historical Park; right, Bancroft Library]

Eliminating curvature on the railroad became something of a stock of local mythology as the narrow gauge progressed southward. The story has often been repeated about the removal of the Lyndon Hotel from the tangent surveyed through Los Gatos in October 1877.[43] Less known was the insistence of a Santa Clara Valley farmer that his well, located in the crosshairs of a surveyor's centerline, was worth not a cent less than $80 in damages if the track should actually pass over it. Charles Silent may have been responsible for the homely answer the farmer received, along with a handful of greenbacks: "Eighty dollars shall not crook the road!"[44]

Even when the railroad entered the mountains in Los Gatos Canyon, its curves would be surveyed no tighter than sixteen degrees, a radius of approximately 359 feet. The tightest curve on the North Pacific Coast, by comparison, was surveyed on White's Hill to a radius of 256 feet. Grades on the SPC were dead level for the first twenty miles and didn't exceed fifty feet of rise per mile in the following ten miles between San Jose and Los Gatos. In the mountains, Julius Smith was under orders not to exceed a grade of 90 feet to the mile, about 1.7 percent; the maximum gradient on the North Pacific Coast was 121 feet to the mile, or 2.3 percent. Compared to the standard gauge Central Pacific, whose grades over the Sierra Nevada reached 2.5 percent, the inclines of the South Pacific Coast were surprisingly modest.

Small refinements added to the integrity of the track design. An eighty-pound iron casting called a head block was installed on stub switches as a clamp to make rigid and hold to gauge both mainline and diverging rails. Head blocks were common practice on Southern Pacific standard gauge switches but rare on West Coast narrow gauge lines in the 1870s. Even smaller details struck the trained observer as an indication that the railroad was well engineered: "The track and roadbed are in excellent condition, and here is evidence of the watchful care over little things which is so important. Thus the bridges and culverts all bear conspicuous numbers, and there are signals at all the tunnels."[45]

No record survives of the nature of the "signals" at the tunnels, or their degree of automation, but the remainder of the railroad was signaled by train order boards at manned depots. Dressed stone retaining walls appear in early photographs of the railroad in Los Gatos Canyon, an indication of careful channeling of creek flow where it threatened to undercut fill or embankment. Other superlatives were used to describe the physical plant in company literature: that the road was fenced along its entire line, that cattle guards were in place at every public grade crossing, and that there was "absolutely no dust" sucked up into moving trains—appurtenances that sounded more as if they were created by marketers than civil engineers.[46]

Even so, newspaper writers inspecting the first increments of SPC trackwork remarked on its extremely solid construction. The *Alameda County Independent,* on December 23, 1876, praised the track as "laid in the best style of art."

The only railroadist early on in the project, Thomas Carter was perhaps responsible for recommending the original South Pacific Coast track standards, but he was certainly responsible for the matching performance standards of rolling stock. Improvements in rolling stock were less visible to the press than trackwork and generated little copy. But it appears that in early 1876 Carter's car-building technology took a step up in several critical performance factors: an increase in load-bearing capacity and a decrease in vibration and jar at high speed, both demands placed on Carter by buyers convinced they should expect nearly the performance they could purchase from a standard gauge supplier. The demand pushed Carter deeper into a competitive paradox: if narrow gauge railroads were going to compete successfully with standard gauge, they would have to perform like standard gauge.

Small design revisions had occurred continuously since Carter first started contracting for cars.[47] But the changes that Carter began engineering in 1876 were not, strictly speaking, revisions. Instead, he undertook what today might be called a change in *platform.* Used in the sense of *computer platform,* the term refers to a component of a product responsible for important features of overall performance. A platform represents the most technical part of a product's design, on which an engineer is likely to spend the most time, energy, and money in achieving some targeted performance goal. By engineering the best performance possible for a given platform, a designer could then replicate the platform across numerous products and be assured of common performance standards and lowest engineering cost while using the platform to support new variations of a product. A modern example is the choice of a microprocessor (386, 486, Pentium) as the foundation, or platform, for designing increasingly higher performance in personal computers.

In the case of wooden car builders, the platform was identified with the truck. True, structural changes in other parts of a car accompanied an increase in size and weight. Carter, for example, added two additional sills to its "four stick" car frames in the time period we're talking about, designing his first six-stick frames. But the design of the truck represented a more concentrated engineering effort. A truck design could be optimized for its own unique performance factors—carrying capacity, tracking, and ability to damp

The Field Notebook: Carter Freight Trucks—Archeological Evidence

Physical evidence of Carter's three distinct truck styles diminishes as we look further back in time. There are at least two complete, operational sets of fifteen-ton Carter freight trucks at Ardenwood Park in Fremont, California, dating from the late 1880s to roughly 1900. There is only one known example of what is believed to be a ten-ton truck, dated 1884. This remnant, found in a creek near Saratoga Gap, California, contains twenty-four-inch wheels, arch bars, and journal boxes, but no remains of the original wood components. For the earliest-generation truck, Carter's primitive eight-ton design, there is today little physical evidence of any kind. A single casting—the body center plate—was found on a twenty-four-foot boxcar thought to have come from the M&SV and is distinctly lighter and smaller than ten- or fifteen-ton counterparts.

Eight-ton parts may exist, though the assertion is unsubstantiated. When the Nevada County Narrow Gauge Grass Valley roundhouse burned in 1915, journal boxes from an eight-ton Carter truck may have been substituted in the rebuilt tender of engine 5; they are in the restored tender today, compatible with what we know to be the dimensions of eight-ton parts approximated from photographs.

The 1978 *Mark's Standard Handbook for Mechanical Engineers* offers a simple formula for calculating the capacity (in pounds) of a modern freight car bearing: bearing diameter × bearing length × 300. The resulting number, times 8, should yield the capacity, in pounds, of the entire car.

However, in the 1870s and 1880s the relationship between bearing size and car capacity was not so formulaic. As the graph below demonstrates, actual measured bearing surface areas from cars of this era were scattered above and below a best-fit straight line. Numerous data points simply don't fall on the line (which would ideally correspond to the *Handbook* formula), indicating considerable variation in engineering design.

Carter's bearing sizes remained fairly close to the straight line:

   8 tons: 15.1 square inches
  10 tons: 16.5 square inches
  15 tons: 24.4 square inches

The eight-ton figure comes from an Interstate Commerce Commission report on NCNG cars published in 1912; the ten-ton figure comes from the remains of a truck found near Saratoga Gap, California; and the fifteen-ton figure is from correspondence between Carter Brothers and the Pajaro Valley Consolidated Railroad, dated 1891.

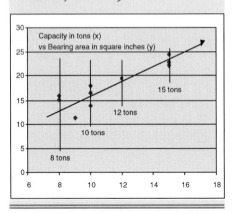

unwanted vibration. To apply the platform concept, the truck became the mechanical foundation on which the rest of the car was engineered. In 1876, Carter designed his first ten-ton-capacity freight truck, upgrading his product line from the primitive eight-ton model first developed in 1874.

To put these changes into some kind of perspective, in 1876 the Baltimore & Ohio had just begun building fifteen-ton-capacity standard gauge boxcars.[48] Even in 1878, two years after Carter completed its first ten-ton-capacity prototype, the *National Car Builder* reported that "the average standard gauge box car weighs 20,000 pounds, and has a carrying capacity of 20,000 pounds, or one ton of paying load to one ton of dead weight. The narrow gauge eight-wheel box car, 24 ft. in length, with swing bolster truck, weighs 10,000 pounds and has a capacity of 16,000 pounds, or $1^3/_5$ tons of paying freight to one ton of dead weight."[49]

That basic configuration of the American freight car changed little in the preceding twenty-five years. As Kirkman, in *The Science of Railways,* noted:

> Until 1878 there was very little change made in the designs and construction of [standard gauge] freight cars. They had increased to about ten tons capacity, the dead weight being nearly as high . . . however it was not until 1880 that any move was made to increase the generally adopted standard capacity (ten tons) of the cars . . . even the Master Car Builder's Association in 1877 deprecated the idea of building cars for carrying more than ten tons of freight.[50]

It is interesting to note that Carter not only matched the average standard gauge boxcar capacity of the day but also lengthened its basic narrow gauge car body to twenty-eight feet, the common length of standard gauge car bodies for the period. Carter's new design, however, failed to duplicate standard gauge performance in one important feature: with narrower width and lower height, the volume of a Carter narrow gauge boxcar was only 60 percent of a standard gauge boxcar of the same length. This limitation was actually viewed as an advantage by early proponents of narrow gauge. By constructing small, lightweight car bodies, Carter achieved the accepted improvement in dead-weight ratio (1.5 tons of paying freight to one ton of dead weight) that narrow gauge champions such as Howard Schuyler believed were central to the superiority of the new technology.

The common fallacy in such an argument was emphasized by George Hilton in *American Narrow Gauge Railroads*: other economic variables, for example, the cost of transshipping cargo to a broad gauge line, would perjure the overall savings a narrow gauge railroad could anticipate purely from its choice of gauge.[51] Although the fallacy applied to most narrow gauge lines, the South Pacific Coast was an exception. For the nine years of its independent operation (1878–1887), it remained one of the most profitable railroads, per mile, of any in California—standard or narrow gauge.[52] In the same period of time, Carter Brothers was to profit in kind.

Over its lifetime as a car builder, Carter Brothers based growth and improvement in its product lines on three distinct narrow gauge freight platforms, each distinguished from the next by the increased capacity of the truck: from 1874 to 1876, eight-ton capacity; from 1876 to about 1886, ten-ton capacity; and finally, from 1886 to 1902, fifteen-ton capacity. Each

change in platform was accompanied by adoption of a new style of freight truck, with a corresponding increase in bearing size (see Field Notebook: Bearing Size Versus Car Capacity).

The design of trucks included other performance factors besides capacity. The Carter ten-ton truck contained one additional feature that the eight-ton product did not: true swing motion. The original Carter eight-ton design featured a framework for installing a swing bolster and coil springs into the slot originally used for rubber springs and a rigid truck bolster. Since the original eight-ton design had the required structural framework, a minimum amount of design effort was required to retrofit the truck for swing motion. In Carter's next-generation truck, the parallel wooden transom beams could actually do the job they were intended for: cradling a swing bolster on forged swing hangers, functionally identical to the Central Pacific's "California truck" of the 1870s. The result was a smoother-riding truck, which some industry advocates believed reduced the pulling resistance of the car on curves as well as wear and tear on the truck itself.[53]

The remainder of the South Pacific Coast's freight equipment, a fleet of more than four hundred cars, would be rated at ten tons capacity or better, and all were equipped with swing motion.

The platform concept could be applied to passenger car trucks as well, although load-bearing capacity wasn't the most important performance factor involved. Ability to track well at high speed, the capability of remaining upright on curves, and reduction in unwanted vibration were all

Carter Brothers twenty-eight-foot, ten-ton-capacity combination boxcar was based on a concept of multiple-use "housecar" at least as old as 1855. Carter produced this narrow gauge version continuously from 1877 until 1898, one of their most successful products; photographed at Agnew by Agent William Fuller, negative number 8, ca. 1890.

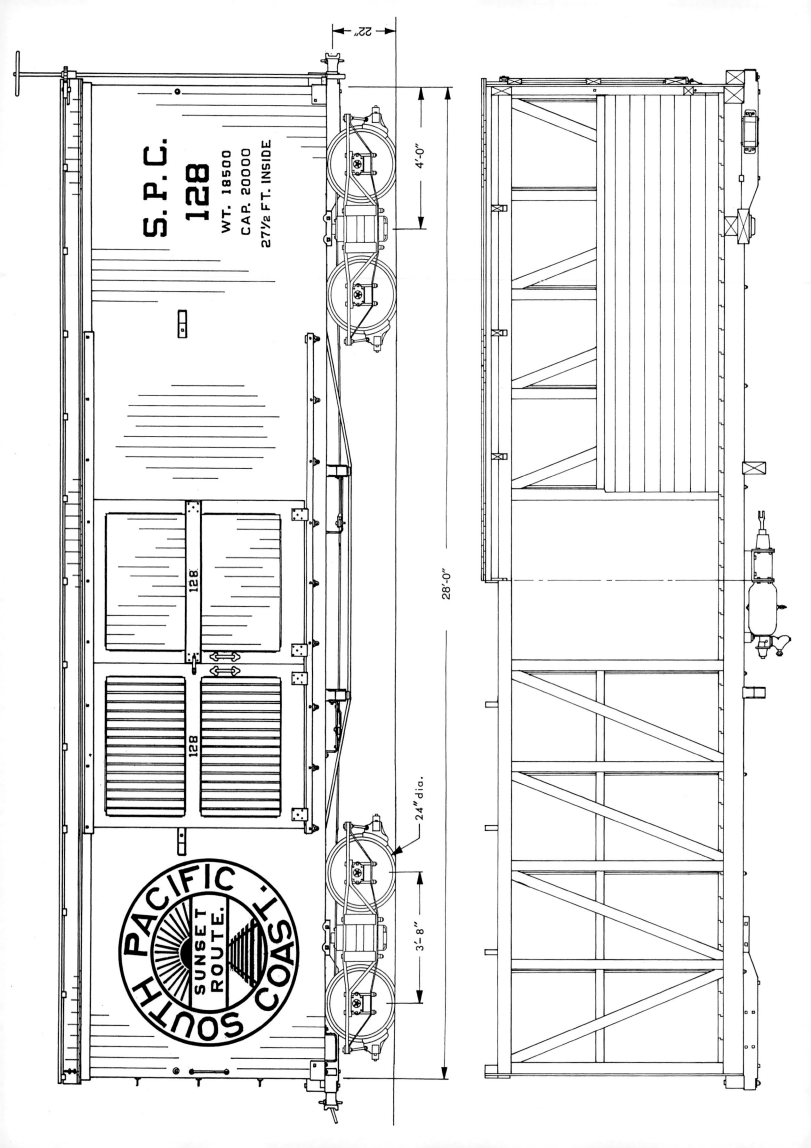

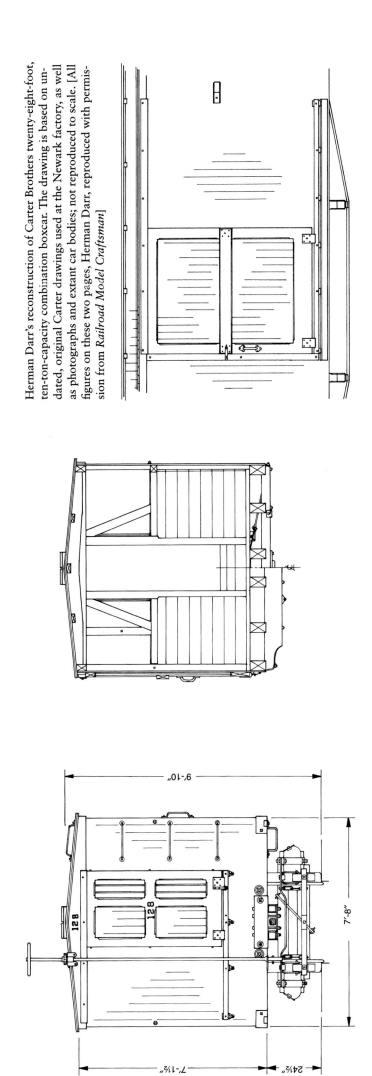

Herman Darr's reconstruction of Carter Brothers twenty-eight-foot, ten-ton-capacity combination boxcar. The drawing is based on undated, original Carter drawings used at the Newark factory, as well as photographs and extant car bodies; not reproduced to scale. [All figures on these two pages, Herman Darr, reproduced with permission from *Railroad Model Craftsman*]

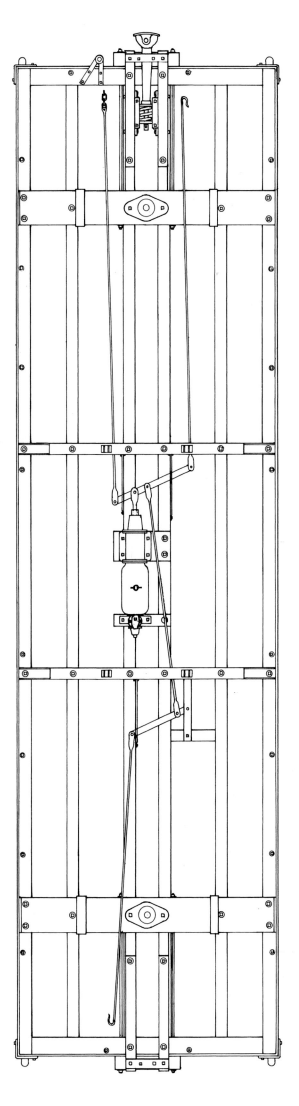

The Field Notebook:
The Carter Ten-Ton Freight Truck

The Carter ten-ton freight truck, first applied to the South Pacific Coast Railroad in 1876 or 1877, included most of the features of a contemporary standard gauge freight truck but in a smaller package. Its statistics included twenty-four-inch single-plate wheels (imported from East Coast manufacturers such as A. Whitney and Sons of Philadelphia, or perhaps Bass and Co. of Indiana) in a 3'8" wheelbase, archbar frame. Journal size was probably 3" × 5.5". But the most unique feature in the truck was the addition of true swing motion. In essence, a pair of fabricated iron swing hangers cradled the truck bolster and allowed it to swing laterally inside a frame that consisted of two transom beams. About ten additional parts were required to add swing motion to a rigid arch bar truck; the added complexity increased cost and production time as well as the difficulty of maintaining the finished truck.

With the ten-ton truck, however, Carter functionally duplicated the Central Pacific's "California Style" truck, a standard gauge swing-motion truck that had been popular with the CP since about 1873 and that might have been Carter's model for the narrow gauge ten-ton truck.

The ten-ton design lasted until about 1886 as a Carter mainstay under its freight equipment, and a number of spin-offs (for example, caboose trucks) are thought to have been derived from the sturdy, mass-produced ten-ton design.

The Carter fifteen-ton capacity truck that followed virtually duplicated many of the ten-ton truck's features, including swing motion, while increasing its capacity by 50 percent.

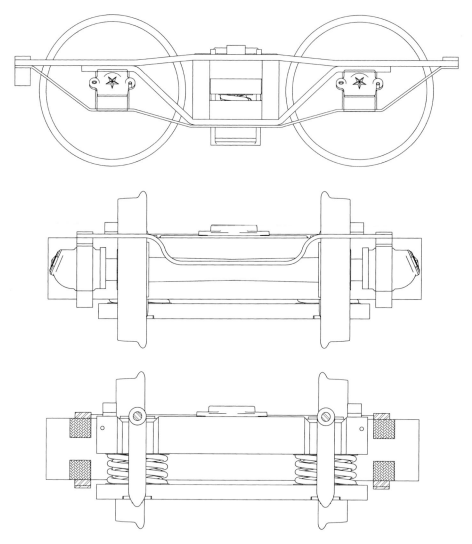

[Curtis Ferrington]

performance features considered critical to good passenger truck design. In 1876, it appeared that Carter committed considerable resources to addressing these problems.

It is perhaps easiest to understand Carter's passenger truck reengineering work of 1876 by comparing the trucks Carter installed under the Monterey & Salinas Valley passenger cars in 1874. The new trucks represented an increase in the wheelbase from four to five feet, adding stability and improving riding quality. The new trucks abandoned the U-shape strap pedestal for a conventional cast pedestal, a change that increased structural support for the journal box. Finally, and most important, the new design evolved from a sixteen-inch-long hanger to one of 7.25 inches, an alteration designed specifically to improve "sway and jar" at high speed.[54]

Swing motion technology was well understood by the industry at large and applied to passenger cars for at least twenty years prior to Carter's efforts at redesign on the South Pacific Coast. Carter's adaptation was to scale down and align each of these features into a narrow gauge version of the

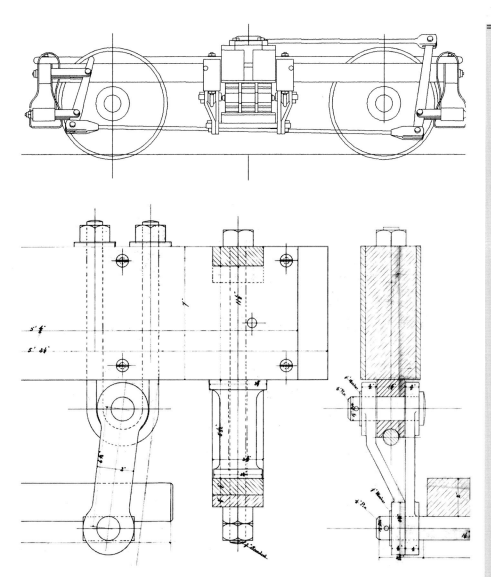

The design of fully sprung passenger trucks was based on a swing bolster pivoted from the bottom of the transom beams (rather than the top, as in freight cars); this stiffened the truck's "lever arm," damping vibration at higher speeds. In the lower drawing, Carter Brothers' original rendition of a passenger truck swing hanger appears; in the upper, the swing hanger is shown adapted to a five-foot-wheelbase South Pacific Coast truck of 1881 vintage. [Top, Michael A. Collins; bottom, California State Railroad Museum]

**The Field Notebook:
High-Speed Swing Motion**

The length of the swing hanger in a swing-motion truck was a crude way for a designer to tune a car's performance to different average operating speeds. The shorter the swing hanger, the more lateral force had to be exerted against the car to cause it to swing. In the narrow gauge passenger car truck designs of Carter Brothers, the version built for South Pacific Coast in 1877–1880 used a swing hanger suspended just seven inches from the bottom of the transom to its pivot point. A low-speed truck (for example, the ten-ton freight truck) used a twelve-inch swing hanger, suspended from the top of the transom beams. With a shorter lever arm, the passenger car truck would tend to exhibit less lateral motion at high speed, in essence damping out unwanted side-to-side oscillation the car would experience at speeds that were often in excess of forty miles per hour.

Industry thinking varied on the choices that Carter made, but since essentially there were just two locations in which to mount the swing hanger (at the top or the bottom of the transom beam), there was little ability to fine-tune the car to match a desired performance goal.

Even so, this strategy may have contributed to the public's impression that the South Pacific Coast enjoyed unusually smooth riding equipment.

truck, a design consistent with parts and tooling that his supply chain could deliver.

Throughout these platform improvements, load-bearing parts increased in cross section. The utilitarian body center plate, for example, the iron casting on which the truck rotated, was designed to be about 30 percent heavier in the ten-ton platform.[55] Materials were upgraded. The gutta-percha springs of 1874, with their "squirm motion," were replaced with high-quality steel coil springs, manufactured by A. French and Co., a spring specialty house.

Carter reengineered the system by taking advantage of improving economics in the overall railroad supply chain. The purchase of heavier rail, for example, was encouraged by prices dramatically falling from $234 per

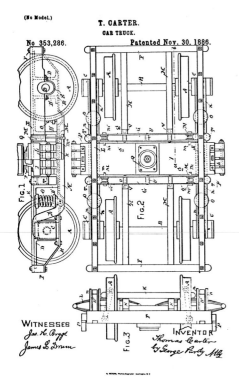

In 1886, Thomas Carter patented refinements in the fully sprung passenger truck by replacing wooden transoms with metal; the patent was actually applied to South Pacific Coast passenger cars built in the late 1880s. The example above shows an unidentified coach, photographed at Santa Cruz sometime after 1893. [Above, U.S. Patent Office; lower, Robert Willey collection]

ton delivered to the Central Pacific in 1865 to $85 per ton on the Monterey & Salinas Valley in 1874, and to $43 per ton on the South Pacific Coast in 1880.[56] Labor rates remained relatively stable throughout the 1870s, giving railroads an economic advantage they could use to upgrade their plants. Carter clearly took advantage of these conditions. Heavier rail allowed higher speeds and higher-capacity bearings, which encouraged upgrading of freight and passenger car trucks.

But as speed and hauling capacity increased, so did the stress and strain on the entire system. Weak points in the system didn't vanish; they migrated and often hid, until experience could be brought to bear on the failure mode of a new design. A good example was swing motion. Applied to a high-capacity truck, the swing hanger itself became the weak link along the load-bearing path through the truck. Found discarded under the car shop floor of the West Side Lumber Co. at Tuolumne, California, several fifteen-ton swing hangers all showed failure in the same way: breaking the forging at the point of the ninety degree bend from overloading.[57] In this case, Carter had pushed swing motion to its limit, installing the lateral motion device on its highest-capacity cars around the turn of the century. The consistent pattern of failure became a catalyst for industry migration away from swing motion as the nineteenth century drew to a close; for the first time in more than a hundred years, car capacity exceeded twenty tons.

The engineering demanded by the new work rivaled Carter's remarkable start-up in 1874. Detailed, part-specific designs consumed Carter Brothers in the early phases of the South Pacific Coast contract. Its focus shifted to choosing and testing materials for parts that met critical design demands for both lightness and strength, finding vendors and suppliers who could provide such parts in quantity at realistic prices, and then proving the value of the design by trial. In passenger trucks alone, the parts Carter redesigned were myriad: pedestals, journals, equalizers, frame pieces, swing motion bearings (upper and lower), swing axles, chafing plates, springs and spring caps, body bearings, and body center plates. Though not as technically demanding as design work in trucks, new designs for a longer car body (twenty-eight feet in the case of freight cars) were on Carter's drawing boards at the same time, accelerating the revision of car frames from four-stick to six-stick.

Evidence of Thomas Carter's technical role in the redesign process comes primarily from a handful of engineering drawings that bear his name, and a patent taken out by Thomas Carter in 1886, more than ten years after the start-up of the South Pacific Coast.[58] The patent clearly leveraged many of the adaptations he created in 1876 and reflected a decade of engineering experience that had followed. The patent description specifies two key refinements to the 1876 style passenger truck. The new design replaced the truck's original wood frame with one of forged iron bar stock, and it extended the bar stock around the axles to perform the original function of the cast iron pedestal. These features addressed strength and flexibility in an area where the truck frame experienced high stress, the junction between wood and metal parts in the original 1876 design.

The patent extended and distilled Carter's almost continuous study of four-wheel passenger trucks since their first application to his products in

1874. The patent represented maturity in his practical, applied knowledge. But its language clearly reflected an understanding of mechanical engineering principles and their application to the unique design features of the narrow gauge passenger car truck. The Carter patented truck was actually built for at least one coach in service on the South Pacific Coast, as well as the Carter parlor car *Ettie* (built for the San Joaquin & Sierra Nevada); this fact is a testimonial to Carter's trust in his own engineering skill and a good example of the relationship between Carter's design and manufacturing experience.[59]

The first phases of Carter's ten-ton reengineering was accomplished under near-laboratory conditions. Since the South Pacific Coast did not begin commercial operation until 1878, for two years there was no schedule to keep, no peak traffic season to support. Instead, for the period between 1876 and 1878, Carter designed, built, and stockpiled cars against the day when Davis would give the order to open the railroad. For two more years, from 1878 until 1880 (the time it took to complete track over the Coast Range and into Santa Cruz), the South Pacific Coast would remain lightly used, fifty miles of nearly flat, manicured roadbed keeping its surface and its alignment like a polished bandsaw blade. On this track, Carter's products ran like well-oiled roller skates. Newspaper stories of the period frequently commented on the unusual (and perhaps unexpected) smoothness of the narrow gauge, as in the observation on December 15, 1877, from the *Santa Cruz Sentinel* that one could "write comfortably sitting down in the cars" at speeds of forty miles per hour.

Although the South Pacific Coast consistently turned a profit over the nearly ten years it was in operation as an independently owned short line, evidence specific to the cost-effectiveness of its rolling stock is mixed. The price of a ten-ton South Pacific Coast car was slightly lower than for the eight-ton cars Carter built for the Monterey & Salinas Valley three years before: $536 for an SPC boxcar versus $575 for an M&SV boxcar; and $449 for an SPC flatcar compared to $490 for an M&SV flatcar.[60] It is harder to cite West Coast prices for standard gauge freight cars, in part because of the high percentage of Central and Southern Pacific freight cars that were built in-house. However, ballpark estimates range from $600 to $800 for a standard gauge boxcar, perhaps 50 percent more expensive than the same narrow gauge product. Even so, car utilization between narrow and standard gauge showed a more dramatic difference than the apparent cost savings in price might suggest. If we compare tons of freight hauled per car for the year 1886, the Southern Pacific system as a whole was using its freight cars at more than three times the level of the South Pacific Coast, to produce very nearly the same earnings per mile.[61] The statistics suggest that cheaper narrow gauge rolling stock represented a questionable long-term competitive advantage.

The performance of Carter passenger cars must be assessed on the basis of speed as well as capacity. On February 21, 1898, a South Pacific Coast locomotive took a two-car train (a baggage car and the "pay car") over the mainline from Alameda to Santa Cruz. The special train was operated as a publicity stunt; the *San Francisco Examiner* chartered it to set records for newspaper delivery to hub cities in northern California and Nevada. In an era when papers orchestrated the news they would later print, the special train captured the public's attention in headlines bannered the following day.

While Engineer Matt Crole was later quoted as saying he "don't like to run her that fast," the *Examiner* reporter watched the speedometer inch up to seventy miles per hour and breathlessly linger there on the long tangents through the marsh south of San Leandro Bay. The train arrived in Santa Cruz two hours and five minutes after it left Alameda, setting the all-time speed record for the "system" that Thomas Carter envisioned twenty years earlier.[62]

Julius Smith and his corps of fourteen civil engineers reached Santa Cruz in mid-December 1876, after several months of hard work in the mountains. Smith announced to the *Santa Cruz Sentinel* (the first of two times) that a preliminary survey over the mountains was finished.[63]

Reports had been circulating since September of a "big tunnel" that would be located somewhere under the summit ridge near Taylor's Pass.[64] Articles linked to Smith provided sketchy details of its location at an elevation of 1,400 feet above sea level, just slightly lower than the elevation of 1,540 feet established for the summit of Taylor's Pass itself. On a modern map, this site was located ten miles southeast of Los Gatos, high up on the canyon wall of Los Gatos Creek. The saddle at the top of the ridge was a steep, narrow col leading to the headwaters of Soquel Creek, a continuous watercourse that reached the ocean at what is today Capitola.

From the frequently clouded-in heights, the mountains revealed their defenses. At Taylor's Pass, the range is only fifteen miles wide, the distance a crow would have to fly between Los Gatos and Santa Cruz. But no continuous stream drained the Santa Clara Valley, on the north side of the mountains, into Monterey Bay on the south. Like a high wall, the summit ridge turned streams along its northern edge, such as Los Gatos Creek, toward San Francisco Bay or the Pajaro River, and streams along its southern edge (Soquel Creek, Burns Creek, Bean Creek, and Zayante Creek) toward the ocean.

Historically, surveyors trying to get a wagon road or railroad directly over the high ridge were forced to tack, much like a sailboat, up one creek until it became too steep to continue and then over (or under) the facing ridge, penetrating into the next canyon, then up or down its watercourse until it became untenable, and so on, crisscrossing the range at a series of right angles to the direction of travel.

Such geography symbolized a long, deep psychic barrier to the communities around northern Monterey Bay. Working from the ridge top, Smith's engineers struck tents in thickets where mountain lions prowled on moonless nights. They used Charles McKiernan's ranch as a supply base and got to know "Mountain Charley" personally. He was a living throwback to the wilderness, wearing a silver skull plate where a grizzly had parted his hair in a near-fatal encounter years before. In spite of the science of levels and transits, barometers and contour maps, Smith could not help but feel that he was intruding on what historian Sandy Lydon called "dark, brooding, mean little mountains."

This was the barrier that had historically isolated Santa Cruz County, and twenty years of nearly continuous civil engineering on its flanks failed to produce a commercially viable railroad route north of the Pajaro River. Experienced surveyors, the brothers Healy, Thomas Wilson Wright, and William J. Lewis knew no practical railroad would ever be able to breast the saddle at Taylor's Pass without difficult gradients. But by tunneling the pass, they could maintain a reasonable grade on the Los Gatos side, and—according to Lewis—an acceptable grade on the steep descent of the Soquel's headwaters. By tunneling Taylor's Pass and following Soquel Creek downstream, only one "tack" was required to cross the mountains. Smith, too, reasoned that one carefully placed tunnel was the key to breaking through the backbone of the mountain. He undoubtedly had Lewis's survey upon which to base his conclusions.

But once into the headwaters of Soquel Creek, a railroad was locked into a sealed pipeline stretching from Summit Ridge to the ocean. The canyon was steep and high. Smith was undoubtedly persuaded to consider alternative routes through the mountains. Davis had spent weeks, in the autumn of 1876, reconnoitering the timber reserves of the San Lorenzo basin and its extension north into the Pescadero basin. Although the Soquel Creek route would reach Frederick Hihn's untapped Soquel Augmentation timber, Davis ordered Smith to consider a way to reach the far larger San Lorenzo timber reserve from essentially the same starting point.

Smith complied. A one-tack strategy quickly turned into a three-tack strategy: one for each additional, unconnected mountain canyon he would have to enter and exit to maneuver the railroad into the San Lorenzo watershed. The summit tunnel under Taylor Pass, already described, would begin the sequence. Then tunneling out of the Soquel Creek Canyon into Bean Creek allowed the survey to pass through Charley Martin's Glenwood property (which included viniculture and lumbering) and through the village of Scotts Valley, the largest community between Los Gatos and Felton. Tunneling out of the Bean Creek watershed, finally, gave a railroad engineer access to the Zayante Creek watershed, which ultimately flowed into the San Lorenzo River, reaching Felton and the established commercial lumbering and fluming operations of the Santa Cruz & Felton Railroad.

Smith described his preliminary results in October 1876. His first tunnel at Taylor's Pass, the critical passage between the Los Gatos and Soquel Creek canyons, would have measured 1,650 feet. The tunnel's location, according to an October 28, 1876, article in the *Santa Cruz Sentinel*, occurred at a point high enough that Smith argued he could breast the second ridge, into Bean Creek, without another tunnel. This alternative survey, Smith contended, could escape the vertical topography of the Soquel Creek headwaters, twist back to the north, and breast the second ridge into Bean Creek with a grade of just ninety feet to the mile.[65] Looking at a modern topographical map of Taylor's Pass, we see that the rugged country Smith faced on the south side of Summit Ridge would have made either option an expensive, technically difficult undertaking. Smith, however, did not have to furnish detailed location and cost work. That would fall to a location engineer, to be hired once the preliminary survey was completed and accepted by management.

In December 1876, Smith's surveyors left the high country with preliminary data, confident they could maintain a ninety-foot descending gradient down Bean Creek and ultimately the San Lorenzo River, all the way to Santa Cruz. Moving his camp to Felton, Smith surveyed the last seven miles to the ocean on the San Lorenzo River bank opposite the Santa Cruz & Felton Railroad. By keeping his line close the river, avoiding the Hogback where the Santa Cruz & Felton had been forced to adopt 137-foot gradients, Smith kept the South Pacific Coast survey to a descent of less than ninety feet to the mile. His work established a technically superior, unbroken engineering standard for the entire railroad.

He proudly announced the results just before Christmas, claiming construction work on the mountain grade would start as early as February.[66]

But by April 1877, the mainline had been graded no further than Los Gatos, and Alfred Davis continued to speak of "options" in the mountain location, once the summit ridge had been breached by the "big" tunnel. Synonymous with business strategy, Davis's options quickly revealed the battle plans he intended to use against his competitors.

For two years, the Santa Cruz & Felton's flume had successfully tapped the San Lorenzo timber reserves above the town of Lorenzo, the ancestral site of Boulder Creek. But by 1877, two years after it opened, the flume was showing considerable signs of wear and tear. It was doubtful it could be counted on to move the high volume of lumber contained in the San Lorenzo and Pescadero basins. Davis, like the original Santa Cruz & Felton investors, had clearly understood the economic advantage a railroad up the San Lorenzo could offer.[67] Superficially in 1876 and in great detail in 1877, Davis spent time and money on the question of reaching Pescadero basin timber by railroad. Clearly, the South Pacific Coast would have to reach Felton first.

The owners of the Santa Cruz & Felton viewed these explorations as a direct threat to their original investment. On November 13, 1876, SC&F's board of directors created the Felton & San Lorenzo Railroad, a competing plan to extend the SC&F along the course of the flume and into the Pescadero basin.[68] The new line's traffic would flow into the Santa Cruz & Felton for shipment to coastal lumber schooners at Santa Cruz. Charlie Gorrill, by then president of the SC&F, was the chief organizer of the scheme, which was clearly a reaction to the competitive threat of the South Pacific Coast.

It was expensive brinkmanship for all players. With the one-tack plan, Davis would have to drill a single tunnel less than a quarter mile in length to reach Soquel. With the three-tack plan required to reach Felton, Davis faced a chilling 2.5 miles of underground construction. At the same time, Gorrill was compelled to reinforce his position with new investments. In April 1877, the SC&F began to beef up rail weight, relaying as much as one hundred tons a month, as well as reducing the worst curves, laying the groundwork for the extension of the railroad toward the Pescadero basin.[69]

The flume, leaky and aging, remained in commercial operation, too expensive for Gorrill to replace.

But instead of a full-scale attack on the summit ridge, Davis inexplicably halted work in the mountains at the onset of the first good weather of 1877. Even more dramatically, he shelved plans to open the existing track between Newark and Los Gatos. The pause was quickly misinterpreted by the press as insolvency. In an August interview with the *Santa Cruz Sentinel,* Davis listed his reasons for the delay, in the process letting slip item six, the most competitively militant option of them all:

1. Construction trains are running too frequently for commercial train schedules.
2. The Los Gatos grain crop is a failure.
3. Due to hard times, the timber market in Alameda County and the Santa Clara Valley is light.
4. Fruit growers have entered into contracts with the Alviso steamer for this season's crop.
5. Travel to-and-from Santa Cruz, by stage, appears too light to justify rapid construction outlay.
6. With a northern terminal at Dumbarton Point and no wharf in San Francisco under the exclusive control of the company, business cannot be conducted in a most satisfactory manner.
7. The road is new and poorly ballasted, forcing slow speeds.[70]

Before Davis could bridge the gap to Felton with the South Pacific Coast, he would have to build an entirely new railroad, the Bay & Coast, into the heart of the Stanford cartel's Pacific Coast terminal.

By the onset of the winter of 1877, the role of the railroadist in constructing the South Pacific Coast had been upstaged by the role of the specialist. Thomas Carter could no longer pretend he personally had the answers to Davis's increasingly complex demands. A growing and varied mix of professionals, among them lawyers, architects, and artisans, were every bit as important to the railroad's progress as civil and mechanical engineers.

The decision to abandon Dumbarton Point, reached in the spring of 1877, was also an acknowledgment that railroading in the Bay Area was a consumer business. To do business, Davis would have to locate the South Pacific Coast's northern terminal facility close enough to San Francisco to directly serve its demographics. An additional twenty-five miles of high-speed mainline became the critical path in competing with Stanford's San Francisco to San Jose schedules. Davis did the math. With a high-speed ferry boat named *Newark* and a mainline extension, incorporated on May 2, 1877, as the Bay & Coast Railroad, he could narrow the gap: a seventy-two minute schedule for Stanford and Co. would be met with a ninety-minute schedule for the narrow gauge between the two largest cities in the Bay Area. It was the opening shot in a ten-year war for control of the Bay Area's passenger market. Over the decade, Davis would shave seconds and minutes off the remaining disparity.

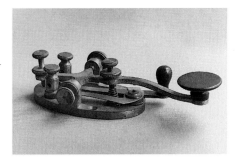

Completely owned by the South Pacific Coast, the Bay and Coast Telegraph Co. charter allowed the railroad's subsidiary to acquire right-of-way for a telegraph line for little additional capital outlay, much like the relationship between fiber optic companies and railroads today. The lower photograph shows the Los Gatos depot telegraph key; both artifacts are from the collection of William Wulf. [Lower, Bruce MacGregor]

Thus, in June 1877 the narrow gauge mainline was surveyed deep into the Central Pacific's stronghold, crossing its old Alameda ferry line at Woodstock before securing a beachhead for a new ferry terminal at Alameda Point (sometimes known as China Point), just one mile south of the Central Pacific's Oakland long wharf.

Alarmed, Stanford and Co. responded to the intruder with a counterattack of injunctions, suits, and mayhem. Notice of legal action began to appear in the press in July 1877, when Central Pacific attorneys solicited and collectivized grievances of property owners. For the following eleven months, Alameda papers routinely tracked the issuing of injunctions, staying of injunctions, and lifting of injunctions in ongoing courtroom actions against the narrow gauge.[71]

Lawyers, not civil engineers, became the new knights of the narrow gauge. Alfred A. Cohen had been instrumental in negotiating Oakland terminal lands for the Central Pacific, but he quit in 1875 over suspicion of misappropriation of company funds. Stanford, Crocker, Huntington, and Hopkins first sued Cohen for the alleged irregularities.[72] Cohen retaliated by suing the railroad for an alleged stock fraud. He brilliantly placed his accusers on trial, trying his suit first in the court of public opinion, appealing to the rising antirailroad sentiment in the state. Cohen won his suit in a San Francisco district court; the Big Four lost theirs. A year later, Cohen was working as an attorney for the South Pacific Coast as the railroad struggled to acquire property and right-of-way in Alameda, Cohen's home town.[73] The affiliation quickly identified the narrow gauge as David marching off to confront the Central Pacific's Goliath.

The legal confrontation gave rise to urban legend. Repeated in twentieth-century literature without any clear provenance, the most violent of the stories told of a crowd gathered on Alameda streets to watch a narrow gauge track-laying gang, perhaps sometime in the summer of 1877. From the back of the crowd, hired thugs first began to taunt the workers, then hurl rocks. Dropping their tools, the track crew bloodied the worst offenders, sent the rest packing, and went back to work. When the bandaged assailants showed up with a lawyer on the doorstep of an Alameda judge, intending to charge the narrow gauge with assault and battery, they discovered his honor wasn't home; nor was the next judge they tried, or the next—all, it turned out, guests of the South Pacific Coast on an excursion timed to whisk the judiciary out of town on the very same weekend it intended to finish its track.

The factual record, however, casts doubt on the tale of the excursioning magistrates. The "excursion" took place on Sunday, December 2, 1877, after the tracks had been securely laid through Alameda streets to open marshland within half a mile of the terminal on China Point. The *Encinal* made no mention of violence on the quiet streets of Alameda that weekend. But the legend persisted, and it contained a nugget of truth: Lawyers, it was clear, would play an increasingly important role in gaining the narrow gauge a foothold inside the Central Pacific's vast terminal complex of Oakland, Alameda, and San Francisco.

The underlying tension in such stories pitted the security of law, order, and property against an urban fear of anarchy. The South Pacific Coast ironically played both roles in its emergence as a *force majeure* in the regional transportation industry. The story of the Patterson shotgun fight is more fact than legend, and it casts the narrow gauge in the role of an advancing army, looting private property in its path.

On the night of July 16, 1877, a small force of armed guards were ordered to stand watch along the southern fence line of George Washington Patterson's eight-thousand-acre ranch near Newark, which lay squarely in the path of the advancing Bay & Coast Railroad. Patterson had operated his ranch since the 1850s with scow schooners, loading hay and grain at a small landing on his own property. He hated the intrusion of an uninvited railroad into the agrarian paradise and refused to negotiate for a sale of right-of-way.

However, Patterson, more than sixty years old at the time, was distracted by his marriage to Clara Hawley, then in her twenties, the daughter of a neighboring family. With track layers approaching his fence line from the Newark side, Patterson reluctantly gave orders for his guards to man the perimeter twenty-four hours a day while he went on honeymoon. Hog Davis, the story continues, quickly seized the advantage. On the night of July 16, the South Pacific Coast's construction boss gifted the guards with a barrel of good drinking whiskey, offering toasts to the future happiness of their boss. The mood changed. Shotguns were leaned against fence posts, and liberal toasts were offered. Sometime after midnight, with the guards sound asleep, the railroad's Chinese gangs cut Patterson's fence and hastily built one mile of track (constructing a small trestle) across Patterson's land. That November, the railroad's lawyers won a condemnation suit, agreeing to pay Patterson $2,094.45 in land value and $294 in property damages to his fence, which the besotted guards had failed to defend.[74] Back in Collins Saloon, Davis no doubt toasted the hair of the dog that bit George Patterson.

The story, however, did not let the narrow gauge escape entirely unpunished. On July 12, 1878—four days short of one year after he had lost the infamous shotgun fight to the narrow gauge—Patterson launched a new scow schooner for service between his landing and the produce markets of San Francisco; he named it the *Broad Gauge*.

Most of the urban legends surrounding the South Pacific Coast concerned its flair for gentrifying travel in the expanding San Francisco Bay Area. Consumer-oriented projects multiplied in the wake of track laying, as with construction of a fleet of ferry boats to connect the Alameda Point facility with San Francisco. By June 1878, the fleet consisted of two boats: the *Newark*, the largest and fastest ferry on the bay (capable of nearly twenty miles per hour), and the smaller *Bay City*. The *Newark* epitomized Davis's gift for combining the practical and the artistic. Local commercial artists, including Denny, Maple, Bush, and Rockwell, were commissioned to paint mural-size California landscapes.

Twenty-nine color panels alone decorated the *Newark* when she was launched on April 18, 1877, and a published catalogue of the paintings was made available to the public as a pocket guide to the collection, much as a museum or a gallery would do.[75] The railroad's promotion of local arts was frosting on the cake. The *Newark*, at 286 feet in length, was the largest

Decorative ice water dispenser and a catalogue of exhibit-quality art were artifacts of early consumerism in the ferry boat trade on San Francisco Bay. The South Pacific Coast service captured superlatives with the Bay's fastest ferry, the *Newark*, in 1876. [Above, Vernon Sappers collection; top left, Bruce MacGregor; bottom left, Baird Archive of California Art, Department of Special Collections, University Library, UC Davis]

The long-standing helmsman of South Pacific Coast ferry boat service, Captain John Leale, retired to write *Recollections of a Tule Sailor*, a classic memoir of maritime San Francisco. His employer issued Leale and his wife an annual courtesy pass on the narrow gauge (shown left). [California Historical Society]

ferry boat on the bay; it cost Davis $200,000, nearly the cost of the entire Monterey & Salinas Valley Railroad. The *Alameda Encinal* paid her tribute on August 11, 1877:

> She is about the size of the Central Pacific Railroad Company's largest ferry-boat, the *Capital*, but has five hundred more horsepower, and is much more pleasantly arranged for passengers. Her make-up and apportionments, as a ferry-boat, leave nothing to be desired. Her powerful machinery, sending her along without effort, her well-arranged and comfortable seats, and her broad passageways, her commodious cabin, with its cheerful upholstery, communicate to the visitor the impression that her owners must have "staying" qualities, and unbounded confidence in the prospects of the country which she is destined to aid in building up.

Architecture, decoration, and ornamentation became increasingly important trademarks for the narrow gauge. The arcade, or covered depot, was a signature of consumer presence in the marketing of public transportation. Steeply pitched gables, topped with finials perched fifty feet above the rails, formed a solid pediment over its track-level galleries. These imposing sheds covered two or even three parallel tracks, and when incorporated into a refurbished terminal at Alameda Point in 1882 they covered eight tracks. The first of the arcade depots was completed in Newark in May 1878, forty feet wide by two hundred feet along the rails.[76] The second was located in San Jose, 50 feet wide by 220 feet long, open for business in August.[77] A third arcade station, again two hundred feet long, was completed in Santa Cruz in 1880. These structures were probably painted a colonial revival yellow with cream trim and a red or green sash accent, the basic body color a close match to the exterior body color of a Carter coach.[78]

Under the gables of the San Jose arcade depot, ornamental sign painters were given an area some six by twenty feet in which to emblazon the railroad's legend, billboarded across nearly the full width of the building in letters as tall as a man: "S.P.C.R.R. Co . . . San Francisco & Santa Cruz."

An Oakland architect named William McDonald was doing design work for Davis in Newark during the spring of 1878 (getting credit for the railroad's new Central Hotel) and may have been the architect responsible for arcade depot design.[79] His skills brought a consistent look and feel to the public that would, beginning on June 1, 1878, see the narrow gauge as the first real alternative to Stanford and Co.

There were other commercial architects working on the South Pacific

The earliest known view of the San Jose arcade depot, dating from the mid-1880s (bottom) offers additional evidence of the South Pacific Coast's flair for public marketing. By the time of Southern Pacific control, in 1904 (just below), the cavernous shed was devoid of advertising, a symptom of monopoly in northern California rail travel. [Top, Ken Lorenzen collection; bottom, California State Railroad Museum]

Below (at top), the South Pacific Coast's San Jose arcade station is portrayed in a bird's-eye view dating from the mid-1880s; beneath that, a broadside for the Alameda Palace Hotel advertises proprietor Abe Beatty's hospitality, dispensed to narrow gauge passengers disembarking at the covered depot. [Both, William Wulf collection]

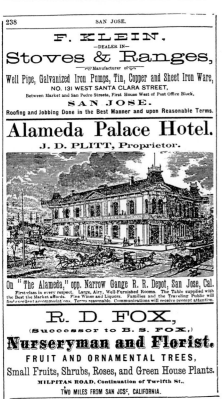

Coast during the Bay & Coast period. William Patton in particular drew attention for his work on a combination downtown Alameda depot and hotel, located at Park and Encinal. The concept of a "grand hotel" at the northern terminal of the railroad was explained in an October 5, 1878, edition of the *Encinal*:

Mr. William Patton, architect, has shown us the plans for the depot, etc., of the South Pacific Coast Railroad Company, to be erected on the northeast corner of Park street and Encinal avenues. The building will have its main frontage on Encinal avenue, 102$\frac{1}{2}$ feet by 57$\frac{1}{2}$ feet on Park street. The waiting rooms, ticket and telegraph office, etc., will occupy the main portion of the lower floor on Encinal avenue, the remainder being designed for stores. The elevation from the ground to the main cornice is 54 feet, with a tower and spire running up to the height of 100 feet. A clock, with four dials 5$\frac{1}{2}$ feet in diameter, will be placed in the tower, and timepieces are to be lavishly distributed about the offices. The two upper stories are designed to be used for hotel purposes, and are to be furnished with all conveniences known to modern architecture. The main entrance to the hotel is in the center of the Encinal avenue front, with private entrance on Park street. A separate building is planned for servants' rooms, connected by a bridge with the second story of the main structure. A commodious cellar, 6 feet in the clear, will be an important feature. The building will be of brick, and will cost approximately $30,000. We learn that the contract for its erection has been awarded to a firm in San Jose, who will begin construction at an early day.

However, when the San Jose contractor, Jacob Lenzen, actually began construction of the facility later the same month, the *Encinal* reported that "the clock tower, we are sorry to learn, will be dispensed with for the present." The three-story hotel, called the Park, was nearing completion the following March. In 1885, the railroad would open Neptune Gardens, an amusement park along the Alameda beach front that advertised its saltwater baths as the "Saratoga of the Pacific." The gardens included a skating pavilion, hotel, a restaurant called Delmonico's, bathing spas, and formal gardens—blended together with a rustic motif characterized by rock fountains and arbored walkways. Together with the Park Hotel, just down the mainline, the narrow gauge had created a destination resort, a small urban center within the urban center of Alameda, just thirty minutes from downtown San Francisco.

Davis's investments in real estate and architecture helped establish a social context for the startup capitalists of the Nevada Bank. They imagined a railroad that did not vanish into the wilderness of forests or the expanse of Central Valley but instead extruded, by line, form, color, and amenity, the elements of the expanding urban center of San Francisco into its newly attached suburbs.

With the opening of the Park Hotel, the railroad's growing list of specialists would include bartenders and innkeepers.

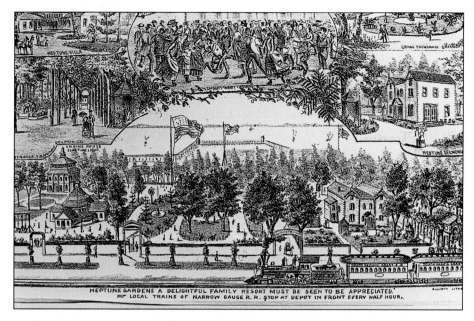

NEPTUNE GARDENS A DELIGHTFUL FAMILY RESORT MUST BE SEEN TO BE APPRECIATED.
LOCAL TRAINS OF NARROW GAUGE R. R. STOP AT DEPOT IN FRONT EVERY HALF HOUR.

With a major seaside resort attracting tourists to its southern terminus, the South Pacific Coast was quick to invent marketing parity at the other end of the line by creating Neptune Gardens, a bayside saltwater spa on Encinal Avenue near the line's northern terminal in Alameda. A theater, restaurant, hotel, skating pavilion, rustic gardens, and saltwater baths crowded together in what narrow gauge advertisements called "the Saratoga of the Pacific." [All, Alameda Historical Society]

Quietly, almost unnoticed in the fanfare surrounding the railroad's extension to Alameda, work on the big tunnel began on the summit ridge under the direction of a new chief engineer, E. H. "Ed" Mix, who replaced Julius Smith in late 1877.

That November, Mix relocated the site of the tunnel two miles closer to Los Gatos. Instead of using Smith's original site, ten miles above the village, Mix placed the mouth of the tunnel just eight miles up the winding course of Los Gatos Creek at a site directly below the col of Morrell Pass. Since the railroad grade climbed continuously along with the bed of Los Gatos Creek, the result of Mix's relocation was to lower the altitude where the tunnel entered the mountain. The relocation therefore increased, to nearly sixty-five hundred feet, the linear distance over which the tunnel would have to penetrate the mountain. Smith's original tunnel would have measured just 1,650 feet, one-quarter the length of his final location.

Unlike Julius Smith, who performed the duties of a survey engineer, Ed Mix was a locating engineer. Mix was responsible for the exact placement of each foot of right-of-way and the engineering of the structures required to support it. Perhaps the ultimate specialist employed by the South Pacific Coast, Mix was hired by Tom Carter to get the track over the treacherous inclines of the Santa Cruz Mountains. His employment signaled the beginning of one of the most complex and costly—and disastrous—railroad construction projects the state ever witnessed.

In such an environment, Thomas Carter himself was forced to specialize. With major engineering responsibilities for new construction now in the hands of Ed Mix, Carter continued the human engineering of the organization that would make the finished system run. He continued to hire the railroad's management team; promoted, demoted, or fired them; and painstakingly groomed the men who would operate the completed railroad.

Shortly after 1880, with the opening of the completed mainline to Santa Cruz, nearly five hundred full-time employees would be required to operate the South Pacific Coast.

Carter rode locomotive cabs with a stopwatch in hand, penciling notes on proposed timetables. He identified bottlenecks in the mainline, one example being the south end of the San Leandro Bay bridge, where ballast regularly subsided into a muddy sink, causing the right-of-way and track above it to sag out of surface. He built up reserves of rolling stock and established tonnage ratings for the line's new fleet of Baldwin 8-18 C class locomotives, although he knew the ratings would be unrealistic for the mountain grades yet to be built south of Los Gatos. He wrote and approved drafts of "Rules and Regulations for Employees," copying liberally from the operating timetables of other railroads. Thomas Carter was probably responsible for nine revisions of the railroad's operating timetable, each increasing the number of train movements, until some forty-six regularly scheduled trains occupied the railroad's track daily.[80]

His work and his life became synchronized to the railroad's master clock, governed by the first rule in the employee timetable: "The clock in the Train Dispatcher's Office, Alameda Point, is the time by which Trains will be run. Conductors and Enginemen will compare their watches with it daily, when practicable."

The escapement of the Alameda Point clock became the metric common to Carter's multiple duties and talents, and a measure of the progress of his career. The clock not only unified rolling stock, track, locomotives, and manpower into a body with one pulse but also measured their acceleration against a backdrop of dirt roads, lumbering freight drays, and tide-bound scow schooners. The clock foreshortened geographic distances, making the forty-four stations that would house the company's business offices virtual extensions of the Alameda Point dispatcher's desk, all synchronized by telegraph once a day to the great clock at Alameda Point. It compressed and standardized the communication that flowed between Carter and his managers, making it possible to parse the business day, and hence cost accounting, into smaller and smaller increments, increasing the efficiency of the ensemble.

It was, of course, a series of refinements that had occurred in the railroad industry at large over the enormous distances and extended time period in which the railroad was the leading edge of American expansion. But somehow, this was different. The same experience was occurring within the scope of the narrow gauge movement, both more concentrated and more visible because of it. To Thomas Carter, it was like watching evolution take place in a test tube, speeded up, rendered in time lapse. With his own set of calipers, rules, and plumbs, he could perfect the entire thing—the system—and strive to accelerate it.

Briefly, until circumstance became something far more chaotic and less predictable, Thomas Carter felt close to the center of a giant clockworks, the animus inside the machine.

Thirteenth and Webster streets in Oakland, ca. 1890s. The seldom-photographed South Pacific Coast number 7, on commute-train assignment up Webster Street, gave the photographer a classic study in nineteenth-century urban railroading. [California State Railroad Museum]

In 1883, South Pacific Coast commute trains ran once every thirty minutes along the mainline in Alameda as well as the Oakland branch. Each line was operated without a turning facility at either extremity, requiring SPC commute engines (for example, number 3 at the top left) to carry full-size headlights on the tender. For commute service, Carter modified its standard coach to include easy-load side seats, with a wide aisle in the section closest to the doors. The dense suburban traffic also required constant maintenance of right-of-way, for example grading and leveling a standard gauge crossing at Thirteenth and Webster in the panorama from the 1890s, below. [Top left, California State Railroad Museum; top right, Stanford University Special Collections; bottom, Frank Trahin photograph, Vernon Sappers collection]

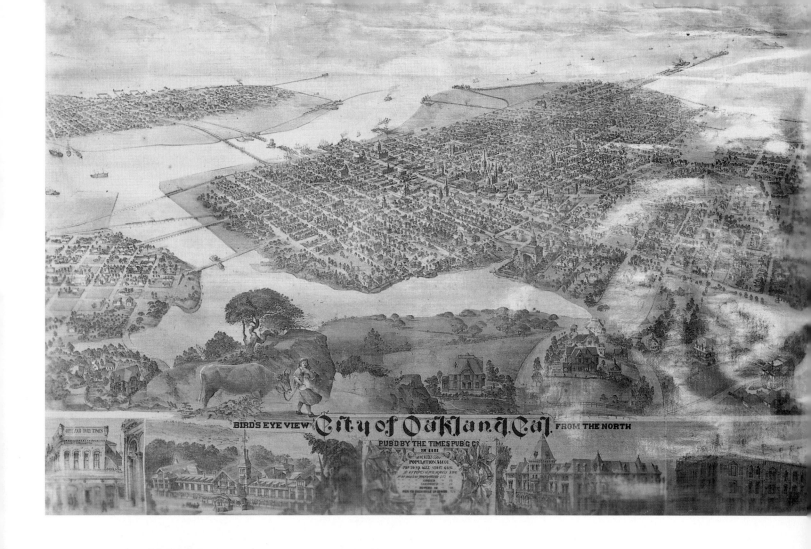

BIRD'S EYE VIEW **City of Oakland, Cal.** FROM THE NORTH

PUB.D BY THE TIMES PUB.G CO.

Thought to have been taken by Oakland photographer Frank Rodolph, the unusual view above shows the San Leandro Bay drawbridge as it appeared about 1885. The map portrays the northern and southern sections of the South Pacific Coast in Alameda, before the "Creek" or estuary was extended to make a complete island. The San Leandro Bay drawbridge appears at the extreme right of the map, just below the "S" in "San Leandro Bay." Details of the South Pacific Coast's Alameda facilities (at the extreme left of the map) included the two-mile-long causeway that led to the railroad's ferry terminal. Tidelands that characterized much of the railroad's East Bay route were the environment for a late afternoon view of the San Leandro Bay drawbridge (above right). [Left, above, John Schmale collection; above right, Alameda Historical Society; below, Kyle Wyatt collection]

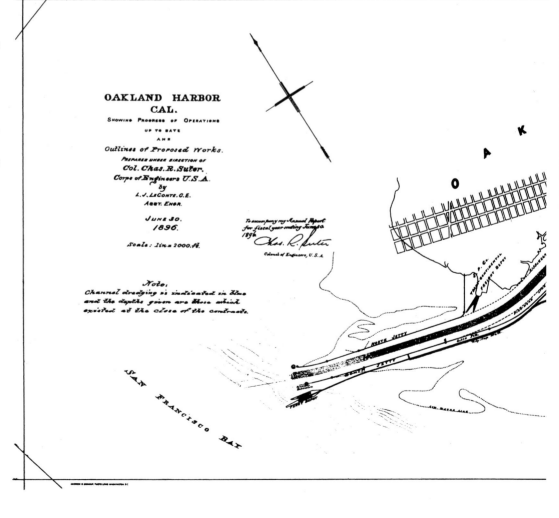

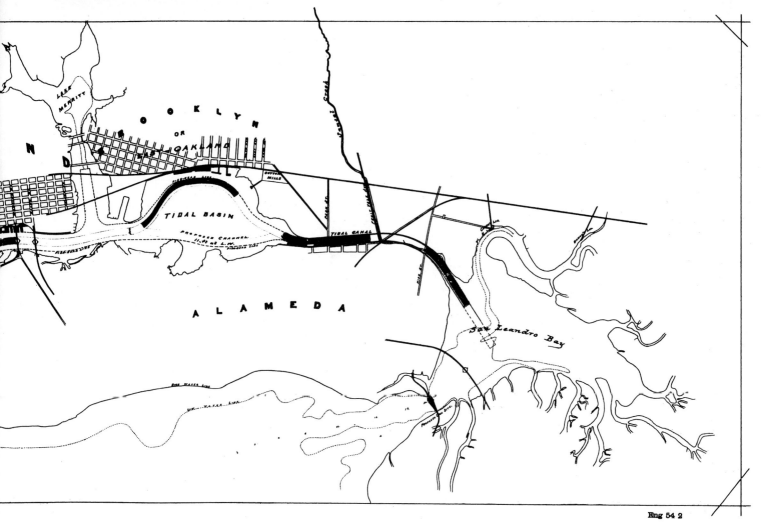

Three evolutionary stages in Carter passenger car design are shown here: at the top, what is thought to be an 1875 Santa Clara Valley Railroad combine, shown as a derelict on the Almaden Branch in 1913; in the middle, SPC coach 2, built in 1876, on Telegraph Avenue in Berkeley; and at the bottom, SPC coach 42, in a Carter Brothers builder's photograph, ca. 1882. The elevations opposite show Michael Collins's reconstruction of SPC coach 39, built to the same design as coach 42 and still in existence at the Orange Empire Museum in Perris, Calif. Both coaches 39 and 42 were built for Oakland-Alameda commute runs. [Top, Vernon Sappers collection; middle, John Schmale collection; bottom, Martin G. Carter collection; opposite, Michael A. Collins]

3 foot gauge,
Size, 8 feet by 36 feet.

SMOKING CAR
Built by CARTER BROS., NEWARK, CAL.

Capacity,
Fifty Passenger

South Pacific Coast No. 39

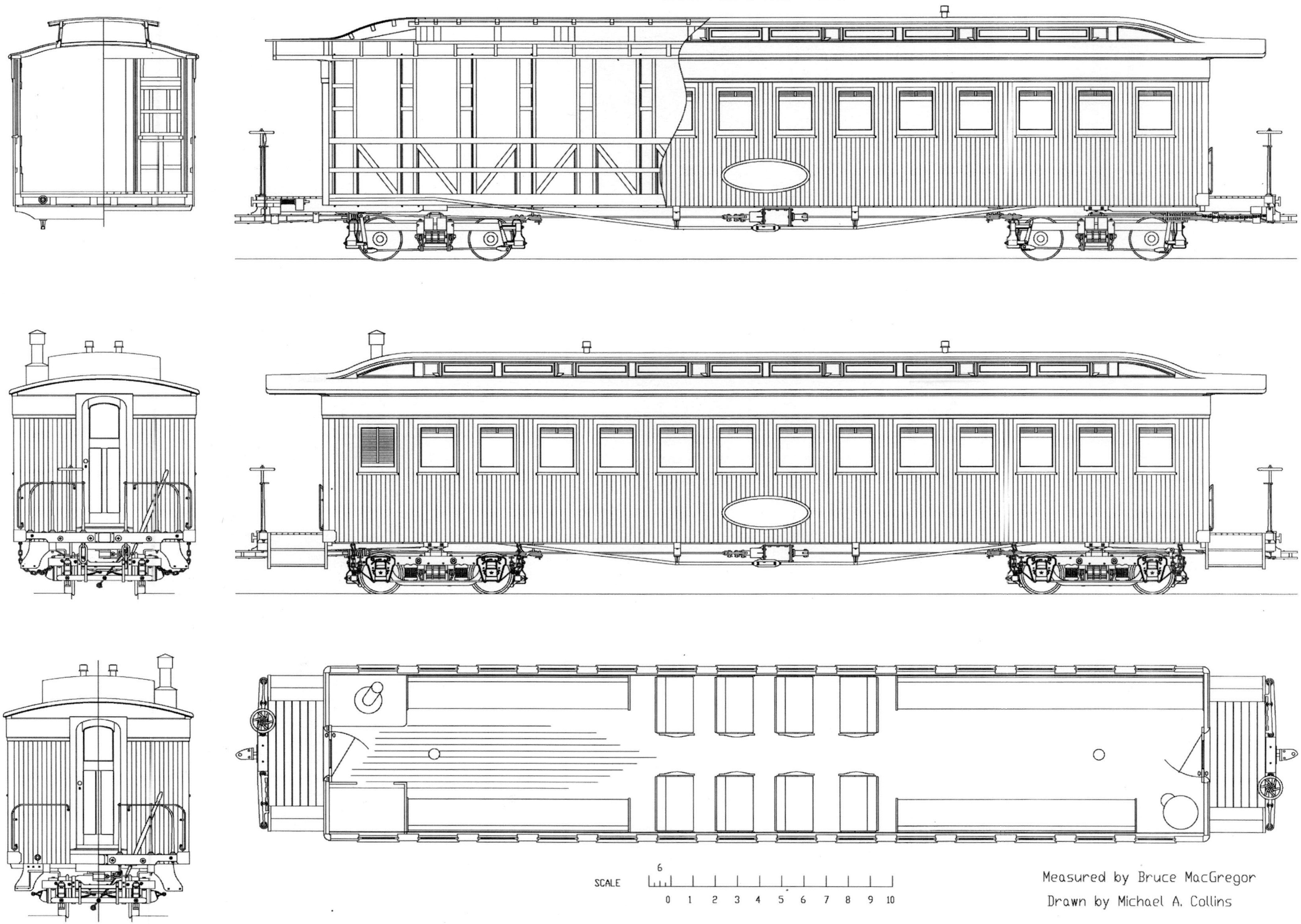

Measured by Bruce MacGregor
Drawn by Michael A. Collins

SCALE

6

0 1 2 3 4 5 6 7 8 9 10

To reform-conscious California, the 1890 Memorial Day wreck acted as an exaggerated reminder of the hazards of narrow gauge railroading, even if the cause of the accident was the gross negligence of South Pacific Coast engineer Sam Dunn, who inexplicably took a loaded passenger train through the open Webster Street drawbridge. Thirteen passengers drowned, trapped in a submerged coach; Dunn somehow escaped the same fate. A Southern Pacific Road foreman named Clement made the glass plates of the wreck's aftermath seen here. As SPC 4-6-0 number 12 pulled the muddy remains of number 3 from the estuary, commute trains continued to roll past on the Oakland Branch. [Above, California Historical Society; others, Vernon Sappers collection]

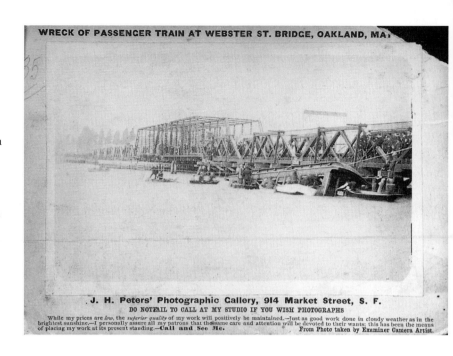

WRECK OF PASSENGER TRAIN AT WEBSTER ST. BRIDGE, OAKLAND, MA

J. H. Peters' Photographic Gallery, 914 Market Street, S. F.
DO NOT FAIL TO CALL AT MY STUDIO IF YOU WISH PHOTOGRAPHS
While my prices are *low*, the *superior quality* of my work will positively be maintained.—Just as good work done in cloudy weather as in the brightest sunshine.—I personally assure all my patrons that the same care and attention will be devoted to their wants; this has been the means of placing my work at its present standing.—**Call and See Me.**
From Photo taken by Examiner Camera Artist.

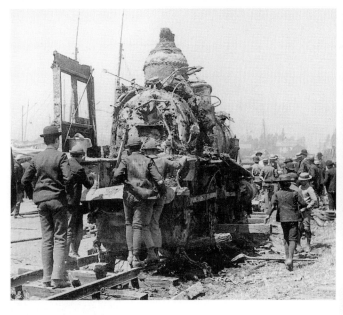

By the 1890s, the narrow gauge was fast becoming a stock of urban legend. In the long process of watching the recovery of South Pacific Coast number 3 from the Alameda Estuary, newspaper reporters remembered the engine had also been involved in the "opening day wreck" of 1880, in which fourteen people were killed in a runaway in the San Lorenzo River Gorge. The locomotive was dubbed "the Hoodo." Outliving the jinx, number 3 was unceremoniously hauled off for repairs in the Newark backshops. [All, Vernon Sappers collection]

South Pacific Coast backshops at Newark, ca. 1890s. Machinist Arthur Biddle turns the forward drivers of 4-4-0 number 15.
[Marge Callow collection]

Newark: The Basis of Business

Until the spring of 1877, the "headquarters" building, the old milker's dormitory built by the Green Point Dairy and Transportation Co., was the only railroad building on the new town site of Newark. There was no railroad track anywhere near it.

This vestige of Newark's birth sat in a small cluster of weathered barns and outbuildings, about six hundred feet south of the county road and about two thousand feet north of the Dumbarton mainline. The board and batten building must have smelled of cows, rancid butter, wood smoke, and leather boots caked with mud from the Dumbarton grade. It had served as a dormitory, cookhouse, storehouse, and field operations point for construction crews since Davis took over the property, and it probably housed Carter's itinerant car crews as they continued to put up batches of flatcar kits delivered to Dumbarton Point from Sixth and Berry. From its weather-beaten vantage, Sam Davis, brother of Hog Davis, watched over the dominion of forty-five hundred windswept acres that his brother had purchased from the Perrins.

Operations at the headquarters building depended on the Dumbarton Point landing for communication and provisions. For the first year of the South Pacific Coast's existence (in which the mainline was extended as far south as San Jose), Dumbarton Point remained the supply base and rail head for the entire project. Two new Baldwin 8-18 C locomotives (numbers 2 and 3) were landed off the deck of barges and set up in the shed at Dumbarton. Car kits continued to be assembled in the same shed. The Bay & Coast Railroad drawbridge over San Leandro Bay was constructed at Dumbarton Point during the summer of 1877 and floated to its final location by barge. The bridge carpenters boarded at the headquarters building, along with track crews and car builders.

Delivery of car kits, probably from Sixth and Berry, continued in Dumbarton's cavernous train shed. Twenty flatcars were completed by May 1876; thirty by January 1, 1877; and seventy by July 1877—evidence that Carter kept Francis Geiser and his crew employed throughout the winter.[1] Food staples, fuel wood, and the regular mail came by way of steamboat to Dumbarton, over the connecting three and a half miles of mainline, to the company outpost in the headquarters building. Throughout the period, Sam Davis kept the Green Point Dairy in operation, and by the fall of 1876 it

First Through Train on Narrow Ga[uge] Newark Mar. 20th 1878.

In 1878, the embryonic site of the town of Newark included the railroad company's Central Hotel (above) and a covered depot (off camera, about four hundred feet to the left), the nucleus of a real estate development whose population didn't exceed two hundred people. When through train service began between Alameda and Los Gatos (above), South Pacific Coast 4-4-0 number 8 paused at Newark, on the northbound leg of the trip, for the earliest known photograph of the town site. The stocky figure directly under the letter "t" in "Coast" at the right edge of the baggage car may be Alfred E. "Hog" Davis. [Arthur Haley collection]

had produced thirty tons of cheese and a thousand gallons of fresh milk. The produce went north from Dumbarton landing by steamer; this is the only record of northbound freight traffic from the landing.

But the Bay & Coast extension made the Newark town site, not Dumbarton Point, the natural conjunction for railroad support functions. The switch for the new mainline to Alameda was located about a mile and a half south of the headquarters building, squarely in the middle of the original Newark town plat. Securely above the tide line, on the uplands of the Green Point Dairy, the switch became the nucleation point for Davis's real estate project, as well as a permanent site for a shop facility.

Surveyor T. P. Wilson's map of Newark, dated 1876, shows features that fixed the location of most of the streets and most of the town's railroad facilities, including the location of the Bay & Coast extension and the first three shop buildings. Work on these buildings did not begin until December 1876 and would not be finished until the following July, which suggests that planning for railroad facilities may have been in place as early as Wilson's surveying work.[2]

The map suggests, in addition, that generous facilities for car manufacture were factored into the plan. The *Alameda County Independent* reported, on July 7, 1877:

> Newark is destined to be the headquarters of the road, for at this place the shops are situated. The dimensions of the shops are as follows: car-shop, 54 × 150; machine-shop, 42 × 150, blacksmith shop, 22 × 34, and the roundhouse is large enough to hold seven locomotives. The car and machine-shops are just having the machinery put in, which is of the most improved pattern. The motive power for running these shops is a large stationary engine in one corner of the machine-shop; it was built by Chas. W. Ewien & Bros., Philadelphia, for the road. The cylinder is fourteen inches in diameter and twenty four inches in stroke; the fly-wheel is nine feet in diameter with twenty inch face, and weighs 3000 pounds; the total weight when in working order is 8000 pounds, and was purchased at a cost of $1350. These also will be in running order in a week or ten days, when Messrs. Carter Bros, who manufacture the cars for the road, will put their workmen at work
>
> . . . . Making the Passenger coaches
>
> which will be finished off inside with black walnut, primavera and tomana, the last two being brought from South America. The seats are iron, with nickle-plated arms and strip over the back, and are finely upholstered in green and crimson velvet. The cars are eight feet broad and thirty six long, with capacity for holding forty-eight passengers. The road will be open for business on or about the first of next year.

The Newark car shop represented badly needed manufacturing capacity for Carter. No additional passenger equipment had been added to the South Pacific Coast roster since August 1876—the month of the last known transfer of cars from Saucelito by North Pacific Coast barge. Since November, at the termination of its lease of the North Pacific Coast's shops, Carter Brothers apparently operated no facility capable of assembling coaches.[3]

Freight car kits continued to come out of the Sixth and Berry facility. But even though the availability of flatcars steadily improved, the fact that no passenger cars were added to the roster between August 1876 and September 1877 is additional evidence that the Sixth and Berry street plant was not equipped for build-in-place manufacture.[4] Lead time for manufacturing passenger cars ranged from three to six months. With pressure increasing on Thomas Carter to open the South Pacific Coast to passenger traffic as soon as the track was completed to Los Gatos, he could not afford to be without this capability for long.

Completion of mainline track to Los Gatos would indeed be accomplished by June 1, 1877. But the backlog on coaches may have added one more reason for Davis to delay opening the railroad. Not only would he have to wait for Carter to build the equipment, he would have to pay for new manufacturing facilities in which to perform the work. As was their practice in Saucelito, Carter Brothers would lease, not buy, manufacturing space. Carter, like Davis, bargained for time.

By December 1876, construction of the shops had begun, consisting of

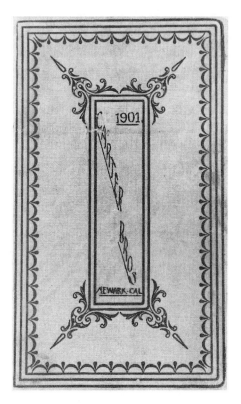

Cover of Carter Brothers Newark factory ledger, 1898–1902, from the A. L. Sunderer family. [Robert Fisher, M.D. collection]

From "Washington Township Illustrated,"
an 1898 newspaper advertising supplement.
[Ken Foster collection]

CARTER'S CAR SHOPS.

CAR building is carried on on an extensive scale at the car shops of Carter Bros., at Newark. The establishment is one of the largest on the coast. Most of the passenger coaches and nearly all of the freight cars of the South Pacific Coast Railroad were built by the firm. Big orders for the San Francisco cable and electric lines have

CAR SHOPS — CARTER BROS. — NEWARK.

also been filled. The firm enjoys a big trade in South America, and makes a specialty of building railroad rolling stock for shipment to that country. Cars for this trade are built complete and painted at the Newark shops, and taken entirely apart for shipment. So perfect is the workmanship that it is not necessary to even repaint or varnish them when they are put together at their destination.

three large buildings: car shop, machine shop, and seven-stall roundhouse. The car shop and machine shop sat on the south end of the seven-acre "railroad reservation." Two tracks wide, 150 feet long, the car shop enclosed space for five or six full-length coaches, with room left over for tooling, subassembly work, and stores. The car shop held 20 percent more floor space than the machine shop, which was an indication of the pressure that car building placed on the overall design of the backshops. With the new space, Carter began to attack the backlog. In this shop building, ten new coaches would be completed by opening day, June 1, 1878.

Conditions at the town site of Newark, however, remained primitive. There was no source of potable water (or boiler water) until an artesian well was sunk near the machine shop. No support services, foundries, or machine shops existed within a six-mile radius. Assuming that Carter continued to rely on the Golden State and Miner's Ironworks for car parts, deliveries still had to reach Carter via steamship at Dumbarton Point, which meant holding raw materials hostage to weather. Until July 1878, no hotel or eating facility existed at the undeveloped town site, forcing Carter's crews to eat and sleep alongside the railroad's track crews in the old Green Point Dairy headquarters building, about two-thirds of a mile from the shops.

The headquarters building was growing crowded. The Sedgely family moved in during the Christmas holiday in 1876. Close friends of Alfred and Sam Davis, John R. Sedgely was hired as an overseer for the new town site; he brought along his wife and son. That winter, Sedgely, along with workmen Peter Kilmartin and John Rogers, began to manage the grading of streets and the setting out of thousands of eucalyptus seedlings, planted as shade trees along the main avenues. Until they were about two years old, the seedlings required watering, a task Sedgely, Kilmartin, and Rogers did religiously.

Sedgely's son, Alfred, was named after Alfred Edward "Hog" Davis; he was fourteen years old when the family moved in. Soon, railroad employees and contractors—and families like the Pauls, who leased local farmland just west on the county road—brought enough children to the project to start a small school; Alfred Sedgely attended classes held upstairs in the headquarters building.[5] Once a milk depot, cookhouse, dormitory, and field engineering office for the narrow gauge, the old headquarters building became the first school in Newark.

By December 1878, six months after the South Pacific Coast opened the line for common carrier service between Alameda and Los Gatos, its rolling stock had reached a total of 14 passenger cars and 160 freight cars. By December 1880, after the line was completed to Santa Cruz and began full-scale operations, its rolling stock would include 40 passenger cars and 320 freight cars.[6] All were manufactured by Carter Brothers. The magnitude of the work was similar to the rolling stock demand of the North Pacific Coast when it opened its Northern Extension into the Russian River in 1877. Both roads would require construction of roughly 300 freight cars in anticipation of opening eighty-mile-long mainlines. But in the case of the South Pacific Coast, the demand for cars would continue after the line was opened. Freight equipment, for example, would reach 428 cars by 1885. The fleet of passenger equipment would number nearly 60.

For Carter Brothers to nearly double the South Pacific Coast's roster in two years, adequate facilities *and* skilled craftsmen had to be found—resources that had been in short supply over the previous two years. Car builders who enjoyed the additional security of full-time or part-time employment with the Central Pacific San Francisco shops would find no similar safety blanket in Newark. In a town that existed for no other reason than to support a new railroad, they would remain sequestered in the drafty old headquarters building, sleeping communally and eating dormitory food. City lights and beer parlors were not a part of Newark's early amenities; just getting back to San Francisco required train fare that was worth two days' wages. On mornings when the bay wind drove rain horizontally across the uplands, Carter's workers grimly trudged two-thirds of a mile from the headquarters building to the car shop at the wye, and the same distance back to supper and bed in the evening.

Familiar faces faded from the scene. Francis Geiser remained in San Francisco as a car repair foreman, working at the Sixth and King Street Central Pacific shop. Alexander Finn, on Carter's Saucelito and Sixth and Berry crews, continued to work in San Francisco as a carpenter. Mary Carter's father, John Larkin, was fifty-five years old in 1877, and while he was living with Martin and Mary after the family moved to Newark he apparently retired from the shops.[7]

Still, Martin managed to pull together the largest crew he ever employed. Fifty workmen were on the payroll at its peak in 1878,[8] thirty in August 1879,[9] twenty-five in 1880,[10] and twenty in September 1882.[11] The 1880 census reported new, mostly younger men on Carter's time rolls: carpenters included E. J. Turner, twenty-six; Charles Meckle, thirty; E. B. Mockberry, thirty-eight; Peter Carlson, twenty-five; Robert Brork, forty-five; and James Mooney, thirty-two; and painters included John Harrington, twenty-two; James Casy, thirty; Louis Mooney, seventeen; James Zotque, thirty-three; George Gibbons, thirty; James Delany, thirty-seven; and William Jacox, twenty-five.[12]

What is striking about this list is that to the best of our knowledge none of these men had worked for Carter before. Old hands would turn up later at Newark (John Nelson, Archibald Hook, Alexander Finn). But in the first three years of activity at the new site, from the summer of 1877 until the summer of 1880, a kind of organizational housecleaning took place, a reordering of the business in which experienced master car builders were replaced by less experienced apprentices and journeymen. A similar change was taking place in the leadership of the firm. A youthful Martin Carter asserted himself as both manager of Carter Brothers and master car builder for the railroad. In addition to the reengineering of its technology, Carter Brothers reengineered its own organization. Soon, that organization would have to learn to make do with considerably less presence from Tom Carter, who had his hands full in the rush to open the railroad.

Newspaper accounts emphasized the accelerated pace of the work, describing pressured working conditions before the June 1878 opening of the Alameda–Los Gatos mainline. In turn, the tempo of new manufacturing helped accelerate development of Newark itself. The arcade depot was under construction in the spring of 1878. The first nonrailroad building erected in the new town site was John Dugan's Newark Hotel, whose construction was timed to coincide not only with the opening of the first segment of the narrow gauge but with the peak of the large labor force in town. Dugan's dining hall opened in May 1878 (while plastering and finish work was going on upstairs in the bedrooms) opposite the arcade depot and a short walk across the mainline from Carter's shop.

A community began to discover its identity. Dugan held the first dance in Newark on June 28, to the accompaniment of Bronson and Daggett's band, and the sounds of waltz music drifted through the backshops until well past midnight. Many of Carter's carpenters now boarded with Dugan, retiring from the dance to clean sheets and private, freshly painted rooms just across the street from their workplace. By the end of the summer, the

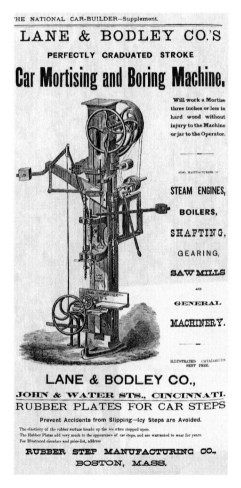

Lane and Bodley Co.'s car mortising and boring machine. [From *National Car Builder*, 1881]

eating hall in the old headquarters building was closed; the building was now far on the outskirts of the activity. Newark, that summer, began to live in its town center.

The original 54' × 150' car shop probably remained Carter's single factory building for the duration of the 1870s.[13]

Machine shop tooling was driven off a railroad-owned boiler located in a 36' × 46' stationary engine house to the rear of the machine shop.[14] The Charles Ewien stationary steam engine in turn directly powered line shafting and the shop's lathes and wheel grinder.[15] An additional $3,000 worth of power tooling was installed in the original car shop in July 1877, driven from a small auxiliary boiler and stationary engine owned by Carter Brothers.[16] An exact list of the car shop's original tooling must be inferred from a January 1, 1899, Carter shop inventory of another era and other business conditions:

buzz planer
2 shaping machines
tenent [sic] machine
morticing machine
drill press
emery machine
grind stone[17]

In comparison to the Virginia & Truckee car shop of a slightly later period, which boasted $10,253 worth of tooling and included a dimension planer, a planer and matcher, surfacer, morticer and borer, shaper, cutoff saw, ripsaw, scroll saw, and numerous other power tools, Carter Brothers seemed minimally equipped.[18] However, two local machine shops (the adjoining railroad machine shop and the Ingraham shop one block away) added to the capability of the Newark facility; under the management of Martin, they could be used virtually as a single shop.

Inside the original car shop, Carter's power tooling crowded onto the shop floor with partially completed car bodies, stock piles of lumber, and cribs of new castings. The building must have offered extremely tight quarters when six full-size passenger cars were built in place at the same time. This was the case on August 2, 1879, when the *Santa Cruz Sentinel* described a facility pushed close to capacity by work for both the home road and a new customer, the Sonoma Valley Railroad:

> In the car shops at Newark, the Carter Bros. are building four first-class passenger cars for the S.P.C.R.R. and likewise two first-class cars and a caboose for the Sonoma road. Thirty men are employed in their construction, each department being carefully superintended by M. Carter, who has under him competent foremen. The cars built at this place are equal to any built in the state. The ornamental woods used in the construction are black walnut, toa and primavera, the two latter being obtained in the South Sea Islands. The upper frame of the coaches is made of ash, and the floors of Oregon pine. It requires two to three months to turn out a car, but if necessity requires, it can be completed in one month. The rolling stock these gentlemen turn out

The Field Notebook: Evolution of the Newark Shops

In July 1877, Carter Brothers moved into a shop building in the new South Pacific Coast Newark yard, just east of the railroad's covered depot (labeled 5 in the diagram below). It was the first of three buildings that would constitute the "Carter compound" in Newark. Called the "car shop" in early descriptions, the long, two-track shed (labeled 1) was architecturally similar to building 4, the railroad machine shop, which was built at the same time. Both (along with the neighboring roundhouse, not pictured) had tall, double-sash windows and distinctive cupolas on the roof. For the next three or four years, the car shop might have been home not only to Carter Brothers but to the SPC-operated car repair facility as well. The railroad owned the buildings and the land they were on. It is likely that Carter simply rented or leased the facilities.

At an unknown date, Carter added two additional buildings as its business expanded. Of plainer design and construction, building 2 probably gave Carter new erection space; building 3 was later referred to in a Carter inventory as "the old paint shop," helping to separate the functions of car erection from car painting. By 1893, all three Carter buildings were in place; five years later, building 3 was gone. By the time of the First World War, all three of the Carter shop buildings were either razed or removed.

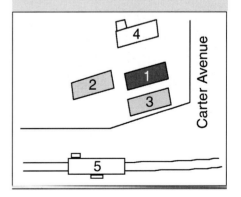

The original 1877 Carter Brothers facility in Newark, pictured top, was located in the South Pacific Coast backshop complex; the Carter erection shop (below) was added later, allowing the original building to become Carter's paint shop. Both photographs, ca. 1913, were made after the shops were closed.

is, scarcely necessary to say, up to the highest standard. All the work is done at these shops, from painting to the ironwork, etc.

Accompanying the national census of 1880 was an addendum called the Industrial Census, intended to profile the fiscal activity of large and small businesses for the year June 1, 1879, to May 31, 1880.[19] Carter Brothers is included in the summary; its activity level is characterized as slowing from the peak production year of 1878. Only three months of the reported year, for example, were spent in "full time operation," while nine months of the year were described as "two-thirds" of full staffing. Still, twenty-five men were on salary during the peak times, earning a total yearly wage reported as $15,000.

The census also reported that on a capital investment of $3,000 (which we can assume represented shop tooling and equipment) Carter turned $25,000 in raw materials, supplies, and fuel, as well as $15,000 in labor, into $30,000 worth of finished goods. On the basis of the belief that Carter manufactured at least $50,000 in retail rolling stock for the South Pacific Coast that year, a reasonable conclusion is that the value of finished goods was underreported.

The Industrial Census also mentions one additional capital item owned by Carter Brothers: some fifty horses, probably the early beginnings of Martin's Nutwood stock farm. Breeding horses would soon become a passion in Martin Carter's life. There was a private half-mile trotting track in the Newark area, owned and operated by H. A. Mayhew on his local ranch. Newspaper articles from 1880 report races between local trotters, with purses of several hundred dollars awarded to horses that turned in a time of 3:25, admittedly slowed on a half-mile track "with tight turns at each end."[20] Carter may have been a regular at Mayhew's track. Within five years, trotters from Carter's own Nutwood stock farm would be running the half mile in 2:04.

By the spring of 1880, on the eve of the South Pacific Coast's opening, it was clear that the entire sum of Carter's production for the previous three years would fall short of demand. Completion of the big tunnels in the Santa Cruz Mountains opened up a floodgate of traffic in finished lumber, lime, firewood, petroleum, and blasting powder. In mid-May 1880, a single South Pacific Coast locomotive manhandled a forty-seven-car freight train from Glenwood to San Jose; it was an early indication of the density of new traffic on the Santa Cruz mainline.[21] Caught off guard, Davis immediately asked Carter to build 150 additional boxcars and flatcars in an attempt to ease the shortage.[22]

By July 1880, the shortfall in rolling stock was so acute that Davis leased unused boxcars and flatcars from the North Pacific Coast, presumably barged to Alameda by the SPC's ferry and car float *Garden City*. Turning to any source of cars he could find, Davis finally leased an order of new Carter freight cars directly from the factory floor and diverted them to mainline service still lettered and numbered for their owner, the Sonoma Valley Railroad.[23]

Carter was at the zenith of its production of mainline narrow gauge railroad equipment.

For more than two years after Davis's original land purchase, until April 1878, there was no public marketing of the company's real estate. An ironic reversal of Davis's original agenda, it was evidence that the president had narrowed his focus to the railroad and its increasingly complex infrastructure. The three shop buildings completed in the summer of 1877, the arcade depot, Dugan's hotel, and a dozen cottages were the only large structures in Newark's core area until February 1879.[24]

Memories of the headquarters building and its unwashable smell remained fresh in the mind of railroad workers; Martin Carter and his crew lived and worked under these conditions for eighteen months. Throughout 1878, the town was still not a town. There was no post office, no store, and (except for the tracks themselves) no developed public highway into the core area. As primitive as Saucelito in 1874, Newark must have seemed more remote, more like a perpetual camp site, exposed to a steady northwesterly wind that blew in off the Bay.

Under Sam Davis's direction, John Sedgely continued to plant blue gum eucalyptus trees in the early winter of 1878. The seedlings were spaced about fifteen feet apart along the main streets in town. During the next two years, Sedgely planted tens of thousands of blue gum seedlings (purchased from P. McKeany's nursery in nearby Washington Corners), each barely a foot tall, delicately ornamented with translucent leaves that looked, in the sapling stage, like rice paper. For the first two summers, he watered the trees by hand and replaced those that died in the adobe-stiffened soil. At a growth rate of two or three feet a year, the blue gums quickly became hedgerows, then a thick curtain, then a forest canopy, landscaping the town.

Sedgely surrounded the shops with eucalyptus and created an arboretum in the railroad wye by the depot, softening the industrial lines of the railroad.[25] A photograph taken of the arcade depot in 1885 shows mature blue gums twenty-five or thirty feet tall, towering above the building's gables, with trunks thickened to nearly a foot. Seen from a distance, the town of Newark was a living cross section of its street map, a parklike precinct whose context (or "suburbanness," as newspapers liked to say) was created not by the natural environment but by landscaping.

Soon, the Pacific Land Investment Co. developed a park within a park. At Cherry and Thornton streets, an open-sided dance hall was constructed on ten acres of land held back from private sale. Called the Pavilion, the park was ringed with eucalyptus and crowned with a fountain built of native stone, fed by a naturally flowing artesian well. By 1880, chartered trains would simmer quietly under the arcade depot while groups of a thousand "rusticaters" strolled to the Pavilion grounds for a picnic, the cough-drop smell of gum trees perfuming the shaded walkways.

With trainloads of crushed rock from deposits in Los Gatos Creek, John Sedgely graded and regraded Newark's streets. The grid of streets soon crosshatched a hundred or so core area blocks, and some 130 farm blocks forming a perimeter around the backshops and town center.[26] On April 22, 1878, more than two years after the original town site was purchased, the Pacific Land Improvement Co. held its first real estate auction, conducted in the comfort of Maurice Dore and Co.'s brokerage house at 410 Pine Street in San Francisco.

Pacific Land continued to appeal to immigrants. Advertisements for the event were widely published in English, German, French, and Swedish. The terms of sale were liberal: one-fourth of the purchase price down in cash, one-fourth in one year, one-fourth in two years, and the remaining fourth in three years, with deferred payments to bear interest at 8 percent. For any buyer constructing a home of at least $800 value within six months of purchase, the second installment would be forgiven.

Discounted commute tickets to San Francisco were offered to buyers at four dollars per month, including ferry transit. Low-cost rail excursion tickets were advertised prior to the auction. The ferry *Newark* made the run from San Francisco to Dumbarton Point for seventy-five cents, round trip, with the brassy music of Walcott's band included in the price of a ticket.

Media reaction to the campaign was generally positive. The *Alameda Encinal* found the development attractive, if a little primitive, when it wrote, on March 28, 1878, that "the view of the surrounding country is clear and extensive, and to those desiring to purchase property we would say, go to Newark and judge for yourself—but take your lunch with you."

Sales, however, were disappointing. It is estimated that fewer than one hundred lots were sold at the April auction (estimated by the number of housing starts that followed during the next six months). Little commercial development existed to support a growing population. By late May 1879, for example, there was still no grocery store in town, and John Dugan's new hotel, the only hostelry, catered largely to machinists, car builders, and painters—sojourners without families. Martin Carter was probably one of its early tenants. Newspaper accounts identified Martin in the role of "superintendent of the works at Newark" as early as December 1877, although it is likely that he was on the scene to oversee the start-up of the shops the previous July.[27]

Martin, however, may have been in a position most of his workmen could only envy. With housing at a premium in Newark throughout 1878, Mary and the two Carter children remained in Saucelito until the spring of 1879, when Martin might have put his carpenters to work on his own residence, or at least on a cottage he could rent from his landlord, Pacific Land Investment. To judge by the date he executed real estate transactions in Saucelito, Martin probably moved his family to Newark in late April. His in-laws, John and Catherine Larkin, both fifty-seven at the time, moved in with them.

The temporary quarters might have been crowded, but the move was a personal milestone for the Martin Carter family. Away from the cheap rooming houses and poisonous air of Tar Flat, he and Mary were at last together, looking forward to settling down. Martin began to take stock of his life; he consolidated his personal wealth. In April 1879, he executed a deed of ownership on his lots in Saucelito, when the Carter home "near the railroad shops" on Easterby Street was rented.[28] In June 1880, Martin filed a legal will, leaving his buggy, harness, furniture, and personal effects to Mary and listing in addition the family cow (still in Saucelito).[29] He also conveyed to Mary the deed to their original house in Sacramento, bringing his real estate portfolio to two homes. Soon, there would be a third.

Martin began to sink roots into the fledgling community. With his son, Thomas Newton, old enough for kindergarten, he was instrumental in raising funds for a permanent Newark public school. A fundraising party on September 12, 1879, drew a crowd of 250 people to a dinner and dance, and a spirited auction[30]: "After supper, a drawing took place for a large cake. This was presented by a Newark lady, who spent the first part of the evening in selling tickets for it, at 50 cents each. Miss Davis was the fortunate winner of the cake. This young lady caused it to be put up at auction and sold for the benefit of the school fund, Mr. William Barry being the auctioneer."

Most of the managers and overseers in Newark took turns buying, and then returning, the same cake. Martin enthusiastically ante'd into the pot, contributing $2.50 to the school furniture fund before handing the cake carefully back to the auctioneer. The dancing continued until four in the morning, with two violinists and a harpist improvising an unlikely medley of a Sailor's Hornpipe, the Scottish Hornpipe, and the Highland Fling. Newark's first permanent school house, built on land donated by the railroad at Dairy and Cherry streets, was under construction the following week.

A modest building boom had finally come to Newark. Its dozen permanent residences, counted in February 1879, became fifty a year later. The Pacific Land Investment Co. added its own hotel in the core area, across the tracks from Dugan's, named the Central Hotel and managed by Sam Marsten. With Brussels carpets laid in the dining room and its own gas lighting system, Marsten's was slightly upscale of Dugan's and attracted drummers, entertainers, land speculators, and probably Tom Carter, who was in need of a room when he took the train down from San Francisco. Newark, a company town born with a support mission for a short line railroad, had graduated from the milker's dormitory to become a small-but-vibrant community. In February 1880, the *Alameda County Reporter* sketched the scene that Martin Carter had helped create:

> Times are quite lively here. Mr. Harker is doing a good business. Mr. Paul is busy stitching away on harness; M. Watkin's hammer is ringing merrily all day; horses to shoe, plows to sharpen, makes the time pass very quickly. The shoe maker is busy pegging away. The S.P.C. Express wagon is going and coming every day with full loads. The plane man is here with his fine planes to sell. The gravel trains are busy putting gravel on the streets. Wagons with beets are going to the Station, and thence their loads are taken to the Sugar Mills, at Alvarado.
>
> Passenger, freight and gravel trains, passing and repassing all the time; steam up at the car shops, where many men are at work building cars, and more men busy painting new cars, and repainting old ones; Messrs. Ingraham & Co.'s large lathes and other ponderous machinery in motion; all with the sawing and hammering of the homebuilders, proclaims Newark as a live town.[31]

In March 1880, adding to his responsibilities as master mechanic, master car builder, and resident manager of Carter Brothers, Martin was named first postmaster of Newark.

On Sunday, June, 9, 1880, Martin became something of a local hero when he rounded up a posse and gave chase to Thomas Brown, who had stolen a locked handcar from the Newark section house and departed south into the face of Train 10, the oncoming San Jose passenger. The incident followed a series of attempts to wreck passenger trains by placing rocks on the mainline at nearby Mowry Station. No arrests had been made, and the threat left the small community with a case of the jitters. Martin had little trouble rounding up volunteers, most of whom were still dressed for church. The posse rode the miscreant to ground three miles south of the shops and found the villainous Brown sitting on the handcar, already set off the track in more than ample time to clear the oncoming passenger train.[32] Catastrophe avoided, Martin did his duty, performing a citizen's arrest and escorting the prisoner to the Centerville jail, where he was booked on charges of grand larceny.

They were heady days at the car shop.

Even while Carter Brothers was located within San Francisco's manufacturing district, it managed the purchase of parts and raw materials through a network of widely dispersed suppliers, including fabrication shops in Tar Flat, foundries in Vallejo and Santa Cruz, Douglas fir wholesalers on Puget Sound, and redwood suppliers from Santa Cruz County. But by 1878 a new kind of supply chain began to take shape. With a permanent build-in-place factory at Newark and its production increasing yearly, suppliers began to move closer to Carter.

By the time of Carter's move to Newark, the small Tay Foundry in neighboring Alvarado had been in business for nearly twenty years and was an available source of small castings. Its foreman, James Graham, would move to Newark in 1883 to start his own foundry. Graham might have made the business decision on the strength of small lots of car castings purchased by Carter from the Tay Foundry in the late 1870s.

With the added incentive of work from the locomotive repair shops, O. P. Ingraham moved his San Francisco works to Newark in April 1879. The machine shop occupied two new buildings in the block just south of Marsten's hotel, a two-story, 40' × 60' fabrication building, and a 40' × 40' foundry and machine room.[33] The *Washington Reporter* gave Ingraham credit for being able to create any metal part "from a lynch pin to a locomotive tire" and described its machine shop as "more complete in its appointments than any other in the bay district outside of San Francisco." Entirely a family-run business, Ossian, Rossini, and Joseph Ingraham settled into the small industrial campus springing up to the south of the narrow gauge backshops.

Ingraham's shop came on line in June 1879, "just in time to repair the thrasher engines" for the fall harvest.[34] Far more important to Davis, the same tooling could turn locomotive drivers—a service Ingraham was demonstrating to reporters as early as March 1880.[35] It is unclear how such work was divided between the similarly equipped railroad machine shop and the commercial works of Ingraham, but there appeared to be business enough for both. Ingraham, in addition, did fabrication work for Carter.

By 1883, Ingraham added a 30' × 40' blacksmith shop to the small industrial complex, equipped with power drop hammers.[36] With the addition of this shop, Ingraham gave Carter a local equivalent of Golden State and Miner's Ironworks, even if the tooling was lighter. Ingraham's shop, just two blocks away from the car factory, further differentiated the support requirements for the narrow gauge work Carter considered his mainstay.

There is evidence that Golden State and Miner's Ironworks in San Francisco continued to furnish castings and metal fabrication for Carter throughout the 1880s. But there is also evidence that GS&M supported primarily standard gauge castings and fabrications—for example, riveted iron car bolsters. As early as 1880, GS&M was supplying such assemblies to Carter for customers that included north coast California logging railroads.[37]

Over time, Carter became more and more dependent on James Graham for patterns and castings. The same castings produced at Golden State and Miner's in the late seventies and early eighties remained a staple in Carter's inventory but migrated, after 1883, into what appears to be a more systematic and centralized pattern warehouse maintained by the Graham foundry. The same part, unnumbered on cars produced in the 1870s or early 1880s, acquired what appears to be a systematic and repeating cast-in number on cars of a later date. An example is the utilitarian truss rode saddle, a small cast iron pad that bore the force of the truss rod against the wood needle beam. Known instances of this part dating from as early as 1881 are unmarked; those from the late 1890s carry a pattern number "20."[38] The list of known Carter parts displaying numbers is in the Field Notebook: Carter Casting Numbers. The apparent sequence suggests that the James Graham foundry began to systematize and maintain Carter's pattern set as early as 1883, thus affording a possible means of identifying and dating extant castings. From Carter's perspective, Graham's presence helped shorten its supply chain and provide maintenance and inventory control over its valuable pattern set.[39]

The most surprising addition to this mix of local suppliers was a lumber retailer. The major Pacific Coast lumber merchants had locations in large cities—Pope and Talbot on Mission Bay in San Francisco (as well as Oakland), and Renton Holmes in Alameda. But by 1880, the *Sentinel* began to report the expansion of a Santa Cruz lumber wholesaler named Elbon and Houck, which set up timber camps to support work on the South Pacific Coast summit tunnel project and announced interest in a Newark retail yard as early as January 1880, as the opening of the South Pacific Coast drew near.[40]

By May 1880, the ex–city clerk of Santa Cruz, E. W. Lucas, was hired to set up Elbon and Houck's lumber yard in Newark, along with a proposed planing mill, raising hopes that Carter would have direct access to a full-service lumber merchant who would furnish not only dimensioned redwood but Puget Sound "Oregon pine" as well. In June and July, Elbon and Houck settled down to business with a sidetrack into the site of the lumber yard near Ingraham's, a spur that passed just fifteen feet to the east of Car-

The Field Notebook: Carter Casting Numbers

Gleaned from castings found on Carter cars built in the 1885–1899 period, casting numbers were usually created by gluing commercially available metal type about three-eighths inch high onto the wood body of a pattern. Hence, the numbers could have been added to existing patterns long after the patterns were created. This suggests that many of the "numbered" Carter patterns are considerably older than the date they were numbered. It is logical that the numbers were created by the James Graham Foundry at Newark, after they took over a prominent role in Carter's supply chain in 1883. The numbering series is incomplete, with gaps that suggest the numbers may have been grouped by type of cars. Numbers 1–20, for example, seemed to be categorized as freight car patterns. Pattern 42 is unique, being nearly identical to an 1875 Kimball pattern, which suggests that Carter absorbed shop inventory from the pioneer builder, perhaps when it occupied the Kimball agricultural implement business at Sixth and Berry streets, in San Francisco.

1: Fifteen-ton-capacity journal box
2: "Star" journal box lid
3: Link and pin coupler
4: Body center plate
5: Truck center plate
6: Brake head
7: Brake shoe
8: Lower swing bearing (truck)
9: Upper swing bearing (truck)
10: Car bearing (brass), fifteen-ton
11: Stake pocket, single bolt
12: Elliptical washer for body bolster truss rod
13: Elliptical washer for truss rod
14: Elliptical washer (small)
20: Body truss rod saddle
28: Disconnect log car, center plate
42: Passenger car pedestal, 1897

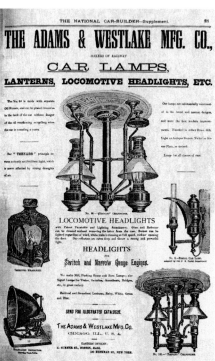

ter's shop. A sale of 150,000 board feet of Santa Cruz redwood accompanied the start-up, although the erection of the planing mill itself was never begun.[41]

The critical mass of suppliers and fabrication shops soon yielded the infrastructure for Carter to expand. Sometime in the early 1880s, two additional shop buildings were added to the Carter works, allowing Carter to separate the painting process from carpentry and assembly.[42] If we recall that painting for first-class passenger cars often took twice the time required to build the car, we see that the new buildings allowed separation of these manufacturing processes and a dramatic improvement in Carter's production time. In three years of active production at Newark, Carter succeeded in creating a small business campus of its own.

There were more than three hundred line items in a complete inventory of parts belonging to a wooden day coach built in America in the late 1870s, representing perhaps some ten thousand individual parts, for which Carter Brothers had to maintain a steady, reliable, and cost-effective supply.[43] For Carter, such an inventory included at least seven types of wood (Douglas fir, ash, redwood, and pine furring on the car's frame and exterior; black walnut, primavera, and tomana on the interior; oak in the trucks and draft timbers). It included single plate wheels and axles hammered from wrought iron, elliptical springs, coil springs, leaf springs, volute springs, brake pullback springs, hand railings, Miller hook patent couplers, and Miller patent buffers. It included tin ventilator boxes, cast iron ventilator frames, varnish, shellac, body paint, putty, glue, window sash, brass sash lifts, dry hoppers, signal cord, signal cord bushings, center lamps, brass baggage racks, glass, screws, lag bolts, and finish nails. And it included brass notice plates for the outside of the doors, bearing the legend "passengers will not stand on platforms" . . . to name just a small fraction of the total.

Over time, an increasingly large percentage of these parts became available through specialty catalogues and railroad supply houses, priced wholesale in bulk. Carter Brothers simply ordered what they needed for a given contract. A sample of Carter components known to have been purchased from supply houses or industry vendors would include both elliptical and spiral truck springs from A. French and Co., Pittsburgh; wheels and axles from A. Whitney and Sons in Philadelphia, or Bass foundry in Indiana, or Taylor Iron Works in New Jersey; iron seat castings from the G. Buntin Seat Co., Boston; dry hoppers by Adams and Westlake, Chicago, and by Post and Co., Cincinnati; brass window latches and lifts, Post and Co.; brass baggage racks, Hart Manufacturing, Detroit; shellac by W. P. Fuller; chrome yellow and golden ochre paints (and an assortment of other colors) by Masury, or Valentine, or W. P. Fuller; finish and polishing varnish by Acme; and finish stucco by Adams.[44]

Other common car parts may have come from vendors whose names can be guessed: lamps were probably manufactured by Adams and Westlake; gilt trim moldings (commercial interior molding finished with gold leaf) probably manufactured by Crerar, Adams and Co., Chicago; compound orna-

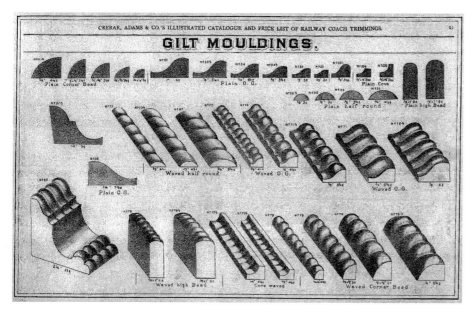

GILT MOULDINGS.

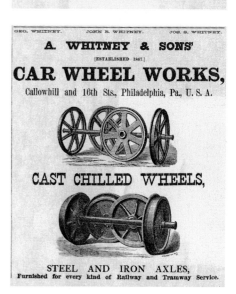

Examples of railroad car supplier advertisements (above) from the *National Car Builder,* 1882–1885; commercial guilt moldings (above left) from Crerar Adams catalogue, undated.

mental clerestory window glass probably manufactured by Western Sand Blast Co., Chicago.[45]

But parts from East Coast manufacturers entailed higher transportation cost, therefore raising the cost of the finished product. To control manufacturing expense, Carter occasionally decided to invest in the skills to craft specialty or decorator accessories. Coach headliners were an example. A commercial headliner, with ornamental designs suitable for lining the ceiling of a first-class passenger car, could be purchased in the vicinity of $150.[46] But in its 1899 inventory, Carter listed a headlining "frame," indicating that they paid their own painter to ornament a thirty-foot-long canvas blank. Headliner decoration was considered high art in the car-building trade, and although no complete examples of a Carter headliner are known to have survived, photographs of new car interiors suggest that Carter did not abridge this visible and quite public tableau. The best known example, the headliner in the private car *Pearl,* built for the Oahu Railway and Land Co. in 1889, was elaborately bordered in blossoms and finials. A photograph is reproduced near the end of this chapter.

Only two groups of parts in a completed Carter passenger car were protected by patent or license agreement: the brake system and the coupling system. The first was the Westinghouse air brake system, manufactured by the company of the same name and costing slightly over one hundred dollars per car, purchased directly from Westinghouse.[47] The cylinders and valves that made up a complete system were not licensed for railroads or car builders to manufacture themselves; car builders simply purchased a complete system (cylinder, valve, hoses, cut-out cocks, and conductor's valves), and installed them as original equipment on new passenger cars. Carter was extremely reluctant to compromise Westinghouse designs or installation standards. When asked to specify freight car brakes as a cheaper substitute for passenger brakes on an 1888 Yreka Railway coach, Carter replied to the railroad "don't think the Westinghouse people will let this Brake be used on Passenger Cars"—an indication of a firm proprietary boundary.[48] In the 1870s, Carter installed straight air w.a.b. systems in its passenger

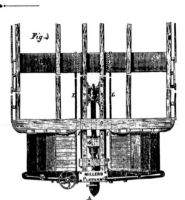
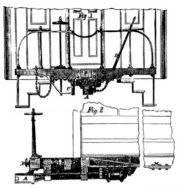

Westinghouse Air Brake Co. straight brake cylinder illustration (above), ca. 1878; Miller Patented Platform ad, ca. 1880 (right). [Westinghouse illustration, collection of Michael A. Collins]

products, consisting of a train line and a single cylinder mounted roughly midships under the car body. An excellent builder's photograph of South Pacific Coast coach 42 survives, of 1881 vintage, clearly showing the straight air system in place on a new Carter coach.[49]

The second proprietary system was the Miller platform and coupler, which, because of its demonstrated ability to resist telescoping in the event of a wreck, was enjoying national popularity in the early 1870s. The Miller system featured not only spring-loaded "hooks," which allowed hands-off coupling and uncoupling, but an improved design of the wooden car platforms that supported the hooks, requiring a complex system of buffers, straps, hangers, springs, and specialized castings to support and strengthen the entire assembly.

None of the Miller parts, however, were as technical or difficult to manufacture as Westinghouse air brake components, and Miller realized early in the life of his business that licensing was a useful tactic in successfully marketing his invention. A hook, for example, could be purchased directly from Miller for $24.50 apiece (or $49 per car) and installed on a new passenger car by a builder or railroad company. However, a railroad could also purchase a license (at $20 per completed mile of track) that would allow it to manufacture the Miller system at far lower costs than Miller would have charged. An example of such in-house manufacturing is a complete home-built hook for $20.00, fabricated for a day coach built in 1879 at the St. Joseph, Missouri, shops of the Kansas City, St. Joseph & Council Bluffs Railroad. The *National Car Builder* reported a cost as low as $16.37 per hook at about the same time.[50]

Undoubtedly, O. P. Ingraham's new hammer shop figured prominently in Carter's ability to make and install Miller hardware sets for the lowest possible price. The South Pacific Coast Railroad could have licensed Miller couplers for an estimated $1,600 (equal to the $20 license fee times eighty miles of mainline track); its eventual count of fifty completed passenger cars would have amortized the licensing fee to only $32 per car. If Carter simply absorbed this cost in its direct charges for parts, it stands to reason that O. P. Ingraham was producing the hooks for less than $17 per pair, or $8.50 per hook, clearly beating Miller's factory prices. There is no direct evidence that this was the price Carter actually paid, but this reconstruction does suggest the leverage that local manufacturing could exert on the cost of even patent-protected railroad hardware. Carter also observed the contractual requirement of placing the cast Miller identification plate on the platform end sill as proof of compliance with the manufacturer's guidelines. The plate was also good advertising; the public had grown to trust the Miller brand name as insurance of designed-in safety.[51]

In this fashion, Carter reduced the cost of raw materials and increased the value of its localized supply chain, ensuring that O. P. Ingraham's business would thrive and in effect making railroad parts cheaper by taking advantage of lower overhead and labor rates.

Carter controlled costs in the most obvious way of all. In 1880, at the time of the Industrial Census, Carter Brothers listed its day labor rate at $1.20 for unskilled labor and $2.75 for skilled labor, lower than in most other light industries covered by the census in southern Alameda County. In contrast, Carter's local supplier of iron castings, the Tay foundry in Alvarado, paid $1.50 for a day of unskilled labor and $3.00 for a day of skilled labor.

Ironically, Carter's finished product typically carried a higher retail price than similar products offered by its eastern competition. By 1879, the average price of a South Pacific Coast Railroad coach was $4,143, about 8 percent higher than the $3,852.20 the Santa Cruz Rail Road paid to Barney and Smith of Dayton, Ohio, for the coach *Theresa* in 1877.[52] But allowing for shipping costs, estimated at $473 for a fully equipped coach, the difference in price favored the Carter product by $182.[53] On this difference, Carter Brothers traded.

No doubt the South Pacific Coast, like the North Pacific Coast before it, enjoyed fringe benefits from having Carter Brothers on the property—for example, by adding on-site car repair capability. But to keep eastern competition out of the picture, it was clear that Carter had to set prices no higher than eastern prices plus shipping, and deliver a comparable product. Carter appeared to enter this high-end passenger car market with impunity, confident of its unique role as a near-monopoly in West Coast narrow gauge car manufacture. It would enjoy this position until about 1884, when John Hammond's California Car Works began production in San Francisco. But even so, Carter still had to compete against the perception that eastern builders were more skilled and offered higher-quality railroad cars.

What exactly, to a growing western market, defined a product comparable to those available from the East Coast? Barney and Smith delivered a thirteen-window coach to the Santa Cruz Rail Road and to the North Pacific Coast as well, thirty-five feet over its end sills, with room for forty-six passengers. The car weighed nine and a half tons and was equipped with Miller couplers; air brakes; and double-sprung, fully equalized four-wheel trucks.[54] Carter delivered a number of comparable thirteen-window coaches to the South Pacific Coast in the 1876–1880 period, 36'4" over the end sills, weighing nine tons, also with seating for forty-six passengers, and also equipped with Miller couplers, air brakes, and fully equalized two-axle trucks. The lighter weight may reflect the use of lighter materials, perhaps Douglas fir instead of yellow pine, in framing Carter's product. But Carter also delivered a number of fourteen-window coaches to the South Pacific Coast in the same time period, 39'10.5" over the sills, similarly equipped but rated at fifty passengers—clearly an enhancement of the smaller car's capacity. The average Carter coach price of $4,143 in this period mixes the shorter and longer types of car, suggesting that Carter got a premium price for the larger.

The traveling public, however, understood the difference between cars, much as it understood differences in house or furniture design, through finish and fashion. The *National Car Builder*, in March 1883, positioned the marketing of new cars in a constantly evolving standard defined largely by ornamentation. After a period of national recession in the late 1870s, in which car ornamentation became unusually plain,

> the reorganization of bankrupt roads and the wiping out of a vast amount of indebtedness, followed by the great iron "boom" of 1878–79, set all the collateral industries of the country on their feet again, and not only revived the demand for fine cars, but enabled the roads to respond to the demand with more alacrity than ever. Veneering not only has become obsolete, but is regarded by many as a cheap device, very nearly akin to sham and deception. Many cars with the old veneer finish are still running, but they have an ancient look. . . . Black walnut has disappeared, and the same may be said of gilt moldings and many things of the doll-baby style of decoration.[55]

A surviving Carter coach of 1881 vintage was considerably out of step with the trends described in this quotation, using both natural black walnut finish and gold-gilt molding on the inside cornice and fascia boards (the interior finish above the windows).[56] Its duckbill-style clerestory roof end was yet another anachronism. By this time, eastern builders had standardized on the bullnose roof end style. The roof end of an 1880 Barney and Smith coach, for example, was designed with delicately reversed curves that added height and complexity to the older duckbill roof end design. Engravings of coaches appearing in the 1879 *Car Builder's Dictionary* displayed both roof styles, marking a transition period in railroad car architecture.

Judging from contemporary illustrations, Barney and Smith cars were more elaborately striped than Carter coaches. The former designed its windows with a double sash, the upper sash rounded (and, in the case of North Pacific Coast examples, inset with etched art glass); the latter apparently treated most of its early South Pacific Coast coach windows with square, single sash.[57]

But the Barney and Smith interior clearly stood out. From the evidence of a surviving example of an 1881 Carson & Colorado coach, the passenger was surrounded by miniature examples of fine cabinet work. Its window posts were executed in fluted hardwoods, climaxed by carved medallions reminiscent of Corinthian columns.[58]

Structural differences between Carter products and those of eastern manufacturers were less obvious to the traveling public than interior decor. Some insight into the mixes of wood used by eastern and western car builders comes from two specifications written in 1889 for a coach ordered by the Port Blakely Lumber Co. (whose holding company, Renton Holmes, was a long-time supplier of lumber for Carter).

Carter bid on the job and ultimately won it, but an unidentified eastern car builder also bid on the work and left behind in Port Blakely's records a detailed specification of the materials it proposed to use:

Car area	Carter Brothers	Eastern builder
Sills	Oregon pine (Douglas fir)	Long-leaf yellow pine
Siding	Redwood	Clear poplar
End sills	Oak	White oak
Platform	Oak or ash	White oak
Interior paneling, doors, sash, and blinds	Cherry or ash	Oak or cherry
Wall posts, bracing	Ash	White ash
Truck frames	Oak	White oak[59]

The differences occur primarily in Carter's use of Douglas fir for sills and redwood for siding, reflecting available Pacific Coast materials. These specifications were made ten years after the initial South Pacific Coast work, but Carter stated in a following letter to Port Blakely that he had been building cars to this specification nine years previously, which gave Carter fair claim to "comparable quality" in materials (if not in cosmetic treatment) between its products and those of established eastern manufacturers.

Ironically, the Port Blakely order described here provoked the opposite reaction from the customer. In a September 9, 1889, letter from the Port Blakely mill to the home office of Renton Holmes in San Francisco, the arrival of Carter's completed cars was not described in positive terms: "Railroad men who examined the pass[enger] coaches say they are very inferior, lightly built, and running gear is lighter. The car purchased [used] from the Lake Shore & Eastern will [surpass] the new [Carter] ones, especially the running gear, and it is stylish and substantially built."[60]

Thomas Carter's vigorous reply, written on September 17, 1889, survives in the Port Blakely collection:

> In reply to your report from your people at the Sound that the two cars just shipped you are too light especially the trucks, will say that the Wheels and Axles and Oil Boxes, pedestal and Journal Boxes are all of the Master Car Builder's Standard and all other parts of the trucks are made in proportion to the weight of the Car. Will further state that we have duplicates of those Cars running on most of the roads in the State and they have given satisfaction. We made a lot of Cars from the same Specification as those for the California Southern nine years ago, and since we have made another lot—about four years ago—and they are still in use, and I was told while in Los Angeles last week that when in collisions and wrecks that our Cars stood as well as any cars on the road. We guarantee that the Cars are heavy enough to stand any kind of usage except going off track and turning over, but with the usual care and treatment they are plenty heavy in all parts for all kinds of use, and if made heavier would only add useless weight.

The Port Blakely letters suggest that Carter was struggling not against differences in hard engineering standards but against public perception of subjective design elements—elements that the Port Blakely correspondent summarized in the word *stylish*. These elements would remain artifacts of a market that West Coast car builders would never significantly penetrate. From the perspective of 1878, when the South Pacific Coast's orders were at their height, the success of Carter's early duckbill coaches was based in part on a captive market, and on the packaging of its products with a broad spectrum of other services, including the ability to repair the same cars it produced (a requirement that occurred annually).

The South Pacific Coast represented a unique customer for Carter. The fleet of forty-five Carter duckbill coaches, completed by the railroad's open-

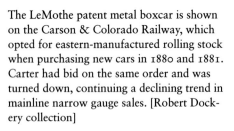

The LeMothe patent metal boxcar is shown on the Carson & Colorado Railway, which opted for eastern-manufactured rolling stock when purchasing new cars in 1880 and 1881. Carter had bid on the same order and was turned down, continuing a declining trend in mainline narrow gauge sales. [Robert Dockery collection]

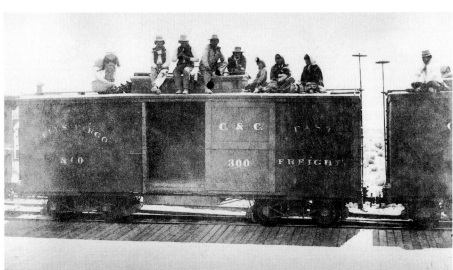

ing in the spring of 1880, would constitute the majority of its mainline passenger roster over the lifetime of the railroad.

Under less artificial market conditions, Carter faced open competition just as any other business did. Going head-to-head with Barney and Smith on a Carson & Colorado bid in 1880, Carter dropped its retail coach price to $3,640, 13 percent lower than its average coach price to the South Pacific Coast.[61]

Barney and Smith won the contract anyway.

Tried and true, Carter returned to craftsman-build manufacturing, and at least for a time stopped producing kits.[62] In the craftsman build (as we saw in Chapter Three), a team of four to six car builders would share detailed knowledge of the entire car, and of its parts and assemblies. Their skill grew from teamwork, and from experience of the fit and interplay of parts, knowledge that might be fragmented and lost under the isolation of assembly-line manufacturing.

The craftsman build was a collection of what might be called *vernacular* skills, unique to wooden car building, unique to the Carter product line, and unique to the practice of the small circle of workmen who began to shape the business coming from the Newark shop. It is difficult to reconstruct these skills, for their practitioners (even those associated with the largest car builders) left few oral histories behind them. The sources that exist—notably William Voss's *Railway Car Construction,* the trade periodical *National Car Builder,* and a printed guide to installation of Miller couplers—suggest that the tradition represented by these craftsmen was rich, complex, and deeply rooted in experience.[63]

A craftsman build of a day coach began with careful selection of raw materials. Douglas fir was the standard choice for longitudinal car parts, such as car sills, wall sills and plates, and clerestory sills and plates. But the vertical pieces (mainly wall posts and bracing) were made from ash, a hard wood able to sustain, without crushing, the compression of tie rods that would splinter softer woods in a small cross-section. The hardest wood in common use, oak, was a prime candidate for draft timbers or end platform decking, but (because of distortion as it weathered) a poor choice for doors. Instead, ash was used in door construction. Finish woods—cherry, black walnut, ash, or the more exotic South American primavera or tomana—were used to create interior panels and molding. Unlike structural members flat sawn in a planing mill, finish material was quarter sawn, orienting its grain structure to minimize shrinkage as humidity varied between summer and winter. Non-varietal woods (often soft pine) were used for furring strips as backing for installation of panels and were referred to collectively as "stuff."

It was critical to use well-seasoned wood throughout the car's framing. Green wood shrank. Even while a car was under construction, a poorly seasoned part would shrink back from the edge of a mortice, causing the entire frame to loosen. Freshly cut braces, posts, or spacers, referred to as sticks, were end-sealed with primer or paint just after cutting, in an attempt to slow the drying process and prevent splitting or checking.

The Carter imprimatur was displayed in various media (from top to bottom): acid-etched glass in the clerestory window, scroll painting on the inside sash of a car door, stenciling on a truck transom, or printing on its business card. [Top, Vernon Sappers collection; middle pair, Bruce MacGregor; bottom, Martin G. Carter collection]

Variations in the well-known Carter "star" cast iron journal box lid may not all have come from Carter; the two lids that do bear Carter's initials (CB SF) show variation in the presence or lack of a casting number and probably came from different foundries. Examples are from the collection of the Society for the Preservation of Carter Railroad Resources. [Bruce MacGregor]

The same logic applied to the frame itself. Longitudinal sills were made from Douglas fir; cross pieces (including bolster and spacer blocks) were hardwood, such as oak or ash, placed under compression by lateral truss rods. Fitting frame parts was a balance between the positive and negative effects of removing volume from the original timber. Creating notches (gaining) allowed an exact plane or volume to be located in rough-cut frame lumber, establishing a datum for accurate location of other parts. Like Lincoln Logs, a set of interlocking gains, cut into mating parts, constituted a system for making the car rigid. Bolsters were gained in this fashion, locking into shallow notches cut (or gained) into the sills. But removing wood also weakened load-bearing timbers. A rabbet was simply a long notch cut into (for example) the corner of a wall post, allowing interior siding to be flush-fitted to the frame. But the rabbet also took structural integrity away from the post. Gains and rabbets, therefore, worked best when minimized. Side sills had to be big enough to provide adequate volume for creating the tenons, which in turn had to be strong enough to join the side sills to the end sills. Car shop wisdom argued that sills were therefore always larger than they needed to be for the loads placed on them. Their size, in other words, was adjusted for the excess of wood removed to create mortise or tenon joints.

Fully aware that gravity would act on the structure they built, car builders knew how to offset sag by introducing camber into the foundation layers of the car. Platforms, for example, were cantilevered off the main car sills by short, auxiliary platform sills. Instead of cutting the platforms sills dead level, a small angle, called camber, was intentionally added to allow the platform to slope upward very slightly, building in leeway for gradual settling. A similar, and more subtle, camber was sometimes intentionally built into the shape of the wall framing, allowing a fraction of an inch of extra height at the ends and middle, offsetting sag in the entire car body before it began. Similar tricks employed gravity to gently pressure parts into

This classic Carter Brothers journal box lid is a reproduction based on originals that probably came from the James Graham Foundry in Newark, adjacent to the Carter factory. In raised lettering, the initials CB SF appear at the corners; in recessed lettering, the casting number 2 appears near the center. [Bruce MacGregor]

some desired orientation. The hole created through the platform end sill to accommodate the Miller uncoupling lever, for example, was inclined slightly away from the vertical, to encourage the lever lean against a ratchet fabricated into the platform railing.

During production, much of the work was laid out with templates. The curves at the end of platform sills, the location of mortices or gains, and the location of drill-outs were all encoded in sheet metal (or inch-thick pine) templates laid over the stock material and then traced, almost always with the sharp point of an awl or scratch tool. Sharp lines gave accurate, precise alignment. Carpenter pencils left a thick trace that invited variation and error. The layout scratches remain today in extant Carter car bodies—perhaps the closest thing we have to the personal signature of their builders.

Fit and function were tested by experience. Before the coach siding was nailed in place, wall framing was leveled by eye. Sag or distortion was corrected by tensioning one or more of the thirteen diagonal body braces, located below each window, a surprisingly accurate way of leveling the horizontal line of the coach. Alignment of a finished truck frame was most easily checked by confirming its tram. The rule of thumb was simple: the distance across each corner-to-corner diagonal had to be exactly the same if the axles were to run true in their bearings.

Many of the tests proceeded by feel, rather than measurement. In installing a Miller coupler, for example, the uncoupling lever (pulled to one side and released) should cause the coupler hook to "snap smartly to the center" if the spring was loaded correctly.

In the world of assembly-line manufacture, tests for quality or uniformity were (like any other step of the assembly process) relegated to individuals who specialized in the testing process alone, performing the same tests over and over. But in the world of the craftsman build, quality was measured by the same people who performed the assembly work. The same car builder who installed the Miller hook coupler knew how the coupler should perform and made sure that it did as he installed it.

The quality of the car was therefore built into its manufacturing process, a measure of the builder's skill born of breadth rather than depth.

The South Pacific Coast Railroad is nowhere to be found in the ponderous volumes of R. G. Dun credit reports. It wasn't just the size of a company that determined an entry in the nationwide credit registry. Far smaller businesses were treated to a detailed investigation into their financial solvency. An interesting example was the San Francisco business of Alonzo Sweetzer, who specialized in manufacturing bird cages. R. G. Dun noted, on April 30, 1874, that Sweetzer was "of temperate habits but gambles and speculates in stocks" and tended to be a "slow pay."[64] The reports were often an investigation into personal habits and character as much as the size of bank accounts. In the case of the South Pacific Coast, which was relying on no public subsidies, trading no shares of public stock, and paying cash whenever it purchased goods or services, R. G. Dun found little reason to investigate either.

Carter Brothers, on the other hand, earned the attention of Dun's reporter because it was buying goods and services on credit and had sustained enough business activity by 1878 to invite inquiry by new creditors, bankers, or other manufacturers, from which R. G. Dun received a fee. The report is brief but remarkably positive for a small startup company doing business in the California recession:

> Thos, M.C. Carter. Carter Bros. Car Builders. March 23/78.
>
> Composed of Thos. Carter, aged 38 & single & Martin aged 33 and married. Thos. Carter states "that they are partners, but on account of his being better known to the trade than his brother he frequently orders goods in his own name. [Banking] Houses in this city can corroborate this statement. Thomas was formerly in the employ of the Central Pacific RR Co, latterly of the [South] Pacific Coast RR Co for the past 2 years has been Supt. of the South Pacific Coast RR Co. for which company the Carter Bros. have been building cars etc. He declines making a full statement of his position, claiming however to own residence in San Francisco worth $20,000 and clear of encumbrances and to have $20,000 in Bank besides stock etc. in works at Newark, Alameda County and not to owe anything of consequence. From parties to whom he refers we learn that they are regarded as worth $30,000–$40,000 safely and probably a good deal more and in this market are prompt pay at Bank, ask no accommodations, own the residence mentioned and it is believed clear of encumbrances. Of Martin but little is known, but Thomas is a cautious, industrious man of considerable ability in his line and regarded as reliable. Are believed safe for any ordinary credit they may require in their line.[65]

Midway through its largest contract at the time of Dun's credit report, Carter's financial performance would only improve over the next two years.

For three years, between 1877 and 1880, Martin Carter was the master specifier for the railroad. In that time period, he directly managed the locomotive repair shops, the car repair shops, Carter Brothers, and the various subcontractors and vendors who supported them. Indirectly, his experience in maintaining and repairing the railroad's growing fleet of cars and engines gave him insight into the rapidly changing demands the railroad would place on new rolling stock.

The responsibilities must have weighed heavily on the thirty-two-year-old mechanic. Nine new engines came on the property from Baldwin Locomotive Works during that time period (the Santa Clara Valley Railroad number 1 bringing the total roster to ten). Two hundred new freight cars were added, all of the new ten-ton design. As the railroad moved further and further into the mountains, the wear and tear on the rolling stock, and the stress it placed on the Newark shops, steadily increased.

Still, his multiple roles gave Martin control over resources that the master mechanic of a larger railroad would have envied. At Saucelito, Carter

Brothers had taken on odd-job repair at the behest of the railroad's master mechanic; now Martin Carter *was* the master mechanic. He could easily fill a labor shortage in the railroad car repair department with excess hands from Carter Brothers. In fact, in the beginning car repair was likely subcontracted to Carter Brothers, making it easy to balance the work force between jobs. Painters could be moved back and forth between new car work and car repair or repainting. Locomotive repair work that could not be scheduled soon enough at the South Pacific Coast backshop was simply moved to O. P. Ingraham, or the reverse, wherever shop time could be found. The dividing line among railroad shop, Carter Brothers, and Ingraham's was largely a bookkeeping formality. Ingraham was an especially attractive resource, since Carter did not have to watch Ingraham's staffing levels to control his own direct costs. Smaller vendors were sought out for the same reason. An itinerant upholstery tradesman was employed at Newark in 1882 to restore the plush on coach seats.

Martin Carter's reengineering efforts soon focused on new motive power designs. His role as master mechanic was like that of a clearinghouse for locomotive performance data, and the changing requirements they implied for new orders. At the same time, Baldwin's own concept of design "platform" was steadily evolving. The sturdy 8-18 C class engine represented, in 1877, a successful three-year-old locomotive design based on a standard platform of four drivers, a four-wheel lead truck, and a twelve-inch-diameter cylinder. One hundred four locomotives of this classification were manufactured by Baldwin between 1874 and 1919, which is testimonial to the flexibility and longevity of the design.[66] The 8-18 C represented a chassis that could take extremely sharp radius curves, while holding in reserve the ability to sustain the speed of a passenger train with a load of one hundred tons or more.

The first two locomotives that Martin Carter specified from Baldwin were both 8-18 Cs, assigned road numbers 2 and 3. But by early summer 1877, the South Pacific Coast's high track standards began to influence follow-up orders. Wanting to leverage the flexibility of the 8-18 C chassis into a higher-performance design, Baldwin created what might be thought of as a half step toward the next platform, labeling the new generation an 8-18$\frac{1}{2}$ C.[67] In Baldwin parlance, the fraction stood for "special class"; the resulting locomotive design was an attempt to increase speed by increasing the length of the engine's stroke. The first two Baldwin "8-18$\frac{1}{2}$ C" machines were sold to South America. Martin Carter ordered the third, fourth, fifth, sixth, and seventh such locomotives, placing the order on August 31, 1877, with his sights set on increasing passenger train speeds on SPC's abundant tangent track and heavy rail.

Each of these half steps in design was accompanied by a slight increase in locomotive weight (44,300 pounds to 45,500, and then to 45,600) and a small increase in heating surface in the boilers (accomplished by adding extra flues to the same basic boiler shell), in an attempt to increase steaming capacity to support longer stroke. Other refinements were noted on the Baldwin order sheets for the special-class engines, such as heavier driving wheel springs, the intent being to damp out vibration at higher speed.

The final pair of engines Martin Carter ordered, South Pacific Coast 9 and 10, would alter the variables in the engineering formula once again, lowering driver diameter to forty-three inches but increasing weight to 50,400 pounds; it was a trade between lower speed and higher tractive force. The changes reflected relatively small variations on a design widely considered successful by American narrow gauge railroads, an attempt on Martin Carter's part to squeeze increased performance out of the higher overall engineering standards of the South Pacific Coast system. But the changes also inched their way toward an upper limit in the 8-18½ C's performance. With the width of the firebox constrained between two pairs of narrow gauge drivers, none of the special classifications managed an increase in the volume of combusting material—a bottleneck that in turn limited their ability to produce more steam. When the South Pacific Coast began revenue service in the mountains, these small variations on the classic 8-18 C would no longer meet the demands for moving freight over the Santa Cruz mountain grades. The dramatic change in operating environment opened the door for newer, larger classes of Baldwins.

Pursuing a new look as well, Carter switched the special engines to a paint scheme of olive green and gold trim, a darker, more sophisticated livery than the garish style of the older locomotives.[68]

Olive and gold would become standard colors on future locomotive orders. Like an anthem, the same colors would work their way onto appliances and furnishings spread widely over the architecture of the railroad, even to the public water coolers on the company's ferry boats.[69]

The Carter monopoly of South Pacific Coast rolling stock, worth nearly a quarter million dollars in retail value by 1880, was interrupted in 1879 by the order of two luxury parlor cars from Jackson and Sharp.[70] In one sense, the order seemed to bestow the pride of the company on an eastern builder who had played no part in the manufacture of its car fleet. At $4,985.01 each, the forty-six-foot cars were the jewels of the railroad.[71] In July 1880, the cars were shipped overland on standard gauge trucks, transferred to narrow gauge trucks at Santa Clara, and delivered to their owners: "they are elegant coaches, handsomely fitted up with all the improvements. The seats consists of luxurious, high-back chairs, with crimson upholstery, 21 in each car."[72]

Called "drawing room cars" on their arrival in July, they bore the names *San Francisco* and *Santa Cruz* in oval name plates and were initially coupled together for special runs. When through passenger service began in May 1880, they were assigned individually to mainline Santa Cruz trains, cut in behind the baggage car (to give the steward access to supplies of ice, liquor, fresh towels, and newspapers stocked aboard when the train left Alameda). Each car apparently contained a double-sized saloon, and a small bar that served as the steward's post. The steward's position was held by a black attendant uniformed much like a conductor—evidence that the railroad's concept of service aboard these cars may have been inspired by Pullman practice.[73] Advertised as a luxury service, the cars would appear on regular through trains to Santa Cruz after the line opened in 1880, but they

In 1879, an East Coast competitor made inroads into the Carter monopoly of South Pacific Coast rolling stock. Equipped with plush swivel seats and a small bar, the pair of Jackson and Sharp chair cars were advertised as luxury "parlor cars" and featured in promotional advertisements for the railroad. The chair car *Santa Cruz* poses on the San Lorenzo River Bridge, behind the train's baggage car. [Fred Stoes collection, courtesy of Rick Hamman]

could be reserved for high-toned trains, say, for the occasional visit of a president, as with Benjamin Harrison in March 1893; or a tour of the line by Leland Stanford and Collis Huntington in 1887.

The parlor cars were the first example of the bullnose roof end style to creep into the South Pacific Coast roster; their presence in the mainline passenger train quickly dated the duckbill architecture and perhaps acted as a catalyst for change. By 1882, Carter would introduce the bullnose roof into its own narrow gauge designs.[74]

There are records of other non-Carter cars infiltrating the South Pacific Coast roster. A pair of coaches manufactured in 1879, numbered 15 and 16 on the roster, have been identified in Southern Pacific records as built by Davis, Howell and Co., a reference to a short-lived railroad supply house

A mixed train on the Boulder Creek branch, ca. 1890, includes coach 15 (on the right), an 1879 product of an obscure West Coast car builder named Davis, Howell. Little is known about this builder, but later records—indicating coach 15 was built by Carter—suggest that Carter Brothers may have been manufacturing OEM-style equipment for other builders. [Donald Duke collection]

listed just two years (1879 and 1880) in Langley's San Francisco business directory. An extant photograph of coach 15, probably taken in the 1890s, shows a thirteen-window coach with duckbill roof proportioned much like a Carter product, with one additional modern feature (rounded window lintels) and one somewhat antiquated feature (board and batten siding). Little is known about the supply house or its partners, or whether Davis, Howell in fact included Alfred Davis of the South Pacific Coast.[75]

The mysterious firm of Davis, Howell and Co. becomes especially intriguing in light of Alfred Davis's demonstrated interest in rolling stock design. The evidence that survives comes from the *Alameda Encinal,* of November 14, 1883. The article explains that he designed a narrow gauge sleeping car "as comfortable as a hammock—hung low to prevent sway," but it fails to explain why the eighty-mile South Pacific Coast would need a sleeper in the first place. The Davis sleeping cars, as far as we know, were never built. Davis, Howell and Co., if it ever intended to compete with Carter Brothers, vanished without a trace after the 1880 listing in Langley's directory.

From the perspective of the tiny car-building concern of Carter Brothers, the intrusion into their near-monopoly seemed to have little lasting impact on the business. Demand for their products continued, perhaps ironically, from Alfred Davis himself. With the exception of the two Jackson and Sharp parlor cars and two Davis, Howell coaches, until 1886 future additions to the South Pacific Coast's passenger car roster would all come from Carter Brothers.

In the autumn of 1880, at the end of the rapid production ramp of South Pacific Coast rolling stock, Martin Carter was able to use part of the profits to purchase acreage in Washington Corners, about four miles from the shops at Newark. The land sat closer to the East Bay foothills than to the bay, on a nearly level plain where wheat grew and cattle pastured. Martin saw the purchase as a chance for a permanent homestead in a rural setting, where he and Mary could raise their children. Over the next four years, he bought adjoining parcels until his holdings spanned about five hundred acres.[76]

On the original parcel, he planned (and perhaps built himself) a home big enough to hold a growing household: Mary's parents; sons Frank and Thomas Newton; and the two Carter children who would be born that decade, Leland and Martin Grover. The chimney on the new, gabled three-story family home would bear the date "1881" in inset masonry, as the cornerstone of the property Martin would name the Nutwood Stock Farm. "The residence," reported a Washington Township subscription testimonial in 1898, "is a massive affair, elegantly furnished . . . lighted with gas and supplied with all modern conveniences and improvements. Here Mr. Carter has surrounded himself with all the comforts and luxuries that capital can secure, or refinement and education demand."

"The ranch," as the family called the homestead, would also be home to the fifty horses that the 1880 Industrial Census listed, and soon Martin developed breeding programs for trotting horses, draft horses, and Hereford cattle—the Herefords imported from New Zealand.[77]

"He was a consummate horseman," his youngest son, Martin Grover Carter, recalled in 1975.[78] "He would stay up all night to tend a sick horse or deliver a foal. He would watch them in the pasture for hours, hanging over the fence." Leland Stanford's East Bay property at Warm Springs was just a few miles away from the ranch, and Carter was soon buying stock from the senator. After Martin's star trotter, John A. McKerron, set a record of 2:04:05 in competition, the Nutwood Stock Farm advertised "sires of early and extreme speed" and began to attract national attention. Acknowledging the legacy of his pioneering car shop, Martin named one of his prize trotters Rapid Transit.

But even after the ranch became a business of its own, Martin still left for the Newark shops before dawn, dressed in a boiled shirt and tie, and seldom returned home until after dark. His boys gradually took jobs in the shops, first on summer vacation from school, filling in at unskilled tasks such as cutting molding on the table saw, or stacking completed parts for carpenters. Martin Grover remembers lifting sticks of sweet-smelling oak out of a vat of boiling water and pushing the softened wood into a jig to form roof rafters for streetcars. Much of Carter Brothers' work in the 1890s focused on streetcars and cable cars, whose roof construction resembled the design of the full-size coaches that Carter had built for the South Pacific Coast.

Martin Grover's oldest brother, Thomas Newton, went to work as a part-time draftsman for his father. The younger Carters grew up as shirttail cousins to the same shop crew that had worked for their father for twenty-five or even thirty years. Martin Grover was especially fond of Archibald

NUTWOOD STOCK FARM.

NUTWOOD Stock Farm, the home of Martin Carter, of the Newark Car Shops, is one of the finest country homes in this section. The residence is a handsome, massive affair, elegantly furnished, lighted with gas and supplied with all modern conveniences and improvements. Here Mr. Carter has surrounded himself with all the comforts and luxuries that capital can secure, or refinement and education demand. Mr. Carter is a breeder of some of the

RESIDENCE — MARTIN CARTER — IRVINGTON.

finest stock on the California turf. He was owner of the celebrated stallion, California Nutwood, sire of Maud C, 2:19; Annie C, 2:25; Albert H, 2:27½; Belle Porter, 2:30 and Nutwood, 2:30. He is also owner of Nutwood Wilkes, by Guy Wilkes, who had a three-year-old record of 2:20½; Rapid Transit, by Director, 2:17 and Long Branch, by Antevolo, 2:19½. The specialty of the Nutwood Stock Farm has been trotting stock and the heaviest Norman horses.

Washington Township Illustrated, an 1898 promotional magazine, featured Martin Carter's Nutwood Stock Farm.

Hook, Carter's foreman and best man at Martin and Mary's wedding in Sacramento in 1873. Hook's wife often made lunch when Martin Grover worked in the Newark shops during summer vacation.

Thomas Carter's nephews grew up thinking of their uncle as a city bloke, and their own father as a country bloke. Martin Grover recalled they didn't see much of Uncle Thomas at the ranch, or at the Newark shops. Their uncle, instead, symbolized the charm and allure of far-off places, of travel, and of the urban pleasures money could buy. Martin Grover and his brother Leland occasionally took the train to San Francisco with their mother, who pointed out the family name on the door transom plates and colored clerestory glass of the cars they rode in. In the City, Uncle Thomas would greet his nephew with a firm handshake and "a big round dollar in his hand." Like a magic trick, the coin slid between palms and disappeared into Martin Grover's pocket.

"We went often," Martin Grover recalled.

One summer day in a year Martin Grover could not remember exactly, Thomas Newton argued with his father, although the point of the argument, like the date, was lost. The oldest of the Carter boys, approaching twenty, "Newt" was independent and strong-minded, and Martin Grover was aware that his oldest brother was unsettled about his future direction in life. His father expected him to continue in the car-building business. Newt was a successful draftsman and was filling in at odd jobs around the shops, gaining experience at the table saw, the joiner, and the drill press while learning the art of drafting, documentation, and design.

But on that day, Martin Grover recalled some eighty years later, Newt's mind was not on the work. Feeding a board through the table saw with his left hand, the work slipped, sending Newt's hand into the blade. He lost three fingers.

That same day, Martin Carter's three sons—including Martin Grover, the youngest—made up their minds to have nothing more to do with the car business. Recalling vividly the sight of blood on the table saw, Martin Grover never went back.

Long before and long after wooden car construction died out as an industry, the term *craftsman's build* was commonly used to distinguish a manufacturing process in which a small group of highly skilled workmen participated in every stage of manufacturing. Unlike assembly-line production, in which the same workman repeated a single manufacturing step over and over, a craftsman's build was entrusted to a small team of workmen who knew how to execute every step in the process. Since they knew the fit and function of every part, they possessed a common awareness of how the quality of one part affected the quality of the entire product. The temperament of a craftsman's build inspired the story of a young car shop foreman who, obsessed with efficiency, cast a critical eye on a slow-moving, gray-haired carpenter who worked on wooden passenger car bodies. Day after day, the old man painstakingly aligned and leveled the heavy, crude beams that made up the frame of a car. Working patiently with a carpenter's square and a wooden mallet, he didn't rest until the crude wooden platform presented a surface as flat as a billiard table. When the foreman confronted the white-haired master car builder about the apparent waste of time, the builder replied, simply, that although it looked as if he were working on the car frame, he was actually doing finish work on interior cabinets. To the incredulous foreman, the master car builder patiently explained his twofold meaning: one, that the square of the car

frame would ultimately determine the square of cabinet work built inside the car; and second, that he was likely to be the carpenter responsible for both.

Although large, successful railroad car manufacturers eventually embraced assembly-line production of wooden cars for the cost savings, the mentality of the craftsman build remained a strong ethic among master car builders. It was a distinctly different approach from how most locomotives were manufactured. The dynamic, interdependent behavior of car parts and subassemblies was due in large measure to the nature of wood, which was the nearly universal raw material from which railroad cars were built. Wooden car construction required an instinctual understanding that wood (unlike metal) was not dimensionally stable. Depending on how wood was cut and dried, its shrinkage or swelling could affect the structural integrity of any part of the car, or the car as a whole. The art of designing and building with wood was the art of understanding how the material reacted to moisture, to the variable geometry of cutting, to methods of drying, and most important to the use to which it was being put. Attempts to standardize the quality of wooden car parts were documented by Kirkman in a 1916 work titled *The Science of Railways,* and were common knowledge among generations of car builders: "Sizes up to 6 inches in width shall measure full when green, and not more than 1/8 inch scant when dry or part dry; sizes

6 to 12 inches in width shall measure full when green and not more than ¼ inch scant when dry or part dry . . . [sills] will admit of sound knots, provided they are not in groups, the mean or average diameter of which will not exceed two (2) inches; pitch; pitch pockets; slight shake; seasoning checks, or other defects . . . will not impair its strength . . . [such sills] . . . must be sawed from sound timber, free from doty or rotten red heart and true to measurements, or at least the measurements at no point on the sill shall be less than the size required." More of an art than a science, careful selection of wood applied to every part in a car and ultimately determined its life expectancy. This knowledge separated wood workers from metal workers and promoted their interchangeable roles in many, if not all, of the steps in wooden car manufacture.

The unique design of railroad cars in turn required unique tooling for execution. In the case of a craftsman's build, most of the implements were hand tools: mortice gauges, calipers, and scribes for laying out; every description of chisel for cutting and shaping mortice and tenons; draw knives for relieving; mallets for seating. The same basic woodworking tools shown here were standard implements for Carter Brothers' carpenters. Limited power equipment—for example, a table joiner and a small, specialized mortice machine—were also present in the Newark shop, but the key criterion for a craftsman's build was not the level of mechanization so much as the ability of a single workman to perform any task in the construction process, from careful selection of wood to fitting together the final part. In approaching car craft in this fashion, Carter workmen ultimately took responsibility for the overall quality of the completed product.

Even as late as 1899, Carter Brothers listed imported hardwoods, for example tamano and primavera, on its shop inventory, shown at the left. Sometimes called "white mahogany" and imported from South America, primavera was a close-grained, light colored wood valued as a finish in car interior walls and panels. Carter's wood inventory routinely included walnut, mahogany, cherry, ash, spruce, redwood, cedar, fir and oak. The variety of woods matched the variety of both structural, and decorative requirements in the passenger equipment Carter produced, for example combination cars for the Monterey & Salinas Valley, shown undergoing restoration in 1978, above. [Left, collection of Robert Fisher, M.D.; above, Bruce MacGregor]

The Carter shop inventory of hand tools (at bottom) dates from 1899, but it contains tools that would have been in common use in car shops of the 1870s. Tools displayed on the frame of a wooden sill flatcar (left) are routinely used in wooden car restoration at Ardenwood Park, in Fremont, evoking a practice that almost died out eighty years before. [Left, Bruce MacGregor; below, collection of Robert Fisher, M.D.]

1	Broad Gauge Skid	20 00
3	Jacks	70 00
16	Hand Screws 8" — 16. H Sc. 10"	9 60
3	12 lb. sledges	6 00
2	Punch Bars	1 60
1	Block, tackle and rope	5 20
2	New Angular Boring Machines 6 75	13 50
1	old "	5 00
4	Carpenters Augers, 1/1", 1/1⅜" 1/1¼" 1/1½"	3 20
4	Carp Augers with brace. 2/7/8. 1/1 1/1⅜	3 75
4	Rip Saws, 1/9" 1/10" 1/15" 1/20	15 00
5	Cross Cut " 1/10" 2/12" 1/15" 1/18"	19 00
2	Shaper Saws 1/5." 1/7"	2 50
2	Band Saws	4 00
2	Set planer knives	8 00
1	Pipe stock and set dies	5 00
5	pr. Pipe Tongs 2/1" , 1/1½" 1/1¾" 1/2"	3.25
1	pr small snips	75
6	#3 S. wrenches; 6. #2. S Wrenches	3 30
18	S wrenches 12" to 33" long. @ 20	3 60
1	" " 3'.3" long. 2 S Wrenches 3. ft. 3@2 00	6 00
1	Claw foot.	30

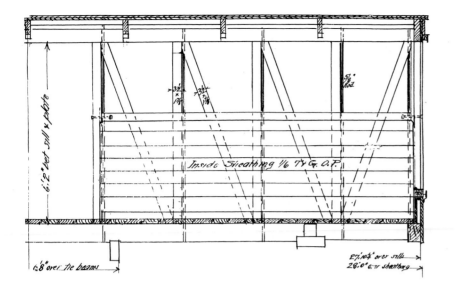

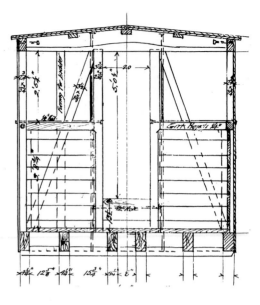

Seen through the computer medium of 3D CAD, the construction of a Carter ten-ton combination boxcar proceeds from left to right, on the basis of original Carter two-dimensional drawings (above and opposite, lower right). Details of freight draft gear are shown opposite (upper right), a simple mechanism that operated through compression of a single draft spring from either direction. Two-dimensional drawings reproduced in this section are not to scale. [Two-dimensional drawings, collection of Robert Fisher, M.D.; 3D drawings, Curtis Ferrington]

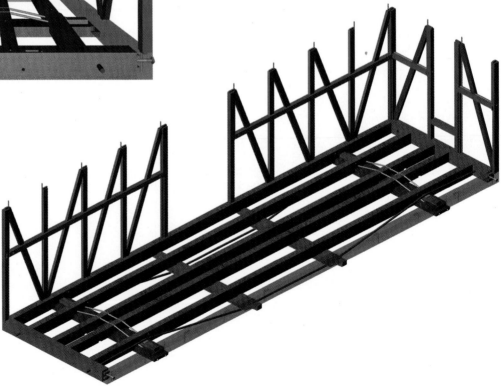

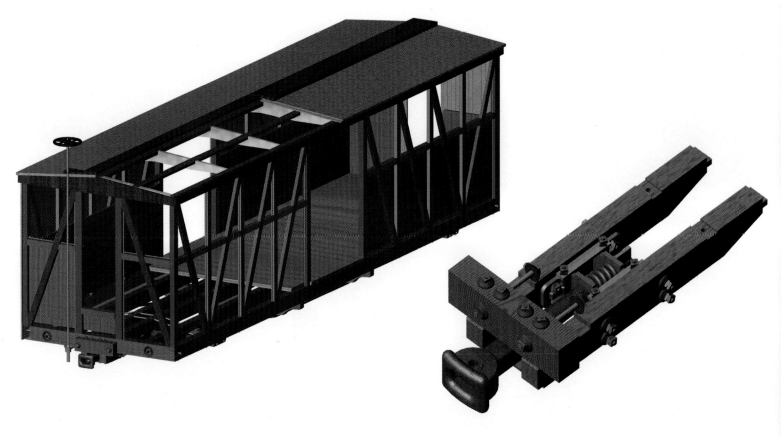

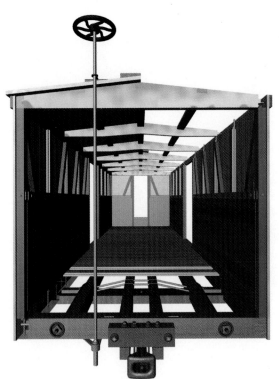

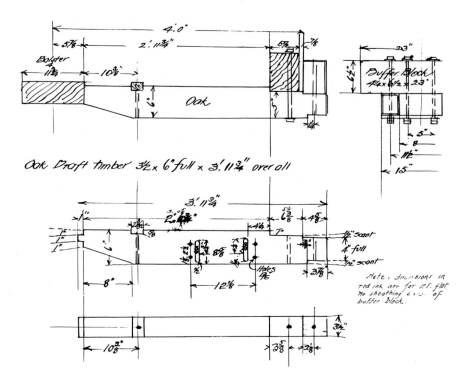

Oak Draft timber 3½ × 6" full × 3' 11¾" over all

Note: dimensions in
red ink are for I.f. flat.
No sheathing over of
buffer block.

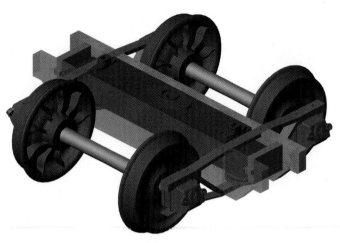
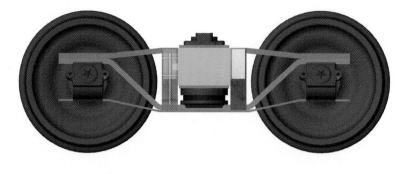

Three-quarter view, elevation, and section of Carter eight-ton-capacity freight truck, showing rubber block springs; and associated 275-pound twenty-four-inch wheel, top half of this page. Ca. 1874–1876. [All 3D illustrations, Curtis Ferrington; wheel drawings, Richard C. Datin collection]

7
24" Wheel

Orig # A 478
N. Patt. # A 478

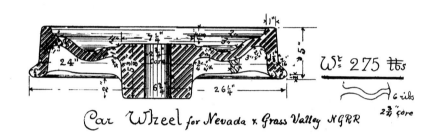

Wt 275 ℔s

6 ribs
2 3/4" core

Car Wheel *for Nevada x Grass Valley NGRR*

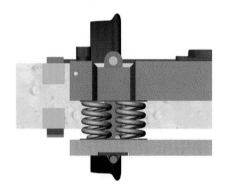
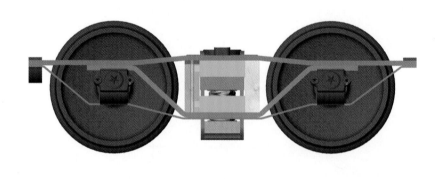

13.
24" Wheel

Orig # A.478.
N. Patt # D.595.

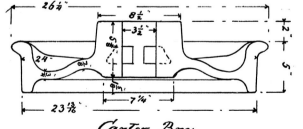

Wt 285 ℔s

Ribs
3 1/4" core

Carter Bros.

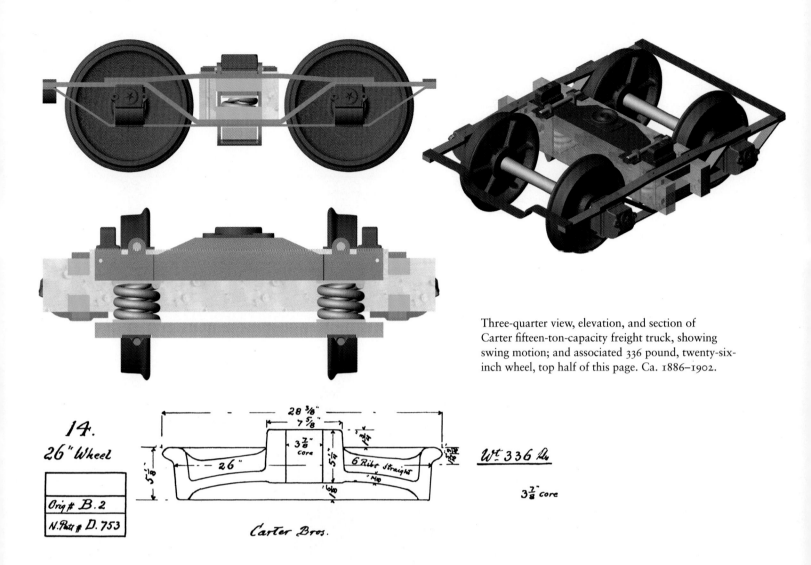

Three-quarter view, elevation, and section of
Carter fifteen-ton-capacity freight truck, showing
swing motion; and associated 336 pound, twenty-six-
inch wheel, top half of this page. Ca. 1886–1902.

14.
26" Wheel

Orig # B.2	
N. Patt # D.753	

28 ⅜"
7 ⅝"
3 ⅞" core
26"
5 ⅛"
5 ¼"
6 Ribs Straight

Wt. 336 ℔.

3 ⅞" core

Carter Bros.

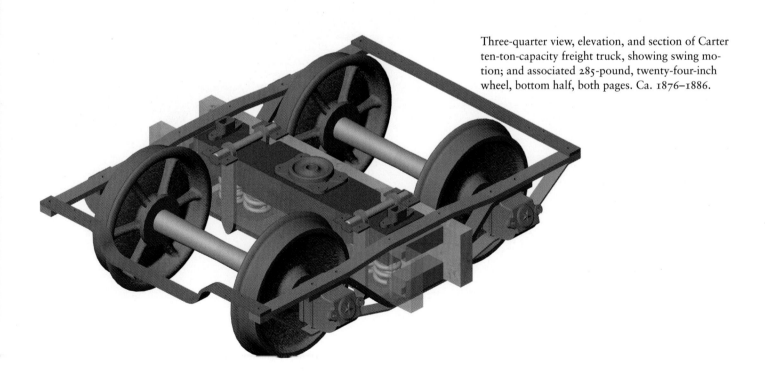

Three-quarter view, elevation, and section of Carter
ten-ton-capacity freight truck, showing swing motion; and associated 285-pound, twenty-four-inch
wheel, bottom half, both pages. Ca. 1876–1886.

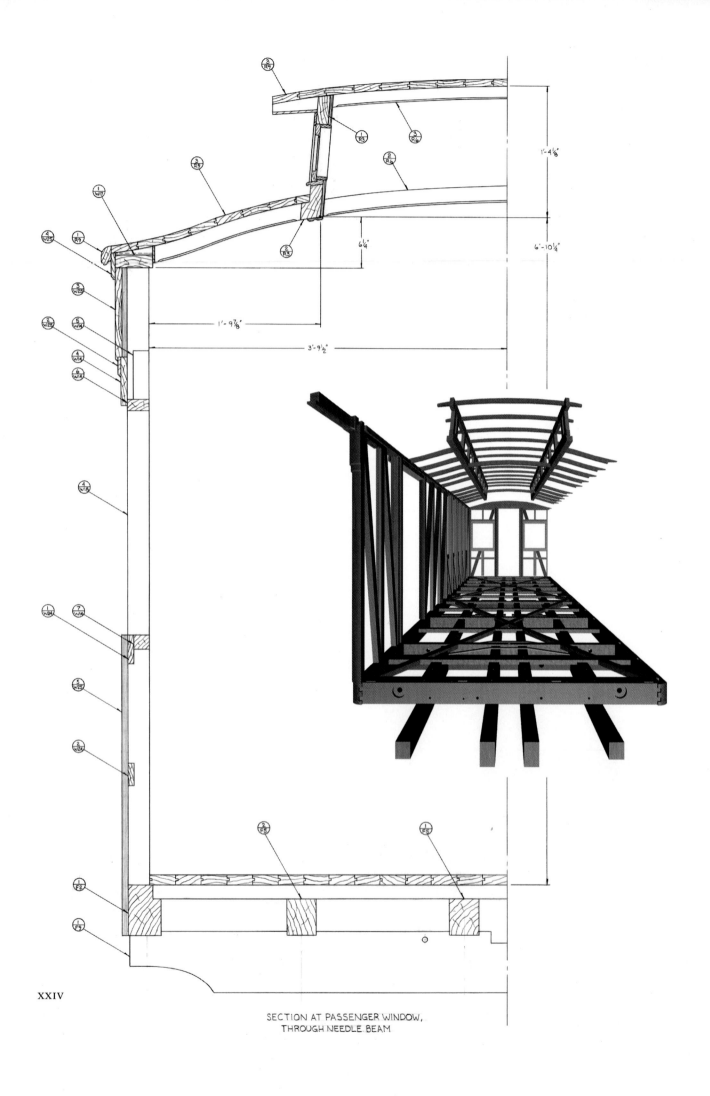

SECTION AT PASSENGER WINDOW,
THROUGH NEEDLE BEAM

XXIV

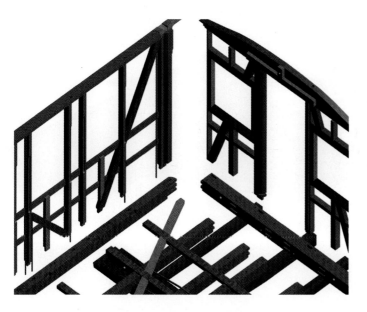

Three-dimensional CAD assembly of Carter Brothers duckbill roof combination car, based on South Pacific Coast caboose 47, built in 1882. Most of the same parts and subassemblies were used in Carter revenue passenger cars of the period. Additional details on caboose 47 appear in Appendix B. [Section drawing, opposite, Dan McGinty; 3D CAD illustrations, Curtis Ferrington]

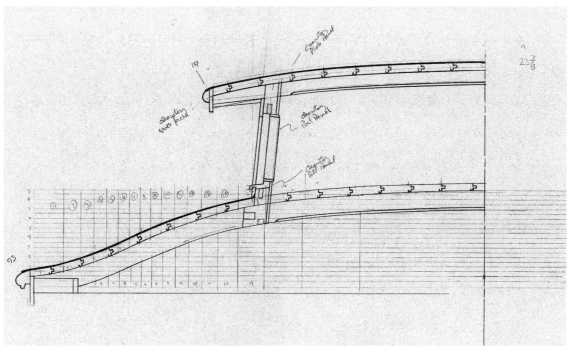

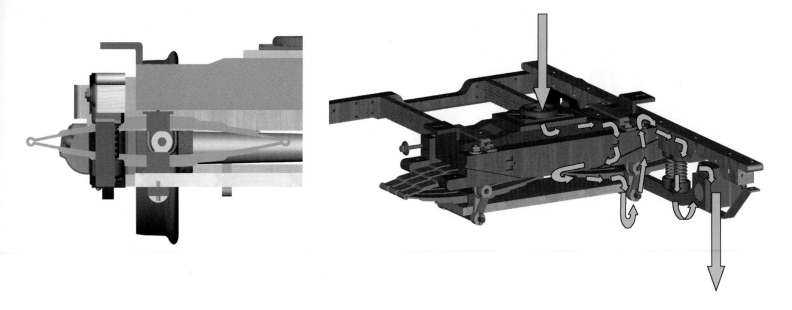

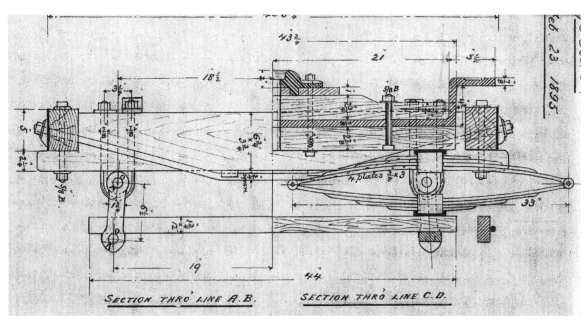

Three-dimensional CAD assembly of Carter-style five-foot-wheelbase passenger truck, as adapted for the South Pacific Coast by the Southern Pacific shops in 1895. The vector drawing at top right traces the path of a car's weight as it is transmitted through the truck, circulating through both leaf and spiral springs, through the swing motion, and finally to the truck bearings and axles. [Above, Richard C. Datin collection; 3D CAD illustrations, Curtis Ferrington]

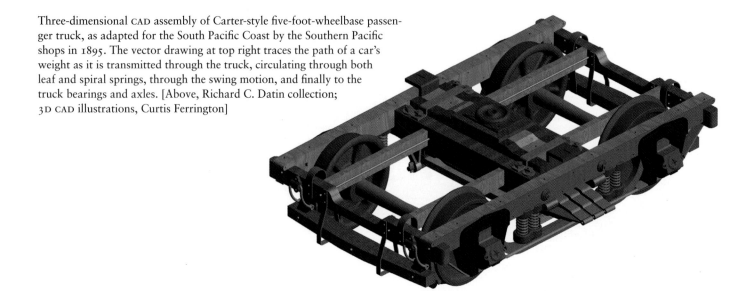

MILLER'S PLATFORMS FOR **RAILROAD** CARS.

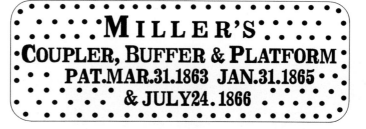

MILLER'S COUPLER, BUFFER & PLATFORM PAT. MAR. 31. 1863   JAN. 31. 1865 & JULY 24. 1866

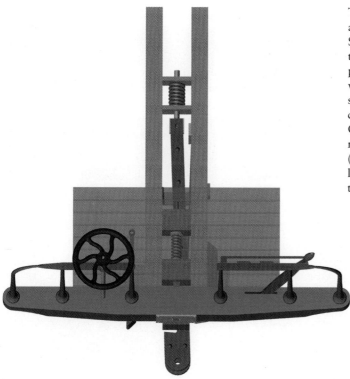

The Miller Patented Coupler, Platform, and Buffer in a 3D CAD series based on Southern Pacific narrow gauge combination car 1010. Southern Pacific licensed the patent from Miller and developed its own version of Miller hardware components suited to narrow gauge passenger cars, including those used on the South Pacific Coast. As proof of legal licensing, the railroad agreed to affix Miller's nameplate (above, right) to each platform. [Above, left, Smithsonian Institution; 3D CAD illustrations, Curtis Ferrington]

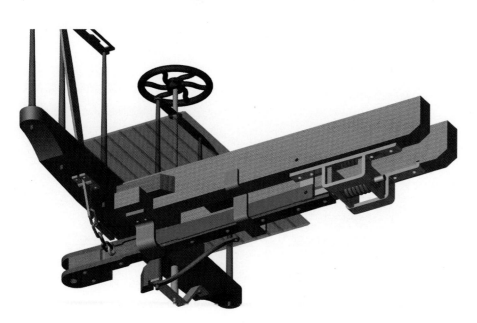

Passenger car hardware found on Carter-built South Pacific Coast duck-bill coaches 23 and 43, ca. 1879–1881, including examples of compound glass from clerestories (above), brass window lifts and bell cord eyes (middle), and brass baggage rack (bottom); hardware from the collection of the Society for the Preservation of Carter Railroad Resources, donated by Henry Welzel. [Bruce MacGregor]

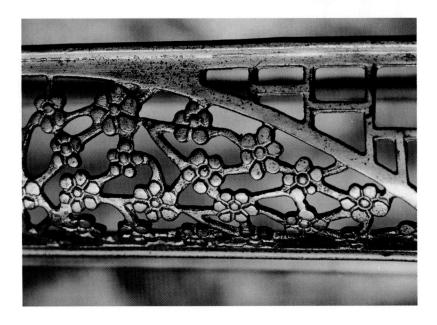

Interior treatments in Carter 1874 Monterey & Salinas Valley combination car, now on display at the California State Railroad Museum, include original and restored polychrome stencils (top) and bulkhead panel and lamp (middle). The restored car interior (bottom) includes a ceiling cloth with a design based loosely on fragments found in the original car. [Bruce MacGregor]

XXIX

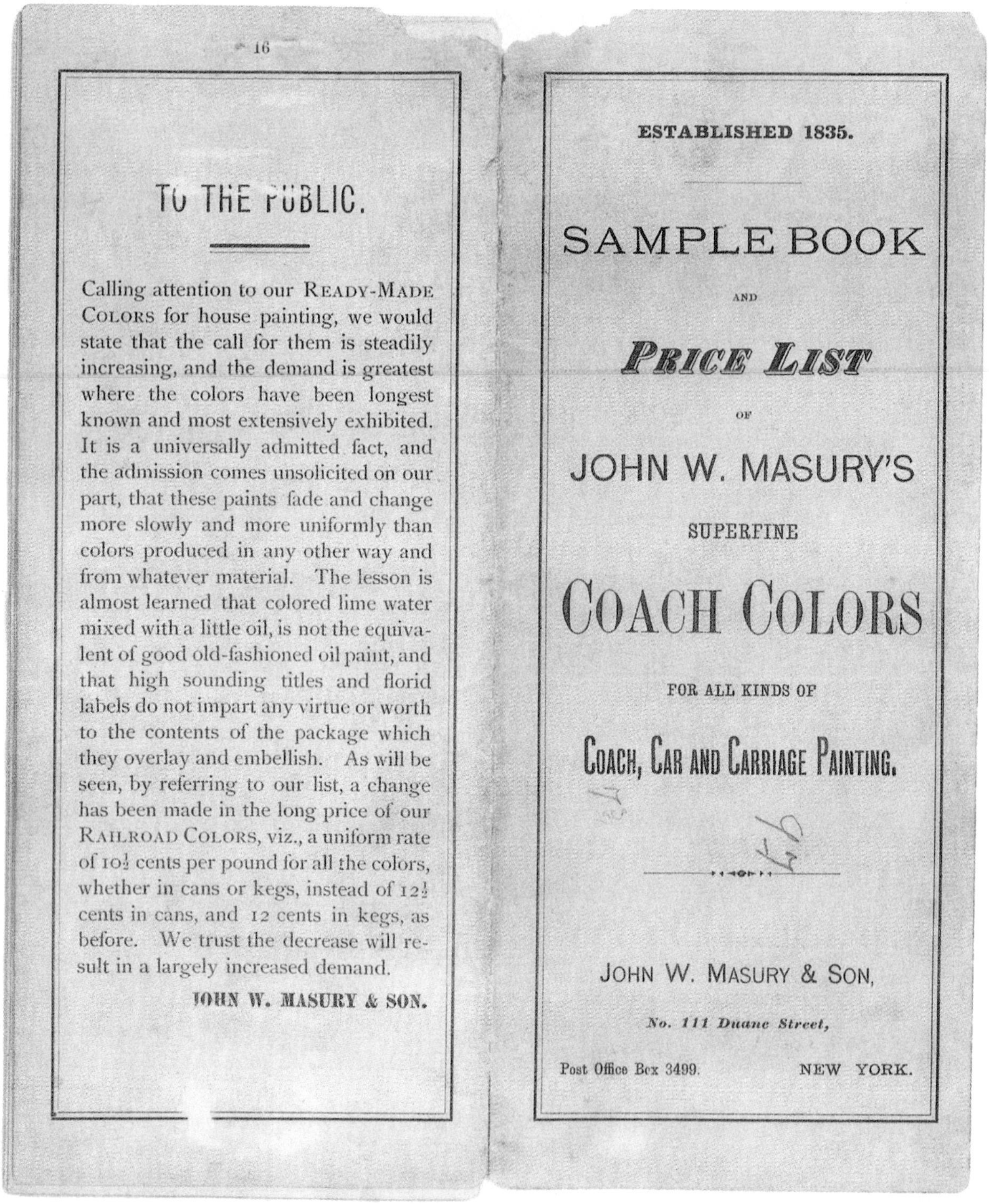

TO THE PUBLIC.

Calling attention to our READY-MADE COLORS for house painting, we would state that the call for them is steadily increasing, and the demand is greatest where the colors have been longest known and most extensively exhibited. It is a universally admitted fact, and the admission comes unsolicited on our part, that these paints fade and change more slowly and more uniformly than colors produced in any other way and from whatever material. The lesson is almost learned that colored lime water mixed with a little oil, is not the equivalent of good old-fashioned oil paint, and that high sounding titles and florid labels do not impart any virtue or worth to the contents of the package which they overlay and embellish. As will be seen, by referring to our list, a change has been made in the long price of our RAILROAD COLORS, viz., a uniform rate of 10½ cents per pound for all the colors, whether in cans or kegs, instead of 12½ cents in cans, and 12 cents in kegs, as before. We trust the decrease will result in a largely increased demand.

JOHN W. MASURY & SON.

ESTABLISHED 1835.

SAMPLE BOOK

AND

PRICE LIST

OF

JOHN W. MASURY'S

SUPERFINE

COACH COLORS

FOR ALL KINDS OF

Coach, Car and Carriage Painting.

JOHN W. MASURY & SON,

No. 111 Duane Street,

Post Office Box 3499.　　　NEW YORK.

In 1877, the John Masury Co. featured a wide pallet of car body and trim colors in its catalogue of samples; Carter was a Masury customer and listed Masury paints on its 1899 plant inventory. The sample chip representing "Car Body Color" (opposite, upper right) is a candidate for the standard South Pacific Coast passenger car finish. The complete line of 1877 Masury car colors is shown on this spread and overleaf. [Catalogue, opposite and overleaf, Randy Hees collection]

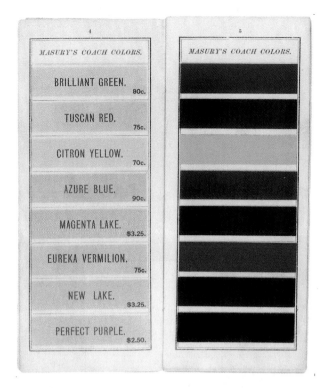

4

MASURY'S COACH COLORS.

BRILLIANT GREEN. 80c.

TUSCAN RED. 75c.

CITRON YELLOW. 70c.

AZURE BLUE. 90c.

MAGENTA LAKE. $3.25.

EUREKA VERMILION. 75c.

NEW LAKE. $3.25.

PERFECT PURPLE. $2.50.

5

MASURY'S COACH COLORS.

6

MASURY'S COACH COLORS.

QUAKER GREEN, Light. 75c.

GOLDEN OCHRE. 40c.

PORTLAND AMBER. 75c.

CARRIAGE-PART LAKE. 75c.

COBALT BLUE. $2.50.

CAR BODY COLOR. 40c.

ENG. VERMILION, Pale.

ENG. VERMILION, Deep.

7

MASURY'S COACH COLORS.

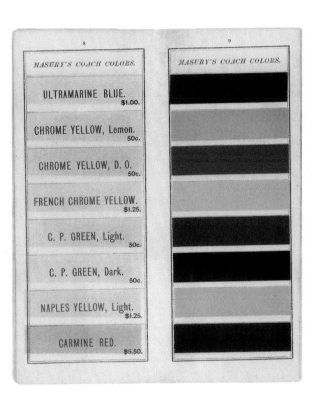

8

MASURY'S COACH COLORS.

ULTRAMARINE BLUE. $1.00.

CHROME YELLOW, Lemon. 50c.

CHROME YELLOW, D. O. 50c.

FRENCH CHROME YELLOW. $1.25.

C. P. GREEN, Light. 50c.

C. P. GREEN, Dark. 50c.

NAPLES YELLOW, Light. $1.25.

CARMINE RED. $5.50.

9

MASURY'S COACH COLORS.

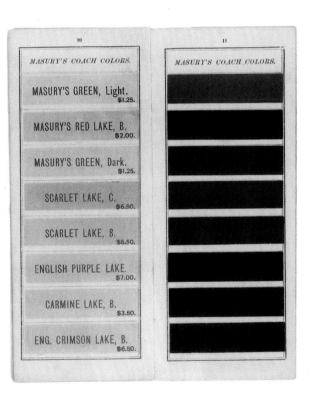

10

MASURY'S COACH COLORS.

MASURY'S GREEN, Light. $1.25.

MASURY'S RED LAKE, B. $2.00.

MASURY'S GREEN, Dark. $1.25.

SCARLET LAKE, C. $6.50.

SCARLET LAKE, B. $5.50.

ENGLISH PURPLE LAKE. $7.00.

CARMINE LAKE, B. $3.50.

ENG. CRIMSON LAKE, B. $6.50.

11

MASURY'S COACH COLORS.

Painting and finishing a wooden passenger car body was a painstaking process involving multiple coats of primer, paint, and varnish. Each step in the process, shown progressing left to right in the schematic below, was often separated from succeeding steps by a week of drying time. The end result was a smooth, high-gloss finish, free from wrinkles. Kevin Bunker's tableau shows the full process applied to Carter's Monterey & Salinas Valley combine, now on display at the California State Railroad Museum in Sacramento. [Right, Randy Hees collection; below, Kevin Bunker]

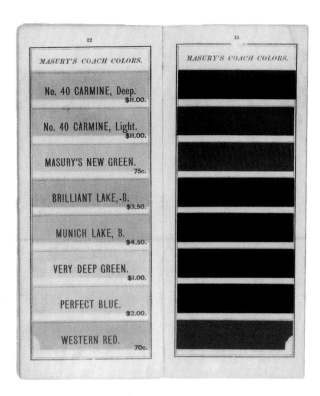

12   13

MASURY'S COACH COLORS.   MASURY'S COACH COLORS.

No. 40 CARMINE, Deep. $11.00.

No. 40 CARMINE, Light. $11.00.

MASURY'S NEW GREEN.   75c.

BRILLIANT LAKE,-B. $3.50.

MUNICH LAKE, B. $4.50.

VERY DEEP GREEN. $1.00.

PERFECT BLUE. $2.00.

WESTERN RED.   70c.

eliminate ornament —too fussy for exterior

corner post ornament like interior as stencilwork — make letterboard similar, reverse colors to best effect.

change vents color to straw

black stripes on batten chamfers

vermilion stripes on panels.

Panels box-striped, (eliminate intermediate vertical stripes.)

use minimal striping on trucks.   wheels unpainted

1. Primer with white lead & raw oil & litharge drier, well-strained. Let dry 5 to 6 days, & sandpaper overall.

2. Second primer coat: 1 part raw oil to 3 parts turp's, bit of Japan as drier — let dry 5 to 6 days.

3. Putty goes on & in all holes, joints, then 3rd coat of primer — or first coat of color if time allows.
   base color applied to letterboard, (crimson vermilion) in boiled oil.

4. First color coat: chrome yellow + golden ochre + white lead — well ground-in together — reduced in turpentine, with small amount of Japan gold size — 3 to 4 days to dry.

5. Second & Third color coats, as above; 3 to 4 drying days for each coat; also apply black color-in-oil to exterior ironwork.

6. Finish color (straw): slight increase of golden ochre, apply with well-brushed work. 3 to 4 days to dry, then rotten-stoned & well-rubbed, cold water washed, chamois-dry.

7. Varnish: 1 part best quality rubbing varnish to 1 part wearing body — 4 days to dry, then rub and wipe down car completely.
   2nd coat varnish after striping, ornamenting & lettering car; let dry 8 days, then cold water wash & chamois-dry to eliminate any water-spotting.
   Last coat: wearing body varnish only; quickly & smoothly laid down. — allow 8 full days drying time — cold water wash & chamois off.

Proposed Paint Supply per car:
est. 5 gals. varnish to 10 lbs. chromium yellow, 3 lbs. golden ochre, 50 lbs. white lead.
15-20 pints turp's, 10 pints Japan size; 2 lbs crimson Vermillion & English crimson-lake.
15 lbs lampblack (for ironwork), 6-8 lbs ivory black (striping & graining).
6 lbs raw umber (for graining) — 20 gals boiled oil & raw oil. Litharge as needed.

8. Doors - passenger   baggage — with windows are to be finished and glazed separate from car: all sash, with blinds, grained as rosewood & mahogany, & varnished front & back.
   Plated window and door hardware - latches, lifts & catches - apply last. Grain letterboard - 3 days drying-time, letter & varnish as above.

9. Roof: Clad with nailed & soldered terne, lye wash and sponge dry in sun. When dry, apply 2 coats litharge primer at same interval as 2nd color coat on car body. Let dry 7 days.
   (& exterior iron & steel)

10. Roof Final color coat: 4 parts golden ochre to 2 parts white lead in raw oil, reduced in turp's. Apply thoroughly & let dry 10 days.

11. Apply 2 coats wearing body varnish over roof, vents & stove jack. Let dry 8 days then cold-water wash & sponge or chamois-off. Car now suitable for 1st trials.

Looking south from the modern location of Thornton Avenue, Newark's covered depot (above) appears in a turn-of-the-century view as the center of the town's "railroad reservation." The original railroad complex included (on the left side of the view) the Carter's shops. Taken at nearly the same location in the 1890s, the view of the Silvey and Munyan General Store includes a glimpse of the original narrow gauge roundhouse at the extreme left. [Both, Marge Callow collection]

The heart of the Newark backshop was a seven-stall roundhouse, constructed in 1877 and
seen at a distance in the portrait
of Silvey and Munyan General
Store (top right). Martin Carter,
appointed master mechanic of the
South Pacific Coast about the
time the shops were built, may
also have been the general contractor for constructing the facilities. The turntable, photographed
in 1913 (top left), closely matches
an 1889 Carter Brothers drawing
for the narrow gauge turntable
they sold commercially (below).
[This page, above: Marge Callow
collection; below, California State
Railroad Museum]

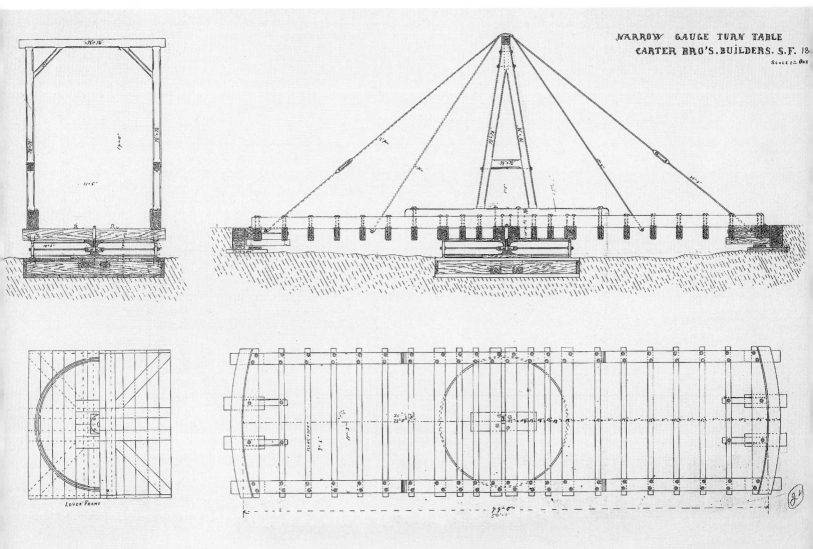

By 1894, Carter Brothers had made a clear break from manufacturing mainline narrow gauge rolling stock to constructing cable and electric cars for street railways. Illustrated above is the only known view of Martin Carter (shown with his three sons) at the Newark plant. During transitional times, a spare parts business, founded on drawings and patterns of original parts (for example, a journal box, below) helped keep Carter solvent. Following Thomas Carter's death in August 1898, Martin wrote a heartfelt letter to a friend named T. W. Grimm, asking for a referral to someone who could "take full charge of a business," but he found no one to fill his brother's shoes. Martin closed the plant in late 1902 or early 1903. [Above, Martin G. Carter collection; below, California State Railroad Museum]

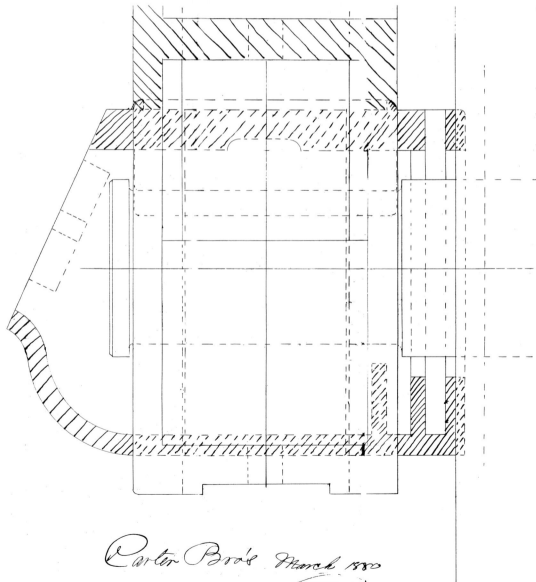

Carter Bro's March 1880

Furniture, ornamental castings, and specialized appliances such as stoves and toilets were manufactured for Carter by established railroad suppliers. The cast iron seat ends (top right) are replicas of seats made by G. Buntin; the egret cast in brass (top middle) was part of a baggage rack vended by Post and Co.; its motif was echoed on a cast iron ventilator door installed in the clerestory (top left), made by an unknown manufacturer. Low-cost manufacturing of cars, such as South Pacific Coast coach 44 (bottom), depended on taking advantage of commodity-priced car hardware. [Bottom: Marvin Maynard collection; others, Bruce MacGregor]

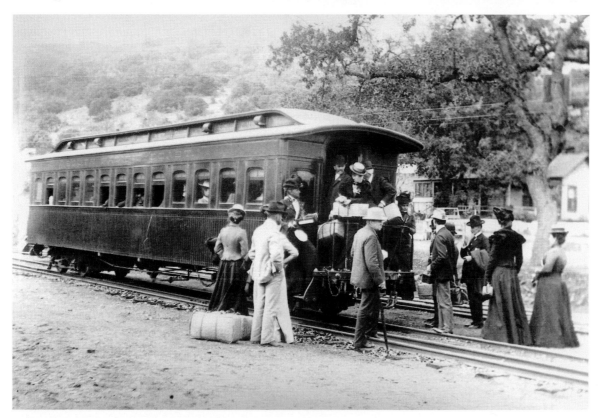

South Pacific Coast coach 22 (above), with its accompanying floor plan (below), was built by Carter on an unusual thirteen-window plan; fourteen-window coaches were more common on the early South Pacific Coast roster (for example, coach 44, opposite below). Both styles shared common design elements in the duckbill roof end and oval number plate, but they differed in window sash treatment, with the shorter car carrying an arch window sash and the longer one a square sash. Fashion, constantly changing with the traveling public, dictated which feature would be adopted. [Above, Marvin Maynard collection; bottom, Malcolm R. Gaddis collection]

FLOOR PLAN OF A NARROW GUAGE COACH

Scale ¼" to 1 ft.   **Sacramento, December 24, 1904.**

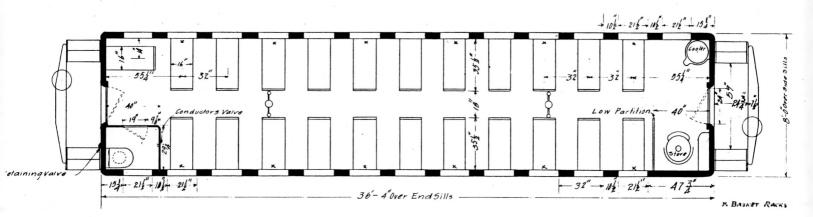

The Arcata & Mad River Railroad was an exception to the three-foot-wide narrow gauge lines portrayed in this book. Its unusual gauge of 3'9¹/₄" derived from a wharf railroad operated in Arcata in the 1850s and eventually expanded to serve the lumber mill at nearby Korbel, whose roundhouse is shown in the view at the bottom of this page. By the 1880s, the A&MR had purchased secondhand Carter equipment, including coach 2 (opposite above, on the right), probably an ex–Santa Cruz & Felton coach. In the same photograph, "the smoker," a Carter coach of unknown origin, sits behind coach 2. The smoker's spartan interior is shown opposite (middle left), photographed in the 1990s. Carter did a healthy business in spare parts with the A&MR, a source of increasing revenue as the 1880s continued, as evidenced by the invoice on the opposite page (middle right). [Opposite, middle left: Bruce MacGregor; all other photographs, John Labbe collection]

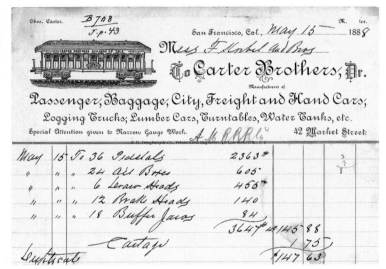

Already displaying an obsolete roof end style, a Carter duckbill coach could be identified on the Sonoma Valley Railroad in the early 1880s (above). Many years later, in the Millerton deadline on the Northwestern Pacific (below), South Pacific Coast duckbill roof coach 5 (middle car) contrasts sharply with South Pacific Coast bullnose roof coach 51 shown at the right. Representing a change in generations of style, Carter built the 5 in 1878, the 51 in 1883. [Above, Phil Ronfor collection; below, Robert Moulton collection]

Carter developed new car designs to serve the high-end narrow gauge market, including construction of elegant chair cars for use by railroad directors and their families. The *Ettie*, shown in a train (above) and in its builder's photograph (below), was the first such car known, built for the San Joaquin & Sierra Nevada in 1885. *Ettie* retailed for $4,265, a premium compared to the $3,500 Carter normally charged for a coach. The *Pearl* (bottom), built for the Oahu Railway and Land Co., probably in 1889, is the second known example of a Carter chair car. [Above, Pat Hathaway collection; below, Holt-Atherton Department of Special Collections, University of the Pacific Libraries]

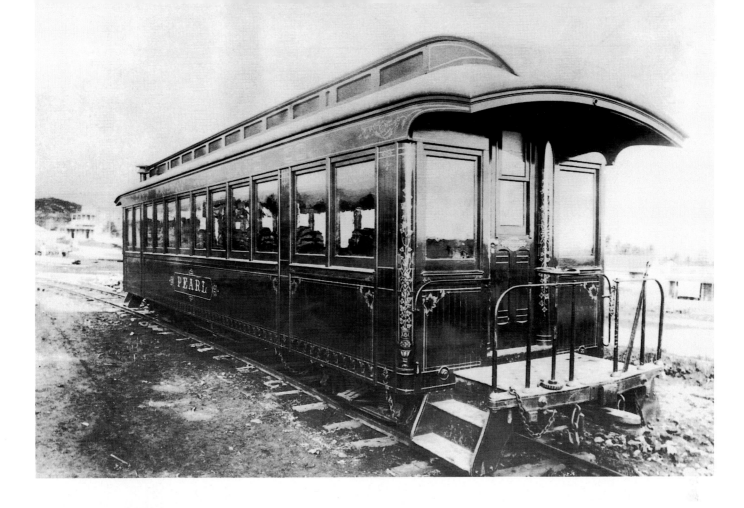

THE POPULAR
Hartley Reclining and Revolving Chair.

HEAD REST DOWN.

REVOLVING CHAIR FOR PARLOR CARS.

The elegant chair car *Pearl* was built in 1889 by Carter for the Dillingham family, owners and directors of the Oahu Railway and Land Co.; it represents a high point in Carter's evolution as a builder of mainline railroad equipment. In service, the *Pearl* occasionally carried Hawaiian royalty and displayed King Kalakaua's crest on a pull blind that can be seen at the far end of the car's interior (opposite), suggesting the photograph was taken not long after delivery. King Kalakaua died in 1891.

South Pacific Coast number 13 and solitary baggage car, photographed in the San Lorenzo River Gorge by John James Riley, shortly after the delivery of the 13 in 1882; from an original stereopticon print in the collection of John Hemmann.

12

Fire and Rain

Work in the mountains quickly transformed the South Pacific Coast into a military operation. Strategy changed to tactics. Instead of a reconnaissance engineer, Davis now needed E. H. ("Ed") Mix, a locating engineer, who came aboard during the summer of 1878. Davis ordered him to run a construction campaign that resembled the field maneuvers of well-trained infantry.

In September 1878, Mix hired Martin, Ballard and Ferguson, the first of a series of large contracting firms, to drill the "big tunnel," which was soon referred to by newspapers as the summit tunnel. A second tunnel, to the south, would be nearly as long. Mix hired additional contractors to support Martin, one being a civil engineering contractor named Osborne, who would grade the rocky, northerly approach to the summit tunnel through Los Gatos Creek Canyon. The primary contractors in turn hired subcontractors—Elbon and Houck, D. H. Montgomery, C. C. Martin, the Morrell brothers, and the Comstock Mill on Soquel Creek, among others—all of whom would provide timber to line the tunnels. By December, most of these subcontractors were operating mills whose entire output would vanish into the bowels of the mountain. Frederick Hihn benefited directly, selling or leasing Soquel Augmentation timber land (one thousand acres each) to Montgomery and Elbon and Houck.[1]

By April 15, 1878, Martin, Ballard and Ferguson had signed contracts for the second longest tunnel, drilled between the Soquel Creek Canyon and Bean Creek Canyon. It would subduct the railroad under the ridge that separated Soquel from Bean Creek.[2] Mix then leapfrogged Osborne's construction crews over the top of the two long tunnels to begin work on shorter tunnels in the Bean Creek watershed. Further south, a contractor named Elliot and Muir went to work grading and tunneling in the San Lorenzo River Canyon.

Ed Mix commanded the army of contractors with his own corps of surveyors and field bosses, men like A. J. Stahlberg and William Drum, who would move into tents near the tunnel site and manage the complex logistics of contract oversight, including payment of contractors on the basis of work completed. Specialized communication links were installed, such as a telegraph line from a surveyor's cabin atop the summit ridge to the two construction camps at the tunnel portals below.[3] Mix moved his family to Santa Cruz but spent most of his nights in a field cabin in the Welsh redwood

Confusion over the number (and
numbering) of SPC's mountain tunnels resulted from the collapse and
daylighting of tunnel 1, near Los
Gatos, probably in March 1878. If
the tunnel had survived, there would
have been nine tunnels on the completed railroad. After the *Santa Cruz
Sentinel* published the revised numbers (shown at the right on the chart
below) in March 27, 1880, there
were just eight tunnels, but occasionally the "old" numbers (shown
in the column on the left) were used
in newspaper articles, which certainly led to confusion. In this book,
in all cases new tunnel numbers are
adopted.

Old	New	
1.	–	"Halfway between Los Gatos & Lexington," 185' long; daylighted Feb.–March 1878
2.	1.	191' long; collapsed; day-lighted in about 1904
3.	2.	"Summit tunnel," Wright's tunnel, or simply Big Tunnel, 6,157' long
4.	3.	Glenwood tunnel, 5,793' long
5.	4.	Clems tunnel, 913' long
6.	5.	Zayante tunnel, 250' long
7.	6.	"Butte Cut" tunnel, 338' long
8.	7.	"Hogback" tunnel, 282' long
9.	8.	Mission Hill tunnel, 918' long

As of March 27, 1880, the total
length of the remaining eight tunnels
on the South Pacific Coast was 2.8
miles long. "New" tunnel 1 was
daylighted in 1904, reducing the
total to seven tunnels prior to the
1906 earthquake.

grove near Felton, the future site of Henry Cowell Redwoods State Park.
From this command post, he made day trips on horseback to assess the
work and maintain a tight grip on nearly a thousand men who were dug
into the hillsides through summer and winter for nearly three years.

The push into the mountains changed Thomas Carter's relationship with
the organization. By 1878, a clear line of demarcation had been drawn, beyond which it was understood that Carter would cede control of the railroad to Mix. At first it was an elastic line, inching its way southward as construction crept through Los Gatos Canyon toward Lexington and the summit
tunnel, giving Mix charge of uncompleted work and leaving to Carter operation of the finished railroad. But by the summer of 1878, the immovable
reality of the big tunnel created a hard line between Carter and Mix. The
incomplete tunnel effectively sealed off the last twenty miles of railroad
from Carter's authority and influence.

Evidence of Mix's impregnable authority survives. By September 1879,
he was using Santa Cruz & Felton trains to dump ballast on unfinished South
Pacific Coast track north of Felton. Although technically under a lease agreement, the SC&F was still functioning as an independent railroad, with its
original management and crew intact. Its superintendent, Captain R. M.
Garrett, scheduled gravel trains up the new mainline with his own crews,
among them brakeman George Colegrove and a conductor named Miller.
On the September evening in question, Miller had no knowledge of a flatcar
of Chinese construction workers descending the grade by gravity at the same
time his own crew was headed upgrade with a loaded gravel train. Gravel
train and flatcar collided on a blind curve, shearing off the locomotive pilot
and giving Mix cause to fire Miller the next day. Garrett's strong objection,
based on the assumption that he had managerial authority over the SC&F
and its crews, was pointless; Mix was the law in the mountains. Conductor
Miller did not report for work the next day.[4]

The South Pacific Coast behaved like two railroads, with two manage-
ments, two cultures, and two standards of conduct. Carter knew Garrett
first as a customer of Carter Brothers and second as his equal-in-rank on
the Santa Cruz & Felton. Sympathetic to his plight, Carter could do nothing about it. Neither could he regain the sense of control he once had over
the railroad. To an engineer who had fine-tuned nearly every part of a complex, interdependent system, the inability to reach into the most complex,
most technically difficult part of the project must have felt like a second
amputated limb.

The location of the big tunnel, the point from which all other details of the
mountain route would have to be reckoned, was the crucial datum in building the last twenty miles of narrow gauge mainline to Santa Cruz. From its
location, all the critical parameters of the railroad—mileage, schedule time,
total cost—and its net competitive advantage against the Southern Pacific
would be figured.

Like his predecessor Julius Smith, Mix at first had to keep two options
open. If Davis ordered the final location of the railroad to go down Soquel

Creek directly to the ocean, for example, the location of the tunnel would remain at Taylor's Pass, the highest and most southerly point the railroad would reach on the summit ridge. A tunnel at this location, projected at a thousand feet elevation, would then penetrate the neck of the ridge at a narrow point. Smith had estimated the length of the resulting tunnel at slightly over a mile—fifty-four hundred feet.[5]

But if Davis chose to retarget the SPC's route to Felton, Mix would be forced to adopt another siting of the summit tunnel. The railroad would have to tack to the west sooner, avoiding the Soquel Creek pipeline and seeking a more westerly course through the ridges. A more complex series of engineering tradeoffs would then be required to position the summit tunnel adjacent to a second long tunnel, which was required to breach the next of three ridges that separated Los Gatos Creek from the San Lorenzo River. The engineering headaches thus doubled. Mix had to locate two tunnels at the same time, carefully reconciling the engineering choices he made for both.

Some of the choices were a given. For example, the long tunnels would have to be drilled with a slight upward slope from each end to avoid flooding the headings during construction. Mix therefore leveled the two tunnel portals but peaked the centers nine feet above the ends, creating a gentle grade of sixteen feet rise to the mile inside the tunnels. In addition, Mix paid close attention to tunnel exit and entry points: if they were too close to the creek in either canyon, he risked flooding the tracks in winter; if too high up on the mountain, the slope became steeper and construction costs more expensive. Ideally, the exit and entry points would both breach the mountain about fifty feet above their respective creek beds—a geometry that Mix identified for the summit tunnel just seven and a half miles up Los Gatos Creek. Having optimized the exit and entry points for the summit tunnel, he then mapped the resulting railroad grade south to an entry point on the second ridge and reconciled anew its fit to the same criteria. Through trial and error, Mix confirmed a new location for the summit tunnel about three miles short of the Taylor Pass site. At an elevation of just 803 feet above sea level, the new summit tunnel would enter the mountain two hundred feet below the old location. But it would therefore penetrate a thicker shoulder of mountain, exceeding six thousand feet in length.

By the fall of 1877, Davis had personally reconnoitered the San Lorenzo and Pescadero basins by horseback, inspecting the region's timber reserves. Accessible only through Felton, the combined resources of the basins were the largest unlogged timber tract in Santa Cruz County. Only the Santa Cruz & Felton's flume (already leaking badly) penetrated the southern end of the basin with any kind of commercial mechanization. By surveying its mainline into Felton, the South Pacific Coast could be positioned to either capture all of the flume's traffic or buy the flume and its parent railroad outright.

The location of smaller timber reserves reinforced the choice. The more northerly location for the big tunnel would still allow the South Pacific Coast to exit the tunnel inside of Frederick Hihn's Soquel Augmentation property, positioning the timber within half a day's delivery to San Francisco lumber wholesalers. The final location of summit tunnel was publi-

The daylighting of the second South Pacific Coast tunnel number one, in Los Gatos Canyon, occurred in 1904 but revealed heavy timber framing used in original tunnel construction in 1877. [Ken Lorenzen collection]

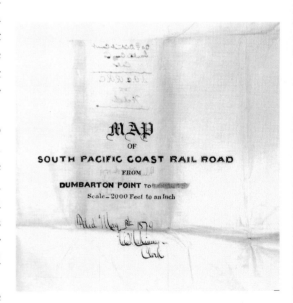

Title block, map of the South Pacific Coast Railroad; the map was used as evidence in *S.P.C.R.R. Co. v. Welch,* a case before the Superior Court of Santa Cruz County, filed May 1, 1879; ink on polished linen, 8'8" × 30". [Museum of Art and History, Santa Cruz]

Fire and Rain 531

cized on September 29, 1878, just a week before reports surfaced in the *Santa Cruz Sentinel* of a meeting between Davis and Hihn. The deal was obvious: Davis wanted Hihn's timber to build his railroad; Hihn wanted Davis's railroad to haul his timber to market.[6]

Mix therefore was forced to take the harder path, and by far the most expensive. In doing so, he increased the length of the railroad's summit tunnel to 6,157 feet, nearly a mile and a quarter, which made it the second longest railroad tunnel in California.[7] Mix also calculated the cost of the revised tunneling project; each and every one of the 6,157 feet would cost Davis an estimated $30. All totaled, the "big" tunnel and its companion tunnel into Bean Creek would cost nearly $400,000 (just $40,000 less than the total cost of the Santa Cruz & Felton Railroad), and would take an estimated ten months to drill. The risks were high. As it turned out, Mix's estimates of both time and dollars were low.

Seven miles up Los Gatos Creek, measured from the town of Los Gatos, Mix selected a steep, narrow alcove for the tunnel mouth and turned the survey stakes into its headwall. The alcove would become the site of Wright's, named for the property owner whose lands the tunnel would pass under. Two small, unnamed creeks drained the center of the alcove. At the onset of the rainy season, starting an excavation in the alcove's wall was like trying to remove debris from a live sluice box.

The first encounter with these sodden hillsides must have been a nightmare. A 6' × 6' drift was started on Hihn's land at the south end of the big tunnel during the last week of December 1878 and "filled up with mud too fast to stop."[8] On the north end, better rock was found, and penetration was more rapid. Mix quickly instituted around-the-clock work shifts, two teams to a shift, terracing the tunnel face so that one team worked the top and the second team worked the bottom, like bunkbeds. But in twenty-four-hour shifts of around-the-clock blasting and clearing, an average of just five and a half feet of rock was cleared each day.

Davis soon understood that at such a rate, the tunnel would take not ten but thirty-six months to complete. At that rate, the opening of the railroad to Santa Cruz would not take place until 1881.

Mix, on the other hand, believed that firmer ground, requiring little or no timber support, would be found deeper in the mountain, which would speed up the work. But in the first thousand feet of tunnel, the heavy timbering continued without interruption through "unconstituted rock." Mix supplied details of the timbering strategy to the editors of the *Mining and Scientific Press* for its June 8, 1878, edition. The article described construction techniques adapted to unconstituted rock, geology that the *Santa Cruz Sentinel* referred to as "rotten sandstone":

> The tunnel is arched at the top and its sides incline slightly from the spring of the arch to the floor. The distance from the crown to the floor is 16 feet three inches. The span of the arch is 13 feet. The width of the floor is 11 feet four inches. The timber is all 10 by 12 inch stuff. The arch is made in six pieces. Each is three feet 10 inches on the top and three feet four inches on the bottom. A flat rod of iron runs through each of these joints, connecting each set of timbers firmly with the adja-

cent ones. Behind the timbers, four by four-inch lagging is placed all around throughout almost the entire length of the tunnel. This is necessitated by the shifting nature of the ground.

Buried treasures were uncovered in the process of excavating the summit tunnel. Fossils resembling periwinkle shells and clams began to appear in deposits of dynamited earth, thrown up in the growing debris pile.[9] Scientists visited the works, collected samples, and pronounced them examples of "tertiary era" fossils.[10] An ancient shark's tooth was collected from the debris of tunnel 3.

By November 1878, with the big tunnel extended more than sixteen hundred feet into the mountain, the color of the debris pile began to darken. The debris soon resembled coal, and it smelled of petroleum.

Of the thousand construction workers toiling on the South Pacific Coast's mountain labyrinth in December 1878, nine hundred were Chinese. It was not the only California railroad construction project to make extensive use of Chinese labor at the time (Southern Pacific's extension across the desert to Yuma probably employed more). The SPC, however, was the most visible Chinese construction project in the state and was often scrutinized by reporters from nearby urban centers as a litmus test of the effects of the anti-Chinese movement on the state's corporations.

The scrutiny was political. In May 1879, when the SPC's construction crews were at their most numerous, the State of California would vote on a new constitution. The draft constitution contained strongly worded statutes condemning the use of Chinese labor and punishing corporations that sought to profit from their toil. The South Pacific Coast was easily labeled as a perpetrator of what proponents of the new constitution considered a crime. When the new constitution was finally ratified in a public election, the narrow gauge was too far committed to its expensive construction project to stop. At the same time, a majority of the state's voters cast legal doubt on its right to continue.

Neither Democrat nor Republican, the Workingmen's Party backed the new constitution in bitter reaction to the high unemployment rate and long-standing business recession of the 1870s. In the northern part of Santa Cruz County especially, the Workingmen's Party found passionate support among laborers, craftsmen, and small businessmen hurt by local unemployment. Founded in February 1878, the Santa Cruz County chapter boasted 266 members, making it the largest in the state outside of San Francisco. The chapter functioned as an economic unit, offering low-cost cooperative retailing (for example, a party-owned dry goods store in Santa Cruz that sold only what it claimed was "white manufactured" merchandise). The Workingmen's Party also offered political retailing, electing thirty-four delegates to the Constitutional Convention and winning four of the six seats on the Santa Cruz Town Council in April 1878.[11]

The Party found a willing mouthpiece in the editor of the *Santa Cruz Sentinel,* Duncan McPherson, who used the paper as a platform to spread racist doctrine far beyond the county's borders. An example of McPherson's invective was this editorial from early 1878: "The Chinamen are an unmitigated curse on this state. They have done a thousand times more evil than good. . . . Chinamen are not citizens in any sense of the word. They do not grant us the miserable boon of letting their heathen carcasses manure our soil, but ship the bones of their dead to the land of Confucius for final interment."[12]

Such rhetoric helped kindle the constitutional debate close to the flash point. On July 13, 1878, McPherson reported an encounter between a Santa Clara County tax collector and the Chinese crews working on the north side of the big tunnel:

> The Santa Clara Echo has the following account of the experience of a Deputy Assessor in collecting the poll taxes from the Chinamen employed in the construction of the Narrow Gauge Railroad in that county: some three or four hundred Chinamen are now employed on the Narrow Gauge Railroad beyond Lexington. A short time ago Fred Farmer, our expert Deputy Assessor, whose ruling passion is collecting taxes from Chinamen, managed to secure the poll-tax from this Mongolian crew, and then watched for an opportune moment to

South Pacific Coast, 1879, Dumbarton Point to Newark. [Museum of Art and History, Santa Cruz]

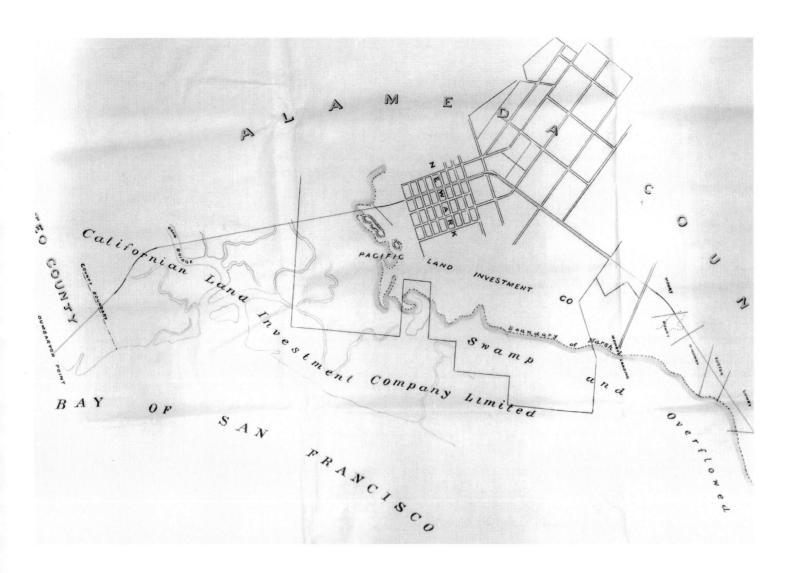

The Birth of California Narrow Gauge

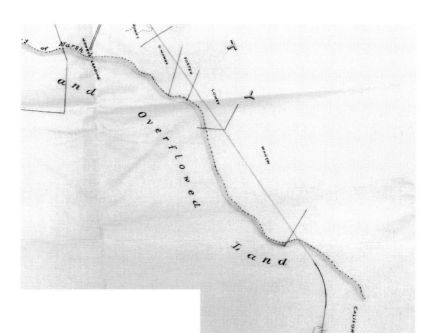

South Pacific Coast, 1879, Newark to Alviso.
[Museum of Art and History, Santa Cruz]

make a raid for the road tax—something John [Chinaman] would as soon pay as take poison. Last Friday, it was ascertained, the Chinaman would be paid off. Immediately Fred put himself in close communication with the paymaster and proceeded with him to the different camps to see the coin dispersed and to relieve the Chinamen of the amount of their indebtedness for the road tax. As soon as Fred's mission was discovered, trouble commenced. The paymaster handed the money out of the wagon while Fred stood by ready to rake in on the spot his share of the coin. One crew indignantly hurled back their money into the wagon, refusing to be paid off with a tax collector staring them in the face, and insisted on receiving their wages at their tents, off the road and down at the bottom of the canyon. Their paymaster complied, and Fred courteously followed. There were thirty Chinamen in the crew. When the money was planked down Fred covered three rolls of twenties with his hand, and delivered thirty receipts. The Chinamen said "no." Fred said "yes." In an instant he was surrounded, and the air was full of picks and shovels and Chinese oaths a yard long. Fred drew forth a persuader in the shape of a six-shooter and with fire in his eye and three rolls of twenties in his hand, made a masterly and backward retreat up the hill to the wagon, besieged by Chinamen all the way.

Overseers and crew bosses in the tunnels routinely carried side arms and worked in pairs. Ed Mix often hired law enforcement officers as foremen, one an ex-policeman from Santa Cruz. The language barrier between management and labor was almost insurmountable. Where words failed to convey meaning, a foreman's fist was a frequent substitute. As the tunnels grew deeper, clashes increased in both frequency and severity. McPherson explained the troubles as motivated by inborn malice the Chinese carried toward their white employers.

In nearly three years of reporting the "great work" in the tunnels, there is just one known example of McPherson's paper affirming a positive relationship between a white man and a Chinese construction worker, a friendship between the telegraph operator, named Cook, and "Jim," a day shift

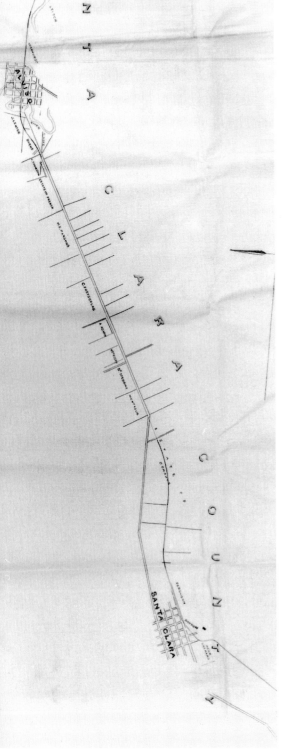

South Pacific Coast, 1879, Alviso to Santa Clara. [Museum of Art and History, Santa Cruz]

laborer working at the north end of the big tunnel. The story, ironically, was told after Jim's tragic death.

By the time the *Sentinel* reported entire gangs of Chinese bolting their jobs for higher wages on the Southern Pacific Yuma extension in December 1878, working conditions in the big tunnel had already deteriorated, confusing cause with effect. It may not have been the promise of higher wages but the fear of a gas leak, first discovered in November, that drove workers to flight. The *Sentinel* first reported the seepage on November 16. By New Year, the flow of gas had increased to the point where a dangerously inflammable concentration of methane could build up at the tunnel heading in a matter of minutes. During a shift change, for example, the fissure would release enough methane into the cavity to displace breathable air. Without an odor, the gas couldn't be detected until workers began passing out.

By January 1879, it became common practice for the foreman to lead his Chinese gang into the tunnel in single file, without light, inching their way nearly two thousand feet from the portal to the pitch black heading. Drawing close to the heading, the foreman would bend close to the ground to light a piece of cotton waste, attaching the flaming wad to a ten-foot iron rod. With the rod extended as far ahead of himself as he could reach, the foreman would lean forward until the flame touched off the accumulated gas, erupting into a ball of fire that illuminated the terrified faces of his crew.

The same editor who condemned Chinese labor and the capitalistic motives for its use also endorsed—even coveted—the results of their toil. Duncan McPherson waxed lyrical in his praise of the commercial growth the South Pacific Coast would bring to the doorstep of Santa Cruz: "Every time we inspect this road, with its great bores, its substantial road-bed, its stone culverts, its walled embankments, its heavy timbers, its powerful bridges, its tasty buildings, its heavy rails, its easy curves, its straight lines, its expensive right-of-way, its smell of money from one end of the line to the other, we say "Hurrah for the Bonanza Kings! Lucky Santa Cruz! Cinch the stock sharps! Set 'em up on California Street! Do not loose your grip till Alameda Point and Santa Cruz are bound together by 52 pound iron."[13]

McPherson's puffery was a personal endorsement of Alfred E. "Hog" Davis, who was by 1879 extremely visible on the streets of Santa Cruz, and whose large corporeal presence amply symbolized the self-made Yankee that Santa Cruz County businessmen considered their archetypal hero. When the scow *Precursor* docked at Santa Cruz in October 1879, a *Sentinel* reporter watched with pride as Davis personally supervised the unloading of a pile driver barged down from Dumbarton Point; it was visible proof that the commanding general was on the front line with his troops.

McPherson found abundant reassurance of the line's leadership in visits from James Fair. Reports that Fair had resigned his position as superintendent of the Consolidated Virginia mine reached the *Sentinel* in July 1878. In the same issue, the paper suspected it was no coincidence that Fair was visiting Santa Cruz with his family. "Business has pleasure by the hand," a reporter concluded, as Fair joined Davis in talks with the management of the Santa Cruz & Felton, the short line Davis would either incorporate into the South Pacific Coast or compete with.

Fair's enormous success in the Consolidated Virginia was a source of assurance to the recession-starved community, incontrovertible proof of the company's wherewithal. Fair's relationship to the railroad was not clear (he did not appear on its 1876 list of incorporators), but his presence gave Davis credibility, on July 13, when he revealed that the narrow gauge was spending $500 a day on its payroll alone and had dispersed, the previous month, $156,000 in payouts to contractors. This "river of money," as Davis called it, appeared to be unending.

James Fair may not have been so sure, or so solvent, as the *Sentinel* believed. Behind the scenes, the exorbitant construction costs undoubtedly became a source of friction between the two capitalists. Fair had quit the Con Virginia shortly before the layoff of 266 of its miners—a sign the press took for "rats deserting a sinking ship."[14] Sharply depressed Consolidated Virginia stock prices mirrored the decline. The river of money was drying up at its source.

At the time of 1878 Fair's visit to Santa Cruz, negotiations between the South Pacific Coast and the Santa Cruz & Felton had not reached the quick conclusion McPherson hoped for. In fact, Charlie Gorrill began to act like Davis's competitor. In February 1879, the SC&F announced a joint rate structure with the Pacific Coast Steamship Co., agreeing to set San Francisco-bound lumber tariffs pro rata in response to the threat of competitive rates from the South Pacific Coast.[15] Gorrill continued to improve the short line's

South Pacific Coast, 1879, Santa Clara to San Jose. [Museum of Art and History, Santa Cruz]

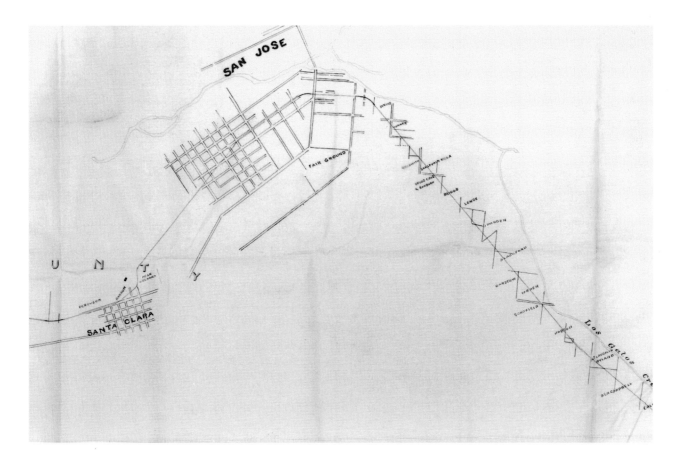

physical plant, installing heavier steel rail on the mainline and adopting the newfangled Bell telephone as a business link between the Santa Cruz and Felton depots.[16]

Larger competitive forces pressed on Davis. The Southern Pacific appeared to be moving stealthily around the south end of Santa Cruz County, infiltrating Monterey Bay in two separate incursions. Ironically, both made use of insolvent narrow gauge railroads as a stepping stone to the backdoor of Santa Cruz County.

It took little imagination, from McPherson's perspective, to foresee the Monterey & Salinas Valley sliding into the Southern Pacific's grasp. In December 1878, Henry Cowell filed suit against Carlisle Abbott for nonpayment of a $32,922.38 loan.[17] Using up every cent of the money, the M&SV was still unable to keep a bridge standing over the Salinas River for more than one winter at a time. While the Southern Pacific inched closer to buying it, the M&SV was kept afloat, literally, by Santa Cruz County credit.

So was the Santa Cruz Rail Road. Like a barometer anticipating the coming economic impact of the South Pacific Coast, the value of the short line's stock dropped from $100 a share at the time of construction to zero by August 1878.[18] What freight the line hauled would soon be diverted onto the SPC's completed mainline. In comparison with South Pacific Coast engineer-

South Pacific Coast, 1879, San Jose to Los Gatos. [Museum of Art and History, Santa Cruz]

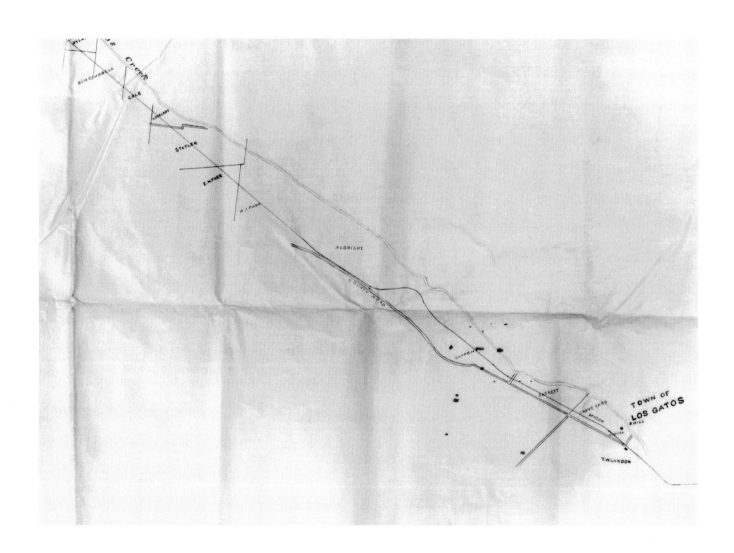

ing standards, the *Sentinel* admitted, "the [SCRR] was indifferently built, and certainly over most objectionable ground, the road being a series of cuts, fills and bridges. Along the beach it was built on sand, and this year, while its earnings have been so much smaller than last year for the same period of time, this section of the road has had to be rebuilt on piles at a cost of $5000."[19]

Still, by July 1878 Hihn had managed to widen cuts, level up sagging fills, and ease curves enough to decrease running time. The improvements gave him the small edge he needed to issue a new, faster public timetable. In turn, the investment Hihn was making (which he attempted to pay for with stock assessments) appeared to counter the company's declining value. The *Sentinel* concluded that the invisible hand of the Southern Pacific was likely at work here too, encouraging Hihn to develop a shorter link that SP could use as a back door into the county. The short-term losses didn't seem to matter as much as the end result. The *Sentinel,* on July 13, rejoiced in the shrinking timetable: "Nearer to thee, San Francisco, we are getting."

Hog Davis could only despair. It would be another year, perhaps two, until the big tunnel was completed. Until it was punched through, Davis would suffer Hihn's duplicity, alternately paying him for tunnel timber off the Soquel Augmentation Rancho and watching the money rematerialize in Santa Cruz Rail Road improvements that would ultimately be used against him by the Southern Pacific. In either event, the time lost in digging the summit tunnel would let his competitors harden their defenses.

South Pacific Coast, 1879, Los Gatos to Summit Tunnel (still labeled as "tunnel no. 3," its original number). [Museum of Art and History, Santa Cruz]

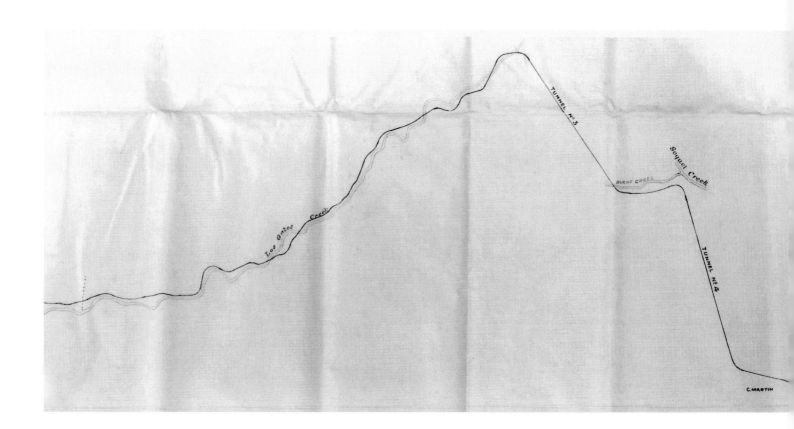

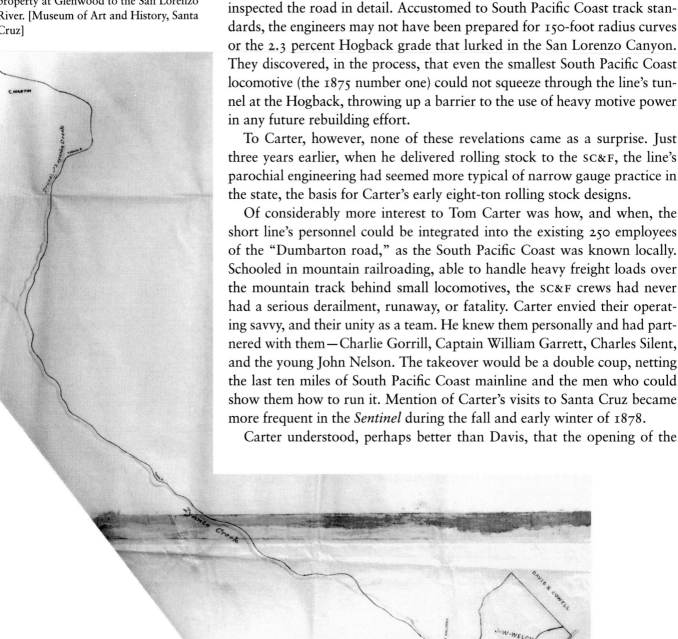

South Pacific Coast, 1879, from C. Martin's property at Glenwood to the San Lorenzo River. [Museum of Art and History, Santa Cruz]

Thomas Carter first crossed over the impregnable boundary into Ed Mix's turf in November 1878. That month, a thaw in negotiations occurred between the South Pacific Coast and the Santa Cruz & Felton. Davis and Charlie Gorrill were at last talking earnestly about merging the two railroads. To assess the SC&F's worth, and also to assess engineering changes that would have to be made to bring it up to minimum operational standards, Davis wanted Carter to take a closer look at the short line.

On Wednesday, November 20, Superintendent Carter and several of Mix's civil engineers crowded into the cab of one of the line's small Porters and inspected the road in detail. Accustomed to South Pacific Coast track standards, the engineers may not have been prepared for 150-foot radius curves or the 2.3 percent Hogback grade that lurked in the San Lorenzo Canyon. They discovered, in the process, that even the smallest South Pacific Coast locomotive (the 1875 number one) could not squeeze through the line's tunnel at the Hogback, throwing up a barrier to the use of heavy motive power in any future rebuilding effort.

To Carter, however, none of these revelations came as a surprise. Just three years earlier, when he delivered rolling stock to the SC&F, the line's parochial engineering had seemed more typical of narrow gauge practice in the state, the basis for Carter's early eight-ton rolling stock designs.

Of considerably more interest to Tom Carter was how, and when, the short line's personnel could be integrated into the existing 250 employees of the "Dumbarton road," as the South Pacific Coast was known locally. Schooled in mountain railroading, able to handle heavy freight loads over the mountain track behind small locomotives, the SC&F crews had never had a serious derailment, runaway, or fatality. Carter envied their operating savvy, and their unity as a team. He knew them personally and had partnered with them—Charlie Gorrill, Captain William Garrett, Charles Silent, and the young John Nelson. The takeover would be a double coup, netting the last ten miles of South Pacific Coast mainline and the men who could show them how to run it. Mention of Carter's visits to Santa Cruz became more frequent in the *Sentinel* during the fall and early winter of 1878.

Carter understood, perhaps better than Davis, that the opening of the south end of the railroad would dramatically change the balance between freight and passenger revenues. With that change would come an entirely different operating environment. As of June 1, 1878, the railroad ran no regular, timetable-mandated freight trains, only a mixed train that picked up and set out freight cars on a leisurely schedule between Alameda and Los Gatos. The overwhelming emphasis was on passenger traffic, much of it local. Thirty-two percent of the train miles on the South Pacific Coast's April 1879 timetable were logged by commute trains alone, operating in suburban Alameda.[20]

Picnic trains added to the early emphasis on passenger revenues. Regularly scheduled picnic trains first appeared in the spring of 1879, running from Alameda or San Jose and terminating at Wright's. On typical weekends, a majority of the line's coaches would be squeezed into the small yard on the bank of the creek opposite the mouth of the summit tunnel. Construction trains, running on a seven-day, twenty-four-hour schedule, had to fight for parking space.

The presence of alcohol quickly added mayhem to the mix. The *Alameda Argus* lamented that the Sarsfield Guard picnic of May 17, 1879

> enjoys the distinction of being the most disgraceful hoodlum affair on record. From the time they embarked on the ferry boat in the morning until they returned at 10 o'clock in the evening, they inspired a reign of terror among all decent people with whom they came in contact. They are represented as having taken San Jose by storm, and word was telegraphed to Alameda during the day for a posse to board the train at Park Street and arrest some of the rioters. . . .
>
> A person who was on the train represents to us that the scene was almost indescribable. The grossest lewdness was indulged in by both sexes and human life was in constant peril by flying missiles and weapons in the hands of the drunken cutthroats. . . .
>
> On Monday morning, one dead man and one with a broken leg were found along the track. At the ferry slip, one or two men fell overboard but were rescued.[21]

The problems with picnic trains multiplied as the weather grew warmer. The thousand San Jose ticket holders who flooded Wright's on June 21, 1879, would have filled twenty coaches, two-thirds of the line's available rolling stock. Arriving just across the creek from the two-acre debris pile that marked the mouth of the tunnel, the violence continued unabated.

When they weren't beating up on each other, the mob eyed the Chinese tunnel crews as a source of entertainment. Carter and his picnic trains added unwelcome stress to Ed Mix's already strained relationship with his crews. More warden than railroad superintendent, Carter ordered his conductors to lock coach doors if passengers grew violent when a train was in motion.

Gorrill's south end crews were not only reinforcements for the immediate battle Carter was fighting, they were also the seasoned troops Carter would need to open the railroad to heavy freight operation. He could not help but feel frustrated when negotiations again stalled between Davis and Gorrill in February 1879, apparently over price. Davis once more ordered Mix and

The J. J. Riley photograph above, ca. 1882, is the only known early view of the south portal of original tunnel three, or Summit Tunnel, by this time renumbered tunnel two after the daylighting of a short tunnel in Los Gatos Canyon. The photograph shows an unfinished wood splitter's mill, perhaps a contract fuel provider for the railroad. Barely across the Santa Cruz County line, South Pacific Coast number 13 and baggage car have entered the Soquel Augmentation Rancho, Frederick Hihn's large timber holdings just one mile from what would later become the Laurel depot. The locomotive rests on the Burns Creek Bridge. [William Wulf collection]

field boss Stahlberg to run transit lines down the eastern bank of the San Lorenzo, trying to convince Charlie Gorrill that the South Pacific Coast could easily afford to detour around the obstinate short line.

But the bluff was beginning to backfire. Davis had to swallow his pride when Mix informed him, in early March, that two tunnels (one twelve hundred feet long) would be required to bypass "the little trick," as Davis was beginning to call the SC&F.[22]

On November 16, 1878, the *Sentinel* reported that excavation at the north end of the summit tunnel, now more than two thousand feet deep into the mountain, had uncovered a new pocket of gas: "At the end of the tunnel on the Santa Clara side of the mountain, the workmen are in rock that much resembles coal, and from the crevices of the rock exudes a gas similar to petroleum gas. The gas is burned every five or ten minutes."

The account differs in one key fact from the later testimony of M. C. Highland, the swing shift foreman on the night of February 12, 1879. Highland remembered that he burned off the accumulating gas "every few hours," rather than "every five or ten minutes" as the *Sentinel* bore witness. If High-land was correct, it was not often enough to prevent a large volume of the deadly, invisible gas from building up at the end of the cavity. On the night of February 12, Highland apparently lit the fuse to a dynamite charge a few minutes before midnight and touched off not the dynamite but an enormous gas pocket:

> On this occasion the gas, and the oil that had gathered at the bottom of the tunnel, both caught fire, the sheet of flame being fearful to contemplate. At the time of the explosion, [Highland] was at work at the face of the tunnel, and immediately fell down, lying on his stomach and placing his hands by the sides of his face. He got up twice and tried to run, but the heat was so intense that he had to lie down and crawl on his hands and knees. Fire above him, fire around him, and a round body of fire from one end of the tunnel to the other.

The tunnel acted like a rifle barrel. Gas exploding in the extreme depths of the tunnel compressed gas closer to the opening, in turn igniting and accelerating the roiling mass toward the portal. Damage, paradoxically, increased further away from the flash point.

> Half way down the tunnel were the two Chinamen who are supposed to be dead. They were in charge of the cars, two in number, which were thrown from the track, and the mule hauling them was carried for a distance of sixty feet towards the mouth of the tunnel. A brace, two hundred feet from the mouth of the tunnel and eight feet above the bottom, was carried seventy feet beyond the mouth of the tunnel . . . the blacksmith shop, half a mile from the place of explosion, was blown to atoms . . . the report was so great that people outside of the tunnel thought the [powder] magazine had exploded.[23]

Highland apparently crawled two thousand feet to the mouth of the tunnel, two wool shirts he was wearing acting as insulation from the flames. The shirts probably saved his life. He dragged himself into the cool night air with most of his hair burned off, his forehead and nose badly blistered.

Most of the Chinese did not make it out of the bore on their own feet. Within minutes, rescuers had stumbled through the smoke to reach the unconscious laborers. At first, the *Sentinel* did its best to sensationalize the aftermath:

> When the mangled and blackened bodies of the Chinamen, five of whom are supposed to be dead, were brought out, a sickening sight was presented. O. B. Castle carried one out and laid him on the bank, the breathing mass leaving the fleshy imprint of a human being in the rescuer's arms, the body breathing through its side as if it had been thrown against some solid substance with great violence.[24]

But the newspaper quickly softened its reporting of the horrors. Perhaps McPherson realized the true danger of what had happened. Chinese workers had frequently died an isolated death from explosion or landslide (or even gunshot) during the South Pacific Coast's work in the mountains. But this was clearly different. The February 12 explosion demonstrated the power

The gas explosions that rocked Summit Tunnel, killing contract Chinese laborers in 1878 and 1879, magnified racial tensions already deeply rooted in California society. Ten years elapsed between the R. E. Wood stereograph (above) taken in the Felton area in 1875 and the Rodolph portrait (top) taken at the northern portal of Summit Tunnel about 1885. But their message was similar: the Chinese carried the White Man's burden. [Above, Dan Matthews collection; top, Bancroft Library]

of a natural disaster sufficient to stop construction altogether. McPherson realized he was no longer reporting isolated deaths but a disaster akin to an earthquake, capable of laying waste the entire tunnel and stopping construction of the railroad.

The *Sentinel* began to distort the truth about what had happened on February 12. By the first of March, the paper gave the impression that all the workers in the tunnel were on the road to recovery: "The report that the fourteen Chinese injured last month have died is not true. Four have gone to San Francisco, ten have remained in camp [at Wright's], ministered by a Chinese doctor."

By March 8, the *Sentinel* managed to turn the explosion into a stock of local humor, when McPherson drew attention to the recovery of foreman Highland: "M. C. Highland, foreman of the fourteen Chinamen not killed at the tunnel explosion, and whom the *Mercury* has killed so often, is on the streets every day, a very lively corpse."

But the truth was hardly a laughing matter. Several of the Chinese workers, removed by the Six Companies to primitive hospitals in San Francisco, took weeks to die from their burns. Not until the following November, after the troubles in the summit tunnel grew worse, did at least part of the truth come out. The *Sentinel* finally admitted, on November 22, 1879, that five workers, all Chinese, eventually died of their injuries.

All the public really knew, in February, was that work at the north end of the summit tunnel had come to an abrupt halt.

In the flickering light of twin bonfires, Dennis Kearney spoke in Santa Cruz on the night of March 15, 1879, flush with renewed zeal for the Workingmen's movement and for the passage of the new state constitution. His remarks echoed the invective he used in the San Francisco sandlot speeches of 1877, castigating the "railroad robbers and the political cutthroats of [California] who have pooled their issues to import long-tailed lepers from Asia."

This time, however, the speech packed more than racist threats. In a June 1878 primary election, Kearney's Workingmen's Party won 51 of the 152 seats at the upcoming California Constitutional Convention, guaranteeing it the leverage to force radical anticorporate and anti-Chinese articles into a new state constitution. If the constitution were ratified by a public vote the following May, Kearney's articles would make it illegal for a California corporation to hire Chinese workers.[25]

Duncan McPherson, probably Kearney's most passionate supporter outside of San Francisco, was forced to confront his own crisis of conscience. The South Pacific Coast Railroad, a vector for the future growth and development of the county, was now facing long delays in its battle to cross the mountains, perhaps a year and a half of additional work in the troubled summit tunnel. While Chinese laborers earned $77\frac{1}{2}$ cents a day in the tunnels, white laborers would command nearly double that figure. Could Davis's river of money make up the difference? Deprived of his army of Chinese laborers, how could Davis hope to finish the tunnel? McPherson clearly became frightened. At the very moment he should have been declaring victory for the Workingmen's agenda, he found himself caught between two ideological extremes. In response, he began to mute his rhetoric. Kearney's speech was reported in the *Sentinel* as "failing to stir a desultory, unenthusiastic audience," the least enthusiastic among them probably Duncan McPherson.[26]

Had McPherson helped kill the goose that might have been about to lay the golden egg? The dark undercurrent of Kearney's visit seemed to provoke a bitter answer. As ratification for the constitution neared, incidents of anti-Chinese violence became more common in Santa Cruz. A mob attack on Chinatown, McPherson knew, would likely torch the whole town.[27]

McPherson's worst fears were coming true. Just three weeks after Kearney's speech, Alfred Davis launched a plainspoken rebuttal against the Workingmen and "the infamous provisions of the new constitution," pointing out that any attack against the state's railroads should be levied equally on the state's "teamsters, stage companies, steamship companies, hotels, brick makers, powder companies . . . milkmen, farmers and printers," all of whom had employed Chinese labor at some point in the past.[28] Davis's inclusion of the powder industry must have struck a particularly painful note with McPherson. The recession was still grimly real, and even with a major earthmoving project passing by its very doorstep, the local California Powder Works had recently closed for lack of orders.

McPherson felt the crisis tighten around him when the new constitution narrowly passed the statewide ratification on May 7, 1879, scrimping a plurality of 11,000 out of a total statewide vote of 145,000. Living in a house divided, McPherson could only watch the outcome escalate into an ironic series of reversals. On June 28, for example, the *Sentinel* reported the suspension of most railroad construction projects in the state until the full meaning of the constitution could be tested. He held his breath, expecting the worst, as the South Pacific Coast announced a reduction in manpower "wherever possible." Reluctantly, McPherson published, on May 24, 1879, the most cynical statement that Alfred Davis had yet uttered: "[Had I] foreseen two years ago what would be the public feeling towards railroads, I would never have built the South Pacific Coast."[29]

Left on the horns of a dilemma, McPherson continued to espouse hatred against the Chinese but spoke not a harsh word against Alfred Davis or his corporation, resolving the apparent contradiction by blaming the Chinese employees, not their employer, for low morality and unethical conduct.

Alfred Davis reconstructed the decision for James Fair while the pair of very large men sat in the back seat of a spring wagon on the road from Felton to Santa Cruz. George Colegrove waited patiently with the reins in his hands, their driver for the day. He was within earshot as Davis reported, in some detail, the events that led up to the final acquisition of the Santa Cruz & Felton.[30]

> Mr. Davis said, "drive out on that point so I can stop a minute. I want to show the Senator where we are." I did. [Davis] stood up in the wagon. "Now," he said, "I call that Constitution Point. That is where we were when the state constitution was adopted. We were undecided whether we would buy up this Felton and Santa Cruz railroad or whether we would build a new road around that side of the river on the east side. I have decided the best thing to do is buy out this little trick (as he called this little Felton and Santa Cruz road) and go down this side of the river."
>
> "Well," Fair said, "why didn't you build it down that side of the river?"
>
> "I didn't want the little trick in the way afterwards. On that side of the river it is limestone rock and on this side it is granite rock. If we have to rebuild it after we buy it, it will be much easier to do than it is on that side of the river. After we get down to about the powder mill we have to go through the powder works and that we can't do. When we get there it drops off. There would have to be a long trestle built to get through and then we would come in on the wrong side of the river in Santa Cruz. So we decided to take this little road and rebuild it."
>
> The Senator said that was all right, he guessed.

But Colegrove missed the obvious implications of the name "Constitution Point." Davis clearly could not afford risking the crucial connection to tidewater if the new anti-Chinese referendum took away the labor he would require to build it. Missing completely from Colegrove's account is the context of the negotiation. Crucial to Davis, at the time, was the strategic importance of controlling the SC&F's lumber traffic coming down the flume, which in turn meant expanding the negotiation with Charlie Gorrill to include not only the railroad but also the flume, the mill, and the timber lands owned by the parent San Lorenzo Flume and Transportation Co.[31] Davis could not afford to hold an eighty-mile railroad hostage to seven miles of the "little trick." Advantage: Gorrill. With all of its engineering flaws, with the irreconcilable need to rebuild its contortionist curves and the far riskier necessity to accept the steep gradients that rollercoastered over the Hogback, Davis would hasten to purchase the Santa Cruz & Felton or risk his entire investment.

Davis would therefore sweeten the offer. Sometime in April or May 1879, he offered Gorrill contracts for South Pacific Coast bridge work in exchange for a successful negotiation on a lease of the Santa Cruz & Felton.

News of renewed dialogue between Davis and Gorrill reached the pages of the *Sentinel* on May 31, 1879, helping to dispel the gloom of the constitutional quandary. No formal announcement of the merger followed, but one week later, on June 14, the *Sentinel* confirmed that work on the 120-foot Howe truss at Big Trees would begin immediately. The bridge would divert the South Pacific Coast mainline from the east bank of the San Lorenzo to the west bank, its southerly abutments located just a few yards from the thirty-pound rails of the Santa Cruz & Felton. The paper made it clear, on July 5, that Pacific Bridge Co. had the contract for the work.

The lease was the first good news McPherson had printed about the railroad in months. Spirits lightened. The weather was warm. On June 14, Ed Mix announced that excavation in tunnel number 3 (referring to the tunnel just south of summit tunnel) had set a record of 509 feet in May, foreshadowing its completion by September. It would be finished ahead of schedule. No gas pockets were ever reported in tunnel 3, and a for a short time it was fashionable for the editor of the *Sentinel* to distract the public, and perhaps himself, from the horrors of the summit tunnel by flaunting progress in the other bores.

Ed Mix personally improved McPherson's disposition, on the evening of June 12, by attending a dance at Wheaton's new bathing establishment on the Santa Cruz boardwalk, appearing unconcerned about the problems on summit ridge as he danced with his wife.

Tension among tunnel workers only increased. Temporarily halted at the twenty-three-hundred-foot mark by the explosion of February 1879, Mix began installing long pipes to convey forced air to the tunnel face, intending to dilute the gas and lessen the risk of an explosion.[32] For three weeks, until nearly a half mile of piping was laid and put into operation, no work took place at the north end of the tunnel.

Even with work on the north heading shut down, fear of gas leaks soon spread to the south heading. With each dynamite blast, the Chinese workers sensed the increasing odds of opening up a gas fissure on the southern end of the tunnel. Nerves grew raw. During the graveyard shift of Saturday, February 22, a foreman named Patrick Daily discharged one of his crew "on account of being lazy," ordering him off the work site. A few hours later, Daily spotted the same worker, trying to blend in with the crew, back at work on the heading. Infuriated, Daily threw the man to the ground, jumped on top of him, and began to pound him with clenched fists. Instantly, Daily

Summit Tunnel crews, March and April, 1901. [Society for the Preservation of Carter Railroad Resources]

was surrounded by the entire crew of seventeen Chinese. With the skill of a javelin thrower, one worker hurled a drill rod at Daily's partner, John Ward, hitting him in the chest. Ward recovered his balance, grabbed a shovel and swung it into the side of the worker's face, knocking teeth out. "It will be remembered," the *Sentinel* told its readers, "that Ward is the individual who some months ago, single-handed, put to flight about a dozen of the subjects of the Flowery Kingdom."

Lamps were quickly smashed out, plunging the heading into darkness. Daily refused to divert his attack from the stowaway worker, leaving it up to Ward to keep the gang at bay. Under considerable pressure to defend the position, Ward quickly discovered that the shovel, swung in a low arc through pitch blackness, could command a central position in the scuffle. His aim, however, was indiscriminate. "Finally," summed up the *Sentinel,* "all the Chinamen who were able to walk were driven out of the tunnel. The next morning out of the seventeen Chinese that were engaged in the melee, only seven were found able to resume work. Daily received a severe scalp wound, probably done with the shovel wielded by Ward."[33]

Chinese crews returned to the north heading in the summit tunnel during the week of May 17, after a shutdown of nearly three months. By June 5, tensions between Chinese workmen and white foremen again reached the boiling point, this time resulting in a fatality:

> Nick Borrosey was herding a gang of Chinamen at work in the tunnel, and finding that one of the lot was lagging in his work, told the China-man to leave the tunnel and go to camp, but the Chinaman refused to obey and was backed by the rest of the gang, some twenty in number. However, as the final result, Borrosey was run out by the gang (as has been the experience with other herders) amidst a shower of picks and drills, which were thrown at him, and Borrosey in his retreat, to defend himself, used his pistol firing several shots, one of which took effect in the neck of one of the pursuers, who will probably die. The Chinamen at work are a vicious lot, are utterly regardless of life, and can throw a drill with great precision. It was a most miraculous escape for Nick. After this little episode, work went on the same, a new "boss" being substituted, who will probably be treated the same way.[34]

As blasting continued to advance the heading, timber crews followed closely behind the heading shifts, assembling a framework of 10" × 12" redwood beams in configurations that depended on the type of rock encountered. In sections through solid granite, no timbering was required. But in softer rock, described by the *Sentinel* as sandstone or sometimes as "loose rock," carpenters crowned vertical redwood posts with hexagonal arcs of tightly fitted compressional pieces, tied together with rods. The timber work was intricate and time consuming, but critical to the integrity of the finished tunnel.

By the first week of July, timber crews had completed a section of cribbing at the eighteen-hundred-foot mark and moved forward into the newly excavated extremity, at least twenty-three hundred feet into the mountain. Compressed air pipes were lengthened to feed forward into the advanced heading. But until the pumps could be turned on, gas seepage to the rear of the new heading began to build up, silently reaching a dangerous level. On Monday, July 14, without warning 250 feet of new timbering was set ablaze like logs atop dry kindling. Two foremen, trapped at the heading when the timbers ignited, had to run the gauntlet of flame to reach safety, barely escaping the dense smoke. Ed Mix ordered the fire sealed off with a makeshift door. Behind the door, the tunnel continued to burn for weeks. The barricade itself went up in flames at least once, and had to be replaced with a new door, installed closer to the portal.

It wasn't until August 2 that workmen even attempted to enter the barricaded section of tunnel. Like a human lifeline, spotters were stationed at intervals to monitor the progress of a foreman and a single carpenter, who walked slowly forward, without lights, toward the eighteen-hundred-foot mark. The last spotter, barely able to see into the murk, watched the foreman and carpenter stagger and then collapse, overcome by gas as they neared their goal. Crews raced in to rescue them, putting their own lives in danger.

Ed Mix ordered more extreme measures, including pumping water through the compressed air lines, attempting to reduce danger of fire. The measures appeared to work. By August 16, the *Sentinel* reported the fire was out. In the section where timbers burned, the roof had caved in, creating a temporary blockade that wasn't completely removed until the week of September 23, a loss of nearly seven months since the February 1879 explosion.

Contractors Martin, Ballard and Ferguson admitted that the delays and work stoppage had cost them more than $30,000.[35] But there had been no fatalities since February, and as the tunnel project entered its third year the contractors reached the last one-fifth of the mountain, leaving just one thousand feet of excavation remaining between the north and south headings. On October 4, the *Sentinel* reported that both heading crews were working in solid granite, an indication that the petroleum and gas deposits were now behind them.

Even with a slower rate of progress through hard rock, the paper estimated the tunnel would be opened by January 1880. The publication of this date is the key to understanding the real pressure that Davis, Mix, and Carter were under, for it was the earliest assurance that commercial contracts for through freight service could be negotiated. Critical business commitments would be based on this date. In the fall of 1879, for example, the Santa Clara Valley Mill and Lumber Co. signed an agreement with a Santa Cruz lumber wholesaler named Hayes and Hubbard, agreeing to deliver regular consignments of redwood to San Jose, via the South Pacific Coast, beginning on January 7, 1880. Wanting to build confidence in the railroad, Davis could only encourage such third-party agreements.[36]

But clearly, such agreements were risky. On October 11, just a week after the paper announced the likely date for opening the summit tunnel, the *Sentinel* confirmed reports that another gas pocket had burst into flame, again igniting timbers and shutting down the work on the north end of the tunnel.

South Pacific Coast switch lock. [Bruce MacGregor]

Of all the narrow gauge men Thomas Carter knew, Captain R. M. Garrett had earned a reputation as one of the best managers in the business. Carter presumably had known Garrett since 1876, when the last lot of Carter Brothers rolling stock was delivered to the SC&F and when Garrett became superintendent and secretary of the short line. Carter and Garrett had been peers ever since. For the intervening three years, Garrett had spearheaded a nearly continuous program of plant upgrades on the SC&F. Heavier mainline rail, a siding to the California Powder Mill, a new yard layout in Santa Cruz (including a new office), and purchase of the second locomotive from Porter, Bell all happened under Garrett's command. Much like Carter, Garrett assumed that whichever railroad won the tug-of-war, there would be prosperity enough for both.

Garrett also hired new employees, among them fireman J. S. Green and conductor George Vass, who in turn enhanced the SC&F's reputation as a well-run, safely operated short line. Given the mountainous terrain through which it operated and the extremely light construction of its track and rolling stock, the safety record of his crew was enviable. In spite of the infamous Hogback grade, there was no recorded incidence of a serious wreck. Except for a handful of derailments involving the line's second locomotive (noted in Fowler Pope's diary), there was hardly a wheel on the ground. The benefit to Carter was straightforward: he would hire the man who hired the Santa Cruz & Felton's exceptional crew.

But Carter was forced to wait. From Davis's perspective, Garrett would be worth more to the South Pacific Coast if he remained on the Santa Cruz & Felton's management after a merger, continuing to lead the short line as it began to interleave its equipment and people with the larger railroad.

Just as the terms of the merger were finally being negotiated by Charlie Gorrill and Alfred Davis, a mishap in June 1879 nearly cost Garrett his life, and Carter his star manager. The *Sentinel* did not report the incident until several weeks after it happened. Apparently a crib of piles, being unloaded from a flatcar, had shifted, catching Garrett off guard and breaking both legs.[37]

Coming close to disaster, the accident ultimately confirmed Carter's belief in Garrett's character. By June 25, the Santa Cruz & Felton's plucky superintendent was being carried "on a stretcher . . . with officers of the SPCRR, to view new construction."[38] By the first weeks of July, Garrett was directing the early stages of a massive reconstruction project while lying prostrate on the stretcher, carried about like baggage on a construction train. But it was clearly Garrett who would manage the day-to-day operation of the Santa Cruz & Felton through its rebuilding phase.

The merger took the form of a lease, leaving the two railroads separate entities each with its own board of directors (although Davis was voted president of the SC&F board on July 22, 1879). The lease allowed Davis to keep the short line's organization, with Garrett as its manager, intact.

Regular train service (both freight and passenger) was immediately suspended between Santa Cruz and Felton, and Garrett began to hire new operating personnel to run construction trains. As recounted in Chapter Ten, George Colegrove came aboard the Santa Cruz & Felton in August as a brakeman, over the objections, or at least the indifference, of Tom Carter.

Coby Lorenzen was hired as a fireman about the same time. In his *Life Story,* Colegrove made the reporting relationships clear: Garrett had hired him and was frequently on site to supervise the work train, but Ed Mix was never far from the scene and was the ultimate authority in a conflict. Colegrove's recounting of the firing of conductor Miller has already been told; it is evidence that Captain Garrett lacked total authority over the Santa Cruz & Felton. Thomas Carter, apparently, had even less authority than Garrett.

The faint outlines of an organizational fault system began to appear. Physically isolated from the Santa Cruz & Felton, Carter appears to have become organizationally isolated as well. Taken at face value, Colegrove's version of his own hiring seems to describe a rift between Davis and Carter, or at least estrangement of their influence and decision making. For Carter, the result was separation from a critical component of the completed railroad. More damaging, perhaps, was the alienation between Carter and Colegrove. When the railroad finally opened its completed mainline, Mix would be gone and Garrett would be promoted to general manager of freight, based in San Francisco, removing two of the organizational layers that separated Carter from the southern theater of operations. Trying to adapt to new reporting relationships, both Colegrove and Carter would finally come face-to-face, still carrying unresolved issues from their August 1879 encounter. A grudge, apparently, was the result.

By the time of Colegrove's hiring, the Santa Cruz & Felton had become an extension of Ed Mix's mountain domain, and in many ways the most complex phase of the South Pacific Coast's construction. Mix moved the contracting operations of Muir Brothers, including roughly three hundred laborers, south from the tunnel projects near Glenwood and into SC&F territory, using Muir to launch a massive rebuilding program.

Two new tunnels would be drilled along the old SC&F alignment. One, first estimated at 400 feet in length, cut through the promontory that bulged out to Butte Cut, a sharp curve that Fowler Pope mentioned in his diary as a spot where south-bound trains occasionally stalled. The second new tunnel, estimated at 270 feet in length, was described in the *Sentinel* on July 26 as being located "beneath" the old Hogback tunnel, an indication that Mix may have been attempting to lower the altitude of the Hogback summit in an effort to shorten the steep grade on the Santa Cruz side. The new Hogback tunnel, however, was ultimately drilled at the same elevation as the old Hogback tunnel, barely fifty feet to its east.[39] It was clear, from a September 13 *Sentinel* article, that the old tunnel would not have provided clearance for a full-sized South Pacific Coast Baldwin locomotive. Mix's first priority, simply, was to widen its clearance, and in the process improve the alignment of track on both sides. By July 19, the South Pacific Coast's one spot, the old Green Point Dairy Baldwin, was barged to Santa Cruz and stood ready to move rail and material north once the new Hogback tunnel was opened.

In the middle of the San Lorenzo Gorge, at the steep, narrow cliff variously identified as "Cape Horn," "the big slide," or the "devil's slide," Mix planned to construct a stone retaining wall to replace the SC&F's "half trestle."[40] The wall was 50 feet high and 150 feet long and would help create a permanent right-of-way at "the point by many considered to be the most

No.401. Felton Big Trees, Santa Cruz Co., Cal.

The stereopticon view of a construction camp (above, left) at the north end of Big Trees grove during the summer of 1879 represents the only known construction photograph of the South Pacific Coast. In the larger view, the same section of track is occupied by rail in September 1879, shortly after the San Lorenzo River Bridge was opened to traffic. [Left, Bill Wissel collection; right, John Schmale collection]

dangerous place on the railroad," as the *Sentinel* summarized the strategy. Heavy work was planned to improve other bottlenecks. The eighty-foot-high trestle above Gharkey's vineyard, at the foot of the Hogback grade, would be replaced by a twenty-five-thousand-yard earth fill, started by Chinese crews in August.

Mix made the decision, by June 1879, to retain the original thirty-pound rail on the Santa Cruz & Felton throughout the rebuilding phase. Once the rebuilding was finished between Santa Cruz and the South Pacific Coast right-of-way near Felton, he would double back and replace the light rail with standard fifty-pound iron as time and manpower became available.[41]

Soon Colegrove's construction train was serving three separate projects: moving heavy new rail from the Santa Cruz wharf to stockpiles at Felton, moving ballast to resurface and realign the newly rerailed track, and moving bridge timbers to the new crossing of the San Lorenzo where the two railroads would join. Completion of the bridge, on September 6, 1879, allowed Santa Cruz & Felton trains to cross over the river onto South Pacific Coast right-of-way for the first time. Colegrove proudly recalled the first train over the bridge: "We pulled up in front of the Big Trees. Johnny Hooper, who kept the trees, came out with a bottle of champagne and treated all hands and chief engineer. Ed Mix was with us and made a little speech and so on."[42]

The splice point between the SC&F and SPC is obvious, even today. Walking the right-of-way from the north, the hiker passes down a thousand-foot tangent through the flank of the Henry Cowell redwood grove, its original first growth trees removed from the right-of-way with the precision of a single, unswerving transit shot. (Eighty dollars shall not crook the road!) But once across the San Lorenzo Bridge, the SC&F's tortured curvature left its signature in the steep canyon walls.

Ever present, Mix pushed Garrett to prioritize use of his men and equipment for construction of new track, north of Felton. To move ballast and fill materials before the rains came, no commercial passenger or freight schedules were maintained on the SC&F between Monday and Saturday. All week long, commercial lumber and freight shipments simply piled up at the flume yard in Felton. Already exhausted from six days of running construction trains, Colegrove and his crew spent Sundays moving the freight to Santa Cruz. Colegrove expressed rancor that Miller had been fired, for now Colegrove had to perform conductor's duties as well as those of brakeman, seven days a week. But the onerous duties were also Colegrove's first promotion, guaranteeing him a permanent job as conductor on the South Pacific Coast.

Garrett was dealing with his own double duties. The flume had gone unrepaired all summer, and by November 1879 it required substantial work. Garrett organized a complete overhaul, including widening of the V planks to increase capacity; he was aware that the flume would play a key role in generating South Pacific Coast revenue when the line opened in January, or perhaps February—a prediction that was now being avoided when management talked to the press. Flume traffic would be the largest source of freight revenue on the new railroad, and Davis clearly had identified it as a critical deliverable once the tunnels were finished.

The task of repairing the eleven-mile wooden structure was not simple. Each succeeding year, as the flume aged, suffered deadfall, and in turn handled increasing traffic, the task of repairing it grew more difficult. Working through bad weather, Garrett in fact would not complete the project until early February 1880, which was considered to be the latest possible date for opening the South Pacific Coast before shipping contracts were in legal jeopardy.[43]

As November began, winter rains held off, giving Garrett and his men the break they desperately needed to finish work on the Santa Cruz & Felton before the big tunnel was completed. Mix appeared confident in Garrett's ability when he departed for the East Coast on November 6; he was not scheduled to return until the first week in December.

Walking on crutches, Captain Garrett gamely held the fort.

It is possible that the Wright's telegraph operator, named Cook, got a single message on the wire about one minute before midnight, November 17, 1879. He was awakened not by the explosion but by a Chinese laborer called Jim, who raced into the depot where Cook slept, shook him from a deep slumber, and warned him that gas had exploded deep inside the mountain. Cook had befriended Jim over the past months, and in this simple act of courage, Jim was returning the favor. Although Jim's English was not fluent, his message was clear—get out while the getting was good.

The Chinese worker did not linger but returned to the mouth of the tunnel where other off-shift workers lit torches and prepared to go to the aid of the workers at the heading. It was the last time Cook would see Jim alive. If Cook succeeded in sending a telegraph message, warning other stations of the explosion, it was brief. Midnight fell. The *Sentinel* chose to dateline its story for the new day, November 18:

Tunnel 3 is situated near this station. From this side the workmen had, up to yesterday, succeeded in penetrating a distance of 2700 feet. A few moments before twelve o'clock last night the force of laborers, consisting of twenty-one Chinamen and two white men, were working upon the face of the tunnel. A blast had been prepared, and the fire was lighted, when with a roar and shock that shook the mountains from base to summit, an explosion of gas occurred. The noise and shock aroused the camp, and before they could be stopped, the other Chinamen, twenty in number, rushed into the tunnel to rescue their countrymen, bearing torches in their hands. At the same time the white men, Perry Hinkle and Thomas Johnson, made their appearance, moving with difficulty, and both terribly burned. They were at once taken to their cabin, and everything possible done to alleviate their suffering. In the meantime, the Chinamen had kept pushing on to the relief of their companions. They had penetrated about 1500 feet from the entrance, when a second report, louder and more intense than the first, shook the earth and wrecked the engine house and sheds within a hundred feet of the entrance to the tunnel. The explosion was followed by a sheet of lurid flame which the great mountain belched forth, consuming everything before it. The engine which ran the blower, which supplied air for the workmen, was fairly blown out of the tunnel, and a group of white men who had congregated at the portal were all more or less injured by the second explosion. Hinkle, the foreman, and Johnson, the car driver, who made their escape after the first explosion, were badly burned about the face and hands, but they will probably recover. Three of the Chinamen taken out this morning will probably die. Ah Wo, who was also brought out this morning, was horribly burned on the chest and stomach, and was taken to one of the cabins, where an hour afterwards he was found with a silk scarf twisted around his neck, dead. The Chinamen who went in this morning after day-light brought out seventeen wounded, and report the others dead. There are probably twenty-four dead bodies in the tunnel now. The gas in the tunnel prevents as yet any search for the bodies, and nothing can be done in that direction until tomorrow morning. Dr. Thorne, of San Jose, arrived upon the ground early, and has worked all day to alleviate the suffering of the wounded. The contractors and employees of the company from the neighboring stations are here and doing everything in their power for the wounded men. Would the scenes within the tunnel and about the entrance be faithfully pictured, it would send a thrill of horror through every reader of the *Sentinel*. The stench of burning flesh, combined with the escaping gas, is almost overpowering anywhere near the portal. The cabins are filled with mutilated Chinamen, some shrieking with the excruciating pain they are undergoing; others praying in their native tongue to their countrymen to kill them and put an end to their suffering, or beseeching the God of Fire to have mercy upon them and cease his torments. In most of the cabins, tapers are burning, the perfume from which serves somewhat to temper the sickening odor of roasted flesh.[44]

No one dared venture into the tunnel until daylight. Unwilling to risk exposed candles or lanterns in the tunnel, crews tilted a large mirror to reflect sunlight into the bore. The mirror offered feeble illumination during the middle hours of the day as the November sun crept briefly above the rim of the canyon.

Picking their way over ground strewn with rock, blown-out lagging, cross timbers, and bodies, search parties penetrated deeper and deeper into the half-mile cavern. Frequently experiencing the effects of residual gas, they considered themselves lucky to make it out alive. H. C. Stillman, a shift foreman leading a small party of Chinese into the semidarkness, turned around just in time to see a Chinese laborer lift a match to a cigar, risking a third explosion. He grabbed the worker's wrist, throwing the match to the ground.

In the half light, Stillman angrily shouted at another laborer, leaning motionless against a 10" × 12" redwood timber and apparently too terrified to go on. Moving closer to urge the worker forward, Stillman realized he was looking at the charred outlines of a corpse, hurled against the timber by the blast and by a quirk left standing upright.

Joining one of the rescue expeditions, telegraph agent Cook identified the body of Jim, found some two thousand feet inside the tunnel. Recalling Jim's warning to Cook the night of the blast, the *Sentinel* published a Faustian epitaph for Jim on November 29, the only personal death notice the paper published for any of the thirty-two Chinese workers who were killed: "his mangled body was brought out yesterday, and nobody but Cook gave a thought to the heroic spirit that dwelt in the clay of the Mongolian slave."

All work in the tunnel, on both the north and south headings, was shut down. The order sent Duncan McPherson closer to hysterics. The California Powder Works had started limited commercial operations, interpreted by the *Sentinel* as good news for the local economy. The bad news was that to conform to the law of the new state constitution, the powder works discharged all Chinese employees.[45] In McPherson's mind, the tunnel explosion could easily precipitate a similar action by the South Pacific Coast, throwing completion of the railroad into uncertainty. Reaching the height of personal frustration, on December 6 McPherson wrote his most hate-filled, racist commentary on the November tragedy: "Laboring men say the Chinese must go. Send them into the oil-gas end of tunnel number 3. They will then wing their flowery way to the Celestial land or hunt the sources of the fires that keep the volcanoes in perpetual motion."

The South Pacific Coast had indeed reached a crisis. While frantic efforts continued to restore the infrastructure at Wright's, no crews returned to the tunnel headings. Larger air compressors, additional piping, and an experimental electric lighting system were all installed at the Wright's end of the summit tunnel by January 3, but the small Chinese crews kept on standby were terrified to enter the tunnel. New Chinese crews arrived by train on January 10, but would not go to work "til the devils they asserted were in the tunnel were driven away, which they proceeded to do by burning incense and plastering Celestial hieroglyphics over the face of the first set of timbers. The next day they went to work as of old."[46]

But the Chinese did not remain at work for long. A slow gas leak continued at the ignition point of the November 17 blast, almost at the exact center of the tunnel. Into this fissure, the contractors drove a metal pipe, channeling the largest stream of gas into an orifice. By lighting the crude lamp, the gas was burned off at its source, creating a perpetual flame at the site of the disaster.

Newly excavated rock continued to smell of saturated oil. Reminders of the fatal blast, including thirty-two graves located somewhere along the mainline just north of Wrights, were powerful devils indeed. Even without subsequent explosions, and even with a pay raise from 77½ cents a day to $1.25 a day—the Chinese crews were loath to stay on the job. The *Sentinel* reported that on January 10, the contractor had succeeded "for the first time in getting two Chinese to the face of tunnel 3. They shook like aspens in a Salinas Zephyr, but faced the music a moment before bolting."

Cornish miners, recruited from the nearby New Almaden quicksilver mines, were hired in early February to replace the Chinese on the northern heading. The extreme measures required to restart the work obscured the fact that the two headings were just 425 feet apart.

Instead, there was a sense, in the numerous small newspaper stories from Wright's that December, that a crisis mentality had come over both management and construction workers. Ed Mix cut short his trip to the East Coast, returning to take charge on December 3. Old infrastructure was speedily replaced. Elbon and Houck cut thousands of unanticipated board feet of tunnel timber, required to quickly replace tunnel lining burned or blown out by the November explosion.

Contingency plans were made for a future gas explosion. An antechamber was planned for excavation somewhere near the mouth of the tunnel, where an entire shift crew could take refuge out of the rifle bore of the tunnel, should methane reach a concentration that could explode again.[47]

The tent camps of retreating Chinese crews were cleared away. The Cornish miners would be housed in wooden cabins; two clusters were erected at Wrights, one near the mouth of the tunnel and another on the opposite bank of the creek, a "big long barracks" that George Colegrove recalled in his *Life Story.*[48] The barracks symbolized Mix's determination to win the battle at any cost.

There was a sense that the railroad's management was fighting a pivotal battle at Wright's that December, one that would ultimately determine the success or failure of the South Pacific Coast, or at the very least predetermine its competitive advantage against the encroaching Southern Pacific. It was now clearly impossible to meet freight contracts like the one signed by Santa Clara Valley Mill and Lumber and Hayes and Hubbard, predicated on a January 1 opening of the railroad. Shortly after the contract should have gone into effect on January 7, 1880, the mill and lumber company brought

Hand-operated South Pacific Coast train order signal at Campbell, ca. 1890s. [Bob Dockery collection]

Hayes and Hubbard into Superior Court in San Jose, suing for nondelivery of contracted lumber.

Literally at the same time, during the first two months of 1880, the Southern Pacific created its first beachhead on the Monterey Peninsula. A luxury hotel, named the Del Monte, was planned to compete for the same tourist business the South Pacific Coast would cultivate in Santa Cruz, just thirty miles north. Foundations for the Del Monte were under construction in February 1880.[49] By that date, the narrow gauge equipment of the Monterey & Salinas Valley had been shipped to Nevada, and the work of standard gauging the line was well under way.

It was clear that all of Davis's managers were feeling intense pressure to open the railroad. Thomas Carter, whose primary role remained managing both revenue and construction trains everywhere on the railroad, very likely shouldered added responsibilities for constructing new facilities. Putting his old skills of contract shop work to good use, Carter may have set up temporary headquarters in the new cluster of buildings erected at Wright's in February. Fragmentary evidence suggests that he personally did site engineering on the new dormitory or cabins intended to house the Cornish miners. The *Santa Cruz Sentinel* did not give details, but it reported, on December 6, that Carter was laid up by a severe case of poison oak, developed from "exposure to undergrowth around summit tunnel."

Thrown into the breach of the battle for summit ridge, Carter began to make his mark on Ed Mix's turf. And it on him.

Wright's, March 20, 1901 [Society for the Preservation of Carter Railroad Resources]

Fire became rain.

Shortly after Christmas, the Muir Brothers succeeded in completing the four-hundred-foot tunnel at Butte Cut on the Santa Cruz & Felton, only to have heavy rains topple the devil's slide down on top of the tunnel's southern portal, sealing the bore. The huge slide also closed the original SC&F alignment around the outside of the tunnel, trapping George Colegrove and his construction train on the Felton side. The slide was enormous, undermining a three-hundred-vertical-foot cross section of canyon wall that extended from the railroad up to the toll road above it. As the rains continued in late December and early January 1880, the devil's slide continued to live up to its name.

Colegrove's construction train worked the slide from the north side, pulling stumps and rocks with chain. A second work train, caught on the Santa Cruz side, cleared debris from the south. Colegrove remembered the intense management pressure to clear the blockade:

> They were rebuilding this part of the road from Felton Junction to Rincon. While rebuilding it, they had cut down a lot of the banks to widen the road. They came into the biggest slide you ever saw on a railroad. Mr. Bowen was superintendent at the time and Mr. Kern was superintendent of the telegraph. It was such a big job that he thought it needed someone on the job to rush it through. The two came there and tapped

the wires and connected them and stayed right on the job for seventeen days.[50]

Whether malaprop or malice, Colegrove confuses Thomas Carter, superintendent at the time of the slide, with F. W. Bowen, who would succeed Carter as superintendent in August 1880.[51] Out of his long-standing dislike of Carter, or from deference to the prejudices of Davis or Mix, Colegrove had begun to write Carter out of the rapidly unfolding climax of the construction of the railroad. His selective memory continued to perpetuate the error for the next six months of his narrative. It appeared that the closer Carter actually got to Colegrove's organization, the more aggressively Colegrove banished him from the story.

Ironically, Colegrove's narrative reveals evidence that Carter was willing to resort to heroics to fulfill his role. In the preceding quote, Colegrove is describing seventeen days that Carter (not Bowen) spent in a six-foot-square telegrapher's shack suspended on an unstable ledge some 150 feet above the raging San Lorenzo River, barely out of range of the worst landslide on the railroad, in more or less a constant downpour. If indeed it was Carter who supervised the work at the devil's slide, then Colegrove has helped build a case that Carter was effectively leading a united organization, personally managing the movement of trains and men through the brutal geography of the Santa Cruz Mountains. It was critical turf for Carter to win before opening the completed railroad, visibility that would position him, finally, to manage the operation of the entire South Pacific Coast. Colegrove continued to narrate the battle of the devil's slide:

> We had about fifty men and two work trains. I was on the Felton side and the other crew was caught on the Santa Cruz side. We were pulling big stumps and boulders that came down out of the slide. As they got it pretty well cleaned out that night it came into rain, or rather they discovered that the bank away up above 300 feet or more had broke loose and there was a big crack. This water that night ran into it and they were afraid it would cave in. They had a watchman there all the time. Sure enough, they had the road open just one day and the trains on this side and the freight train passed through to Santa Cruz. It [the slide] came in that next night and blocked it again. We were seventeen days more opening it again. That time I was caught on the Santa Cruz side and could be home nights.[52]

The *Santa Cruz Sentinel* corroborated most of Colegrove's story, suggesting, however, that the closures may have lasted longer than Colegrove remembered. From the first indications of trouble at the devil's slide, noted by the paper on December 27, it was almost three full months before the *Sentinel* reported the blockade broken.

The paper acknowledged the breakthrough on Sunday, March 21. By rotating the line's two locomotives, nine trains, each heavily loaded with lime and lumber, escaped from the Felton flume yard that day and made it safely down the canyon to Santa Cruz.[53]

On April 2, although no mention was made of the devil's slide, the *Sentinel* noted that a locomotive, apparently one of the SC&F's Porters, hit a log somewhere in the canyon, disabling itself. In the same article, the *Sen-*

tinel reported the first use of South Pacific Coast's one spot, perhaps as replacement power for the crippled Porter. The story may testify to the first time a Baldwin machine operated over Santa Cruz & Felton right-of-way. The heavy engine's progress, however, was quickly curtailed. Storms continued to dump rain in the already saturated mountains. Rock again came avalanching down the devil's slide during the week of April 10, blocking the mouth of the new tunnel at Butte Cut and shutting the railroad down for the second time.

Storms continued through April, causing widespread damage across the mountains. Slides and treefall closed the track between Felton and Glenwood. Washouts undermined fill between Los Gatos and Alma. As late as May 1, seven hundred men, the majority Chinese, continued on the South Pacific Coast's construction payroll, suggesting that Davis was willing to risk violating the state constitution rather than jeopardize the opening of the railroad. One hundred fifty laborers, 21 percent of the force, were assigned to day and night shifts on the devil's slide, peeling back layers of rock like dead skin in the effort to clear the mouth of the Butte Cut tunnel. By that time, Carter's temporary telegraph post at the big slide would have been an active station for nearly six months.

During the long, wet winter he was in residence on the south end of the railroad, Tom Carter's most critical accomplishment was winning the trust of the men who had operated the Santa Cruz & Felton. He had personally gotten to know Porter, Green, Tucker, and Lorenzen. By standing sentry duty at the most hazardous spot on the railroad, Carter safeguarded the crews while they ran loads down the 137-foot Hogback grade—the steepest grade on the completed South Pacific Coast—without an accident.

Even in Colegrove's account, Carter was seen to reward his men for their performance. Referring to the time of transition to new management, Colegrove paraphrased compliments from the "Superintendent": "The superintendent gave me a pretty good record, saying that I was on that run for three years and a half and never had a wheel on the ground. I never broke drawhead or never had an accident for three years and a half. He thought that was a very good record for the way we had to do the work."[54]

Carter tendered promotions for the alumni of the pioneering short line. Coby Lorenzen earned his stripes as a fireman and later an engineer on the completed South Pacific Coast. Captain Garrett accepted the position of chief freight agent, departing Santa Cruz for a new home in San Francisco on April 24. His knowledge of the south end flume traffic would be invaluable in managing the flood of freight that the railroad would move northbound, once the big tunnel was finished. The day Garrett left Santa Cruz, Benjamin Charles Gadsby, painter of the first narrow gauge cars manufactured in Santa Cruz, finished lettering the South Pacific Coast express wagon that would soon serve the freight business of the completed railroad.[55] George Colegrove would be given a permanent position as a conductor on the South Pacific Coast, a promotion that Carter ultimately had to approve.

Yet bad blood lingered in the critical weeks that north end and south end crews first melded together as a team, revealed in jokes the northern road crews told at the expense of their south end counterparts, an unconscious

The Field Notebook: The Making of a Timetable

"Useful Information for Railway Men," a small engineering handbook published by Ramapo Wheel and Foundry in New York in 1880, contains an early example of a spreadsheet used as a prestudy for an operating timetable. A simplified example, based on only a portion of South Pacific Coast timetable no. 10 of 1881, is shown below. Time is plotted on the horizontal axis, and stations on the vertical (unlike our simplified example, the distance between rows would be made in proportion to the distance between stations). With this grid, a train movement is represented as a line whose slope is proportional to the train's speed. Southbound trains are plotted with a slope from upper left to lower right; northbound trains have the opposite slope.

This "operational diagram" was extremely useful for showing the meeting point of two trains (where two lines cross) and allows planning for the location of passing tracks. When the South Pacific Coast was planning its first operating timetable, a diagram such as this was likely used by Tom Carter as a development tool.

	3	4	5	6	7	8	9	A.M.
Station								Station
Alameda Pt.								Alameda Pt.
Park St.								Park St.
Mt. Eden								Mt. Eden
Alvarado								Alvarado
Newark								Newark
Alviso								Alviso
Agnews								Agnews
San Jose								San Jose
Los Gatos								Los Gatos
Alma								Alma
Wrights								Wrights
Glenwood								Glenwood
Felton								Felton
Big Trees								Big Trees
Summit								Summit
Santa Cruz								Santa Cruz
	3	4	5	6	7	8	9	A.M.

release of tension masking the joining of two dissimilar cultures. When twenty-two-ton Baldwins from the north end and ten-ton Porters from the south end finally began to mix on the sidings at Felton, the *Sentinel* reported crews exchanging invitations to race.[56] Colegrove, too, recalled an attitude of superiority from the first northern road crews he met on the job.

Perhaps the tension was a symptom of doubt—from Mix, Davis, or perhaps even Carter, apprehensive about the next disaster lurking in the mountain corridor, communicated through what indiscretion, what ill-advised display of anger or contempt, we can only guess. The reverse may have been true: perhaps Carter himself was finally exposed to Colegrove's resentment, no longer insulated behind an abstract organizational boundary line drawn through the summit tunnel. Intangible elements corroded team work: Colegrove's pride, Tom Carter's distrust of politics, Davis's insecurity around his own authority.

Two railroads became one. Sheltered from the spring storms, the two summit tunnel crews, Cornish on the north and Chinese on the south, finally blew a hole between their headings during the week of March 13. On Saturday, March 20, Ed Mix, Captain Garrett, C. B. Younger,[57] and a *Sentinel* reporter rode with a Santa Cruz & Felton engine crew to the south end of the tunnel. The March 27 *Sentinel* recorded their historic walk-through:

> after lighting candles, rolling up pants bottoms, expressing some misgivings . . . the yawning bore was entered, the explorers moving in single file. Some places were found to be dry, others wet, and once in a while feet were heard splashing in water four to ten inches deep. In one section the cross timbers in the bottom of the tunnel were seen to be broken, the pressure from the sides and top having been so great as to crack them off like pipe stems. But little lagging was found to be lacking. Tunnel 3 is a credit to E. H. Mix. He determined its length, located its portals, and fixed its grade. The center of the tunnel is 9 feet higher than the ends, furnishing drainage. The variation in line is one inch, the difference in length $1\,^3/_{10}$", while the grade is perfect. The tunnel took 27 months to complete, and was begun in December, 1877.

Mix, Garrett, Younger, the *Sentinel* reporter, and a passenger named F. Adams walked silently past the gas flame that still burned like a memorial in the center of the mountain.

At last, long strings of rolling stock, manufactured by Carter's own firm to designs he had drafted with his own hands, sat laden with timber and split stuff in the Felton flume yard. Two generations of Carter cars filled the sidings and house tracks, the new ten-ton-capacity designs and the older eight-ton cars built for the Santa Cruz & Felton five years earlier. The sc&f's 1876 coaches already looked anachronistic alongside the newer, longer duckbill models that had worked their way southward through the mountain barrier. The Felton yards, in the spring of 1880, housed a museum of Carter products and technology, as well as a showcase for its expanding product line. For the first time, through a complex schedule of Carter's own devising, the cars would move north, using the long tunnels to reach the San Francisco Bay Area over the shortest commercial link ever created between the two manufacturing regions.

Personally and professionally, Carter reestablished a presence in the small but commercially vibrant kingdom of Santa Cruz County. He regained ground ceded to local manufacturers in 1874, monopolizing the manufacture of rolling stock operating within county borders. His rival, Ed Mix, was scheduled to depart for Portland, Oregon, in early June 1880, when Tom Carter alone would manage the unified leases, mergers, and subsidiaries that made up the South Pacific Coast Railroad.

There is uncertainty about the date on which through freight trains began to roll under Carter's authority, but the *Sentinel* suggests that Monday, May 10, 1880, marked the first commercial through freight traffic over the South Pacific Coast.[58] Stray rainstorms persisted in the mountains, but the devil's slide had been stable for several weeks (a watchman, taking up the telegraph key where Tom Carter allegedly stationed himself, stood watch twenty-four hours a day) and the backlog of loads at Felton was filling the flume yard to overflowing. For the first time, the flume lumber traffic would move north, not south, under the authority of South Pacific Coast Employee Timetable number 6.[59]

Carter and Davis were spotted on the sidewalks of Santa Cruz on May 12, keeping a close eye on the crucial first few days of the start-up. Carter had given thought to the problem of mixing north and south crews. Freight operation, once it began, was choreographed to keep south end crews on the south, and north end crews on the north; it was a deliberate effort made to focus the experience where it was needed. The meeting point, as Colegrove explained, was Glenwood, roughly the midpoint in the mountains:

> We got the track all in shape and the slides all cleaned out and opened her up on the fifteenth of May, 1880. All trains started out on time. We had our time cards. Every fellow was on the job. They gave me the Santa Cruz to Felton local. That was the train that ran from Santa Cruz up to Felton and took what freight there was. Our work was to switch out all the loads that were going west and take them around to New Felton. Then we would couple in with the freight train, the new freight train, and help them up to Glenwood. Then we would take all the empty cars we could find at Glenwood that the other train had brought up and left there. We would fetch them down and distribute them in the Felton yard so they could be loaded. In the afternoon we would switch out what freight there was for Santa Cruz. We would leave there about half past four for Santa Cruz and had about another hour of switching to do. My train was a mixed train between Santa Cruz and Felton, freight and passenger. On Sundays it was a straight passenger train. It made two round-trips to the Big Trees and back every Sunday.[60]

Colegrove's assigned train was still using the SC&F's tiny Porter, Bell engines when this tour of duty started. Primarily a switching assignment, Colegrove's crew could easily make up trains with a light engine in the Felton yard, awaiting the arrival of a heavier Baldwin road engine to boost the assembled string up to Glenwood   with Colegrove's engine acting as a helper on

Stately caboose 3 was built by Carter in 1880 to meet the demands of heavy freight service in the Santa Cruz Mountains. Except for its roof-mounted marker lamp, the car is almost indistinguishable from a combination passenger-baggage car. Caboose 3 was photographed in San Jose in 1904. [Ken Lorenzen collection]

the rear of the train. But the rise in elevation between Glenwood and the summit tunnel was just ten feet, making the drainage gradient in the tunnels (fifteen feet rise per mile) the steepest grade remaining to be overcome.[61] Early northbound freights departing Glenwood for San Jose routinely handled the combined loads singleheaded.

For example, during the week of May 16, 1880, forty-seven loaded cars left Glenwood behind a solitary Baldwin 4-4-0; this was a remarkable feat, even considering the light gradient. If its cars had been loaded to just 50 percent of their rated capacity, such a train weighed at least 500 tons. On a grade of twenty feet to the mile, just slightly steeper than the gradients in the tunnels, Baldwin rated a narrow gauge 8-18 C class locomotive at 310 tons maximum load.[62] Handling such a train through the twin summit tunnels required skill, and a certain amount of luck.

It was like railroading inside a sewer pipe. That May, rains saturated the mountains, penetrating deep into reservoirs of decomposed rock. Even after the storms cleared, the land remained full. Long, heavy freight trains, struggling up to the mouth of summit tunnel on dry rail, entered a cavity that, in the dim light of the oil headlamp, appeared to be awash from thousands of broken shower heads dripping from its vaulted ceiling.

Like trying to gain traction on sheet ice, the engine's wheels slipped wildly on wet rail. Shutting down the throttle with his left hand, the engineer had to reach for the sand valve with his right, inching it open, timing the sand to start pouring in front of the drivers just a moment after the power was shut off. The sequence of his moves was critical. Sand hitting the rail in front of a spinning driver could cause the wheel to grab the rail on a power stroke, shattering the wheel's spoked casting. The engineer knew the correct sequence like breathing: throttle in, sander out. Briefly, in between sand and throttle, he would feel the machine relax. Slowly, a notch at a time, he widened the throttle back out. Feeling the power return to the cylinders, he listened for the sharp cutoff in the sound of the exhaust that would tell him the wheels had locked onto the rail, grabbing briefly to walk the train forward, only to spin wildly out of control again, and again.

Pulling the throttle in and out like a trombone, the engineer hunted for a sweet spot where throttle, Johnson bar, and sand all magically balanced, preserving what little adhesion was left. But on wet rail, the sweet spot was elusive. Moving at ten miles per hour when it entered the tunnel, the forward speed of the train quickly eroded to eight miles an hour, then five, then barely a walk. A thousand feet into the tunnel, daylight no longer penetrated, which forced the fireman to reconnoiter their forward speed by holding a brakeman's lantern up to the passing bulwark of timber.

Freight conductor at Felton, 1904. [Ken Lorenzen collection]

The locomotive's fire began to throb as the engine slipped, drafting hot gases through the flues like a blowtorch. Already operating very close to its maximum pressure, the boiler inched toward supercritical. Safety valves, lifting at about one hundred and sixty pounds of pressure, erupted like the lower registers of a pipe organ, the sound literally turning to vibration deep in the vertebrae. The real danger was now the risk of losing volumes of live steam, and power, out the safety valves at the moment the engineer needed them the most.

The monkey shifted to the fireman's back. Unable to reduce the mass of burning firewood, the fireman struggled to cool the boiler. First, he increased the flow of water coming from the crosshead pumps. But as speed dropped, so did the volume of water the pumps could supply, until the pumping pressure was no longer adequate to force water through the boiler's check valves.

In desperation, the fireman resorted to the engine's single injector, a Sellers number 3, mounted on the engineer's side of the boiler. The injector was optional equipment on Baldwin locomotives of the period, regarded as experimental by engine crews; designed as a supplement to the engine's crosshead pumps, it was intended for use when the engine was standing still. To crack the injector open when the engine was moving, the engineer or fireman would have to open the starting valve and then crank out the steam feed, counting on the device to prime and inject. If the prime failed, the process would have to be repeated, the fireman straining to hear the whomp of cold water propelled through the injector's nozzle. Watching the steam gauge drop, struggling to regain balance between fire, feedwater, and throttle, the fireman felt as if he were riding on the back of a barely controlled explosion.

As the speed eroded even further, draft through the firebox began to reverse its flow, sucking dark, sulfurous smoke back into the cab through the firebox door. Wreaths of black smoke from the stack curled back over the engine, wrapping it in a dense dark cloud trapped in back of a cylinder of air compressed by the hydraulic action of the entire train, stroking like a giant piston into the bore of the tunnel. There was little choice but to go on. Breathing through their handkerchiefs, running blind into a ball of smoke lit from the inside by the engine's headlight, the crew stuck to their posts as the engine clawed its way up the twenty-seven hundred feet of upgrade to the center of the tunnel and the summit of the railroad.

There, in the middle of the mountain, the gas lamp that marked the 1879 tunnel disaster would appear out of the stinking darkness like a lighthouse, identifying the top of the climb in the pale fire of the mountain's own furnace. One by one, the cars crossed over the top, their slack turning and running back into the locomotive, registering in the engineer's backbone like a drum solo.

Thus the South Pacific Coast moved the loads north.

There was, briefly, euphoria in Santa Cruz. On Sunday, May 9, 1880, the Reverend Trefren, pastor of the Methodist Church, delivered a lecture on "The opening of the South Pacific Coast, its influence on the financial, social and moral interests of Santa Cruz."

The railroad's financial influence was certainly positive. Alfred Davis announced, during the same week, that he was raising the wages of white railroad laborers from $1.75 a day to $2.00 a day, and that no Chinese need apply. During the week of May 22, he announced a reduction of the tariff on lime from forty-two cents a barrel (the old rate by steamer) to thirty-six cents a barrel by train.

An emissary from the town, blacksmith Elihu Anthony, approached Davis about a celebratory banquet.

During the same week, the city of Hollister also sent an emissary, seeking commitment from Davis to extend the narrow gauge mainline through the Salinas Valley in exchange for a promise to ship Hollister's grain by narrow gauge for the next five years.

A stage coach, the last "probably forever," the *Sentinel* eulogized, arrived in Santa Cruz from San Jose on May 14. Duncan McPherson could hardly believe the words he saw printed in his own paper.

It was noted in later testimony that Robert Elliott's train broke in two not once but twice on the mountain grade that Sunday morning. A passenger on board described the hair-raising experience in the *Watsonville Transcript* of May 25:

> Going up from San Jose in the morning we ran very fast, considering what curves are made. Once the coupling between two of the flat-cars was broken and the strain came on the two chains which extended between them. This soon split the timbers of the end of the car and let the car loose. The train was stopped and the trouble fixed up. Before we

reached the picnic ground another car was partly torn off in the same manner.

Elliott's train ran doubleheaded from Alameda, Baldwin number 9 coupled to Elliott's own Baldwin number 3. The doubleheader led a picnic special destined for Big Trees near Felton, carrying members of the San Francisco Independent Rifles.

From such testimony, evidence mounted that Robert Elliott was unfamiliar with the handling of trains on the mountain. "A temperate man, a few years short of thirty," the *Sentinel* later indicated, Elliott had been an engineer on the north end of the South Pacific Coast for four years. But that Sunday, May 23, 1880, was his first trip to Felton, and apparently his first solo with a locomotive on the mountain grade. Tom Carter was in Felton that afternoon, and an inquiry into the break-in-two, if it occurred, would have taken place shortly after Elliott's train arrived. No mention was made in the newspaper that management was even aware of the mishap.

George Colegrove, meanwhile, recalled nearly forty years later that he arrived in Felton at 9:30 in the morning on his regular run, the Santa Cruz & Felton Local, train 18. Colegrove remembered that his train, powered by one of the ten-ton SC&F Porter, Bell locomotives, sat on a siding at Felton after completing its switching. It ran as a mixed train, and on this day, anticipating overflow picnic crowds, Colegrove carried two coaches in his consist.

Colegrove and his engineer, William Porter, expected to take the local back to Santa Cruz at 3:30 P.M., departing southbound as regular train number 29. There was a long midday lull in between arrival and departure times. Local Santa Cruz picnickers recalled seeing Porter in the Big Tree grove at lunch time, mingling with the crowd. Also around noon, Bob Elliott's train pulled into the siding next to Colegrove's local. The doubleheader then split into two sections. Engine 9 would take the coaches and a few members of the Independent Rifles to Santa Cruz. Elliott's engine, number 3, would stay with the flatcars in Felton, awaiting the return of the 9 that afternoon.

Sometime after twelve, Colegrove received news of a change in plans. New orders were issued, probably while Colegrove and Elliott sat next to each other on adjoining Felton sidings. George Colegrove kept a copy of the new train order in his personal effects for the rest of his life, perhaps as proof that he bore no responsibility for what followed, the infamous event of Sunday, May 23, 1880, that would become known as the Powder Mill wreck.

The new orders made it clear that Colegrove would no longer command train 29. Instead, the order required Colegrove and Porter to take their locomotive and coaches back to Santa Cruz later in the evening. Colegrove's original train number, and departure time, were given to Elliott.

The order was signed simply "Colegrove" and "Wm R. Porter," but in addition it bore the countersignature "Correct T.C.," indicating that Tom Carter had personally seen and approved the change. Carter's initials are strong evidence that he was sitting by the telegraph key in the Felton depot when the order came through the wire from the dispatcher in Alameda. It also suggests (although it does not prove) that Carter orchestrated the switch.

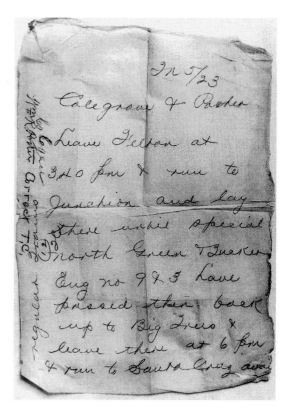

Train order issued to Conductor George Colegrove and Engineer Bill Porter on May 23, 1880, prior to the catastrophic "opening day wreck." Tom Carter initialed the order on the left edge. [George Hildebrand collection]

Terrible and Fatal Railroad Accident near Santa Cruz, May 23, 1890.

Artist's recreation of the "opening day wreck," in the San Lorenzo River Gorge near the site of the Powder Works, May 23, 1880. Eyewitness reports suggest that the artist drew on factual accounts in reconstructing details of the wreck, including South Pacific Coast number 3 running backward—a dangerous practice for a 4-4-0. [University of California, Santa Cruz, Special Collections]

In his *Life Story*, Colegrove pointedly blamed the dispatcher, physically located in Alameda, for the change, but he also implicated the rivalry that existed between crews from the north and south:

> Mr. Dispatcher [A. H. Walker], thought he was going to save maybe ten cents or so, so he sent orders to this new crew to run in my place down to Santa Cruz in the afternoon . . . in place of letting me and my crew and the two coaches go, they let this other crew go, who had never been over the road at all . . . they got the orders and read them. This other . . . crew from the other side was kind of inclined to make fun of us. We had a smaller engine than they had and they had been working a little longer on [the north] side and they were a little more experienced.[63]

Colegrove also offered what could be the only real clue about why the change was made. His Porter, Bell engine was too light to help the Independent Rifles special back up the grade from Santa Cruz to Felton. Without the help of engine 3, which was at that moment sitting on the siding at Felton, Elliott's original train was stuck in Santa Cruz at the bottom of the Hogback grade. Colegrove second-guessed Walker's mistake: "What they should have done was to deadhead that engine [number 3] down there to help the excursion train up and let us run our own train on our time. The accident would not have happened."[64]

Newspaper accounts verify that Tom Carter remained at Felton as the afternoon wore on.[65] But Colegrove minimized Carter's role; in fact, he erased him entirely from the story, which is the second unexplained mystery in the events surrounding May 23. Instead of deferring to the highest authority in the railroad's operating department (its superintendent), Colegrove suggested that he personally took matters in his own hands to protect the safety of his regular train.

Colegrove's version began with an interrogation. Colegrove asked Elliott's conductor, Sam Bones, if he had ever been down the Hogback grade. Bones answered that he had not. Colegrove then remembered lecturing Bones about the dangers of the grade. He finally insisted that he himself—not Walker and not Carter—asked his brakeman, Howard Antrim (whose name is also spelled Anthrum in newspaper accounts) to accompany Elliott on his engine as a pilot.

Using an experienced pilot was a common management prerogative, done deliberately to familiarize a new train crew on the mile-by-mile realities of an unfamiliar stretch of track. Given the last-minute switch in orders, it seems unreasonable that Colegrove would have taken this kind of supervisorial responsibility, with the railroad's superintendent present. Where was Tom Carter? What did he say to Colegrove? Why didn't Colegrove mention Carter anywhere in the three double-spaced, typed pages he devoted to describing the events of May 23?

Far from being absent from the scene, Tom Carter was sitting by the Felton depot telegraph at the same moment Colegrove himself was sitting by the Felton depot telegraph, thirty seconds before 4:00 P.M., when news of the disaster reached Felton from Santa Cruz. Minutes later, Tom Carter, Bill Porter, and station agent Joe Aram commandeered Colegrove's locomotive and raced down the San Lorenzo River Canyon to be first on the scene. If Carter was indeed present throughout the afternoon, was it Carter, not Walker, who took away Colegrove's normal assignment? Did Colegrove remember, and hold against Carter, the rebuff of his first application for work in 1879? Was the resentment shared by Carter, forming the basis for a grudge? Did they fight? Why, simply, did Colegrove erase Carter so completely from any kind of presence that day—including a presence he could later have blamed for what happened?

Colegrove claimed he was in the Felton depot at thirty seconds before 4:00 P.M., and that he remembered the time because it "lacked seven minutes and a half of my train being due in Santa Cruz," which would have described train 29, the Santa Cruz & Felton Mixed, scheduled to arrive at the downtown Santa Cruz depot at 4:07 P.M. But at that exact moment, neither was George Colegrove where he was supposed to be. The train order he signed specified he should be waiting for the return of the double-header at "the Junction," two miles west of Felton station, departing Felton under orders at 3:40 P.M. But in his memoirs, he stuck to a contradicting story, insisting he was in the Felton depot, sitting in a chair next to operator Aram, when the fateful message came through at precisely thirty seconds before 4 P.M. Why would he sign an order he didn't follow?[66]

Robert Elliott, meanwhile, was preparing to depart Felton with Baldwin number 3, running tender-first for Santa Cruz with the remaining three flatcars from the Independent Rifles special. It was commonly accepted practice in railroading that an American-type locomotive was not to be run backwards for any distance, with any load, especially through tight curves. Lacking a rear trailing truck, the 4-4-0 format had no provision for guiding its driving wheels around a curve when running in reverse, thus risking derailment. The mistake nearly cost Elliott his life.

Obvious risks clearly were being taken, yet no one besides Colegrove seemed aware of the danger. Sam Davis (President Davis's nephew) climbed onto the cab of Elliott's engine for the ride into Santa Cruz; evidence of young Davis's confidence in the safety of the operation.

What really went wrong after Elliott departed Big Trees with some three hundred picnic goers, moving into the sultry depths of the San Lorenzo River Canyon? Testimony suggests Elliott left Felton on time, and passengers remember nothing unusual about the train's speed until it reached the top of the Hogback, marked by a short tunnel. The *Watsonville Transcript* continued its May 25 report:

> About the middle of the tunnel the speed perceptibly increased and I exclaimed "Good God! . . . is the engineer crazy? If he goes at this rate we'll have a smash-up, sure. The cars were swaying then so that it was impossible to stand still on them and they were so crowded that many were standing between the seats. As we emerged from the tunnel we struck a sharp curve. The engineer whistled "down brakes," but the brakemen had to collect fares and were away from the brakes, and before they could reach them the front end of the second car left the track, turning to the right against the bank.

A mile of steep downgrade separated the tunnel from the site of the derailment, and in the estimated minute and a half it took the train to descend the mile, Elliott became fully aware that he had a runaway on his hands. Yet witnesses agreed that the critical signal, one short blast demanding down brakes, was not heard until the train almost reached the bottom of the mile-long descent, nearly out of control.

Elliott remembered that he called for brakes twice, once when he exited the tunnel and once near the bottom of the mile-long descent, when, he testified, "I repeated the signal, with the same unsatisfactory result." If they heard the signals, the brakemen were unable to squeeze past the standing crowds to reach the brake wheels in time. Accelerating rapidly, the train shot across the wagon road above the Powder Works, and into a series of reverse curves. As the engine pitched into a thirteen degree curve to the left, Elliott felt a violent shudder run through his locomotive. "The engine seemed to lift itself," he later described the sensation. Desperate to regain control, he managed to seize the reverse lever and pull it back, sending the engine's drivers into a backwards spin. The engine settled back onto the track, narrowly avoiding going over on its side. But either the engine's momentum or the action of reversing on a downgrade may also have caused the poorly ballasted track to shift under the heaving weight, kinking the rail at a joint. Somehow Elliott's engine traversed the kink; the flatcars behind did not. The first car derailed, hitting the rocky bank to the right of the train. The impact sheered off the side sill and probably the intermediate sill of the flatcar, letting passengers plummet through the disintegrating floor. The impact sent most of the passengers on the second flatcar flying through the makeshift railing, and into a rock wall. With both of its trucks still on the rails, unable to stop, the third flatcar plowed through the stunned and prostrated passengers left scattered on the tracks from the first two cars, maiming, mutilating, and killing.

It took Elliott's engine between three hundred and five hundred feet to stop, dragging the remains of the train behind it. Howard Antrim raced back on foot to assess the damage. Horror-struck by what he saw, he returned to tell Elliott they must go for help. Antrim uncoupled the engine, and jumped into the cab. They were at the downtown Santa Cruz depot before 4:00 P.M. Thirty seconds before four, lacking seven minutes and a half of the scheduled arrival time of train 29, the Santa Cruz operator was telegraphing the message that Colegrove, Aram, and Carter picked up in the Felton depot— proof, in Colegrove's mind, of "how fast they were going."

Commandeering Colegrove's locomotive, with William Porter at the throttle, within minutes Aram and Carter appeared at the wreck site. One of the three, likely Aram, climbed the nearest telegraph pole, spliced a portable key into the wire, and sent messages to the Alameda dispatcher for a relief train. Aram then telegraphed to Colegrove, still at the Felton depot, to bring bridge gangs down to clean up the wreck. Many of the laborers were still at the Big Tree grove, celebrating with the Independent Rifles. Colegrove tried not to spread alarm as he quietly asked them to come along.

An almost manic energy followed the accident. A relief train, with Elliott at the throttle, brought doctors from Santa Cruz. Crowds gathered at grade crossings and at the depot, frantic to know the fate of friends or loved ones. The Santa Cruz skating rink became a temporary morgue. The Ocean House, Wilkins House, and the Germania Hotel became hospitals for the injured. By eight that evening, acting County Coroner John Davenport convened an inquest at the skating rink, asking a hastily convened jury to view the bodies and prepare for a weeklong hearing to determine cause of death. The initial death toll thus became known that night. Fifteen passengers died at the site. Fifty more were seriously injured.

That night, Colegrove and his crew labored by torch and lantern to clean up traces of the wreck. They had nearly finished their labors by nine in the evening, when the Independent Rifles special crept slowly past the wreck site on its way north. By the next morning, little sign of the wreck remained. Photographic evidence suggests that Colegrove's crew left the track in better condition than it was in before the incident. By the time Coroner Davenport's jury visited the site on Monday, bringing along a photographer, the two-inch kink in the rails was nowhere to be seen, and the track had even been completely ballasted, thus making it impossible to verify the physical evidence that witnesses would later testify they observed immediately after the wreck.

Still, Davenport's jury patiently listened to testimony and gathered evidence for nearly a week after the accident. It finally returned a verdict on Monday, May 31. In fact, the jury returned three separate, contradictory opinions. The fragmented and incomplete evidence divided the jurors. There were few answers to the unresolved mysteries, only a growing consensus that human error had played a decisive role in the catastrophe. The

[Top left two photographs, Alan Young collection; others, William Wulf collection]

majority of the jury attributed the wreck to "unforeseen causes, and that the same are to us unknown," in essence failing to find blame. A single juror, Benjamin Knight, faulted engineer Robert Elliott for incompetent handling of the locomotive. But three others, influential members of the Santa Cruz community, placed the blame on Thomas Carter, finding "that the General Superintendent of the road is blamable for the make up of the train, and entrusting the same to young men, and to some extent inexperienced, neither of whom in the discharge of such duties had before passed over that section of the road."

The minority report was endorsed by jury member Elihu Anthony, who, just two weeks before, had approached Alfred Davis with a community invitation to a banquet, intended to celebrate the opening of the South Pacific Coast.

Instead of the banquet, funerals and lawsuits followed.

No known transcript of the inquest survived, in which Thomas Carter might have been heard to speak in his own defense. His testimony in front of the coroner's jury, although referred to by the local newspaper coverage of the investigation, was not directly quoted, nor was he apparently interviewed by the press following the adverse finding of the jury. Davis remained in town for at least a week to attend to what today would be called damage control, and here and there in the *Sentinel*, in the testimony of railroad men at the inquest, can be heard Davis's influence and money at work. The railroad, for example, picked up all funeral and embalming expenses for the dead, the hotel bills for the injured, and their transportation back to their homes. Much was made of the fact that Davis's nephew had voluntarily ridden in the cab of Elliott's locomotive, a sign of trust and assurance that the president's family believed in the safety of the railroad and continued to after the disaster (although none aboard the locomotive cab suffered any injuries).

As June began, the story rippled through San Francisco papers and even-

The Santa Cruz County coroner's jury, convening at the site of the "opening day wreck" one day after it occurred, brought with it an unidentified photographer, who recorded the stereopticon images (opposite and above). The railroad appears to have cooperated with the jury's investigation, spotting locomotive number 3 on the curve where Engineer Elliott had stopped the runaway (above). The photographs also show evidence that the railroad may have hastily reworked the track after the wreck, erasing evidence of a kink in the rail. [Above, Alan Young collection]

tually to the *Sacramento Record-Union,* which was owned by Stanford interests and which chastised not only the South Pacific Coast but the whole principle of narrow gauge railroad design: "We have already intimated a doubt as to the safety of travel on narrow gauge railroads, where the curves are sharp and frequent.[67]

But none of the accounts dwelled on Thomas Carter, or attempted to interview him, or even interviewed others about him.

For ten weeks after the wreck, he vanished from the news. Then, without a word of explanation or display of self-vindication in any known published account, Thomas Carter quietly resigned the superintendency of the South Pacific Coast on August 18, 1880.

Less than two weeks later, his brother Martin resigned the position of master mechanic.

Like the wooden ship's spar in the novel *Billy Budd,* the telegraph pole that Joe Aram climbed on Sunday, May 23, 1880, remained something of a landmark in the depths of the San Lorenzo River Canyon. As with the relic of the hanging of the young foretopman in Herman Melville's story, the telegraph pole marked the scene of a tragedy and the loss of innocence for the world that remained behind—the beneficiary, and victim, of the increasing velocity of life.

Years later, Santa Cruz residents who barely remembered the wreck would pass by the aging redwood pole on a train and hear someone in the coach remark about the deaths of friends or loved ones at the site. Perhaps the storytellers themselves were unsure of the details; perhaps they assigned to the square wooden beam the role of solitary witness in the deep, cloud-wreathed gorge of the San Lorenzo.

J. J. Riley's stereopticon image (above) of South Pacific Coast number 13 in Los Gatos Canyon, ca. 1882. The image is reproduced from an original print, clear enough to show the railroad's stone retaining wall, built near creek level. Below: Los Gatos Creek trestles, and the Alma depot, were photographed in the same canyon. [Above, John Hemmann collection; below left: Bob Dockery collection]

The earliest known images of the mountain out-post of Wrights are the upper two photographs on this page, taken by Frank Rodolf prior to July 4, 1885, when a fire destroyed "old Wrights," located on the east bank of Los Gatos Creek. The panorama below was also taken before the fire; it shows little development of commercial business on the west bank of the creek, near the depot, water tank, and tunnel. [Above and right, Bancroft Library; below, William Wulf collection]

By the time of the 1890s panorama at the left, "new Wrights" was flourishing on the west bank of Los Gatos Creek, providing a town site for two hotels and a general mercantile store in addition to the railroad facilities. Fruit dryers and vintners, in the surrounding hills, teamed their produce to the railhead at Wrights for loading into narrow gauge combination boxcars. [This page, Bob Dockery collection]

In the late 1870s, freight operations on the South Pacific Coast used Glenwood yards as a marshaling point for carloads of lime, lumber, and produce coming from the flume yard at Felton, the Santa Cruz yards, the California Powder Works, or Doherty's Lumber Mill. Short trains of loaded cars— four, five, or six at a time—were moved up the steep mainline grade north of Felton (shown below in 1904) or the even steeper grade up the San Lorenzo River Canyon and assembled at an elevation of 891 feet above sea level in the Glenwood yards, shown in the panorama at the top about 1885. From Glenwood, the summit of the railroad was just 3 1/2 miles north and twenty-five feet higher in elevation, making it an easy climb for freight trains moving Santa Cruz County products to the north. From the beginning, northbound freights out of Glenwood were singleheaded. [Top, Rick Hamman collection; below and opposite below, Ken Lorenzen collection]

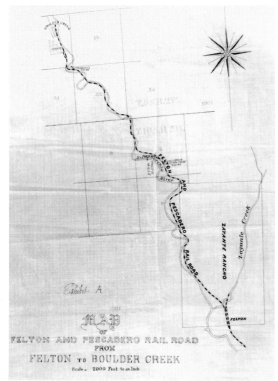

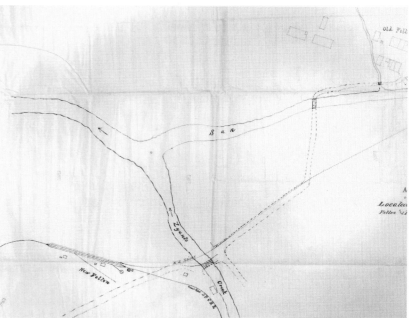

An aging relic by 1884, the original Santa Cruz & Felton flume was torn down and replaced by the Boulder Creek Branch, a winding, seven-mile-long extension of the mainline at Felton, shown in the maps above and on the facing page. The tiny Santa Cruz & Felton locomotive *Felton*, however, lived on as the Boulder Creek switch engine and was soon dwarfed by newer narrow gauge Baldwin locomotives (top). [Top, Ken Lorenzen collection; both maps, Museum of Art and History, Santa Cruz]

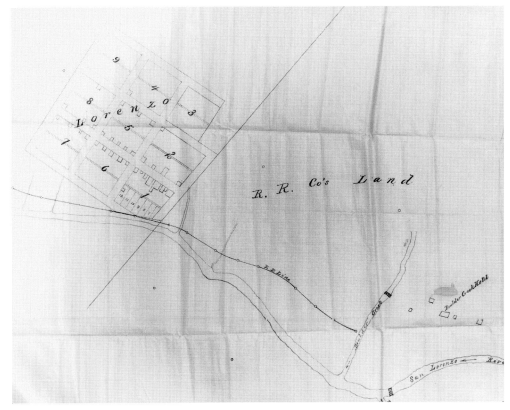

Second-generation narrow gauge
locomotives, such as South Pacific
Coast number 13 (above), set
records for moving freight out of
the Santa Cruz Mountains. In
1902, the 13 led seventy-two cars
downgrade from Boulder Creek
to Felton, the longest train ever
operated on the railroad and a testimonial both to the railroad's
physical plant and the crews that
operated it. Routinely, the largest
engines took a single cut of cars
from Felton to Glenwood and continued on with the section to San
Jose in a train known to crews as
the Boulder Creek night freight.
[Above, John Schmale collection;
below, Museum of Art and History, Santa Cruz]

The San Lorenzo River Bridge, near Felton, marked the southernmost point where South Pacific Coast civil engineers surveyed a high-performance right-of-way, including grades of 90 feet per mile and curves of 360-foot radius; south of the bridge, the SPC was forced to adopt grades and curves of the Santa Cruz & Felton, including 137 feet per mile and curves of 250-foot radius, artifacts of an earlier generation of rail-roading. The Howe truss bridge was built to South Pacific Coast design by the Pacific Bridge Co. in 1879. [Below, Frank Rodolph photograph, ca. 1885, Bancroft Library]

—⊱ VIEWS of the SOUTH PACIFIC COAST RAILROAD. ⊰—

South Pacific Coast promotion became a powerful incentive for patronage through lithographs such as the one above, entitled "View of SPCRR, 1882," from *The Wasp* of December 22; the direct result were long picnic trains parked on the Gharkey pier in Santa Cruz, the first practical day trips from San Francisco to the beach at Santa Cruz. [Above, Bancroft Library; right, John Schmale collection]

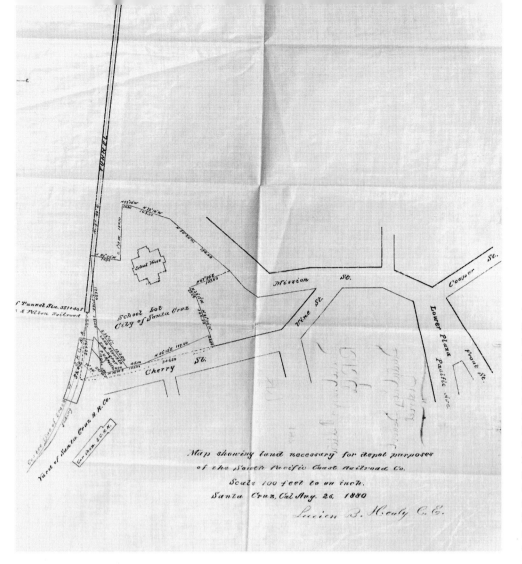

Map showing land necessary for depot purposes
of the South Pacific Coast Railroad Co.
Scale 100 feet to an inch.
Santa Cruz, Cal Aug. 26, 1880
Lucien B. Healy C. E.

The final architectural flourish in the South Pacific Coast's southern expansion was the Santa Cruz arcade depot, a miniaturized version of the larger covered depots of San Jose, Newark, and Alameda. Lucien Healy, the Santa Cruz & Felton's original chief engineer, filed the location map for the depot in August 1880, just three months after the South Pacific Coast was opened. Photographs of the depot are rare, but the view below, taken from inside the cavernous shed, shows a sample of its architectural detail against the backdrop of the Mission Hill Tunnel. The tunnel itself was engineered by Healy in 1876. [Left, ink-on-linen map, Museum of Art and History, Santa Cruz]

flatcars and one passenger car for the second—hardly a windfall.[4] Any business that advertised "Special Attention given to Narrow Gauge Work" was, in 1880, not exactly cutting edge—a failure of Carter's original business plan to address dramatically changing conditions in the railroad supply market as the decade of the 1880s began.

What we know about Carter Brothers during this pivotal period comes not from authoritative factory records but from a patchwork of newspaper stories, government reports, the files of customers, and—in one important case—the exaggerated testimony of Thomas Carter himself. At best, the sources are fragments of a complete picture. The *Newark Enterprise,* for example, which was launched during the wave of optimism that greeted the town's beginnings as an industrial center, was in operation for less than six months. In June 1880, it suspended publication. One single issue of the *Enterprise* survives. From this issue, and from scraps of reassembled records, we glimpse Carter's business in rapid transition. Tom Carter's subscription biography, published in Lewis's *Bay of San Francisco,* boasted that the decade of the eighties began with "the biggest single order" of Carter cars, 175 freight cars ordered by the three-foot-gauge Oregonian Railroad. But the contract has yet to be documented in another source, leaving its superlatives open to question and its role in Carter Brothers survival perhaps another example of Thomas Carter's gift for hyperbole.

In truth, large orders were few and far between. The South Pacific Coast, for example, eventually added more than two hundred additional Carter freight cars and thirty Carter passenger cars to its 1880 total, but it took six years to do so. More typical was the short line work for the San Joaquin & Sierra Nevada Railroad, an initial order Carter filled for fifty-two freight cars and one caboose in 1882, delivered at Lodi, California. So parsimonious was this short line that instead of buying passenger cars from Carter Brothers, it simply converted one of the flatcars to a coach using its own shop at Woodbridge, California, ordering window blinds from Carter in an apparently misbegotten attempt to save money.

In 1883, shortly after the Lodi work, a new competitor, John Hammond, opened the California Car Works in San Francisco and ended the period of Carter's unique West Coast monopoly.

It took a certain amount of boldness, creativity, and imagination to bolster the good name of Carter Brothers, not to mention its credit rating, in such a business environment. Smaller, more specialized market segments were courted, including logging equipment, horse cars, cable cars and electric cars, and by 1882 cars for the offshore trade. The earliest known example of Carter foreign sales occurred in the summer of 1882, when thirty boxcars, five flatcars, and three passenger cars were kitted for the Champerico & Northern Transportation Co. of Guatemala.[5] Orders for the Hawaiian Islands occurred at about the same time, including the magnificent chair car *Pearl.* John Carroll's early guidance in kit manufacturing eventually lit the trail to Mexican markets, although no reliable chronology for this business has ever been established.

As the Carter Brothers business matured, so did a spare parts aftermarket, swelled by logging lines in need of replacement parts and castings required for home-built disconnect trucks. Standard gauge clients were found, including the California Southern and the Eel River & Eureka. Carter Brothers diversified into real estate, buying parcels of land in the New Almaden area in 1887, as the South Pacific Coast extended a branch line southward from Campbell.

Much of this new business bears the earmark of Thomas Carter's instinct and stamina. But it was Martin who may have kept Carter Brothers alive long enough for Thomas to get a new grip on the handlebars. Plant records extant from the 1890s show Carter Brothers doing millwork, interior molding, scrollsawing, window casings, door sash, and table legs for furniture—all for local businesses, schools, and residences within Washington Township. Within a radius of four or five miles from the Newark plant, Martin found customers for shop time. Just as the Central Pacific Sacramento shop had turned banisters for the state capitol when railroad work went slack, Martin Carter filled the needs of the local building trade, using the same craftsmen he relied on to build rolling stock. A "ranch" account was a permanent line item in the car shop books, recording shop time put into carpentry for the Nutwood Stock Farm. Unfortunately, these plant records do not cover the years before 1898, but they do suggest a pattern of activity dating from the early years of the Newark shop. Martin's Irvington home may have been built by car shop craftsmen in 1881. The water tank that sat in back of the house bears an uncanny resemblance to the narrow gauge water tanks seen on the South Pacific Coast, North Pacific Coast, and Nevada County Narrow Gauge. Martin became his own customer. Probably on a shoestring, and even more likely on Martin's own cash reserves, the plant stayed open.

Again, what facts illuminate Thomas and Martin's relationship during this period come not from contemporary letters or diaries but from publications of a later period. By 1896, the *San Francisco Call* was having a field day with the details of a hot and cold romance between Thomas and Mollie Redmond, a seamstress Carter met during his seclusion following the Santa Cruz wreck. The press described Mollie as "a plump and pretty brunette" and as a practical business woman whose relationship with Thomas had, by the late 1890s, deteriorated to lawsuits filed for breach of promise of marriage.[6]

By the time of the sensational press, Thomas Carter and Mollie Redmond had struggled with the off-and-on relationship for almost fifteen years (accounts varied), meeting for the first time in perhaps 1880 or 1881. At the time, Carter had just turned forty. Mollie was a worldly twenty-four.[7] The couple courted in the quiet retreat of Byron Hot Springs, a mineral bath and resort near Livermore where Carter retired to soak his leg and his bruised ego. The only commercial health resort operating near the Bay Area, Byron Hot Springs was a three-hour train ride from San Francisco, located in the treeless foothills of the Livermore Range. "They spent many hours full of shade and bright sunshine and seductive moonlight alone together, and out of those meetings of the happy summer time long ago grew the romance whose closing chapter was filed yesterday in court," the *Call* surmised on June 16, 1896, after Mollie had sued for breach of promise.[8]

The stepdaughter of an alcoholic, Mollie Redmond was raised a Catholic, watched over by an uncle named James Horen. After her father's death, she

North Pacific Coast Railroad

Researchers Kevin Hassing, Kyle Wyatt, George Pitchard, Allen Tacy, Kevin Bunker, Don Marenzi, Herman Darr

The extremely sketchy information about early NPC passenger cars is based on four "knowns" and numerous inferences. Knowns are two express cars built by Carter in Nov. 1874 (*Marin Journal*, Nov. 5, 1874); a total of twelve Kimball passenger cars delivered prior to Sept. 1875 (original contract cited by R. G. Dun and Co. Credit Reports, California 16, p. 370, dated July 10, 1874); delivery of a Kimball private car in Sept. 1875; and arrival of Barney and Smith coaches 15, 16, and 17 in Aug. 1876 (*Reno Evening Journal*, Aug. 25, 1876). These sparse facts created a majority of the "symbol" lines in the table. Car numbers, however, were added to the symbol only if photographs (showing design elements such as roof lines or trucks) provided reasonably positive identification of a car as Carter, Kimball, or Barney and Smith. These design elements are summarized in the Comments column. Other data (length, weight, capacity) were then added to a car number by linking it to later published tables, for example, Northwestern Pacific (NWP) rolling stock listing of 1910. The resulting NPC roster, ca. 1874–1880, is one of the most speculative in this appendix.

Car category	Symbol	NPC road number/name	Builder	Builder's date	Length over sills	Weight	Capacity	Retail cost	Comments
Express	NPC-a		Carter	Nov. 1874	Nov. 5, 1874, *Marin County Journal* article refers to 35' length, but unclear over what			$1,800?	The earliest known NPC photographs of passenger equipment show BME (baggage-mail-express) cars with duckbill roof end; full clerestory roof, two baggage doors, one express door between; no letter board; see photograph in Kneiss, *Redwood Railways*, behind NPC no. 6 at San Rafael B Street Station; two Carter cars are referred to as "express" cars in newspaper and are candidates for these two early NPC BME's
Express	NPC-b		Carter	Nov. 1874	35'?			$1,800?	Similar or identical to NPC-a; both NPC-a and NPC-b built without air brakes or Miller couplers; all Kimball equipment used air and Miller
Combine?	NPC-c	3?	Kimball	Dec. 1874	34'6½"	27,000		$3,400–$3,600	Eight windows per side, single baggage door; to NWP 801; includes 4' wheelbase truck (common to Kimball NPC cars); combine configuration verified in 1912 photo; may have been converted from what was originally a coach
Coach	NPC-d	4?	Kimball	Dec. 1874				$3,400–$3,600	Twelve windows per side, board and batten siding, oval number plate, Miller hook coupler; duckbill roof end; possibly shown in photo of 1882 wreck of NPC locomotive no. 9 near San Rafael

Car category	Symbol	NPC road number/name	Builder	Builder's date	Length over sills	Weight	Capacity	Retail cost	Comments
Coach	NPC-e	5?	Kimball	Dec. 1874	34'5"	26,500		$3,400–$3,600	To NWP 733 as early as 1888; many Kimball car roof styles were altered, also board and batten changed to narrow car siding; some evidence from NPC cash books that Carter Brothers performed this work in 1888–89; NWP 733 is an example of such alteration
Coach	NPC-f	6?	Kimball	Dec. 1874				$3,400–$3,600	Possibly destroyed in North Shore "funeral train wreck" of June 21, 1903
Coach	NPC-g	7?	Kimball	Dec. 1874	34'5½"	28,000		$3,400–$3,600	Twelve-window car; 4' wheelbase trucks; to NWP 702; retired Oct. 5, 1923
Coach	NPC-h	8?	Kimball	Dec. 1874	34'5½"			$3,400–$3,600	Twelve-window car; sold Aug. 29, 1909, to Nevada California Oregon Railway and then to Huckleberry Railroad in 1976; by 2003, the only known remaining NPC Kimball car
Baggage-mail-express	NPC-i		Kimball?	Apr. 1875?					A total of three BMEs are on roster by Dec. 1875; two are presumed to be Carter (NPC-a, -b); this third BME presumed to be Kimball; origin of NPC-i is assigned to this role; no clear correlation to known photographs
Coach	NPC-j		Kimball	Apr. 1875?				$3,400–$3,600	
Coach	NPC-k		Kimball	Apr. 1875?				$3,400–$3,600	
Coach	NPC-l		Kimball	Apr. 1875?				$3,400–$3,600	
Coach	NPC-m	13?	Kimball	Apr. 1875?				$3,400–$3,600	There is evidence that this car number was "backfilled" with a later Carter car dated 1882 (see Stindt, Dunscomb roster in Northwestern Pacific); the same NPC road numbers may therefore be populated with multiple cars over a thirty-to-forty-year period
Coach	NPC-n	14?	Kimball	Apr. 1875?	34'5½"			$3,400–$3,600	Twelve-window car; 4' wheelbase trucks; to NWP 708; retired May 1927

Santa Cruz Rail Road (continued)

Car category	Symbol	SCRR road number/name	Builder	Builder's date	Length over end sills	Weight	Capacity	Retail cost	Comments
Rack cars		Two cars	SCRR shops?	?					Possible modification of flatcars for hauling sugar beets
Horsecar	SCRR-f	1	SCRR shops	Aug. 1875					Horsecars included in 1881 inventory of SCRR rolling stock, for bill of sale to SP
Horsecar	SCRR-g	2	SCRR shops	1876?					
Open horsecar	SCRR-h	3?	SCRR shops	1876?					

Santa Cruz & Felton Railroad

Researchers David Eggleston, Randy Hees

The railroad and all its rolling stock were leased by the South Pacific Coast in 1880. Poor's directories of the 1880s listed the equipment separately but noted the line was leased to the SPC. It is clear that the boxcars received SPC numbers in 1880, and we assume the flatcars did also. The passenger cars (and the locomotives), however, were never incorporated into the SPC roster. The railroad also owned eight "other" cars: four dump cars, two handcars, and two pushcars. Primary source: California Board of Commissioners of Transportation annual report, Dec. 1877, as well as contemporary copies of the *Santa Cruz Sentinel*.

Car category	Symbol	SC&F road number	Builder	Builder's date	Length over end sills	Weight	Capacity	Retail cost	Comments
Coach	SC&F-a		Carter	June 1876	29'?			$2,300	First-class car, ten windows, board and batten siding; two stove jacks, longitudinal seating; to Arcata & Mad River Railroad no. 2, prior to 1917
Coach	SC&F-b		Carter	June 1876	29'?			$1,600	Second-class car, nine windows without sash or glass; board and batten siding; longitudinal seating; thought to have been converted to first Boulder Creek depot, ca. 1885
Flatcar		Thirty-four cars, probably 1–67 odd numbers	Carter	1875–76	24'	8,000	Eight tons	$507	Delivered as kits and assembled in Santa Cruz; delivered in three orders: ten flatcars, July 1875, fourteen flatcars, Jan. 1876 (at the same time as six boxcars; this order is reported as twenty flats in some sources), and ten flatcars, Apr. 1876
Boxcar		Six cars, probably 2–12 even numbers	Carter	Jan. 1876	24'	9,000	Eight tons	$651	Assembled from Carter kits in Santa Cruz, using castings from the Amner, Morton foundry in Santa Cruz

Nevada County Narrow Gauge Railroad

Researchers Herman Darr, Greg Maxwell

A small roster, and comparatively stable traffic conditions, contributed to a fleet of rolling stock that changed little during the 1870s. One exception is the NCNG's inventory of unused car material, noted in the California Board of Commissioners of Transportation annual report for June 30, 1876, which cited $8,575.15 in "extra car material," assumed to be unassembled car kits left over from the initial Carter order in 1875. Perhaps a strategy for holding extra rolling stock in reserve, this material might have been adequate for assembling a dozen (or more) additional flatcars or boxcars. Only one such car is noted on this roster, boxcar 32, built in the railroad's Grass Valley shops in 1876. Additional home-built cars may have followed.

Car category	Symbol	NCNG road number	Builder	Builder's date	Length over sills	Weight	Capacity	Retail cost	Comments
Combine	NCNG-a	1	F. E. Canda and Co.	1875	36'			$2,500	Seven-window combine
Coach	NCNG-b	2	F. E. Canda and Co.	1875	36'2"			$3,700	Twelve-window coach
Combine	NCNG-c	3	F. E. Canda and Co.	1875	36'			$2,500	
Coach	NCNG-d	4	F. E. Canda and Co.	1875	36'2"			$3,700	
Flatcar		Fifteen cars, 1–29 odd	Carter	1875	24'		Eight tons	$533	
Boxcar		Fifteen cars, 2–30 even	Carter	1875	24'		Eight tons	$707	
Boxcar		32	Carter/NCNG shops	1876	24'		Eight tons		Built from unassembled Carter kit material a year after initial boxcars were built; may have been additional unused Carter kit material; but unclear when, or if, this material was used

Santa Clara Valley Railroad

The Santa Clara Valley placed an order for rolling stock with Carter Brothers in Nov. 1875. Carter may have only partly filled the order, completing a few flatcars before the SCV collapsed in Jan. 1876. The railroad and all the rolling stock were taken over by the South Pacific Coast by Mar. 1876. There is some confusion over what was ordered. One contemporary newspaper account reported only two passenger cars and two baggage cars; however, a combine may have actually been delivered first, eventually used as a depot at Le Franc on the Almaden branch. The order also included pushcars, pumpcars, and iron cars. We have included the SCV cars apparently ordered from Carter with the South Pacific Coast equipment but have identified them in the Symbol column with codes starting with "SCV."

Car category	Symbol	SPC road number/name	Builder	Builder's date	Length over sills	Weight	Capacity	Retail cost	Comments
Coach	SPC-d	6	Carter	1878					Second-class car; burned Alameda Mole fire, Nov. 20, 1902
Coach	SPC-e	7	Carter	1878					Second-class car; sold NWP July 20, 1907
Coach	SPC-f	8	Carter	1878		21,700 (on NWP)			First-class car; sold NWP July 20, 1907; scrapped Oct. 1934
Coach	SPC-g	9	Carter	1878	39'11"				Second-class car; sold to OWR&N (Oregon-Washington Railroad & Navigation) May 20, 1912
Coach	SPC-h	10	Carter	1878					Second-class car; burned Alameda Mole fire, Nov. 20, 1902
Coach	SPC-i	11	Carter	1878	39'10"				Second-class car; burned Alameda Mole fire, Nov. 20, 1902
Coach	SPC-j	12	Carter	1878					Second-class car; burned Alameda Mole fire, Nov. 20, 1902
Coach	SPC-k	13	Carter	1878					Second-class car; scrapped Sept. 1913
Coach	SPC-l	14	Carter	1878	39'10 1/2"	21,700 (on NWP)			Second-class car; to NWP Feb. 10, 1908
Baggage-mail-express	SPC-m	3	Carter	Aug. 1878					Listed in Railway Equipment Register, July 1887 as baggage car; scrapped Sept. 1912
Baggage-mail-express	SPC-n	4	Carter	1878	35'	25,000			Originally built as a mail car; to NWP 650, Feb. 14, 1908; retired 1930
Coach	SPC-o	15	Davis and Howell (Carter?)	1879	38'	22,500 (on NWP)			First-class car, perhaps built by Carter Bros. under contract; NWP later reported that Carter was the builder; to NWP 705, July 20, 1907; thirteen windows, rounded window sash, duckbill roof; board and batten siding
Coach	SPC-p	16	Davis and Howell (Carter?)	1879	38'				Similar or identical to SPC-o; to NWP July 20, 1907
Combine	SPC-q	17	Carter	1879?					
Combine	SPC-r	18	Carter	1879?					
Coach	SPC-s	19	Carter	1879					First-class car; burned, Alameda Mole fire, Nov. 20, 1902

South Pacific Coast Railroad (continued)

Car category	Symbol	SPC road number/name	Builder	Builder's date	Length over sills	Weight	Capacity	Retail cost	Comments
Coach	SPC-t	20	Carter	1879	36'4"				First-class car; scrapped Sept. 1913
Coach	SPC-u	21	Carter	1879					First-class car; burned Alameda Mole fire, Nov. 20, 1902
Coach	SPC-v	22	Carter	1879	36'7"				First-class car; thirteen windows, duck-bill, rounded top window sash; to N&C July 15, 1907, to NCNG June 11, 1934, as coach 7; scrapped 1940
Coach	SPC-w	23	Carter	May 1880	39'11"				Second-class car; to OWR&N Jan. 30, 1907, as N-15; some parts salvaged (in collection of Society for the Preservation of Carter Railroad Resources)
Coach	SPC-x	24	Carter	May 1880					Second-class car; burned Alameda Mole fire, Nov. 20, 1902
Coach	SPC-y	25	Carter	May 1880					Second-class car; to NWP, burned in Sausalito fire Sept. 26, 1909
Coach	SPC-z	26	Carter	?					Second-class car; possibly converted to combine 26 after listing as coach in 1888; burned Alameda Mole fire, Nov. 20, 1902
Coach	SPC-aa	27	Carter	1880					Second-class car; converted to standard gauge work car, Nov. 27, 1909
Parlor	SPC-bb	San Francisco	Jackson and Sharp	1879	42'			$4,985	Built 1879, received in 1880; burned, Alameda Mole fire, Nov. 20, 1902
Parlor	SPC-cc	Santa Cruz	Jackson and Sharp	1879	42'			$4,985	Built 1879, received in 1880; to N&C 17, Aug. 9, 1909; to Lake Tahoe Railway & Transportation Company (LTRy&T) 17, ca. 1910, razed near Truckee, ca. 1927
Baggage-mail-express	SPC-dd	5	Carter	Aug. 1880					Listed in Railway Equipment Register July 1887 as baggage car; listed as baggage-mail, 1903; set aside at Wrights, Dec. 31, 1909; fragments intact on Summit Road, 1968
Baggage-mail-express	SPC-ee	6	Carter	Aug. 1880					Listed in SPC records July 1887 as baggage car and mail; gone from Railway Equipment Register by 1902
Baggage-mail-express	SPC-ff	7	Carter	Aug. 1880					Two baggage doors per side; square door lintels; to NWP 8, July 20, 1907; burned Sept. 1907 in Sausalito car house fire

Car category	Symbol	SPC road number/name	Builder	Builder's date	Length over sills	Weight	Capacity	Retail cost	Comments
Caboose	SPC-gg	3	Carter	1880	36'8"				Last caboose to carry a caboose number; body to Santa Cruz roundhouse; seven-window duckbill combine; equipped with Miller hook by 1904
Coach	SPC-hh	28	Carter	1880					Second-class car; probably burned in Alameda Mole fire, Nov. 20, 1902
Coach	SPC-ii	29	Carter	1880		21,700 (on NWP)			Second-class car; fourteen windows per side; to NWP coach 24, July 20, 1907
Coach	SPC-jj	30	Carter	1880					Second-class car; burned, Alameda Mole fire, Nov. 20, 1902
Coach	SPC-kk	31	Carter	1880	39'11"				Second-class car; to OWR&N, May 20, 1912
Caboose	SPC-ll	32	Carter	1880	30'				This is the first caboose to carry a passenger car number; first known listing as caboose, Mar. 1888; deleted July 1894 from Equipment Register
Coach	SPC-mm	33	Carter	Mar. 1881	39'11"				Second-class, first of series of twelve coaches (nos. 33–44) built for Oakland commuter service; fourteen-window duckbill roof cars, three-section seating (benches on ends, walkover seats in middle of car; same for numbers 34–43); see Michael Collins drawing of SPC 39; burned, Alameda Mole fire, Nov. 20, 1902
Coach	SPC-nn	34	Carter	Mar. 1881	39'11"				Burned, Alameda Mole fire, Nov. 20, 1902
Coach	SPC-oo	35	Carter	Mar. 1881	39'11"				Burned, Alameda Mole fire, Nov. 20, 1902
Coach	SPC-pp	36	Carter	Mar. 1881	39'11"				Burned, Alameda Mole fire, Nov. 20, 1902
Coach	SPC-qq	37	Carter	Mar. 1881	39'11"				Burned, Alameda Mole fire, Nov. 20, 1902
Coach	SPC-rr	38	Carter	Mar. 1881	39'11"				To OWR&N, Feb. 20, 1912
Coach	SPC-ss	39	Carter	Mar. 1881	39'11"				Laid aside Dec. 31, 1909; preserved at Orange Empire Museum, Perris, California

South Pacific Coast Railroad (continued)

Car category	Symbol	SPC road number/name	Builder	Builder's date	Length over sills	Weight	Capacity	Retail cost	Comments
Coach	SPC-tt	40	Carter	Mar. 1881	39'11"				Burned, Alameda Mole fire, Nov. 20, 1902
Coach	SPC-uu	41	Carter	Mar. 1881	39'11"				Burned, Alameda Mole fire, Nov. 20, 1902
Coach	SPC-vv	42	Carter	Mar. 1881	39'11"				Known Carter builder's photo; burned, Alameda Mole fire, Nov. 20, 1902
Coach	SPC-ww	43	Carter	Mar. 1881	39'11"				To OWR&N, no. N-13; some parts salvaged (in collection of Society for Preservation of Carter Railroad Resources)
Coach	SPC-xx	44	Carter	Mar. 1881	39'9½'				Last of twelve-car coach series (nos. 33–44), to N&C, July 18, 1907; to LTRy&N no. 14, 1910; presumably razed near Truckee
Caboose	SPC-yy	45	Carter	Apr. 1882	30'				This and next three cars, five-window duckbill roof combines; no. 45 deleted July 1894 from Railway Equipment Register
Caboose	SPC-zz	46	Carter	Apr. 1882	30'				To N&C 456, Oct. 27, 1907
Caboose	SPC-aaa	47	Carter	Apr. 1882	30'				To N&C 455, Oct. 27, 1907; detrucked at Keeler, California, 1913 (preserved by Society for the Preservation of Carter Railroad Resources, Ardenwood Park, Fremont, California; see Appendix B)
Caboose	SPC-bbb	48	Carter	Apr. 1882	30'				To N&C 1, Oct. 27, 1907; to SP 1, to SP 400, burned 1949
Boxcar		2–20 even	Carter	1876	24'	9,000	Eight tons, later converted to ten-ton		Ordered by the Santa Clara Valley Nov. 1875; converted to ten-ton capacity
Boxcar		22–90 even	Carter	1879–80	28'	10,000	Ten tons	$536	Possibly a series of orders added to the SPC roster between 1879 and 1880; average price of seventy boxcars on hand by end of 1881; cited in California Board of Commissioners of Transportation

Car category	Symbol	SPC road number/name	Builder	Builder's date	Length over sills	Weight	Capacity	Retail cost	Comments
Boxcar		92–102 even	Carter/SC&F	Jan. 1876	24'	9,000	Eight tons, later converted to ten-ton		Built by the Santa Cruz & Felton from kits; incorporated into SPC roster 1880; same six cars listed under Santa Cruz & Felton roster, but note increase to ten-ton capacity under South Pacific Coast ownership
Flatcar		1–19 odd	Carter	1875, 1876	24'	8,000	Eight tons		Ordered by the Santa Clara Valley Nov. 1875, originally eight-ton capacity; by 1888, however, cars in this number series are all 28' long, ten-ton capacity flatcars, suggesting that original Santa Clara Valley 24' cars were either scrapped or converted by SPC
Flatcar		21–139 odd	Carter	1876	28'	9,000	Ten tons	$449	Price is an average for 235 flatcars on hand at the end of 1881; cited in California Board of Commissioners of Transportation report
Flatcar		141–199 odd	Carter	1877	28'	9,000	Ten tons		
Flatcar		201–419 odd	Carter	1878–1880	28'	9,000	Ten tons		A total of 210 flatcars on hand at end of 1880; average weight 4.25 tons unloaded

Appendix B: South Pacific Coast Caboose 47

The small fleet of four South Pacific Coast cabooses, constructed by Carter Brothers at Newark in 1882, resembled miniature versions of duckbill roof passenger cars; in fact, their wall, roof, and sill structures were almost identical to the anatomy of Carter coaches 33–44, built the previous year. But as cabooses, cars 45–48 had spartan interiors, link and pin couplers (instead of Miller type couplers), and a leaf-spring version of a freight truck. A rectangular hole was cut in 47's clerestory roof to accommodate a four-aspect marker lamp, and a tool box was slung under its frame like a pack saddle, where jacks, chains, and pinch bars could be stored for use by train crews.

One of this caboose series still survives. After a sale to Southern Pacific's Nevada & California Railroad in 1907, caboose 47 changed numbers to 455 and served a brief career on the Mina-to-Keeler run. Retired in 1913, 47 wound up as a goat shelter in Keeler, Calif., shorn of most of its metal hardware and nearly mummified by the desert heat. There, it was rescued in 1978 by Richard Datin, the Mission Peak Heritage Foundation, and the Society for the Preservation of Carter Railroad Resources, and preserved at Ardenwood Park in Fremont for future restoration.

One of the first steps in the restoration process was to create an extremely detailed set of D size mechanical drawings, covering nearly every part and assembly on the car body. Dan McGinty, a high school junior when the project started, spent four years creating the document set, and it remains today the most detailed, complete technical specification of a Carter car in existence. Only a portion of McGinty's extensive drawing set is reproduced on the pages following, but they represent all of the subsystems of the car body: frame, walls, and roof. Drawing page numbers (called sheet numbers) begin with the letter of the car's subsystem shown in that drawing—W for wall, R for roof, F for frame. Cross-references between drawings are provided by either circles, pointing to detailed drawings of wooden parts; or diamonds, pointing to drawings of metal parts. For both circles or diamonds, the bottom number indicates the referenced sheet number, while the upper number indicates the figure number within that sheet. Only parts or assemblies actually present on the original car body were drawn; missing parts (for example, trucks) have not been included. The drawings are not reproduced to scale.

In the photograph below, dating from the 1890s, one of the few clear views of caboose 47's trucks is reproduced, illustrating the leaf spring Carter freight truck applied to cabooses and to small, second-class passenger cars.

Today, caboose 47 represents two important legacies from the pioneer car builder: 47 and its three sister cabooses were the last duckbill roof cars that Carter built for the South Pacific Coast (and perhaps for any railroad). By 1882, the bull-nose roof end was adopted by Carter as more in step with current fashion. Forty-seven was also the last caboose to turn a wheel on the South Pacific Coast; it is easily identified in a photograph taken at Agnew, Calif., sometime in 1908 and labeled as the last train on the narrow gauge. [Marvin Maynard collection]

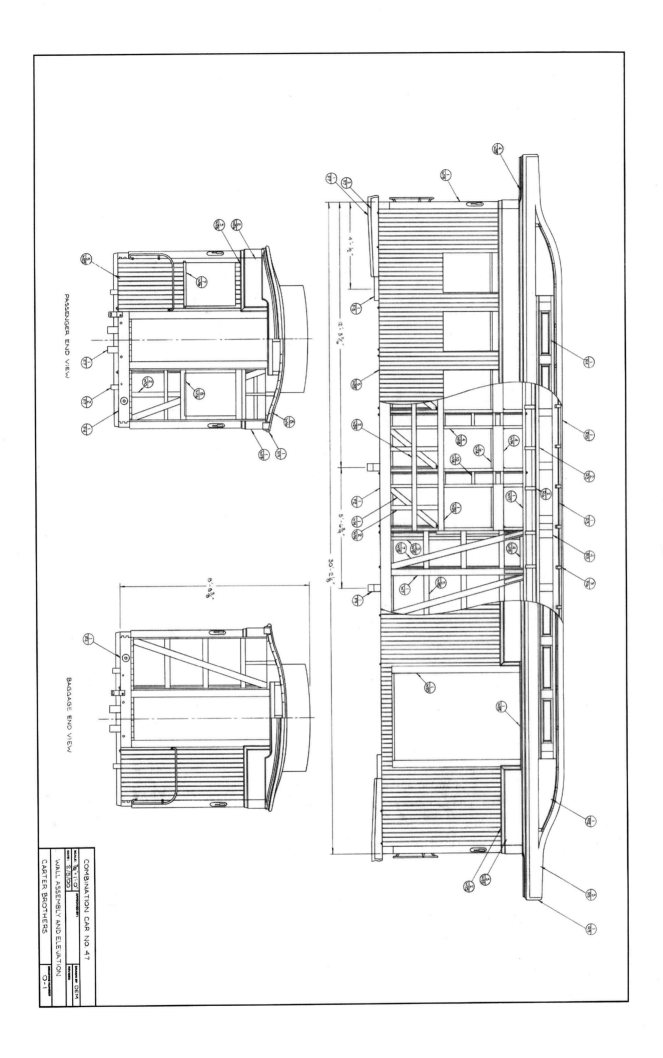

PASSENGER END VIEW

BAGGAGE END VIEW

COMBINATION CAR NO. 47
WALL ASSEMBLY AND ELEVATION
CARTER BROTHERS

SCALE: ¾" = 1'-0"   DRAWN BY: DEM
DATE: 2/5/00
DRAWING NUMBER: O-1

603

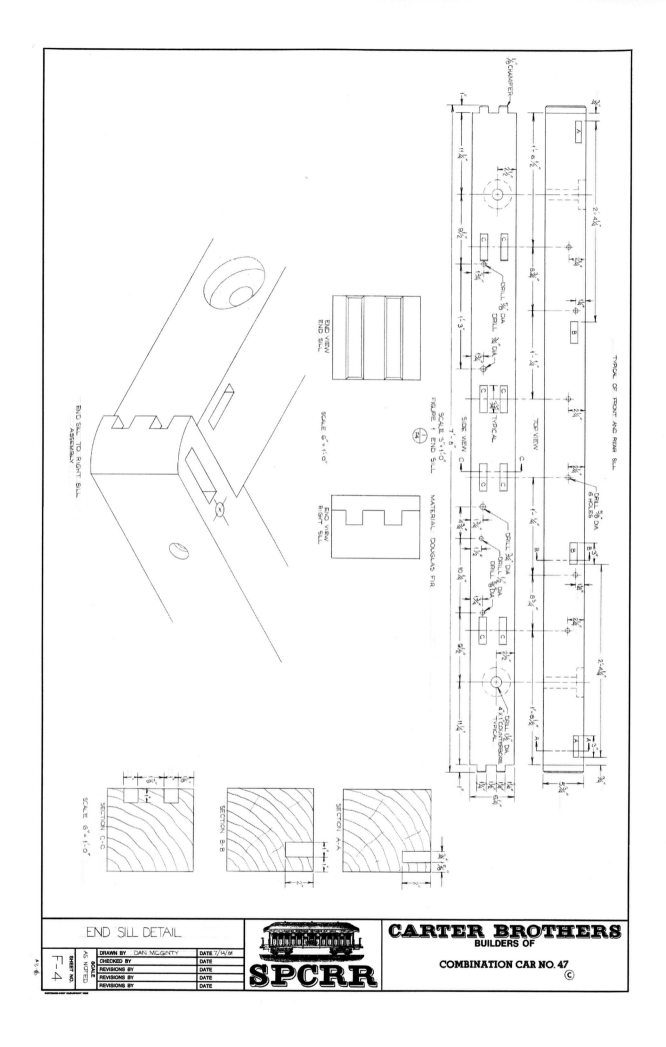

END SILL DETAIL

DRAWN BY	DAN McGINTY	DATE 7/14/81
CHECKED BY		DATE
REVISIONS BY		DATE
REVISIONS BY		DATE
REVISIONS BY		DATE

SHEET NO. F-4
SCALE AS NOTED

CARTER BROTHERS
BUILDERS OF

COMBINATION CAR NO. 47
©

SPCRR

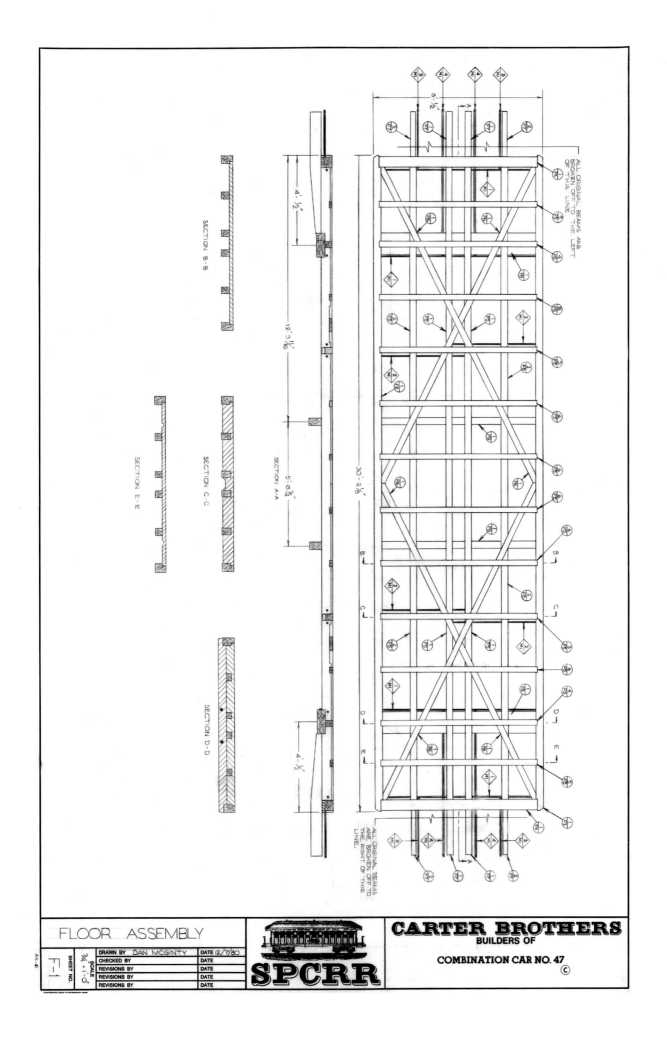

SECTION B-B

SECTION C-C

SECTION E-E

SECTION A-A

SECTION D-D

ALL ORIGINAL BEAMS ARE BROKEN OFF TO THE LEFT OF THIS LINE.

ALL ORIGINAL BEAMS ARE BROKEN OFF TO THE RIGHT OF THIS LINE.

FLOOR ASSEMBLY

DRAWN BY	DAN MCGINTY	DATE 12/7/80
CHECKED BY		DATE
REVISIONS BY		DATE
REVISIONS BY		DATE
REVISIONS BY		DATE

SCALE ¾" = 1'-0"

SHEET NO. F-1

SPCRR

CARTER BROTHERS
BUILDERS OF

COMBINATION CAR NO. 47
©

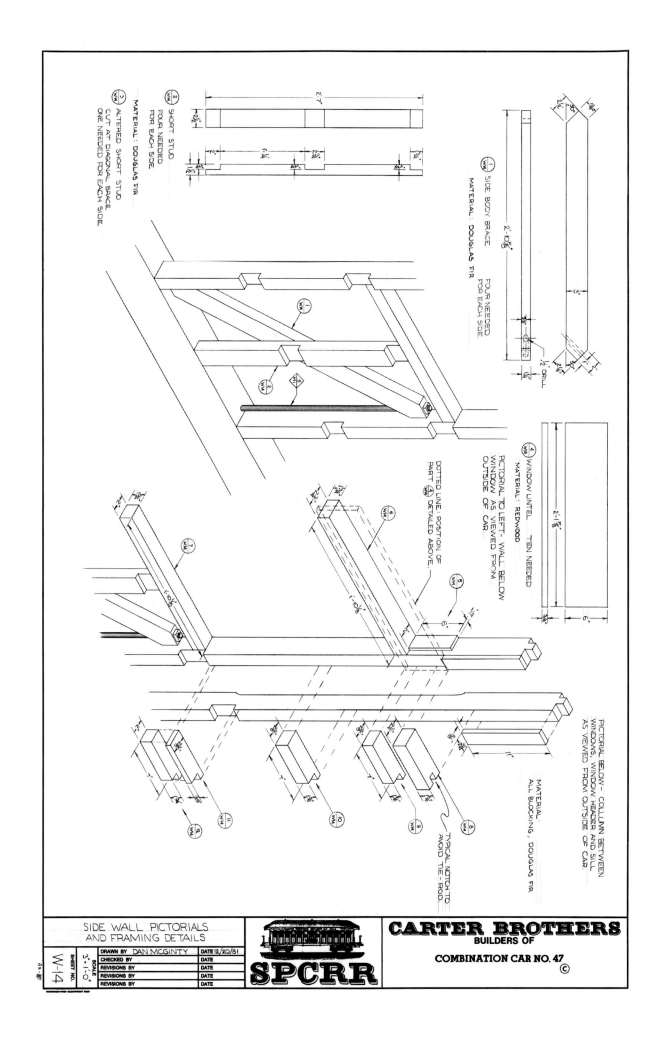

SHORT STUD
FOUR NEEDED
FOR EACH SIDE

MATERIAL: DOUGLAS FIR

ALTERED SHORT STUD.
CUT AT DIAGONAL BRACE.
ONE NEEDED FOR EACH SIDE.

SIDE BODY BRACE
MATERIAL: DOUGLAS FIR   FOUR NEEDED
FOR EACH SIDE

WINDOW LINTEL   TEN NEEDED
MATERIAL: REDWOOD

PICTORIAL TO LEFT - WALL BELLOW
WINDOW AS VIEWED FROM
OUTSIDE OF CAR

DOTTED LINE: POSITION OF
PART 4 DETAILED ABOVE.

PICTORIAL BELOW - COLUMN BETWEEN
WINDOWS, WINDOW HEADER AND SILL
AS VIEWED FROM OUTSIDE OF CAR.

MATERIAL:
ALL BLOCKING, DOUGLAS FIR

TYPICAL NOTCH TO
AVOID TIE-ROD.

½" DRILL

SIDE WALL PICTORIALS
AND FRAMING DETAILS

DRAWN BY	DAN MCGINTY	DATE 12/20/81
CHECKED BY		DATE
REVISIONS BY		DATE
REVISIONS BY		DATE
REVISIONS BY		DATE

SHEET NO.
W-14

SCALE
3"=1'-0"

SPCRR

CARTER BROTHERS
BUILDERS OF

COMBINATION CAR NO. 47
©

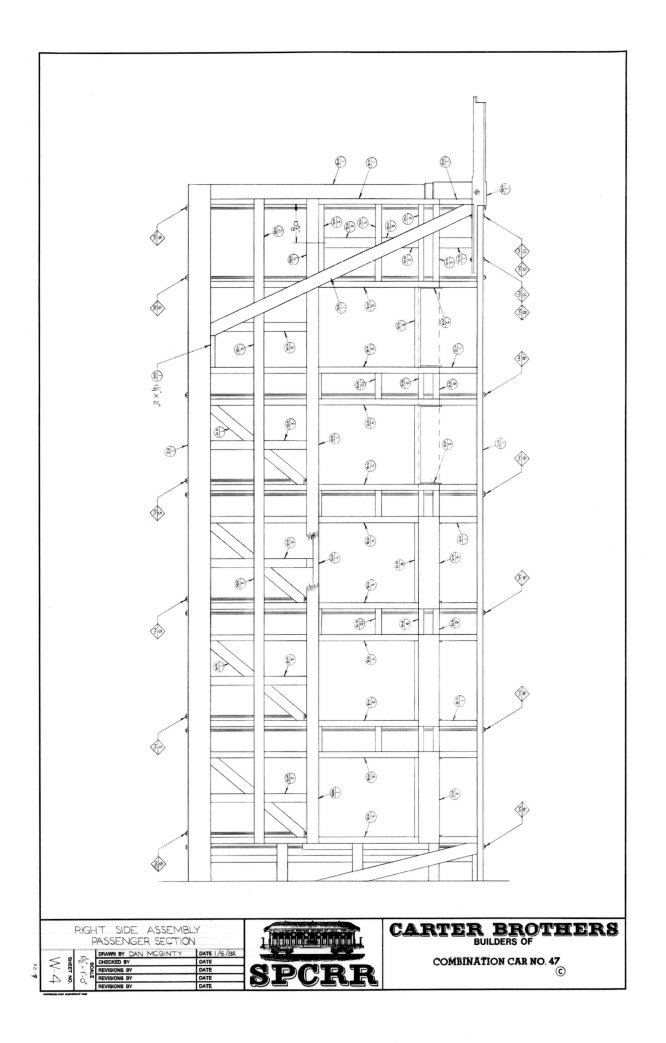

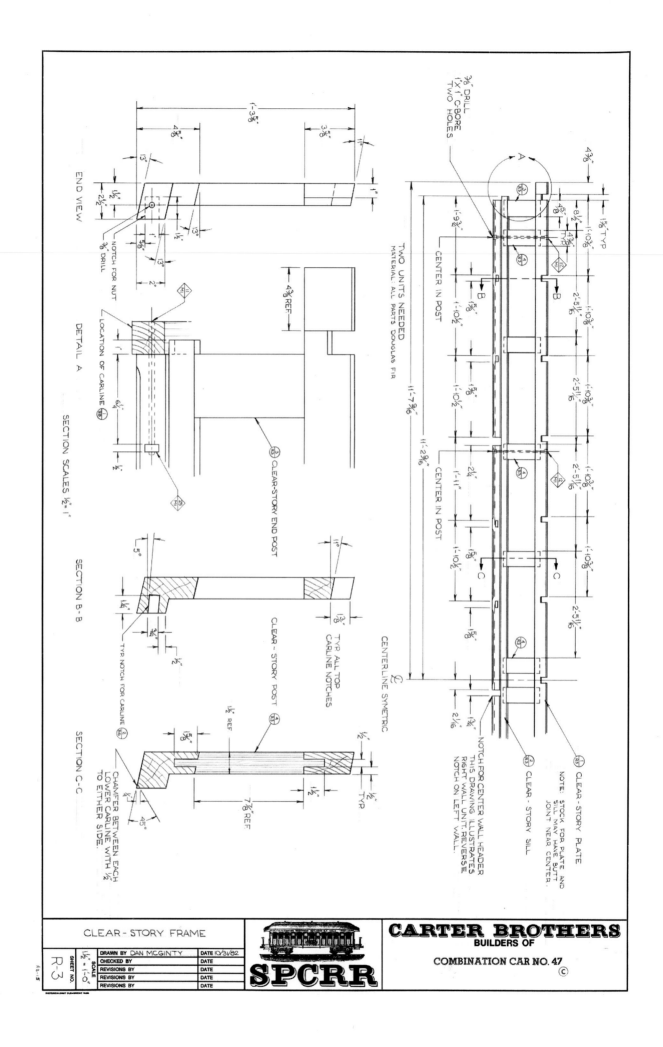

END VIEW

DETAIL A

LOCATION OF CARLINE

SECTION SCALES ½" = 1"

SECTION B-B

SECTION C-C

TWO UNITS NEEDED
MATERIAL: ALL PARTS DOUGLAS FIR

CLEAR-STORY END POST

CENTERLINE SYMETRIC

TYP ALL TOP
CARLINE NOTCHES

CLEAR - STORY POST

CENTER IN POST

CENTER IN POST

CLEAR-STORY PLATE
NOTE: STOCK FOR PLATE AND
SILL MAY HAVE BUTT
JOINT NEAR CENTER.

CLEAR - STORY SILL

NOTCH FOR CENTER WALL HEADER
THIS DRAWING ILLUSTRATES
RIGHT WALL UNIT. REVERSE
NOTCH ON LEFT WALL.

TYP NOTCH FOR CARLINE

CHAMFER BETWEEN EACH
LOWER CARLINE WITH ½
TO EITHER SIDE.

NOTCH FOR NUT
DRILL

DRILL
1"X 1" C-BORE
TWO HOLES

CLEAR - STORY FRAME

DRAWN BY DAN McGINTY   DATE 10/31/82
CHECKED BY   DATE
REVISIONS BY   DATE
REVISIONS BY   DATE
REVISIONS BY   DATE

SHEET NO. R-3
SCALE ½" = 1'-0"

SPCRR

CARTER BROTHERS
BUILDERS OF

COMBINATION CAR NO. 47

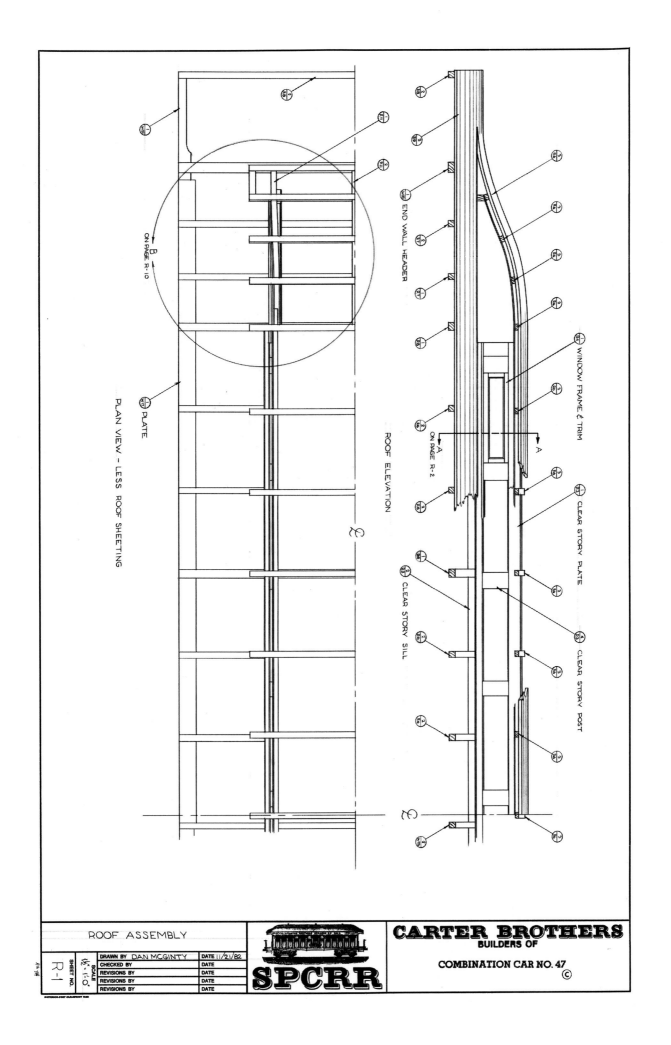

PLAN VIEW - LESS ROOF SHEETING

ON PAGE R-10

B

PLATE

ROOF ELEVATION

END WALL HEADER

ON PAGE R-2

A

A

WINDOW FRAME & TRIM

CLEAR STORY PLATE

CLEAR STORY POST

CLEAR STORY SILL

ROOF ASSEMBLY

DRAWN BY DAN McGINTY   DATE 11/21/82
CHECKED BY   DATE
REVISIONS BY   DATE
REVISIONS BY   DATE
REVISIONS BY   DATE

SHEET NO.
R-1

SCALE
1½" = 1'-0"

SPCRR

CARTER BROTHERS
BUILDERS OF

COMBINATION CAR NO. 47
©

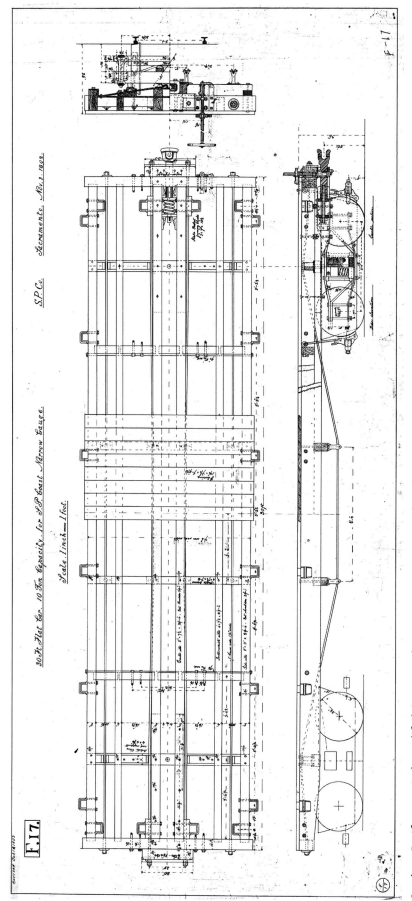

Southern Pacific extensively modified Carter car designs once its Sacramento shops began to supply new rolling stock to the South Pacific Coast in the late 1880s; an example is this thirty-foot narrow gauge flatcar, equipped with rigid archbar trucks and steel bolsters, as drawn by the Sacramento shops in 1892. [Richard C. Datin collection]

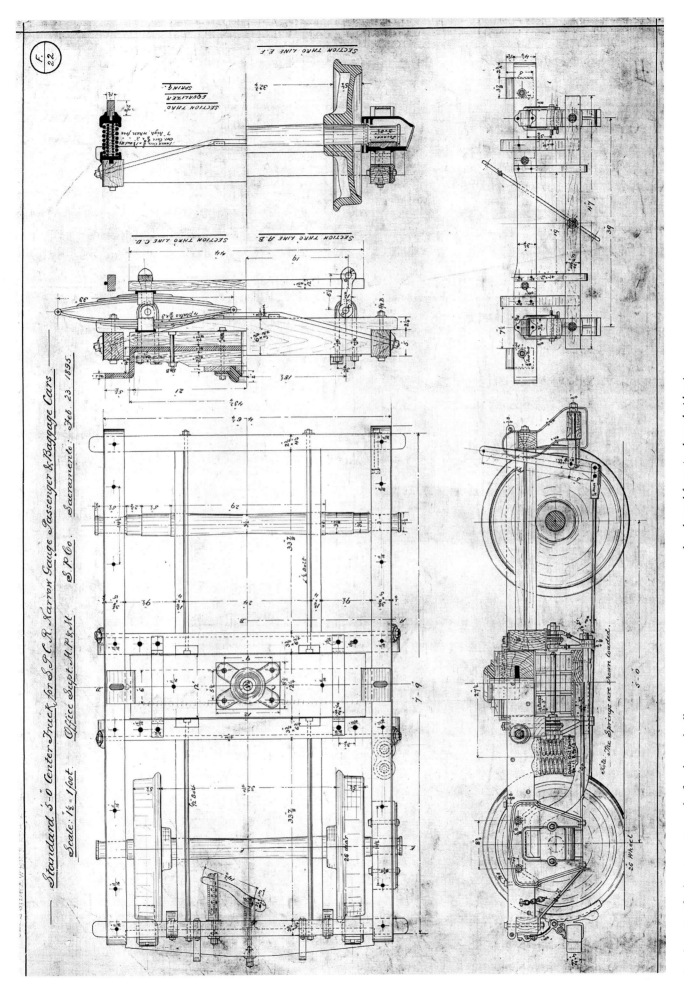

Southern Pacific drawing, 1895, of a five-foot-wheelbase narrow gauge passenger truck, adapted from (and nearly identical to) a Carter Brothers passenger car truck applied to its products since the late 1870s. [Richard C. Datin collection]

Perhaps the most versatile of all the cars portrayed in this book, the narrow gauge combination boxcar has been illustrated in Carter's eight-ton capacity version (ca. 1874) and ten-ton capacity version (ca. 1877). After the Southern Pacific leased the South Pacific Coast, the SP's Sacramento shops began to build a twenty-ton capacity version in November 1891. Shown here in schematic, this final stage in the car's evolution was thirty feet long and included rigid arch bar trucks, a replacement for Carter's original swing motion design. Examples of the twenty-ton capacity car operated on the South Pacific Coast until the line's standard gauging in 1908. Not reproduced to scale. [Herman Darr collection]

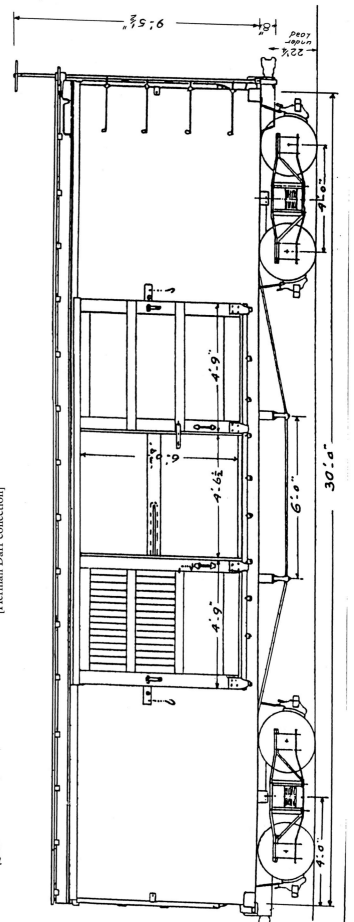

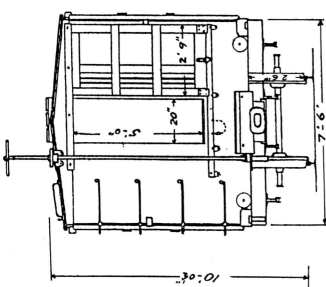

Chapter 1

1. The date of the Carters' emigration, 1848, was noted in a subscription biographical sketch that Thomas Carter gave to the editors of *The Bay of San Francisco: A History,* vol. 1, Lewis Publishing, 1892, p. 498. However, emigration records reconstructed from the J. and J. Cooke passenger lists have identified seven members of a Carter family arriving in Grosse Isle on the ship *Superior,* out of Londonderry, on September 7, 1847. The seven include a Margaret (mother) and a Thomas (child). However, the Cooke lists omit four names of the Carter family of this narrative: Thomas (father), John (child), Margaret (child), and Martin (child). The Cooke lists note the family emigrating from County Leitrim, Ireland, bordering the western Ireland counties but not adjacent to Galway County, which was identified in Thomas Carter's obituary as his birthplace (see note 6 for this chapter). Hence it is not possible to conclude on the basis of this evidence alone whether the Cooke lists have identified the Carter family of our narrative. However, if these records do identify Thomas Carter's arrival in Canada, it means the family arrived at the height of the cholera epidemic, in 1847. Conditions on their ship would have been extreme. Records indicate that 71 of the *Superior*'s 366 passengers died either en route or on Grosse Isle itself after the *Superior* docked. The author is indebted to Doris Drolet-Dube and Andre Charbonneau of Parks Canada, and to Lissa Mckee, for bringing the Cooke lists to light.
2. John F. Maguire, *The Irish in America,* London: Longmans, Green, 1868, p. 135.
3. Maguire; extracts from the diary of Gerald Keegan, p. 137.
4. Robert O'Driscoll and Lorna Reynolds, *The Untold Story: The Irish in Canada,* Toronto: Celtic Arts of Canada, 1988.
5. Maguire, p. 138.
6. There is conflicting evidence about the county of Tom and Martin Carter's birth; Galway is named in Thomas Carter's obituary in the *San Francisco Call,* Aug. 31, 1898. Genealogical research conducted in Primary Evaluation land records suggests that the Killanin, Rahoon, and Kilcummin parishes of western Galway had the largest number of surviving families with the Carter surname in 1855, seven years after the Thomas Carters left Ireland, but there is no conclusive proof of Thomas Carter's place of birth (research conducted by Eileen O'Byrne of the Hibernian Research Co. at the author's request and reported by personal letter on Feb. 16, 1999).
7. Ages of family members in 1848 are estimated from Martin G. Carter, M.D., biographical sketch in, J. J. McGroarty, *California of the South: A History,* vol. 5, Chicago: Clarke, 1933–35, p. 666; Martin Grover Carter biographical notes, typescript, from an interview by the author and John I. MacGregor in Los Angeles, and *The Bay of San Francisco,* p. 498.
8. Kerby A. Miller, *Emigrants and Exiles: Ireland and the Irish Exodus to North America,* Oxford University Press, 1985, p. 297.

9. 1871 Canadian census records.

10. Miller, p. 292.

11. See also Martin Grover Carter's biography in McGroarty.

12. *The Bay of San Francisco,* p. 498.   14. *Santa Cruz Sentinel,* Apr. 11, 1874.

13. *Petaluma Argus,* Feb. 17, 1872.   15. *San Francisco Call,* Aug. 31, 1898.

16. John H. White, Jr., *The American Railroad Freight Car,* Johns Hopkins University Press, 1993, p. 139.

17. *San Francisco Call,* op. cit.

18. Miller, p. 322.

19. *The Bay of San Francisco.*

20. Correspondence from Merideth Carter-Fish (Martin Carter's great-grand-daughter) to the author, Dec. 21, 1999.

21. The patents were for improvements to railroad truck designs; the first, U.S. patent no. 353286, granted on Nov. 30, 1886, provided for lowering the effective center of gravity of a passenger car by modification of the truck design; the second, U.S. patent no. 341877, granted May 18, 1886, applied the concept of swing motion to a single-truck log bunk, an attempt at improving its riding qualities.

22. Miller, p. 327.

23. *The Bay of San Francisco,* p. 498.

24. *Niagara Falls Gazette,* July 14, 1860. The article notes that the new clerestory design was applied to New York Central sleeping cars and represented a major improvement over "ventilators on the side," which blasted passengers with a stream of cold air.

25. *Biographical and Portrait Cyclopedia of Niagara County, New York,* Samuel T. Wiley and W. Scott Garner, eds., Gresham Publishing, 1892.

26. *Niagara Falls Gazette,* Oct. 3, 1860.

27. On May 1, 1852, Judah created a commercial flier advertising his services for "engineering, surveying, leveling, estimation, etc, and to furnish Plans and Estimates for, and build Suspension Bridges of all kinds." The flier is reproduced in the Railway and Locomotive Society's *Bulletin* 156, along with a discussion by Ralph Greenhill about the myths and facts surrounding Judah's brief career in Niagara Falls. The location of his home is suggested by a copy of the insurance policy, from the Merchants Insurance Co. of Buffalo, dated June 24, 1851, now in the collection of the Niagara Falls Library. In the policy, the house is located "on the bank of the Niagara River, in the village of Belleview," the former name of Suspension Bridge. Judah's wife, Anna, later described the house as having a spectacular view of the falls and river. At the time they lived in it, Roebling's suspension bridge was under construction.

28. The Sacramento Valley Railroad is generally credited with being the first steam-operated, passenger-carrying railroad to offer scheduled service west of the Rockies. However, earlier, more specialized railroads existed in the West, for example, the horse-drawn predecessor of the Arcata & Mad River, and a portage railroad at Cascade Locks on the Columbia River.

29. *Sacramento Union,* July 4, 1855.

30. *Niagara City Herald,* Dec. 21, 1861.

31. Interview with Martin Grover Carter, Los Angeles, 1975, by author and John I. MacGregor.

32. Ibid.

33. In an article published on Jan. 29, 1862, the *Niagara Falls Gazette* noted that the railroad shops in that town would close on Feb. 1, 1862.

34. *Niagara Falls Gazette,* Jan. 8, 1862. The Canadian Great Western Railroad

ran from Suspension Bridge, N.Y., to Detroit, and the *Gazette* estimated that three quarters of its revenue was generated from American business. The railroad's apparent need for a "loyalty oath" from its employees, many of whom were American, was viewed in the Niagara Falls press as unwelcome.

35. *Niagara Falls Gazette,* Nov. 5, 1862.
36. Entitled "An Act to provide for the enrollment of the militia, the organization and discipline of the National Guard of the State of New York and for the public defence," passed Apr. 23, 1862, and contained provisions for the draft.

Chapter 2

1. James Ambrose Carroll diaries, 1855 through 1859; Sacramento Archives and Museum Collection Center.
2. A year earlier, in 1854, the predecessor of the Arcata & Mad River Railroad started construction of a horse-drawn tram on the pier at Arcata, Calif., near Eureka. Even though it began construction one year later, the Sacramento Valley Railroad ranks as the first freight and passenger carrying steam railroad in the state.
3. Carroll diary, Feb. 27, 1856; the width of the side sill is called out in Carroll's diary, and the depth is estimated from typical practice of the period.
4. White, *The American Railroad Freight Car,* p. 219.
5. Evidence that Davenport and Bridges was the manufacturer of early Sacramento Valley rolling stock is based on *The Transaction of the California State Agricultural Society,* published in Sacramento in 1892, describing Sacramento Valley Railroad coach number 4 (on display that year at the state agricultural fair) as having been built in Cambridge, Mass., in 1854, at a cost of $2,300. It was not stated who the manufacturer was, but Davenport and Bridges was the only railroad car manufacturer in Cambridge at the time.
6. John Ambrose Carroll's employment by Davenport and Bridges remains conjectured, but a John Carroll (without middle initial) is listed as a carpenter in the 1852 *Cambridge Directory and Almanac,* published by John Ford, also editor of the *Cambridge Chronicle* (research in Cambridge business directories by Richard Pitter, through Wendell Huffman).
7. Wendell W. Huffman, *The Placerville Branch of the Southern Pacific,* 1998, unpublished manuscript, p. 42.
8. Huffman, "Railroads Shipped by Sea," *Railway and Locomotive Historical Society Bulletin, 180,* Spring 1999, pp. 7–30.
9. Huffman, *Placerville Branch,* p. 400. It is not known if the San Francisco contractor engine had steamed or simply been stored.
10. *Sacramento Union,* Feb. 11, 1865. The actual income is estimated. "From the total income received," the *Union* wrote, "the sum of $600 is deducted for family expenses, and also the actual amount of house-rent paid." The published figure, $1,268, ought to represent the balance of John Carroll's income for 1865.
11. White, pp. 442–43; Charles Davenport's truck patents included swing motion (1841) and metal arch bar side frames (1844).
12. *Cambridge Directory and Almanac,* 1849–1854; p. 25 for 1847–48; courtesy Richard Pitter.
13. *Sacramento Union,* Jan. 18, 1861.
14. *Folsom Telegraph,* June 10, 1865.
15. Huffman, *Placerville Branch,* p. 103.

16. Original in the California State Railroad Museum collection. Although undated, the "What I Want" memo suggests that the first money Judah borrowed was made available in January 1860.

17. *Preliminary Survey for the Pacific Railroad: Report of the Chief Engineer,* Stanford University Library.

18. Letter from Lester Robinson to J. Mora Moss, Mar. 4, 1861; in the J. Mora Moss Collection, Wells Fargo History Room, Wells Fargo Bank, San Francisco.

19. William J. Lewis's long career as a civil engineer in California included surveys for the Pacific & Atlantic Railroad, for the predecessor to the San Francisco & San Jose; for the first railroad from Benicia to Marysville; for the first Western Pacific from San Jose to Sacramento; and for an extension of the SF&SJ to Gilroy (*Daily Alta California* and *San Francisco Times* of July 9, 1883, reported two days after Lewis's death).

20. Huffman, *Placerville Branch,* p. 191.

21. *Sacramento Union,* Feb. 18, 1865. The listed income is only a partial figure; using the guidelines described in note 10, Thomas Carter's income is listed as $200 in the *Union* inventory. Six hundred dollars is understood to be added for living expenses, suggesting a gross income of perhaps $1,000 per year.

22. Huffman, *Placerville Branch,* pp. 97–98.

23. Judah's survey work in the summer of 1861 was "final" only in the sense that it selected the Donner Lake route over other alternative crossings of the Sierra Nevada. For the next five years, sections of Judah's original survey would be relocated—the largest being a route east of Dutch Flat along the American River, not along the Yuba River, as Judah had planned.

24. Report of the U.S. Pacific Railway Commission, 1887, p. 4531.

25. Mileage on Sacramento Valley locomotives referred to in the *Folsom Telegraph* on Oct. 21, 1865.

26. *Telegraph,* June 17, 1865.

27. An article in the *Telegraph* dated Apr. 25, 1868, describes two additional lathes being added to seven existing ones in the machine shop, leading to the conclusion that the seven lathes were part of the original shop equipment. The *Telegraph* lists shop capabilities on June 24, 1865.

28. Huffman, *Placerville Branch,* pp. 205–6.

29. Huntington letters, Hopkins to Huntington, Feb. 21, 1866.

30. *Folsom Telegraph,* Jan. 27, 1866.

31. *Telegraph,* Oct. 13, 1866.

32. Huffman, *Placerville Branch,* p. 98.

33. The original dictionary is in the Martin G. Carter collection.

34. San Francisco business directories list Casebolt as a "Coach and Car Builder" as early as 1862; his obituary repeats the undated story that Casebolt built the first cars "used in San Francisco" (*Call,* Sept. 24, 1892); this is a possible reference to the four steam dummies built for the Market Street Railroad in 1860, allegedly the first railway rolling stock built in San Francisco.

35. *San Francisco Daily Alta California,* Mar. 13, 1866.

36. *San Francisco Bulletin,* Nov. 5, 1874.

37. *Bulletin,* Oct. 29, 1875.

38. *San Francisco Town Crier,* Aug. 19, 1876.

39. In 1873, San Francisco's street railway system used 163 horsecars, 1,391 horses, and 598 employees to service seven companies operating 30.5 miles of track (*San Francisco Bulletin,* Apr. 1, 1873).

40. *Bulletin,* Nov. 24, 1871.

41. A history of major foundries and ironworks is compiled in the *Bulletin* of Apr. 29, 1872; at the time of Carter's imagined walk, in the fall of 1868, all of the foundries mentioned would have been in operation under the names found in the text of the *Bulletin* article.

42. A brief history of the early iron foundries in San Francisco is in the *Bulletin* of July 9, 1875.

43. The description of Miner's Foundry is from an unidentified newspaper article of the 1860s, reproduced in part in *Archeology of the SF-480 Terminal Separation Rebuild Project,* p. 129; see also *San Francisco Bulletin,* Oct. 23, 1871.

44. The first locomotive built by Union Iron was the *California,* for the San Francisco & San Jose Railroad in 1865.

45. *San Francisco Bulletin,* June 12, 1873, and June 3, 1876.

46. See the *San Francisco Bulletin* of Oct. 23, 1871, for a list of Risdon's wheel customers; they included the Central Pacific and Southern Pacific railroads.

47. The story of Palmer Cox's background appeared in the *San Francisco Alta,* Jan. 31, 1874.

48. Miller, *Emigrants and Exiles,* p. 321.

49. Typical prices of a working-class San Francisco restaurant are reviewed in the *San Francisco Bulletin* of Nov. 2, 1875. Carter's imagined lunch at the Miner's is reconstructed from that article.

50. Nancy Olmsted, *Vanished Waters: A History of San Francisco's Mission Bay,* Mission Creek Conservancy, 1986, p. 41.

51. 1867 San Francisco directory identifies Carroll as a car builder on the Potrero & Bay View Railroad, with shops at 627 Sacramento and residence at Kentucky near Butte.

52. The earliest R. G. Dun credit report on "Kimball Carriage & Car Mfg Co." is dated November 1869 and in estimating the expense of constructing the Fourth and Bryant factory says "they must have gone to an expense of, say, $250,000."

53. George Lyman, *Ralston's Ring,* Scribner, 1937, p. 227.

54. R. G. Dun and Co., California [accounts], p. 376.

55. *San Francisco Trade Circular* (undated), quoted in *Sketches of Leading Representative Men of San Francisco,* 1875, sketch of Capt. R. L. Ogden.

56. *San Francisco Bulletin,* Oct. 7, 1871.

57. White, p. 146.

58. Langley's San Francisco Directory, 1869–70.

59. The date of Mary Carroll's death is uncertain, but she does not appear with John Carroll in the U.S. census records of 1870. His four children are listed living with him in Portland, Oregon, when he is employed by the Oregon Central Railroad.

60. Thomas Carter was naturalized in the District Court, Sixth Judicial District, in Sacramento on Sept. 18, 1868 (vol. C, p. 123, Naturalization Records).

61. The manuscript census records of 1870, taken in Portland, Oregon, list Carroll's birthplace as New Brunswick. Both previous and subsequent voter registration records list his birthplace as Maryland. There is no record of Carroll's naturalization.

62. Olmsted, p. 42. The grant was actually divided into a 60-acre subgrant, donated to the participating railroads; a 58-acre subgrant, sold to the railroads; 4 acres leased to the railroads; and an additional 28 acres donated for right-of-way, making a total of 150 acres of Mission Bay land.

63. Mileages tabulated from *Report of the Board of Commissioners of Transportation to the Legislature of the State of California,* Dec. 1877.

64. See, for example, the *Carson City Daily Appeal* of June 14, 1868.

65. *San Francisco Bulletin,* Jan. 29, 1872.

66. Letter from Mark Hopkins to Collis Huntington, May 31, 1865, in the Huntington papers; it is likely that Hopkins consulted Ben Welch before in effect suggesting company policy governing the purchase of wood for building rolling stock.

67. White, p. 453. Kyle Wyatt has argued that the Allen truck, also known as the "California truck," made its first appearance on the Central Pacific in 1872, several years after Carter left the Sacramento shop, a likely assumption since the recession drove Central Pacific orders for new equipment to a virtual standstill in the period 1869–1872. It is also likely, however, that Carter witnessed the conditions that led to the trial of the Allen truck. The design of the California truck contained many of the structural elements of Carter's later three-foot-gauge adaptation, including swing motion, which appeared on the South Pacific Coast Railroad as early as 1876.

68. The names of Central Pacific shop employees are taken from 1870 U.S. Census records correlated with the 1869 Sacramento city directory. The names listed in the text appeared in both listings.

69. *Petaluma Argus,* Feb. 17, 1872.

70. Peter Donahue sold the San Francisco & North Pacific to the California Pacific on Apr. 13, 1871, after the Cal P began construction of a parallel right-of-way near Santa Rosa. A comprehensive history of the Cal P up to the time of the European bond holder suit is given in the *San Francisco Bulletin* of Aug. 7, 1874. See also Gilbert Kneiss, *Redwood Railways,* Berkeley: Howell North Books, 1956, p. 34.

71. *California As I Saw It: First-Person Narratives of California's Early Years, 1849–1900,* part 10, "Recollections of a Newspaperman: A Record of Life and Events in California," by Frank A. Leach.

72. Central Pacific equipment roster, Oct. 1875, sections on the California Pacific Railroad, pp. 72–74, California State Railroad Museum collection.

73. Vallejo Directory, Kelley and Prescott, 1870, p. 292.

74. At the time, Donahue was a trustee of the affiliated Southern Pacific, which minimizes the chance that he would launch a serious competitive threat to the Stanford organization.

75. From Lucinda Woodward, *A Documentary History of California's State Capitol,* Sacramento: Joint Committee on Rules, 1981.

76. Interview with Martin G. Carter, by the author and John I. MacGregor, in Los Angeles, 1975.

Chapter 3

1. North Pacific Coast Journal no. 1, Dec. 1871–Dec. 1874, reported full salaries paid to George Black for Feb. and Mar. 1872. The journal is in the Southern Pacific Collection, Department of Special Collections and University Archives, Green Library, Stanford University, and hereafter referred to as Journal no. 1.

2. The White's Hill survey actually adopted had a grade of 121 feet to the mile for more than four continuous miles; "Board of Commissioners of Transportation to the Legislature of the State of California, December, 1877" (hereafter referred to as "Board of Commissioners Report, 1877"), p. 426.

3. The length of the White's Hill tunnel, as completed, was 1,250 feet, indicating Black's location did not climb as high as the final location. Fred Stindt,

The Northwestern Pacific Railroad, published by Stindt and Guy Dunscomb, 1964, p. 119.

4. Black attached detailed cost estimates to his letter of resignation, including line-item costs for land purchase, earthwork, rail, culverts, fencing, structures, rolling stock, and ties.

5. The original Austin Moore purchases in the Rancho Bodega are detailed in the deed conveying the property from A. D. Moore to the Russian River Land and Lumber Co., dated Sept. 2, 1875, filed in the Sonoma County Recorder's Office Book of Deeds, pp. 300–53. The author thanks Harry Lapham for research into Russian River Land and Lumber Co. deeds.

6. The first known instance of Black's work on the North Pacific Coast was reported in Journal no. 1 on Feb. 9, 1872. He reported extensive field hours in the same journal by Mar. 21.

7. References to the "Dutch Bill" timber reserve, or region, occur in early North Pacific Coast records—for example, the Feb. 24, 1873, entry in NPC's Journal no. 1 referring to surveyor John Wade beginning work on the "Dutch Bill section" of the railroad. The nearby village of Howards, later Occidental, was also referred to as Dutch Bill's; see *Marin County Journal,* Oct. 6, 1876; after 1877, however, Moore's timber preserve is more commonly referred to as the Russian River Land and Lumber Co.'s holding.

8. *Saucelito Weekly Herald,* Nov. 18, 1871.

9. *Weekly Herald,* June 17, 1871.

10. *Weekly Herald,* July 6, 1872. The incident occurred at the height of Stanford's efforts to secure a San Francisco terminal for the Central Pacific.

11. SF&NP track was in operation to Cloverdale, north of the Russian River, by Apr. 15, 1872, barely five weeks before Black's resignation. See Stindt, p. 13.

12. The full text of Moore's "apology" was dated Aug. 8, 1872, and published in the *Saucelito Weekly Herald* on Aug. 24.

13. Journal no. 1, for Dec. 16, 1871, p. 1. The 935 stock subscriptions include 100 shares for A. D. Moore, 50 for William Tillinghast, and 50 for Samuel P. Taylor. In the next six months, fewer than 50 additional shares were sold (for example, Warren Dutton's 25 shares on Jan. 24, 1872).

14. Journal no. 1, pp. 1–38, show a total of four stock assessments.

15. Construction activity for the summer of 1872 is reflected in an entry for Journal no. 1, on Aug. 21, 1872, reporting twenty-one men employed on grading for a total monthly payroll of $466.66.

16. The *Marin County Journal* of Apr. 6, 1876, noted that the county bond monies, totaling $160,000, were not actually delivered to the railroad until that month, rendering the subsidy useless to Austin Moore's efforts at fundraising prior to the opening of the line to Tomales.

17. *Saucelito Weekly Herald,* Aug. 12, 1871, and Sept. 23, 1871.

18. George Hilton, *American Narrow Gauge Railroads,* Stanford University Press, 1990, pp. 171–75.

19. Hilton, p. 174, quoting Howard Schuyler in the *Railroad Gazette,* Mar. 1871, p. 360.

20. Hilton, pp. 174 and 176; within its own ads, the company's name was inconsistently spelled "Billmeyer & Smalls" or "Billmeyer & Small."

21. Jackson and Sharp have been given credit for manufacturing the first two-truck, eight-wheel narrow gauge cars, designed and built under the direction of Superintendent William S. Auchincloss; *Railroad Gazette,* Mar. 23, 1872, p. 129.

22. Hilton, p. 176.

23. Stephen Powers, letter to the editors of the *Railroad Gazette,* May 9, 1874, pp. 171–72; the list of proposed California narrow gauges was included in Powers's summary.

24. F. A. Hihn, as reported in the *Santa Cruz Sentinel,* Sept. 7, 1872; Hihn advocated a San Francisco–San Diego narrow gauge system while laying the political groundwork for the eighteen-mile-long Santa Cruz Rail Road.

25. Journal no. 1, dates and amount of assessment noted between Dec. 16, 1871, and Apr. 22, 1873.

26. Journal no. 1; advance payment on bond hypothecate accounts began on Apr. 30, 1873, with $65,000 and extended (usually monthly) to Oct. 22, 1874, totaling $335,000.

27. Journal no. 1, Feb. 24, 1873.

28. Payments on interest dated May 1, 1875, in the NPC Cash Book no. 2 indicate that Falkner and Bell held bonds on the San Rafael & San Quentin Railroad, which the North Pacific Coast controlled by Mar. 1875.

29. Renton Smith would, by 1875, reorganize as Renton Holmes. The names are used inconsistently in the NPC financial record books; for our purposes, the company is referred to as Renton Smith for activities taking place in 1874 and Renton Holmes thereafter.

30. Referred to as "Mr. Lemon" in all known *Marin County Journal* references from the time of the NPC's construction, he is probably the same James M. Lemon who performed contract grading on the Vacaville Extension Railroad in Mar. 1875; see, for example, the *Vallejo Chronicle* of Mar. 25, 1875.

31. *Saucelito Weekly Herald,* Apr. 12, 1873.

32. Journal no. 1 indicates that sounding work on Richardson Bay may have been in progress between Jan. 6 and Mar. 7, 1873, the dates of hire for the boat of Charles Forrest. However, on Mar. 31, the Journal records a payment to Thomas Cassidy for two days' "work at Saucelito with Mr. Carter, sounding," which suggests that the final profiles of Richardson Bay were made during the week of Mar. 30–Apr. 4, 1873, consistent with the report in the *Herald.*

33. On Apr. 12, 1873, the *Herald* noted that engineer Smith and two surveyors had duplicated Carter's earlier soundings, working on-site on Thursday, Apr. 10, and "gave a result nearly identical" to Carter's the previous week. Apparently, Smith was a cautious engineer.

34. The Duncan timber contract, paid in part on July 10, 1873, is interesting for two reasons: first, Duncan was paid partly in railroad stock, which was an incentive for what later became Duncan's commitment to move his mill to the railhead when the NPC reached the Russian River; second, no attempt was made to use Austin Moore's nearby sawmill, or timber holdings, for the same purpose.

35. *Saucelito Herald,* Apr. 26, 1873.

36. The William Henry Gorrill papers, hereafter cited as the Gorrill papers, include correspondence, clippings, day books, and ephemera; they are at the Center for Archival Collections, Bowling Green State University, in Ohio.

37. The Smith bridge design was patented on July 16, 1867, by Robert W. Smith.

38. Letter from William Henry Gorrill to Addie Walker, from San Jose, Jan. 29, 1870; Gorrill papers.

39. The original Smith design has been compared to a Warren truss, which relied on wood diagonals for both compression and tension; it is a revision of the Howe truss, which uses heavy metal rods for tension members (John Stutz, in a conversation with the author on Apr. 6, 1999).

40. Robert W. Smith incorporated the Smith Bridge Co. in 1870 and soon was

overseeing construction of seventy-five bridges a year all over the Midwest. Able to centralize his business, he concentrated on production-style tooling, inventing machines for shaping and planing the timbers that went into his truss design. He franchised the design all over the United States, granting Henry Gorrill's Pacific Bridge the exclusive West Coast rights (Gorrill Papers).

41. William Henry Gorrill to Addie Walker, from San Francisco, Jan. 7, 1870 (Gorrill papers).

42. William Henry Gorrill diary, Mar. 28, 1870 (Gorrill papers); the names of Carroll and Kidder, as well as Sam Montague, were included after Henry's visit to Sacramento, presumably to the Sacramento shops of the Central Pacific.

43. William Henry Gorrill to Addie Walker, July 3, 1870 (Gorrill papers).

44. *Scientific Press,* Apr. 1871.

45. Examples include the San Lorenzo River Bridge, designed by Carter in 1874 (see Chapter Six), and at least one of three South Pacific Coast drawbridges (see Chapter Nine). The sole surviving Carter bridge elevation shows one of the South Pacific Coast drawbridges but includes no detail of the truss design; photographs, however, substantiate that the bridges named here were built to the Howe truss concept.

46. Journal no. 1, Aug. 22, 1873.

47. The first entry in Charlie Gorrill's diary referring to contractual work at Saucelito is on July 18, 1873; the last, indicating payment of crews with money from Grim, is on Dec. 16 (Gorrill papers).

48. Carter next appears working as a bridge design engineer on the Santa Cruz Rail Road in Apr. 1874. His professional activities between July 1873 and Apr. 1874 are open to speculation.

49. *Saucelito Herald,* May 10, 1873.   51. *Journal,* July 24, 1873.

50. *Marin County Journal,* Apr. 10, 1873.   52. *Journal,* Sept. 18, 1873.

53. As late as July 31, 1873, the *Marin County Journal* reported that the "planed stuff for the draw in the bridge" was ordered but had not yet arrived from Puget Sound, indicating the railroad's continuing intention to complete the drawbridge.

54. Journal no. 1, entry for July 17, 1873.

55. Schuyler's remarks were made on the occasion of a successful holing through the White's Hill tunnel and were recorded in the *Marin County Journal* on Mar. 12, 1874.

56. Journal no. 1, summary of account balances for June 8, 1874.

57. Monies spent are from Chief Engineer's Report, North Pacific Coast, Sept. 30, 1873, pp. 26–27; total monies collected are estimated from NPC Journal no. 1, Dec. 1871–Sept. 1873.

58. Since no cash books survive for the period, we may surmise that other spending was going on during the winter of 1874 but simply remained undocumented; however, in the three years spanned by Journal no. 1, at no period of time was its recorded activity as sparse as in the first six months of 1874, when, as noted, only one entry per month (Howard Schuyler's salary voucher) appears in Apr. and May. This suggests a virtual standstill in contractor activity and is the primary evidence for believing that Carter had no car building activity at Saucelito until at least July 1874.

59. A reference to the contract appears in R. G. Dun and Co. Credit Reports, California 16, p. 370, dated July 10, 1874. It states that "at present they [Kimball] have very little work on hand except a contract to build 12 narrow gauge cars for the North Pacific Coast Railroad." An article of nearly the

same date, July 16, 1874, in the *Marin County Journal* also describes the contract. It remains unclear what car types were included, but at least one baggage car and one combine may have been included with coaches.

60. Schuyler estimated NPC passenger car prices in the Chief Engineer's Report to the board of directors on Sept. 30, 1873. He listed twelve passenger cars: four first-class coaches at $2,500 each, five second-class coaches at $2,000 each, and two baggage cars at $1,800 each, totaling $25,400. In the same report, Schuyler also listed the total current contract liability to Kimball at $29,400, suggesting that an additional $4,000 had been obligated to Kimball for flatcars. However, Schuyler's estimate does not explain Kimball's $43,840.75 actual balance for passenger cars sold to the NPC, as summed from 1874 and 1875 ledgers, journals, and cash books. A better fit comes from adding $3,600 for each of eleven coaches, $1,800 for one baggage car, and $5,000 for the private car *M.S.L.* delivered in Sept. 1875. This total is $46,400, reasonably close to the balance quoted here. Of the three prices, those for coaches and the *M.S.L.* are quoted from newspapers; the price of baggage cars is adopted from Schuyler's 1873 Chief Engineer's Report.

61. *San Francisco Call,* Sept. 27, 1874.

62. The only extant North Pacific Coast Kimball coach, believed to be number 8, is located today at the Huckleberry Museum in Flint, Michigan. Its construction reveals just four 4" × 6" car sills manufactured at a time when industry standard was six sills. In addition, coach 8 reveals a number of construction features similar to those found on Wason cars, such as unique details of window sill framing.

63. Estimates of the cost of rolling stock to equip the line come from Schuyler's Sept. 30, 1873, report to the board of directors and total $258,025. At the time of this report, however, it is likely that only ten flatcars had actually been purchased from Kimball, and probably just five of those actually delivered.

64. The crucial impact of painting on car production schedules was noted by the *San Francisco Newsletter* on Oct. 10, 1874: "The passenger train between Saucelito and San Rafael will not run before November 1, because Kimball will not be able to complete painting of cars." A thorough paint job took at least eight weeks, most of the time to allow for adequate drying between coats.

65. Reported in the *Marin County Journal,* Aug. 28, 1873.

66. The report of Carter's taking the rolling stock contract occurred in the *Journal* on July 9, 1874; by July 16, the paper reported ten flatcars were "on hand," suggesting that Carter could not have built them. Earlier, on June 8, 1874, NPC's financial journal no. 1 reported $5,323 having already been spent on "freight cars," presumably under the terms and conditions of the Kimball contract. We can estimate that at $425 each, the money was adequate to build twelve flatcars, nearly the ten reported on July 16, 1874.

67. Lyman, *Ralston's Ring,* p. 228.

68. R. G. Dun and Co., California 16, p. 370; credit report on the Kimball Carriage and Car Co., Oct. 24, 1873.

69. See, for example, *San Francisco Call,* Feb. 2, 1875 (rickshaws) or Feb. 6, 1875 (scow schooners), or the *Bulletin,* May 27, 1874 (tug boat).

70. Henry Fairfax Williams papers, in Bancroft Library; see the entry for Aug. 26, 1874.

71. A number of local newspaper sources on the *Siempre Viva* were compiled by John White in "George P. Kimball: A Pacific Coast Car Builder," *Railway and Locomotive Historical Society Bulletin,* spring 1978, vol. 138; these in-

clude the *Alta California* on May 17, 1871, and the *Pacific Rural Press* on May 27, 1871.

72. R. G. Dun and Co., California 14, p. 376.

73. *San Francisco Bulletin,* Jan. 18, 1872.

74. "Restoration Feasibility Investigation on Nine Selected Passenger and Freight Cars," Virginia & Truckee Collection, Nevada State Museum (Stephen Drew, for Short Line Enterprises, June 1981, p. 64).

75. Correspondence between R. L. Ogden of Kimball and H. M. Yerington of the Virginia & Truckee, Feb. 3, 1873 (Special Collections, University of Nevada Library).

76. List of suppliers and vendors comes from the *San Francisco Bulletin,* Jan. 18, 1872.

77. Schuyler's Chief Engineer's Report, dated Sept. 30, 1873, lists the rolling stock required to complete the railroad:

four passenger engines	@ $8,500	135 platform cars	@ $425
three freight engines	@ $10,000	5 stock cars	@ $500
three freight engines	@ $12,000	20 box cars	@ $500
four first-class pass cars	@ $2,500	10 combination cars	@ $600
five second-class " "	@ $2,000	10 hand cars	@ $200
three baggage cars	@ $1,800	10 push cars	@ $50

The total number of passenger cars (twelve) matches the apparent total for the Kimball contract, which, at this date, might already have been awarded. However, prices for passenger cars, reflected in Schuyler's report, appear to be considerably lower than those in the press, which quoted $3,600 for a coach.

78. On Sept. 14, 1874, Latham would purchase an additional 1,137$^1/_2$ shares, bringing his total for the year to 4,387$^1/_2$ shares.

79. R. G. Dun and Co., California 17, p. 34.

80. The location of Austin Moore's original mill was on Knowles Ravine, located 3$^1/_2$ miles upstream from the original Duncan's mill near the mouth of the Russian River.

81. The first of Latham's timber purchases was apparently a deed executed between the Russian River Land and Lumber Co. and Latham on Sept. 9, 1875, and recorded in the Sonoma County Recorder's Office. Other timber land sales to Latham in the same area would continue over the next two years (research courtesy Harold Lapham).

82. Journal no. 1, pp. 215–16, lists A. P. Wood's track-laying activity extending from the Saucelito shop area to the station of Fisherman's, on Tomales Bay. It is likely that he is responsible for laying the entire mainline from the Saucelito shops to Tomales.

83. Renton Smith became Renton Holmes sometime in 1875, both names referring to the holding company operating the Port Blakely mill on Puget Sound.

84. On Nov. 30, 1874, NPC Journal no. 1 reports $696.11 spent under Carter's account 45, "for materials used in building cars," and includes almost nineteen thousand board feet of redwood. This material would have been used in Carter's construction of roughly forty boxcars and two express cars.

85. Journal no. 1 is at Stanford University Special Collections; all other ledgers and cash books are in the collection of the CSRM.

86. *Marin County Journal,* Oct. 14, 1875, lists 100 flatcars and 40 boxcars on the roster; also "Board of Commissioners Report, 1877," for North Pacific Coast Railroad year ending June 30, 1876, p. 164, listing 150 freight cars total. The two express cars are assumed to be the first two baggage-mail-

express cars on the railroad (see roster in Appendix A), although little is known about them, other than a *Journal* announcement on Nov. 5, 1874, that Thomas Carter has completed "two splendid express cars" in the Saucelito shops. Although later newspaper accounts attribute the line's early baggage cars to Kimball, we assume that the first baggage cars on the railroad were these cars.

87. The key assumption in estimating these prices is that the ratio of Carter flatcar to boxcar prices remained constant; on the basis of 1882 Carter prices to the San Joaquin & Sierra Nevada, cited in its cash book (preserved by the CSRM), that ratio is $410/$525 = 0.78. The retail value of each type of car is then calculated as a percentage of the $51,000 total value of the folio. The express cars are estimated to have cost $1,800 each, the price quoted by Howard Schuyler in his 1873 Chief Engineer's Report.

88. Summary of new rolling stock quotations for the Carson & Colorado, mid-1880 (Carson & Colorado Collection, University of Nevada Special Collections). Carter's freight charges for a flatcar were $30 in addition to the $450 purchase price, or $480 total. A complete Barney and Smith flatcar, including shipping, was estimated at $492.80. Carter undoubtedly kept that pricing in mind when it set its own prices. Other than the NPC work, the lowest known price for a Carter flatcar was $375, charged to the Pacific Coast Railway in a contract signed July 31, 1884 (contract in the Oregon Improvement Co. Collection, Manuscripts and University Archives, University of Washington Libraries).

89. As of Jan. 1, 1875, the *Marin County Journal* reported the North Pacific Coast had seventy-five freight cars on its roster, sixty-five of which were probably Carter products. In round numbers, this represented almost half of Carter's incomplete car contract.

90. Carter's labor cost per car is also corroborated by a separate cash book entry for 1876, noting a credit to Carter of $35 per car for assembling flatcars from kits. The context of this work is explored in Chapter Five.

91. Flatcar part inventory and estimates of cost:

Name of Part	Est. Cost	Source
Castings	$22	@ .03/lb.; *National Car Builder,* Feb. 1881, p. 71 (hereafter, NCB)
Lumber, per 1,000	$42	*San Francisco Bulletin,* Mar. 2, 1874
Draft springs	$3	Carter 1898 plant inventory
Oak	$3	NCB
Paint	$2	NCB
Truss rods	$22	@ .04/lb.; NCB
Fasteners	$15	NCB
Wheels, axles	$117	Cash books, SJ&SN RR (from Huntington and Hopkins Hardware, vendor, 1881)
Arch bars	$20	NCB
Truck springs	$5	Carter 1898 plant inventory
Brasses	$5	Carter 1898 plant inventory
Misc.	$10	Includes shipments of raw materials
Labor	$34	10% of estimated retail price
Total	$300	

92. The fact that the shop account, 269, carries a lower account number than the new car accounts (561 and 566) suggests that the shop activity

represented by account 45 never really ended but simply changed accounting numbers, to 269, and so predates the new car contract.

93. The North Pacific Coast Saucelito shop journal, in the collection of the Northwestern Pacific Railroad Historical Society, begins on June 4, 1875, and covers shop activity through Oct. 31, 1875; the volume then jumps to Jan. 31, 1878, and includes car and locomotive maintenance activity through Nov. 1, 1878.

94. As examples, "Material furnished car department in July [1875]: $5.18" and "Freight car repair, material furnished in August [1875]: $76.24." Numerous other entries, in the same time period, are clearly attributed to Carter (for example, "Bridge repair, materials furnished by T. Carter as per his bill— 6/30/75: $6.50").

95. The best example is a set of ten drawings prepared to document a ten-ton-capacity combination boxcar, believed to have been drawn in the 1890s at the Newark factory by a part-time draftsman named Sunderer. Portions of this drawing are reproduced in Chapter Eleven.

96. See a drawing of a Carter standard gauge truck pedestal for the Eel River & Eureka Railroad, 1883 (CSRM).

97. On the basis of the earliest known date that John Kidder was involved in the M&SV (Mar. 10, 1874), the date of receipt for steamship tickets to begin survey work.

98. The Great Register of Marin County, 1868–1878, Saucelito entries.

99. "Board of Commissioners Report, 1877," p. 150 (author's collection).

100. *Monterey Weekly Herald,* Sept. 5, 1874.

101. Early Denver & Rio Grande boxcars by Billmeyer and Small actually had dimensions slightly smaller than the "24-foot" standard; eight-wheel boxcar 2001, for example, measured 23'7" long over the buffer sills and six feet wide over the side sills (White, *The American Railroad Freight Car,* p. 205).

102. See elevation and plan views from *Engineering,* Dec. 11, 1871, reproduced in White, p. 205.

103. *National Car Builder,* Dec. 1878, 9(12).

104. 1874 Carter dimensions were measured from the extant Nevada Central boxcar body at Boulder City, Nevada, on Mar. 1, 1992, by Randy Hees, John Stutz, Craig Robinson, and the author; ca. 1874 Billmeyer and Small dimensions come from two Eureka & Palisade boxcar bodies, one measured at Boulder City, Nevada, on Mar. 1, 1992, and the second at Eureka, Nevada, in Aug. 2001, by Greg Maxwell. The two sets of E&P boxcar dimensions were consistent.

Component Name	1874 Carter 24' Boxcar	Ca. 1874 Billmeyer and Small 24' Boxcar
Side sill	4" × 8½"*	3½" × 7"
Center sill	3¾" × 8¼"*	3½" × 7¼"
End sill	5" × 8½"*	5½" × 4¾"
Bolster	5½" × 9½"	4" × 12"*
Wall post	2" × 2¾"	2" × 2¾"
Wall plate	3" × 4¼"*	2¾" × 4¼"
Wall diagonals	1½" × 2¾"	1¾" × 3½"*
Corner post	2½" × 3½"	3½" × 3½"*
Roof end cap	2¾" × 8"	2¾" × 8"
Carlines	2¼" × 8"*	1⅝" × 8"

* indicates larger cross section

In the critical area of frame sills, the average part sizes for Carter were generally larger than for the equivalent Billmeyer and Small part. Carter used Douglas fir for all of its parts; Billmeyer and Small used southern yellow pine, materials comparable in strength.

105. Billmeyer and Small's cushion drawbar system, first introduced on the Denver & Rio Grande, never became popular on western roads.

106. For a discussion of the evolution of swing motion truck design, see White, pp. 451–56.

107. Hilton, p. 176.

108. White, p. 453.

109. Sources for minimum radius: on the NPC, "Board of Commissioners Report, 1877," p. 415; for the M&SV, manuscript survey of the line from Monterey to the Salinas River Bridge, in the David Jacks papers (Henry E. Huntington Library).

110. Ibid., p. 135.

111. Two patents exist in Thomas Carter's name: an improvement in passenger truck design, dated Nov. 30, 1886 (U.S. Patent Office no. 353,286); and an improvement in a single-truck logging bunk, dated May 18, 1886 (U.S. Patent no. 341,877).

112. Virginia & Truckee Railroad correspondence for the Carson & Colorado Railroad, June 4, 1880 (University of Nevada Special Collections).

113. There is photographic evidence that some of the early Carter 24-foot NPC boxcars were constructed as ventilator boxcars, or "double door" boxcars, intended for either dry goods or fresh produce. In particular, see the 1875 view of "The Junction," or San Anselmo, with a new combo boxcar pictured on the left edge of the photograph.

114. The origins of the ventilator-style boxcar predate Carter's design by at least twenty years. In 1855, for example, a similar twenty-five-foot standard gauge design was built for the Illinois Central (White, p. 173). The number of Carter ventilator boxcars built for the North Pacific Coast is estimated from Schuyler's Chief Engineer's Report, Sept. 30, 1873 (see note 77 of this chapter). At the time it was written, no freight cars had been delivered to the line, but Schuyler's listing of the target quantity of cars proved to be remarkably close to the number of completed cars later reported on the roster.

115. Journal no. 1, Oct. 15, 1874, p. 192.

116. The *Marin County Journal,* on Oct. 14, 1875, cites the need for "300 freight and flat cars," while the *San Francisco Bulletin,* on Oct. 29, mentions the need for an additional 250 flats and 60 boxcars. Actually, far fewer cars were eventually purchased.

117. Mining and Scientific Press, Mar. 6, 1875; however, the *Vallejo Chronicle* noted on Mar. 20 that castings for NPC car work were still coming from the original Vallejo Foundry. It remains unclear at what point (if any) Carter took delivery on McCormick parts from the new San Francisco facility, rather than the original Vallejo Foundry.

118. *Marin County Journal,* Jan. 31, 1878, notice of $15.87 unpaid property taxes on Saucelito property of Martin Carter.

Chapter 4

1. Rodman Wilson Paul, "The Great California Grain War: The Grangers Challenge the Wheat King," *Pacific Historical Review,* Nov. 1958, pp. 331–49.

2. *Salinas City Index,* Apr. 30, 1874.

3. Op. cit., p. 337.

4. Kidder biographical data compiled from Gerald Best, *Nevada County Narrow Gauge,* Howell North Books, 1965; also Kidder's handwritten biographical sketch, in Bancroft Library manuscript collections; and articles from the *Carson City Daily Appeal,* for example on Apr. 25, 1868. This last source was made available through Richard Pitter.

5. *Solano Republican,* various issues from Jan. 23, 1873, to Apr. 1, 1874; *Benicia Tribune,* various issues from Oct. 25, 1873, to Feb. 7, 1874.

6. *Railroad Gazette,* May 9, 1874, pp. 171–72.

7. See Frederick Shaw, *Casey Jones' Locker,* San Francisco: Hesperian House, 1959. Shaw's name appeared as draftsman on an elevation of California Central Narrow Gauge baggage car number 12. Calling out Carter Brothers as its builder, the drawing has remained unexplained, since no known rolling stock orders were ever placed by the CCNG, nor was any track laid atop the grade that Kidder started in 1873. However, the trucks in Shaw's drawing bear a strong resemblance to the U-pedestal style trucks described in this chapter, which leads us to speculate that Shaw's drawing is based on evidence now lost.

8. Paul, p. 341.

9. Total mileage computed from Central Pacific and Southern Pacific mainline and branch track within California as of June 30, 1876, for a total of 1,098 miles; see "Board of Commissioners Report, 1877."

10. Paul, p. 345.

11. Ibid., p. 346.

12. *Salinas City Index,* Apr. 30, 1874.

13. *Santa Cruz Sentinel,* Jan. 3, 1874.

14. This figure ($260,000), presented as the total for constructing the railroad, was published in the *Monterey Herald* on Oct. 10, 1874; however, on Oct. 3 the *Herald* reproduced a letter from Kidder to Dr. A. S. Taylor of Santa Barbara, in which cost estimates for the railroad were broken down into various categories; this summary gives a total of slightly less than $218,000. One discrepancy between the two figures may be the purchase of land and right-of-way, not itemized in the letter to Taylor.

15. "Board of Commissioners Report, 1877," p. 151.

16. David Jacks papers, Huntington Library, vol. 7, Daily Journals and Diaries, 1874; entry dated Apr. 1, 1874.

17. *Castroville Argus,* Apr. 25, 1874.

18. *Monterey Democrat,* Mar. 21, 1874. "Brenham" may have been a misspelling of "Brennan and Co.," which operated coastal steamers in the late 1860s.

19. Minute Book of the Monterey & Salinas Railroad, Dec. 30, 1867; in collection of the Monterey County Historical Society in Salinas, California.

20. Early CP rates on grain shipment from Salinas are quoted in the *Monterey Herald,* Oct. 10, 1874.

21. Op. cit.

22. Minute Book of the Monterey & Salinas Railroad, 1868–1871; some of the three thousand lines of subscription are entries in behalf of the same name.

23. Anonymous to David Jacks, Oct. 4, 1872, in David Jacks collection, Stanford University Special Collections.

24. Ibid., various dates, 1868–1871.

25. Articles of Incorporation of Monterey and Salinas Valley Railroad, filed in the office of the Secretary of State, Mar. 5, 1874, book 6, p. 130. In this document, the official title of the company is referred to both as "Rail Road" and as "Railroad."

26. The Six Companies, closely aligned with six Chinese families, acted as both contract labor agents and benevolent societies for the largely male Chinese population of California; see Sandy Lydon, *Chinese Gold,* Capitola Book Co., 1985, p. 130.

27. "Description of Right-of-Way, Monterey to Salinas River, of the Monterey & Salinas Valley Narrow Gauge Railroad," a five-page, handwritten manuscript in the David Jacks papers; the last six miles of right-of-way to Salinas City would apparently not be finalized until the week of June 13, according to the June 20, 1874, *Monterey Herald,* and are not included in the "Description of Right-of-Way."

28. David Jacks papers, Daily Journals and Diaries, Mar. 30, 1874.

29. Ibid.

30. David Jacks papers, Ledger A, 1873–1875, p. 116, Feb. 23, 1875.

31. Op. cit., Nov. 16, 1875.

32. Op. cit., undated entry for 1874, prior to Aug. 25.

33. *Santa Cruz Sentinel,* Mar. 28 and Apr. 11, 1874.

34. *Sentinel,* June 10, 1874.

35. Robert Joseph Trusk, *Source of Capital in Early California Manufacturers, 1850–1880,* University of Illinois, 1960, Table X, p. 208, comparison of total capital investment in manufacturing by county, 1870; of a total of fifty-three counties, only forty-three are ranked, due to incomplete data.

36. *Santa Cruz Sentinel,* Apr. 11, 1874.

37. *Sentinel,* Mar. 28, 1874.

38. *Sentinel,* July 11, 1874.

39. Trusk, Table X, p. 208.

40. We know for certain only that the Monterey car shop foreman, Frank Geiser, was on the job in Monterey by June 1874. This does not preclude the possibility that John Carroll or Martin Carter might have been present earlier, possibly to help set up the factory.

41. *Monterey Democrat,* Mar. 21, 1874.

42. See note 27.

43. The dollar value standing to be lost because of the rail procurement problem comes from David Jacks's own estimate, cited in his "accounting" of his and Abbott's performance at a board meeting in June 1876 (*Monterey Democrat,* June 24, 1876.

44. *Salinas City Index,* May 23, 1874.

45. *Monterey Herald,* May 30 and June 6, 1874.

46. *Herald,* June 20, 1874; a commercial ad for the Shades Saloon, located at "Main Street near its junction with Alvarado Street," suggests that Main Street and *Calle Principal* were one and the same.

47. From a letter from Jacks to D. R. Ashley, Feb. 22, 1868, reproduced in A. E. Bestor, "David Jacks of Monterey, and Lee L. Jacks, His Daughter," Stanford University Press, 1945.

48. *Monterey Herald,* June 13, 1874.

49. James Miller Guinn, *History of the State of California and Biographical Record of Santa Cruz, San Benito, Monterey and San Luis Obispo Counties,* Chapman Publishing, 1903, p. 420.

50. California Industrial Census, June 1, 1879, to May 31, 1880, manuscript supplement to the 1880 U.S. Census (California State Library). The *Oakland Tribune* of Sept. 13, 1882, describes the Carter factory as employing twenty men; however, the paper notes it could employ as many as fifty, if adequate skilled labor were found.

51. Letter from E. E. Morgan and Sons to John Markley, secretary of the M&SV RR, reprinted in the *Monterey Herald* on Aug. 22, 1874; the letter is undated but refers to receiving correspondence from the M&SV dated "the 10th inst.," referring presumably to Aug. 10, 1874.

52. The first mention of a twelve-hundred-foot wharf, instead of the original thousand-foot structure, is made in the *Monterey Herald* on June 5, 1874.

53. *Monterey Democrat,* July 4, 1874.

54. *Herald,* Aug. 15, 1874.

55. *Herald,* July 4 and July 11, 1874.

56. The price of the combines was reported at $2,800 each in a letter written to the *Petaluma Argus* by John Markley, later superintendent of the M&SV, and published in that paper on Dec. 4, 1874.

57. California Board of Transportation Reports, 1876–77, for the Santa Cruz & Felton Railroad. However, the prices quoted may not have been Carter's contract prices, since there is evidence that trucks for both of these cars were manufactured locally in Santa Cruz. See Chapter Six, "Santa Cruz Supply Chain."

58. That Carter took special pains with his first production passenger cars strongly suggests the existence of photographic documentation. However, the absence of a commercial photographer in Monterey during 1874 may have negated the chance of photographs being taken. See Peter E. Palmquist, with Lincoln Kilian, *The Photographers of the Humboldt Bay Region, 1865–1870,* published by Palmquist, 1986, particularly in reference to C.W.J. Johnson's studio locations in 1874 (p. 88).

59. Whether called Colonial Revival yellow or not, paint manufacturers of the day used a variety of trade names for roughly the same color. John Masury, for example, called out a similar color as "car body color" in an 1877 paint sample book.

60. Board-and-batten siding shows up on a handful of other Carter passenger cars whose ancestry cannot be traced. One example is a combine shown in a photograph of the South Pacific Coast Railroad; see the author's *Narrow Gauge Portrait, South Pacific Coast,* Glenwood Books, 1975, p. 155.

61. The comparison is based on South Pacific Coast Railroad coach 39, built by Carter in 1881 and currently in the Orange Empire Railway Museum collection at Perris, California.

62. Only one narrow gauge Kimball coach survives to shed light on their design and construction, and it has been extensively rebuilt. Believed to be NPC coach 8, the car body has been restored by the Huckleberry Museum of Flint, Michigan. Its framing is notable for having just four sills, each 4" × 6", which is minimal even by narrow gauge standards of the 1870s.

63. "Report of the Chief Engineer of the Nevada Central," inventory of equipment, Feb. 24, 1880 (Stokes collection, University of Nevada Archives).

64. The primary evidence comes from photographs taken of one of the combines at the Battle Mountain, Nevada, Central Pacific freight house, and can be dated as earlier than the fire that destroyed the freight house (prominent in the photograph) on Apr. 3, 1880; one combine had arrived at Battle Mountain by Dec. 20, 1879, and the second by Feb. 2, 1880 (dates from the *Battle Mountain Messenger* of Dec. 20, 1879, and Feb. 7, 1880, respectively). Therefore, at the time of the photographs, the cars could not have been on the Nevada Central more than fourteen weeks.

65. *Santa Cruz Sentinel,* June 20, 1874.

66. Sharon L. Edaburn, "Monterey & Salinas Valley Railroad Combination Car

#1 Research and Restoration Report," CSRM, Nov. 1979, pp. 58–59 (hereafter referred to as Edaburn to distinguish it from other restoration reports cited in endnotes).

67. A clerestory duckbill frame member, thought to be original because of paint samples, contained this evidence; the author's examination of original parts was conducted at the CSRM, with Kevin Bunker, in 1999.

68. Op. cit., pp. 30–34.

69. Edaburn, p. 35.

70. A match to Pantone 141–2; see Edaburn, p. 51.

71. Research and restoration of the polychrome stencils is credited to Kevin Bunker; this description comes from Bunker's reconstruction of his manuscript notes, which are in the CSRM library though currently uncatalogued.

72. *Monterey Herald,* Nov. 6, 1875, as well as Edaburn. Further evidence comes from John Markley's letter to the *Petaluma Argus,* dated Dec. 4, 1874, mentioning that the car was originally equipped with seventeen seats. With this many seats, there would have been room for a stove or a bathroom, but not both. Mike Collins's mechanical drawing of the car, reproduced in this chapter, shows one possible configuration for the seventeen-seat, "as built" version of the car.

73. The *C. S. Abbott* is described in the "Baldwin Locomotive Works Specifications for One Engine Class 8-18 D, Monterey & Salinas Valley Railroad," June 18, 1874; the *Monterey* is described in "Specifications for One Engine, Class 8-18 C, M&SV RR," Nov. 28, 1874 (California State Railroad Museum microfilm of Baldwin order records, from originals in DeGolyer Library, Southern Methodist University).

74. *The Narrow Gauge Locomotives: The Baldwin Catalog of 1877,* University of Oklahoma Press, 1967, p. 18. The rating is stated in terms of 840 gross tons' capacity on level track.

75. *Monterey Herald,* Sept. 19, 1874.

76. The satiric version of the "first excursion" was published in the *Herald* under the title "Pleasant Papers No. 4," on Sept. 19, 1874, and signed by "Sottice," probably a pseudonym.

77. Loose letter from Morgan and Sons to David Jacks, dated Aug. 6, 1874, found in Jacks's Ledger A, 1873, 1874, 1875 (David Jacks papers).

78. *Monterey Herald,* op. cit.

79. Account entries for the sale of wood to the M&SV total $578.25 by Nov. 4, 1874 (David Jacks papers, Ledger A, p. 116).

80. *Herald,* Oct. 31, 1874.

81. *Herald,* Oct. 17, 1874.

82. The *Herald* identified the project as the Hollister & San Juan Railroad in its Nov. 7, 1874, issue. This proposed narrow gauge connection with the Monterey & Salinas Valley Railroad was never built.

83. *Herald,* Oct. 31, 1874.

84. Paul, p. 349.

85. Loose receipts, David Jacks papers, Huntington Library.

86. David Jacks papers, Ledger A, p. 161, entry for Feb. 23, 1875.

87. *Monterey Herald,* Mar. 18, 1876.

Chapter 5

1. The entry was recorded on Oct. 6, 1875, in Cash Book no. 2, under "bills payable."

2. North Pacific Coast Saucelito shop record book; see, for example, entry for May 1, 1878.

3. Baldwin Locomotive Works specification on North Pacific Coast number 9 (microfilm copy at California State Railroad Museum, original in DeGolyer Library).

4. Kneiss, *Redwood Railways,* p. 72; Kneiss's description of the private car seems to add factual details to the *Marin County Journal* article of Sept. 16, 1875, although no citation is provided.

5. For example, see the *San Francisco Daily Evening Bulletin,* Dec. 11, 1876.

6. Three entries from NPC Cash Book no. 2 are totaled: Mar. 31, 1875, balance, Bank of British Columbia loan, $231,666.66; same date, balance for London and San Francisco Bank loan $435,000; and Apr. 22, 1875, balance on French Savings and Loan Society loan, $150,000.

7. NPC Ledger no. 2, account 291, "Roadbed & Track RR Extension" in the period July 1875 to Mar. 1877, totaled $458,420.09.

8. The first NPC record of John Wade doing survey work in the Dutch Bill area was on Feb. 24, 1873, in Journal no. 1 (Stanford University Special Collections).

9. NPC Ledger no. 2, pp. 291–94, reporting on aggregate costs of roadbed, track, and bridges, for "Railroad Extension."

10. The delivery of the last four Kimball cars sometime in the spring of 1875 is evidenced by NPC Cash Book no. 2, Nov. 12, 1875: note to Kimball Co. for $3,654.97; and Dec. 13, 1875, note to Kimball for $3,764.59. These amounts are close to the reported retail price of these cars ($3,600), adding perhaps incidentals or transportation charges.

11. This interesting breakdown of Carter's finished and unfinished work is from the *San Francisco Bulletin*'s Jan. 6, 1875, edition, on the opening of the first division of the NPC. It is interesting also because it suggests that of some 150 freight cars reported on the roster by July 31, 1875, only 125 may have been Carter's, which suggests that the remaining 25 cars may have been Kimball's. Other accounts suggest Kimball built just 10 NPC flatcars.

12. This work corresponds to the first order of flatcars for the Santa Cruz & Felton, which the *Santa Cruz Sentinel* notes on June 18, 1875, were under construction at Saucelito.

13. A variety of woodworking jobs are credited to Carter in the Saucelito shop book records from 1875, including fabrication of crossing signs, water tank construction, and freight car repair. But numerous charges, including the repair of a baggage car (billed on June 30, 1875) are not attributed to Carter's account. Among them are freight car repairs on July 31, 1875, charged to the "car department," which suggests that an in-house woodworking department was employed in parallel with Carter's contracting services.

14. *Marin County Journal,* Apr. 6, 1876.

15. The length of this tunnel has also been reported as 1,710 feet, on a sign fixed to the portal timbers; see Stindt, *The Northwestern Pacific Railroad,* p. 120.

16. California Commission on Transportation, report of 1875–76, and 1876–77.

17. An 1875 photograph of NPC track at San Anselmo shows evidence of crimping at joints on a curve, using spiked rail brace castings in place of angle bars as a means of keeping rail in line on curves.

18. The *Marin County Journal* of Feb. 15, 1877, notes that fifty-five-pound steel rails were being used to relay track on the south end of the NPC, near San Rafael. The paper added: "these rails have the new anglebar joints, and make the smoothest possible road."

19. *Journal,* Dec. 14, 1876. The earliest known Latham transactions for timber

lands in the area are deeds of land from O. A. Olmsted on July 15, 1875, and from Meeker on July 16, 1875, all lands on the original Rancho Bodega that would be incorporated into the Russian River Land and Lumber Co. holdings.

20. At the first stockholder's meeting of the Sonoma Lumber Co., on Apr. 28, 1877, Latham held 493 shares of stock, compared to 492 held by James Streeten, the firm's other principal owner (Sonoma Lumber Co. minute books, Bancroft Library).

21. *San Francisco Bulletin,* Dec. 1, 1874.

22. *Resources of California,* Mar. 1877 edition.

23. NPC Cash Book no. 2, Mar. 31, 1875, and Apr. 22, 1875.

24. *Marin County Journal,* Oct. 14, 1875.

25. *Journal,* Oct. 22, 1875.

26. Revenue computed from the "Board of Commissioners Report, 1877," specifically for the years 1875–76 and 1876–77; the NPC rated paper as class two freight and charged 8 cents per ton mile.

27. Ibid., p. 427.

28. Ibid., p. 167; see also the *Journal,* Oct. 14, 1875, citing the revenue for the first five months of operation at "about $18,000 per month."

29. NPC Ledger no. 2, pp. 291–94, various accounts relative to "Extension."

30. See, for example, Kneiss, p. 48, or more recently Allen Tacy, "A Number One Question," in the *Northwesterner,* Spring 1991; both Kneiss and Tacy emphasized the poor steaming qualities of NPC number 1, attributed to a "straight" style boiler lacking the "wagon top" steam reservoir of later Baldwin designs.

31. The sale of NPC's number 1 to L. E. White Lumber has long been a source of conjecture for locomotive historians. The notice of sale in the NPC cash books occurs on Jan. 3, 1882, recording the sale of the engine to L. E. White for $6,000. The author is indebted to Doug Richter and David Spohr for research on number 1's sale to White.

32. The Saucelito shop record book is now in the collection of the Northwestern Pacific Railroad Historical Society, covering locomotive, car, and physical plant repairs for the North Pacific Coast in the periods June–Dec. 1875 and Jan.–Dec. 1878.

33. Saucelito shop book, various entries, pp. 24–29; all expenditures reported are attributed to account 67, except painting the engine, which is attributed to account 38.

34. The *Mining and Scientific Press* reported, on July 3, 1875, that the change in name from H. J. Booth to Prescott, Scott had occurred shortly after Booth's retirement on June 8, 1875.

35. Original rigid wheelbase taken from Baldwin order sheet for *Saucelito,* serial number 8-18-D7; the revised rigid wheelbase is the residual spacing between the middle and last driver pairs, assuming that spacing did not change during the rebuilding work.

36. Conversation with Kyle Wyatt, curator, California State Railroad Museum, on the basis of his research on A. J. Stevens.

37. Op. cit.

38. Mason order sheet for builder's serial number 537, North Pacific Coast's number 2, the *San Rafael.*

39. NPC Cash Book no. 3, p. 101; voucher to Burnham, Perry, and Williams, $22,291.50, for three locomotives, purchased Apr. 4, 1877. The average price of these engines is $7,430.50, a considerable reduction over the engine's nominal $8,000 retail price.

40. Art Wallace, "Mr. Mason's Marvelous Machine," in *The Bear Trap*, Summer 1996.

41. Researching NPC first number 3, *Tomales*, is complicated by the fact that the builder's spec sheet, allegedly documenting the first number 3, describes an 0-6-6 standard gauge Mason bogie bearing factory number 563. As the engine appeared in the spec sheet, it was delivered on July 26, 1876, as standard gauge Galveston, Harrisburg & San Antonio Railway number 22, the *Dixie Crosby*. It is unclear whether the various specifications called out on the sheet were modified from different dimensions when the same engine was allegedly the narrow gauge version built for the North Pacific Coast.

42. *Marin County Journal*, Sept. 17, 1874.

43. Baldwin Locomotive Works specification sheets, or register of engines (from a microfilm at CSRM based on an original at the Smithsonian). *Moscow* was a light class 4-12 C (identical to *Tyrone*) intended for switching at the mills; *Madrona* and *Freestone* were class 8-18 Cs intended for mainline service.

44. Mason's spec sheet for the *Bully Boy*, assigned shop number 584, cites the delivery date as June 9, 1877.

45. Specific reference to the *Bully Boy*'s pulling capability occurs in the *Marin County Journal* for July 12, 1877, but see also the *Journal* of Mar. 8, 1877: "new engine on order to handle 12 cars; those now on the run can handle just 6."

46. *Bully Boy* weight from letter of Eliot Sparks to William Mason, Dec. 7, 1878, and tractive force from A. Bray Dickinson, *Narrow Gauge to the Redwoods*, Los Angeles: Trans Anglo Books, 1967; Baldwin 8-18 C weight from Sparks letter, and tractive force from Dickinson.

47. The likely delivery date is suggested by the *San Rafael Weekly Herald* of Nov. 2, 1876; "The NPC RR," it wrote, "have just received three new engines from the East."

48. See, for example, "North Pacific Coast Railroad Locomotive #12, 'Sonoma'" restoration report by Richard N. Katz (California State Railroad Museum, Feb. 5, 1979, pp. 5–6).

49. Maintenance expenses for the *Sonoma* from the Saucelito shop book, various entries in 1878.

50. *San Francisco Bulletin*, Apr. 25, 1876.

51. *Bulletin*, Oct. 29, 1875.

52. CSRM Collection, North Pacific Coast Railroad Ledger no. 2, p. 361.

53. NPC Cash Book no. 2, Nov. 13, 1876, voucher to Barney and Smith for $562.92, represents an incremental charge for installation of Westinghouse air brakes on new passenger equipment.

54. The first batch of three cars, numbers 15, 16, and 17, was reported in the *Reno Evening Gazette* on Aug. 25, 1876; the delivery of the second batch of three cars was reported in the May 11, 1877, *Railroad Gazette*, with no mention of road numbers.

55. *Marin County Journal*, Dec. 21, 1876.

56. San Francisco & North Pacific service into San Rafael began in June 1879.

57. NPC Ledger no. 2 recorded $23,964.76 spent on the "Moscow Bridge" at Duncan's Mills, over a period listed as Feb.–Dec. 1877.

58. *Journal*, Mar. 8, 1877.

59. *Journal*, Feb. 15, 1877.

60. *Journal*, Nov. 1, 1877.

61. *Journal*, Mar. 4, 1875.

62. Cash Book no. 3, dated Apr. 15, 1878, reported a payment of $21.00 to San Francisco photographer Thomas Houseworth, in support of pending publication in *Resources of California*.

63. The *Santa Cruz Sentinel*, Jan. 18, 1873, cited redwood selling at $20 per

thousand board feet. On Nov. 30, 1874, the North Pacific Coast *Journal*
no. 1 reported selling Carter redwood siding at $30 per thousand, which may
also reflect the cost of surfacing rough-cut material into car siding (*Journal*
p. 203).

64. North Pacific Coast *Journal no. 4,* dated Dec. 31, 1882, reporting twenty-five
cords of wood burned in the shop at a cost of $3.50 per cord.

65. NPC Cash Book no. 3, Jan. 20, 1877; this loan may have been used to pay
off part of Latham's earlier loans from the London and San Francisco Bank,
the Bank of British Columbia, and the French Savings and Loan Society.
However, Cash Book no. 3, on Feb. 1, 1878, indicates that Latham paid the
Nevada Bank loan in full.

66. NPC Cash Book no. 3, Feb. 25, 1878: "Amount received from A.D. Moore
for his proportion of the balance of $75,000 due on Co's note, date 6/19/75,
this proportion having been assumed by J.G. Eastland: $1342.50." The size of
the original note was $176,768.84, from an entry in Cash Book no. 3, dated
Aug. 10, 1878.

67. In *Redwood Railways,* Kneiss gives an accounting of NPC indebtedness:
London and San Francisco Bank, $400,000; Société Mutuelle des Épargnes
(French Savings and Loan Society), $160,000; Clay Street Bank, $300,000;
Latham estate, $600,000; total $2.4 million (p. 82).

68. *Marin County Journal,* Apr. 11, 1878.

69. *Railway Age,* vol. 3, p. 228, May 2, 1878.

70. For this reason, contemporary western narrow gauge lines were known to
inventory separately eastern-manufactured wheels and those made locally;
see Santa Cruz Rail Road inventory included in "Bill of Sale, F. A. Hihn to
the Pacific Improvement Co., April 1881" (in Frederick Hihn Archives,
Record Books, vol. 3, pp. 393-419). In that account, seventeen pairs of Whitney wheel-axles are called out separately from other (locally manufactured)
wheel-axle pairs on hand.

71. Kimball bankruptcy records, Federal Archives, San Bruno, California, case
2531, location 1022D–1023C, boxes 1–88.

Chapter 6

1. *Santa Cruz Sentinel,* Dec. 20, 1873.

2. *Ibid.,* Dec. 12, 1878.

3. Hilton, *American Narrow Gauge Railroads,* pp. 87–117.

4. Ibid., p. 90.   6. Ibid., Mar. 28, 1874.

5. *Sentinel,* Mar. 7, 1874.   7. Ibid., Jan. 3, 1874.

8. Obituary of Michael O. Boyle, "A Long Life Ended, Death of M. O. Boyle,
Santa Cruz Pioneer," *Santa Cruz Surf,* Feb. 25, 1890.

9. *Santa Cruz Sentinel,* Feb. 7, 1874.

10. Ibid., Apr. 11, 1874.

11. Ibid., Aug. 8, 1874.

12. Typescript of autobiography of Titus Hale, archives of the Pajaro Valley
Historical Association, Watsonville.

13. Transcript, *Santa Cruz Railroad Company* v. *Board of Supervisors of Santa
Cruz County,* before the Supreme Court of the State of California, Case
6287, Oct. 1878; testimony of F. A. Hihn, p. 67, folio 198, 199.

14. Comparison of construction costs is based on four narrow gauge lines completed by July 1876: SCRR, $15,129 per mile; M&SV, $16,052 per mile; NCNG,
$19,939 per mile, and North Pacific Coast (on the basis of fifty-one com-

pleted miles to Tomales), $45,560 per mile; "Board of Commissioners Report, 1877."

15. W. W. Elliott, *Santa Cruz County, California, Illustrations,* Wallace W. Elliott and Co., 1879.
16. *Sentinel,* June 1, 1872.
17. *Sentinel,* Nov. 22, 1873.
18. *Sentinel,* Sept. 14, 1872.
19. See "List of Stockholders of Santa Cruz Railroad Company," in "Board of Commissioners Report, 1877," p. 173.
20. Ibid., p. 179.
21. *Santa Cruz Sentinel,* Feb. 5, 1877.
22. "Report of the Eighth Industrial Exhibition of the Mechanics Institute of the City of San Francisco," Sept. 7, 1871, p. 154.
23. Op. cit., Jan. 31, 1876.
24. *San Francisco Bulletin,* May 22, 1873.
25. *Santa Cruz Sentinel,* Nov. 14, 1868, refers to 69,350 barrels of lime transported in the previous ten months.
26. Conversation with Sandy Lydon, May 22, 1997.
27. *Sentinel,* Mar. 8, 1873.
28. *San Francisco Bulletin,* May 22, 1873.
29. Historian Ron Powell has assessed Hihn's total Soquel Augmentation Rancho holdings at 15,464 acres, of which 2,513 acres—nearly all timbered in the 1860s—were located in the area referred to in 1880 as the Summit, or at a later date Laurel.
30. *Sentinel,* Jan. 6, 1866.
31. The projected San Lorenzo Rail Road is described in detail in a prospectus by engineer Robert Harris, dated Apr. 29, 1869; details of the location are provided in the narrative engineering survey of M. L. Stangroom, dated May 2, 1871 (both documents in Stanford University Special Collections).
32. Ibid.
33. *Santa Cruz Sentinel,* May 1, 1869.
34. *Watsonville Pajaronian,* Mar. 24, 1870; the quote is attributed to the paper's editor, C. O. Cummings.
35. Letter from Stan Stevens to the author, Apr. 14, 2000; Stevens's conjecture is based on a reading of a letter by "Seyante," a pseudonym, published in the *Santa Cruz Sentinel* on Jan. 13, 1866, in which Seyante offers evidence of the superiority of a rail route up the San Lorenzo River, over a route advocated by Hihn in a letter to the *Sentinel* on Jan. 6, 1866. The style of the two letters, Stevens points out, is similar.
36. David Lavender, *The Great Persuader,* Doubleday, 1969, p. 290.
37. Ward McAfee, *California's Railroad Era,* Golden West Books (San Marino, Calif.), 1973; see chapter nine of that book for a general discussion of the antisubsidy movement in the 1870s.
38. For an excellent summary of Hihn versus Davis and Cowell, see Rick Hamman, *California Central Coast Railways,* Pruett Publishing, 1980, pp. 84–7.
39. *San Francisco Bulletin,* May 22, 1873.
40. *Santa Cruz Sentinel,* Dec. 16, 1871.
41. *Watsonville Pajaronian,* Sept. 19, 1872.
42. *Santa Cruz Sentinel,* Apr. 6, 1872.
43. *Sentinel,* Dec. 21, 1873.
44. *Sentinel,* Apr. 12, 1873.
45. *Sentinel,* May 24, 1873.
46. Wendell Huffman, "Rival Rails," unpublished manuscript, Nov. 1997, p. 91.
47. Stanley D. Stevens, *A Researcher's Digest on F. A. Hihn and His Santa Cruz Railroad* (Frederick Hihn Archives, University of California, Santa Cruz, Special Collections, 1997, pp. 144–61).

48. Ibid., p. 160.

49. *Sentinel*, Aug. 16, 1873.

50. See "List of Stockholders of Santa Cruz Railroad Company," pp. 173–76, in "Board of Commissioners Report, 1877."

51. The estimate is based on the cost of one additional Howe truss bridge, at $4,000, plus the cost of an additional two miles of grade and track required to create the "horseshoe" through Aptos, estimated to total $12,000 on the basis of costs for land, gradation, and rail (summarized in "Board of Commissioners Report, 1877," p. 180).

52. Charles Davis's son, Calvin, also had a middle initial "W," giving both father and son identical initials. The opportunities for confusing father and son in the printed record are therefore numerous.

53. The reference to "Master Mechanic" was used to describe Carter in the Mar. 28, 1874, *Sentinel*; the reference to "Architect of the Road" came from the Apr. 11, 1874, *Sentinel* feature story excerpted in the text.

54. A reference to George Hyde Bliss, owner and proprietor of the Ocean Villa resort on the eastern bluff of the San Lorenzo River near where the railroad bridge was built.

55. The San Lorenzo Howe truss measured 150.5 feet in length, the Soquel truss 105 feet, Aptos Creek 100 feet, and Valencia Creek 105 feet; the Pajaro River Bridge consisted of three Howe truss spans of 150 feet each (bridge statistics from "Board of Commissioners Report, 1877," p. 183 and p. 443).

56. See, for example, the *Santa Cruz Sentinel*, Apr. 17, 1875.

57. The weight and cost of the *Betsy Jane* are found in the Santa Cruz Rail Road's Annual Report of Dec. 31, 1874: five tons, $4,200. Its builder, long speculated to be a San Francisco foundry or machine shop, remains unknown; however, the *Santa Cruz Daily Surf* noted on Feb. 4, 1887, that Hihn ordered a narrow gauge locomotive from Risdon Iron Works for use on his Aptos Creek logging operations; this is a possible clue to the manufacturer of the *Betsy Jane* thirteen years earlier.

58. Hihn established the date of completing the first five miles of railroad in testimony before the District Court in Santa Cruz (reference in *Santa Cruz Railroad Company* v. *Board of Supervisors of the County of Santa Cruz*, Oct. 1878, p. 19, folio 55).

59. See, for example, *Santa Cruz Sentinel*, Dec. 12, 1874.

60. William Henry Gorrill's diary, entries for Jan. 6 and 7, 1874.

61. The relative size of Santa Cruz lumber merchants is indicated by assessed values published in the *Sentinel* on July 11, 1874: Huntington and Comstock, $6,970; George Gragg, $9,024; and George Treat, $53,829.

62. *Santa Cruz Sentinel*, Dec. 19, 1874.

63. Transcript from Supreme Court Case 6287, Oct. 1878, *Santa Cruz Railroad Company* v. *Board of Supervisors of the County of Santa Cruz*, p. 71, folio 210.

64. *Santa Cruz Sentinel*, July 11, 1874; this request for bids specifically named the San Lorenzo River wagon bridge in Santa Cruz; clearly, it was normal practice for a contractor to manage its own bid process for raw materials.

65. See, for instance, *Sentinel*, Nov. 13, 1875.

66. Ibid.

67. This count assumes that Amner did no casting work for the two M&SV passenger cars; the assumption is based on the lack of reference to passenger car parts in the *Sentinel*. If Amner did parts for the combines, the M&SV car count should be fifty.

68. *Sentinel,* Sept. 13, 1873.

69. Santa Cruz County deeds, vol. 15, pp. 305ff. Grantees include Charles Silent and other principals of what later became the Santa Cruz & Felton Railroad. Grantors included sixteen landowners in the San Lorenzo basin; Davis and Cowell are noticeably absent from the list.

70. *Sentinel,* Aug. 15, 1874.

71. Flume capacity would be considerably upgraded over a period of five years. With the addition of more water sources near the head of the flume, the *Sentinel* noted 116,400 board feet of lumber delivered in a nine-hour period on June 14, 1881—nearly three times the delivery capacity the flume exhibited when it opened in 1874.

72. Santa Cruz County Book of Deeds, dated Feb. 23, 1875, vol. 24, pp. 33–49, filed Feb. 20, 1877, and recorded Mar. 29, 1877; the author is indebted to Stan Stevens for identifying this revealing deed and bringing it to light.

73. Santa Cruz & Felton manuscript survey, vol. 24, pp. 32–43, in the Santa Cruz County Book of Deeds; this survey covers only the SC&F right-of-way on Cowell and Davis lands and stops short of Santa Cruz city limits. The tightest curve listed in the survey is forty-one degrees, equivalent to about a 155-foot radius. The "Board of Commissioners Report, 1877," lists the "curve ending a slide" and then the St. Charles Hotel curve as the two tightest on the railroad, at 146.6 feet and 118 feet in radius respectively (pp. 189, 450).

74. Minimum rail weight for operation of a Porter, Bell Class C narrow gauge 0-6-0 was between twenty-five and thirty pounds per yard. See Hamman, *California Central Coast Railways*; Pruett, p. 88.

75. The *Sentinel* identifies him as "F. E. Williams" on Nov. 6, 1875, but the Great Register identifies "Benjamin Franklin" Williams as "Superintendent, Railroad," and registering to vote on Aug. 28, 1875. It is assumed that the same individual is listed in both sources. The Great Register's version is adopted in the text.

76. *Santa Cruz Sentinel,* Mar. 20, 1874.

77. *Ibid.,* Mar. 27, 1874; the long, detailed description of the flume was signed "W," probably for R. E. Wood, who reported its construction as a journalist and as a photographer.

78. "Board of Commissioners Report, 1877," p. 191; "Rev. Gorrill" probably refers to Charles's brother R. W. Gorrill, known as Winnie, at the time a resident of San Francisco.

79. *Santa Cruz Sentinel,* Apr. 17, 1875.

80. *Sentinel,* May 15, 1875.

81. *Sentinel,* July 17, 1875.

82. *Sentinel,* Apr. 3, 1875.

83. *Sentinel,* Mar. 13, 1875.

84. *Sentinel,* Feb. 27, 1875.

85. *Santa Cruz Railroad Car Counts,* 1873–1878, unpublished manuscript compiled by David Eggleston, Sept. 1994.

86. Stevens, p. 132. Logan's first name may have been spelled "Huestis."

87. *Santa Cruz Sentinel,* May 8, 1875.

88. The passenger car in question was really classified as a second-class coach in the Santa Cruz Rail Road's Annual Report for the year ending Dec. 31, 1875. It had nine windows on a side, end platforms, one stove, and two wall-mounted side lamps inside. The description is based on a photograph by Carleton Watkins taken on the Capitola bridge, ca. 1877.

89. Labeled "car house" on an 1877 Sanborn fire insurance map.

90. *Santa Cruz Sentinel,* Aug. 14, 1875.

91. *Ibid.,* Mar. 10, 1877; H. W. Logan is named as a subcontractor to J. T. Boyle.

92. The photograph dates from construction work on the Loma Prieta Railroad on Aptos Creek, a project that took place in the period July–Nov. 1883, after the Santa Cruz Rail Road was standard-gauged.

93. Inventory from Hihn record books, vol. 3, pp. 393-419; bill of sale of the Santa Cruz Rail Road to the Pacific Improvement Co., Apr. 23, 1881; in the Frederick Hihn Archives, University of California, Santa Cruz, Special Collections, and provided through its curator, Stan Stevens.

94. "Board of Commissioners Report, 1877," for the Santa Cruz & Felton Railroad, p. 452; for the Santa Cruz Rail Road, p. 446.

95. *Santa Cruz Sentinel*, Dec. 30, 1876. The article does not reveal to *which* car, or which manufacturer, the faulty wheel belonged.

96. Evidence from a detailed comparison of voter registration records suggests that some of the carpenters in the suspected M&SV labor pool may have remained in Monterey County. Santa Cruz historian Stan Stevens identified a list of carpenters registered in Santa Cruz County prior to 1874 but subsequently registered in Monterey County. They include George Ulmer Collins, age thirty-two, registered in Monterey on Aug. 23, 1875; Obed Wilson Felker, forty-one, registered in Monterey on Sept. 1, 1875; and Henry Forrest, forty-nine, registered on Aug. 25, 1875 (from correspondence between author and Stevens, Nov. 20, 1997).

97. James Cutter appears in the Santa Cruz County Great Register of Voters, registered on May 1, 1871, and at the time forty-eight years of age. However, in ads for his pharmacy appearing in the *Santa Cruz Sentinel* on May 8, 1875, his name is spelled James M. *Cutler.*

98. *Sentinel,* May 15, 1875. This article anticipates the arrival of car material by May 21 and predicts the opening of the Santa Cruz & Felton by July 1. In fact, the line didn't open officially until Oct. 3, 1875.

99. The exact count of SC&F cars, by car type, is not clear from contemporary newspaper accounts. The July 10, 1875, *Sentinel* article notes ten flatcars arrived; the Dec. 11 article notes twenty flatcars arrived; yet the Jan. 22 article notes a total of just twenty-four flatcars and six boxcars on the railroad. By July 1876, the "Board of Commissioners Report, 1877" (p. 189) notes forty freight cars total, consisting of thirty-four flatcars and six boxcars (p. 450).

100. Carter time rolls, June 1899; manuscript in the collection of Robert Fisher, M.D.

101. See *Santa Cruz Sentinel,* Dec. 18, 1875, for consignee lists aboard the steamer *Santa Cruz;* included are "27 pair, car wheels."

102. Ibid., Nov. 13, 1875.

103. Hihn referred to Spreckels's $125,000 loan as a mortgage; see California Supreme Court transcript, *Santa Cruz Railroad Company* v. *Board of Supervisors of the County of Santa Cruz,* Oct. 1878, p. 71, folio 212.

104. Stevens, p. 96.

105. *Santa Cruz Sentinel,* Mar. 18, 1876.

106. The first Baldwin on the line, 8-18 C-19, named the *Pacific,* was ordered on July 14, 1875, according to Baldwin records. However, the engine was not delivered until May 7, 1876, almost ten months after the order was placed. Numerous alterations to her specification sheet may indicate revisions to the original order while Baldwin waited for payment. In contrast, *Jupiter,* ordered from Baldwin on June 16, 1876, was delivered in the week prior to Sept. 30, 1876, representing just slightly over three months of factory time for construction.

107. The resolution of the bond injunction, in favor of the Santa Cruz Rail Road, is described in the *Sentinel,* Feb. 26, 1876.
108. "Board of Commissioners Report, 1877," p. 452.
109. *Santa Cruz Sentinel,* Nov. 25, 1876, which spelled his name "Hewston Logan."
110. Ibid., Nov. 6, 1875.
111. See Charles S. McCaleb, *Surf, Sand, and Streetcars: A Mobile History of Santa Cruz, California,* Interurban, 1977, p. 104.

Chapter 7

1. Lydon, *Chinese Gold,* Capitola, 1985.
2. *Santa Cruz Sentinel,* July 10, 1875.
3. Letter from Lucien B. Healy to F. W. Pope, May 23, 1875, in the collection of Fowler Pope's great-grandson, Norris Pope.
4. Fowler's mother was Betsy Pope (sometimes spelled "Betsey"), seventy-nine years old in 1870; brothers were Horace W., age forty-six; and Joseph, also forty-six at the time of the 1870 census.
5. *Santa Cruz Sentinel,* Aug. 26, 1876.
6. Ibid.
7. Letter from F. W. Pope to his wife, Hattie, from Pittsburg Landing, Jan. 27, 1883 (Norris Pope collection). Fowler's employment at the Loma Prieta lumber company was noted in his obituary in the *Danville* (Vermont) *North Star,* in Nov. 1897.
8. Santa Cruz County Recorder's Office, "Map of F. W. Pope's Building Lots", filed Feb. 1, 1878, by H. E. Makinney, recorder. These are the same lots referred to in note 68 of this chapter.
9. Elliott, *Santa Cruz County, California, Illustrations.*
10. The first typescript of the Pope diary was created by Barbara Clark for the Santa Cruz Museum of Art and History.
11. James M. Tucker was forty-eight at the time of the 1880 census.
12. The term *cone* refers to the cast iron deflector inside the smokestack, designed to catch sparks.
13. William Francis Waterman, forty-nine years old, registered to vote in Santa Cruz County on July 23, 1880, blacksmith, native of Maine (Santa Cruz County Great Register of Voters).
14. According to the *Sentinel* of Jan. 1, 1876, a severe storm ended just four days previous, causing suspension in the railroad's operation because of landslides. Regular operation resumed two days prior to the Jan. 1 article.
15. Refers to a latch or fitting that held the spark-arresting screen in place at the top of the locomotive's smokestack.
16. George Tickner Gragg was owner and operator of Gragg's planing mill, a retail lumber outlet on Pacific Avenue in Santa Cruz, also specializing in scroll sawing, wood stair parts, moldings, and trim. Pope frequently spells his name "Gregg."
17. Alfred Baldwin, sixty-four, shoe dealer, registered to vote in Santa Cruz County on May 29, 1880 (Great Register of Voters).
18. In 1875, when the Santa Cruz & Felton opened, the California Powder Works was still hauling powder to Santa Cruz by wagon and team. A connecting spur between the mill and the SC&F would not be built until Dec. 1877.

19. The California Board of Commissioners of Transportation, in its report for the period ending June 30, 1876, lists twenty-four trestles on the railroad, totaling 4,694 aggregate feet. The exact location of bridge 15 is unknown, but it was somewhere around the midpoint of the railroad, perhaps near Rincon.

20. Apparently the first water supplies on the railroad were open tanks to collect rain water. Permanent wells or pumps would not go into operation until July 1876, when SC&F chief carpenter Alanson Burgess erected a pump-fed tank at Felton near the flume yard.

21. "Sawmill flat" was the name given to Rincon in the days when Davis and Cowell supplied cord wood from the sawmill, delivered over the so-called shuttle road discussed in Chapter Six to its lime kilns, which were located on the modern site of the UC campus; it was still a reference point in the Davis and Cowell contract with the Santa Cruz & Felton on Feb. 23, 1875.

22. The "big slide" probably refers to the one described by the *Sentinel* on Mar. 18, 1876, affecting the railroad, wagon road, horse-drawn tram, and flume of the California Powder Works.

23. Daniel Quimby Moulton, forty-eight, registered to vote in Santa Cruz County on Sept. 11, 1880 (Great Register of Voters).

24. Here, Pope seems to be differentiating between Carter flatcars, assembled on the Santa Cruz pier in May and June ("old flats"), and those assembled in Dec. ("new flats"). As far as we know, the two groups of flatcars were identical.

25. The *Santa Cruz* had a similar stall on opening day, Oct. 3, 1875, when Pope stopped dead on the 137-foot grade with three flatcars. The *Sentinel* of Oct. 9, 1875, reported much the same scenario as occurred in the "Butte Cut" stall; starting from 100 psi, Pope allowed pressure to build until the gauge registered 130 pounds. Pope then opened the throttle and successfully started the train.

26. William R. Porter, thirty-four at the time of the 1880 census, was employed as superintendent of the Santa Cruz & Felton in 1875, after quitting a position on the Santa Cruz Rail Road; Porter doubles in other roles, including locomotive engineer and conductor, during the period of SC&F service.

27. The term *chalk rock* refers to stone excavated from the Mission Hill tunnel; the rock was unstable and prone to collapse, as the tunnel had to be substantially timbered throughout its entire nine-hundred-foot length.

28. Probably a reference to Lucien Healy, surveyor of the SC&F.

29. The St. Charles Hotel, near Lower Plaza on Pacific Avenue, was the SC&F's main Santa Cruz station until the opening of Mission Hill tunnel in Oct. 1876. It was also, apparently, the legal limit of steam locomotive operation north of the downtown section along Pacific Avenue, thanks to a city ordinance restricting Pacific Avenue to horse operation only.

30. It is interesting to read Porter, Bell and Co.'s specification for the SC&F's second engine, in light of Pope's comments; clearly, a heavier set of front engine springs were considered important to the second order. See Field Notebook: The SC&F's Porters, in Chapter Six.

31. A reference to the "Johnson bar," or reverse lever, in locomotive cab.

32. Charles Clark Garcelon, thirty-nine, registered to vote in Santa Cruz County on Sept. 2, 1880, occupation "Railroad Superintendent," and also locomotive engineer on the Santa Cruz Rail Road.

33. The term *top of the hill* refers to the modern location of Rincon, also called Summit on South Pacific Coast Railroad timetables in 1880. From Rincon it was downgrade in both directions, and a siding there was a means of storing

part of a train when a crew was forced to "double the hill," or take a train up to the top in two or more sections.

34. *Umner's* apparently refers to Amner, Morton's foundry on Water Street, a short distance south of the SC&F's Mission Orchard engine house.

35. Benjamin Charles Gadsby, thirty-six, merchant, registered in Santa Cruz County on May 29, 1880 (Great Register of Voters).

36. Probably a reference to Alfred Russel Imus, 1849–1895, liveryman and policeman in Santa Cruz, owner of a homestead on the north side of Santa Cruz where the SC&F entered the San Lorenzo Canyon.

37. Dr. F. E. Bailey, Santa Cruz physician; Ann is Anna Pope, Horace's wife, thirty-four at the time of the 1870 census (June 17, 1870, manuscript census).

38. The *Sentinel* makes little mention of the "railroad war," noting, on Apr. 1, that "steps are being taken to enjoin [the SC&F] from doing further work at that point, by the officers of the Santa Cruz Railroad." This work was primarily the laying of a temporary spur up Chestnut Street to the southern mouth of the Mission Hill tunnel. By Apr. 15, the *Sentinel* noted that rock from the tunnel excavation was being removed via this spur. On Apr. 22, the paper said the tunnel was being excavated from both ends.

39. Mike Costello was a friend of Fowler Pope's and an occasional substitute fireman for Tucker (for example, see diary entry for July 26).

40. Real estate agents Hinds and Hoffman.

41. Capt. R. M. Garrett was superintendent and secretary of the SC&F as of June 30, 1876. "The Big Trees landing" was on the west side of the San Lorenzo River, opposite today's location of Henry Cowell State Park. A footbridge led from the SC&F's platform (called Big Trees Station) over the river to Big Trees Grove itself, which, in 1876, was private land belonging to the Joseph Warren Welch family. The post-1880 location for Big Trees station was within the Big Trees Grove, located on the South Pacific Coast Railroad mainline on the east side of the San Lorenzo River.

42. Refers to John Carter, stockholder and one of the original investors in the SC&F. No known relation to Thomas or Martin Carter.

43. Weltden Perry England, forty-five, registered to vote on May 20, 1880, with his occupation given as gunsmith and machinist, "also bell hanging and repairing of water pipes attended to"; located downtown on Front Street; *Sentinel,* Feb. 14, 1874.

44. For the week ending May 18, 1876, the *Sentinel* reported the SC&F hauling to Santa Cruz 209,450 feet of lumber, 2,285 barrels of lime, 3,800 broad gauge ties, 3,150 narrow gauge ties, 6,000 feet of tunnel lumber, 11,000 shakes, and 113,000 shingles; to Felton, it hauled 81,457 pounds of general merchandise.

45. The SC&F opened with twenty-pound-per-yard rail installed on the mainline; by spring 1876, fifty-pound-per-yard rail was being laid in its place on tight curves and at the Summit (Rincon) tunnel. At the same time, curvature was reduced.

46. Pope never does reveal the story he hears from Healy, but continues to hold Bill Porter in disdain for as long as he works for the railroad. Porter, on the other hand, continues to work for the SC&F through its merger with the South Pacific Coast in 1879 and is employed as an engineer when the South Pacific Coast opens in 1880.

47. The California Powder Works used water power from the San Lorenzo to turn its machinery, but when water levels dropped in the summer months, the SC&F may have been called upon to deliver firewood.

48. There was also a reference to "Mobry" in the Aug. 24 entry (not reproduced in this chapter).

49. Probably a reference to Alanson Burgess, lead carpenter on the Santa Cruz & Felton in the period of Pope's diary.

50. Edmund James Cox, cashier, Santa Cruz Bank of Saving and Loan, forty-two years old, registered to vote in Santa Cruz County, May 22, 1880.

51. Unlike the Carter freight equipment, delivered as kits to the SC&F in 1875, we infer from this entry that the two Carter passenger cars arrived assembled and operational.

52. Three Burgesses—perhaps a garbled reference to two individuals—are listed in the 1866–1875 Great Register of Voters: Ammi Austin Burgess, age twenty-five, occupation lumberman; Amnu Austin Burgess, age twenty-five, laborer; and George Everett Burgess, age twenty-eight, laborer. All were from Maine. Newspaper accounts refer to Alanson Burgess as the lead carpenter on the Santa Cruz & Felton Railroad, but it remains unclear if he is one of the three Burgesses listed in the 1866–1875 Great Register.

53. Judge John B. Bias, twenty-seven, registered to vote in Santa Cruz County on Sept. 13, 1880; occupation was given as cooper, with Moulton and Bias.

54. At the time, the SC&F was operating on Time Table no. 1, with train 1 being the first morning northbound run from Santa Cruz to Felton, and train 2 being the first return trip from Felton to Santa Cruz; in the afternoon, trains 3 and 4 repeated the routine.

55. The term *foaming* in a steam locomotive refers to boiling water entering the dry pipe where live steam is siphoned out of the boiler for delivery to the cylinders. The cause may be an overly full boiler or possibly contaminants in the water (such as high mineral content). Foaming not only cripples a locomotive's power but can potentially introduce water to the cylinders, which may cause a cylinder head to blow out.

56. Clearly a reference to William Porter, and an ironic counterpoint to Pope's own derailment on Oct. 10, which he emphatically claimed was "not my fault."

57. Once poured into a bearing, babbit metal is usually planed, much like wood, to the approximate desired contour of the axle. Once planed as closely as possible to the final contour, the surface is "run in" to the true contour by routine use.

58. For the year ending June 30, 1877 (including half of 1876), the California Board of Transportation reported that the SC&F owned just six boxcars; this conflicts with the account that ten boxcars were in Pope's train on Sept. 6, 1876.

59. Normal running time between Santa Cruz and Felton was one hour, according to Time Table no. 2, in effect Nov. 20, 1876.

60. This event also marks the end of SC&F freight operations to the wharf via Pacific Avenue. Shortly afterwards, the Pacific Avenue line was converted to horsecar operation by a new corporation, whose board of directors was essentially the directorate of the SC&F. The incorporation, called the Pacific Ave. Street Railway Co., is noted in the *Sentinel* on Oct. 21, 1876. The line is extended to the beach near the SC&F's pier (*Sentinel,* Apr. 28, 1877). The second horsecar on the line arrived, noted the *Sentinel,* on June 2, 1877, which suggests that the rolling stock for the line was purchased from a vendor outside the county.

61. Probably Daniel's Transfer Co., in Santa Cruz.

62. The "new engine house" was located adjacent to the new beach yard and warehouses, on Washington Street at the base of Blackburn Terrace. This

location became the site of the South Pacific Coast's first Santa Cruz round-house sometime after 1880. Also in Nov. 1876, construction foreman Burgess was finishing a 30' × 75' warehouse for the sc&f in the same area, adjacent to the pier.

63. Anachronistic reference to personal belongings or effects, as in "trappings."

64. Fowler Pope's birthday, as evidenced by his death record at the Santa Cruz County Recorder's Office: "Pope, Fowler W., age at death 69 years, 0 months, 0 days. Birthplace, Vermont. Married. Occupation: engineer. Death date: 10/31/97 at 221 Mission Street. Buried at IOOF Cemetery, Santa Cruz. Cause of death, heart disease."

65. The *Sentinel* continued to describe dramatic cost-cutting measures on the sc&f through Dec. 9, 1876, when it noted that both railroads in town "have reduced expenses to the lowest possible figures. No unnecessary work is being done."

66. The *Sentinel* of Oct. 18, 1876, notes completion of the Pajaro River Bridge on the Santa Cruz Rail Road and indicates it is ready for service. Pope's mention, on Nov. 14, of the "first train over the Pajaro Bridge" must have signified the first *passenger* train to use the span.

67. Perhaps a reference to William Thomas Cope, Santa Cruz merchant, married in 1878 to Katherine Charlotte Hihn, first-born child of Frederick Hihn.

68. The lots Pope sells "over the river" probably refer to a block of real estate the *Sentinel* identifies as "Pope's Addition," on Pine Street between Soquel Road and Broadway. Constituting approximately three acres, by 1878 the County Recorder's Office shows Pope's land partially subdivided into eleven building lots.

Chapter 8

1. The first locomotive constructed in the Central Pacific's Sacramento shops was 4-4-0 number 55 (the second by that number), in 1873.

2. Henry Fairfax Williams papers (hereafter designated HFW papers), Apr. 29, 1871 (Bancroft Library).

3. HFW papers, Mar. 20, 1873.

4. William Gouverneur Morris and H. C. Bennett, "The Manufacturing Interests of California," an essay reprinted in the *Report on the Eighth Industrial Exhibition of the Mechanics' Institute of the City of San Francisco*, 1872, p. 181.

5. Ibid., p. 187.

6. See North Pacific Coast cash books for Sept. 15, 1875 (Renton, Holmes interest) or Nov. 9, 1875 (McCormick and Lewis interest).

7. HFW account books, for "ground rent" on block 17, principal and interest due on a loan from auctioneers H. M. Newhall and Co., dated Dec. 28, 1872.

8. Even by 1873, the view from the Kimball building to the southwest looked across empty, filled lots in an unbroken sweep to the shore of Mission Bay, just two blocks away (observation from a line drawing entitled "Bird's Eye View of the City and County of San Francisco, 1873," by Gray and Gifford; Bancroft Library).

9. HFW account books for Sept. 15, 1869; June 22 and Nov. 15, 1870; and Jan. 14 and Feb. 2, 1871. The final transaction is in behalf of James Grave, a sub-contractor who frequently performed filling and grading on the underwater lots of Mission Bay.

10. HFW papers, Sept. 1, 1872.   13. HFW papers, Apr. 16, 1874.

11. HFW papers, Feb. 12, 1872.   14. *San Francisco Bulletin,* May 21, 1872.

12. HFW papers, Jan. 10, 1873.   15. *San Francisco Alta,* Aug. 16, 1867.

16. HFW papers, Aug. 13, 1872, in a conversation with foundryman J. N. Risdon.

17. Ibid., Apr. 28, 1872.

18. *Daily Alta California,* Mar. 9, 1868; see also McAfee, *California's Railroad Era.*

19. *Daily Alta California,* Aug. 17, 1872.   21. HFW papers, Apr. 26, 1872.

20. HFW papers, Mar. 21, 1872.   22. HFW papers, May 16, 1872.

23. Efford and Hall's salt works was actually a newer example of earlier solar salt producers in the bay. John Plummer established his Crystal Salt Works in 1857 about a mile south of the Efford and Hall works.

24. The earliest recorded name of Dumbarton Point was "Potrera Point," designated on Capt. F. W. Beechey's 1827–28 map of San Francisco Bay. The designation "Potrero Point" was common through 1874; the name Dumbarton Point was first applied by J. Barr Robertson as part of the California Land Investment Co. operations sometime in 1874. Green Point was the name of a separate landing, two miles south of Dumbarton Point at the mouth of Mowry Slough.

25. Consistent use of Mission Bay block numbers appears on various city maps of the period, for instance the 1870 map of the City and County of San Francisco, reproduced in part in Olmsted, *Vanished Waters.*

26. HFW papers, Mar. 8, 1877.

27. HFW papers, June 10, 1874.

28. HFW papers, Feb. 1, 1872.

29. The main branch of the harbor seal colony was located on Mowry Slough, about two miles southeast of Dumbarton Point. The area is still a pupping ground for harbor seals today, protected by the San Francisco Bay National Wildlife Refuge.

30. HFW papers, Sept. 16, 1870.

31. HFW papers, Feb. 27, 1875; the town site referred to in this diary entry is the first location for Newark, as chartered under the Newark Town and Land Association in 1875. From this early survey, a survey map by G. H. Thompson, entitled "Map of the Lands of the Newark Land Company," was published in Apr. 1875; my estimate of original acreage in the town site (three thousand) is on the basis of this map.

32. J. Barr Robertson was listed in Langley's Directory as "Director, California Land Investment Company, Ltd, London; office 320 Pine, rm 57, 1875–1879. Residence, Occidental Hotel, San Francisco, 1875–77."

33. Letter to J. M. Walker, Sept. 21, 1874, in letter books of J. Barr Robertson (Bancroft Library).

34. Ibid.

35. Carry Peebles, a Santa Clara Valley farmer who planted the first successful strawberry crop in the valley, was also the president of the first San Jose and Alviso railroad scheme; *San Jose Mercury,* May 23, 1868.

36. Op. cit., Nov. 14, 1874.

37. There were actually two town-site incorporations associated with the early development of Newark: the first, the Newark Town and Land Association, was legally created on Dec. 16, 1874; the second, the Newark Land Co., was created on Feb. 12, 1875. The first had nine directors, the second five, apparently a reflection of internal disagreements on the original board of directors. Henry Fairfax Williams and J. Barr Robertson were incorporators of the second organization, but not of the first.

38. HFW papers, Dec. 12, 1874. A subscription of $300 was paid to Charles Peters on this date.
39. HFW papers, Mar. 30, 1875.
40. A letter to J. M. Walker on Sept. 7, 1874, refers to a crew of ninety men working on ditches and levees in the vicinity of Dumbarton Point (letter books of J. Barr Robertson).
41. *San Francisco Call,* Dec. 18, 1874.
42. Letter to J. M. Walker, June 2, 1875 (letter books of J. Barr Robertson).
43. The 1878 dimensions of the Dumbarton Point wharf come from Thompson and West's 1878 Atlas of Alameda County; there are no known photographs of the facility prior to 1880.
44. No further information on the exact location of the first depot in Newark has ever come to light. Its dimensions don't appear to match any prominent railroad buildings constructed two years later by the South Pacific Coast Railroad.
45. Affidavit of N. C. Efford and W. C. Hall, May 23, 1876, in Transcript of Appeal, *Noah C. Efford* v. *The South Pacific Coast Railroad Company,* Supreme Court of California, docket 5218.
46. *Santa Cruz Sentinel,* Oct. 9, 1875.
47. *Oakland Tribune,* Oct. 25 and Nov. 4, 1875.
48. *San Francisco Bulletin,* Nov. 8, 1875.
49. *San Jose Argus,* Nov. 6, 1875. The number of cars ordered varies slightly, depending on which newspaper account is consulted; for example, the *Argus* cites "2 first class passenger cars, 2 second class passenger cars, 2 baggage express cars, 10 box, 10 flat, one hand car and one iron car," a total of 28 units of rolling stock. This count contrasts with 27 units reported in the Nov. *6 San Francisco Bulletin.*
50. See, for example, NPC Journal no. 4, for Dec. 31, 1882, listing twenty-five cords of wood consumed in the shop stationary engine at $3.50 per cord.
51. Letter books of J. Barr Robertson, Dec. 27, 1875.
52. *San Jose Mercury,* Jan. 27, 1876. The article notes that the locomotive "is being fitted out in San Francisco"; the engine would not actually be delivered to Dumbarton Point until Mar. 1876, after the South Pacific Coast Railroad had taken control of the project.
53. *San Francisco Bulletin,* Sept. 14, 1875.
54. Oscar Lewis, *Silver Kings: The Lives and Times of Mackay, Fair, Flood, and O'Brien,* Knopf, 1947.
55. The reference is apparently to A. Paraf, a San Francisco inventor and chemist. Little is known about Paraf, but he applied for a patent on a new "fluxing compound" through Dewey and Co., San Francisco patent agents, in 1875. Notice of the granting of the patent appeared in the *Weekly Solano Republican* on Sept. 9, 1875.

Chapter 9

1. Letter from Kimball to the V&T Railroad, Jan. 7, 1873; transcribed copy from Charlie Siebenthal collection.
2. *Territorial Enterprise,* undated but just subsequent to Nov. 21, 1874, when four reconstructed Kimball cars returned to service; published in "Restoration Feasibility Investigation on Nine Selected Passenger and Freight Cars," 1981.
3. Ibid., p. 106.

4. R. G. Dun and Co., California 16, p. 370.
5. Ibid.
6. Henry Fairfax Williams (HFW) papers, Aug. 25, 1874.
7. R. G. Dun and Co., California 16, p. 370.
8. The lease of the original Fourth and Bryant works to the Cornell Watch Co. factory appears to have taken place in Feb. 1875; by this time, Ralston was using the larger portion of the building for furniture manufacture for the Palace Hotel. Ralston was a principal owner of both businesses (R. G. Dun and Co., California 16, p. 370, dated Feb. 19, 1875).
9. HFW papers, Feb. 10, 1875.
10. HFW papers, Apr. 24, 1875; in this entry, Austin Moore shows interest in a portion of block 12, located at the mouth of the Channel Street inlet at the current site of China Basin. It is unclear whether he actually purchased or leased the space.
11. Mission Bay blocks, of which number 21 is an example, apparently had no numerical scheme for subdividing. The lot Williams leased to Eugene Soule in Jan. 1875 was described by Williams on Jan. 15 as "60 feet on Berry St. running through to King for $100 a month." This lot was at the extreme southwest end of block 21.
12. R. G. Dun and Co., California 18, p. 158.
13. These dimensions conflict with those published in the *Mining and Scientific Press* (see next note), which reported the building as 90 by 220 feet in exterior dimension. The building's size, therefore, remains unknown.
14. *Mining and Scientific Press,* San Francisco, Apr. 17, 1875.
15. *San Francisco Bulletin,* Apr. 25, 1876.
16. *Frank Roney's San Francisco: His Diary—April, 1875–March, 1876*; quoted in Neil L. Shumsky, *The Evolution of Political Protest and the Workingmen's Party of California,* Columbus: Ohio State University Press, 1991.
17. R. A. Burchell, *The San Francisco Irish, 1848–1880,* University of California Press, 1980, especially pp. 65–70.
18. Op. cit.
19. R. G. Dun and Co., California 20, p. 146.
20. *Mining and Scientific Press,* Mar. 6, 1875.
21. It is difficult to establish dates for the entrance of Cornell Watch and California Furniture into the old Kimball building at Fourth and Bryant, but the *San Francisco Bulletin* of Sept. 4, 1875, gives clues: West Coast Furniture, it claims, was established "within the last year," while Cornell was established "towards the close of last year." Both of these occurrences happened well before Ralston's death, and probably after the initial investigation of the Sixth and Berry location by Ralston and Williams in Aug. 1874.
22. R. G. Dun and Co., California 20, p. 370. The citation, made on July 10, 1874, mentioned a "greatly strengthened" impression that Ralston, not Kimball and Ogden, was in control of the business.
23. "Restoration Feasibility Investigation . . ." p. 108.
24. *Mining and Scientific Press,* July 10, 1875.
25. *Central Pacific and Leased Railroads: Locomotives, Cars, Steamers, Barges,* office auditor M. P. and M. Department, June 1, 1878 (Guy Dunscomb collection). Counted in this total are coaches, sleepers, baggage, postal, express, and emigrant cars.
26. *San Francisco Bulletin,* Jan. 17, 1876.
27. Told to the author by Cal Palmer in an interview, Grass Valley, California, 1991.
28. HFW papers, Mar. 12, 1874.

29. In his diary, Williams notes on Aug. 5, 1874, a large purchase of Mission Bay land on blocks 23, 24, and 30 by John Nightingale, attorney for Ben Richardson, a trustee for the "Lumber Association." This lumbermen's combine represented several individual companies and had financial support from the Central Pacific Railroad.

30. Williams notes that an agreement with the Gorrill brothers was reached on Oct. 10, 1874, for space on block 21.

31. Langley's advertised its cutoff date in the Jan. 6, 1877, *San Francisco Bulletin*.

32. Both photographs were taken by Eadweard James Muybridge from atop the Mark Hopkins mansion on Nob Hill; the first was taken in the fall of 1877, the second probably in June 1878 from the same location. Both are thought to show the cluster of Kimball agricultural implement buildings at Sixth and Berry streets, which became the Carter works.

33. R. G. Dun and Co., California 18, p. 158. This citation, dated May 23, 1876, also gives the month and year of Soule's bankruptcy petition: Feb. 1876.

34. White, *The American Railroad Freight Car*, p. 141.

35. Reproduced in "Carson and Tahoe Lumber and Fluming Co., Lake Tahoe Narrow Gauge Railroad Locomotive No. 2 'Glenbrook,'" found in "Restoration Feasibility Investigation . . . ," p. 15.

36. "Restoration Feasibility Investigation . . . ," p. 239.

37. Best, *Nevada County Narrow Gauge*, p. 13.

38. "Report of Chief Engineer J. H. Bates on the Survey of the Nevada County Narrow Gauge Railroad," Aug. 3, 1874 (copy in collection of Searles Memorial Library, Nevada City, Calif.).

39. Best, p. 200; this freight car roster asserts that boxcars 2–30 (even numbers only) were Carter products of 1875–76, while boxcar 32 was assembled in the Grass Valley shops in 1877. A 1912 California Public Utility Commission roster notes car 32 was built in 1876, probably from Carter kit material.

40. *Grass Valley Union*, undated reference, in Juanita Kennedy Browne, *A Tale of Two Cities and a Train*, Nevada County Historical Society, 1987, p. 15.

41. For example, see the *Nevada City Daily Transcript*, Aug. 29, 1875; other rumors circulating in the contemporary press suggested that the Nevada Bank management had withdrawn $2 million in currency from the Bank of California, precipitating the crisis.

42. HFW papers, Feb. 20 and 24, 1877.

43. HFW papers, Nov. 5, 1877.

44. "Board of Commissioners Report, 1877," pp. 210 and 457.

45. Carter bids on work for the Carson & Colorado, in 1880, appear to offer cars complete at the factory (Virginia & Truckee Railroad memo, June 4, 1880, University of Nevada Special Collections).

46. San Francisco city directories (Langley's and Vandall's) for 1876–77 show at least two Martin Carters: one a laborer, with residence at 108 Mason; another a teamster, residing at Five Mile House. In addition, there is a Carter with no first name (as seen in the text), listed as "machinist, foot of Sixth," residence Excelsior Hotel. The same directories list four Thomas Carters: a tailor by that name, whose residence was the Union Hotel; another Thomas, car builder, office 17 Drumm, residence 625 Minna St.; Thomas O., farmer, with an office in room 33 of the Merchant's Exchange; and Thomas S., a machinist with Johnson Clark and Co., residence 643 Stevenson.

47. See, for example, the *Nevada City Daily Transcript*, Sept. 21, 1875.

48. William Issel and Robert W. Cherny, *San Francisco, 1865–1932*, University of California Press, 1986, p. 125.

49. Walton Bean, *California: An Interpretive History,* R. R. Donnelley and Sons, 1968, p. 190.
50. *The Wasp,* Nov. 17, 1877, p. 242.
51. The Workingmen's movement was national in scope. In July 1877, railroad strikes in the East gave Dennis Kearney and other organizers a national theme on which to focus local issues and local militancy. The result, the Workingmen's Party of California, became the most visible and successful political outgrowth of the movement (op. cit.).
52. Bean, p. 193.
53. Quoted from Kearney's speech in Santa Cruz in Mar. 1879, cited in Lydon, *Chinese Gold,* p. 126.
54. From the *San Francisco Monitor,* Apr. 17, 1869, cited in Burchell, p. 4.
55. Ibid., p. 7.
56. Ibid., p. 54.
57. See the cover of the Mar. 17, 1885, *Wasp,* cartooning Chinese and Irish workers pushing the same float during a St. Patrick's Day parade.
58. HFW papers, Mar. 17, 1877.
59. R. G. Dun and Co., California 16, p. 495.
60. Ibid.
61. "Board of Commissioners Report, 1877," p. 201.
62. *Vallejo Chronicle,* May 20, 1875, reporting on the interest of the Vacaville Extension Railroad in a "train of passenger coaches made for the California Pacific, before it sold out, as a specimen of [Kimball's] workmanship, and which has ever since lain idle."
63. R. G. Dun and Co., California 18, p. 158.
64. Bankruptcy filing against the Kimball company, July 27, 1878 (Federal Archives, San Bruno, Calif., case 2531, location 1022D–1023C, boxes 1–88; material researched by Randy Hees in Sept. 1996).
65. Op. cit.
66. Municipal Reports, City of San Francisco (History Room, San Francisco Public Library).
67. *San Francisco Bulletin,* Jan. 4, 1877.
68. 1884 Coast Survey Map is reprinted in part in Olmsted, *Vanished Waters,* p. 46.
69. John Leale, *Recollections of a Tule Sailor,* San Francisco: G. Fields, 1939.

Chapter 10

1. There is no record of the payment of this debt. The assumption, however, is based on the *Oakland Tribune* story of Nov. 4, 1875, stating that eleven flatcars were delivered to the project. The amount of the money owed to Carter is figured from eleven flatcars valued at $475 each, the total extent of Carter's kit deliveries to the Santa Clara Valley Railroad prior to Jan. 1, 1876.
2. *San Jose Mercury,* Jan. 6, 1876.
3. *Alameda County Independent,* Jan. 29, 1876.
4. J. Barr Robertson to Walker, Feb. 11, 1876 (letter books of J. Barr Robertson, Bancroft Library).
5. Ibid., Mar. 6, 1876.
6. Deed of transmittal, Edward B. Perrin and B. B. Minor to Alfred E. Davis, recorded in the County of Alameda on Mar. 4, 1876, in California Supreme Court, docket 5218, *Noah C. Efford* v. *The South Pacific Coast Railroad,*

1876. Perrin stated in affidavit that the sale of the original sixteen hundred acres had taken place on Mar. 3, 1876, for "more than the sum of one hundred thousand dollars in United States gold coin."

7. Robertson to Walker, Apr. 12, 1876.

8. In other land purchases, Davis routinely employed a professional searcher of records, named Gustave L. Mix, to search for the title of any land Davis intended to buy. See California Supreme Court docket 5218, cited in note 6.

9. E. L. Beard was a pioneer Washington Township landowner and agriculturalist who patented (probably in 1867) the wetlands that were ultimately purchased by the California Land Investment Co.; as Robertson's letter indicates, Beard was compensated (at least in part) with stock in the investment company.

10. *Alameda County Independent,* Mar. 20, 1880. In spite of the paper's promise that the Dumbarton line would be "laid with lighter rails," there is no evidence that the rail was replaced. Maps dated 1884 show the track removed for the entire three miles from Dumbarton Point to Newark.

11. The story is recounted in the memoirs of Edward Bosqui, self-published, San Francisco, 1904.

12. Alonzo Phelps, *Contemporary Biographies of the Pacific States,* San Francisco: A. L. Bancroft, 1881.

13. *In Memoriam: Alfred E. Davis, a Member of the Society of California Pioneers,* presented at the society's meeting on June 3, 1907, following Davis's death, by a committee consisting of J. P. Bering, Henry Palmer, and S. M. Collins (the Silas Collins of Collins Saloon).

14. Langley's San Francisco Directory, 1866, p. 678.

15. Lewis, *Silver Kings,* pp. 128–29.

16. Incorporation date for the Allison Ranch Mining Co. is Mar. 5, 1869; Alfred E. Davis is listed as one of the three original incorporators. The *Grass Valley Union,* Dec. 1898, describes A. E. Davis as the mine's owner in "the late 1860s" but identifies James Flood and John Mackay as its subsequent owners, which suggests that Davis would have been acting as the agent or representative for Flood and Mackay after the "Big Bonanza" of 1875.

17. Ibid.

18. In 1876, Vandall's San Francisco Directory lists Thomas Carter's address as 625 Minna Street, but this listing was at least three city blocks away from A. E. Davis's address on the same street, and it was probably three years after Davis's move to Nob Hill.

19. "The Manufacturing Interests of California," reprinted in *Report on the Eighth Industrial Exhibition of the Mechanic's Institute of the City of San Francisco,* 1872. 1870 rankings by net manufacturing revenue include San Francisco County (first), Santa Clara County (second), Santa Cruz County (fourth), and Alameda County (eleventh).

20. Lewis, p. 217.

21. Op. cit.

22. The reference to San Mateo County in the original incorporation papers of the South Pacific Coast is to a small area in and around Dumbarton Point that was, at the time, geographically part of Alameda County but annexed through a boundary line that cut across the bay from Ravenswood Point to San Mateo County. Today, Dumbarton Point and its adjoining lands lie totally within Alameda County.

23. Travel times for the period given in the *Santa Cruz Sentinel,* Sept. 1, 1877.

24. "Board of Commissioners Report, 1877," p. 213.

25. North Pacific Coast Cash Book no. 2, entry dated May 3, 1876: "received

from SPC for use of *Tiger* & barge transferring cars and locomotive from San Francisco & Saucelito to Dumbarton Point on April 30, $500."

26. On Nov. 4, 1875, the *Oakland Tribune* noted eleven flatcars assembled at Dumbarton Point; this is evidence that Carter started assembling kits on the property three months before the South Pacific Coast controlled it.

27. *Alameda County Independent,* May 13, 1876.

28. According to the Feb. 19, 1876, *Alameda County Independent,* Bartling was included in the reorganized board of directors of the South Pacific Coast Railroad; however, by the official incorporation date of the railroad, Mar. 4, 1876, Bartling's name vanished from its list of officers.

29. *Alameda County Independent,* May 13, 1876.

30. Evidence that fifty-pound rail was first laid on Dumbarton Point comes from a Mar. 20, 1880, article in the *Alameda County Independent,* noting that the rails to Dumbarton Point are being taken up for reuse on the new Oakland branch. "The rails are heavy," the article notes, "suitable for heavy traffic." Since fifty-two-pound rail became a standard on the South Pacific Coast, it is likely that anything lighter would have been rejected for use on the high-density commute operation of the Oakland branch.

31. "Board of Commissioners Report, 1877," p. 307.

32. Louis Ruschin, *Pioneers of Newark: The Sedgely Family,* a typescript intended for publication in the *Township Register* to commemorate the opening of the Dumbarton highway bridge in 1926. In this article, the two-story dormitory is described as "surrounded by large barns and sheds, and a cookhouse," all of which was removed except the dormitory itself. Ruschin locates the building a thousand feet west of the railroad crossing, on the modern Mayhews Landing Road in Newark.

33. Carter might also have designed the Santa Clara Valley Railroad's partly completed drawbridge over Beard's (or Jarvis) Slough about a mile east of Dumbarton Point. This bridge was completed and placed in operation by the South Pacific Coast by the end of Apr. 1876.

34. *Alameda County Independent,* July 8, 1876.

35. The *Mining and Scientific Press* of Feb. 9, 1884, identifies Golden State as the foundry for parts for 120 Carter Brothers logging cars, built for the California Redwood Co. Drawings of castings for California Redwood fitting this description are included in the Graham Hardy collection at CSRM and labeled "Castings for 60 Kimble Car trucks, California Redwood Company . . . Dec 1883"; other parts represented by drawings in the set are intended for the Eel River & Eureka Railroad and labeled "Carter Brothers"; it is likely that the entire set of drawings came from the Golden State and Miner's Foundry. "Kimble" refers to the owners of the California Redwood Co., rather than to the Kimball car works.

36. *Alameda County Independent,* Sept. 9, 1876.

37. *Independent,* Sept. 23, 1876. On this date, the paper noted the setting up of SPC Baldwin locomotives number 2 and 3 at Dumbarton Point.

38. The first known reference to Julius H. Smith in connection with the South Pacific Coast occurred in the *Santa Cruz Sentinel* on Oct. 28, 1876. The paper identified his residence as San Francisco, and his occupation as civil engineer.

39. From right-of-way map filed in the court action of *SPCRR* v. *Welsh,* May 1, 1879, in the Municipal Court of Santa Cruz. The map shows primary landowners between Dumbarton Point and a location just south of Big Trees station, where the South Pacific Coast merged with the separate business entity of the Santa Cruz & Felton Railroad.

40. *Santa Cruz Sentinel,* Feb. 10, 1877. The lumber yard was probably Farmer's Lumber and Wood Yard, located near the Alameda in San Jose. During construction of the railroad, a part of the lumber yard was integrated into the spc's San Jose engine house facility.

41. *Ninth Annual Report of the Board of Railroad Commissioners of the State of California,* for the year ending Dec. 31, 1888 (p. 294), lists 496 permanent employees for the South Pacific Coast; in 1878, with the mainline to Santa Cruz not yet open, a conservative estimate suggests the railroad may have begun operations with half of its ultimate employee population.

42. *The Life Story of George L. Colegrove, Pioneering California Stage Driver and Railroad Man, as Told by Himself,* an unpublished typescript, p. 111.

43. *Santa Cruz Sentinel,* Nov. 3, 1877.

44. *Sentinel,* Apr. 21, 1877.

45. From "A Trip on the South Pacific Coast in 1882," *Railway Age,* July 20, 1882, pp. 395–96; reprinted in *Railway and Locomotive Historical Society Bulletin* no. 132, pp. 86–92.

46. Specifications on track and right-of-way are drawn from a company advertising pamphlet titled "S.P.C.R.R.—Shortest, Quickest, Best," dating from the 1880–1882 period, now in the collection of the California Historical Society. See also the comments of spc superintendent A. H. Fracker on the use of eight-foot ties (standard gauge length) in "A Trip on the South Pacific Coast in 1882" and the *Alameda County Independent* of Dec. 23, 1876, citing similar engineering standards for very early spc track work.

47. One example is the shift from body-hung brake beams, visible on eight-ton-capacity m&sv boxcars built in Monterey, to truck-hung brakes, seen on eight-ton-capacity boxcars built for the Nevada County and North Pacific Coast railroads. The motive probably originated from differences in curvature on the three railroads.

48. White, *The American Railroad Freight Car,* p. 194.

49. "The Narrow Gauge Convention," *National Car Builder,* Dec. 1878, 9(12).

50. Kirkman, *The Science of Railways, Cars, Their Construction and Handling,* Chicago: Cropley Phillips, 1916, p. 644.

51. Hilton, *American Narrow Gauge Railroads,* pp. 70–71.

52. Earnings per mile for the South Pacific Coast in 1887 were $8,896.49; earnings per mile for the Southern Pacific Co. (including the Central Pacific and leased subsidiary lines in California, Nevada, and Arizona) were $7,326.91 for the same period (*Eighth Annual Report of the Board of Railroad Commissioners of the State of California,* for the year ending Dec. 31, 1887).

53. White, p. 452.

54. Swing hangers were configured in two ways. In the first, swing motion would be suspended from the top of a truck transom beam to create a longer "moment arm" that in turn promoted faster oscillation at any given speed; in the second version, a swing hanger suspended from the bottom of a transom beam featured a shorter moment arm that stiffened the swing motion, creating slower oscillations for a given speed. The second version therefore was common in passenger car truck designed specifically to provide more lateral stability at higher speeds.

55. Calculation based on measuring the weight of an extant eight-ton body center plate, from the surviving m&sv boxcar, at twenty pounds, and the weight of an extant ten-ton body center plate from Towle Brothers Lumber Co., at twenty-nine pounds; both parts in the collection of the spcrr at Ardenwood Historic Farm, Fremont, California.

56. *Monterey Herald,* Oct. 3, 1874, and *Santa Cruz Sentinel,* Jan. 24, 1880.

57. The swing hangers in question were examined by the author in Tuolumne, California, in 1985. Most likely they came from Carter fifteen-ton, twenty-four-foot flatcars and were in service on the West Side Lumber Co.

58. "U.S. Patent Office, in the name of Thomas Carter, of San Francisco, California, Car-Truck." Patent no. 353,286, dated Nov. 30, 1886, application filed Aug. 12, 1886. Other features of the same patent were lowering the car's center of gravity and adapting hollow metal transom beams. The resulting truck, with the exception of the bolster, was of all-metal construction, a departure from the substantially wood-framed Carter truck designs of the 1870s.

59. Evidence for application of the truck appears in a photograph of an unidentified coach pictured in front of the Santa Cruz depot, taken in the 1890s; the photograph is reproduced in this chapter.

60. "Reports for the Railway Companies in 1881," Board of Railroad Commissioners of the State of California, p. 499.

61. *Eighth Annual Report of the Board of Railroad Commissioners of the State of California,* for the year ending Dec. 31, 1887, pp. 152, 153 (Southern Pacific) and p. 215 (South Pacific Coast). The comparison is based on reporting of tons of freight hauled by each railroad for the year (SP 980,443,574, SPC 9,054,080); that year, South Pacific Coast's freight car fleet numbered 428, but Southern Pacific's freight car count can only be estimated since off-road cars were involved in handling its traffic. The SP's freight car count is estimated at fourteen thousand cars for the year in question.

62. *San Francisco Examiner,* Feb. 21, 1898; the publicity stunt was staged by the *Examiner* in conjunction with other high-speed runs over the Southern Pacific—for example from Oakland to Reno—all staged to deliver copies of the newspaper in record time. The *Examiner*'s subsequent story doesn't specifically identify Carter cars on the train, but the baggage cars known to be in service on the SPC at the time were all built by Carter.

63. *Santa Cruz Sentinel,* Dec. 16, 1876.

64. The names Taylor's Pass, Morrell Pass, and Burrell Pass were often used interchangeably. In 1880, J. B. Burrell, H. C. Morrell, and James Taylor were all neighbors along the modern location of Morrell Road, near the summit of the Santa Cruz Mountains at its junction with Highway 17.

65. *Santa Cruz Sentinel,* Nov. 28, 1876.

66. Ibid.

67. *Santa Cruz Sentinel,* Jan. 5, 1878, reconstructs Davis's early interest in the Pescadero Basin survey, although the timeline it suggests is vague.

68. *Sentinel,* Nov. 18, 1876.

69. *Sentinel,* Apr. 14, 1877.

70. *Sentinel,* Aug. 4, 1877.

71. An example is *Mienecke* v. *The Bay & Coast Railroad,* noted in the *Alameda Encinal* on Mar. 16, 1878. The suit was brought by Charles Mienecke against the railroad for laying a track on the street in front of his Central Avenue (Alameda) residence.

72. See Lavender, *The Great Persuader,* pp. 302–3.

73. For details of the Cohen action against the Central Pacific, see Lavender.

74. Third Judicial District Court Proceedings, Alameda County. Order of Condemnation no. 4111, filed Nov. 30, 1877, Judge S. B. McKee presiding.

75. "Catalogue of Paintings on the Steamers *Newark* and *Bay City,* on the Ferry Lines of the South Pacific Coast Railroad Co.," an original card from the Baird Archive of California Art (Department of Special Collections, University of California, Davis).

76. *Alameda County Independent,* May 25, 1878; the article spoke of the depot

as "under construction," but with the line open for passenger business on June 1, completion could not have been far off.

77. *Santa Cruz Sentinel,* Aug. 24, 1877.
78. Kevin Bunker, "A Historic Color Scheme for the Ardenwood Train Station," prepared for the East Bay Regional Park District, May 14, 1986; paint samples are based on research on the surviving Agnew depot, believed to have been built by the South Pacific Coast in 1877.
79. *Sentinel,* Apr. 26, 1878.
80. This summary is based on operating timetable no. 10, issued Apr. 4, 1881, the first timetable produced under the supervision of F. W. Bowen, who replaced Thomas Carter.

Chapter 11

1. *Alameda County Independent,* July 7, 1877. The conclusion that at least some kit building took place on Dumbarton Point after March 1876 is based on only two known shipments of assembled cars from Saucelito, the first by NPC car float on Apr. 30, 1876, and the second on an unspecified date in Aug. of that year. The shipments included some passenger equipment, leaving room for fewer than twenty assembled freight cars. The count of freight cars on the SPC reached eighty by July 1877, including seventy flats and ten boxcars.
2. Ibid. Starting date for construction of the shop is suggested in the *Alameda County Independent,* Dec. 23, 1876.
3. The *Independent,* on Sept. 1, 1877, notes "four fine passenger coaches, . . . built by Messrs. Carter Bros. at Saucelito and transferred to Dumbarton by barge." By this date, the Carter facility in Newark would have been in operation just four to six weeks, not enough time for Carter Brothers to have produced the cars on site.
4. Counts of passenger equipment in the *Independent* show consistent stock-on-hand: "six passenger cars," Dec. 23, 1876; "4 passenger coaches, 2 baggage [cars]," July 7, 1877; "4 fine coaches," Sept. 1, 1877 — the latter count omitting baggage cars.
5. "Pioneers of Newark: The Sedgely Family," typescript of an article published by the *Washington Township Register* on or prior to Sept. 1, 1926.
6. "Board of Commissioners of Transportation Report for the South Pacific Coast Railroad, 1880"; the entry, however, is broken down into 45 boxcars, 210 flatcars, and 65 "other" cars. The latter category may represent already obsolete eight-ton freight cars from the Santa Clara Valley Railroad, as well as work equipment.
7. Census records for 1880 list John Larkin, fifty-eight, living with the Martin Carters in Newark, no occupation given.
8. *Oakland Tribune,* Sept. 13, 1882, reported in the *Washington Corners Reporter,* date unspecified.
9. *Santa Cruz Sentinel,* Aug. 2, 1879.
10. Industrial Census records, schedule 3, Manufactures; Products of Industry in Washington Township, in the County of Alameda, State of California, from June 1, 1879 to May 31, 1880, from the U.S. Census Records in the California State Library (hereafter, "Industrial Census records").
11. *Oakland Tribune,* Sept. 13, 1882.
12. 1880 U.S. Census records; inhabitants in Centerville Precinct, County of Alameda, collected on June 16, 1880.

13. Evidence supporting the construction date of the two additional Carter shop buildings is sketchy, but a photo dated 1885 apparently shows one of the two new buildings in place.

14. *Alameda County Independent,* July 7, 1877.

15. Only one photograph taken inside of the Carter shops is known to exist. It shows a small, floor-mounted stationary steam engine. The photograph dates from the turn of the century, and it is not clear that this power source was in place during the 1880s.

16. Industrial Census records.

17. Stock taken Jan. 1, 1899, Newark shop, Carter Bros. Car Manufacturers; see complete text of inventory in Appendix (collection of Robert Fisher, M.D.).

18. An inventory of Virginia & Truckee tooling for June 30, 1917, appears in Stephen E. Drew, "An Historical Overview, Virginia & Truckee Railroad, Carson City Enginehouse and Shops," Oct. 1990.

19. Industrial Census records.

20. *Alameda County Reporter,* June 15, 1880.

21. *Santa Cruz Sentinel,* May 22, 1880.

22. *Sentinel,* July 17, 1880.

23. Ibid.

24. *Alameda County Reporter,* Feb. 10, 1880.

25. The earliest recorded period of planting eucalyptus was reported on Aug. 24, 1878, by the *Alameda County Independent.* The scope and location of the first eucalyptus plantings in Newark are indicated by an 1896 map of Washington Township, in which individual trees are distinguishable.

26. T. P. Wilson map of the Town of Newark, "showing villa lots" and farms, 1876 (author's collection).

27. *Alameda Encinal,* Dec. 8, 1877.

28. Quit claim deed between Sausalito Land and Ferry Co. and the Martin Carter Estate Co., Nov. 5, 1909, filed in the Marin County Recorder's Office. Note the change in spelling: the original form *Saucelito* had by this time been replaced with the modern *Sausalito.*

29. Last will and testament, Martin Carter, June 6, 1880, executed in Newark, California.

30. *Alameda County Reporter,* Sept. 13, 1879.

31. *Reporter,* Feb. 28, 1880.

32. *Reporter,* June 5, 1880.

33. *Santa Cruz Sentinel,* Apr. 26, 1879.

34. *Washington County Reporter,* June 7, 1879.

35. *Oakland Tribune,* Mar. 5, 1880. The same article notes that in addition to turning locomotive drivers, Ingraham's machine works was turning out both iron and brass castings for railroad use.

36. A reference to Ingraham's "hammer shop" is in the *Oakland Tribune* of Dec. 24, 1879.

37. This inference is based on a surviving collection of ten Carter Brothers drawings believed to have all come from the Golden State and Miner's foundry, variously dating between 1877 and 1891. The preponderance of drawings, if taken as a statistical sample of GS&M's work for Carter, seem to indicate a majority of standard gauge hardware. One possible conclusion is that GS&M was tooled for heavier fabrication work than Newark's local machine shops, making it Carter's preferred choice for standard gauge orders (Graham Hardy collection, now at CSRM).

38. Early 1880s examples are from the restored car *Silver State* at the CSRM; later

examples, ca. 1898, are from West Side Lumber Co. parts in the collection of the SPCRR, at Ardenwood Historic Farm in Fremont, California.

39. With the exception of part numbers 28 and 42, examples of numbered Carter castings are held today by the Society for the Preservation of Carter Railroad Resources, at Ardenwood Historic Farm.

40. *Santa Cruz Sentinel,* Jan. 31, 1880.

41. *Sentinel,* June 12 and July 24, 1880.

42. Evidence for a new paint shop building comes from Carter's Jan. 1, 1899, inventory, which cites a $250 inventory of lumber and sash from the "paint shop (removed)." By this time, photographs confirm that the building had been torn down. The date of the shop's construction, however, remains unknown.

43. Number of part names in a contemporary day coach estimated from Matthias N. Forney, *1879 Car Builder's Dictionary,* Dover reprint, 1974, pp. 242, 301, 359, and 421.

44. Makers of car fittings and hardware are identified from labeled parts on South Pacific Coast duckbill coaches 23 and 43, whose remains were salvaged by Henry Welzel in 1971 and preserved in Puyallup, Washington; paint brands are from the Carter shop inventory of Jan. 1, 1899; wheel vendors are identified by a Carter "Specification for Passenger Cars and Combination Passenger and Baggage Cars . . . " (ca. 1889), calling out materials and features of cars bid for the Port Blakely Co., found in Special Collections, University of Washington; springs are identified from extant 1881 Carter passenger car trucks under the car *Silver State,* at CSRM.

45. Names of commonly used suppliers appeared in the *National Car Builder* at various dates from 1877 to 1882.

46. Crerar, Adams and Co. catalogue, ca. 1870s, Chicago, p. 74; original from collection of William Wulf.

47. Cost of a narrow gauge Westinghouse brake system estimated from the price of a standard gauge W.A.B. system, cited in the *National Car Builder* in its Dec. 1880 issue, p. 184. The price was $103.83.

48. Letter from Carter Brothers to F. A. Autenrieth, secretary, Yreka Railroad, July 13, 1888; from the collection of the Yreka Western Railroad.

49. Commentary on W.A.B. systems and sales guidelines in a letter from Dave Garcia to the author, Dec. 28, 1998.

50. Kansas City, St. Joseph & Council Bluffs Railroad costs for Miller hooks reported in the *National Car Builder* in Dec. 1880; the lowest reported price found, $16.37 per hook, was reported in the same publication in Feb. 1881.

51. Only one known photograph clearly shows the Miller badge plate in place on a Carter product: the *Pearl,* the private car built for the Oahu Railway and Land Co. The plate labeled the car as equipped with "Miller's Coupler, Buffer & Platform" and summarized the patent dates, extending back to Mar. 1863.

52. Santa Cruz Rail Road, first-class coach price from "Board of Commissioners Report, 1877," p. 180; South Pacific Coast Railroad first-class coach price from average of fourteen coaches (aggregate retail value, $58,000) from *Ninth Annual Report of the Board of Railroad Commissioners of the State of California,* 1878, p. 463.

53. Shipping costs are estimated at $1.97 per thousand pounds of finished coach weight, f.o.b. Chicago to San Francisco; rates from Carson & Colorado bid estimates on new rolling stock summarized in a memo dated June 14, 1880, on Virginia & Truckee stationery, from its office in Carson City, Nevada; original from Yerington papers, Special Collections, University of Nevada.

54. Details of the Barney and Smith coach come primarily from the Graham Hardy edition of Flemming's *Narrow Gauge in America,* an engraving entitled "Narrow Gauge Passenger Car, Building by Barney & Smith Manufacturing Company, Dayton, Ohio." This is believed to be Barney and Smith's first narrow gauge coach, built in 1875, and a close match to the North Pacific Coast cars sold in 1877.

55. *National Car Builder,* Mar. 1883, entitled "Passenger Car Ornamentation," p. 84.

56. Evidence was found in the extant car body of South Pacific Coast coach 39, built in May 1881 by Carter, for the railroad's new Oakland branch. The car body is preserved at the Orange Empire Museum in Perris, California. Although paint research on the car has not been completed at the time of this writing, preliminary sampling indicates an interior featuring natural wood finish with gold leaf molding.

57. Data on this point are sketchy, but photographs of SPC coaches before 1880 show square window sash finish in both thirteen- and fourteen-window versions; however, coach 22, reportedly built in 1879, was a thirteen-window version with a number of upscale features: arched top window sash, art glass in the clerestory windows, and more elaborate striping.

58. Carson & Colorado coach 5, built by Barney and Smith in 1881; preserved at Orange Empire Museum.

59. Port Blakely Collection, University of Washington, Special Collections; box 95C, folder 11 contains Carter's specification, and that of an unidentified eastern builder.

60. Ibid., box 84.

61. See note 53.

62. Kit-based construction was used after 1880, as with standard gauge freight cars for the Alameda & San Joaquin Railroad, built in Lathrop, California, in 1897; Dan L. Mosier and Earle E. Williams, *History of Tesla, A California Coal Mining Town,* Mines Road Books, 1998.

63. William Voss, *Railway Car Construction,* originally published by R. M. Van Arsdale, New York, 1892; reprinted by Newton K. Gregg, Novato, California, 1975; *National Car Builder,* 1874–1882 consulted, published by James Gillet and L. F. Dinsmore, New York; "Particular Directions for Constructing Miller Platforms: Carpenter Work," date and publisher unknown but thought to have come from E. Miller and Co., New York (original in the Smithsonian Museum).

64. R. G. Dun and Co. California 16, p. 495 (Baker Library, Harvard School of Business).

65. R. G. Dun and Co. California 20, p. 146. This is the only entry for Carter known in the extant R. G. Dun credit books in the Baker Library.

66. Baldwin Locomotive Works, serial list of locomotives constructed by class, pp. 148–49 (Stanford University Special Collections).

67. Baldwin also created two other subclasses of the same basic design, labeled 8-18$\frac{1}{4}$ C and 8-18$\frac{1}{3}$ C; p. 10, ibid.

68. The South Pacific Coast chose Baldwin paint style "1" for engines 2 and 3 and switched to paint style "49" for engines 4–8 (Baldwin color and style book, in Stanford University Special Collections).

69. A South Pacific Coast ice water dispenser from the ferry *Encinal,* in the author's collection, displays the olive and gold livery described in the text.

70. *Third Annual Report of the Board of Railroad Commissioners,* dated Feb. 1881, gives value of South Pacific Coast passenger cars as $120,634.85, and value of freight cars as $121,382.42.

71. Ibid., p. 325.

72. *Alameda County Reporter,* July 31, 1880.

73. Evidence for this conclusion comes from two sources: the memoirs of George Colegrove, who noted a "negro porter" on the car during a special run for John D. Rockefeller (undated); and a photograph of a wreck involving the mainline passenger train, running with a parlor car, in 1901. The view was taken shortly after the wreck and shows passengers and crew standing by the derailed train; it includes a single, uniformed black employee, presumed to be the chair car porter.

74. Among the earliest known examples of the Carter bullnose roof end are two cars built for the San Joaquin & Sierra Nevada Railway: the 1882 combination car that would become Southern Pacific 1009 (later SP narrow gauge 401); and the coach *Ettie,* built in 1885, later becoming Southern Pacific coach 1011.

75. South Pacific Coast coaches 15 and 16 were identified as "Davis, Howell & Co." cars, built in 1879, in the deposition of E. W. Chapin in a lawsuit against the Southern Pacific, dated 1898; however, Northwestern Pacific records list the builder as Carter.

76. The core parcel purchased by Martin Carter was the ranch of J. T. Walker, which appears on the 1878 Atlas of Alameda County as a tract about two miles southeast of Mowry Station and a mile southwest of Washington Corners (later called Irvington).

77. *Oakland Tribune,* Jan. 22, 1884.

78. From a transcript of an interview with Martin Grover Carter in Los Angeles, by Bruce MacGregor and John I. MacGregor, 1975.

Chapter 12

1. *Santa Cruz Sentinel,* Dec. 22, 1878, gives the names of railroad timber contractors, several of whom purchased timber land from Frederick Hihn; D. H. Montgomery, for example, bought a thousand acres of redwood for $13,000.

2. *Sentinel,* Apr. 13, 1878. "Work to begin immediately," the paper noted.

3. *Sentinel,* Aug. 2, 1879.

4. *The Life Story of George L. Colegrove,* p. 114.

5. *Santa Cruz Sentinel,* July 28, 1877.

6. Locating the summit tunnel was described in the *Santa Cruz Sentinel* on Sept. 29, 1878; the report on Davis's meeting with Hihn was printed in the *Sentinel* on Oct. 6.

7. The Southern Pacific's San Fernando Tunnel, completed in 1876, was 6,966 feet long; the South Pacific Coast's summit tunnel, completed in 1880, was 6,200 feet in length.

8. *Sentinel,* Feb. 16, 1878.

9. *Mining and Scientific Press,* June 6, 1878, p. 361.

10. Ibid.

11. Lydon, *Chinese Gold,* p. 120.

12. Ibid., p. 122.

13. *Santa Cruz Sentinel,* Oct. 25, 1879.

14. The first speculation about falling revenues from the Consolidated Virginia was mentioned in the *Sentinel* on July 20, 1878; the *Sentinel* reported the layoff of miners on Nov. 16, 1878.

15. *Sentinel,* Feb. 1, 1879.

16. *Sentinel,* July 20, 1878.

17. *Monterey Weekly Herald,* Dec. 24, 1878.

18. *Santa Cruz Sentinel,* Aug. 3, 1878.

19. *Santa Cruz Sentinel,* Aug. 10, 1878.

20. From Time Table no. 4, Apr. 1, 1879; commute train mileage based on seventeen trains operating in both directions between San Francisco and High Street, Alameda; mainline train mileage based on seven trains operating in both directions between San Francisco and Wrights, California. Even with completion of the mainline to Santa Cruz in 1880, the ratio of commute train miles to total train miles dropped just 1 percent, to 31 percent.

21. *Alameda Argus,* May 24, 1879.

22. Mix's report that two tunnels would be required on the east bank route down the San Lorenzo (on the opposite side of the river from the Santa Cruz & Felton) appeared in the *Sentinel* on Mar. 1, 1879.

23. *Santa Cruz Sentinel,* Feb. 15, 1879; author's comment about the blacksmith shop adapted from *Watsonville Pajaronian,* Feb. 20, 1879.

24. Ibid.

25. Bean, *California: An Interpretive History,* p. 195.

26. *Santa Cruz Sentinel,* Mar. 15, 1879.

27. Santa Cruz violence following the Kearney speech is discussed in Lydon, pp. 126–27.

28. *Santa Cruz Sentinel* transcript of the remarks of A. E. Davis, made on Apr. 12, 1879, and printed on Apr. 26.

29. *Sentinel,* May 29, 1879.

30. *The Life Story of George L. Colegrove,* p. 117.

31. The *Sentinel* noted on Feb. 5, 1876, that Lawrence Archer, assemblyman from San Jose, had introduced a bill in the state legislature making it possible for the Santa Cruz & Felton Railroad to purchase the San Lorenzo Flume and Transportation Co. This bill would, in effect, have allowed the parent and child companies to merge.

32. *Sentinel,* Feb. 8, 1879.

33. *Sentinel,* Mar. 1, 1879.

34. *Sentinel,* June 7, 1879.

35. *Sentinel,* Aug. 2, 1879.

36. Superior Court, County of Santa Clara; *Santa Clara Valley Mill & Lumber Co.* v. *Hayes & Hubbard.*

37. The first known report of the incident was made in the *Sentinel* on June 14, 1879, and simply noted that "Captain Garrett had his legs broken several weeks ago by a pile falling on them."

38. *Sentinel,* June 28, 1879.

39. Both Hogback tunnels were subsequently daylighted. Extant physical evidence of the two tunnels today shows a cut roughly seventy-five feet in width, with the tracks of the modern standard gauge tourist line, the Santa Cruz, Big Trees & Pacific Railroad, passing along the east (river) side of the cut.

40. *Sentinel,* Aug. 2, 1879.

41. On June 14, 1879, the *Sentinel* mentioned "the intention of the SPCRR to use 30 # rail in reconstructing the Felton road"; however, by Nov. 11, the paper makes it clear that fifty-pound rail is being substituted.

42. *The Life Story of George L. Colegrove,* p. 113.

43. *Santa Cruz Sentinel,* Feb. 7, 1880.

44. *Sentinel,* Nov. 22, 1879.

45. *Sentinel,* Feb. 21, 1880.

46. *Sentinel,* Jan. 10, 1880.

47. The "antechamber" plan was mentioned on Nov. 29, 1879, but it is unclear whether the chamber was actually excavated.

48. *The Life Story of George L. Colegrove,* pp. 116–17; also, *Engineering News,* vol. 34, no. 28, Nov. 28, 1895, p. 359, indicates such a boarding house in a

map of Wrights. It was located on the San Jose side of the Los Gatos Creek bridge, between the mainline and the creek, and was approximately 25 feet by 110 feet in dimension.

49. *Santa Cruz Sentinel*, Feb. 14, 1880.

50. Op. cit., p. 129.

51. Davis hired Bowen from the Sacramento Division of the Central Pacific, where he was employed by the pay department; *Railway Age*, Sept. 9, 1880, p. 472.

52. Op. cit.

53. *Santa Cruz Sentinel*, Mar. 27, 1880.

54. *The Life Story of George L. Colegrove*, p. 130.

55. *Santa Cruz Sentinel*, Apr. 24, 1880.

56. *Sentinel*, May 23, 1880.

57. Charles Bruce Younger was a prominent Santa Cruz attorney, with a residence on Laurel Street in 1879; see *Santa Cruz County California Illustrations with Historical Sketch, 1879*, Elliott and Co., 1879; 1997 reprint, Santa Cruz Museum of Art and History, edited by Stanley D. Stevens.

58. *Sentinel*, May 8, 1880; this article states that the first SPC freight train would leave "Monday morning next," which would have been May 10; the first passenger timetable was published on May 15. However, in his *Life Story*, George Colegrove recalled that the line did not open until May 15—though he was often in error about exact dates. The date of the first commercial operation of the completed eighty-mile system is thus in contention by several days.

59. The oldest known surviving South Pacific Coast timetable covering the completed Alameda–Santa Cruz mainline is Employee Time Table no. 7, dated May 29, 1880. Freight operations over the completed line, however, began in early May, which suggests that timetable no. 6 was the earliest one to govern the completed railroad.

60. *The Life Story of George L. Colegrove*, pp. 130–31.

61. The elevation at Glenwood is 891 feet; the elevation at the south end of the summit tunnel is 901 feet, and the distance between them 2.75 miles. However, a good part of this distance was filled with the mile-long Glenwood-Laurel tunnel, whose portals were at the same elevation and whose midpoint was raised nine feet above the end points. Thus the steepest portion between Glenwood and the middle of the summit tunnel was the fifteen-foot-per-mile gradient within the tunnel itself, engineered into the tunnel's design for drainage.

62. Baldwin Locomotive Works; *The Narrow Gauge Locomotives*, p. 11. Note that these performance specifications were intended to be conservative, reflecting less-than-ideal conditions.

63. *The Life Story of George L. Colegrove*, p. 125.

64. Ibid., p. 128.

65. The details of the wreck as reported by local newspapers are drawn largely from the *Watsonville Transcript*, May 23, 1880; the *Santa Cruz Courier-Item* of May 26; and the *Santa Cruz Sentinel*, May 23.

66. Transcribed nearly fifty years after the accident, *The Life Story of George L. Colegrove* contains numerous errors and inconsistencies in its description of the May 23, 1880 wreck. For example, Colegrove cites the date of the wreck as May 15 (p. 124); he refers to the Hogback grade as 126 feet to the mile (p. 125) when in fact it measured 137 feet to the mile; he refers to the runaway train containing two flatcars when it contained three (p. 125); he notes "old man Sam Davis" (Hog Davis' brother) riding on the engine when it was in fact Davis' nephew Sam, at that time 33 years old (p. 126), who was aboard.

Colegrove's omission of Tom Carter from the scene, and his failure to explain why he didn't depart Felton with his own train at the time the dispatcher specified in a written order, have already been mentioned. While Colegrove roundly condemns dispatcher Walker for sending an inexperienced crew down the grade, inferring blame for a run-away train, he asserts (p. 126) that the cause of the wreck was a kink in the rail, warped by the heat of the late afternoon sun. Colegrove ignores the inference that even a train moving at safe speeds would have risked derailment on damaged track. Taken together, the inconsistencies cast doubt on Colegrove's memory, or veracity, or both.

67. *Sacramento Record-Union,* undated, as quoted in the *Santa Cruz Sentinel,* June 19, 1880.

Afterword

1. Hilton, *American Narrow Gauge Railroads,* p. 88.
2. *Third Annual Report of the Board of Railroad Commissioners, State of California,* for the year ending Dec. 31, 1880, p. 302.
3. Ibid., p. 294.
4. The Oregon & Nevada contract was filled in the late summer of 1882.
5. Reports from the Consuls of the United States, no. 96, Aug. 1888, Washington, D.C.: Government Printing Office, pp. 263–68.
6. *San Francisco Call,* June 16, 1896; the breach-of-promise suit was filed in the San Francisco Superior Court on June 15, for $50,000, against Thomas Carter.
7. She is listed as Mary E. Redmond, twenty-four years old, in the 1880 census. Her occupation is dressmaker, working for and residing with Miss A. M. Kind at 1017 Market St., San Francisco.
8. However, in a June 17, 1896, *Call* article, James Horan disputed the story of how they first met, suggesting that it was in San Francisco and that meetings at Byron Hot Springs did not take place until roughly 1890. Since lawsuits had been filed between Mollie Redmond and Thomas Carter at this point, Horan cannot be considered an objective witness.

Index

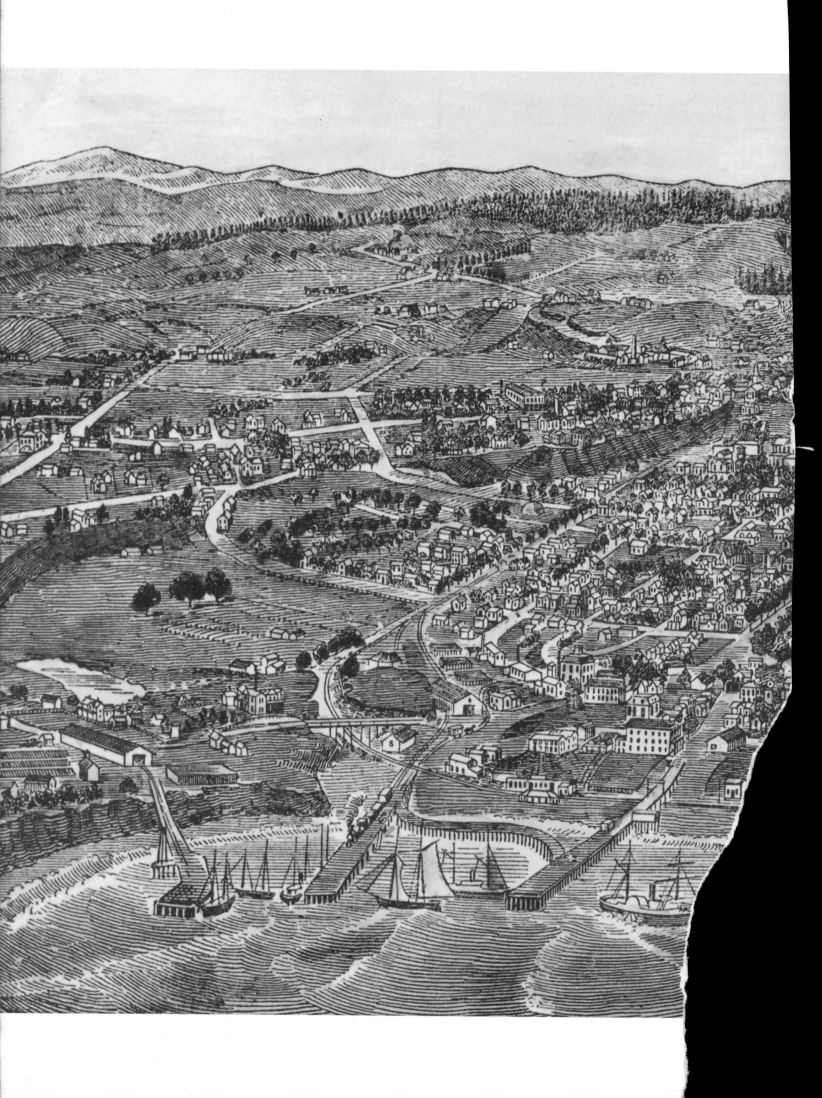